The Wicked Waltz
and Other
Scandalous Dances

The Wicked Waltz and Other Scandalous Dances

Outrage at Couple Dancing in the 19th and Early 20th Centuries

MARK KNOWLES

McFarland & Company, Inc., Publishers

Jefferson, North Carolina, and London

LIBRARY OF CONGRESS CATALOGUING-IN-PUBLICATION DATA

Knowles, Mark, 1954–
The wicked waltz and other scandalous dances : outrage at couple
dancing in the 19th and early 20th centuries / Mark A. Knowles.
p.   cm.
Includes bibliographical references and index.

ISBN 978-0-7864-3708-5
softcover : 50# alkaline paper ∞

1. Ballroom dancing — History — 19th century.   2. Ballroom
dancing — History — 20th century.   3. Ballroom dancing — Social
aspects — History — 19th century.   4. Ballroom dancing — Social
aspects — History — 20th century.   I. Title.
GV1751.K66   2009   793.3'3 — dc22   2008053221

British Library cataloguing data are available

On the cover: Ballroom dance ©2009 Pictures Now;
ornate border and marble background ©2009 Shutterstock

Manufactured in the United States of America

*McFarland & Company, Inc., Publishers
Box 611, Jefferson, North Carolina 28640
www.mcfarlandpub.com*

To my sister,
Anne Knowles Snell,
with all my love and gratitude

Acknowledgments

Many kind and talented people supported me in the writing of this book. The waltz section of this book was written as part of my master's thesis. I would like to thank the staff at Antioch University, McGregor whose friendly advice and assistance made the process of getting my degree a fulfilling experience. I would especially like to acknowledge my two faculty advisors, Barry Cavin and Dan Reyes, who supported and encouraged me. I would also like to thank the members of my committee, Lynn McMurrey, a man I greatly admire and loved talking with, and my committee chair, Dennis Castellano, a dear friend, who guided me throughout the program with enthusiasm and integrity.

I was fortunate to have the very best instructors in my program. It was an honor to study with Jon Saari. The research and reading I did with Larry Billman was instrumental in the writing of this thesis and I appreciate his help. Alex Romero was, as always, an inspiration. I was so blessed to have him as a mentor and friend. I danced the waltz with Theresa Hayes at the Grand Victorian Ball, as part of my studies. I'll never forget that experience nor the help and constant support she has always given me. She is an amazing woman and a brilliant educator whom I admire and respect.

I was fortunate to be able to attend both the "Sonomama Improvisation as Life Practice," and the "Waltz Improvisation as Life Practice" workshops given by Cheryl Cutler, my first dance teacher. To be able to return to the classroom to study with her was an answer to my prayers. The work that she does with Randall Huntsberry is inspiring, and I will always be grateful for the profound experiences I had studying with these two passionate individuals. The information that I gained at the waltz workshop was especially pertinent to this book, and many of the ideas and insights that I have written about were initially introduced in discussions with Ms. Cutler and Dr. Huntsberry. I love these people and thank them for sharing their hearts with me so freely.

The staff at the Huntington Library in San Marino was of great service, and the research I did in the lovely surroundings of that institution was among the most pleasant times I spent during the process of writing this book. Many other kind and capable librarians at libraries around the country have also assisted me.

At La Salle High School in Pasadena, where I have had the honor of teaching for many years, my research was aided by Kathleen Peck and Delia Swanner. The late Annie Johnston gave me her copy of the *MLA Handbook* and always met me with a hug to ask how my book was coming along. Pat Bonnacci, the principal of La Salle, awarded me a grant for further study which allowed me to finish my Masters. Richard Grey and the staff and faculty have been kind and supportive. My departmental chair, Jude Lucas, and my fellow dance teacher, Nancy Evans Doede, have been especially understanding and helpful. My students at La Salle have kept me young and passionate about dancing.

My students at the American Academy of Dramatic Arts/Hollywood were instrumental in the inception of this book, and I will always think of them with fondness and gratitude. I have shared a lot of waltzes and Charlestons with these talented young men and women. The students at Occidental College and the University of California, Irvine patiently listened to my ramblings as I was discovering new topics while writing this book, and asked many pertinent questions that crystallized my thinking. Even my young tap students at Ballet Petit Performing Arts Center in La Canada have kept me going.

My spiritual and my physical well-being has been guided by Dr. Asa Hershoff, Dr. Kevin Michael, and Dr. Sailing Michael. They have kept me healthy and on track.

My friends have been there through this whole process. Alison England Sam kept me laughing and reminded me to trust. Rob Risko and Tom Robinson kept me company and kept me sane. Tom provided great advice over many meals at *Chipotle* and also helped with computer issues.

My partner of twenty-three years, Don Keller, believed in me, and loved me, and urged me to express myself. Before he was ill, he proofread the first part of my manuscript, offered editorial advice, and kept the computer up and running. He passed away during the writing of this book, but he continued to be with me when I was able to return to writing. He was a rare and precious gift in my life, and he is still my greatest teacher.

My mother and father inspired a love of learning in me from the start. They always expressed interest in my ideas and treated even my craziest ideas with respect. They filled the house with books and, more importantly, with love. I felt them over my shoulder as I wrote this book. My siblings, Nancy, Rex, and Trudy, and their families, continue to love me, listen to my ideas, and support me in all my endeavors. My sister Anne is my kindred spirit. She recognizes orchidity when she sees it, and knows when *Little Men* or *Pride and Prejudice* are called for. We were "Masters buddies"— laughing, bouncing ideas off each another, seeing *Blue Jacket*, racing to the lilac bush, and stressing out together. She proofread every page of this manuscript twice. She gave me so much more than just suggestions and editorial advice. She gave me hope and confidence and lots of love.

I love you all more than tongue-can-tell.

Contents

Tell me now, Mother mine, are you willing to send
Your girl to the Pit for the demons to rend?
Well, if not, then beware of the lure of the DANCE.
There the Devil will catch her if given a chance.

Lulu Agnew Singer
(From "The Lure of the Dance")

Preface

For the past fifteen years, I have been on the faculty at the American Academy of Dramatic Arts in Hollywood, California. As part of the curriculum in my Movement for the Actor I & II, I teach a Charleston and a Waltz. Besides learning the dances, my students are expected to research the historical events, styles, fashions, slang, etiquette, and any other pertinent issues of the period surrounding these two dances. As I watched these eager young actors dive into their research, my own interest in the history of these social dances grew.

After the pleasurable experience of researching and writing my second book *Tap Roots: The Early History of Tap Dancing*, I decided that fully researching the dances that I taught at A.A.D.A. (as well as a few others) could be equally satisfying. I've been interested in anti-dance literature for many years and have fed my e-bay addiction by trying to track down anti-dance tracts and "No Dancing" signs. Above my bedroom door is one of my favorites—"No Ragtime or Tango Dancing Allowed." I knew it was time to write a book about this subject.

In 2001, after I had decided to earn my Masters in Visual and Performing Arts, I approached my advisory committee with the idea of writing my thesis on social dancing and anti-dance reaction to it. They readily agreed, but suggested I limit my writing to the Waltz. In 2003, I completed my thesis, and the first part of this book was born. Family illnesses, the deaths of loved ones, and a busy schedule teaching, directing, and choreographing prevented my finishing the rest of the book until recently.

This book is not an attempt to teach people how to perform these dances. It is not a dance manual. It is merely an effort to gather as much material as possible from many varied sources so as to shed a little light on how these dances reflected their times and how society reacted to them.

The Wicked Waltz and Other Scandalous Dances opens with a brief overview of anti-dance sentiment from around the fourth century up to the present day. It then focuses on couple dances of the nineteenth and early twentieth centuries—a period of widespread social, political, and economic change. Around the world during this time, monarchies decayed and fell, and a rapidly growing middle class emerged. With the growth of industrialization and free enterprise, the focus on capitalism increased. These changes led to a disruption of established class structures and a restructuring of society as more and more people moved into urban areas. As cities grew, so did the sense of discontentment with traditional social values and the way these values were expressed. Social dancing, as both a symptomatic and constitutive kinesthetic expression, reflected this tumultuous period in history and revealed the shifting social ideologies of the day.

The first section of the book starts with an investigation of the history and development of perhaps the most beloved and most maligned social dance to come out of this volatile period in history—the waltz. Like other couple dances that swept the world, the waltz was surrounded by controversy. It evoked indignant reactions from religious leaders and other self-appointed arbiters of social morality who sermonized against the corrupting influence that social dancing had upon the decency and health of those who danced. Anti-dance sentiment to the waltz grew in direct proportion to its rising popularity.

In addition to exploring the cultural and historical roots of this couple dance and its subsequent evolution, this book will examine the impact the waltz craze had upon fashion, music, leisure time, and social reform. It will also give an overview of the violent opposition to the dance and the proliferation and function of both anti-dance and courtesy literature.

The last three sections of the book will explore these same issues as they relate to other dance crazes of the early twentieth century–Ragtime Dances (such as the Turkey Trot, Grizzly Bear and Bunny Hug), the Tango, and the Charleston. The book concludes with a look at the concepts of order and disorder as they are revealed through dance.

Social dances reflect the lifestyles, culture, and class of the people who perform them. It is as if that particular period of history is somehow mirrored in a kick, a turn, or a twist of the body. How society reacts to these dances likewise exposes the standards, beliefs and morals of that era. At times, these reactions may seem humorous to us today. Sometimes, they are touching — sometimes shocking. They are always revealing.

It is my hope that in exploring the "wicked" waltz and other "scandalous" dances, this book will give some insight into the fascinating periods of history in which these dances held the world in their power.

1

Overview of Anti-Dance Sentiment

"The dance is a quagmire of wreckage. It's as rotten as hell,"[1] said evangelist Billy Sunday summing up the belief of those who thought that dancing — whether the waltz, the turkey trot, the tango, or the Charleston — was wicked.

People have criticized dancing as long as people have danced. They deemed it inappropriate because it crossed boundaries of acceptable behavior for a certain class or gender; sometimes race was a factor. Critics warned that dancing was unhealthy, that it caused physical debilitation. Furthermore, they called it frivolous — a waste of time and money that easily led to financial ruin.

Perhaps, the most common attack was that dancing broke sexual taboos. One critic observed, "Dancing is the perpendicular expression of a horizontal desire."[2] It led to temptation. It was indecent and immoral.

"Don't go to that dance," Bill Sunday warned. "It is the most damnable, low-down institution on the face of God's earth.... It causes more ruin than anything this side of hell."[3]

Early Antecedents of Anti-Dance Sentiment

Perhaps the most vociferous opponent to dancing in Western cultures has been the Christian Church. Church sanctions against dancing date to the fourth century. Although the primitive Christian Church utilized dance in many of its services and accepted it as an important sacred ritual,[4] church leaders grew concerned when both sexes started to participate and "mixed" dancing crept into certain practices. The hierarchy of the Church warned that holy rites were corrupted by the inclusion of women who tempted male participants into licentious behavior. Matters were further complicated because early church members believed that because humans were created in the image of God, the devil was frightened away by the naked human body. In the midst of the dance, therefore, celebrants often ripped off their clothes. Church leaders grew increasingly concerned about the number of religious rituals that were deteriorating into sexual orgies.

These leaders viewed the mixture of dancing and women as a dangerous combination. The proof, they said, was in the Scriptures. Salome's dance before King Herod led to the beheading of John the Baptist. The Bible was explicitly clear. When women and dancing mixed, wickedness resulted.

The Church made both women and dancing the targets of continual attacks in its attempts to control behavior and regulate social conduct. These attacks were based on

> two fundamental premises: first, dancing is evil because it is the work of the devil, who is ever out to tempt the devout Christian to sin or forbidden behavior; and second, as inheritors of the opprobrium of the creation story, women are the agents of the devil.[5]

The early church fathers launched vociferous attacks against dancing. St. Augustine was a particularly vocal opponent, although he reluctantly admitted that in certain controlled situations sacred dance could sometimes be appropriate. St. Chrysostom was not so forgiving. He said, "For where there is a dance, there is also the Devil. For God has not given us our feet to use in a shameful way but in order that we may walk in decency, not that we should dance like camels."[6]

In the Middle Ages, the first ecclesiastical summas, or penance books for confessors, were issued. Used as a means to control the populace, these books defined sins in detail and prescribed corresponding penances. Many contained admonishments against dancing. The *Summa Astensis*, written in 1317 by Astesanus de Asti, stated "that watching the dancing 'of lascivious women' can progress from venial to mortal sin if one studiously fixes attention on the dancers."[7] Furthermore, women "would be sinning mortally if they intended to incite themselves or others to lust, or if they danced habitually, even though free of corrupt intention."[8] The *Summa Astensis* was one of the first pieces of anti-dance material to detail three major themes that would later run through subsequent anti-dance literature: the motive or intention of the dancers; their frequency of participation in the dance; and the resulting effects or consequences of their dancing.

In 1429, the *Destructorium Vitiorum,* written by Fabritius, issued strong indictments against the dance. This book remained extremely influential and popular throughout the fifteenth and sixteenth centuries. In it, Fabritius stated,

> The entring into the Processions of Dances, hinders men from ingress into the Heavenly procession; and those who Dance, offend against the Sacraments of the Church. First, against Baptism; They break the Covenant which they made with God in Baptism; wherein they promised, to renounce the Devil and his Pomps; but when they enter into the Dance, they go into the Pompous Procession of the Devil.[9]

Fabritius reiterates another important theme among anti-dance critics—that the devil is the originator of the dance.

Reaction in the Renaissance and Elizabethan Era

During the Renaissance there were two significant developments in social dancing: the appearance of the first dance teachers and choreographers in the guise of professional dancing masters, and the simultaneous advent of instructional dance manuals. These two advancements brought with them the notion of dancing as a courtly art. With sufficient effort and training, one could achieve grace. Dancing was blended with manners and proper behavior, and it was generally believed that orderly movement was moral and disorderly movement was not. "Order and morality went hand in hand with courtesy and polish on the dance floor."[10]

Because hiring a dancing master or purchasing an instructional manual required money, dancing ability became a means to distinguish social class. The writers of courtesy literature in the Elizabethan period fostered this notion by reminding ladies and gentlemen that dancing reflected the order of society and functioned best when there was a separation of social classes. The powerful and the privileged should shun the disorderly dances of the common folk and dance only proper, orderly dances appropriate to their rank. By doing so, they were not only cultivating themselves, but also cultivating a better society. For a gentleman and a lady, proper dancing was a civic duty.

Despite the fact that many in the Elizabethan era viewed orderly dancing as a means of expressing moral, ethical behavior, many still denounced it as an evil, immoral pastime. Printed in 1527, Henri Cornelius Agrippa's *Of Vanitie and uncertaintie of Artes and Sciences* included vitriolic denunciations against dancing. This influential book was reprinted and consulted as late as the eighteenth century. It introduced an important theme that became part of the battle cry of future adversaries of the dance: dancing was a vain and idle pastime. It was an absurd waste of time and energy, and those who participated in it were nothing more than strutting peacocks. Agrippa concluded, "daûsing is the vilest vice of all."[11]

During the Elizabethan period, opponents to dancing continued to warn of its sensual and lascivious nature. John Calvin said dancing was nothing more than an "inticement to whoredom."[12] Detractors urged that those who refused to stop dancing should at least forswear fast, excessive, and disorderly movements, especially because violent motions were associated with drunkenness and debauchery. One should exercise control over the passions. Discrete, sober, prudent, and restrained movement was required if one must dance. In the early 1500's, Juan Luis Vives, counselor to Catherine of Aragon at the court of Henry VII, wrote a book entitled *Instruction of a christian woman*. In his book, Vives reiterated the typical warnings about dancing: it incited lust and led to a loss of chastity. Vives particularly implored all virgins to avoid dancing.[13] He also voiced a practical and immediate concern — the hopping and shaking movements in dancing caused extreme fatigue and therefore prevented dancers from going to church.[14]

Many denounced dancing because its movements were viewed as ridiculous. Proponents argued that careful study with a dance master could remedy this problem. Others, such as Lambert Daneau, a Reformed Church pastor and professor of theology, replied that taking time to study unsightly movements was absurd and vain, and that a Christian had enough to do to resist the world's temptations without wasting time "studying the art of publicly making an ass of oneself."[15]

During the mid to late 1500's, the rise of Calvinism in England brought with it more virulent attacks against dancing. As tensions between Protestants and Catholics grew, objections to dancing merged with objections to the doctrines and practices of the Catholic Church. Papists were accused of supporting dancing, further proof of its wickedness. The anti-dance sentiment of these Protestant reformers culminated in strong negative reactions to dancing by the Puritans, who eventually brought these beliefs to America.

Opposition to Dancing in the United States

The first known anti-dance treatise written in the United States was Increase Mather's "An Arrow Against Profane and Promiscuous Dancing Drawn out of the Quiver of the Scriptures" (1665).[17] Mather was fervently opposed to members of the opposite sex dancing together. He wrote, "But our question is concerning *Gynecandrical Dancing*, or that which is commonly called *Mixt or Promiscuous Dancing, viz.* of Men and Women (be they elder or younger persons) together: Now this we affirm to be utterly unlawful, and that it cannot be tolerated in such a place as *New-England*, without great Sin."[17] Mather was also opposed to Maypole dancing and wrote in a later tract, "It is an abominable shame, that any Persons in a land of such Light and Purity as New-England has been, should have the Face to speak or think of practising so vile a piece of Heathenism."[18] The theme of dancing as a heathen and barbaric practice would later be used to justify attacks against the Charleston and ragtime dances, such as the turkey trot, that were derived from African sources.[19]

Although dancing was not outlawed entirely in Puritan New England, several pieces of legislation against dancing were enacted to curb civil disorder and prevent pagan practices. These laws were strictly enforced. In 1641, a man named David Owls from Salem, Massachusetts, was ordered to pay a fine of twenty shillings or spend time in the stocks for disorderly behavior when he was caught dancing in his own home. In Connecticut, in 1678, white citizens were strictly forbidden to attend any Native American dance ceremonies "because it encouraged the natives in their 'Divill worship.'"[20]

At the end of the seventeenth century, Cotton Mather, son of Increase Mather, issued a tract entitled "A Cloud of Witnesses; Darting out Light upon a Case, too Unseasonably made Seasonable to be Discoursed on." This booklet was specifically written to warn against the dangers of dancing. In it, Mather addressed "People of Quality" and warned them that even if they hired the most sober and modest dancing master to teach their children poise, they were still going against Christian virtue and fostering vanity. Mather reiterated many of the typical themes of prior anti-dance writers: dancing was aligned with the devil; it was a wasteful stewardship of time and energy; it was vain and artificial; it was inappropriate for women; and of course, it led to lust. Mather wrote in capital letters, "A CHRISTIAN OUGHT NOT TO BE AT A BALL."[21]

During the eighteenth century, as urban areas in America expanded and more people immigrated to the United States seeking economic rather than religious freedom, opinions towards dancing gradually shifted. New educational theories began to support the use of dance as a valid method of learning grace and composure, and by the middle of the eighteenth century in New England, it became increasingly popular to educate young ladies and gentlemen at schools in the art of dancing. Social dancing was especially popular and prevalent in the Southern states where members of the upper classes had both wealth and leisure time, and gravitated toward more aristocratic forms of amusement.

In Virginia, dancing was viewed as a worthy form of recreation for the elite as well as the servant and slave classes. Dancing was deemed a necessary ingredient in the education of every gentleman and was used at such respected institutions as William and Mary College to teach gentle manners and deportment. Balls were a common occurrence on plantations and in Southern cities such as Richmond, Williamsburg, Savannah, and Charleston. Many influential people, including Thomas Jefferson and George Washington, openly expressed their love of dancing.

Despite a more tolerant attitude towards dancing in the South, tensions still existed between supporters and detractors. Oliver Hart, a Baptist minister in Charleston, published a sermon entitled "Dancing Exploded." He argued that dances were the work of the devil and that many were "extremely immodest and, incentiveness to uncleaness."[22] They "murdered" time and also represented frivolous stewardship of money. Hart warned parents that sending their children to a dancing master was sinful because it wasted money that could have been used for charitable purposes. He admonished, "Think how dreadful it will be to have the blood of your dear children's souls crying against you, in the day of judgement."[23]

The dawning of the nineteenth century brought with it an increase in the popularity of dancing as well as an increase in the number of anti-dance tracts. "As Americans struggled to define themselves, tensions developed between European ideals for gentlemen and ladies, on the one hand, and republican, as well as denominational, ideals for citizens and Christians, on the other."[24] The role of women in dance was particularly in question and issues concerning gender and beliefs about the rights of women elicited complex reactions. A deluge of American anti-dance literature was written by white, Protestant, male evangelists and clergy who held rigid traditionalist views about the roles of women in society. These men admonished women that dancing always led to pernicious ends. Simultaneously, there was a growing number of books on etiquette that offered conflicting advice about dancing, citing its value in teaching grace and gentle deportment, and its ability to enhance one's chances of advancing in society, and therefore, making a good match.[25] As women's issues became more prominent, a few female authors joined the ranks of those who wrote about the evils of dance. The first woman to do so was Hannah More, an Englishwoman whose writings on the subject were widely read in the United States. She preached against the frivolity of dancing and attempted to expose the folly of following the dictates of polite society.

During the nineteenth century a new theme emerged in anti-dance literature — the idea

THE DANCE OF DEATH.

"The Dance of Death" from the anti-dance book *The Modern Dance* by Jas. H. Brookes (date unknown).

that dancing was wrong because it ran counter to the intellect and dissipated the mind. Detractors argued that, as an idle pleasure, dancing offered no useful stimulation of the thinking faculties and was "merely a 'mechanical art which requires but little exercise of the understanding,' [and] proficiency in it indicates virtually no intellectual excellence or improved understanding."[26] This concept was also expressed in writings that did not necessarily oppose dancing as such. In St. Louis in 1888, for example, the *Social Mirror* stated,

A young lady should not attend parties and balls while engaged in educational pursuits. The proper serving of two such masters as learning and the gay world, is an utter impossibility, especially at the age of seventeen, when the fascinations of a ball possess charms that are never experienced in after years. Going to school is an old, well tried experience, going to a ball is a new and delightful one, and it is not hard to tell which would engross the entire thought of a young girl.[27]

Opponents to dance concluded that since dancing did not improve the mind, it reflected the lowest of human expressions and was really nothing more than base animal sensuality. Therefore, according to the Bible, it was a "work of the flesh"— something that was strictly prohibited.

American perceptions regarding the use of money also evoked anti-dance sentiment. As an entertainment, dancing provided no goods or services; therefore, the concepts of necessity versus frivolity, work versus play, and stewardship versus waste came into play. Opponents to dance railed against the wastefulness of dancing. Paying for dance lessons, or buying lavish ball gowns and other dance-related paraphernalia was considered extravagant; money could better be used to feed one's family or help the poor. Tensions heightened between those who argued that dancing played a necessary part of the lives of the ideal gentleman or lady, and those who stated unequivocally that dancing had no part in the life of the ideal Christian.

The Second Great Awakening,[28] which occurred during the first few decades of the nineteenth century, brought with it increasing ire against dancing as well as a new theme in anti-dance literature— that dancing operated in direct opposition to the spirit of revivalism because it excited and therefore misdirected the senses. Evangelist Charles Grandison Finney, a nationally prominent revivalist, stated, "Diverting excitements, if strong and permanent, will prevent a revival. Hence, it has always been the policy of Satan to keep the church, and if possible the ministry, in a state of worldly excitement."[29]

After the War of 1812, a growing dissatisfaction with European tastes and concepts led the

An early twentieth century postcard that pokes fun at the extravagance of dancing.

American people to search for their own artistic expressions—ones that could express national ideals in a uniquely American way. New forms of entertainment emerged that catered to the tastes, needs, and desires of the common man and woman. The blackface minstrel show was the most important entertainment form to result from this cultural process, becoming the preeminent form of American entertainment for the major part of the nineteenth century. Minstrelsy brought with it new rhythms and styles of dancing, as well as new reasons for dance opponents to express their outrage.

White minstrels confiscated and then theatricalized African-American dances, bringing

THE HABIT OF DANCING WILL NOT AID US
TO RESIST OTHER TEMPTATIONS.

This illustration found in Jas. H. Brookes' anti-dance treatise *The Modern Dance* (189–?) suggests that yielding to the temptation of dancing can lead to other transgressions such as drinking, gambling, and attending the theatre.

about a synthesis of both white and black cultural elements. The new hybrid introduced many important forms into theatrical dancing that were later absorbed into social dancing as well. The use of syncopation, improvisation, poly-rhythmical body movements, and animal mim- icry are just a few examples of the African-American influence upon popular social dances of the time. Dance detractors strongly objected to these innovations because they were associated with black culture, which was judged as primitive, savage, and sensual.[30]

In addition to the rise of minstrelsy, other "worldly" amusements became more accessible to the American public at this time. Classical ballets were presented in major metropolitan areas and European dance stars began touring the United States. Ballet star Fanny Essler[31] had an enormously successful two-year American tour that began in 1840. She was showered with flowers, inundated with rave reviews, and met with adulation wherever she danced. Young male admirers surrounded her in droves. Nightly, they unhitched the horses from her carriage and pulled it themselves from the theatre back to her hotel. She was invited to dance at the White House for President Martin Van Buren and was escorted around town by Van Buren's son. Con- gress even adjourned whenever she was in Washington in order to see her perform.

Conservative moralists were outraged at these improper displays. Minister and orator Henry Ward Beecher heavily criticized the dancer. In 1843, he exclaimed, "We cannot pay for honest loans, but we can pay Essler hundreds of thousands for being an airy sylph!"[32] Ralph Waldo Emerson on the other hand, called her dancing "religion." Camps were divided. Oppo- nents of dancing saw stage dancing as a perpetrator of vice and one of the "unfruitful works of darkness,"[33] whereas proponents saw it as a civilizing, cultural advancement.

During the first third of the nineteenth century, as the United States was seeking to estab- lish its own identity as a republic independent of European ideals and manners, dance oppo- nents latched on to a new theme in their attempts to ban social dancing. Dancing was unpatriotic. They urged true Americans to shun the fancy clothes and courtly airs typically used at dances and reminded them that by attending balls, they were not only imitating aristocratic behavior, but also alienating and demoralizing other members of the democracy by spending money friv- olously instead of helping their brothers in need. In 1828, one commentator remarked,

> The Fancy ball has been a source of unparalleled aggravation to the poor, and cannot but arouse them to a deeper sense of their own poverty, wretchedness and misery, thereby adding another agonizing pang to their sufferings; and also reflect upon the conduct of those whose object it should be to alleviate (as far as their power lies) their condition; instead of giving them new cause to regret their deplorable fate.[34]

Those who opposed dancing declared that a true member of a democratic republic had a social responsibility to help his fellow citizens. Spending time and money on idle pleasures such as dancing was therefore not only wasteful, but also unpatriotic. Excessive, ostentatious displays ran contrary to public spirit, and planted the seeds of disharmony, despair, and dissipation.

After the Civil War, a new theme was introduced into anti-dance literature that specifically associated dancing with the evils of prostitution. A growing number of dance opponents pointed out that most prostitutes attributed their downfall to having once attended a dance. One of the classics of anti-dance literature, *From the Ball-room to Hell*, by T. A. Faulkner,[35] claimed, "It is a startling fact, but a fact nevertheless, that two-thirds of the girls who are ruined fall through the influence of dancing."[36] The author argued that he himself had personally interviewed two hundred prostitutes, and one hundred and sixty-eight of them swore that they were led into prostitution because they attended a dancing school or went to a ball. He summed up his findings by stating, "To close the doors of the brothel, close first the doors of the dancing school."[37]

Faulkner's *From the Ball-room to Hell* is the quintessential piece of anti-dance literature. It utilizes many of the common themes found within the genre. The book warns that dancing always results in ill health and ruined reputation; that it is a wasteful stewardship of time and

Showing that frequenting the dance hall can lead to unwanted pregnancy, this illustration carried the caption "The tragic climax of this young life was not reached in one step, but led there by easy stages through the fascination of the dance hall." From *From the Dance Hall to White Slavery; The World's Greatest Tragedy* by H W. Lytle and John Dillon (1912).

money; and that it is an expression of the barbaric and uncivilized. The bottom line-dancing is the work of the Devil who uses women to seduce men into lust. These themes and others were used as cannon fodder to battle the sin of dancing.

With the rapid expansion of urban centers in the United States at the turn of the century and the growing need for avenues of recreation, a new phenomenon appeared — the public dance hall. Frequented by working men and women, these venues fostered an atmosphere of permissiveness where unchaperoned strangers met and danced together. Dance opponents saw them as hotbeds of vice and launched sustained attacks against them. They stated, "The dance hall is the nursery of the divorce courts, the training-ship of prostitution, and the graduation school of infamy."[38]

Critics cautioned that dance halls were used to snare unsuspecting women into the white slave trade and lives of prostitution. Many books were written to expose the tragedy of innocent women lost to sin in the dance hall. In *Fighting the Traffic in Young Girls; or War on the White Slave Trade*, author Ernest Bell wrote, "One of the fascinating allurements of city life to many young girls is the dance-hall, which is truly the ante-room to hell itself. Here indeed, is the beginning of the white slave traffic in many instances."[39] Lester Bodine, superintendent of compulsory education in Chicago said, "More girls enter the White Slaver's mart through the portals of the disorderly dance hall than through all other agencies."[40] An investigation by the Municipal Vice Commission of Chicago reported that seventy-five percent of the city's 5,000 prostitutes "attributed their downfall in a greater or lesser degree to the public dance hall."[41] Social activist Jane Addams, founder of Hull House in Chicago said, "The dance hall is a canker that the community must eradicate to save its future generations."[42]

This illustration, entitled "Dangerous Amusements — The Brilliant Entrance to Hell Itself," contained the caption "Young girls who have danced at home a little are attracted by the blazing lights, gaiety and apparent happiness of the 'dance halls,' which in many instances lead to their downfall." From *Fighting the Traffic in Young Girls or War on the White Slave Trade* by Ernest A. Bell (1910).

Critics warned that the dangers inherent in the lewd, grasping embrace of such dances as the turkey trot, the grizzly bear, the bunny hug, and the tango were heightened in the contexts of the public dance hall; and because most dance halls were connected with saloons, liquor added to the menace. In the dance hall, unscrupulous men could ply unsuspecting women with liquor, hug them close in a lewd manner, and trot or tango them around until they fell into the devil's snare.

As the world moved into the twentieth century, the syncopation of ragtime and jazz spawned a host of new dances, highly charged with a wide array of both positive and negative perceptions. Animal dances stampeded across the globe, and so did opposition. Tangomania and the Charleston craze evoked strong responses. Critics sneered at these dances' questionable origins. Moralists found their movements obscene. Many just thought they were downright awkward and ugly. When reporter Tom Sims saw the Charleston for the first time, he described the movements:

> If you have a corn on eevry [sic] toe, put on some tight shoes some damp day and you are doing the Charleston.... Watch dad when he gets the bill for wife's fall hat. He will do a Charleston step.... Don't worry when the cook drops a plate. Take off your shoes and learn a Charleston step on the pieces.... Ever stand on a red hot stove with a dozen eggs in your hand. It is a Charleston step.... The Charleston was invented by some timid soul jumping from a snake and landing on a porcupine.[43]

When the jitterbug became the dance of the day, most critics were not so worried about issues of morality as issues of safety. In 1939, the *Fresno Herald* reported that the Rainbow Ballroom had enacted a ban on the dance. "Not only did it inflict bruises," the owner of the dancing establishment claimed, but "flying feet would also cut women's stockings."[44]

In the 1960's concern about the twist elicited warnings from the Society of New Jersey Chiropractors who called the dance "a potentially hazardous torque movement causing strains in the lumbar and sacroiliac areas."[45] The home safety director for the Greater New York Safety Council was more direct. She said, "Stop twisting!"[46] Resistance to the twist also came from those around the world who saw the dance as sexually suggestive. Igor Moiseyev, the director of the well-known Russian folkdance troupe commented, "[The twist] expresses dirty feelings, dirty instincts, and poverty of thought and spirit."[47] Some countries banned the dance.

In the 1970's the "Disco Sucks" movement was born. On April 30, 1979, the *Penn State Daily Collegian* reported on a campus protest of about 200 students calling themselves the LSD or "Let's Stop Disco." They chanted anti-disco slogans and smashed and burned disco

Dance hall sign from the first decade of the twentieth century forbidding the dancing of "freak dances."

albums. One student who was interviewed stated, "Disco music's one of the three major attacks on American security along with paraquat and Ronald Reagan. It breeds mindlessness in the leaders of future generations."[48] Two Chicago DJs organized "Disco Demolition Night" in Comiskey Park in Chicago on July 12, 1979. In between a double-header between the White Sox and Detroit Tigers, the crowd threw their disco records towards the infield like Frisbees and shouted "Disco Sucks!" Several fires and small riots erupted and the baseball field was destroyed in the process. The fracas got so out of hand, the White Sox forfeited the second game.

Opposition to dance continued into the 1980's especially in certain fundamentalist groups. In 1984, preachers in Mesquite, Texas, warned their listeners that "allowing dancing was just one step on the road to topless waitresses."[49] "Dirty dancing" and the lambada were considered too risqué by many when they became popular.

In the present day, many high schools ban freaking, grinding, and other dances that simulate the sex act. Some schools have equipped chaperones with flashlights to expose inappropriate movements, while others have eliminated school-sponsored dances entirely. In Los Angeles, C-Walking, or Crip Walking was banned in most high schools because of its gang connotations.

So it has been throughout the history of social dancing and so, it seems, it will continue. Critics complain. And, the dance goes on.

PART I. THE WALTZ

2

Origins of the Waltz

Social dances shift from one trend to another as rapidly as society itself changes. As physical manifestations of how individuals interpret, emotionalize, and respond to their environment, these dances often challenge the status quo and are met with fear and resistance. This response certainly greeted the most celebrated social dance of the late eighteenth and the nineteenth centuries: the waltz. Today this enduring social dance is considered elegant, restrained, and sedate, but when it was first introduced, "genteel society was shocked by the intimacy implied by the waltz's embracing position."[1] Throughout its history, the waltz has been met with the gamut of emotions from joy, pleasure, attraction, and obsession, to shock, indignation, hostility, and outrage. From its beginnings, the waltz was revolutionary.

Although its roots are somewhat obscure, dance historians believe the waltz probably evolved out of either the sixteenth-century court dance called the volta, or the Austrian folkdance called the ländler.[2]

The Volta

The volta[3] (lavolta) was part of a group of Renaissance court dances called galliards[4]—energetic dances that utilized hops, turns, kicks, and jumps. Performed in triple meter, galliards served as "after-dances" which traditionally followed slow, stately, processional pavanes.[5] Popular between 1550–1650, the volta was not only the most athletic and controversial of the galliards, but also the only court dance of the period that was performed by a couple in a closed embrace.

When dancing the volta, partners held each other tightly and matched steps to heighten the centrifugal force as they twirled around in a series of 3/4 turns. The dance's signature move was a leap in which the man lifted the woman into the air and spun her around before setting her down again.

Done in six beats of music in 6/4 or 6/8 time, the footwork of the volta actually consisted of only five steps, with one count held as the man lifted the woman into the air in the leaping move called a caper.[6] The dance was commonly known as the cinque pas, cinque-pace or five-step.[7] In England it was known as the sinky-pace, or the sink-a-pace. Popular in the Elizabethan court, it was one of Queen Elizabeth's favorite dances.[8]

The caper required precise execution. The man held his partner tightly around her waist, and lifted her into the leap by placing one hand on her back and his other near her crotch, on the bottom of her busk, a rigid piece of bone, wood, or metal that was used to stiffen the front of the corset. Pivoting on one foot and revolving on his own axis, the man lifted his other knee under the lady's buttocks and propelled her into the air. The woman used her right hand to press down on her partner's shoulder and her left to hold down her skirt "lest the swirling air should catch them and reveal her chemise or bare thigh."[9] In his book *Orchésocraphie*, first published in 1589, French cleric and dance-manual author, Thoinot Arbeau,[10] gave instructions for the proper way to perform a volta. He wrote,

Early twentieth century postcard depicting Queen Elizabeth dancing the volta with the Earl of Leicester. The queen is being lifted by her busk; her hands are positioned to prevent her skirts from flying up.

[I]f you wish to dance the lavolta (volta) ... you must place your right hand on the damsel's back, and the left below her bust, and, by pushing her with your right thigh beneath her buttocks, turn her....[11]

Moralists of the day considered the dance shamelessly obscene because of the suggestive embrace and the revealing glimpses of feminine leg, despite the woman's attempts to keep her flying skirts held down. In his tract, *Gottseliger Tractat von dem ungottseligen Tantz* in 1592, Johan von Münster wrote,

> In this dance the dancer with a leap takes the young lady — who also comes to him with a high jump to the measure of the music — and grasps her in an unseemly place.... With horror I have often seen this dance at the Royal Court of King Henry III in the year 1582, and together with other honest persons have frequently been amazed that such a lewd and unchaste dance, in which the King in person was first and foremost, should be officially permitted and publicly practiced.[12]

Johann Praetorius also denounced the volta in his book *Blocksberg-Verrichtungen*, (*Practices of Witchcraft*), which was published in 1668. He wrote,

> a new galliard, the volta, [is] a foreign dance in which they seize each other in lewd places and which was brought to France by conjurers from Italy.... [It is a] whirling dance full of scandalous, beastly gestures and immodest movements.... [The volta] is also responsible for the misfortune that innumerable murders and miscarriages are brought about by it."[13]

One critic suggested that the volta "...should really be looked into by a well-ordered police force and most strictly forbidden."[14]

The vigorous movements of the volta were considered not only indecent, but also injurious to one's health. In her book, *Dancing Through Time*, dance historian Allison Thompson quotes one eyewitness who pointed out the hazards of dancing the volta. "Some haue broke their legs with skipping, leaping, turning, and vawting."[15] She mentions an archbishop who actually broke his neck while attempting the dance. It was so athletic that "elegant ladies of the court needed to change their under-linen during an evening of court festivities which included the vigorous volta (la volta)."[16]

The volta is believed to have originated in the Provençal courts of southeastern France sometime during the late eleventh to twelfth centuries when troubadours were developing the idea of courtly love.[17] Thoinot Arbeau, who provided the clearest description of the dance, stated that the volta began in Provence, but earlier records spoke of the dance as if it were Italian. The most probable explanation for this disparity is that the French version of the volta migrated to the courts of Northern Italy and was introduced to other courts throughout Europe when the Provençal troubadours[18] fled southern France during the first two decades of the thirteenth century while trying to escape the slaughter of the Albigensian Crusades.[19] It is likely these troubadours took the volta with them as they searched for safety during those turbulent times.

Dance historians are confident that the volta was eventually brought back to France by way of Italy when Catherine de Medici married into the French royal family in the sixteenth century.[20] Her love of dance and her use of French and Italian dancing masters to stage court entertainments resulted in the popularization and documentation of the volta.

Introduced in Paris around 1556, the volta reached the pinnacle of its popularity during the reign of Henri IV (1589–1610). It remained in vogue for about one hundred years, fading out shortly after 1636. The dance was enjoyed by the aristocracy but was not often danced by the common folk. There is conjecture among dance historians that Henri IV's prudish son, Louis XIII (1610–1613), who was heir to the French throne, considered the dance indelicate and therefore forbade its use at court, bringing about the volta's eventual demise.

By the beginning of the 1600's, the volta had grown tamer and had lost its more athletic qualities. Large steps and hops were transformed into smooth, polished glides. As with other dances of this period, the volta became more subtle and dignified, following the smooth manner, or "*douce manier,*" which became "the guiding principle of dance"[21] during this time.

Curt Sachs, in his book *World History of Dance*, points out that as social dances began to change during this time, there were also transformations in dance rhythms. In the first part of the sixteenth century, most dances were performed in 4/4 time, the tourdion, galliard, and volta being the only exceptions. Toward the end of the 1500's, most court dances were altered to 3/4 time. Sachs suggests that these rhythmic changes were dictated by

> the great inclination of the baroque to seek expression rather in breadth than in height. A visit to any picture gallery will show that in the seventeenth-century rooms the broad form appears more frequently than the high form, and that the fashions of this period are wide, full skirts, millstone ruffs, and broad-brimmed Rembrandt hats. The new rhythm is essentially a manifestation of the same tendency.[22]

The volta died out by the middle of the seventeenth century and by the eighteenth century, its exuberant, lusty nature was replaced by the controlled codified formality of the minuet.

The Ländler

The ländler (länderer, länderli, länderische tanz) was one of several alpine, turning folk dances that were popular in Germany, Bavaria, Austria and Bohemia. These couple dances, all performed in a close embrace while rotating, were grouped together under the generic name of *Deutsche* (*deutsche Tänze*) or "German dances." Each type of dance was identified either by the particular aspects of the dance such as the dreher ("spinning top"), weller, spinner (also characterized by turning), or schleifer (sliding), or by a geographical location indicating where the dance was most popular, such as the steirer from Styria or the ländler, which derived its name from *das Landl,* meaning "the little country" referring to *Landl ob der Enns*, the name for upper Austria.

The ländler originated as the last section of a dance called the schuhplattler. The schuhplattler, mentioned in Latin writings as early as 1000 A.D., came from the Tyrolian region in Bavaria. It was part of a distinctive group of dances called "shoe clapping" dances, in which the body was hit percussively to create highly complex syncopated rhythms. Dancers slapped their thighs, knees, buttocks, feet, and cheeks, and hit the leather shorts they traditionally wore, using every possible part of their own anatomy and at times even hitting the other dancers in an effort to create unique sounds. These movements were derived from ancient animal dances and mimicked the mating or fighting of the native Bavarian black grouse. There were two basic versions of the dance: one performed by two men, which symbolized the fighting of two birds, and the second, a male/female version, in which the man imitated a strutting cock, wooing the woman with his dancing.[23] In this couple version, the woman played the demure hen, teasing but also repulsing the man's attentions. Although it was a couple dance, the two partners rarely touched until the very end when the man finally won over the woman with his virtuosity, and they moved together in the waltz-like ländler.

The earliest written reference to such a German courtship dance was in the year 1023 in a poem by Ruodlieb, although couple dances certainly existed well before this date. In his poem, Ruodlieb described how the man courted the woman during the dance, both partners imitating the movements of birds.

The young man jumps up, and towards him moves the girl,
He is like a falcon, and she glides like a swallow.
No sooner are they near to each other than they are already parted.
He tries to grasp her lovingly, but she flies away,
And no-one who watches this couple is able,
In dance, springing and gestures, to better it.[24]

During the ländler, the couple moved together in a slow waltz step. The dance was traditionally performed with the man's hands on the woman's waist and the woman's hands on his shoulders, although the dance contained other figures such as the lady twirling under the man's arm or swerving behind his back. The dance was performed to 3/4 time music, usually to the accompaniment of singing or yodeling, or sometimes to the playing of a fiddle and alpine wind instruments.[25] The lilting melodies and use of wide leaping intervals in the music, especially evident in yodeling, gave rise to deep swinging movements and lifts in the dance. As with the signature movement of the volta, the climax of the original version of the ländler involved the man tossing the woman vigorously in the air before bringing her gently back down to earth at the end of the dance.[26] Dance historians believe this leaping movement originally grew out of

This engraving shows the type of rambunctious couple dance that evolved into the waltz. "Dance of German Peasants." From *A History of Dancing: From the Earliest Ages to Our Own Times* by Gaston Vuillier (1898).

ancient fertility rites and was used to implore the divine to bring a rich harvest. It was believed that the height that the woman's skirt reached as she leaped into the air determined the height to which the corn crop would grow, and therefore, while performing the dance, the man attempted to toss his partner as high as possible.

As with the volta, German folk dances such as the ländler were met with outrage and indignation by the self-proclaimed arbiters of social morality. The close embrace and the rapid turns that left limbs exposed and dancers dizzy were a constant source of controversy. As early as 1404, in Ulm, a ban was imposed upon dancers to prevent them from such intimate contact. It decreed that henceforth couples could only dance in single file. In 1494, Sebastian Brant commented on the immoral nature of turning dances in his satirical poem *Das Narrenschiff*. He wrote,

> There dance the priests and monks and laymen,
> The cowl must also range behind;
> And there they run and whirl about,
> So that one sees their naked legs.[27]

As the Reformation swept Germany, the battle against immoral dancing reached unprecedented proportions.[28] In 1543, clergyman Melchior Ambach published *Von Tantzen/Vrtheil/Ausz heilger Schrifft und den alten Christlichen Lerern gestalt.* In it he wrote," [Dance is] a surrender to lust, a consent to vice, an encouragement to unchastity and a sport that offends all pious persons."[29] An equally violent condemnation came from the Pastor at Schellenwalde, Florian Daule von Fürstenberg, who wrote,

> scandalous, shameless swinging, throwing, turning and allurements of the dance devils, so swiftly and at great height, just as a farmer swings his flail, that the skirts of the damsels, lasses and servant-girls sometimes fly above their girdles or even over their heads.... Those who delight in seeing lewd things are very pleased at such swinging, falling and flying clothes, laugh and are merry, for they see a very pleasant romantic view.[30]

Such protests led to several legal prohibitions. One restriction issued in 1554 declared, "In the evening dances, every one shall refrain entirely from whirling and turning or throwing about the damsel or dancer, and from dancing only in hose and doublet."[31] In Vienna, the city that later became known as the center of the waltz craze, an ordinance was passed in 1572 which warned,

> Ladies and maidens are to compose themselves with chastity and modesty and the male persons are to refrain from whirling and other such frivolities. Whichever man or fellow, woman or maiden will turn immodestly in defiance of this prohibition and warning of the city fathers will be brought to jail.[32]

As late as 1760, attempts were made to ban the ländler. Stern warnings were issued from church pulpits against doing any "German waltzing dances" in the streets, and the bishops of Wurzburg and Fulda issued decrees prohibiting gliding and waltzing. Despite such bans, the waltz grew in popularity. In 1765, the author of *Faust*, Johann Wolfgang von Goethe, "then a student at Strassburg, felt obliged to learn it, for without knowledge of this dance, it was impossible to enter the highest social circles."[33]

The evolution of German peasant dances owes much to the growth of the burgher middle class in Germany. As market towns were developing in the eleventh century along important trade routes, a class of affluent tradesmen began to emerge. By the twelfth century, these wealthy members of society were controlling city affairs and by the thirteenth and fourteenth centuries, were forming powerful guilds. These guilds began to take in members from the upper patrician classes as well as tradesmen and farmers who were gaining in wealth. This middle class of burghers helped the evolution of new cultural expressions during the High Middle Ages, including new dance forms that combined the slow sedate processionals of the upper class with the rustic, energetic turning dances of the peasants. Eventually the sedate parts became more energetic and the turning dances became more refined. These new dances were disseminated throughout Europe through trade-links, and the dances known as *deutsche* to the Germans came to be known outside of Germany as *allemandes*.[34] *Allemande*, meaning "German dance," became a generic term used to describe several types of dances that were popular from the fifteenth until the nineteenth centuries. These dances were believed either to be of German origin or to at least contain characteristics and qualities that were considered German. By the mid–eighteenth century, the term was generally used to denote dances that were done in a close embrace. In 1762, Italian ballet master Giovanni Gallini described such a dance.

> The Germans have a dance called the *Allemande*, in which the men and women form a ring. Each man holding his partner round the waist, makes her whirl round with almost inconceivable rapidity: they dance in a grand circle, seeming to pursue one another: in the course of which they execute several leaps, and some particularly pleasing steps, when they turn, but so very difficult as to appear such even to professed dancers themselves. When this dance is performed by a numerous company, it furnishes one of the most pleasing sights that can be imagined.[35]

The term "*allemande*" was used in many different countries to describe a wide variety of dance movements.[36] One version, popular in Paris in the 1760's and 1770's, was characterized by a series of interlaced hand positions.[37] In this figure, which was later incorporated in many contre-dances, partners moved past each other, passing under their joined hands and turning behind their partner's back. Vestiges of this version of the *allemande* are still part of American square dancing vocabulary as the "allemand right," or "grand right and left."

Towards the middle of the 18th century, another word was brought into general use in reference to peasant spinning dances. The word, *wälzen*, meant "to revolve," "to turn," "to roll" or "to wander," and at first was only used as a descriptive verb.[38] The word eventually began to be used as a present participle describing the spinning movement. Finally, people began to use *wälzen* as the name of the dance itself. The etymology of *wälzen* can be traced to the Old High German *walzan* and the Old Norse *velta* that meant "to turn or to revolve." Its roots come from the Latin *volvere*, to turn around, and *vertere*, to turn.

The Use of Folk Dance by Aristocratic Society

Dance historians point out that the acceptance of folk dance forms by aristocratic society was not unexpected or unusual in German culture. German nobility had used folk music and folk dancing in court entertainments for centuries.[39] Mosco Carner states in his book, *The Waltz,*

> The old Hapsburg monarchy was a feudal State in which the Emperor and the aristocracy owned large estates all over the country. There was thus a close contact between the Austrian peasantry and the ruling classes, and it was inevitable that the music and dances of the peasants should have found their way into the Emperor's palace and the rich mansions of Viennese society.[40]

The tradition of using folk themes in German court entertainments dates to the seventeenth century when the Emperor and his family, dressed in peasant garb, appeared in theatrical productions and acted out scenes from peasant life. These dramatic scenes were interspersed with folk songs and dances such as the ländler.[41] The boisterous ländler, which had been danced by peasants in heavy shoes and boots outside on the ground, was taken over and refined by the nobility, who performed the movements in satin dancing slippers on the polished surface of the drawing room floor.

"The Waltz in the Tyrol" after a lithograph. From *A History of Dancing: From the Earliest Ages to Our Own Times* by Gaston Vuillier (1898).

Another factor that greatly influenced the acceptance of folk dance forms by the upper classes in Germany and elsewhere was the publication in England of John Playford's dance manual, *The Dancing Master*,[42] and the subsequent rise in popularity of English country dancing. First introduced from England to France at the end of the seventeenth century, these country dances spread to Germany soon after.

Playford's collection of folk dances consisted of round dances, couple dances, and dances for eight, but the majority were contre-dances that were usually performed in two facing lines by several dancers. English contre-dancing[43] defied the class-conscious artifice and formal technique of the minuet by introducing figures that intermixed dancers regardless of station. The natural simplicity of the contre-dance steps revitalized social dancing which had stiffened into complex fashion shows and conventionalized expressions of court etiquette[44] with no physical contact other than the slight touch of the fingers from a distance. The contre-dance's democratic approach shattered the hierarchical rigidity of the minuet, and English contre-dancing became all the rage in ballrooms across the Continent.[45]

In an effort to further utilize rural dances as source material, aristocratic society was soon drawn to the energy, vigor, and heady eroticism of the closed couple German spinning dances.[46] Eventually the waltz replaced contre-dancing in popularity in the parlors and drawing rooms of the wealthy. In 1800, J. H. Katfuss wrote,

> [The waltz] has now become such a general favourite and is so fashionable that no one can any longer be reconciled to the English dance without it, for practically all English dances are usually mixed with two turns of the waltz.[47]

The waltz was danced and accepted by all levels of society regardless of rank, pedigree, or income.[48] One Bavarian citizen of the period commented,

> The people here are excessively fond of the pleasure of dancing; they need only hear the music of a waltz to begin to caper, no matter where they are. The public dance floors are visited by all classes; these are the places where ancestors and rank seem to be forgotten and aristocratic pride laid aside. Here we see artisans, artists, merchants, councilors, barons, counts and excellencies dancing together with waitresses, women of middle class, and ladies. Every stranger who stays here for a while is infected by this dance malady.[49]

The waltz became so popular that in March 1792, the *Journal des Luxas und der Moden* informed its readers that "waltzes and nothing but waltzes are now so much in fashion that at dances nothing else is looked at; one need only be able to waltz, and all is well."[50] In 1797, a journalist commented that the waltz "was as common and contagious as a cold in the head."[51]

3

Development and Dispersion of the Waltz

The Romantic Movement

In order to fully understand the pervasive popularity of the waltz, it is necessary to examine this simple social dance in the context of an historical, ideological, and social perspective. At the end of the eighteenth century, a social trend called the Romantic Movement rebelled against the conventional rules, well-ordered symmetry, and emotional restraint that characterized the classicism of the previous era. The Romantic Movement placed emphasis on the spontaneous unpredictability of individual expression. Fostered by the egalitarian ideals of the French Revolution, the primary tenets of Romanticism were

> a return to nature and to the belief in the goodness of man. Most notably expressed by Jean Jacques Rousseau — with the subsequent cult of "the noble savage," attention to the "simple peasant," and admiration of the violently self-centered "hero"; the rediscovery of the artist as a supremely individual creator; the exaltation of the senses and emotions over reason and intellect.[1]

The Romantics believed that art was meant to educate, enlighten, and entertain the masses, not just satisfy the privileged few. Social rank and status no longer dictated participation in the creation or consumption of art. Artistic expression became linked with equality and social justice. Ruth Katz, in her article "The Egalitarian Waltz," stated,

> [Romanticism] enshrined the concept of the uniqueness of individual expression and the struggle against the very principle of tradition, authority and rule. Whereas the pre-revolutionary middle class saw art as one means of expressing identification with the aristocracy and aloofness from the lower classes, in the post-revolutionary period it began to think of art as individualistic and idiosyncratic, a "matter of taste" which might vary among different people, different times and different places.[2]

Artistic expressions no longer had to be sanctioned and legitimized by royal patronage, or validated by the aristocracy. As a rapidly growing middle class struggled to find its identity, art, music, literature, and dance became ways to express rebellion against authority and establish cultural independence.

On the dance floor, the influence of the Romantic Movement was expressed in several different ways. A revolt against the symmetrical formality of the minuet led to a passion for softer curvilinear lines. For proponents of the dance during this period, "...angular lines were condemned and only curves were considered worthy of admiration."[3] In 1821, Thomas Wilson, a prominent dancing master, wrote,

> Straight lines are useful but not elegant; and, when applied to the Human Figure, are productive of extremely ungraceful effect. With persons of taste, and true judges of beauty, the gently flowing Serpentine and Curved Lines, form the acme of grace, and have always been considered most beautiful.[4]

Wilson recommended that dancers should be sure to remember that even presenting a dropped glove to a lady, offering a dance card to be signed, or lifting one's fan were opportunities to demonstrate grace and elegance by doing so with a curved arm.

The principles of Romanticism stressed that dancing was actually an expression of the quality of one's soul, and therefore provided an opportunity to reveal one's nobler sensibilities. Grace, propriety, elegance, and simplicity were all attributes to be admired in the dance. Awkwardness, pretentiousness, and arrogance were looked upon with disdain.

The desire to rediscover the natural, unspoiled, and unaffected led the Romantics to look towards the unembellished purity of by-gone days. They began to delve into their own traditional folk sources. Nationalism flourished.[5] Folk songs became popular, and such peasant dances as the ländler were in demand.

Although this Movement started in the middle classes, the ideals of Romanticism soon began to spread to both a disintegrating aristocracy and an industrial lower class that was gaining power. Barriers that had previously prevented the crossing of class lines were destroyed and those of lower status were granted the same accessibility as those of impeccable pedigree.

The simplicity and freedom inherent in the waltz made it an ideal artistic expression for this ideological milieu. The waltz did not require hours of meticulous study under the guidance of a trained dancing master. Anyone could learn the few basic steps and be free to interpret the dance as he or she saw fit. The waltz was truly a "revolutionary" dance that provided all classes an opportunity to prove worth based upon skill, not upon rank in society. "The beautiful commoner, if she waltzed very well, would be invited to dance with the prince."[6] The waltz became the great equalizer.

> The dancers surrender their worldly identities upon entering the "society of the dance" where individuals take on new roles and where recognition is accorded not by virtue of one's status in the larger society, but by virtue of one's performance in the dance.... The emphasis is on the participation of all, and on the equality of all, while rewarding achievement within the dance itself rather than status one brings to the dance from "the world outside."[7]

The Vienna Congress

The potency of the waltz as a symbol of a new society was reflected at the Vienna Congress, held in the Austrian capital from September 1814 to June 1815. Over one hundred thousand foreigners including six sovereigns and more than seven hundred diplomats, along with their families, domestic staffs, secretariats, courtiers, and camp followers, descended upon Vienna for one of the most important international political gatherings in the history of Europe.[8] The Congress opened with a series of lavish balls and for the remainder of the assembly, the waltz reigned supreme.

To foreigners not yet familiar with the new dance craze and its scandalously intimate embrace, the impropriety of the waltz must have seemed intimidating. Yet despite these misgivings, representatives knew that to succeed in the delicate negotiations of the Vienna Congress they had to participate in the endless round of balls and entertainments that dominated the affair. Viscount Castlereagh, the foreign minister of Britain, hired a dancing master to teach him the waltz and rehearsed with a chair as his partner when his wife wasn't available.

As political intrigue and international rivalries stalled the critical business of dividing and reapportioning Europe after the first defeat of Napoleon,[9] competitions sprang up to ascertain which governmental delegation could give the most lavish and impressive ball. Princess Catherine Bagration, the mistress of the Russian Czar, arranged for a select gathering of only two hundred of the most elite at her brilliant ball.[10] The Emperor of Austria, Francis I, and his wife,

Maria Ludovica, hosted one memorable gathering at the palace for as many as ten thousand guests.[11] Although he had to raise taxes by fifty per cent in order to defray the cost of such lavish entertainments, the Emperor and his wife continued to give balls at the Hofburg palace at least once a week until Lent.[12] The saying of the day became, *"le Congrès ne marche pas, il danse,"* meaning "the Congress doesn't advance, it dances."[13]

The Vienna Congress provided perhaps the most effective propaganda for the waltz. The dance spread rapidly through the Continent as the huge number of diplomats and their staff returned home and carried the rage of Vienna back to the capitals of Europe.[14] Despite many vehement protests against it, the waltz was almost universally adopted by high society and its conquest of the fashionable world was virtually guaranteed. The pervasive feeling among devotees of the dance was "One need only be able to waltz and everything is all right."[15]

Dancing Palaces

The waltz's wide appeal led to the demand for appropriate dancing venues, and soon assembly halls were converted into ballrooms, and new dancing palaces sprang up across the Conti-

A dancing master plays for a waltzing couple. The title of the engraving indicates the passion with which society took to the new dance. "The Fashionable Mania," after Carle Vernet. From *A History of Dancing: From the Earliest Ages to Our Own Times* by Gaston Vuillier (1898).

nent. Perhaps the most opulent were erected in the birthplace of the waltz — Vienna. The ball-rooms there were unequaled in splendor and size, and "...the rivalry between these establishments became so acute that audacious directors spent considerable sums on satisfying the taste for luxury which they themselves had rashly aroused in their patrons."[16]

The Mondschein Hall was one such famous ballroom.[17] Used for dancing as early as 1772, at first waltz parties at the Mondschein were prohibited by police because of the immodest nature of the dance. Despite these early restrictions, the Mondschein eventually became one of the most popular places for dancing during the height of the waltz craze in Vienna. Playwright Adolph Bäuerle described a typical night of waltzing there.

> The Mondschein Hall made an immortal name for itself by the mortality of young people dancing nothing but the *langaus* [a frenzied two-step version of the waltz]. It was the fashion to be a daring dancer. The man had to waltz his partner from one end of the hall to the other with the greatest possible speed.... The circle had to be made six or eight times at a breathless pace with no pause. Each couple tried to outdo the others, and it was no rare thing for an apoplexy of the lungs to end the madness.[18]

The Sophia was named after the Archduchess Sophia and was first built as a Russian steam bath. Later a swimming pool was added and then a magnificent ballroom and concert hall. The ballroom was so large that police attempted to shut it down for fear the ceiling would collapse. The owner, Franz Morawetz, petitioned the Emperor and received imperial permission to open the dancing palace. The ceiling that had so worried authorities did cause a surprise at the first waltz — it opened and thousands of rose petals were showered down upon the astonished crowd.

The Sperl,[19] which opened in 1807, was another well-known dancing palace. The ballroom there was so large that one end of the room was barely visible from the other. "At Sperl's there were soft rugs, palm trees, flowers, mirrors, a dining room 'with many hundreds of candles,' a winter-garden, and a large park."[20] In 1833 Heinrich Laube wrote, "An evening and half the night at Sperl's is the key to Vienna's sensuous life, which means Vienna's life."[21] A venue for many of the city's most important balls, Joseph Lanner and Johann Strauss I often played there.[22] The Sperl eventually became the artistic home of Strauss and the site where he premiered many of his waltzes. Heinrich Laube, who frequented the establishment during the heyday of the waltz, recounted his memories of an evening at Sperl's.

> In the middle of the garden on the orchestra platform there stands the modern hero of Austria, *le Napoléon Autricheien*, the musical director, Johann Strauss. The Strauss waltzes are to the Viennese what Napoleonic victories were to the French....[23]

The Tivoli Pleasure Gardens, which opened in September of 1830, was another popular spot for waltzing. The gardens contained a spectacular colonnaded dancing pavilion that overlooked all of Vienna. One of the added attractions at the Tivoli was a toboggan-like chute with four tracks that allowed sixteen carriage-type cars mounted on sledges to speed excited patrons up and down. Johann Strauss I wrote a waltz entitled the "Tivoli Slide Waltz" to commemorate the roller coaster–like ride, and humorously featured in his music a sliding effect a few bars before the coda. The popularity of the pleasure gardens led to such souvenirs as Tivoli hats, Tivoli watches, and even Tivoli rockets.[24]

The Dianabad was originally an indoor swimming pool, the first such in all of Europe. During the winter months the pool was covered over with a large dancing floor. The Dianabad grew more popular after the mid–nineteenth century as other more opulent dancing palaces had closed. On February 13, 1867 the younger Johann Strauss premiered a number there sung by the Vienna Men's Choral Society. The waltz, although not a complete failure, did not meet with the same public adulation that usually greeted the composer's work. Strauss commented, "The waltz was probably not catchy enough."[25] The piece, entitled *The Blue Danube*, later became Strauss' most famous and successful piece.

The largest and most magnificent pleasure dome was the Apollo Hall, the center of the waltz craze in Vienna from 1808–1812.[26] The Apollo had five large ballrooms and forty-four other public rooms, in addition to three glasshouses, thirteen kitchens, an artificial waterfall, a lake with live swans, and flowers and trees that bloomed year round. Everything in the Apollo was done on a grand scale.[27] One chandelier in the dining room held 5,000 candles. The musicians were tastefully hidden so that as the elite of Vienna swirled around the floor, the melodic strains of the waltz seemed to float down from the sky itself. Opened on January 10, 1808 to celebrate the engagement of the Emperor Francis I to his third wife, Princess Maria Ludovica d'Este, the Apollo Palace could accommodate up to 5,000 patrons.[28] The entrance fee for the inaugural soirée was 25 guilders, an exorbitant sum in those days. The dancing hall catered to the wealthiest citizens of Vienna, and it was not unusual to see gentlemen there lighting their cigarettes with hundred-guilder notes. There was no lack of willing dance partners at the luxurious Apollo Hall, well known as the best place to find the highest-paid prostitutes.

Dances were also given at the imperial palace. At the Hofburg, when masquerade balls were given each year at Carnival time, special birthing chambers were set aside for woman who were pregnant but did not want to miss the chance to waltz. Irish singer Michael Kelly told of this obsession to waltz in his book *Reminiscences* published in 1826. He wrote,

> The people of Vienna were in my time dancing mad ... the propensity of the Vienna ladies for dancing and going to carnival masquerades was so determined, that nothing was permitted to interfere with their enjoyment of their favourite enjoyment — nay, so notorious was it that for the sake of the ladies in the family way, who could not be persuaded to stay at home, there were apartments prepared, with every convenience for their accouchement, should they be unfortunately required.[29]

In the spring of 1832 alone, at least 200,000 people attended the several hundred balls that were given in Vienna. This was half the population of the city, including infants and the elderly. Tens of thousands more waited outside for hours just to watch attendees arrive.

The Waltz in England

Dance scholars conjecture that the waltz was first introduced in England around 1790, and was regarded primarily as a country dance. Often inserted as an embellishment to contre-dances or cotillions,[30] this form of the waltz involved the intertwining of arms in the old allemande style and did not yet utilize the embrace that later sparked such vehement reaction from the more prudish elements of society. The closed position version of the waltz did not appear in England until the second decade of the nineteenth century. The dance was probably brought there by aristocrats who had traveled to the Continent, seen the latest fad during their travels, and returned home to share it with their fellow members of society. In all likelihood, the English waltz came by way of France,[31] even though the two countries were at war with each other at the time. The dance is first documented as being performed at Almack's Assembly Rooms in London around 1812.

At first the English were extremely reticent to accept the scandalous dance, yet "...in the course of time, the waltzing mania, having turned the heads of society in general, descended to their feet, and the waltz was practiced in the morning in certain noble mansions in London with unparalleled assiduity."[32]

The dance only gained widespread public notoriety after one of the leading trendsetters of London society, Countess Lieven, the wife of the Russian ambassador, created a huge sensation

"A Ball Under the First Empire" after an engraving by Bosio in the Bibliothéque Nationale. From *A History of Dancing: From the Earliest Ages to Our Own Times* by Gaston Vuillier (1898).

by dancing the German novelty at Almack's in the summer of 1814 during festivities to celebrate Napoleon's defeat.[33]

Almack's Assembly Rooms

Almack's was "the seventh heaven of the fashionable world"[34] and the most exclusive gathering place in London. All polite society aspired to be part of the entertainments there.[35] Admission to balls was strictly regulated by a committee of seven women,[36] who instituted the practice of holding exclusive balls every Wednesday night during the Season.[37] The women, Lady Castlereagh, Lady Cowper, Lady Sefton, Mrs. Drummond-Burrell, Princess Esterhazy, Countess Lieven, and Lady Jersey, who headed the council, maintained absolute control over the proceedings, including who would receive tickets to the grand affairs, what the attendees would wear, what time the ball would start, and, for young ladies, who their dancing partners would be. An introduction to one of the patronesses and her approbation was mandatory for any who wished access to the ultra-fashionable establishment. Only a privileged few were admitted, and the women made sure that Almack's remained a place "into whose sanctum the sons of commerce never intrude."[38] Tickets were so hard to come by that three-fourths of English nobility was denied entrance. In his memoir *The Reminiscences and Recollections of Captain Gronow*, the Grenadier Guard reported,

> Many diplomatic arts, much finesse, and a host of intrigues, were set in motion to get an invitation to Almack's. Very often persons whose rank and fortunes entitled them to entrée anywhere

else were excluded by the cliqueism of the lady patronesses; for the female government of Almack's was a pure despotism and subject to all the caprices of despotic rule: it is needless to add that, like every other despotism, it was not innocent of abuses.[39]

The seven patronesses of Almack's exercised stringent control and insisted that their every rule was obeyed to the letter. They were so powerful in London society that even the Duke of Wellington, the popular national hero who had vanquished Napoleon at Waterloo, was refused admission on two separate occasions: once when he arrived in black trousers instead of knee breeches, and once when he was seven minutes late to a ball.[40]

It is no wonder that the introduction of the waltz at the most exclusive venue in the city, danced by Countess Lieven, one of the patronesses of Almack's, guaranteed that all of London would take notice. Although the waltz began to appear more frequently at balls in London after being given the stamp of approval from the powerful and influential Madame de Lieven,[41] not all of England embraced the naughtily intoxicating dance. In the summer of 1816, *The Times* commented with horror on the inclusion of a waltz at a ball given by the Prince Regent.

> We remarked with pain that the indecent foreign dance called the "waltz" was introduced (we believe for the first time) at the English Court on Friday last. This is a circumstance which ought not to be passed over in silence. National morals depend on national habits: and it is quite sufficient to cast one's eyes on the voluptuous intertwining of the limbs and close compressure of the bodies, in their dance, to see that it is indeed far removed from the modest reserve which have hitherto been considered distinctive of English females. So long as this obscene display was confined to prostitutes and adulteresses we did not think it deserving of notice; but now that it is attempted to be forced upon the respectable classes of society by the evil example of their superiors, we feel it a duty to warn every parent against exposing his daughter to so fatal a contagion.... We owe a due reference to superiors in rank, but we owe a higher duty to morality. We know not how it happened (probably by recommendation of some worthless and ignorant French dancing master) that so indecent a dance has now for the first time been exhibited at the English Court; but the novelty is one deserving of severe reprobation, and we trust it will never be tolerated in any moral English society.[42]

One particularly vocal opponent of the waltz was the Romantic poet, Lord Byron. In his sarcastic poem "The Waltz; An Apostrophic Hymn," published in 1816[43] under the pseudonym Horace Hornem, Esq., Byron presents strong arguments against the waltz's promiscuous nature. Near the end of his poem he writes,

> But ye — who never felt a single thought
> For what our morals are to be, or ought;
> Who wisely wish the charms you view to reap,
> Say — would you make those beauties quite so cheap?
> Hot from the hands promiscuously applied,
> Round the slight waist, or down the glowing side,
> Where were the rapture then to clasp the form
> From this lewd grasp and lawless contact warm?[44]

Historians have conjectured that perhaps Lord Byron's opposition to the waltz was also colored by the fact that he was born with a clubfoot and was therefore unable to enjoy the dance himself.[45]

There were several proponents of the dance in England. Thomas Wilson, a dancing master who wrote several popular dance manuals, strongly proclaimed the efficacy of the waltz.[46] In his book, *A Description of the Correct Manner of Waltzing*,[47] published in 1816, he reassured his readers that the waltz was "generally admitted to be a great promoter of vigorous health and productive of an hilarity of spirits." He explained that the waltz, as danced in the cooler climate of England by persons with self-control, did not have the same "attitudes and movements" that made it questionable in "warmer and lighter climates." Therefore, he declared, the English waltz was "not an enemy of true morals."[48]

Queen Victoria

In 1837, with the death of her uncle King William IV, eighteen-year-old Victoria Alexandrina was crowned Queen of Great Britain and Ireland, and Empress of India, thus ushering in the period of history most associated with the waltz — the Victorian age.

In preparation for her future role in society, Victoria had received weekly lessons as a young girl in the art of dancing. She attended her first public dance at age fourteen at a juvenile ball given in honor of her birthday by her uncle the King at St. James' Palace. Her dancing instructor, Madame Boudin, was present to guarantee that the young Princess made no mistakes.[49]

The princess continued regular dancing lessons and was thrilled at the age of sixteen when her German cousins visited England because etiquette demanded that a princess only dance with other members of royal blood. Victoria was finally able to practice her waltzing with a male partner.

Two years later, Victoria's coronation festivities included three State balls. The opening ball had music provided by Johann Strauss himself, who composed a special waltz that included the strains of "God Save the Queen." The new Queen had to be content to watch while others waltzed that evening. Even though the gathering comprised the aristocratic elite of London, "there was still no arm fit to encircle the Queen's waist in a waltz."[50] The celebrations surrounding Victoria's ascension to the throne in 1837 and her marriage to Prince Albert[51] a few years later included a flurry of parties and balls. Costume balls were a particularly popular staple of

"A Group of Waltzers" from a print of the restoration period. From *A History of Dancing: From the Earliest Ages to Our Own Times* by Gaston Vuillier (1898).

high society during this period, and elaborate disguises were used to add a sense of mystery and excitement to an evening's entertainment.[52] Queen Victoria herself gave many fancy dress balls. In 1842, she and her husband Prince Albert gave a Plantagenet Ball and the couple appeared in costume as Queen Philippa and Edward III. Victoria wore a jeweled bodice studded in diamonds valued at over 60,000 pounds. She stayed in the ballroom dancing until quarter to three in the morning. In 1845, the royal couple gave a Royal Costume Ball and guests were required to arrive in outfits from the period between 1740–1750. In 1851, they held a Restoration Ball.

The Queen's love of dancing sparked a renewed interest in dancing among the social elite and created a favorable environment for the introduction of new dances. There was also a simultaneous surge in interest in the folk cultures of Central Europe, especially Poland. These forces combined and soon a dance that had originated in Bohemia found its way to England via France. This dance was the polka,[53] and although for a while polka mania swept the world, it could not replace the waltz in overall lasting popularity.[54]

Throughout her reign, Queen Victoria maintained a love of dancing, and it was said she was especially enamored with the waltz. In particular, the Queen loved waltzing with her husband Prince Albert who was recognized by all as an expert dancer. From the beginning of Victoria's long reign and during her idyllic marriage to the German Prince Albert, society witnessed a growing trend towards sentimentality and an idealistic regard for women. It was a commonly held belief during this period that only the pious, virtuous qualities of woman, in the form of a wife, mother or sister, could overcome the baser qualities of indelicate, uncouth, insensitive man. These ideas spilled over into the ballroom where it was believed that correct dancing and proper etiquette allowed a woman to exert her influence over a man's baser qualities. There was a deluge of courtesy literature that suggested that dancing "develops the inherent power of the female sex, when clothed with the polite accomplishments, to correct and reform ... restoring man to his original dignity and usefulness"[55]

This Victorian sentimentality was also tempered by a strict view of morality; with the rise of literature supporting the value of dancing, an equal number of tracts appeared denouncing it as a breeding ground for improper passions and an opportunity for rash extravagance.

The Waltz in the United States

The waltz made its initial appearance in the United States around 1790, the same year it was first seen in England, but as in England, it did not really gain the public's full attention until after the turn of the century. Some sources state that the waltz was first performed by Lorenzo Papanti[56] in 1834 at a demonstration given at Mrs. Harrison Gray Otis' Beacon Hill mansion in Boston, Massachusetts.[57] According to some accounts, Boston society was shocked by the "indecorous exhibition."[58] Papanti (sometimes spelled Papatino) was a successful dancing master who taught the children of Boston's elite. He was described as "a tall, skeleton thin, fiery tempered Italian Count."[59] In *Boston and the Boston Legend*, Lucius Beebe states, "All good Boston children went to Papanti's, where his lean figure, glossy wig and elegant patent leather dancing pumps, and above all his pointed fiddle-bow, used both as an instrument of correction and harmony, struck terror to all juvenile hearts."[60]

Around the turn of the century, as the structure of society began to change, social dancing in the United States began to evolve. Strongly influenced by an influx of French dancing masters who fled to America after the French Revolution, new forms of dance, such as the contre-dance, began to appear and older forms, such as the gavotte, minuet, and cotillion fell out of vogue. By the mid–nineteenth century, the quadrille and the waltz had replaced the contre-dance in popularity.

Believed to be a depiction of Papanti's Ballroom at 23 Tremont Street, in Boston. From the music cover "Tremont Quadrilles," Henry Prentiss publisher, no date.

Until the middle of the nineteenth century, standards for theatrical dancing and social dancing were not separated into different categories. A person who studied social dancing with a dancing master was classically trained in the ballet arts and learned specific, intricate choreography for each dance. This type of training was reserved for the elite few who had enough money and free time to take lessons; as a result, dancing masters prospered under the patronage of the wealthy. With the disruption of class structures during the nineteenth century, this system changed and the dance teacher's livelihood was threatened.

The growth of the mail order business and advancements in transportation, such as the invention of the steamboat, and the rapid expansion of the railroad system, fostered widespread dissemination of dance paraphernalia. Ready-made ball-gowns, shoes, ballroom decorations, and dance manuals were now available to a wide cross-section of citizens. The growing accessibility of printed instructional guides compounded the threat to the normal functions of a personal teacher.

In response, dancing masters searched for new ways to approach the teaching of dance. Starting around 1840, American dance instructors began to realize that the rapidly growing population in urban areas included a large middle-class that was not only seeking entertainment, but also looking for ways to advance socially. Dance teachers saw promising commercial opportunities in this expanding part of the population. They redirected their focus away from the technical aspects of dancing, and they began to stress how dancing could be used as a civilizing and educational pastime. "To expand their clientele, dance teachers began to emphasize the moral, physically corrective, and novel aspects of their arts ... [showing that] learning to control the parts of the body was morally valuable...."[61] Dancing masters now stressed that proper protocol in tandem with sufficient training could create "morality in motion."[62]

Dancing masters banded together to form professional trade groups that worked to codify social dance forms such as the waltz. These unions hoped that by setting uniform standards they could insure a steady stream of future students who would need to be well-tutored in the morally correct and proper styles.

Developments in American Social Dancing

In the United States, four important trends took place after the end of the Civil War that influenced the development of social dancing. First, as mentioned earlier, dance teachers professionalized, forming trade organizations to foster their cause. In 1879, The American Society of Professors of Dancing was founded, and four years later, The American National Association of Masters of Dancing, United States and Canada, was formed. A third trade organization, The Western Association Normal School, Masters of Dancing, was founded in 1894. These groups provided an aura of acceptability and legitimacy to social dancing. Members worked hard to eradicate the onus attached to such dances as the waltz. They were largely responsible for the spread of the dance in America and the eventual acceptance of the waltz as valid aesthetic expression.

The second trend was the introduction of physical education programs into public schools. This innovation came about from an increasing interest in educational methods sparked by the Chautauqua Movement.

Started in upstate New York in 1874 as an outgrowth of a proposal presented at a Methodist Episcopal camp meeting, the Chautauqua Movement was a powerful forum for discussing and improving educational principles and methods. The initial proposal, introduced by John Heyl Vincent and Louis Miller, suggested that secular as well as religious instruction be included in the summer Sunday school. This simple suggestion developed into an eight-week summer institute that offered courses in the arts and humanities and attracted thousands of participants.

The Chautauquans offered home study courses for those who could not attend in person, and eventually the Movement grew to include community organizations across the country. The Movement fostered educational reforms and sponsored a series of touring lectures by leading artists, politicians, and authors. In 1886, the Chautauqua School of Physical Education was founded by William G. Anderson, and provided courses to physical education teachers in a codified and stylized movement curriculum. The Chautauqua Movement brought an increased awareness of the healthful, moral benefits of dancing and helped to bring about the integration of dance into the American educational system.

The third trend involved an increasing emphasis on the use of posture and gesture in the study of elocution and a growing appreciation of physical expressions. These things were aided by the introduction of the Delsarte System to America.

Created by French acting and singing teacher Françoise Delsarte (1811–1871), the Delsarte System consisted of a set of rules and principles of dramatic gestures that coordinated the voice with the body. Officially called "Applied Aesthetics," the two basic cornerstones of Delsarte's philosophy were the Law of Correspondence and the Law of Trinity. The Law of Correspondence stated, "...to each spiritual function responds a function of the body; to each grand function of the body corresponds a spiritual act." The Law of the Trinity in Delsarte's own words was, "...the unity of three things, each of which is essential to the other two, each co-existing in time, co-penetrating in space, and co-operative in motion."[63]

"The Waltz" after Gavarni. From *A History of Dancing: From the Earliest Ages to Our Own Times* by Gaston Vuillier (1898).

The Delsartian System was introduced to America by Steele MacKaye, who added exercises of his own that he called "Harmonic Gymnastics."[64] The popularity of these exercises quickly spread across the United States, and a growing number of Americans began advocating their use as a means to improve one's health and posture, and add to one's natural grace.

In the 1890's, many women's colleges offered classes in Delsarte's techniques, paving the way for the inclusion of dancing as a part of their curriculum as well. More and more, the modern woman of the day was expected to put on her bloomers and improve herself by learning Aesthetic movement.

When Delsarte's teachings were all the rage in the United States, a host of products bearing his name came out including Delsarte corsets, Delsarte cosmetics, Delsarte gowns, and even a Delsarte wooden leg. The System had many followers, including Emma Dennis, mother of modern dance pioneer, Ruth St. Denis. Modern dance icon Ted Shawn suggests that the principles of Delsarte underlie all of American modern dance.

The last trend to influence social dancing in nineteenth century America was a revival of nostalgic dances and a renewed interest in dances from other countries. A growing appreciation of America as a melting pot of cultures led many educational reformers to advocate the teaching of folk and national dances in schools. Dance was legitimized as it was included in the American educational system. This acceptance sparked a renaissance in social dancing. More and more Americans began to see dance as a viable form of emotional and interpretive expression.[65] The cries of critics remained unabated, but the popularity of social dancing continued to grow.

As Americans struggled to establish a national identity and create national norms, cultural stereotypes resulted which emphasized correct outward displays of the body. Conformity to these notions in dress, manner, and attitude was seen as a sign of good character; deviation from them was seen as uncouth and improper. Controlled body movements were prized as attributes of a civilized, moral person.

> Physical expressions of moral lessons were also acted out in real life by assigning body movements certain cultural meaning. Restrictions of movements (such as that between the rib cage and pelvis, thus presenting the torso as a single unit) and the rigid prescription of gender roles (for example, stereotypical ways that men physically displayed strength and independence and that women exhibited dependency) affected how dancing was perceived and to be performed. Clothing proper to the occasion of dancing supported preferred body movement patterns.[66]

The Boston Waltz

One version of the waltz that became particularly associated with the United States was the Boston Waltz,[67] or Boston Dip, a popular form of the valse à deux.[68] During the Boston Waltz, dancers did a slight dip or plié and then held the second and third beats of the measure. Prominent dancing instructor, Melvin Ballou Gilbert explained the beginnings of the dance:

> [The Dip] was originated by the late Russ B. Walker, in December 1870, and christened "Glissade Waltz." Harvard men were among its first patrons, and directly it was called the "Cambridge Waltz," and retained it soubriquet during its first season. The sinking or dipping movement accompanied the forward and backward step in each measure, and shortly after its popularity became established, extreme dipping became general, being carried to that extent which savored of vulgarity....[69]

In his book *The Boston Dip*, published in 1871, Fred W. Loring reported his impression of the dance in verse form. He wrote,

An early twentieth century Italian postcard by Giovanni Nanni entitled "Valse Boston."

The progress of society
Is ever on the stride;
Bar-rooms are generally closed,
Policemen have no pride;
And though we have not reached the point
When bolts are laid aside,
Yet the giddy and immoral waltz
Has ceased fore'er to glide.

No more do dancers float along,
They frantically skip;
They tumble as if sick upon
A very buoyant ship;
The gentle clasp around the waist
Has now become a grip,
And round and round the couples bob, —
It is the Boston Dip.

One way to dance it thoroughly
Is much champagne to sip;
Or, — rub your boots with orange peel
Till they are sure to slip;
Or, — imitate a horse
When startled by a whip, —
In all these ways you'll meet success,
When you attempt the Dip.[70]

Even though most professional dancing masters thought the Boston Dip somewhat vulgar, and not true waltzing,[71] they realized that the majority of the American public found it irresistible. In the January, 1898 issue of *The Director*, the editors commented, "The Dip still continues to be popular, and a refusal, on the part of a dancing master, to properly teach it, resembles a case of a man 'biting off his nose to spite his face.'"[72]

The Boston Dip is credited with being the first waltz performed with parallel feet, a departure from the balletic turnout that had characterized all other prior styles of formal social dancing. The turning in of the feet and the constant dipping were significant innovations in social dancing, and foreshadowed ragtime dances like the turkey trot and bunny hug that later became the rage during the first decades of the twentieth century. However, because the Boston stopped the flow of traffic on the dance floor and also took up more space, it eventually faded from the spotlight and most Victorian dancers returned to the original Viennese valse à trois temps.

4

---·-·-·-·-·---

Fashion and Music of the Waltz

During a century of waltzing, ladies' fashions changed frequently from decade to decade. Fashion magazines from Paris, as well as books on etiquette and deportment, clearly defined what to wear, when to wear it, and the vital importance of dressing correctly. Strict adherence to the rules of style reinforced a person's place in the social structure.

While the Vienna Congress was being held, the fashion of the day dictated that women wear gowns made of thin, gauzy material that clung to the body. These diaphanous, form-fitting, columnar dresses were gathered under the breasts in the French Empire style and were often slit up to the thigh with only the thinnest shifts underneath them. Following the Romantic aesthetic, dancing dresses presented a natural, casual look to underscore the delicate, feminine qualities of a woman. Freed from the constraint of panniers and the heavy formal costumes of the previous century, these new styles allowed much greater freedom on the dance floor.

Although fashions during the first two decades of the nineteenth century were designed to imitate the flowing drapery of Greek or Roman statues, most women continued the practice of wearing corsets to assist them in achieving a thinner silhouette. Many of the ankle-length gowns of this period still had trains or demi-trains, but etiquette books of the day discouraged them for dancing dresses because they were "too cumbrous an appendage to dance."[1]

Despite the apparent simplicity of such ball-gowns, the actual cost of these garments and the jewels that adorned them was enormous. Viennese dressmakers scrambled to provide a seemingly endless supply of new outfits as the Congress progressed; even the very wealthy became concerned about the extravagance. One police agent who reported on the proceedings commented, "Ladies cannot manage on their ordinary budgets, and husbands are already reduced to adding another sizable deficit to their accounts."[2]

For men during this period, trousers gradually replaced knee breeches except at official court functions—an innovation that afforded greater freedom of movement on the dance floor.[3] Men's fashions remained fairly static through the remainder of the century with only minor alterations in form, although gentlemen were expected to follow the latest dictates of style however subtle. In 1836, *The Laws of Etiquette* stressed the importance of dressing properly, warning gentlemen that they must be careful to avoid any faux pas when dressing. The author advised his readers, "Before going to a ball or party it is not sufficient that you consult your mirror twenty times. You must be personally inspected by your servant or a friend."[4]

In the first decades of the nineteenth century, wigs were abandoned in favor of natural hair, carefully and meticulously modeled after Greek or Roman hairstyles. For both men and women, footwear became lighter with lower, less precarious heels. Most women's shoes for the first two decades of the century were flat and made out of satin, silk, or soft, supple leather. A conscientious lady often took extra pairs of slippers with her to a ball because the first pair rarely survived much dancing. One etiquette manual of the day reminded readers, "the massacre of one's shoes had to be borne with stoicism."[5] When the Empress Josephine discovered a hole in one of her dancing slippers after only one wearing and complained to her shoemaker, he responded, "Ah I see what the problem is, Madame, you have walked in them."[6]

From the 1820's to the 1830's, the waistlines of women's dresses gradually dropped; skirts became fuller and longer with numerous petticoats underneath; and large commodious sleeves were attached to a form-fitting bodice. Women wore short, heavily boned corsets that cinched the waist tightly. As the 1830's moved into the 1840's, a growing number of etiquette books warned of the dangers of lacing one's corset too tightly.[7] *The Art of Good Behavior* (1845) stated, "No woman who laces tight can have good shoulders, a straight spine, good lungs, sweet breath or is fit to be wife or mother."[8] One Englishman commenting on the current fashions wrote,

> The Parisian fashions of the day are carried out to their extreme, detestably ugly as they are. Really the modern European (and American) costume gives a woman the appearance of something between a trussed fowl and an hour-glass ... she is compressed in the waist, and puffed out above and below it, to such an extreme that one expects her to break off in the middle at the slightest touch.[9]

As the nineteenth century reached its midpoint, skirts continued to increase in size with several stiffened petticoats underneath providing a bell-like shape to the garment. The lines of these dancing dresses were intentionally kept simple, and fashion dictated minimal ornamentation that was "meant to symbolize the inner purity and sincerity of the wearer."[10] Despite this attempt at simplicity, women were often not able to dress themselves; bodice and sleeve designs and binding corsets inhibited arm movement. In the 1850's and 1860's, skirt size continued to expand, at times reaching a circumference of more than twenty feet. The bottoms of ball gowns

"The Waltz" after a lithograph by J. David. From *A History of Dancing: From the Earliest Ages to Our Own Times*" by Gaston Vuillier (1898).

were only prevented from dragging on the floor by an ever-increasing number of petticoats, supported by crinoline hoops.[11]

Crinolines began to flatten in the front during the 1860's, and emphasis was placed on adding extra fabric to the back of the dress. Smaller hoops were sometimes employed instead of full crinolines to lift only the back portion of the dress. This development eventually led to the advent of the bustle and the popularity of long trains around the 1870's, and provided new challenges for dancers.[12] Etiquette books suggested that perhaps a lady might want to forgo strict adherence to this latest fashion trend rather than risk tearing her dress while dancing. Further warning was given to the gentleman to avoid stepping on a lady's gown at all costs, and to be aware that assisting a woman with holding her dress up while dancing was a serious breach of decorum.

Throughout the Victorian period, gentlemen were expected to wear white gloves while dancing so that their hands wouldn't stain a ladies dress with perspiration.[13] Etiquette recommended that they carry an extra pair in case the first became soiled. The true gentleman would never offer his hand to one of the fairer sex with less than pristine gloves.[14]

Women also always wore gloves to every ball; in fact, a language of glove flirtations developed in which a lady could convey the most complex communications to a man through delicate gestures with her gloves. For example, biting the tips of gloves signified, "I wish to be rid of you very soon." Twisting them around the fingers meant, "Be careful, we are being watched." There also was an equally complex language utilizing fans, handkerchiefs, and parasols.[15]

When attending a ball, the proper Victorian woman required a number of accessories and accoutrements. These articles always included a dance card with attached writing pencil. Each dance card listed the order of dances for the evening along with the composer, with spaces beside each number for listing the lady's partner for that particular dance. The dance card came in a variety of shapes and sizes, and each had a decorative cord attached to allow it to hang down the front of a lady's skirt and free her hands for dancing. The admission to balls in Vienna was always higher for women than for men in order to cover the cost of manufacturing these *ballspenden,* as they were called in Austria.

Another common accessory for a lady attending a dance was a skirt-lifter, a tong-like apparatus that was attached by a string to the waistband of her dress. The skirt lifter had a metal clip that was used to grab the hemline of the skirt and to manage her train. A lady also often carried a hand cooler, a chilled glass egg that was held to prevent unsightly and unfeminine sweaty palms and to avert "passing fevers." Another common accessory was the posy holder, or *bouquetier,* a small container for flowers that was either worn on the hand by means of an attached ring, or released and suspended on a delicate chain down the skirt. The wide variety of posy holders ranged from those that were mass-produced to specially commissioned ones made out of precious metals and jewels. Nosegays were commonly used to ward off unpleasant odors and as a means of covert communication. As with fans, parasols, and gloves, there developed a Victorian language of flowers; each variety of flower signified a different meaning, explained in one of the many floral dictionaries available at the time. For example, roses signified love, whereas ivy meant only friendship. *Collier's Cyclopedia of Commercial and Social Information and Treasury of Useful and Entertaining Knowledge* from 1882 explained,

> Flowers have a language of their own, and it is this bright particular language that we would teach our readers. How charmingly a young gentleman can speak to a young lady, and with what eloquent silence in this delightful language. How delicately she can respond, the beautiful little flowers telling her tale in perfumed words; what a delicate story the myrtle or the rose tells! How unhappy that which basil, or yellow rose reveals, while ivy is the most faithful of all.[16]

Complex conversations were held with simply the exchange of flowers. A bouquet of amethyst, meadow lychnis, and moss rosebud signified, "You're so clever! I admit, I love you!"

whereas one composed of vine, great bindweed, common almond, and mimosa meant, "You were drunk and misled me. How thoughtless of you! I can't handle such behavior."

In her fascinating book, *From the Ballroom to Hell: Grace and Folly in Nineteenth-century Dance*, dance historian Elizabeth Aldrich points out that there was a direct correlation between fashions created for dancing and the dance itself. She writes,

> At the end of the eighteenth century skirts were full and the tempo of the waltz was rapid. The tempo slowed down after the first years of the nineteenth century and a lady's dress was tubular and narrow. The slower tempo of the "Slow Waltz," described by Thomas Wilson in 1816, complemented the architecture of the narrow skirts. Fuller skirts, which began appearing at the end of the teens and reached their height of fullness in the fashions of the 1830s through the early 1860s, paralleled the increasing tempo of the waltz and also complemented the circular nature of the whirling dance. As full skirts gave way to the trains and bustles of the later 1860s through 1880s, whirling rapid circles yielded to a more pendulum-like box-step waltz.[17]

In the United States, several factors contributed to the growth of the dance fashion industry. Technological advancements, such as the invention of the sewing machine by Elias Howe, the Jacquard loom, which made lace, and the Mays sewing machine, which provided ready-made shoes, made dressing in style more affordable for the everyday woman, and provided access to the latest styles in dance apparel for those who were not able to buy expensive, professionally-made gowns. New technologies in the printing industry and an expanding rail system provided easy access to inexpensive fashion magazines that carried the latest Paris designs. Factory-made fabrics also gave many American women the opportunity to make affordable, yet stylish dance clothing.

The Music of the Waltz

To perform the original version of the Viennese waltz, also called the *valse trois temps*, the man stepped across the woman, tracing a curvilinear path on the floor, as she swiveled on her own axis. The couple executed one half-turn on these first three steps, causing them to rotate 180 degrees. They then completed the turn on the next three steps, as the man swiveled on his axis and swung the woman across him. Traditionally, the waltz started with the man facing outward from the center of the ballroom. Beginning on his left foot, he spiraled his partner clockwise, always ending up facing outward again after every six steps. As the couple rotated together clockwise, they moved around the ballroom floor among the other dancers counter-clockwise.

In the book, *Revolving Embrace: The Waltz as Sex, Steps and Sound*, Sevin H. Yaraman points out that the circular movement of the Viennese waltz was reflected in the music that early nineteenth century composers specifically created to accompany the popular dance. These composers kept their music fairly simple to correlate with the simple waltz steps, and like the dance, it was organized into six count sections with the second three counts echoing the first three. The first beat of each measure was accented with a heavy bass note followed by the remainder of the chord on the two next beats. This underlying um-pah-pah rhythm continued throughout. Each measure of three counts, as well as each two measure phrase of six, corresponded to the undulating feeling of the dance.

The circling of the couples around the dance floor was reflected in the overall organization of the music, which was highly repetitive and cyclical, and propelled dancers into an ecstatic altered state through the narcotic effect of endless repetition.

When dancing the *valse trois temps*, the Viennese slightly anticipated the second beat of the dance, a custom that heightened the swinging feeling and added a sense of passion and urgency to the waltz. This anticipation was also mirrored in the music. In addition, breaks in

"The Waltz" by Percy Macquoid. From *Dancing* by Mrs. Lilly Grove (1901).

the phrasing required the dancers to slightly vary their rhythm in order to stay on the beat. These syncopations required sensitive timing, and true aficionados of the waltz knew that "only a born-and-bred Viennese can do [the waltz] properly because 'it's all a matter of feeling.' Either you have it or you don't — in which case no one can help you."[18]

The Birth of Waltz Music

The musical form of the modern waltz had its birth at the end of the eighteenth century and is most associated with the city of Vienna. Barges floating down the Danube River from Linz in Upper Austria to Vienna carried musicians on board to entertain the passengers. Usually comprising only one or two violins, a guitar, and a bass, these itinerant, self-taught musicians, known as Linzer Fiddlers, specialized in ländlers, waltzes, folksongs, and popular tunes. To earn extra money, they played in the beer-gardens, wine taverns, inns, and fairs found along the river, while waiting for their barges to return.[19]

Most of these establishments had dance floors, and on holidays and Sundays, were thronged with the lower classes from the city. The rural musicians, who lacked training and technique but had energy and strong rhythm, found a receptive audience who welcomed the danceable feel of the *Linzer Schiffsmusik*.[20]

Development of the Waltz Musical Form

The demand for new waltzes led to a prolific outpouring of compositions in triple time by many composers. The number and variety of these waltzes is indicative of the dance's enormous popularity and Vienna's love of music.[21] At first these waltz tunes were fairly primitive in form and were based on old ländler melodies.[22] They consisted of eight bars of music, followed by a second eight bar section, which was generally a repeat of the first section transposed up a fifth. This practice was so common that Austrian poet Nikolaus Lenau wrote a poem entitled "Styrian dance," in which he sarcastically pondered if life in heaven would be "just higher by a fifth,"[23] than life was here on earth.

In 1786, Spanish composer Vincenz Martín y Soler included a simple ländler at the end of the second act of his opera, *Una Cosa Rara*. In the opera, the four main characters performed a dance to the tune, and when the work premiered in Vienna, the number created an immediate sensation. The waltz made *Una Cosa Rara* such a hit that Mozart's *Figaro*, which was on the scheduled repertoire that year in Vienna, was abandoned. However, recognizing the waltz's growing appeal, Mozart jumped on the bandwagon; he included a waltz in his opera *Don Giovanni*, which premiered the following year in 1787.

Mozart was passionately fond of dancing the waltz himself. As court composer, he created many orchestral dances in triple time. Several of these dances included authentic folk songs or contained melodies modeled on ländler tunes. Mozart's dances were harmonically refined, sophisticated, and often humorous, but despite his musical genius, he never truly developed the waltz form. However, Mozart and his contemporary, Martín y Soler, began a trend that continued throughout the nineteenth century, leading to the creation of some of the most beautiful opera music ever composed.[24]

Hayden, Beethoven, and Schubert also wrote waltzes. Hayden composed several sets of orchestral dances and often insinuated ländler-like dance music by subtly transforming traditional minuet forms. In 1766, he included the first known waltz specifically written for piano in his sonatina "Mouvement de Waltze." Beethoven enjoyed inserting Austrian flavored folk tunes into his compositions, but like Mozart and Hayden, he never truly developed the waltz form. Franz Schubert created many beautiful waltzes for piano, and a few for string orchestra, which were alternately labeled as ländlers, Deutschers, or walzers. Schubert's waltzes were slow, with each beat of the bar stressed as in the rustic ländlers. Mozart, Hayden, Beethoven, and Schubert wrote their waltzes specifically to accompany dances and not as concert pieces.

Hummel was the first to compose waltzes for piano, intended purely as concert pieces. One such waltz was *Deutsche Tänze*, Opus 28, which he was commissioned to write for the grand opening of the Apollo Hall in Vienna. Hummel's waltz compositions tended to be heavily reminiscent of the slow, plodding ländler; however, they were musically important in the development of waltz music because these early experiments in concert-style piano music culminated in the works of Weber, Chopin, Brahms, and Liszt.

It was Weber's 1819 *Aufforderung zum Tanz* (*Invitation to the Dance*) that truly elevated the music of the waltz from the ballroom to the concert hall. The first important milestone in the development of the waltz musical form, Weber's composition tied several waltzes together and included a formal introduction and thematic coda. This form was imitated by both Joseph Lanner and Johann Strauss I, who elevated waltz music to its highest degree.

Joseph Lanner and the Strauss Dynasty

Joseph Lanner was born on April 12, 1801, the son of a glove maker who worked in Oberdöbling, near Vienna. His musical talent was apparent at an early age and by the time he was twelve, he was playing violin with a popular dance band led by Ignaz Michael Pamer,[25] himself a prolific composer of ländlers and waltzes. Lanner left Pamer's orchestra at age seventeen to form his own trio of two violins and a guitar. The group became so successful that in 1823 he added a fourth member, a twenty-five year old viola player named Johann Strauss.[26] The meeting of Lanner and Strauss led to a collaboration that significantly influenced the development of waltz music.

Lanner's group expanded to a quintet, then to a string orchestra, and eventually to a full classical orchestra with woodwinds and percussion. This musical group became so popular with Viennese audiences that Lanner eventually split the orchestra in two and put Strauss in charge of one half.

The two musicians were the closest of friends, sharing housing, debts, girls, and even their shirts.[27] Eventually though, professional jealousies erupted between Lanner and Strauss. The Viennese public, who delighted in gossiping about the two young musical stars, speculated that the trouble was caused when Lanner introduced new waltzes under his own name that had in fact been composed by Strauss. Others said the split resulted from Strauss stealing Lanner's girlfriends. Whatever the cause, the two parted ways in 1825 after having a very public free-for-all one night on the bandstand at a popular dance hall where they were performing.[28] The fight was widely covered in all the papers, and because "in Vienna during the waltz age all emotions were expressed in waltz themes,"[29] Lanner commemorated the event by writing a humorous composition called "Trennungs-Waltzer," or the "Separation Waltz" which echoed in musical themes a drunken brawl even down to the sounds of people hiccupping.[30]

After leaving Lanner's orchestra with sixteen of Lanner's musicians, Strauss formed his own orchestra in 1826. Soon both orchestras were competing with each other as the most popular purveyors of waltz music. The citizens of Vienna, as well as foreign tourists, all longed to hear Lanner's and Strauss's intoxicating melodies and to dance to their prolific outpouring of waltzes. Frederick Chopin, who at age twenty-one had come to Vienna hoping for recognition for his own musical skills, sadly remarked, "Lanner, Strauss and their waltzes dominate everything."[31]

A rather shy man, Lanner did not share Strauss's fiery temperament and driving ambition.[32] Whereas Lanner seemed content with local fame, Strauss longed for international recognition, and one year after forming his own orchestra, he organized a long tour throughout Germany. The following year, in 1836, he took his twenty-five-member group to Belgium, Holland, Northern Germany, and the Rhineland, and in 1837 traveled to France and England. Strauss's music created a sensation wherever he went. He became an international celebrity and his name became a household word. "Men everywhere smoked Strauss pipes and women drank tea from Strauss cups."[33]

As the tour continued, however, Strauss's homesick musicians rebelled against the relentless schedule and demanded to return to Vienna. Strauss suggested instead that the orchestra tour America. They turned him down and grudgingly agreed to return to Southern France. Still discontented, the musicians rebelled in Rouen and refused to play. A hurt Strauss refused to speak with the musicians for several weeks, yet the tour continued. In Scotland, November rains made the whole orchestra sick. The band members recovered but Strauss did not. He continued to push himself as they played in city after city. His fever and cough worsened; after a doctor gave him opium to help with the cough and he fainted several times, he realized the tour could not go on. The grueling schedule had resulted in a complete breakdown. He collapsed several times on the way back to Vienna and in Strasbourg had to be taken to the hotel where he was unconscious for four days. In Linz, he had another relapse. He ran out into the street in delirium, collapsed, and had to be carried back inside. Newspapers reported he was dying. Few believed he would survive the rest of the trip back home, but Strauss insisted on going back to Vienna. When he finally arrived there, friends rushed to inform his wife Anna that her husband would die within hours. The family gathered and waited for his death, but Strauss survived.

He never completely recovered from the breakdown, but as soon as he was able to get up out of bed, Strauss reorganized his orchestra. He made his first public appearance after his illness at Sperl's dancing palace on January 13, 1839. Vienna welcomed him back with a ten-minute ovation.

Addicted to overwork, Strauss soon had another collapse. As part of his treatment, he decided to move away from his family into an apartment of his own so he would be away from the noise that he complained his children made.[34] He was particularly irritated by his eldest son and namesake, Johann Strauss II. The boy wanted to pursue music against his father's wishes. Despite his father's resistance, the boy secretly studied violin with his mother's help and by age nineteen became his father's chief competition.

Johann Strauss II was born on October 25, 1825, one month after his father had broken away from Joseph Lanner's orchestra. His father, a difficult and moody man, was rarely at home because he was either playing in Vienna or touring abroad. The boy was raised by his mother Anna and remained close to her throughout his life.[35]

In 1844, Johann Strauss II formed his own orchestra but had difficulty finding a place to debut the group. The proprietors of the leading establishments in Vienna were leery of offending the young man's powerful father. Eventually his mother arranged for her son to play at Dommayer's Casino. The announcement of the premier created a furor in Vienna as curious citizens gossiped about how the nineteen year-old upstart was challenging his father, the reigning waltz king of Vienna. The hottest news in the waltz-crazed city was Strauss versus Strauss. Johann Strauss Sr. was quoted as saying, "Goodness, now the lad wants to write waltzes of which he hasn't the faintest idea! It isn't even easy for me, after all these years, to create something new in eight or twelve bars."[36]

The new orchestra, led by the younger Strauss, premiered on Tuesday October 15, 1844, and all of Vienna fought for tickets. "Dommayer's had never seen anything like it. The police got nasty when important individuals made too free with their elbows. Women got hurt and fainted...."[37] The ballroom was packed to capacity, mostly with supporters of the elder Strauss, although he was not there himself. Instead, he had sent two of his friends to spy on the proceedings. The young Strauss appeared on the stage and, despite a bad case of stage fright, began to conduct his orchestra. One of his father's spies started to hiss trying to instigate others in the audience to follow his lead. Instead, the crowd politely applauded after the first number. For his second piece the young Strauss played one of his own compositions. The surprised crowd loved it and made him repeat the number four times. Other numbers were so well received they had to be repeated nineteen times and as the evening progressed, the crowd was completely won over. When Strauss played one of his father's most popular compositions at the close of the musical soiree, many in the audience began to cry. The next morning Strauss's spy reported back. He told the fuming patriarch, "The rascal was terrific."[38]

The elder Strauss refused to speak to his son for two years. Finally on June 23, 1846, Johann II gathered a small group of musicians from his orchestra and went to his father's house. They stood beneath his window and began to serenade the older man with his own waltzes. The father was moved by his son's attempts to reconcile, and the two finally embraced. When Johann I suggested his son join his orchestra as concertmaster, the younger Strauss respectfully declined. A truce was reached though, and both men continued to compose and perform, each with his group of rival supporters.

Five years later, Johann I died at the age of 45. He was buried next to his friend Joseph Lanner. Two days after the burial of his father, Johann II conducted his father's orchestra in a memorial concert; however, several of his father's musicians refused to play under the son's baton. The citizens of Vienna were even more partisan and once again divided into rival camps. One group accused Johann II "of failing to show filial piety" and the other argued "he had been forced into a struggle with the dead."[39] There was serious talk of boycotting the young man's music. In an effort to pacify the warring factions, Johann II issued a statement explaining that since his father's death, he was now responsible for supporting his grieving mother as well as his siblings. He added, "I feel my dear father's influence is with me. It leads me to the spirit that mourns at his grave. I shall show myself worthy of him."[40] The citizens of Vienna were placated and soon the matter faded from the public's interest. The members of the elder Strauss' orchestra were invited to play or resign. They choose to play and eventually both orchestras were joined together.

Johann took over all of his father's duties and continued his own. He was in constant demand, performing every evening, conducting and composing at a superhuman pace, all the while running a large business enterprise. A special coach was hired to whisk him from engagement to engagement. His popularity was unsurpassed. One writer of the period commented, "No foreigner left Vienna without having heard Strauss's waltzes under the composer's direction. To miss such an event would be like going to Rome without seeing the Vatican."[41]

In 1853, Johann collapsed from overwork. From his sickbed, he asked his brother Josef to take over the family legacy. The shy, melancholic young man protested, "I couldn't replace you. I don't even play the violin." Johann responded, "It doesn't matter. You have the Strauss personality. You will conduct with the baton. Meanwhile, you'll learn to play the violin."[42] Josef reluctantly agreed. At first the critics were understanding but unenthusiastic. Then an insightful Josef, aware of the Viennese public's demand for original works, not only presented his father's and brother's compositions, but also successfully composed and conducted his own. The Strauss dynasty continued and Josef eventually went on to create 222 pieces, many of which are ranked as some of the most beautiful waltzes ever written.

Unlike the relationship between father and son, there was no jealousy or rivalry between the two Strauss brothers. As Johann began to recover, the siblings sometimes alternated conducting the family orchestra. When Johann resumed touring, Josef often accompanied him and ran the business part of the organization.

In 1870, Josef was asked to conduct in Poland. The young man traveled to Warsaw, but difficulties developed when seven of his musicians didn't arrive from Vienna. Their Polish replacements presented problems in rehearsal, especially the first violinist, and Josef had to cut several bars of music that were causing problems in one piece. The first three performances went smoothly, but during the fourth performance, the violinist forgot the music that was cut and there was musical chaos. Josef, who already suffered from frequent fainting spells, was overcome and collapsed on the stage, fell down four steps, and suffered a severe concussion that put him into a coma. Josef's wife and his brother Johann rushed to Warsaw to be with him; he finally recovered consciousness after a few days. They carefully took him back to Vienna, where Josef died on July 22 at the age of forty-three.

The Strauss organization was kept together after Josef's death by the third brother, Eduard, also an accomplished conductor and composer. Although he never reached the artistic heights of his two siblings, Eduard was another link in the Strauss dynasty that helped to spread waltz music across the globe.[43]

During his life, Johann II remained the most influential and celebrated member of the Strauss family. He was an international celebrity; posters announcing his concerts sometimes showed the Waltz King sitting on top of the globe with his conductor's baton held as a scepter. During his American tour in 1872, concerts were given to crowds of over 100,000.[44]

The composer was treated with such adulation that women kissed the seams of his coat and begged for locks of his hair. Strauss' valet provided the "authentic Strauss" hair that he actually clipped from a dog, until he feared the black Newfoundland would end up completely bald.[45]

A prolific composer, Johann Strauss II penned more than 500 waltzes, including the memorable "Blue Danube" (1866) and "Tales From the Vienna Woods" (1868), as well as numerous other dances and marches.[46] He also composed 16 operettas, including *Die Fledermaus* (1874), *Eine Nact in Venedig* (1883), and *Der Zigeunerbaron* (1885). Johann Strauss' music was more lyrical and refined than his father's. He brought the artistry of the Viennese waltz to its zenith adding sophisticated rhythms, unique melodic inventions, and rich orchestral colorings.

As the nineteenth century came to a close, the waltz lost its shining star. Johann Strauss II died on June 3, 1899.[47] After working on a score for *Cinderella* one afternoon, he closed his eyes and died peacefully in his sleep. Less than an hour after his death, the news quickly spread throughout Vienna. At a benefit concert being held that day at the Stadtpark pavilion to raise money for a monument to honor Joseph Lanner and Johann Strauss I, Eduard Kremser, the conductor, received the news of Johann II's death on the podium while in the middle of a number. He stopped the orchestra immediately and without any explanation to the audience, began instead to conduct *The Blue Danube* waltz. The audience rose to its feet and wept.

Johann Strauss II was buried three days later. His violin was carried in the funeral procession on a velvet pillow behind the casket. All of Vienna lined the streets to honor him.

The enduring worldwide popularity of waltz owes a debt to this family of musicians who for eighty years dominated the hearts and minds of society.[48] The buoyancy and beauty of their music continues to evoke the very spirit of the waltz.

5

Reaction to the Waltz

As the waltz found its way into salons and drawing rooms, polished floors and light dancing slippers replaced the rough barroom floors, outdoor fields, and heavy hobnailed footwear which had been a part of earlier versions of the German spinning dance. These changes in venue and fashion resulted in considerable accelerations in the tempo of the dance. Traditional hopping and skipping steps were replaced with gliding steps so that the swift turns could be executed more easily. In 1797, the *Journal des Luxas und der Moden* stated that the Viennese waltz "surpassed everything in headlong speed."[1]

Such rapid turns required new ways of holding one's partner. The traditional manner in which the ländler was performed, with the man's hands on the woman's waist and the woman's on his shoulders, changed as both placed their hands on their partner's torso.[2] In 1800, one eyewitness described this new method of waltzing.

> The man placed the palms of hands gently against the sides of his partner, not far from the armpits. His partner does the same, and instantly with as much velocity as possible they turn round, and at the same time gradually glide round the room.[3]

Medical Objections

As the speed of the waltz increased, objections to it also increased. Enemies of the dance alerted the public about the detrimental effects that too much spinning had upon a person's health and well-being.

> [T]oo much dancing, especially waltzing, is as injurious to the soundness of the mind as to the health of the body and contributes, apart from other physical effects, not a little to the weakness of the mind and the resulting despondency ... this violent movement, destroying both body and mind, is unfortunately much beloved by almost the entire female sex.[4]

Opponents of waltzing thought that women were in particular danger from participating in the dance because of their "delicate constitution."[5] One critic warned women that the waltz's "rotary motion is injurious to the brain and spinal marrow."[6] Another cautioned, "A lady should never waltz if she feels dizzy, It is a sign of disease of the heart, and has brought on death."[7] In his book *Exercises for Ladies* (1836), Donald Walker alerted his readers,

> abandon waltzing, on account of its causing too violent emotions or an agitation which produces vertigo and nervous symptoms ...its rapid turnings, the clasping of the dancers, their exciting contact, and too quick and too long a succession of lively and agreeable emotions, produce sometimes, in women of a very irritable constitution, syncopes, spasms and other accidents which should induce them to renounce it.[8]

Physicians warned of over-exertion and over-heating. While some touted the benefits of exercise achieved by doing a few waltzes, others cautioned that participants should use restraint. In 1888, a newspaper in Wisconsin explained how Edward Scott, author of *Dancing and Dancers,* had estimated "the distance actually waltzed by the belle of the ball room." The paper revealed to its "fair and fragile reader" that if she went six times around an average size ballroom it would equal a circuit of 480 yards. "But you are turning nearly all the time, say on an average, once in every yard of onward progress, and the circumference of a circle is rather more than three times its diameter, which will bring each waltz to over three-quarters of a mile, or at least fourteen miles for the ten waltzes."[9] The implication was clear — fourteen miles in a heavy ball-gown was overdoing it.

In his book *The Social Dance*, Dr. R. A. Adams stated,

> Visit the dancing woman the day "after the ball is over;" hear her weak voice, and look into her listless eyes; note her general lassitude, observe that she has scarcely any life left in her, and you will get some idea of the physical effects of the dance.... In a certain Western city, after quite a discussion with a frail young woman of 22, she acknowledged that it required at least three days for her to recover from one night's dancing.[10]

Anti-dance writers admonished their readers that overexertion from waltzing, in combination with other dangers inherent in the ballroom, created a perilous mix. In his book *May Christians Dance?* James Brookes wrote:

> If heated rooms, and sumptuous feasting, and whirling round and round, and jumping up and down until two or three o'clock in the morning, and then sudden exposure to the cold air, followed by a day of slumber or ennui, tend to promote health, the physicians are all in the dark with regard to hygienic laws, and my own observation has greatly deceived me.[11]

Dr. R. A. Adams stated that according to his statistics, "...the longevity of a habitual dancer is 25 years for the female and 37 years for the male."[12]

The article "Concerning Round Dances," published in *Harper's New Monthly Magazine* in April of 1866, gives a detailed explanation of the deleterious effects of dancing in a crowded ballroom:

> It needs no extensive physiological knowledge to teach us that the maintenance of health depends upon the fulfillment of two conditions — adequate aëration of the blood, and proper ablation of effete tissue. Both of these desiderata are effected by the agency of oxygen, which not only revivifies that portion of the blood which has made the circuit of the body, but aids in making new from the chyle freshly added; and combining with the carbon resulting from textural waste, is breathed forth as carbonic acid. Now, in a crowded ball-room, we have, above, a multitude of lights, burning each its share of this all-important gas, and below, several hundred human beings, who, under the stimulus of violent exercise, are undergoing more waste, and consequently consuming more oxygen, and creating more poisonous carbonic acid. After a while, this latter is produced in such excess that our dancers, instead of getting rid of their own detritus, are actually inhaling that of others.[13]

The article also warned of the added threat when a hostess used a "crash," a cloth that was sometimes spread over the dancing floor.

> [F]urther incentive to disease is hospitably provided by ball-givers in the form of a "crash" — a maleficent linen cloth which is spread over the carpets to afford a smooth surface for the "many twinkling feet" of pallid victims. From the excessive attrition of this fabric the air is soon filled with a mist of floating lint, whose minute particles whiten one's coat, permeate one's hair, irritate one's eyes, and, worse than all, clog one's organs of respiration with a tenacious coating.[14]

The article blamed the prevalence of bronchitis in nine out of ten sufferers among the fashionable set on the "pernicious lint-dust" from "crash" cloths. The death of a musician was even attributed to it.

Despite warnings, the popularity of the waltz continued to grow. The dance seemed almost irresistible to those who fell under its spell. The euphoria created by the rapid rotations of the waltz was one of the most vital parts of the thrill — the thrill of losing control. But it was this

The allemand arm position of the center-left couple indicates an early form of the waltz. To the left of that couple, the woman's precarious position suggests that she is suffering from vertigo because of spinning. "The Cyprians' Ball at the Argyle Rooms," after an engraving by Robert Cruikshank. From *A History of Dancing: From the Earliest Ages to Our Own Times* by Gaston Vuillier (1898).

very point that so terrified those who sought to protect ethical and moral standards because, in addition to the physical damage caused to the mind and the body by the constant spinning, it was thought that this motion scrambled the brain, and destroyed what little moral sense the waltzer may have had. The waltz's real danger was that the vertigo made the dancer fall back into lust.

Moral Objections

In the journal of his travels through Germany, Hungary, Italy, and France in 1798–1799, Ernst Moritz Arndt documented the new style of waltzing he had witnessed:

> The dancers grasped the long dress of their partners so that it would not drag and be trodden upon, and lifted it high, holding them in this cloak which brought both bodies under one cover, as closely as possible against them and in this way the whirling continued in the most indecent positions; the supporting hand lay firmly on the breasts, at each movement making little lustful pressures; the girls went wild and looked as if they would drop. When waltzing on the darker side of the room there were bolder embraces and kisses. The custom of the country; it is not as bad as it looks, they exclaim; but now I can understand very well why here and there in parts of Swabia and Switzerland the waltz has been prohibited.[15]

Close physical contact between members of the opposite sex, often between virtual strangers, would have been unthinkable in a public forum before the advent of the waltz. The closed dance position shattered all previous ethical standards and allowed dancers to have what must have seemed, at that period in history, a highly erotic experience. The sensual thrill was heightened because it exposed, in public, the most intimately private relationships.

The firm embrace was not only an arbitrary preference for those executing the fast turns of the waltz, it was also an absolute necessity. Without mutual cooperation, the couple could be pulled apart by the centrifugal force of the dance's many revolutions. Eye contact was also essential to orient one's self in relation to one's partner and lessen the vertigo. This intense face-to-face proximity, mixed with the danger of spinning madly in a room full of other moving couples, made the waltz an erotically exciting and irresistible experience. "In this sense the waltz may have represented a world in which only the senses were operative, a world which was void of responsibility, an experience of self and self-involvement, an escape from reality and a surrender to the moment...."[16]

Moralists did not stand for it. "In addition to the associate dissipation, late hours, fashionable dressing, midnight feasting, exposure through excessive exercise, exertion, improper dress, etc., it can be shown most clearly that dancing has a direct influence in stimulating the passions, and provoking unchaste desires, which too often lead to unchaste acts and are in themselves violations of the requirements of strict morality...."[17]

The Dance Hold

A major concern was the way in which the man held his partner.[18] One of the leading dance masters of the day, Allen Dodworth[19] explained,

> The manner of holding is, however, of very great consequence, as what is seen in this is frequently used as a measure of character. In this is its greatest importance.... To hold closely has many objections without one advantage. It is indelicate (vulgar might be a better word). It reflects unpleasantly upon the characters of the dancers. It prevents freedom of motion. It is ungraceful in appearance. And as it is always in favor with the vulgar and vicious, it ought to be frowned upon by the cultivated.... In conclusion, let it be remembered that purity of thought and action may be conspicuous in waltzing as in any other situation in life; that the gross waltz grossly, the vicious viciously, the refined and innocent innocently and in a refined manner.[20]

Dodworth recommended that the gentleman rest his hand lightly on the lady's back "so that air may pass between, as in some cases the close contact induces perspiration and may leave a mark upon the lady's dress."[21] *True Politeness, A Hand-Book of Etiquette for Gentlemen. By an American Gentleman* (1847), also admonished gentlemen not to hold a woman too tightly while waltzing. It stated, "If a lady waltzes with you, beware not to press her waist; lightly touch it with the open palm of your hand, lest you leave a disagreeable impression not only on her *ceinture*, but on her mind."[22]

Dancing masters were well aware of the public's perception of the waltz position.[23] They assured them that professional dance teachers taught only the proper hold and worked to prevent indelicate embraces on the dance floor. In *The Director*, the first American magazine devoted to dance, a letter from New York dancing master A. E. Bournique stated,

> It has been for some time a matter of anxiety on the part of dancing masters to preserve the dignity and grace of the round dances. While pupils are with us it is simple enough, for we can insist upon propriety and good form. After they leave the dancing schools and take up fads it is more difficult to influence them. The college fellows, who are given to frolics, are largely responsible for the present evils. They have got bad habits, and everywhere one sees examples of young men and women dancing in a manner that should make them blush.[24]

Mr. H. W. Beck agreed. He responded,

> The vulgar position has been one of my worst enemies in teaching dancing. I find these attitudes are assumed by college boys and girls more than any other persons. They are constantly trying to originate something "new and odd," and they do so much to the detriment of good form, breeding and grace. I am very strict about the position dancers assume.... I am a member of the American Society of Professors of Dancing and I will aid them to the best of my ability in correcting the "hugging habit."[25]

The editor of *The Director*, and President of The American Society of Professors of Dancing,[26] Melvin Ballou Gilbert, was particularly troubled by improper variations in the waltz hold.

The proper way.

The extended arms, and the lady's hand grasping the gentleman's arm, are not in good taste.

The lady's head too close, the extended arms and bad attitude of hand very objectionable.

Extremely vulgar.

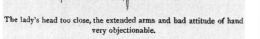

Four illustrations demonstrating the proper waltz hold. Taken from *Dancing and Its Relation to Education and Social Life* by Allen Dodworth (1888).

The so-called side position, where the lady is held to the right of the gentleman instead of in front, is at once the most dangerous enemy of social dancing, retaining as it does the bad features of the other false positions, and adding to them by seriously interfering with freedom of movement. The position of the gentleman's right arm as it is held resting across the lady's breast should be at once condemned as indelicate, and reflecting unpleasantly upon the character of the dancers, many times wrongfully. It being in especial favor by the low and vicious it ought to be frowned upon by the cultivated, remembering that purity of thought and action may be noticeable in dancing as in any other situation in life.[27]

In order to curb complaints against the unseemly dance hold, the American Society of Professors of Dancing issued a decree at its twenty-first annual meeting in 1898:

Hugging while waltzing is under the ban. The decree has gone forth from the men who teach waltzing that no more hard pressure shall be permitted during the process of the fascinating whirl. Reprimands are in store for all young men or young women either, who persist in hugging in the dance.[28]

The aspect of hugging in the dance was especially abhorrent to detractors because throughout an evening of waltzing, couples could change partners several times. The impropriety of intimate contact with a stranger — someone who might not be related by either blood or marriage, was a disturbingly blatant example of the lascivious nature of the dance. It created an uproar among opponents of the waltz. In *Across the Dead Line of Amusement*, author Henry Stough wrote,

No woman has any right to allow a man not her father, her son, her brother, or other blood relative, any liberties with her person, and no man has any right to take such liberties with any woman not his mother, his wife, his daughter, his sister, or other blood relative. Such liberties indulged in promiscuously in a public dance hall or a private parlor are bound to engender familiarities that eventually breed contempt among people, both young and old. Married people cannot grant such liberties to others than their life partners without the same results.[29]

Stough told of a Philadelphia army officer who saw a waltz and remarked, "If I should see a man offering to dance with my wife in that way, I would horse-whip him."[30]

Critics admonished that the temptation was too great. Waltzing in the arms of a stranger inevitably led to a woman's downfall.[31]

The girl whose blood is hot from exertion and whose every carnal sense is aroused and inflamed ... is led to the ever-waiting carriage, where she sinks exhausted on the cushioned seat. Oh, if I could picture to you the fiendish look that comes into his eyes as he sees his helpless victim before him. Now is his golden opportunity. He must not miss it, and he does not, and that beautiful girl who entered the dancing school as pure and innocent as an angel three months ago, returns home that night robbed of that most precious jewel of womanhood — virtue![32]

Those who did not totally disapprove of waltzing all together strongly insisted that a woman should at least take special care to only dance with suitable partners. *The Illustrated Manners Book* in 1855 declared, "A woman especially ought to be very sure that the man she waltzes with is one worthy of so close an intimacy."[33] Mme. Celnart wrote in *The Gentleman and Lady's Book of Politeness*, "The waltz is a dance of quite too loose a character, and unmarried ladies should refrain from it altogether, both in public and private; very young married ladies, however, may be allowed to waltz in private balls, if it is very seldom, and with persons of their acquaintance."[34]

Defenders of the waltz tried to avert possible protests by mandating that the gentleman not encircle the lady's waist with his arm until dancing actually commenced. They also insisted that at no time should a gentleman's bare hand touch any part of his partner's anatomy. Therefore, gloves were absolutely required while dancing. If for some unforeseeable reason the gentleman did not have his gloves, he was to place a handkerchief in his hand to prevent improper skin-to-skin contact with his partner.

A cartoon from the *London Illustrated News* dated February 23, 1889 entitled "Waltzers and Waltzing." It shows the plight of Gertie, who suffers the indignities of dancing with many unsuitable partners until she finds Jack who can actually waltz.

In addition to disgust with improper contact between partners, many also disapproved of the exhibitionistic nature of ballroom fashions. Unlike daywear, ballgowns were often décolleté. Corsets lifted the bosoms until they almost spilled out over the bodice and upper arms and shoulders were frequently exposed. In his book *May Christians Dance?* James Brookes was shocked at the shameful display of the fashionable female dancing the waltz. He wrote:

> [Women] with dresses so shamefully low in the neck that the bosom is exposed, and with dresses so short that in "the voluptuous movement of the waltz" the limbs are fully exhibited to view only covered with flesh-colored stocking and drawers, while young men make comments during the entertainment or afterwards upon the comparative shapeliness of the "fine legs" revealed to their gaze.[35]

T. A. Faulkner, author of *From the Ballroom to Hell,* wrote,

> To be sure, one not accustomed to such scenes would consider them [women] anything but respectably dressed, with their nude arms and partially exposed breast, and tightly clinging skirts which more than suggest the contour of body and limb. But society and fashion demand such dress; vile men demand it; for them the waltz would be spoiled of half its pleasure if the woman was not nearly as nude as she dare be.[36]

PART II. THE ANIMAL DANCES

6

Origins of the Animal Dances

The first decade of the twentieth century brought with it a barnyard full of dances. Each week, it seemed, a new dance was invented, usually based on the movement of some beast or bird and christened after that creature. Dancers did the turkey trot, the bunny hug, the horse trot, the crab step, the fish walk, the snake dip, the eagle rock, the chicken scratch, the kangaroo kant, the wiggle worm, the grizzly bear, the fox trot, and a host of other dances.[1] Animal dances were the ragtime rage, and the local dance hall was a veritable zoo.

Most of the dances were based on the one-step, or trot, as it was also called, a fairly simple movement in which one step was taken on each beat of music. The fun came with how the dancers embellished it. Imitating the characteristics of whatever animal the particular dance was named for, dancers would flap their arms, shake their shoulders, bob their heads, hop or slide or stomp their feet, or wiggle their backsides. The elegant, erect posture of previous couple dances gave way to the slouched, hunched-over gait of a lumbering animal, and the smooth circular motions of the waltz gave way to the jerky movements of ragtime trotting.

Origins of the Animal Dances

Animal dances can be found in the rituals of many primitive cultures. During these magical rites, dancers pantomimed the movements of animals, believing that by imitation they could harness, control, and incorporate an animal's strength, agility, speed, and cunning. Animal dances were used during initiation rites, fertility rites, courtship rituals, funeral rites, and hunt rituals.

The origins of the animal dances of the ragtime era can be traced to African ritual dances. Many mimetic African dances used animal movements, and dance historians believe that the slaves who came to the United States from Africa brought these dances with them and later developed them. Several plantation slave dances utilized animal mimicry—the buzzard lope, the camel walk, snake hips, the fish tail, the pigeon wing, and the eagle rock are just a few examples. The use of gliding and sliding steps, centrifugal movement of the pelvis and hips, swinging movements, polyrhythmic body movements, improvisation, and a crouched body position are all traits of African dance. Certainly the syncopation used in ragtime music is an identifying feature of African music. By the time ragtime came into vogue, most of the authentic tribal movements had evolved to a point that the original ritual steps were difficult to identify. Nevertheless, the traces of authentic African dance were visible in the popular social dances of the 1910's.

In 1914, an article in the *New York Times* stated, "the 'rag' is a dance of the most primitive peoples and of the most ancient times. There are those that assert the dance was brought from Africa...."[2] The connection to African-American dance is also suggested in the sheet music of "Texas Tommy Swing" published in 1911. The Texas Tommy was one of the first ragtime dances and was the progenitor of the turkey trot and grizzly bear. The sheet music, printed in the form of a newspaper, contained the following story:

"The One Step" by artist Lester Ralph, an early twentieth century postcard.

The rhythm of the Grizzly Bear, the inspiration of the Loving Hug, the grace of the Walk-Back and the abandon of the Turkey-Trot all blend in the harmony of the Texas Tommy Swing, which was really the parent of all the others. The dance originated more than forty years ago among the negroes of the old Southern plantations.... Southern darkies brought the dance and a suggestion of the melody to San Francisco several years ago, and there upon the Barbary Coast it was rounded into perfect harmony.[3]

The Barbary Coast

Most historians trace the first public use of ragtime dances to the dance halls, dives, and brothels of the Barbary Coast in San Francisco, California. An article in *The Anaconda Standard*, dated February 11, 1912, explained that after the San Francisco earthquake of 1906 destroyed the city's bars and dance halls, new Bohemian resorts sprang up along the beach. When insurance money began to pour in, the beach resorts flourished.

Most of these halls employed singers, "coon-shouters," Ethiopian or lighter, who weaved through their audiences keeping time with shoulders and arms and heads to the syncopations of the orchestra. They loked [sic] as much as anything else like cake walkers without partners. There was nothing systematic about their gestures or gyrations. They walked and swayed and undulated in individual style, keeping perfect time to the piano and drums. Well, one night in the "Eye-wink"—it may have been—or at any rate in one of these halls, a girl excited by champagne, started up facing the singer and imitated him, keeping at a distance from him but performing rock for rock, sway for sway, every one of his motions. Her name is lost to fame, but she was the first turkey trotter of the female sex. The next night she did it again, but this time clasping arms with the singer. They danced pretty well apart (as the turkey trot should be danced), his right arm under her left so as to force her shoulder upward and induce the dragging of feet that is necessary to a precise rendition.[4]

The article further explains that as the town began to rebuild, other dance hall managers recognized the commercial value of the turkey trot and hired couples to perform it for visiting tourists whose "dollars were cast liberally upon the polished floors as largess for the most skillful performers."[5] The dance became more "systematized," and then, "somebody hit upon an appropriate name—turkey trot—having in mind the waddling and wing flapping of a dignified old gobbler."[6]

In his lectures, Professor Oscar Duryea of the "American Society of Professors of Dancing" theorized that rag dancing had probably developed because sailors who visited the dance halls along the Barbary Coast still had their "sea legs." When female dance hall hostesses tried to teach the sailors the two step, the men would waddle "one-step-at-a-time." Duryea announced, "That was the first one-step that was ever danced."[7]

Dance historians Jean and Marshall Stearns suggest that the Texas Tommy and other rag dances were performed at a club called Purcell's[8] as early as 1910. The nightspot, located on the north side of Pacific Street between Montgomery and Kearny Streets, was owned by Lew Purcell, an ex–Pullman porter, and had only a bar, a few tables and chairs, and some rough benches that surrounded a dance floor. Although it was the only Black cabaret on the Barbary Coast, it did not allow African Americans in as customers. The club catered to a tough crowd, and shootings there were frequent. The club next door to Purcell's, Spider Kelly's, took extra precautions and installed a sheet-iron boiler plate behind their bar to block any stray bullets that might come through the adjoining wall. Purcell's had the reputation of being the hottest spot to hear ragtime and jazz. The club attracted many celebrities wishing to experience the nightlife of the Barbary Coast. Al Jolsen and Sophie Tucker both visited to the club, and it was there at Purcell's that Anna Pavlova first learned the turkey trot. "All the new dances came from Purcell's, which hired the best colored entertainers from coast to coast."[9]

In his book *The Barbary Coast,* historian Herbert Asbury claims that both the Texas Tommy and the turkey trot were given birth in a dance-hall near Purcell's called the Thalia. Located on the same side of the street as Purcell's, the Thalia was the biggest dancehall on the Pacific Coast.[10] Its large dance floor, in the center of a barn-sized building, was cordoned off on each end and had double tiers of balconies on each side where patrons could sit and drink. To the far right of the entrance was a separate higher balcony where members of society who were slumming could sit without being bothered by the club's regular customers. One of the big attractions at the Thalia was the final dance of the night, a "Salome dance," that took place at about one o'clock in the morning and featured the women who worked at the club. "The 'Salomes' danced and strained and twisted, received a faint spattering of applause, and then, throwing coats or loose gowns over their scant costumes, joined the throngs of dancers in the comparatively conservative steps of the Grizzly Bear, the Bunny Hug, and the Texas Tommy."[11]

Four years after the San Francisco earthquake of 1906, at least three hundred dance-halls and saloons were crowded in the six block area around Pacific Street.[12] Nicknamed "Terrific Street," the millions of lights that lit up the outsides of these nighttime resorts could be seen for miles. The newly re-built dance-halls of the Barbary Coast became a major tourist attraction in the city. At night Pacific Street alone became so crowded that it was almost impossible for automobiles to squeeze through to drop off customers. These resorts were specifically designed to attract sightseers and were marketed to entice, entertain, and shock visitors. Almost all establishments had "slummers balconies" that were nightly filled with gawking spectators ogling the debauchery with delight. Although slummers reveled in seeing the low-life, "the principal attraction was the dancing. The whole Barbary Coast was dance-crazy, and practically every dive of any pretentiousness was a combination dance-hall and concert saloon, offering both theatrical entertainment and an opportunity to trip the light fantastic or to watch it being tripped."[13]

Celebrities who were in San Francisco were always sure to visit the area. Sarah Bernhardt, for example, stopped in whenever her tours played the city, "declaring that she had found it more fascinatingly wicked than Montmartre."[14] Ballet superstar, Anna Pavlova, claimed "she had obtained many ideas for her own dance creations by watching the gyrations of the light-footed Barbary Coasters."[15] Pavlova herself took the dance floor in one dive and performed the turkey trot. As news of the event was reported on the wires, papers around the country described the naughty trot and carried sketches of the ballerina doing the dance. Shortly afterward, the turkey trot began to appear in roof-garden shows in New York. Pavlova, who felt that she had been instrumental in propelling the dance into the public's notice, later regretted doing the dance. As one paper reported, "[Pavlowa] gave the dance its first impetus. That's why she feels impelled to fight it.... [She] detests the Turkey trot because it is neither beautiful nor graceful, and it is apt to be unmannerly."[16]

In addition to the more elaborate dance-halls located in San Francisco's Barbary Coast, fifty or more nickel dance-halls, as they were called, existed near the area. Women were allowed in free, but men were charged five cents for five minutes of dancing. No liquor was sold and there was no other entertainment. Hoping to present themselves as somewhat respectable establishments, these dance-halls frequently posted signs forbidding immoral behavior, such as the following:

ADMISSION
Only on the Following Rules and Conditions:
Turkey Trots, Couples
With Their Heads
Together, Walking,
Bowerying, Dipping, Or Gentlemen Introducting
Themselves to Ladies in the Hall

STRICTLY PROHIBITED!
Introducers on the Floor.[17]

In reality any man, no matter what sort of character he was, and any woman, even if she was under-aged, was admitted. Pimps frequented these low class dives and used them as recruiting grounds for the brothels in the Barbary Coast. The nickel dance-halls were really nothing more "than supply depots for the red-light district."[18]

Although most historians agree that ragtime dances originated in the lower class dance halls of San Francisco, some sources state that the Texas Tommy, bunny hug, grizzly bear, and the turkey trot began on the other end of the social spectrum, at the Fairmont Hotel in 1911. This is probably not the case because newspaper articles that mention the dances pre-date this year. However, it is known that an African-American by the name of Johnny Peters is often credited with being one of the first to develop the ragtime dances in the first decade of the twentieth century in San Francisco. Peters reportedly brought the dances to San Francisco from the South sometime in 1911. After Peter's first dance partner Mary Dewson became ill, he found a new partner, Ethel Williams, considered by some to be the top female American dancer of that era.[19] The two frequently presented the Texas Tommy and other ragtime dances at the Fairmont.

Other Explanations

As ragtime dances grew in popularity and spread across the country, conservative members of society reacted to their connection to the brothel and seedy dance hall. One commentator wrote, "One trouble with the turkey [trot] is the fact of its origin. It sprang from the lowest strata — the smoke-reeking, beer-stained resorts of San Francisco's beach, where iron-lunged singers hurled their voices against the wall paper."[20]

Articles appeared that attempted to trace the turkey trot, grizzly bear, bunny hug, and other dances to more noble roots. Many said the dances were derived from classical sources. One such article in the *Milford Mail* in Milford, Iowa stated, "The movements which make up the turkey trot are traced to the savage dancing of Romulus."[21]

Historian Léon La Farge traced the grizzly bear to an ancient Greek bear dance. He claimed it originated in the city of Brauron and was a springtime dance done to honor the goddess Artemis. The ritual was performed to appease the goddess' wrath when a young female devotee killed her pet bear. Young girls performed the dance, some dressed in saffron robes and others disguised as bears. The dancers imitated the movements of a she-bear, circling around an image of the goddess.

The *New York Times* reported La Farge's claims and stated, "This discovery of the illustrious lineage of a dance thought to be of American origin, is causing people to regard it with increased respect and interest. It is now hoped that records of the turkey trot may be found in Egyptian inscriptions, or the bunny hug among the brick tablets of Assyria,"[22]

Others agreed that the lineage of the animal dances sprang from ancient roots. *The San Antonio Light* ran an article on September 14, 1913, that stated that the turkey trot could be traced to the Kukis people of Northern India, who introduced the dance in Pompeii:

> Long before the Christian era, before there were any gods on Mount Olympus or vestal virgins dancing in Rome, the Kukis of Assam were dancing the turkey trot with knees bent exactly as they are now by those who dance it.... It was during the reign of Emperor Augustus Caesar in A.D., 79, that a famous Egyptian named Arbaces went to live in the city of Pompeii, then a prosperous Roman town of 20,000 people nestling at the base of the great volcano Vesuvius. Arbaces had just arrived from a triumphant siege in Asia, where he had overthrown the savage Kukis of Assam and taken the country in the name of Caesar.... Arbaces brought the tribe of Kukis and their quaint religious dances for the entertainment of their [Pompeii's visiting dignitaries] guests.

The dancing fad of the Kukis and their esthetic evolutions soon caught the fancy of the sport-loving and amusement-seeking public, and it was not long before everybody was sliding, gliding and swaying to the rhythmic motion of the savage dance.[23]

Professor Edward Davidson, a Washington dancing master, announced in a lecture on the history of dancing in 1912, that the turkey trot was "one of the holy of holies in the religion of the Murats."[24] According to the professor, the primitive tribe of head-hunters, living in the north of Borneo, had used ritual dance for over five hundred years to honor the rain god. When drought affected the community, members of the tribe danced the "trot" around an image of the rain god day in and day out until rain came.

Davidson explained that this same turkey trot was later introduced in dancing schools in Italy and Portugal as early as the late 1700's, but when the Italian, Spanish and Portuguese clergy raised an outcry against the "heathen dance," it fell from favor. He pointed out that traces of the turkey trot could still be seen in the folk dances of Italy, Spain, Portugal, France, and Switzerland. Davidson said that the turkey trot was then introduced to the United States in 1880, by Giovanni Casini, an Italian who traveled to San Francisco's Barbary Coast.

Most commentators of the day, however, were skeptical that the ragtime dances had their origin in classical dance. They asserted that such dances were too uncouth to claim such highbrow pedigree. As one writer put it, "Some learned persons have endeavored to blame the modern dances on the ancient Greeks, which is very unkind. Probably the Greeks never would have countenanced such vulgar perversions of a beautiful art. No, the Greeks are not responsible."[25]

Some commentators suggested implausible explanations for the origins of ragtime. One, for example, stated that the turkey trot was actually a cowboy dance. In 1907, he claimed, some tourists from the East visited a "small cattle town in the far west" during roundup. The tourists saw cowboys dancing in the local saloon. According to the author of the article, that dance was the turkey trot. "The younger members of the party found at once what they had sought for years, a new dance; the step was varied, also the contortions...."[26] The tourists returned to New York and, after practicing the dance, introduced it in Newport during the next spring season.

Another journalist claimed that the turkey trot was invented around 1911 in Pennsylvania in "the rathskellers of Harrisburg."[27] There, in the state capitol, "...a number of the legislators and flunkies perfected the dance and put their stamp on it in a way that has made it popular and enchanting."[28] The article also related that "the Sultan of Turkey sent his agent to Harrisburg to see if a modified style of the Turkey Trot could not be used in his harem with his regular oriental music."[29]

7

Development and Dispersion of the Animal Dances

From the saloons, dives, and dance halls of the Barbary Coast in San Francisco, animal dances made their way to metropolitan centers in the East, such as Chicago, and New York.[1] An article entitled "Origin and Spread of the Vivacious 'Turkey Trot'" that appeared on February 11, 1912 in a Montana newspaper, *The Anaconda Standard,* explained how the trot made its way back East:

> It was along the Barbary Coast, as San Francisco calls its collection of dance halls and dives, that Mabel Hite and Mike Donlin discovered the turkey trot. They were in vaudeville out there and looking for new ideas. They were taught how to perform the dance and brought their knowledge eastward to Chicago. In May 1910, the Donlins were guests of honor at a party in the Hotel la Salle given by Frances Demerest, Joe Smith, her husband; Jack Gardner and other New York stage folk. In the middle of the supper the Donlin family got up and illustrated the turkey trot, much to the amusement of the company. Smith, a producer of dances, at once spotted the commercial possibilities of the freak. He asked Miss Hite to be careful about showing it around when she got to New York, because he thought it would be the hit of a Broadway musical show. Then Miss Hite was made the star of "A Certain Party" and George C Tyler of Liebler & Co. put on the turkey trot at Wallack's. Within a week the town was talking about the novelty. You met everywhere people who rocked their shoulders and dragged their feet.[2]

The Joe Smith mentioned in the above quote supports this story in a letter to the editor he wrote to the *New York Times* dated January 17, 1914. "The turkey trot I first put on the stage, and the first time it was danced was with the late Mable Hite and Mike Dolin in a 'Certain Party' production at Wallack's Theatre over three years ago."[3]

The musical *A Certain Party,*[4] opened on Broadway on April 24, 1911 and was choreographed by Joseph C. Smith.[5] The end of the second act featured Mabel Hite,[6] Mike Donlin,[7] and a group of chorines dancing to a number called "The Turkey Trot"—probably the first official use of a ragtime dance on the Broadway stage.

Smith was not only a choreographer, but also a well-known exhibition dancer himself. Son of America's first premier male ballet dancer, George Washington Smith, he claimed to have been the first to introduce both the turkey trot and the tango to American audiences. In his letter to the *Times*, Smith states unequivocally that he was "...the first to introduce the turkey trot."[8] He also says he rightfully can "claim the start of all this dancing."[9] As a performer Smith appeared in many Broadway shows, but it is important to note that in 1912, he was in the cast of *Over the River,*[10] a show which some dance historians credit with introducing the grizzly bear to Broadway audiences.

Some credit Smith with also helping to spread rag dancing's popularity throughout Europe. In June of 1911, Smith and his wife, Frances Demerest, were sailing to Europe when they encountered a group of college athletes who were traveling to England to compete in an international meet. The young collegians saw the Smiths performing the turkey trot one evening in the salon

Joseph C. Smith with an uncredited partner. From *The Tango and Other Up-to-Date Dances* by J. S. Hopkins (1914). In the original caption for this picture, Smith is listed as the "Originator of the Tango."

and begged Smith to teach them the snappy dance. According to the account, "for the rest of the voyage everybody aboard from bridge to stokehole turkey trotted enthusiastically."[11]

After arriving in England, Smith met with British theatrical producer George Edwardes, and suggested that he include the trot in his newest musical, *The Quaker Girl*. "Mr. Edwardes leaped at the suggestion and at once Joe Coyne and Gertie Miller began rehearsing the trot."[12] After that,

> Smith went to Paris and taught the dance to Adelaide La Petite and Hughes. Then the turkey trot jumped the Alps and got hold on the Italians, hurdled the Pyrenees and made a splash with the Spanish. The Germans took it up and Berlin began to trot. Away up north in St. Petersburg the fad attained popularity. Vaudeville sets abroad utilized it. Ethel Levey at the Alhambra and Bessie Cayton turkey trotted industriously and the London papers said it was very quaint. Joe Smith came back to New York with more money than he started with, but he didn't get the rest he was after. He had been too busy teaching the trot.[13]

Shortly after *A Certain Party* opened on Broadway, syncopated rag dancing sprang up in other shows on the Great White Way. Florence Ziegfeld presented "Lillian Lorraine doing the Texas Tommy, a full sister of the turkey trot"[14] in his *Follies*. According to *The Anaconda Standard*,

> Mr. Ziegfeld, tacking about the Barbary Coast one night seeking new follies for his New York productions, observed in one of San Francisco's most widely known resorts, "The Midway," a pair of mahogany finish dancers, rocking over the waxed floor in time to the syncopated beat of snare drums and piano. He saw at once that here was a real novelty, something that would make the dead watch at any Broadway show sit up and take a new interest in life. So he hired the dark dancers to teach the turkey (for such it was) to his merry Follies.[15]

Around the same time, dancers Jim Lane and Edna Hunter performed the turkey trot in Louis Werba's & Mark Luescher's production of *Little Miss Fixit*.[16] Soon, there were "dozens of musical comedy and vaudeville teams that took up the dance."[17]

Lobster Palaces and Cabarets

At the end of the nineteenth century and during the first years of the twentieth century a number of nightlife offerings sprang up in metropolitan centers. In New York City, in the area that would later become known as Times Square, several upscale restaurants were opened. In 1897 Delmonico's moved to Fifth Avenue and Forty-fourth Street and re-opened. The same year the Palm Garden at the newly built Waldorf-Astoria opened on Thirty-fourth. Sherry's opened the following year across the street from Delmonico's. Other opulent restaurants included Bustanoby's, Churchill's, Martin's, Maxim's, Murray's Roman Gardens, Rector's, Reisenweber's, and Shanley's. Called lobster palaces, a reference to the lavish late-light lobster dinners, these sumptuous eateries featured ostentatiously decorated interiors, gourmet food, top-notch service, and an opportunity for society to enjoy conspicuous consumption in its most glorified manner.

In late 1911 and in the first months of 1912, in response to the economic slump that was affecting local businesses, some of these New York establishments began experimenting with offering light entertainment while dining, in hopes of attracting customers.[18] The idea had first been introduced in the spring of 1911. Two former vaudeville performers, turned producers, had seen cabaret shows while in Paris and hit upon the idea of opening one of their own in the States in the heart of the theatre district. Henry B. Harris and Jesse Lasky introduced their Folies Bergere Theater which offered an intimate cabaret show from 11:15 P.M. to 1:00 A.M. after their full-scale revue had finished. Their theatre/restaurant failed but the concept caught the eye of a number of the lobster palace owners who were looking for new ways to bring in new business.

During the dance craze of 1912 to 1916, these restaurants met the demand of a ragtime-hungry public; owners cleared away some of the center tables and installed dance floors. "Dancing not only offered diners the opportunity to participate in their own entertainment but also enshrined the dance floor as a central part of the entertainment style of the cabaret."[19]

The rise of cabaret society exerted a powerful influence on the development of social dancing by moving it out of private homes and ballrooms and into the public sphere. Restaurants that offered entertainment attracted a clientele that came from different classes and economic backgrounds. The moneyed members of New York's old families mingled with bankers, businessmen, and theatrical luminaries to enjoy the food, watch live entertainment, and trip the light fantastic themselves. As the business of Broadway mushroomed during this period, tourists who flocked to the Great White Way to see shows also wanted to experience a bit of the high life in one of Times Square's elegant eateries.

George Rector, owner of one of New York's most popular restaurants during this time, spoke about the necessity of installing a dance floor in his place: "All they wanted to do was dance, and we accommodated them with a dance floor that measured thirty feet by twenty. The entire 1,500 all tried to dance on this postage stamp at the same time."[20] Rector recalled, "...the diners would drop their knives and napkins the minute the orchestra broke loose, and stampede for the dancing area. It looked like an elephant dancing on a butcher's block. The couples were jammed back to back, elbow to elbow, and cheek to neck"[21]

The crowded dance floors of these cabarets effected an important change in social dancing. The limited space caused dancers to move more informally as they tried to avoid other couples. The turned-out classical foot positions of previous dances were replaced by a more natural stance, with the feet facing forward. The close proximity of other dancers also brought about the most visible, and to critics, the most shocking change — the close, hugging-type hold. Unlike the ballrooms of the past, there was no dancing master calling out figures. Dancers could improvise and express themselves freely. The strict rules of etiquette that had hobbled the ballrooms of the nineteenth century were gone. Within the cabaret setting, couples could dance the entire evening together without changing partners.

Around 1912, restaurant owners began experimenting with afternoon tea dances, known as thé dansants, or sometimes as tango teas. These tea dances were immensely popular, especially with women, many of whom claimed to be shopping or visiting friends, while secretly slipping in to dance without the knowledge of parents or spouses. The danger to their reputations added to the excitement. The management of these establishments often hired professional male partners called gigolos to dance with unescorted women. The most popular gigolos were Latins, their ethnicity considered many of the period to be a sign of their sensuality. Many lower-class Italian and Jewish men made good livings after claiming to be Latin.

By World War I the tea dance had become a staple of hotels, cabarets, and roof-top gardens. The *New York Times* described the phenomenon of "tea dispensed to the accompaniment of ragtime."[22] The article explained how the hotel tea dance was first promoted by two women in the summer of 1913. Some were scandalized by the notion, but the practice proved to be so popular, "the dancing rooms were soon opened in many other hotels."[23] The public's desire for more and more places to dance led the *Times* to remark,

> [N]ow only the first few hours of the day are kept sacred for sleep; with the result that we have the luncheon dance, the tea dance, the supper dance, and the dance that begins at 1 o'clock in the morning and keeps going as long as people want to stay up. So numerous have become the places where one may go and rhythmically stretch one's nether limbs with respectable and self-respecting folk keeping company that to visit them all would fill months of afternoons and evenings.[24]

One commentator was convinced that soon the dance craze would do away with sleep altogether. He remarked, "We are already accustomed to the dance at the afternoon tea; how long will it take before we are threatened by the dance at the breakfast coffee?"[25]

Exhibition Dancing

Responding to the public's voracious appetite for dancing during this period, theatrical producers began to feature exhibition dance acts in their shows. Broadway musicals always seemed to include a specialty number, even if it had nothing to do with the plot. Vaudeville ballroom dance teams were also in demand. Following the trend, restaurant and cabaret owners rushed to hire the top exhibition ballroom dancers to satisfy their dance-hungry patrons. These dancers typically performed two or three sets a night, after which the audience themselves got up on the floor and tried out the latest steps they had just seen. Dance teams used the popular social dances of the period and stylized them in a theatrical way to appeal to their audiences, thus modifying and refining them. They also invented new dances that found their way in to the social dance vocabulary that is still used today.

There were many favorite ballroom luminaries during this period. Joan Sawyer,[26] nicknamed the "queen" of exhibition dancing, was perhaps one of the most highly paid and successful female dancers. She had many partners including Maurice Mouvet, John Jarrot,[27] Benne Dixon, Carlos Sebastian, George Raft, and in vaudeville, a young Rudolph Valentino.[28] Sawyer appeared in several New York cabarets, such as the El Fey, Louis Martin's, and the Jardin de Danse. In 1914, she was hired by the Shuberts to be general manager and hostesses of The Persian Garden, a dance club on top of the Winter Garden building. There she presented her wildly popular Persian Garden tango, as well as her own creations, the Aeroplane Waltz, the Three In One, and a dance she named after herself called the Joanelle. In 1913, Sawyer with her partner Lew Quinn reportedly introduced the rhumba to American audiences.

Another well-known ballroom dancer was Mae Murray,[29] whose "performances were heralded as much for their dramatic postures and lavish clothing as for their dancing."[30] Murray traditionally danced with a long scarf draped around her neck, a practice soon imitated by many other female ballroom dancers. Murray had supposedly traveled to Paris to study the latest dances, and upon her return to the United States, enjoyed success dancing in New York's most exclusive nightclubs such as William Morris' Jardin de Danse. She eventually served as mistress of ceremonies at the Folies Marigny rooftop garden cabaret above the Forty-fourth Street Theatre in 1914. The club was a popular nightspot and had a dance floor that could hold up to ninety couples at once.[31] Murray did her exhibition dances there every night throughout the spring of 1914. She had many partners, although her most famous pairing was with Clifton Webb.[32] The duo usually opened their act with the Brazilian maxixe, followed by Mae Murray's own version of the hesitation waltz. They closed with a dance called the Cinquante-Cinquante, a dance similar to the Half and Half, made famous by Vernon and Irene Castle. For their encore, Murray and Webb did the Pavlowa Gavotte, a dance created by Anna Pavlowa. In addition to their run at the Folies Marigny, Mae Murray and Clifton Webb had great success touring vaudeville.

Webb had previously partnered another popular dancer, Bonnie Glass. Glass had seen Webb at the Jardin de Danse when he was out dancing socially. She auditioned him and he joined her act. They became a well-known exhibition team on the club and vaudeville circuits, and the two were romantically linked. Although he had training as a show dancer, he learned ballroom from his partners. He had performed in musical comedies as a young man, but he did not gain real notice as a performer until he began dancing in cabarets. In addition to dancing in clubs,

Joan Sawyer and Carlos Sebastian dancing the Maxixe. From *The Tango and Other Up-to-Date Dances* by J. S. Hopkins (1914).

John (Jack) Jarrott and Louise Alexander. From *The Tango and Other Up-to-Date Dances* by J. S. Hopkins (1914).

Webb became a sought after performer in major revues and musicals. "Critics marveled at Webb's versatility; in these shows and others that followed he demonstrated his penchant for both straight exhibition ballroom and comic-eccentric dances. Webb, in fact, often resisted the label of ballroom dancer, since his dancing covered such a broad range, but clearly his ballroom prowess brought him the recognition he needed to further his career."[33]

After Clifton Webb and Bonnie Glass dissolved their partnership, she hired another male dancer to fill his spot—Rudolph Valentino. Throughout 1915 and 1916, the team billed as "Bonnie Glass and Rudolpho," did their act at the Montmartre Café, a club that Glass managed. They also toured across the country on the Keith vaudeville circuit eventually ending up as the headliners at the Palace Theatre in New York.

The husband and wife ballroom team of John Murray Anderson[34] and Genevieve Lyon were an exceptionally popular act in cabarets and revues. Anderson ran one of the top dance schools in New York and, at one point, employed Martha Graham as one of his teachers. The couple served as advisors on the book *Social Dances of Today*, an instructional dance manual written by Margaret and Troy West-Kinney and considered to be one of the most important social dance teaching aids of the period. After his wife died in 1916, John Murray Anderson left exhibition ballroom dancing and became an enormously successful producer, director, author, lyricist, lighting designer, and theatrical entrepreneur, working in vaudeville, in the circus, on the Broadway stage, and in films. He also ran an acting school in Manhattan that included among its students Lucille Ball and Bette Davis.

The Dolly Sisters[35] were identical twins who danced with many male partners separately, but created the greatest sensation when they performed a tandem act with each other. Favorites of the cabaret set, they were ballroom dancers who commanded the public's adoration with their beauty and unique duo and trio dances. They performed at William Morris' Jardin de Danse. In the finale of their act there, they danced with Carlos Sebastian while wearing pony masks. He was dressed as a ring master and maneuvered them around the stage as they trotted a one-step.

The two most famous teams—Maurice Mouvet and Florence Walton, and Vernon and Irene Castle—became international celebrities, icons whose every move affected the tastes and fashions of the day. E. B. Marks compared the two couples; "...the Castles were a sprite and a steel spring; Maurice and Walton were a tiger and a woman."[36]

Maurice Mouvet,[37] often referred to as simply Maurice or Monsieur Maurice, was born in New York City to parents of Belgian extract. He had swarthy, exotic good looks; many thought he was Latin and therefore something of a womanizer. His association with the apache dance furthered the perception that there was something slightly dangerous and passionate about him. In reality he was a proponent of grace and restraint when performing.

Mouvet is sometimes credited with introducing many of the major rag dances to America although he himself always maintained that he did not. In a letter to the editor of *The New York Times* on January 25, 1912, he declared, "I have not brought to America that dance they call the 'turkey trot,' not the 'grizzly bear,' not the 'bunny hug.' In fact, until I arrived here I did not know of these dances...."[38] Mouvet also asserted he did not teach these dances. He did introduce many new dances though, including the junkman rag and the Brazilian maxixe. He was also a major innovator of the American tango.

Maurice Mouvet first gained notoriety in 1907 when he introduced his version of the *danse des Apaches*[39] at the Café de Paris in Paris. A violent dance that mimicked a street fight, the apache dance was associated with the lower class street gangs of Paris. Mouvet claimed to have learned this "Dance of the Underworld" from the original gang members known as the "Gunmen of Paris."[40] Although he was not the first to introduce the dance to the United States, Mouvet became the dancer most associated with the dance and was its chief proponent.[41] He did the dance with all of his various partners, but when he performed it with Florence Walton[42] the audi-

Maurice Mouvet and Florence Walton. From *The Tango and Other Up-to-Date Dances* by J. S. Hopkins (1914).

ences went wild. Always part of their cabaret act, the dance was performed only for late-night customers at the cabaret. "[It] began with a slow waltz and concluded with a death-defying spin, in which Walton clutched her arms around her partner's neck and whirled around him like 'a floating sash.'"[43]

Mouvet was first partnered with Walton in 1911 when Florence Ziegfeld hired them for his production of *The Pink Lady* at the New Amsterdam Theatre. The two married in 1911 and became one of the most successful ballroom exhibition teams, rivaling Vernon and Irene Castle.[44] Mouvet and Walton eventually divorced in 1920. His next partner was Leonora Hughes, but she left the act to marry Argentine millionaire Carlos Ortiz Balsualdo in 1925.[45] Mouvet then teamed up with Barbara Bennett, sister of movie star Constance Bennett. They separated within the year and Mouvet hired Eleanor Ambrose, daughter of a Kansas City oilman, to replace her. In 1926, the two were wed in Paris and danced at the St. Moritz until consumption forced Mouvet to move to the Alps for his health.

Vernon and Irene Castle

Society dancers Vernon and Irene Castle[46] were perhaps the most emulated and influential ballroom couple of the era. In 1915, the *Dramatic Mirror* referred to the husband and wife team as "our supreme ballroom artists, possessing distinction, intelligence, delicacy of dance, and what is termed in the varieties—class"[47]

The Castles first achieved success in the summer of 1911 in Paris where they performed in a sketch for the French musical stage. The revue's initial opening was postponed many times, but finally occurred in March, and the Castles included the grizzly bear in a number they did at the end of the show. According to Irene Castle, her mother had sent her clippings from the newspapers that described the grizzly bear. She recalled, "We decided, as a finale to the show, to introduce French audiences to the latest American dance furor. Unfortunately we had not seen the latest American dances and had only the vague newspaper descriptions to go by."[48] Although the Castles improvised the dance, the response was overwhelming:

> If the American version was rough, ours was even rougher, full of so many acrobatic variations that I was in the air much more often than I was on the ground. The French audience was enthusiastic. They stomped their feet and clapped their hands and yelled "Bravo." They stood up at the end of the number and cried out "greezly bahr" until we appeared again."[49]

Despite their success, they decided to quit the revue because of the wretched conditions at the theatre. Two months after leaving the show, the couple was completely broke. They were then approached by Louis Barraya, who offered them an opportunity to dance at the Café de Paris, the most luxurious supper club in France. The first night, Irene Castle performed in her wedding gown because it was the only garment she had that resembled evening clothes. Her gown had a train and Irene had to pin it up to keep from tripping on it. The dress forced the couple to tone down their moves. In addition, the dance area was miniscule, "like dancing in the aisle of a Pullman car."[50] The couple quickly won over the audience with their restraint and refinement, qualities that would become the hallmark of their dancing.[51] As their fame grew, the couple was invited to dance at private soirées, sometimes as many as three a night, before ending the night with their performance at the Café de Paris.[52]

In 1912, with their reputations preceding them, they returned to the United States. They brought with them a letter of introduction from Louis Barraya, owner of the Café de Paris in Paris, personally addressed to Louis Martin at the Café de l'Opera in New York. They presented the letter and when asked their rate, they demanded the exorbitant fee of three hundred dol-

Vernon and Irene Castle. From *The Tango and Other Up-to-Date Dances* by J. S. Hopkins (1914).

lars a week to perform at the club. Initially, an outraged Martin refused, but within a few days offered them a contract.[53] Included in the deal was a suite of rooms on the fourth floor of the club where the Castles lived. Every night the Castles danced and audiences flocked to see them.

The Castles' charm and polish as they glided across the floor made them favorites with upper class society, and hundreds clamored to see them perform and to take lessons from them. In 1913, with the help of literary agent and socialite Elizabeth Marbury,[54] they opened Castle House, a dance studio with mirrored ballrooms.[55] Located across from the Ritz Carlton Hotel, the exclusive dancing school catered to the most elite clientele and served as a gathering place for young socialites interested in learning the intricacies of the latest dance steps. New York's most prominent matrons, among them Mrs. Stuyvesant Fish, Miss Elsie De Wolfe, and Mrs. W. G. Rockefeller, embraced the young couple, becoming patronesses of the school and inviting them to dance at their private soirées.[56] In addition to Castle House, the couple's connections with the upper echelon led them to open their own cabarets— in late 1913, the Sans Souci; in 1914, Castles in the Air; and in 1915, Castles-by-the-Sea. They performed at their own clubs, but also in other venues across the country, appearing in musical comedies,[57] vaudeville, regional tours, cabarets and restaurants. They appeared in a newsreel entitled *Social and Theatrical Dancing* in 1914 and the following year starred in their own film biography, *The Whirl of Life.*

With the franchising of their name, stores carried everything from Castle corsets and cigars to Castle cosmetics and clothing. They became spokespersons for Victrola records and record players and issued Castle dance records featuring the Castle House Orchestra led by jazz pioneer James Reese Europe.[58]

Irene Castle became one of the most written about women of the day, her every move setting new fashion trends. Her sense of style and views on fashion caused many to dub her "the best dressed woman in America." She advocated for less binding clothes for the modern woman declaring that as dancing came to the forefront in present society, it demanded more sensible styles for women.

> She believed that the power of the dance would force cruel corsets, tight shoes, hats like peach baskets, heavy petticoats, and stiff-boned collars to give way to easy-moving skirts with slits in them, collarless frocks, and subtly cut, free-falling gowns.[59]

When she cut her hair after getting appendicitis, she set in motion a trend in hair-styles that ten years later became the trademark of the flapper in the 1920's. The Castle clip led millions of women to bob their hair.[60]

Because of their refined elegance and decorum, the Castles helped remove many of the negative reactions to modern social dancing. They were instrumental in combating ragtime's connections to lower-class origins and the animal dances' association with vulgarity and impropriety. The Castles made dancing an acceptable, respectable pastime, and they graciously reigned over the dancing craze that captured the world during the second decade of the twentieth century.

The couple authored dozens of articles on dance, fashion, and etiquette. Their instructional best-seller, *Modern Dancing*, was one of the first books to cover modern ballroom dancing. In addition to refining many rag dances, they invented the Castle Walk,[61] the half and half, the innovation, and other dances. They made fashionable the glide, the hesitation waltz, and the maxixe, and in 1914, when they appeared on Broadway in Irving Berlin's *Watch Your Step,* they popularized the foxtrot. Some sources credit them with inventing it.

Dance Madness at All Levels of Society

From 1910 to 1917, dance fever gripped the world. All levels of society were either dancing or talking about it themselves. No one was immune from the influence of ragtime. And, if one

Vernon and Irene Castle. From *The Tango and Other Up-to-Date Dances* by J. S. Hopkins (1914).

wanted to be up-to-date, one had to tango and trot. As one commentator pointed out, "...what's to become of the poor boob who doesn't dance? Social outcast, poor fellow."[62]

As more and more thronged dance halls, clubs, and ballrooms, the demand for new material grew. Dances were created with stunning rapidity. Every week, it seemed, a new dance was introduced. The headline in one newspaper reported, "Dancing Masters are in a Quandary Over What Bird or Beast to Imitate in Search of a New Dancing Sensation."[63]

In his book, *Maurice's Art of Dancing*, Maurice Mouvet mentioned a typical cartoon that appeared in 1914:

> Young man meets his friend rushing breathlessly from studio of well known dancing teacher:
>   Young man: "Where are you going in such a hurry, Tom?"
>   Tom (frantically): "Oh, for Heaven's sake, don't stop me! I must get to the *thé dansant* before the newest step I just learned has become completely old-fashioned."[64]

In addition to catching high society's fancy, dancing also played an important part in the lives of working-class youth, especially young working women.[65] Thousands of day-laborers, factory workers, shopgirls, and secretaries flocked to the local dance-hall, which became the primary cultural and social center of lower and middle class workers. By 1910, over 500 dance halls had opened in New York City. In the lower East Side alone, a dance hall could be found every two and a half blocks.

Dance halls played an important role in the lives of these young workers, offering them a place to meet others of the opposite sex in a safe, but un-chaperoned atmosphere. Meeting at the dance hall was considered "modern." It challenged the old stereotypes about the roles of men and women, and promoted new attitudes about leisure, sexuality, modernity, and personal identity. "Many young women, particularly the daughters of immigrants, came to identify 'cheap amusements' as the embodiment of American urban culture, particularly its individualism, ide-

A 1910 postcard of a ballroom in Santa Cruz, California.

ology of consumption, and affirmation of dating and courtship outside parental control."[66] The growth of the dance hall industry was synonymous with the emergence of the new American woman: modern, independent, strong, and sexual.[67] For women who were subjected to the grind of working in the labor force during this era, dancing provided an escape, a chance "to forget rattling machinery or irritating customers in the nervous energy and freedom of the grizzly bear and turkey trot...."[68] Many young working-women saw dancing as an opportunity to find a husband. Some saw it as a means of moving up in the world. By following the habits of society's elite—doing the kinds of dances that were in vogue and imitating the fashions of the day as best they could—they thought they could somehow improve their social status and perhaps, in the process, attract a man of higher social standing. Dancing represented hope for many young women trapped in the drudgery of a mundane existence.

Keeping current with the latest trends in dancing was almost a requirement. Many factory workers viewed it as a way to forge friendships among each other, recounting the previous evenings pleasures with one's fellow workers, and demonstrating and practicing the latest steps during breaks. Management often ignored discreet discussions on such topics, but usually discouraged outright demonstrations on company property, fearing they might adversely reflect on the company's image.

The most well-known case in point occurred at the Curtis Publishing Company in Philadelphia. Sixteen employees were terminated after they were found practicing the turkey trot on the third floor of the *Ladies Home Journal* building during their lunch break.

> The 16 were discovered at the noon hour engaged in this terpsichorean specialty, much to the disgust of Edward Bok, the editor, who promptly informed the superintendent of the department that the company could dispense with the services of the girls who could so far forget themselves as to engage in such dances even among themselves.... In the meantime there will be no more "turkey trots," "bunny hugs," or "grizzly bears," at least while Mr. Bok is in the building.[69]

Although the girls felt they were treated unfairly because the event occurred during their lunch hour, and some of them asked to be reinstated, the editor did not budge from his decision.

More and more working girls embraced the trotting dances as a way of expressing their independence and modernity. As the girls mimicked the dances, fashions, and habits of the upper classes, the upper classes became concerned that these working girls, who had not had the advantage of a proper upbringing and therefore did not understand restraint, were falling victim to the dance's darker nature.

8

Fashion and Music of the Animal Dances

The second decade of the twentieth century brought with it a period of frenetic change as the world moved into the modern era. Industrialization mushroomed and with it labor unrest. In the United States, the emergence of the middle class brought dramatic social changes as Americans looked for ways to express their newfound affluence. Seeking excitement and modernity, people saw new fashions, new music, and new dances as symbols of social standing and success. Progressive education, rights for minorities, prohibition, socialism, birth control, and women's suffrage were the hot topics of the day.

In the midst of this social unrest, the world was plunged into the Great War. Countries were forced out of isolationism and onto the international stage. Naïve traditions and outmoded values were challenged. The world was changing, and so were its dances. The waltz was set aside and trotting took its place. A leading psychologist of the day saw "grave dangers in the universal craze for sensuous dances." He warned, "No one can doubt that true dangers are near wherever the dancing habit is prominent ... overemphasis on dancing has usually characterized a period of political reaction, of indifference to public life, of social stagnation and carelessness. When the volcanoes were rumbling the masses were always dancing."[1] And the masses were dancing — keeping in step with the infectious rhythm of ragtime.

Ragtime Music

Ragtime was at the height of its popularity between 1899 and 1918 and is considered to be "the first truly American musical genre."[2] It was basically created from a combination of European musical forms and African dance rhythms and syncopations. The harmonic and tonal structure of ragtime was also influenced by the march, first introduced in minstrel show cakewalks and walk-arounds and further popularized with military bands at the turn of the century. Ragtime differed from the basic cakewalk march in its use of syncopation; the bass hand kept a steady metrical beat, but the melody emphasized offbeat accents.[3] "The ultimate (and intended) effect on the listener [was] actually to accentuate the beat, thereby inducing the listener to move to the music."[4]

Ragtime began primarily as instrumental dance music. As it grew in popularity, composers began adding lyrics to the syncopated melodies. Ragtime was then disseminated through sheet music. The new musical style flourished, aided by the growth of the music publishing industry, which simplified ragtime, so the buying public could play it more easily.[5] Tin Pan Alley was born and ragtime songwriters flooded the market with new tunes.

One of the earliest published ragtime songs, "La Pas Ma La," was composed by African American minstrel dancer and comedian, Ernest Hogan,[6] in 1895, and was accompanied by a comedy dance step which consisted of a walk forward and three hops back. An article in the *Spirit Lake Beacon*, which appeared on February 2, 1906, spoke of the song and dance:

The author of the new dance was Ernest Hogan, who afterward gained a measure of fame for other songs he composed, but when asked what his initial effort meant he said "ragtime." Ernest Hogan is the "father of ragtime," for "Pas-ma-la" was the first effort of this kind that ever attracted general attention.[7]

Hogan also wrote and published the hit "All Coons Look Alike To Me,"[8] which sold over one million copies and started a craze in "coon songs"—a genre of racially derogatory songs.[9] Hogan was heavily criticized by members of his own race for writing the song, and he expressed deep shame for having fostered negative stereotypes. Composer E. B. Marks wrote, "Hogan died haunted by the awful crime he had unwittingly committed against the race."[10]

The coon song, although today recognized as racially divisive and deeply offensive, was largely responsible for bringing ragtime to a larger, more diverse audience and helping to fuel the ragtime dance craze by popularizing ragtime music.

There were many important ragtime composers, including Scott Joplin, Tony Jackson, Jelly Roll Morton, Willie Bloom, Ben Harney, and numerous others—too numerous to mention here. One in particular though is closely identified with helping to popularize the animal dance craze—Irving Berlin.

In 1911, when the young composer was invited to join the Friar's Club, he presented as part of his initiation entertainment a song called "Alexander's Ragtime Band." The tune eventually became one of the biggest ragtime hits of its day. The same year, Berlin wrote a song that became the anthem of the animal dance craze—"Everybody's Doin' It Now." Part of the lyric read,

> Honey, honey, can't you hear?
> Funny, funny music, dear
> Ain't the funny strain goin' to your brain?
> Like a bottle of wine, fine
> Hon,' hon,' hon,' hon,' take a chance
> One, one one, one little dance
> Can't you see them all swaying up the hall?
> Let's be gettin' in line
>
> Ev'rybody's doin' it, doin' it, doin' it
> Ev'rybody's doin' it, doin' it, doin' it
> See that ragtime couple over there
> Watch them throw their shoulders in the air
> Snap their fingers, honey, I declare
> It's a bear, it's a bear, it's a bear, there![11]

In 1912, Berlin's song was used in the Broadway production of *Over the River*, a show many historians credit with introducing the grizzly bear to the general public. The production also featured other ragtime dances. In a review of the show, The New York Times reported, "...all the dances from the turkey trot to the tango, are exposed to the eye, by no less person than Maurice [Mouvet], (direct from the Café de Paris and Louis Martins.)"[12]

Not all musicians embraced the new ragtime musical style. Edward B. Perry, a classical musician of the period compared rag to "a dog with rabies."[13] Another critic said it was like a cheap crime novel "full of bangs and explosions, devised in order to shake up the overworked mind."[14]

The American Federation of Musicians adopted a resolution against ragtime dancing and went on record as against the publication and distribution of ragtime music declaring that it would have a degrading effect on public morals and impugn the art of music in general. Union members of Local 309 in Fond du Lac, Wisconsin called the new music disgusting and called for a total ban. They also cited concerns that if ragtime kept growing in popularity, it would decrease their work because many of the members had trouble playing ragtime.

EVERYBODY'S DOING IT NOW

Everybody's doing it,
  'Till they wear out hide and hair.
They don't care for anyone
  When they do the Grizzly Bear.

EVERYBODY'S DOING IT NOW

Everybody's doing it
  With a motion that's a lot.
You move your body sidewise
  When you do the Turkey Trot.

EVERYBODY'S DOING IT NOW

Everybody's doing it
  On the carpet, floor and rug.
They will do it anywhere,
  If it's the Bunny Hug.

EVERYBODY'S DOING IT NOW

Everybody's doing it:
  You'll have to take it from me
That you must hug and squeeze me tight
  When we do that Texas Tommy.

Many blamed the dances of the day on the music. *The La Crosse Tribune*, stated, "...ragtime music is responsible for ragtime dances, and if the charge is true it constitutes another indictment against the degeneracy of melody."[15]

Some songwriters of the period reacted to the onslaught of ragtime songs and dances by publishing anti-rag songs. "My Anti Rag-time Girl" was one such attempt to combat the trend. Written by Elsie Janis, the 1913 song honored the pure young girl—"the kind your mother would have liked to have you know,"[16] who shunned ragtime dances. The chorus of this song was,

> She won't do the Bunny Hug,
> nor dance the Grizzly Bear,
> She hasn't learned the Turkey Trot
> and somehow doesn't care.
> For chasing round the restaurants
> she doesn't care a fig,
> She can't tell a Tango
> from a Can Can or a Jig
> She don't wave her shoulders
> when the band plays "It-chy-koo;"
> The "Wedding Glide" don't make her senses whirl.
> But bet that she's right there
> on some sweet old fashioned air,
> Like "Genevieve, sweet Genevieve."
> She's my little Anti Rag-time Girl.[17]

Ragtime's widespread appeal was perhaps due to its cross-cultural use of both European and African traditions, a combination that resulted in a purely American sound. It was "a rural folk music transposed to an urban and industrial context, where its machine-like rhythms became an expression of lost innocence of bygone days and ways."[18] Most importantly, it was danceable.

Ragtime Fashion

When the *Ballets Russes* presented *Scheherazade* in Paris in 1910, Orientalism came into vogue and dame fashion responded. Espoused by designer Paul Poiret, this Eastern influence was evidenced by the use of full pantaloons or flowing skirts topped with long tunics tied with a sash. The wearing of turbans or bandeaus with feather spikes, also insinuated the Asian influence. During this period waistlines were generally high, just under the bustline, and narrow skirts with short draping overskirts were also popular. Referred to as lampshade skirts, these overskirts were sometimes wired to hang like a lampshade from the waist.

By 1914, hobble skirts came into fashion. These dresses also drew heavily upon Eastern influences, with the tight bottom hems of the skirts suggesting the bottoms of harem pants. They usually measured only about three feet around at the bottom, and at times were so narrow, walking in them was almost impossible. Some women actually tied their legs together with cord, fearing that the skirt would split if their stride were too wide.

Some articles of the day suggest that trotting dances were initially shaped by the short, jerky steps that women had to utilize while wearing a hobble skirt. Fashion icon Irene Castle initially wore a hobble skirt herself while dancing, but found it so difficult to move in, she quickly adopted simple, free-flowing gowns. When the new dresses proved to be much more comfort-

Opposite: **These 1912 postcards comically represent four of the most popular animal dances of the day. The title of the series is from Irving Berlin's ragtime anthem "Everybody's Doing it Now."**

Early twentieth century British postcard of a ragtime couple.

able to move in, Castle also began wearing similar styles for her everyday wear. Newspapers remarked that she resembled a noble French Revolutionary heroine. Because of her enormous popularity with the public, she did indeed lead something of a revolution in women's fashion. By the summer of 1913, many women were abandoning the constricting hobble skirt and started experimenting with the Grecian-inspired "Castle frock."

As dance mania gripped the world, fashion struggled to keep up. Trains were eliminated, and to allow freedom of the legs and make movement easier, the split skirt was introduced. Conservative factions reacted with horror.

Two girls wearing slit skirts were walking down the street in New York City with two of their friends when they were heckled by other girls. The insults resulted in a brawl in which "many cheeks were scratched and much hair was pulled." The scuffle finally resulted in the police being called. The four girls were arrested along with the fifteen-year-old who started the catcalls, Miss May Gross. All five were put in the patrol wagon, which "gave the four a splendid chance to pummel their critic, and they were busily engaged in making the most of this when the police pried them apart."[19]

In Annapolis, Maryland, a bill was introduced in the House of Delegates that prohibited the wearing of slit skirts. The bill included instructions that "money collected from fines for violating its provisions shall be used to 'educate girls how to dress decently.'"[20] In Richmond Virginia, Blossom Browning was fined twenty-five dollars and driven out of town after she appeared in a slit skirt on the city streets and "startled Mayor Ainslie and Chief of Police Werner."[21] Miss Browning told the court that the gown was in fashion and had been purchased at a licensed department store, and besides, she liked it. When that defense failed, she informed them that the slit in her skirt had been basted shut, but that the stitches had ripped. The Mayor and Chief of Police testified that her pretty little ankle proved otherwise, and Miss Browning was ordered to pay the fine and was driven out of Richmond.

The Chief of Police of Louisville, Kentucky issued orders calling for the arrest of any woman who wore a slit skirt who didn't also have a protective undergarment covering the leg. He stated, "A number of women have been appearing upon the streets in Louisville in dresses which the laws of decency forbid, and I believe this is disorderly conduct ... where a flagrant exposure is made it is the duty of the police to make arrests."[22] The Chief also commented, however, that he didn't think it would do much good because "women who have the 'nerve' to appear on the streets in slit dresses will not mind 'a little thing like a Police Court trial.'"[23]

The Rev. H. T. Walsh called the slit skirt dresses "monstrosities" and announced from his pulpit at the Church of Our Lady of Mercy in New Britain, Connecticut that he would refuse communion to any woman who approached the alter in such garb. In Atlantic City, Mrs. Charles Lanning appeared on the beach in a bathing suit that had long skirt with slits on each side. Passersby began to throw sand at her until a crowd of two hundred men had surrounded her. The lifeguards "formed a flying wedge and broke through the mob"[24] only to find Mrs. Lanning lying unconscious on the ground with the crowd still pelting her with sand. She was rushed to the hospital with the crowd following her "to get another glimpse of the suit."[25] After the victim had recovered and was released, she saw the huge crowd gathered outside the hospital and promptly fainted.

Opinion was divided. Although some women viewed the new styles as scandalously improper, many responded to the new freedom offered by the slit skirt and quickly embraced the changes. Even some men supported the reforms. When citizens started a campaign to bar the slit skirt in Kansas City, Missouri, the head Judge of the Criminal Court Ralph Latshaw issued this statement: "There is nothing immoral in the slit skirt, diaphanous gown, or any other present form of women's attire. Narrow skirts and trim figures do not mean immorality, as some insist." The judge added, "The women of to-day have only one idea in view — to dress in a man-

An early twentieth century postcard of a turkey trotting couple. The lady wears a fashionable hobble skirt and a Dutch cap made popular by Irene Castle.

ner that appeals to men. Well hasn't it always been so?"[26] Nevertheless, as a concession to modesty, Irene Castle suggested combining the split skirt with a plaited petticoat underneath. Thus, when turning or dipping the legs would be free to execute the figures of the dance, but still remain chastely covered. She added, "The openings in a skirt of this sort can be fastened with tiny glove-snaps, so that on the street the wearer may appear to have the usual narrow costume, while at the same time she has a practical one for the daily *thé dansant*."[27]

In addition to slits, the overall silhouette of gowns was also altered because of demands of the dance. Tight sleeves constricted range of motion and so soft loose blouses with full sleeves became popular. Collars were eliminated and gowns became lower cut in both the front and back to offer greater freedom. Choice of material was also affected. Softer, lighter, more diaphanous fabrics were used.[28] Castle said, "...the demand of the women who dance is, 'Give me something soft and light.'"[29] In her book *Modern Dancing* she reminds her readers,

> The costume for the modern dances is a very important feature. A gown that is stiff or bunchy in its lines and does not fall softly will make even the most graceful dancer seem awkward and uncouth, and no amount of skill in stepping intricate measures can obviate the ugliness of a pump slipping off at the heel in the pretty dips or twirls of the dance.[30]

In addition to changes in fashion silhouettes, innovations in undergarments were also brought about by the new ragtime dances. Stiff whale-boned corsets were abandoned and one-piece combination bloomer/brassiere and softer elastic girdles were worn instead. Irene Castle stated, " ...all these precautions as to the outward gowning are wasted if you continue to wear the long, stiff corsets ... no amount of grace, no amount of clever training, and no amount of the knowledge of the most intricate steps will help you to dance charmingly unless your corset has 'give' in it and allows you to move with supple ease and comfort."[31] She recommended the Castle Corset, which supported, yet conformed to the natural figure. Because under petticoats were typically made of chiffon or similar filmy material, light or colored stockings that matched the shoes or gown were substituted for the dark heavy stockings worn in the previous era. Stockings were adorned with colored gems, lace, embroidery, "and, of course, all kinds of clocks and butterflies to draw attention to a slender foot and ankle."[32]

As hemlines inched slightly upward, shoes became a prominent fashion item. For dancing, shoes had to be comfortable and fastened securely. Castle herself usually wore either pumps tied with ribbons, or soft leather boots that reached up to just below the knee. She recommended that the average woman wear "...a pump with a moderate heel, fastened about the ankle with ribbons which cross the leg several times." She said, "This gives the impression of the Greek dancing-sandals, and also accentuates the slenderness of the ankles."[33]

In 1913, in Boston, a unique "dancing pump made only for use in executing the tango, turkey trot, bunny hug or a few other of the fancy dances that are raging around the country in high popularity"[34] appeared on the scene. First introduced on the campus of Harvard University, the shoe featured a rubber inset to prevent slipping on the dance floor. An article in the *Lowell Sun* in Lowell Massachusetts explained, "Directly beneath the spot where the ball rests there is a lump of corrugated rubber which looks like the half section of a goose egg. This, firmly fastened to the sole of either foot, permits the wearer to tango or trot to his heart's content without fearing the sort of catastrophe which is commonly preceded by pride."[35] The non-skid shoes cost $10.00 a pair.

Irene Castle's influence sparked many fashion innovations. In 1914, after being photographed wearing riding jodhpurs, fashionable women added them to their everyday wardrobes. She also initiated the fashion of wearing Dutch bonnets. Perhaps her most lasting influence was when she cut her hair before having her appendix removed, and women around the world started bobbing their hair. Those that kept their hair long, adopted simpler coiffures because they didn't "become untidy when dancing."[36] Picture hats also fell victim to the dance. As Irene Castle declared, "Big hats are unpleasant to dance in."[37]

In 1914, with the outbreak of World War I, hemlines began to inch up largely due to shortages in fabric. As women entered the workforce, overskirts and tunics also became fuller, and confining underskirts were eliminated, creating a simpler, freer silhouette. Waistlines dropped to the natural waist. By 1915, skirt length had risen above the ankle and was hailed as patriotic, earning the name "war crinoline" by the fashion periodicals.

9

Reaction to the Animal Dances

On August 24, 1913, the *Oakland Tribune* featured a commentary in its society section entitled "Suzette's Views on Society and Dancing." The column's society writer observed,

> Anything connected with dancing is of instant interest. No one seems ever to tire of the subject. All over the world the dance is on. Everybody dances. The "dasante" has swept Europe. It has invaded New York. In cafes and cabarets the professional dancers no longer hold the center of the stage — they are simply crowded on side — everybody is a professional — for every one thinks he can dance well. It is quite, as a clever woman writes from New York, "Everybody Trots."[1]

Between 1911 and 1914, when the ragtime dances were at the height of their popularity, it did indeed seem that everyone was trotting. One paper reported, "If you happen to be staying late in a Broadway restaurant, you will see couples totting on their way to the coat room, trotting while the hat boy earns his tip, trotting as they are helped into their wraps and finally trotting across the sidewalk into a taxi to the high amusement of the policeman. Possibly they resume trotting as soon as the taxi deposits them at their homes."[2]

Society embraced the syncopated dances at balls, at tea dances, and at late night roof-top gardens; the working class flooded dances halls to dance the turkey trot, the bunny hug, and grizzly bear. The dances were also a staple on Broadway, in vaudeville, and at cabaret performances. The syncopation of the new dances was infectious. Newspaper accounts of the day were full of anecdotes about who was dancing what and where. The *New York Times,* for example, reported on the delayed departure of a train at Union Station when two stars of the Boston opera danced the modern dances on the station platform. No one seemed to mind. "The conductor with his right hand raised to give the 'high ball' sign, stood rigid, the fireman let his steam go down, and the porters dropped the suitcases and all stared and smiled while the two songbirds tripped daintily through a maze of baggage trucks and mail bags."[3]

Meanwhile, physicians, psychologists, and commentators sought to explain why this dancing craze held so many in its thrall. Some blamed the rhythm.

> The turkey trot appeals to that primitive instinct, that universal sense of rhythm which is part of the fiber of our being.... Just feel the rhythm. One, one, one, one, one, one.... Just stand up, bend your knees a little, relax your muscles and let yourself go. Can you keep still? Doesn't some primitive sense of rhythm in you leap out in response to the beating summons? One, one, one, one, one, one, one, one.... That is why the one-step — call it turkey trot, tango, grizzly bear, horse trot, what you will — will live.[4]

Others blamed the growing social unrest of the time.

> The dancing epidemic which the country is witnessing recalls in some respects the dancing mania of the middle ages.... The ragtime and turkey trot manias appear to be contagious in much the same way that the medieval manias were.... These neurotic phenomena have been asserted to widespread neurasthenia due to unrest and other pathological social conditions.... The instinct to dance is a very primitive one, and through the dance certain emotions find outlet and expression. There is a normal and an abnormal phase to the subject, however, and we are inclined to think that it is the latter that finds exemplification in ragtime and trotting.[5]

Whatever the cause, the ragtime rage grew and grew, as did reaction against it.

Etching entitled "Father Learns the Turkey Trot" by Wm L. Jacobs.

Anti-Ragtime Sentiment

Freak dances, as ragtime dances were also called, evoked strong emotional reactions from those who watched them and those that danced them. As with all social dances, there were defenders and detractors. Most who railed against trotting did so because they objected to its shady origins. To many it was simply ugly. The close hold and jiggling of the body employed during the dance drew the most ire, causing the out-spoken adversaries to pronounce the modern dance vulgar, if not downright immoral. The dance was seen as "a reversion to the grossest practices of savage man ... based on the primitive motive of orgies enjoyed by the aboriginal inhabitants of every uncivilized land."[6] After seeing the new dances, one critic lamented that it had struck "sex o'Clock in America."[7]

Anti-rag voices rang out. Vincent Wehrle the Catholic Bishop of Bismarck, when asked his view of modern dancing, said, "The dances and entertainments which people prefer are always a reflection upon their moral standard. When they are anxious to strut like turkeys, they must have something in their moral makeup which is kindred to the pompous conceited turkey."[8] Henry Beets of the Christian Reformed Church in Grand Rapids, Michigan contended, "No one has ever been able, by means of the modern dance, to dance himself 'Nearer my God to Thee,' but statistics have proven that many have gotten nearer to the devil by means of it."[9] The Canon of St. Paul's Cathedral in London said that modern dances such as the turkey trot were "Evils which flourish unrebuked."[10] Dr. A. M. Williams, presiding elder of the Columbus Methodist District, stated that the turkey trot was surely the "gait to Hell."[11] A bishop in the Episcopal Church was perhaps the most vitriolic. He stated, "The venom of the serpent is in it [the dance]. The taint of its birth, the virus of its constitution, is ineradicable. It is evil, only evil, and that continually."[12]

Thomas S. Byrne, the Bishop of Nashville, not only preached scathing sermons against freak dancing, but also ordered an announcement read from every pulpit under his authority that anyone who continued to "indulge" in the vile modern dances would be denied the Sacrament of penance, stating that it "would be useless for them to go to confession in hope of obtaining absolution."[13] Cardinal Basilo Pomili, Vicar General of Rome and representative of the Pope, even went so far as to call for a Papal ban on all modern dances.

In the United States, the most well-known voice raised against dancing was evangelist Billy Sunday. "The dance is one institution I'll rip from hell to breakfast and back again for lunch," Sunday ranted. "Nothing causes the ruin of more girls than the damnable rotten dance."[14] Sunday's colorful exhortations about the "hotbed of immorality" known as the modern dance were heard by millions of Americans between 1906 and 1918. He said, "The dance is simply a hugging match set to music,"[15] adding "The dance is the dry rot of society. I say it is immoral.... Don't you go to that dance.... I say young girl, don't go to that dance; it has proved to be the moral graveyard that has caused more ruination than anything that was ever spewed out of the mouth of hell."[16]

Outrage was not limited to the clergy. Britain's upper crust was appalled at the scandalous excesses seen on the dance floors in London. They feared "that if adopted these dances would soon reduce the ballrooms to beer gardens."[17] One matron emphatically stated, "I will not have the 'turkey trot' or 'bunny hug' in my house. Anyone dancing them would never be invited again. It is simply a foolish craze for notoriety that prompts people to invent these absurdities. The inventors must be bad dancers themselves."[18] *The Washington Post* reported on May 24, 1913:

> Mrs. Rexford Parsons, a prominent London hostess, caused a society tempest by telephoning to those who had planned dinner parties to precede her splendid dance at the Ritz-Carleton Wednesday, that if the tango, the turkey trot, or any other transatlantic freak dances should be attempted, the cassano orchestra would immediately cease playing. In spite of many notable absentees, Mrs. Parsons was applauded at the ball as a champion of the right.[19]

As ragtime became more popular in England, outrage mounted against those "nasty American hug-dances." The most ardent opponents proposed an Anti-Ragtime League "that would effectively stamp out the craze for these new dances."[20] Efforts were mounted to ban the dances outright.

Similar actions were taken around the globe. In Berlin, the police arrested and fined any person caught turkey trotting. The dancing masters of Greater Berlin, who were behind the campaign, reported good success in ridding the public dance halls of offending dances, but were concerned that upper levels of society "were still indulging privately in the contortions."[21] The Panamanian Government barred the Turkey Trot. The International Academy of Dancing Masters in France declared "these epileptic evolutions to be hostile to good society,"[22] and in Paris the tango, turkey trot, and grizzly bear were barred.

Bans were also widespread in the United States.[23] The Chief of Police in New Haven, Connecticut issued orders to shut down any public dances where the grizzly bear and turkey trot were performed. Officials in Chicago called the new dances a disgrace, stating, "Their names alone are enough to condemn them."[24] All wiggling dances in the Windy City were banned. The Mayor of Boston mandated that a matron and policeman be on guard at every public dance hall to see that the turkey trot, tango, and dances of similar ilk were not attempted. He threatened to revoke the license of any establishment that allowed the dances. Chief of Police John W. Ryan of Dallas, Texas mandated that the turkey trot, grizzly bear and bunny hug "would not be permitted in local dancing halls." The Chief announced, "You must be able to see daylight between the dancers. Promiscuous hugging in dance halls will not be tolerated in Dallas. The young girls must be protected."[25] In New York City, Mayor Gaynor barred the turkey trot, bunny hug, wiggle worm, and other dances which he said were "threatening the morality of Gotham society."[26]

After a personal investigation of various dancing venues, he concluded that New York dancers "were exceeding the speed limit."[27] He drew up a bill that he submitted to the state legislature to rid the state of the wicked dances.

New York City was serious about ridding itself of freak dances. The Southern Hotel in Manhattan was raided and the proprietor and manager were arrested. All 600 registered guests and lodgers were ordered to vacate the building within forty-eight hours, and the establishment was closed because of reports of "extremes in dancing...."[28] Wilson's Dancing Studio on the corner of Broadway and Forty-sixth Street, was raided and nearly a hundred people were arrested for indecent and immoral dancing.[29]

When a guest introduced the turkey trot at a ball given at the Naval Academy in Annapolis, the Superintendent of the Academy, Captain John Henry Gibbons, responded swiftly by announcing a series of four new Naval regulations:

1. None of the modern dances are to be performed at the United States Naval Academy under any circumstances.
2. The midshipmen must keep their left arm straight during all dances.
3. A space of at least three inches must be kept between the dancing couple at all times.
4. Midshipment [sic] must not take the arm of their partner under any circumstances.[30]

Any infraction of the rules by cadets would be met with severe disciplinary action. Captain Gibbons announced, "Naval officers who ought to know declare that under these rules turkey trotting and similar dancing is impossible."[31]

The stigma associated with ragtime dancing was so pervasive that, in an effort to avert what he called a national scandal, President-elect Woodrow Wilson canceled the Inaugural Ball fearing that guests might do the turkey trot, bunny hug, or grizzly bear. Wilson ordered the cancellation, he said, because he feared that no matter what steps were taken to prevent such dances, "they were almost certain to appeal to some of those attending the function, who would manage to have their way."[32]

Social Reformers

Progressive reformers viewed ragtime dancing as a threat to the moral well-being of the masses. In Chicago, Jane Addams, founder of Hull House settlement, criticized the dance hall. In her 1909 book *The Spirit of Youth and the City Streets* she wrote that it was a place where "improprieties were fostered." Addams lamented the lack of proper supervision for young women eager to find entertainment. She said, "The public dance halls, filled with frivolous and irresponsible young people in a feverish search for pleasure, are but a sorry substitute for the old dances on the village green in which all of the older people in the village participated. Chaperonage then was not a social duty but natural and inevitable."[33]

Leading the fight against immoral dancing among the working classes in New York was Belle Linder Israels. She founded an organization called the Committee on Amusements and Vacation Resources for Working Girls. The group was one of the most active opponents of the turkey trot, bunny hug, grizzly bear, and other "hugging dances." Formed in June of 1908, the group began its battle by conducting a survey of public amusements available to the working class youth of New York City. The investigation revealed that nine out of every ten young working women said that going to the dance hall was their favorite pastime, and that over 150,000 youths frequented local dance halls each week. Capitalizing on the dreadful reputation of dance halls at the time, one opponent called the dance hall a "muck-raking, maiden-murdering, man-destroying institution."[34] Members of the Committee used this information to attract outside

The caption on this 1914 postcard insinuates the less-than-savory nature of the turkey trot.

support. They actively campaigned to eradicate vulgar dances, believing that such dancing, mixed with the readily available alcohol sold at these establishments, was a recipe for promiscuity. Girls who tripped the light fantastic on the dance hall floor, they believed, inevitably tripped right into the brothel. Even the most innocent of young girls could unwittingly fall into the trap of impropriety in the unchaperoned, unregulated, and sexually charged atmosphere of the local dance hall. In her article "The Way of the Girl," Mrs. Israels wrote,

> [N]o girl comes to the dance hall night after night and remains what she was when she began coming there. You cannot dance night after night, held in the closest of sensual embraces, with every effort made in the style of dancing to appeal to the worst that is in you, and remain unshaken by it. No matter how wary or how wise a girl may be — and she has enough things in her daily life in factory and store to teach her — she is not always able to keep up the good fight. It is always a matter of pursuit and capture.[35]

Because prostitution and white slavery were potent topics of debate during this period, the Committee received wide support. Upright citizens of good moral character realized that to battle the evils of modern man, they had to address the root of the problem — modern dances. One critic was overhead to remark, "The closing of the red light districts as a means of correcting immorality, while permitting the modern dances to flourish is like aiming a popgun at a battleship."[36]

In a circular published after their dance hall investigation, the Committee's following plea was included:

> The attention of the Committee on Amusements and Vacation Resources of Working Girls of New York City has been directed to the widespread diffusion of certain forms of dancing and its contribution to delinquency. After investigation our committee has reported that conditions on this regard challenge the immediate consideration of all who are interested in the welfare of young men and young women. We need your co-operation in our efforts to suppress tough dancing, which, according to our investigators is being practiced to an alarming extent. We feel that once the public conscience is aroused to the gravity of the situation means will be adopted whereby all dancing of this character will be prohibited.[37]

In addition to fighting for the removal of tough dances from the dance hall, the Committee on Amusements and Vacation Resources for Working Girls also fought to remove improper dancing from the ballrooms of the wealthy. Israels and her army of reformers were concerned that if members of high society performed the dances, they would legitimize them. Therefore, the Council reminded the smart set that the upper echelon must set an example for those less fortunate. Mrs. Israels argued,

> The "turkey trot" and the "grizzly bear" can be and are danced very prettily by some girls in the younger set, but that the difference between their manner of dancing them and that which can be witnessed in the rowdy dance halls is only one of degree, and that innocent participants can slip almost unconsciously from one extreme to the other. The working girl who seeks the dance hall for her amusement is tremendously interested to read in her newspaper that Mrs. So-and-So's debutante daughter has danced the "grizzly bear," and urges this fact as the reason why she should continue to indulge in it; without realizing at all that there are "grizzly bears" and "grizzly bears."[38]

Because of its inherent dangers, Mrs. Israels stated that even modified forms of freak dances should be discouraged. She warned,

> It is this milder form of the dance that is being taught to the unsuspecting. The positions and movements of the dance, no matter how slight they may be, are pernicious.... We urge the importance of recognizing the distinction between legitimate dancing and this hideous perversion, which generally speaking, is not dancing at all, but a series of indecent antics to the accompaniment of music.[39]

The Committee held conferences to educate members of society about rough dancing.[40] Their first, held at Delmonico's, featured a demonstration of the turkey trot, the Gaby glide, and other current dances, highlighting the more objectionable aspects of each. One of the dancers demonstrating was a young man named Al Jolsen, who was performing at the Winter Garden. He and his partner Florence Cable showed the eager crowd the scandalous dances. The bunny hug brought gasps from those watching. The turkey trot was presented in its most extreme form, a variation called "The Shiver"—a dance that was said to send shudders through those gathered to watch the demonstration. The audience, consisting of society matrons, settlement workers, and city officials, were titillated and suitably shocked by the performance, and Jolsen and his partner were apparently met with thunderous applause.[41]

The second conference, held in the ballroom of Mrs. Charles B. Alexander's mansion on Fifth Avenue was attended by prominent socialites and featured mostly folk dances that were used as examples of "the more dignified and graceful method of dancing."[42] The committee predicted at the conclusion of the second conference that during the next winter's season, "the perversions of the dances of to-day" would be replaced by "the stately minuet."[43] Mrs. Israels commissioned the young ladies attending "to carry forth the message and to assist in establishing a standard of beautiful dancing."[44]

The Committee exercised tremendous clout in the fight against improper dancing. After their attempts to censor the dances proved largely futile, they decided to attack the problem by regulating the dance halls instead. The Committee worked in tandem with the Bureau of Licenses, "having the dances declared disorderly conduct, so that the license could be revoked as a penalty for the very appearance of the dance."[45]

The Committee was able to get a bill introduced into the State Legislature, which called for the licensing and regulation of public dancing academies. In addition to prohibiting the sale of liquor at such establishments, it held the proprietor responsible for any displays of indecent or improper dancing. The law went into effect in September of 1909. When dance academy owners challenged the law in court, the Committee responded by introducing similar legislation regulating dance halls. It quickly became law. Inspectors were assigned to investigate dance halls, and any owner who tolerated "tough dancing" was threatened with forfeiture of his license.

Refining Ragtime Dances

Despite the battle to exterminate ragtime dances, they flourished. When banning them outright failed, efforts were made to replace the objectionable dances with more acceptable ones, or at least tone them down.[46] On September 27, 1913, the *Lincoln Daily News* in Lincoln, Nebraska ran an editorial that urged its readers to work on refining the modern dances, not eradicating them:

> It [the turkey trot] has its dangers. To attempt to avoid the dangers by forbidding the dance itself is folly. To attempt to eliminate the dangers by wise counsel, temperate restriction and constructive suggestion, is the bounden duty of parents and guardians, and all upon whom rests the responsibility for directing the development of the present day young person. Control the turkey trot, do not try to stamp it out.[47]

Along these lines, there was a movement to standardize freak dances to eliminate any objectionable features from them. Uriel Davis, creator of the horse trot and several other dances, proposed a central clearing house in which dances would be approved and then distributed to various studios around the country.[48]

Vernon and Irene Castle, perhaps the leading proponents of refining rag dancing, urged restraint and decorum while dancing. In the forward to their 1914 book *Modern Dancing*, they stated, "...dancing, properly executed, is neither vulgar nor immodest. But, on the contrary, the personification of refinement, grace, and modesty." They continued, "Our aim is to uplift danc-ing, purify it, and place it before the public in its proper light."[49] The Castles listed various "sug-gestions for correct dancing," such as; "Do not wriggle the shoulders," "Do not shake the hips," "Do not twist the body," Do not flounce the elbows," "Do not pump the arms," and "Do not hop-glide instead."[50]

The couple's influence upon changing dance styles is evident in an article that appeared in *The New York Times* on January 31, 1913, entitled "Turkey Trot Must Glide." The article reported that Mrs. Sadie George took Mrs. Blake to court claiming Mrs. Blake's guests had danced the turkey trot and caused her ceiling to fall in. Mrs. Blake's lawyer defended his client stating that the turkey trot was now a gliding dance and therefore was not intended to produce noise. He testified, "...your honor, my client and her guests were just learning to turkey trot, and the con-volutions they indulged in may have produced a racket. However, they have learned how to do it now, and from this [point] on they will glide. Then there won't be any noise." The judge responded, "Well. If your client knows how to glide now, let her glide out of court, but she must remember that any more turkey trotting must be of the gliding kind." The article concluded, "Mrs. Blake glided immediately and Mrs. George swept out after her."[51]

The most powerful lobby for changing rag dancing was that of professional dancing teach-ers. The Academy of Dancing Masters in Paris, for example, set down the "Ten Commandments of Dancers." Reacting to what they viewed as "frivolous influences which have lately invaded society ballrooms" in the form of "the 'turkey trot,' the 'grizzly bear,' and other freak dances from America,"[52] the Academy created a "Dancers' Decalogue." The rules were sent to all prin-cipal dancing schools in America to be prominently exhibited. The ten rules were as follows:

1. Have beautiful movements and you have beautiful thoughts.
2. Correctness of carriage gives correctness of mind.
3. The drawing room dance should be a silent expression of courtesy and not a series of unseemly movements without order of taste.
4. The mental effect of dancing should be a feeling of gentleness, politeness, and respect, and not of coarseness.
5. A coarse gestures is more harmful to the mind and often inspires more bad thoughts that vulgar speech.
6. Discipline your muscles and always maintain correct attitudes toward intimate friends.
7. Young man, hold the lady by the waist. Do not press her, but hold her respectfully. Young woman, do not rest altogether on your partner in dancing. Keep a pleasing, gra-cious, but correct attitude and you will be respected.
8. Let your intelligence, goodness, and politeness be known by your movements.
9. Physiology should always correspond closely with psychology.
10. Dance like a civilized being and not like a savage.[53]

Part of the appeal of rag dances was the close hold employed while dancing. Partners could squeeze each other so tight there was not even enough space between them "for the Holy Ghost."[54] The American National Association of Masters of Dancing continually made efforts to clean up rag dances and to replace them with "keep-your distance dances." In their annual meet-ing in New York in January of 1920 they announced that they "count[ed] upon the support of moth-ers, fathers, daughters, sons, dance hall proprietors, dancing teachers and hostesses—and if necessary the police department—to exterminate the 'half Nelson,' 'body hold,' 'shimmy lock,' and other imported ballroom grips which are practiced by some dancers." They suggested hand-ing out cards to offenders with the pre-printed phrase on it—"you will please leave the ball."[55]

Since the close hold employed during rag dances caused the most criticism, some savvy businessman created an invention to remedy the offending hug. Called a bumper, the contraption consisted of padded poles that extended out from a belt, and when strapped around the woman's waist, prevented the man from getting too close. A similar apparatus consisted of two metal belts held together with a nine inch bar to teach dancers the correct distance to have between them when dancing.[56]

In addition to the attempts made to refine earlier rag dances such as the turkey trot, grizzly bear and bunny hug, there were concerted efforts to do away with them entirely and create others to take their place. The creators of these replacements promised they would be "...jolly, but neither ugly nor vulgar, as the others are."[57]

New dances sprang up almost weekly, and were snatched up by a dance-hungry public. Exhibition dancers and cabaret performers, seeking to cash in on the dancing craze, created most of the newer steps. The trend was commercially lucrative for dancers and choreographers who often simply shuffled around existing steps and gave the new combination a name. Uriel Davis[58] capitalized on the craze by forming "Uriel Davis Modern Dancing Studios, Inc." which operated studios across the United States and offered to teach the latest steps. Davis is most famous for creating the horse trot,[59] but he also originated a number of other dances including the tiger, the fish walk,[60] the dream tango, the seasick dip (or seasick step), the deedleum minuet, the Bulgarian canter, the college chum schottische, the Baltimore Rag, the grape juice wallow, the roseda waltz, and the Davis fox trot.[61] Davis was the darling of social circles in Washington, New York, Boston, Philadelphia and Newport, and as such, also invented social games and novelties. In articles of the day he is sometimes referred to as the "originator of freak dances."[62]

Other innovators, including the Castles, Maurice Mouvet, and Ned Wayburn, also created new dances to the syncopated beat of ragtime. In 1911, Wayburn choreographed the Gaby glide for a play entitled *Vera Violetta*.[63] It was created specifically for popular actress and dancer, Gaby Deslys.[64] She performed the dance with partner Harry Pilcer.

In the summer of 1914, vaudeville actor Harry Fox[65] introduced the fox trot[66] at the Jardin de Danse on the rooftop of the New York Theatre in Ziegfeld's *Danse De Follies Cabaret*. His version of the dance was a fast, jerky trot done to ragtime music. A more refined fox trot was presented by Oscar Duryea to the public on September 3, 1914, under the auspices of the American Society of Professors of Dancing. In Duryea's tamed-down version, gliding or sauntering took the place of the more strenuous trotting utilized by Fox.

A booklet put out by Columbia Gramophone Company entitled "How to Dance the Foxtrot" and written by Joan Sawyer who was listed as "Originator of this Season's Most Popular Dance" included a letter inside its front cover. Dated November 23, 1914, the letter read in part, "The Fox-trot was originated and danced first by me at my Persian Garden in New York and later in vaudeville...."[67] It is signed by Joan Sawyer.

W. C. Handy said that Vernon and Irene Castle originated the foxtrot:

> Jim Europe [James Reese Europe], head of the local Clef Club, was the Castle's musical director. The Castle Walk and One-Step were fast numbers. During breath-catching intermissions, Jim would sit at the piano and play slowly the Memphis Blues. He did this so often that the Castles became intrigued by its rhythm, and Jim asked why they didn't originate a slow dance adaptable to it. The Castles liked the idea and a new dance [the foxtrot] was introduced....[68]

Irene Castle herself stated, "It was Jim Europe ... who suggested the foxtrot to us, and for all I know he invented it."[69]

Medical Objections

In his book *The Modern Dance*, anti-dance advocate M. F. Ham mentions an article in the *Houston Chronicle* that told of the newest disease called "Turkey Leg," threatening the coun-

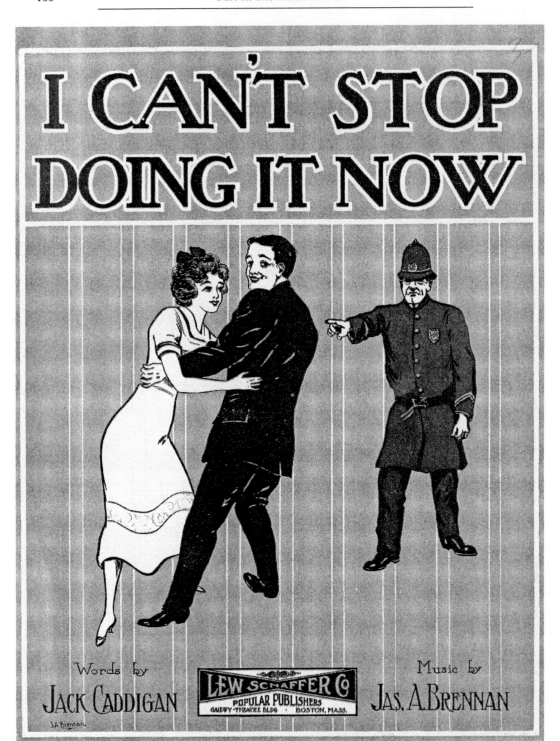

The cover of this 1913 piece of sheet music of the ragtime tune "I Can't Stop Doing It Now" shows a couple dancing the Grizzly Bear despite warnings from a policeman that the improper dance must stop.

try. "High society, the kind that dwells in Newport, has it. Houston, if it turkey trots too much, may get it. And Houston mothers as well as Newport mothers have of recent date become worried. Doctors to the turkey trotting rich say that the only cure is to shake your leg or get it pulled several times daily."[70] The ailment was widespread. In the summer of 1913, *The Fort Wayne Sentinel* reported that in Philadelphia it was a virtual epidemic:

> Medical men in this city who have been called on to treat so many society men and women suffering from an inflammation of the muscles of thigh that has been caused by excessive "turkey trotting," say the ailment is due to what they term "sartoritis," getting its name from the longest muscle in the body, the sartorius. Many of the patients have had to keep off their feet until the injury had healed. The women were all affected on the right leg, while the men were bruised or strained on the left leg. Surgeons say this is because the turkey trot is a one-step affair and following the steps of the dance the women bear down on the one side and the men on the other.... Society folk have termed the affliction "turkey leg."[71]

"Turkey leg" was not the only medical complaint lodged against trotting. Irene Castle recalled that a medical maelstrom erupted when she had her appendectomy. Although half of the physicians who voiced opinions claimed that dancing was therapeutic, the other half insisted that ragtime dancing was actually the culprit and "had damaged [her] appendix and caused the attack."[72] Dancer Preston Gibson, one of the leaders of Washington society, also blamed his appendicitis on his zeal for doing the trotting dances. "Formerly an ardent admirer of the turkey trot and kindred dances,"[73] Gibson called for a ban on what he now saw were wicked dances. Some doctors attributed "sciatica, rheumatism, hip disease, neuritis, neuralgia, paralysis, and other terrifying ills"[74] to ragging.

In Philadelphia the rag was banned from aristocratic ballrooms because "the fascination of the 'turkey trot' and other demure dances" had caused "some of the most notable debutantes in Philadelphia society to faint from exhaustion."[75] In Yonkers, New York, seventeen-year-old Helen Paulsen broke her leg while doing the turkey trot. The trot itself was not really the cause, but rather some rotten floorboards on her front porch where she was learning the dance from a friend. Her foot went through one of the boards, she tripped, and consequently broke her leg. The paper that reported the incident informed its readers, "Miss Paulsen has resolved to let the turkey trot and its associate dances alone."[76] In one tragic case, a young bride in Atlantic City died from internal hemorrhaging after doing the dance. "Over-exertion from doing the turkey trot with friends in her home caused Mrs. Agnes E. Day's death Saturday night."[77] Mrs. Day experienced an intense pain in her side while dancing and "it was later discovered that she had ruptured a blood vessel."[78]

In 1912, William Milburn Dye, a Methodist minister, issued a warning to those who were tempted by a trip to their local dance hall, stating that recent statistics confirmed that dancing was not only injurious to the health, but also fatal. He declared, "Habitual dancers die at an average early age, men 31, and women 27."[79]

People were so passionate about dancing ragtime that violence often erupted. In Middletown, Connecticut, a small riot occurred when several hundred dancers were not allowed to tango and turkey trot. "Decorations were torn down, furnishings broken and the electric light wires disarranged by the crowd."[80] In New York, a Mrs. O'Leary discovered her eighteen-year-old daughter Gladys and twenty fellow members of the Harlem Girls' Social Club rehearsing the turkey trot, grizzly bear, and bunny hug in her home. Mrs. O'Leary had provided sandwiches, cakes and lemonade for the girls and was setting the refreshments on a table in the corner of the parlor when she witnessed the dances. According to the account in the papers,

> Mrs. O'Leary rapidly underwent the emotions of surprise and astonishment, which were superseded by anger that knew no bounds, especially when the girls laughingly told her they would give an exhibition with young men at the coming ball of the club. On this the matronly spirit of

Mrs. O'Leary burst its bonds, She chased the whole bevy from the room. In anger they defied her. The Celtic spirit rose quickly. She pulled the hair of the girl nearest her and booted another. Then followed screams and an all-round fight. The suffragette spirit in the girls developed, and they piled onto Mrs. O'Leary, while Gladys stood in the background fright-stricken. Mrs. O'Leary proved the victor. The girls were routed, some with bruised and discolored eyes and others minus "rats" and other indispensables in the line of women's goods. Policeman Alexander was attracted by cries of "Murder!" and "Help!" and upon the demand of the club members, excepting Gladys of course, placed Mrs. O'Leary under arrest.[81]

Mrs. O'Leary was arraigned on multiple charges, but they were eventually discharged. When the mothers of the other girls heard about the incident, they placed a ban on the dances.

On March 27th, 1913, in Grants Pass, Oregon, Ed Spence, the owner of the club "Holland," was stabbed eleven times after trying to enforce his "no animal dances allowed" rule upon a couple caught doing the bunny hug. In West Virginia, a woman shot three people to death when the band at a local dance played "waltzy music when she wanted ragtime."[82]

In Prussia, a Colonel criticized a General for allowing his daughter to dance the turkey trot with an officer at a military ball. The General challenged the Colonel to a duel to the death with sabers, and the Colonel was fatally wounded in the head. In a similar incident, an Austrian officer challenged a young American, who had danced the trot with his daughter, to a duel. As a result of incidents like this, Swiss hotels began to prohibit the turkey trot and bunny hug.

Ragtime dance mania was considered a madness and a threat to mental health. Dr. S. Grover Burnett, the former president of the University of Missouri medical school, declared in an interview on January 26, 1915, that "insanity is increasing in the United States." He warned, "...many of the cases of insanity developed in the United States within the last few years may be traced to modern eccentric dances as a causal source, [and] one-tenth of the insane of this country have lost their minds on account of troubles which may commonly be traced to modern dances."[83]

PART III. THE TANGO

10

Origins of the Tango

Fashions, like waves, sweep over continents. Sometimes it will be a dance, sometimes a food, sometimes a song, sometimes a freak of fashion, sometimes a game; but the year 1913 might be called "The Tango Year," for the dance has provoked more conversation and evoked more clothes and teas and music than anything else. The Tango danced itself into favour in America with the dawn of 1913; it is dancing at the height of its prosperity all over Europe with the close of the same year.[1]

The tango, long associated with passion and desire, swept like wildfire across Europe and America at the same time that animal dances were trotting their way into the news. Tangomania grabbed the world and brought with it equal parts of outrage and acclaim.

Etymology of the Word "Tango"

The etymology of the word "tango" is somewhat shrouded in mystery. Most historians trace the word directly to African origins and point to its use in various dialects to mean "a closed place," "a reserved place," "a circle," or "any private place to which one must ask permission to enter."[2]

Some suggest that the word is merely onomatopoeic and echoes the beating of a drum. It has also been suggested that perhaps "tango" is a phonetic alteration of the name of the Yoruba god of lightning and thunder, Shango.[3] In Cuba, for example, blacks who spoke the Yoruba language wrote the name of the deity as *Sango*. They pronounced the first "s" like a Spanish "s," therefore articulating the deity's name to sound like "tango."

Gladys Beattie Crozier, in her 1913 dance manual *The Tango and How to Dance It*, stated that the word,

[S]aid by some to be derived from the word "Tangonette"—a special variety of castanet used in dancing—when translated actually means "I touch," being the first person singular of the Spanish verb "tangir," meaning "to touch" and doubtless chosen as a title for the dance owing to the somewhat close proximity of the partners.... This gives further proof, if further proof were needed, of the undoubted Spanish origin of the dance.[4]

Other sources have pointed to the word's connection to Spain. According to some, its first known use can be traced to Isla de Hierro, one of the Canary Islands owned by Spain, and located off the coast of Africa. It is also well documented that the word was brought to Argentina from Andalucía, Spain in the middle of the nineteenth century and was used to reference a specific type of music.[5]

Other writers have suggested that the term can be traced to the Portuguese because it is closely related to the Latin verb *tangere*, "to touch."[6] Historians who support this theory believe the term was brought to Argentina by blacks when they were transported there during the slave trade. The word was assimilated into pidgin Portuguese when slaves learned the word from their captors. It is known that the word was widely used on the island of São Tomé, a center of the Portuguese slave trade.[7]

The first written use of the word "tango" can found in a document signed by the Spanish governor of Louisiana in 1786. It mentions "los tangos, o bailoes de negros," translated as "the tangos, or dances of the blacks." In 1803, the *Real Academia Española* dictionary listed the word "tango" as a variant of *tángano*, which was defined as "a bone or rock used to play the game bearing the same name." The same year, the *Archives of the Holy Inquisition in Mexico* contained a reference to the "ancient tango" and stated that it was a Mexican song.[8]

Crozier states that a dance called the tango was common in Cuba when the island was still a colony of Spain. When Cuba was fighting for its independence, the families of revolutionaries "took refuge in Jamaica, where they introduced the Tango under the name of 'the Spanish dance' or 'Cuban Dance.'"[9]

The word "tango" appears to have been fairly commonly used throughout Latin American although its meanings varied. Most often the word signified "a gathering of blacks to dance to drum music" but it was also used as "the name the Africans gave the drum itself."[10] It eventually came to have two commonly accepted meanings: first, as a place for dancing for either slaves or free blacks, and second, as the dances themselves.[11]

Whatever the exact derivation, most agree that the word "tango" probably indicates slave connections, and therefore can be traced to African origins.[12] In his book *Dictionary of the Dance*, W. G. Raffé states that the tango can be traced to a North African ritual dance of the Shango (or Xango), and that it was an important part of the New Year Feast celebration. The tribal dance consisted of twelve parts dramatizing twelve stories.[13] Raffé suggests that a form of this ritual dance made its way to Spain and then to Argentina.

Others have had different theories as to the origin of the tango. In their book *Modern Dancing*, Vernon and Irene Castle stated,

> The Tango is not, as commonly believed, of South American origin. It is an old gipsy dance which came to Argentina by way of Spain, where in all probability it became invested with certain features of the old Moorish dances. The Argentines adopted the dance, eliminating some of the reckless gipsy traits, and added to it a certain languid indolence peculiar to their temperament.[14]

Writer Gladys Beattie Crozier agreed. In 1913, she wrote,

> [T]he suggestion that it [the tango] originally started as a gipsy dance and was carried by the gypsies into Spain, and thence by the Spaniards to the Argentine, where, by reason of its slow, dreamy movements, so specially well suited to a hot climate, it became firmly established as a national country dance, seems the most probable solution to the mystery [of the origin of the dance].[15]

As with the animal dances, there were attempts to distance the tango from its "savage" African roots and associate it with more "refined" classical origins. Jean Richepin[16] of the Académie Francais declared that the tango was derived from ancient Greek rituals—"war dances of the Ancient Thebans."[17] He stated, "Pindar, Homer, Socrates, and Sophocles were exponents and practitioners of the dance. The antiquity of the tango can be proved from figures in the British Museum and from the tombs of Thebes."[18] Richepin elaborated, "The tango was well known to the ancients. You can see it in the British Museum, where figures of ancient Thebes are dancing the tango, clothed only in a belt of gold thread. The Egyptians and Chaldeans had a similar dance in which there were mathematical and metaphysical and mystical features."[19]

In Milford Iowa, *The Milford Mail*, reported on November 19, 1914, that the tango was actually of Japanese descent.

Opposite: From a series of 1914 Russian tango postcards.

The tango did not originate in Argentine. It came from Tango, Japan, a district on the southern shore of Wasaka bay down on the west coast, where it originated some 300 years ago in the city of Hashidate.... The music for the Japanese tango was strummed on an instrument known as the stamisen. When Argentine borrowed the dance from Japan and gave it plenty of advertising, they discarded the stamisen and hired brass bands.[20]

The Early Development of the Dance

By the mid–nineteenth century, about one fourth of all the inhabitants of Buenos Aires were black. Mainly living in the inner-city parishes, these African-Argentines developed their own styles of dance. One in particular was the *candombe*. A fusion of African drum rhythms peppered with European elements, the *candombe* involved intricate footwork and ended with "a final section combining wild rhythms, freely improvised steps and energetic, semi-athletic movements."[21] The dance is primarily associated with Uruguay, and is believed to have had its genesis in and around Montevideo during the early colonial days of that country, but it also developed in black communities in Buenos Aires and in other cities in South America.[22]

Dance historian A. H. Franks states that the origins of the *candombe* can be traced to an African dance known as the *tangano*. African slaves brought the dance to Cuba and Haiti during the first part of the eighteenth century. Descendants of these slaves later migrated to the River Plate area in South America, bringing the *tangano* with them. The dance absorbed European influences and became known as the *candombe*. The *candombe* contained the earliest seeds of the tango.

Another dance, the habanera, arrived in Buenos Aires around 1850, brought there by black slaves who were originally taken to Montevideo.[23] This rhythmical dance developed on the plantations of Cuba, and combined African-inspired bent knees and undulating hips done in a European dance position similar to the waltz. Recognizable because of its distinctive bass line — a dotted eighth note followed by a sixteenth and two eighth notes, this type of syncopation stresses every other beat.[24] The habanera played an important role in the development of the tango, as well as other dances such as the canyengue, the milonga, the maxixe, and the samba.

Around 1870, the milonga appeared as the popular dance of the day in Buenos Aires. Sometimes called "the poor man's habanera,"[25] the milonga grew out of the African tradition of mock battle. The dance was like a ritualized duel, a theme later utilized by dancers as stylized competition and taunting while doing the tango.[26] According to the authors of the book *Tango! The Dance, the Song, the Story,* "There has never been any real doubt about the importance of the *milonga* and the *habanera* in the tango's immediate ancestry. It seems fairly clear that the *milonga* actually *was* the embryonic form of the tango before the new dance was finally given a name."[27]

Development of the Tango in Early Buenos Aires

In 1880, Buenos Aires became the capital of Argentina. Drawn by dreams of wealth, thousands flooded to the city from rural areas. Most prominent were the nomadic cowhands of the Argentine Pampa, known as *gauchos,* and Afro-Argentines descended from seventeenth century slaves. In Buenos Aires, they mixed with immigrants from Spain and Italy who brought with them their own rich cultural heritage.

Most settled in the poorer areas of the city — the sprawling suburbs, known as *barrios* and *arrables* where the main industry was the city's slaughterhouse. A common site was the figure of the *compadre* who herded cattle from the Pampa to the slaughterhouse. A more urban version of the *gaucho*, the *compadres* nevertheless retained some qualities of the *gauchos* such as "fierce independence, masculine pride, and a strong inclination to settle affairs of honour with knives."[28] Young street toughs from the poor slums called *compadritos*[29] adopted the *compadres* ways—mimicking their speech patterns, and imitating their outfits, although often in an exaggerated way. Their traditional manner of dress consisted of a "slouch hat, loosely tied handkerchief, high-heeled boots, and knife casually tucked into belt."[30] These rowdy young men played an important part in the birth of the tango.

A man who called himself Viejo Tanguero, translated as "Old Tangoer," wrote an article published on September 22, 1913 in *Crítica*, Buenos Aires' first mass-circulation popular newspaper, that stated the tango was created as a parody dance by young *campadritos*. He wrote that *compadritos* had a habit of frequenting Afro-Argentine dances. One time they saw a candombe-like dance that the blacks called the tango. These young ruffians took the dance back to *Corrales Viejos*, the slaughterhouse district in the southern *arrabal* of Buenos Aires, and in the low-class dives and brothels[31] they began interpolating aspects of it into the milonga. This variation of the popular milonga soon found its way to other districts in the city.

Tanguero's story is confirmed by author Ventura Lynch who wrote in 1883, "the milonga is danced only by the *compadritos* of the city, who have created it as a mockery of the dances the blacks hold in their own places."[32]

The *compadritos'* dances were traditionally athletic, robust, and masculine. The African-Argentine dances were sexually provocative and laced with elements of violence; they utilized jerky motions that interpolated stops in which the dancers held a pose and menacingly stare at others.[33] In the overcrowded slums of the city, these various cultural influences cross-pollinated, eventually creating a fusion of styles.

> The distinctive features of the new dance-form came entirely from the *compadritos'* parodistic borrowings from the African-Argentine tradition—in particular the so-called *quebradas* and *cortes*. The *quebrada* was simply an improvised, jerky, semi-athletic contortion, the more dramatic the better, while the *corte* was a sudden, suggestive pause, a break in the standard figures of the dance, not in itself a particular movement so much as a prelude to a *quebrada*. The true novelty, as the embryonic tango slowly took shape, was that the *cortes* and *quebradas* were incorporated into dances in which the partners danced *together*, not, as in the African-Argentine "tango," apart.[34]

In addition to African influenced dances, the *compradritos* took other common dances of the day, stylizing them to create a hybrid fusion of styles. According to tango historian Jo Baim, "Much of the creation of the tango dance grew out of the *compadrito* society's unique treatment of the polkas, mazurkas, waltzes, and quadrilles known to everyone. The goal was exaggerated style, highly ornamented with filigrees and *refaladas* (ornamental steps) of various kinds."[35] The melding of European and African styles was apparent in another vitally important way—the dance hold. "Candombe was danced apart whereas polka and habanera were danced in embrace position. In translating the break patterns of African apart dancing into embrace dancing, the compadrito (as well as other vernacular stylists) were gradually creating their own empirical choreography."[36]

Around 1900, another dance emerged, also important in the early development of the tango—the canyengue. The native or Creole dance or *tango criollo* of the Argentine-born *compadritos* and creolized Italian immigrants was usually danced upright. The canyengue, however, was done in a deep bend with the bodies of the dancers leaning against each other. Tango scholar Robert Farris Thompson states, "...it is possible to suggest a composite translation for canyengue: the oldest form of tango dance, where one melts to the music; taking short steps, keeping knees bent, and leaning on the chest of one's partner."[37] According to Thompson, the leaning, the dips, and the deep bending knees employed while doing the tango can all be traced to African roots.[38]

Tango on the Early Argentine Stage

Around the 1860's, the tango was a common feature on the Buenos Aires stage, especially in a form of burlesque called the *sainete proteño*. These farces were typically one act plays that utilized large casts, featured local talent, and had plots based on the *compadrito* society and how it dealt with the flood of immigrants. One theme that was used was the *duelo crillo*, or a duel between an immigrant and someone born in Buenos Aires, also known as a creole.

In early Buenos Aires, street duels were common as social tensions escalated between immigrants, in particular the Italians,[39] and the creole *compadritos*. The *duelo criollo* was "highly ritualized, and the type of knife chosen and the type of wounds inflicted indicated the level of respect or disrespect each fighter had for his opponent. Eventually, the tango replaced the knife, and the level of respect was indicated by the tango's lyrics and the complexity of tango steps."[40]

The short vignettes in the *sainetes,* such as depictions of the *duelo criollo*, as well as other themes, helped to preserve early tango lore. They allowed tango poems and lyrics that had previously been passed down orally to be written down. The plays created tango personalities; their success and popularity, in turn, heightened the popularity of the dance. In addition, the *sainetes* introduced a broad spectrum of Buenos Aires society to tango language and style. By the end of the 1800's, the tango was so well known to all classes that it was not uncommon for upper-class men to venture to the lower class establishments to experience the dance.

The early tango often conjured up an image of a smoky brothel where intertwined couples danced the tango in an atmosphere of lust and danger. The dance was full of raw energy, lasciviousness, and drama, and the stereotype of the pimp acting out control of his prostitute through the dance is still a lasting archetype. Some reputable historians question whether the tango really began in the bordellos of Buenos Aires, but many point out that the tango certainly had its birth in rougher neighborhoods of the city.[41] As the dance was developing, the sensuality of the tango convinced most who saw it or danced it, that it must have had less than higher class origins. Its association with the whorehouse or *quilombo*, as it was called in Argentina, lingered, and the tango always maintained an air of impropriety.

Respectable society in Buenos Aires shunned the tango initially, fearing that any connection with it would lead to moral contamination and scandal. The wealthy sons of the Argentine oligarchy might go slumming, but their parents would never allow the voluptuous dance at any of their own social functions. By the early 1900's, however, as knowledge of the tango spread throughout the capital city and then abroad, most middle and upper classes began to accept the dance[42] and proudly to claim it as an expression of Argentine culture. Many tango venues opened, and dance halls, cafés, cabarets, and tango bars flourished.[43] As the upper classes embraced the dance, the style of the tango evolved from the exaggerated flourishes used by the *compadritos* to a smoother, more refined and serious dance.

11

Development and Dispersion of the Tango

Throughout the nineteenth and early twentieth centuries, Argentine high society traditionally sent its sons to Europe to take the grand tour and do those things young men must do when they come of age. For many Argentines this meant a great deal of time spent in the supper clubs and cabarets of the Paris demimonde, especially in Montmarte. Though they could learn nothing new about dance in society ballrooms, they found surprising developments in the lower-class clubs. The Parisian demimonde had a dance called the Apache, and in it the Argentines claimed to find a spirit kindred to that of the tango. A mutual exchange of steps and styles ensued, and thus the tango found its way to Paris.[1]

Paris was ripe for the invasion of the new dance. In 1909, Diaghilev's Ballet Russes thrilled and excited Paris audiences, sparking an interest in things foreign and unusual. Rag dances and syncopated music from America had introduced Parisians to jazz. In the tango, Parisians found the epitome of sensuality, exoticism, and innovation.

When wealthy young men from Argentina introduced the dance to their Parisian hosts, the risqué, aggressive nature of the dance intrigued and titillated the more modern-thinking French. Unlike the acrobatic French Apache which had piqued earlier interest, but was too dangerous to actually attempt, the naughty tango was accessible. It was a dance even a socialite could do. Learning the sensuous moves from a handsome, wealthy Latin man only added to its appeal.

The tango also found its way to Paris by other means. Entertainment agents from France had discovered the tango while visiting Buenos Aires. After hearing the new music and seeing the provocative dance, they signed Argentine orchestras and dancers to perform in clubs and cabarets in Paris.[2]

Although the music was an instant hit in Paris and in other towns in France, the overtly sexual aspect of the dance, as it was first presented in French cabarets, shocked as many as it intrigued. Efforts were made to tone down the tango to make it more appropriate and accessible. Some were rather disappointed in the results. As one writer of the day put it, "In Paris the true Argentine "tang" which gave the dance its somewhat tigerish air of energy, latent, though unexpressed, is in the most fashionable dancing sets being daily more and more eliminated ... with the result that the dance in certain Paris sets shows some signs of degenerating into a languid, characterless crawl — which seems a pity."[3]

Most people welcomed the newly refined, but still somewhat risqué dance. American ballroom dancers Vernon and Irene Castle observed, "...from a rather obscene exhibition, which is still indulged in by certain cabaret performers, it bloomed forth a polished and extremely fascinating dance, which has not had its equal in rhythmical allurement since the days of the Minuet."[4]

In 1908, the tango made its first appearance in a theatrical review in Paris, and two years later Professor B. G. Bottallo, the director of the Academy of Dance and Deportment, "officially" demonstrated it at the Sorbonne. The Professor danced with French cabaret sensation Mistinguett. The much-beloved music-hall performer, who later became known for her tangoing abilities, helped propel the dance to greater heights of popularity among the Paris upper classes.[5]

In his book *Maurice's Art of Dancing*, exhibition ballroom dancer Maurice Mouvet claims

Early twentieth century Italian postcard depicting the tango, by artist Giovanni Nanni.

that he was "the first professional to perform this dance [the tango] in Paris,"[6] when he danced it with his partner Leona at the Café des Ambassadeurs. Mouvet explains that he had learned the tango from a group of South American boys who frequented Maxim's and first introduced the daring dance there. Mouvet explained that he was able to learn the dance so thoroughly because he danced with the young men themselves when they could not find female partners. According to Mouvet, the same-sex partnering resulted in "a good deal of critical comment both among the dancers and spectators."[7]

Whoever first officially presented the dance in Paris may never be known, but it is clear that soon the tango took the city by storm. "Paris went completely mad about it. 'La Ville Lumiere' was dubbed 'Tangoville' ... and for months Tango dancing, Tango dress, Tango teachers, and Tango teas [were] the only topics in the Gay city."[8] Dance studios grew wealthy as socialites rushed in for daily lessons. Male instructors were particularly in demand, especially if they were handsome, exotic-looking Latins, or at least men masquerading as such. Many young, ambitious men from Buenos Aires traveled to France to work as tango instructors, drawn by the lure of easy money. One was heard to remark "We love dancing with this ruined old French nobility."[9] Other men, who could not claim Argentine roots, quickly learned the tango and simply manufactured their own exotic heritage.[10]

The city was flooded with dancing masters. One of the most successful instructors was Ludovic de Portalou, Marquis de Sénas, an ex–Hussar who helped start the famous restaurant Maxim's. He had learned the tango while visiting Buenos Aires and became known around Paris as "Le Roi du Tango," or "The King of the Tango."

The tango influenced everything from French cuisine to French couture. Even the banana was renamed *La Banane Tango* by virtue of its yellow color — a shade associated with the tango.[11] The dance became a popular subject with top artists, who captured the tango's dramatic poses in everything from paintings to postcards. A special "Tango Train" was put together so aficionados of the dance could keep tangoing while traveling between Paris and Deauville during the summer. The Palais de Glace featured a tango on ice skates. Tango contests and competitions were a common occurrence.[12]

> There were tango teas held between four in the afternoon and seven, where the public, for an entry fee of up to five francs including tea and sandwiches, could dance to their heart's content. There were also champagne-tangos, surprise-tangos, charity tangos, dinner-tangos, and of course tangos in nightclubs, then spreading like wildfire to cater to the dance craze.[13]

Many of the large town homes along the Champs Elysées were converted to clubs to meet the growing demand for tango venues. The craze reached such a fever pitch that some leading socialites arranged to have one mansion set aside exclusively for a popular tango teacher so he could give lessons to members of the smart set. The class drew so much attention that tickets had to be issued for those wishing to attend the classes: "Blue for women of the most exclusive society circle, pink for other women, and white for men."[14]

One of the most ardent supporters of the tango in Paris was writer and dramatist Jean Richepin. On October 13, 1913, Richepin, a member of the prestigious French Académie des Beaux Arts, gave a lecture defending the tango. Later that same year on December 30, 1913, the city was treated to a play about the dance written by Richepin and his wife, Cora Laparcerie. Entitled *Le Tango*, the drama opened at the Athénée Theatre in Paris, with sets and costumes by fashion icon Paul Poiret. The plot revolved around a young couple unable to consummate their marriage until they discover the secret of sexuality by dancing the tango. Oddly enough, the message of Richepin's play conflicted with his lecture for the French Académie des Beaux Arts, which argued that there was nothing intrinsically erotic in the tango. Audiences were shocked by the subject matter and even further inflamed because in the production women played the roles of both the husband and wife. Critics hated the play and subsequent articles accused Richepin of merely writing the *Le Tango* in an attempt to make money off the popularity of the dance.

Dancer and writer Victor Silvester stated that the person most responsible for helping to popularize the tango in the Europe was French entrepreneur and dancer Camille de Rhynal.[15] In 1907, Rhynal was at the Imperial Country Club in Nice with a gathering of friends who were intrigued with the tango but found its movements too overtly provocative. Rhynal and the others, who included Grand Duchess Anastasia of Russia, worked together to remove any "objectionable features." The revamped, refined dance proved a success in Nice, and from there was transported to Paris, "where the presence of genuine Argentine tango orchestras — specially imported by beady-eyed musical agents — ensured that the dance was a hit."[16]

The Tango Spreads Through Europe

As the tango craze grew in France, word of the dance filtered to other metropolitan centers in Europe. Around 1910, the British first heard of the daring new dance. After the summer of 1911, when English tourists vacationing in France returned home, they began requesting the dance they had seen abroad. The same year, the *Dancing Times* ran photographs of the tango. In February of 1912, George Grossmith, who had learned the dance while visiting Paris in the winter of 1911–1912, performed a tango with partner Phyliss Dare at the Gaiety Theatre in the West End, in a musical called *The Sunshine Girl*. The show, which ran for a year was a huge hit, and caused a host of other companies to quickly add the tango to their productions.

Shortly afterward, afternoon tango teas came into vogue, and London, like other cities across Europe, was gripped by tangomania. By 1913 and into 1914, practically every hotel and restaurant offered *thés dansant* and most prominent society hostesses offered private tango teas in their homes. The Savoy Hotel offered a special tango dinner each evening.

Trying to top the ordinary tango tea, the manager of Murray's organized a super-tango tea. An article in the *New York Times* described the event: "The super-tango tea ... consists of a formidable programme which is a mélange of tableaux vivants, ultra-modern dances, ragtime, and the added novelty of a fashion parade of mannequins showing the latest Parisian creations." Although the attendees did not dance themselves, they could enjoy a presentation of the latest dances to the "strains of a negro banjo band, followed by coon songs and then a fashion parade with couture all based on a Chinese theme." The show was presented in a supper club decorated with Chinese scenery to resemble a room in "the palace of Benevolent Blessings." African-American songs were used to connect the segments of the Asian-themed program.[17]

The tango infiltrated every level of British society, from the wealthy to the working classes. Even street urchins danced the tango on London's street corners for pennies. Viscount Haldane, the Lord Chancellor of London, lamented that low numbers of enlisted men in the Territorial Army was largely due to young men preferring to spend their time doing the tango, rather than serving their country. The topic of the tango crept into almost every conversation; one society woman was overheard to remark, "I don't see why the women of England are making such a rumpus over suffrage when they have the Tango to argue about."[18]

Germany also went mad over the new dance. Tango teas and classes offering instructions in the dance popped up around the country. When an American paper asked its foreign correspondent to write an article about "the subject uppermost in the German people's mind,"[19] he submitted a piece about the tango. In October of 1914, *The New York Times* reported on a afternoon tango tea offered by one department store in Berlin. "Judging by the throngs which attended the opening tea this week," the article read, "the innovation will prove a bigger attraction than bargain sales...."[20]

The Jardin de Danse, atop the New York Theatre, was one of the many famous nightspots where couples tangoed the night away. From *The Tango and Other Up-To-Date Dances* by J. S. Hopkins (1914).

Tangoists were horrified when Kaiser Wilhelm II issued an unexpected edict in 1914, forbidding his uniformed officers from doing the dance or even attending private functions where the tango was performed. The Kaiser's orders effectively banned the dance from being performed by members of high society because officers in uniform were *de riguer* at every social function. The tango faltered, but Germans still demanded the dance. Despite the Kaiser's edict, the tango continued to proliferate outside of official court functions.

In Russia, Tsar Nicholas II ordered a demonstration of the tango after he was informed that two of his nephews, "had been involved in an incident in a fashionable nightclub in St. Petersburg, 'where a new perturbing dance was revealed.'"[21] The grand-dukes showed their uncle the tango and "perhaps surprisingly—he liked it."[22] One magazine in St Petersburg ran the headline "Everybody's Dancing the Tango." The article included instructions on how to do the dance as demonstrated by Phyllis Dare, who had recently grabbed Britain's attention doing the tango in *The Sunshine Girl.*

The tango also invaded Spain and Italy. Spanish King Alfonso XII favored the tango, although the more conservative members of his court expressed contempt for the dance. In Rome, "...impoverished young aristocrats, whose noble blood made them disdainful of more useful employment, suddenly found their vocation as tango partners."[23] In the early months of 1914, two members of the nobility demonstrated the dance for Pope Pius X. The pontiff thought the tango nothing more than "barbarian contortions of Negroes and Indians."[24] The Vatican issued a circular calling the tango "offensive to the purity of every right-minded persons,"[25] but despite efforts to suppress the dance, the tango craze swept through Italy.

The Tango in the United States

The tango hit the United States full force in the winter of 1913–1914. As in the metropolitan centers of Europe, cities across America were swept up in tango madness—tango teas and tango classes were everyday occurrences. On February 16, 1914, the *Oelwein Daily Register*, in

Oelwein, Iowa, ran an article, "Tango Mania Has New York in Its Grip" that summed up the situation:

> Nothing matters nowadays but the tango.... Truly it can be said these days that Milady Butterfly dances through life. From the moment she wakes until she drops exhausted in her fluffy nest of a bed her day is just a continuous round of dancing. After breakfast the more ambitious of her will migrate to the studio of a dancing master, usually a young man of foreign importation and unpronounceable name whose dexterous movements in the tango and the maxixe cast a spell nightly over the feminine portion of his audiences in some big eating and dancing palace. Here she will cheerfully surrender 25 of papa's good, honest American dollars for one hour's private instruction in the intricacies of the latest variety of the tango.... After a hasty luncheon at home she sprinkles a drop of tango perfume on her tango frock, adjusts her tango veil over her freshly powdered little nose, grabs her tango bag, and hikes off to an after-luncheon dancing class, where she whirls and twirls in joyous abandon. Then after a thé dansant in any one of the numerous gorgeously appointed places devoted to this fad, she joins the merry throng on the ballroom floor of a dinner dansant restaurant, where she dances away until the wee hours of the morning.[26]

After conquering New York, the tango quickly spread across the America. *The Lincoln Daily Star*, in Lincoln, Nebraska, reported on October 5, 1913:

> Tango-itis, in cyclonic velocity, is sweeping across the country, and almost the entire world for that matter. And like a storm, it sweeps everything before it ... go where you will, it is impossible to get away from it. If people aren't dancing it, they are talking about it. The prevalence of the dance and its universal adoption in some form, exceeds in popularity anything ever introduced into the social world.[27]

A paper in Fort Wayne, Indiana also reported on the dance craze:

> Boston is at present in the throes of Tangoitis. The craze was a little belated in reaching there, but the city has a bad case of it. Philadelphia and Washington are inclined to frown on the Tango, but Cleveland is receiving the dance with enthusiasm. Baltimore is divided against itself. The police will not allow the Tango to be danced in public, but it is at present at most private affairs. Reno is tired of it. Things move fast in Reno.[28]

The dance was so popular in New Orleans that dance halls sprang up like weeds in the French Quarter, earning that section of town the title "The Tango Belt." In Los Angeles, vaudeville theatres inserted extra intermissions between the acts so members of the audience could tango up and down the aisles and out into the foyer.

In Sheboygan, Wisconsin, a society column in *Sheboygan Press*, on December 18, 1913, gave the following advice to citizens of its fair city who wanted to keep up with the trend. In addition to learning to do the dance, one must also know how to properly pronounce it. The columnist wrote, "Another word — you must never forget to hold on to the A in tango as long as though you had forgotten for the moment what came next."[29]

To keep up with the public's demand for more and more places to dance, some cities resorted to imaginative solutions. In Atlantic City, the local trolley company introduced the "Tango Car," which was outfitted with a parquet floor for dancing. Those in the know predicted that the new "'Tango on wheels' promise[d] to be one of the most popular diversions of the season."[30] In Chicago, some members of society created a similar novelty called the "Tango Special," a freight train car specially outfitted as a ballroom with waxed floors "so that the dance may continue while the train is traveling fifty miles an hour."[31] The train was created so partiers could attend Mardi Gras in New Orleans and dance all the way down to the festivities. In Toledo, Ohio, the Rotary Club put together a similar tango car with "the intention of tangoing from Toledo to Texas" on their way to the annual Rotary convention in Houston.[32]

At the end of 1913, Gladys Beattie Crozier's dance manual, *The Tango and How to Dance It*, was published in England. The book appealed not only to fans of the dance, but also to those

Tangoing on the Beach, Atlantic City, N. J.

"Tangoing on the Beach, Atlantic City, N. J.," an early twentieth century postcard.

curious about the latest rage. It helped begin the process of standardizing the dance which had been a hodgepodge that "boasted as many steps as there were days of the year."[33]

In March of 1914, Irene and Vernon Castle published their *Modern Dancing* in the United States which codified tango steps. The popular young exhibition dancers suggested that perhaps society's negative reaction to the tango actually sprang from its difficulty. They wrote,

> The Argentine Tango is unquestionably the most difficult of the new dances. Perhaps that is why some people still maintain that they "do not like it." Others, never having seen it, declare it "shocking." On broad general principles it is human to disapprove of that which is beyond our understanding or ability.... And so for a long time society looked askance at the Tango.[34]

The Castles reassured their readers that although it was rumored that the tango required mastering up to one hundred and sixty different figures—"enough to terrify the most inveterate dancer"[35]—their method was composed of only six fundamental steps. In addition, the book's publisher Elizabeth Marbury assured readers in the introduction that the tango as taught by the Castles was refined and suitable. She wrote, "There is in it no strenuous clasping of partners, no hideous gyrations of the limbs, no abnormal twistings, no vicious angles."[36]

The outbreak of World War I dampened the enthusiasm for the tango, although the dance did reemerge again full force in the 1920's renamed the "New French Tango." During the war years, Argentina began releasing films that featured the dance. The first film in 1915, was *Nobleza gaucha*, followed by *Flor de Duranzo* and, in 1917, *El tango de la muerte*, a film whose subject was solely the tango. After the end of the Great War, Hollywood released a silent film in which Rudolph Valentino danced with Beatrice Dominguez. Valentino's mesmerizing tango in *Four Horseman of the Apocalypse* glamorized the dance and gained the Latin idol instant celebrity, insuring his place in tango film history and earning him the nickname "Tango Legs."

12

Fashion and Music of the Tango

On April 12, 1914, *The New York Times* reported, "The clothes of the day cannot be fashioned without due regard to the requirements of the dance."[1] The tango, perhaps more that any other social dance in modern history, changed styles and influenced fashion trends.

At the annual meeting of the National Association of Clothiers in 1914, attendees were happily informed, "the tango craze was helping the clothing business, for all of the men who had been 'bitten by the tango bug' were purchasing dress suits and tuxedos."[2] The dancing gentleman had to be in style. Author Gladys Beattie Crozier suggested that due to the many venues for dancing, gentlemen could properly wear anything from traditional formal wear to tweed suits worn with brown boots for afternoon dances in the country, although "in town, ordinary calling dress-black morning coat, dark grey striped trousers, and a black waistcoat, with a white piqué slip in it, and black boots—[was] *de rigueur*."[3] She acknowledged that "Grey suits, with cutaway coats, are also sometimes seen, and they look both smart and cool for dancing."[4] The most ardent tangoists began adopting dinner jackets cut longer in the Argentine style known as "fumadero tango." The type of jacket afforded more freedom through the arms and shoulders, so tangoing was easier.

When the tango was featured at fancy dress balls that required costumes, Mr. Percy Anderson, "the famous authority on the subject,"[5] suggested that gentlemen dress like a Spanish or Argentine peasant, or a Spanish gypsy. The Spanish peasant outfit consisted of a black suit with a short Eton-type jacket, tight, black knee-breeches, white shirt and stockings, and a black straight brimmed hat, the kind usually associated with Valentino, worn low over the eyes.

As an Argentine peasant the gentleman was to wear a chamois leather coat with big fancy buttons, black velvet knee breeches, and brown leather gaiters with leather fringe down the sides of the leg. A red cashmere shirt and a white or red sash peeking out underneath a leather belt provided a splash of color. For headgear, a red handkerchief was tied around the head, with the ends hanging over the left ear, topped off with a wide straw hat with an upturned brim.

The gentleman's Spanish gypsy costume was the most dramatic. This consisted of a white shirt, brown velvet knee pants, "gaping at the outside of the knee and tied with leather thongs (very narrow),"[6] a bright orange sash around the waist, and a brown Spanish shawl decorated with bobbles, casually thrown over the shoulder. The tango dancer wore a bright orange handkerchief tied tightly round his head, with the warning from Mr. Anderson that "the orange material must *not* be silk."[7] Two important props finished off the look — a knife tucked into the sash and a lighted cigarette dangling from the tango dancer's mouth.

Women's Fashions

The tango changed women's fashions in many ways. Silhouettes became simpler and waistlines rose "to eliminate the harsh line of the hips."[8] The idea was to have one free-flowing line of material that draped from the bustline to the ankles. As fashion icon Irene castle explained,

"This lends a supple ease to every movement of the body and tends to improve, from the artistic standpoint, the various measures of the dance."[9] Marthe Urban, French ballerina and leader in the Paris fashion world, said, "To dance the Tango one must be free from embarrassing influences— as far as dress is concerned."[10]

One way this was accomplished was the use of softer, lighter materials, such as chiffons, crêpes de Chine, or taffetas in the construction of women's garments. Stiffer, bulkier materials were eliminated because "they have a habit of wrapping themselves about one's feet at the most inconvenient moment, making it almost impossible to move."[11] The appropriate dance-frock needed to flow. As Irene Castle put it, "...the demand of the women who dance is, 'Give me something soft and light.'"[12]

The freedom afforded by lighter, simpler garments was augmented by new designs in corsetry. "The tango corset should be the start and foundation of your tango toilette de luxe. The accepted model is of silk tricot and but one bone in the front and back. It allows the figure full play and yet is so admirably constructed that it confines and holds well in its proper place any undue embonpoint."[13] Irene Castle reaffirmed the importance of wearing the proper corset while tango dancing:

> All these precautions as to the outward gowning are wasted if you continue to wear the long stiff corsets decreed by fashion when she dismissed our hips and other curves. No amount of grace, no amount of clever training, and no amount of the knowledge of the most intricate steps will help you dance charmingly unless your corset has "give" to it and allows you to move with supple ease and comfort.[14]

Of course, Mrs. Castle recommended the Castle corset made entirely of elastic and "designed especially for dancers."[15] Around 1913, the first girdle came into use and was named the "Tango."

Perhaps the major fashion innovation brought about by the tango concerned the most prevalent trend of the day — the hobble skirt. To dance the tango, women needed their legs to be free. Tight hobble skirts made modern dancing awkward, unsightly, and even dangerous. To accommodate the tango, skirts became fuller. As one paper reported,

> The first debt of gratitude the devotees of the fashion world owe to the tango is the additional width in the skirts. For the past two years the designers have been endeavoring by pleats and drapery to let in a little more fullness, but enter the tango, and presto change — the wider skirt is demanded.... Because it was impossible to execute many of the more intricate steps in the restricted skirts of yesteryear, the tango enthusiasts clamored for wider skirts.[16]

Slits in the skirt were also introduced. To prevent too much leg from showing, a pleated underskirt, petticoat, or bloomers were worn underneath. Culottes, called tango trouserettes, became the most popular choice for tangoing. In "New Customs, New Costumes," an article published in the *New Oxford Item*, in New Oxford, Pennsylvania on February 2, 1912, the fashion reporter explained,

> While the idea of "trousers" may seem startling at first; they are really modest garments, for they conceal the legs, and even the ankles, in a way that they have not been enveloped for years, not since the good old days when pantelettes made hoop skirts modest.... They solve the problem for the tango dancer in an ideal manner: they are voluminous when the wearer is in action and slinky when the body is in a state of rest.[17]

Tango trouserettes came in a variety of styles. Some came almost up to the shoulders, others fell from the waistline, and still others were attached with garters at the knees. Generally made of a light material, such as chiffon, and often trimmed in lace, the garments were sometimes so full they appeared to be skirts.[18]

> Over these trouserettes the skirt is draped in almost any desired style. For tangoing, the rounded fronts have been found successful, more so than the back slashing, though both are often seen.

When the side slashing is selected, both sides are generally slit, and volants of lace are inset in the openings.[19]

Lingerie, especially stockings, was dyed to match the petticoat and often decorated with lace, jewels or other adornments. One fashion reporter explained that in all cases, "tango stockings are agleam with spangled flora and fauna."[20] Irene Castle wrote, "There are filmy stockings with anklets embroidered in colored gems, lace-encrusted hose with silver embroideries, and, of course, all kinds of clocks and butterflies to draw attention to a slender foot and ankle. Any of these may be worn without violating good taste...."[21]

Long, difficult-to-maneuver trains were eliminated. "The fashions of 1914 have done away with it, because — you could not dance in a train!"[22] Because tangoists danced morning, noon, and night, more formal evening gowns that did feature a small train were designed so they could "be clamped up under the drapery of the skirt in a most satisfactory way."[23]

As in ragtime fashions, long tunics were often worn over the dresses. Overdresses, such as those in the lampshade style were common. Because of the focus on Orientalism, wide obi-like sashes and kimono sleeves were in style. One popular tango style was the Minaret tunic.

> Over the draping there is almost sure to be a Minaret tunic.... The newest Minaret tunics bear a close resemblance to the skirts of a ballet dancer, and like skirts of the ballet dancer they are cut so full that they stand out without wiring or boning of any kind. One, two, three, and even four layers of net are now being used, and wonderful blending of colors are possible.[24]

Color was an important part of the fashionable tango outfit. Brighter, more garish colors came into vogue.

One effect of the tango's enormous popularity was the introduction of the "couleur tango" — an orangish yellow hue that became popular in the fashions of the day. Legend has it that the color actually resulted from a mistake. A silk manufacturer accidentally botched some satin he was dyeing. When the garish color wouldn't sell and sat for weeks in his shop, he finally put the material on sale, but hit upon the idea of advertising it as "Satin-Tango." Immediately the fabric was snapped up and his customers demanded more. Unfortunately the poor fellow had lost the formula for the tint. Seeing a chance to cash in on the craze, other manufactures quickly came out with their own versions, claiming that they offered "la véritable couleur tango" or "true tango color." Many variations resulted from light yellow to dark reddish orange.

Although tango orange was the most popular shade for tango enthusiasts, other rich colors also came into vogue. "The dark red shades, the dregs of the wine, and the rich green colors are particularly well liked for tango frocks...."[25] The tango title was also conferred on other hues, virtually guaranteeing their success. In an article entitled "Tango Styles in Riot of Color," the *Oakland Tribune* reported on March 12, 1914, "Everywhere one hears 'tango.' Tango green, tango purple, tango rose...."[26]

The most ardent female tango dancers even dyed their hair in the latest tango colors.

> First and topmost of all is the new tango hair which is of the best hectic of hues dubbed tango red. Perfectly good tango hair may also be done in other equally riotously radiant shades such as cobalt blue, mauve, nile green or orange. Then your tango dyed locks should be done in the tango coiffure which means that it must be loosely waved, drawn neatly back from the face and the back hair fastened and tucked under at one side of the head with a jeweled tango comb or two jeweled tango pins.[27]

Small hats made of tulle or lace replaced wide picture hats because "Big hats are unpleasant to dance in."[28] Earlier headgear featured hats worn at an angle adorned with long horizontal aigrette feathers. The tango made imbalanced hats impractical. Instead, small hats, often tri-corners, were placed in the middle of the head. The placement of feathers also changed because the quick head turns of the tango made horizontal feathers a danger to the partner, who

"Le Tango," a 1914 Parisian postcard by artist Xavier Sager.

could accidentally be blinded.[29] One single aiglette was worn vertically. Another popular option was the little lace cap fashioned after the Dutch style popularized by Irene Castle. Russian head-dresses were also used. Coiffures became simpler as Mrs. Castle remarked, "because they do not become untidy when dancing."[30]

The dancing craze sparked the tango shoe, a low heel with crossed straps at the ankle, to hold the shoe securely on the nimble foot. Shoes made for dancing the tango were also length-ened at the toe "to exaggerate the long deliberate steps"[31] of the dance. To add further pizzazz and catch the attention of admiring spectators, the tango shoe was frequently adorned with rhinestones.

> [T]he favored tango slipper is the cothurne with its jeweled tango slides and buckles. Next in favor to the cothurne is a plain satin slipper with a rhinestone buckle and the newest variation to be sprung in the buckle ornamentations line are tiny jeweled tassels fastened at the instep which bob and sparkle seductively at every tango twist and turn.[32]

Snap and sparkle were important in tango fashion and not restricted to the fleeting glimpse of a jeweled heel or shoe buckle.

> It is with [not] just these fascinating and expensive touches that the jewelers get in the dance. They have you by the ears with lovely long and bobbing tango eardrops, glistening with semi-precious gems that scintillate with every toss and quiver of a lovely head. Charming waist-long strands of vari-colored tango beads they offer also and their latest chef d'ouevre is the tango ring. It is of a large design, the dimensions of a dinner ring, barbarically Oriental in effect and always composed of sparking stones that fail not to catch the light and twinkle even as the twinkling toes. These rings show up well on either fair hand whether it be the one coyly held out stiffly at right angles to the body in the tango partner's or the one that rests coyly upon his manly tango shoulder.[33]

To stay fresh and well put together after such continual dancing, the *valise de salon* became a must-have for the true tangoist. The little carrying case might contain a fresh collar, hand-kerchiefs, and other conveniences. The dancer could easily transport the portable toilette from morning instruction to afternoon tea dance to evening dinner dance. Some suggested that if the tango craze continued to grow, "hostesses may soon have to provide a series of tiny toilette cabinets even with baths, where exhausted dancers may recover from their weariness and renew their fresh appearance."[34] And after freshening up, the lady tango dancer was given this final, vital piece of advice, "Of course, as the last essence of tango perfection you must spray your hair and hanky with the newest Tango perfume and there you are a finished Tango product."[35]

The social reporter of the *Evening Chronicle* in Marshall, Michigan, summed up the all-encompassing fascination with tango fashions of the day:

> Just because everybody's mad about tango, they must needs have their wardrobe rebuilt to meet the requirements of the aforesaid tango. So they wear tango slippers, tango corsets, tango gowns and tango lingerie. And that's not all. They wear those things in the original tango shade. For it's tango, tango, tango, and nothing but tango from alpha to omega. So far, no one can predict just how far the tango craze will effect [sic] milady's wardrobe; but if it has so violent an effect upon her wardrobe as it has upon her festivities, it will be all tango, wholly tango, and nothing but tango. For that's the last word of the hour. And the world has apparently gone tango mad.[36]

Tango Music

The music of the tango developed from a rich variety of sources similar to those of the dance. Rhythmical elements were contributed from African influences and rural Argentine dances, and the Cuban Habanera contributed European elements found in French contradance.[37]

The earliest tango music was generally improvised. Untrained musicians interacted with the complex and often unpredictable steps of the dancers, and as movements were repeated and new ones invented, melodies that matched the rhythms were created. These songs were eventually refined.

Primitive tango bands, often trios who experimented with the form, developed the music into its distinctive sound. Historians often refer to these early musicians as the *Guardia Vieja* or "Old Guard." The various combinations of players might include flute, clarinet, violin, harp, or guitar.[38]

The large influx of Italian immigrants to Buenos Aires at the turn of the century brought with them other instruments such as the accordion and the mandolin that soon augmented early tango bands. The Italianization of the tango also included the melodic influence of Neapolitan songs. The ideal combination of sounds eventually evolved into a tango orchestra comprised of six players: two violins, a double bass, a piano, and two bandoneóns.[39]

The arrival from Germany of the accordion-like bandoneón contributed the most characteristic sound of tango music.[40] The instrument had been invented in Germany in the mid 1800's and was used by poor communities as a substitute when they could not afford a church organ. When the instrument was introduced in Argentina, it was originally used for playing polkas and waltzes, but soon was accompanying the early forms of the tango. Because of the technical difficulty of playing the bandoneón, many players could not keep up with the rapid steps employed by early dancers moving to the driving beat of African-influenced rhythms. Dancers were forced to slow down to accommodate players and so the languid feel of the tango developed.

In the 1880's, tango music moved away from pure improvisation as composers began writing simple piano pieces for publication. By the 1890's musicians were publishing more structured, complex, and fully developed forms that eventually evolved into true tango music as it is known today.

> With the new century the musical tradition took on a definite life of its own. In fact while the dance lost much of its original fierce, aggressive, erotic character (as it more or less had to do in order to be accepted in the ballrooms of the world), the music that went with it gradually became richer and more sophisticated — became, in fact, a tradition in popular music in its own right.[41]

The invention of the phonograph and improvements in recording technology were instrumental in helping spread the music of the tango. Angel Villoldo, sometimes called the "Father of the Tango," is credited with recording the first tango in Paris in 1907. In 1911, Columbia Records hired Vicente Greco and his sextet to put out tangos. Juan Maglio, known by the nickname Pacho, also recorded tangos that were enormously popular.

Around this same time the tango song began to develop with words set to the popular tango tunes of the day. Many of these early songs contained lyrics that referred to the early disreputable origins of the dance. Many notable singers became associated with the tango. Perhaps the most renowned was Carlos Gardel,[42] whose tango singing would secure him a place as "Latin America's greatest popular singer of the twentieth century, and the tango's supreme legend."[43]

13

Reaction to the Tango

As the tango grew in popularity, those who opposed the dance sought to eradicate it. In November of 1913, the *New York Times* reported that in Germany, in addition to threatening his officers with immediate dismissal if they did the tango or fraternized with any people who did, the Kaiser warned members of the Royal Opera House ballet against participating in any charity entertainments where tango competitions were included.[1] Orders were issued in the Austro-Hungarian army that "officers in uniform are not allowed to dance the tango."[2] Shortly after the Kaiser's ruling, the King of Bavaria also put a ban on the tango, calling the dance "absurd."[3]

The most far-reaching condemnation came from Rome; the Vatican issued a circular calling the tango "offensive to the purity of every right-minded person."[4] In December of 1913, reports appeared in papers around the globe that a toned-down version of the tango had been presented in a demonstration before Pope Pius X so he could judge whether or not it was still immoral.[5] Many waited breathlessly to hear the Pope's verdict. After seeing it, the Pontiff remarked that if the tango were made a penance for sins, it would be "looked upon as sheer cruelty."[6]

In January of 1914, Cardinal Cavallari, Patriarch of Venice, issued the following statement regarding the tango; "It is everything that can be imagined. It is revolting and disgusting. Only those persons who have lost all moral sense can endure it. It is the shame of our days. Whoever persists in it commits a sin." Cavallari then ordered that absolution be denied "to those who, having danced the tango, do not promise to discontinue the practice."[7]

Several French bishops joined in the attacks against the tango and urged the Cardinal-Archbishop of Paris, Cardinal Amette, to join them in the crusade to eradicate the immoral dance. It was hoped that if he did, "it would prove a death blow to the tango in real Parisian society, although it may not affect the somewhat nondescript cosmopolitan agglomeration which forms its fringe and seeks to pass itself off as the real thing."[8] Monsignor Amette, agreed, and on January 11, 1914, the Primate of France published a scathing attack on the tango, calling it "...by its nature indecent and offensive to morals."[9] He admonished other clerics to keep the wicked dance in mind when hearing confessions and called for a complete ban of the dance. Many members of society reluctantly shied away from the tango. One "professor of dancing"[10] sued Cardinal Amette for his lost income after the decree. The tango teacher said that after the Prelate's decree against the dance, he lost several pupils from fashionable circles.

In Paris, the battle between supporters of the tango and those who detested the dance grew to epic proportions. On February 16, 1914 an article appeared in the *Mercure de France* calling the tango "une danse de filles publiques,"—"a whores' dance." It stated that the tango "led to drunkenness and murderous brawls" and that it was "a sure path to indecency, authorizing poses and movements which make the body of the purest woman look infamous." The article added that young people performing the tango "were acting like monkeys from the Andes."[11]

Around the same time, the President of France, Monsieur Poincaré, prohibited the tango from being danced at palace functions. The tango was even banned at the Argentine Embassy in Paris. The minister plenipotentiary to Paris, Enrique Rodriguez Larreta stated:

> The tango is in Buenos Aires a primitive dance of houses of ill repute and of the lowest kind of dives. It is never danced in polite society nor among persons of breeding. To Argentine ears it awakens the most disagreeable feelings. I see no difference whatsoever between the tango that is danced in elegant Parisian dance halls and that which is danced in the basest nightspots in Buenos Aires.[12]

Eventually, municipal authorities drew up a decree banning the tango. By April 12, 1915, five tango teachers were issued decrees of expulsion from the capital city for disobeying a ban against the dance. Paris, the city that was most identified with the start of the tango craze, now turned its back on the dance.

In England, the tango also created furor. Several leading London hostesses came out against the dance. The Duchess of Norfolk said, "In my opinion such dances are not desirable; for the tango in itself and in the comments that it leads to is surely foreign to our English nature and ideals, of which I hope we are still proud."[13] Others joined her in condemning the dance:

> Lady Coventry does not think it desirable that the tango should be danced at social functions. Lady Layland-Barratt considers it an immodest and suggestive dance, altogether impossible for any girl of refinement or modesty. Lady De Ramsey strongly disapproves the tango and would never let it be danced in her house. Lady Beatrice Wilkinson says: "Never having seen the tango danced, I am not in a position to give an opinion. If, however it is anything like the horrible dances of negroid origin which have for the moment ruined English ballrooms, I very strongly object to it.[14]

Initially, Queen Mary herself heartily disapproved of the dance, although her prejudice against the tango changed after she witnessed a private demonstration by Maurice Mouvet and Florence Walton. The couple showed how the dances should be done in polite society.[15]

In Luxemburg, one newspaper refused to accept any advertisements that even mentioned the tango, including "advertisements for lessons in this dance, announcements of any functions where it is to be danced, and even notices where tango music and the score of one or the other of the half dozen tango operettas may be seen and purchased."[16]

Even in Argentina, the birthplace of the tango, many people opposed the dance. One paper reported, "...it is not considered very nice even to mention the dance among respectable people of that land—the land of the tango.... It is looked upon as something terrible, unmentionable. There is an ironclad ban against it in polite circles."[17]

Moral Objections to the Tango

The Rev. Charles A Eaton, the pastor of the Madison Avenue Baptist Church in New York City said,

> It is a craze, a form of nervous degeneracy. It has been stimulated, first, by unwholesome social conditions, and, second, by commercialism. People of all walks of life seem to have abandoned their common sense, their sense of self-possession, and in many cases their morals. Instead of using the dance as a modest and beautiful means of recreation, it has degenerated into a sort of civilized "snake dance." I don't know what the parents of our country are thinking about. They throw their children to the crocodiles as the Indian mothers used to do, but the former without any religious motive. They are consumed by an itch for social advance, and they think the only way to get into society is to dance in.[18]

The management of one large dance hall went so far as to hang the effigy of "a most disreputable-looking" dancer in its front window. Over it was a sign that read: "We have got him, the dirty miserable Tango. This is a respectable dance hall, you CANNOT dance the TANGO here."[19] The window also included anti-tango quotations from the ballerina Anna Pavlova.

In Chicago, the city council wanted two questions answered: "What is the tango?" and "When is it immoral?"[20] They ordered Mayor Harrison to create a "tango committee" to monitor anyone who attempted the dance in cabarets and theatres and to provide suggestions for creating a tango ordinance.

The Dean of All Saint's Episcopal Church in Spokane, Washington barred all members of his parish from dancing the tango. The Very Reverend W. C. Hicks sneered at the dance saying, "Two young people interlocking knees and putting their chests together and then pushing each other across the floor with a duck-like walk are not dancing."[21]

The Cardinal of New York did not call for an outright ban of the tango, but did make it known in no uncertain terms that "the tango is degrading and he has resolved to do all he can to discourage it."[22] In March of 1914, men and women from the Salvation Army invaded several restaurants where patrons were doing the tango and exhorted the dancers to "pause and reflect that there was also a serious side of life."[23] Evangelist Bob Jones declared that New Yorkers were tangoing themselves "on the brink of hell," adding, "the only difference between Manhattan and hell is that Manhattan is surrounded by water."[24]

The clergy's virulent opposition to the dance led some members of high society to rethink the dance. The New York Junior Auxiliary recalled 600 invitations to one of their events out of fear the tango would be done. The Knights of Columbus also barred the tango from its annual ball at Madison Square Gardens, even going so far as to appoint a censoring committee of 150 to patrol and make sure no one tried the dance.

Despite exhortations from the pulpits across the country, true tango fanatics refused to give up the dance. *The New York Times* reported on February 1, 1914 on one humorous incident that took place in Atlantic City. It stated, "Warfare on the tango took a new turn here to-day when Mrs. Lillian Boniface Albers, soloist of St. Paul's Methodist Episcopal Church choir, received the alternative of giving up the dance or resigning her place in the choir. She resigned immediately."[25]

When Cleveland barred the teaching of the tango, dancing teacher Asa Anderson sued the city. At the trial, he asked to demonstrate the dance with one of his pupils before the judge to prove the dance's harmlessness. The judge did not make a final ruling immediately but did give his "nod of approval" to the dance. He later ruled "...the tango as taught by Anderson is perfectly moral and can be so danced." In his opinion, Judge Vickery added, " Every beautiful thing may be vulgarized. But because some dancing is vulgar, we could not bar all dancing."[26]

Citing indecency and immorality as reasons for banning the dance, several American Universities barred the tango, including Kansas University, The University of Wisconsin, the University of Vermont, Notre Dame, and Yale to name just a few. Harvard prohibited the tango from being danced by any member of the track team stating that the dance "does not tend to make outdoor athletes."[27] It also banned the tango in its chemical laboratories after thousands of dollars worth of equipment were damaged by students jarring the floor while tangoing in the science classrooms.

High schools and other institutions of learning also barred the tango. Some teachers in Pittsburgh were not happy when the school board declared that dancing the tango "left the teachers in poor condition physically to teach the day after."[28] When they prohibited the dance, the teachers went on strike, giving the school board an ultimatum — if they could not tango, they would not teach.

The tango also affected the workforce. In 1913, Stanley W. Finch, head of the National Social Welfare League stated that the dance was having a crippling negative economic impact upon business. Finch revealed that he had heard from several businessmen around the U. S. who complained that the craze was getting out of hand. One wrote to him and lamented, "The tango has

Le Tango

A 1914 French postcard by Xavier Sager that captures the scandalous sensuality of the tango.

taken such a grip upon our best employees that their capacity for work is cut in two. They go out and dance the newfangled twists half the night; the next morning they have none of their former vigor, and the result is that the whole business suffers greatly because they are no longer able to turn out their accustomed amount of work."[29]

Tango Pirates and Pickpockets

At the height of the tango craze in the United States, *The New York Times* ran an article that contained the following photo caption: "Afternoon Dances Develop a New Kind of Parasite Whose Victims Are the Unguarded Daughters of the Rich." The parasite referred to was the tango pirate — a dancing lothario who bilked money out of young women at *thé dansants*. This new breed of thief had to be an excellent dancer and elegantly dressed to the nines.[30] *The Times* reported, "During the Fall, Winter and Spring these young fellows invariably wear a silk hat, usually tilted at an angle of forty-five degrees. In the Summer they wear, before dark, the most fashionable straws. And cutaway coats. And spats— always spats. I have seen fifty of them and never one without spats."[31]

A tango pirate, also sometimes called a social gangster, flattered his victim, seducing her with words and the latest tango moves, but usually not having sex with her, "knowing the moment she has broken with her family his avenue of profit is cut off. He doesn't want the girl; he wants her money."[32] In addition to the titillation of dancing the tango with a handsome, dangerous young man, these naïve young women were frequently introduced to drugs, typically, cocaine. Many tango pirates were users themselves. *The Times* went so far as to claim, "...all of these tango pirates are victims of the cocaine habit, or in its advanced stage, the heroin habit."[33]

The problem was widespread in large cities and articles and editorials appeared advising parents to keep their daughters away from tango teas. They were warned, "...no girl can spend her afternoons in the cafés and escape with her money — or her reputation, even if she survives with all else.[34]

One tango pirate case that captured the attention of the press and the public involved nineteen-year-old heiress, Eugenia Kelly. The daughter of a prominent New York banking family, Miss Kelly began to frequent the "'trotteries' of the gay white way."[35] She struck up an acquaintance with a tango pirate by the name of Al Davis.[36] He was an older married man and a professional dancer, and Eugenia lavished him with jewelry and other expensive gifts. Miss Kelly's mother, concerned with Davis' "continued pernicious influence"[37] and troubled by Eugenia's late-night forays, feared that the cabaret life was "seducing her daughter into a life of modern evil."[38] The distraught mother petitioned the courts "to have Eugenia declared incorrigible and remanded to her care or jailed."[39] On May 21, 1915, detectives arrested the young girl. During the trial, the judge sided with the young girl's mother, and warned Eugenia to give up the "Broadway crowd."[40] After three days of fighting against the prosecution's case, a rebellious Eugenia learned that she might lose her ten million dollar inheritance and reluctantly repented.[41] She stated before the judge, "I was wrong and mother was right.... I realize now that I was dazzled by the glamour of the white lights and the music and the dancing of Broadway."[42] The District Attorney who worked on the case commented, "...in all my experience I have never met with such a case as this. It is awful when you think how these Broadway parasites can fasten upon young women and filch from them their estates."[43]

Another notorious tango pirate case involved the murder of thirty-five-year-old Mrs. Elsie Lee Hilar of Brooklyn, who was strangled at the Hotel Martinique on March 15, 1917, and robbed of $2,500 worth of jewelry.[44] The Kelly and Hilar Cases proved to critics of the tango that the dance and the men who did it were inherently dangerous. The tango not only threatened the sanctity of the home, but also one's life.[45]

The police classified similar types of criminals prevalent at the time as "tango pickpockets." Like tango pirates, tango pickpockets were people of questionable character who were given access to ballrooms simply because they were good dancers.

> Thus an attractive young woman, who for some weeks frequented the exclusive society of a dancing club where she was believed to be a Russian Princess, turned out to be lady's maid, while a number of ex-waiters, ballet dancers, and circus performers playing the roles of Argentine millionaires have enjoyed unlimited hospitality in some of the best social circles on the strength of their skill in the tango.[46]

Masquerading as someone of a different class may have been distasteful, but the real problem was that "...many of these pseudo-aristocrats have been taking full advantage of the complicated attitudes which the tango and its kindred dances involve to pick pockets and purloin jewelry."[47] The victims didn't notice the thefts because they were concentrating so hard on executing the intricate steps of the tango.

Because of these dangers as well as questions about the decency of the dance, politicians and office holding officials lambasted the tango. In 1914, the Massachusetts state legislature considered a bill making it a crime to dance the tango. The penalty for breaking the law was a $50.00 fine for the first offence and six months in jail for the second. Mayor Fitzgerald of Boston issued orders for a policeman and matron to stand guard at every dance hall to see that the tango was not danced. He announced that any establishment that allowed the dance would have its license revoked.

Mayor Gaynor of New York, in an effort to curb improper behavior at tea dances, tried to do away with the tango. He said some *thé dansants* had gotten so out of hand they had become "lascivious orgies,"[48] although André Bustanoby defended the dances at his well-known establishment declaring that tango teas were really a necessity. "The afternoon dance is necessary because so many women eat rich foods and pastry, and they get fat if they don't take some exercise. Here they dance and grow graceful and slim."[49] Another restaurant owner prevented inappropriate behavior on his dance floor with a unique method. He explained, "If any people offend," he said," we turn the spotlight on them and make them behave."[50]

Medical Objections

As tangoitis infected more and more of the population, an article in the *Journal of the American Medical Association* purported that the tango and other modern dances were "potentially harmful amusements."[51] It stated that middle-aged dancers should not "fail to observe that nice, long word 'potentially'.... In fact, if you are a man you might paste it in your hat. And if you happen to be a woman, you might pin it — somewhere."[52] The esteemed journal also warned that "elderly dancers were in danger of putting too great a strain on a dilated heart or an arterio-sclerotic artery,"[53] and that dances like the tango could aggravate kidney trouble. As a side note, the *Journal* added, "Insomnia may haunt what is left of the night after one has danced most of it away."[54]

Reporting on the journal's findings, *The New York Times* stated that middle-aged men should entertain extra caution when dancing with young girls "who aren't any more troubled with high blood pressure than a feather is that floats around on the wind."[55] The paper also declared that "dancer's heart" was "already talked of among professionals,"[56] and that it was a common occurrence for some cabaret dancers to faint after performing.

Many ailments were attributed to the tango. *The New York Times* reported on a new disease affecting Paris called "fallen stomach." The paper said that the malady was a "fashionable ailment, the effect of too much tangoing"[57] and resulted when people danced too soon after eating. To combat the problem, the following treatment was prescribed: "Immediately after eating lie down for half an hour with the legs in the air, at least higher than the body."[58] Some knowledgeable physicians suggested that Paris salons "would have to be provided with bars and railings on which guests not entirely recovered may be able to place their feet at proper angle with the body after dinner."[59]

In Berlin, Dr. Gustave F. Boehme diagnosed a new disease he called "tango foot." The syndrome resulted from over-stretching the muscles of the foot and leg while dancing the tango. In an article in the *Medical Record* Dr. Boehme, a neurologist at the West Side German Dispensary and Hospital said the "new affliction [was] due entirely to our love of the aesthetic and the joyous."[60] Symptoms include pain in the front of the leg, the lower part of the calf, and the ankle, and other joint problems.

The doctor stated that "the foot symptoms are precisely the same as seen in the wage earner who operates a foot-power sewing machine,"[61] indicating that whereas the repetitive stress on the extremities from constant tangoing may have caused the problem, "...simple cessation from dancing is all that is necessary"[62] for curing the disease. The doctor also had various lotions that he recommended to reduce swelling.

Another concern was "tango face." The editor of the *Photographic News*, Carl E. Akerman, said that the tango was causing wrinkles to appear on women's faces because they were taking the pastime too seriously.

> The tango face is a real menace to the good looks of the American woman. It is characterized by deep, dark hollows under the eyes, by indentations from the nose to the corners of the mouth, by a number of fine lines on forehead and on cheeks, and finally by a wooden smile, unmoved and meaningless.[63]

Akerman added, "The real reason why many women tango dancers have such a strained, unnatural expression is because they are constantly trying to look proper while doing what they secretly believe is improper. The set smile means that they are endeavoring to look happy when they have lost all spontaneous pleasure and are only craze driven."[64]

Announcing his finding at the convention of the National Association of Photographers held in Atlanta, "...as proof he added the fact that photographers find increasing difficulty in making satisfactory pictures of feminine tangomaniacs."[65] Reporting on Akerman's findings, the *Waterloo Times-Tribune*, in Waterloo, Iowa, concluded, "The tango has been blamed for almost every conceivable mishap from broken arches to broken homes, but perhaps the most portentous charge against it of all is now being brought against it. For an excellent authority, the tango is accused of spoiling the beauty of the American woman."[66]

Miss Marguerite Lindley, an expert in physical economics, noted that the backward bend and the quick side dip in the tango were injurious to the health and "may do great harm."[67] Unhealthy situations were exacerbated by "late hours, nerve strain and excessive exercise in tight clothes."[68] Some suggested that because of all the new steps they had to learn, women were suffering from too much strain on their brains.

Tango madness certainly took its toll. On the night of February 6, 1913, a Parisian tailor named Guenard began throwing furniture out the window of his fourth floor apartment onto the street below, nearly hitting passersby. The man looked out the window to the stunned crowd below and shouted," I must have room to dance the tango." *The New York Times* reported, "When the police arrived Guenard was seized after a struggle. He was found to have become insane."[69]

There were reports of serious injuries and even death associated with tangoing. Professional dancer Ida Crispi broke her arm while doing a variation of the Argentine tango called the Yankee tangle when she fell near the end of the dance. In his memoir, *They All Sang*, Edward Marks wrote of Henry Blossom, librettist of *Mlle. Modiste*, who broke his leg dancing the tango. Mrs. Ethel Fitch Conger also broke her leg, and planned to seek legislation against the dip.[70] Joseph E. Bishop broke his arm, sprained his ankle, and suffered internal injuries because of the tango. Forty wedding guests were dancing the tango at his wedding when the hall collapsed. His bride's injuries were so severe, doctors expected her to die.

One high school student collapsed and died after dancing the tango for seven straight hours. In Louisville, Kentucky, Emma Schuchman, "tangoed to death."[71] The seventeen-year-old died of heart failure in the middle of the dance floor. Thirty-three-year old John Noyes Failing also died from heart disease on the dance floor while dancing at a weekly meeting of the Progressive Tango Club. As proof of how dangerous the tango was at any age, Marks wrote of a 102-year-old man who died within a week of his first try at the tango.[72]

Death by tango also made its way into the courts. Daniel Spencer who was charged with manslaughter in the untimely death of William H. Brown was later released when Miss Ollie Thompson testified that Brown had actually lost his life as a result of dancing the tango. She revealed that Brown was "tangoing with her, when he struck his head against a door, knocking a panel out."[73] After demonstrating to Judge Ely and the court how the accident happened as they danced, Spencer was acquitted.

Perhaps the most notorious tango case to hit the courts was that of the murder of dance instructor Mrs. Mildred Allison-Rexroat near Chicago. The young woman had divorced her first husband, Mr. Allison, and left her three children to pursue "the lure of the gayer life of tango dancing."[74] She met Everett Rexroat, a farmboy who had come to Chicago to learn the tango himself, and the two courted on the dance floor, eventually marrying. They soon split because Mildred realized she didn't really love Everett "but simply was danced into marrying him."[75] Alone and struggling to make a living, Mildred started teaching tango at a Chicago dancing academy. Then the shadowy Henry Spencer came into the picture. An unemployed cigar clerk, Spencer took tango lessons from Mildred. He soon became obsessed with the young divorcée and started stalking her. He suggested that Mildred form a tango class in the nearby town of Wheaton. On the night of September 13, 1914, he lured her out of the city on the pretense of showing her the ideal location. Spencer choked and then shot Mildred, leaving her body on the railroad tracks. Her corpse was found when it was struck by a passing train near Wayne, Illinois. The body was so mutilated, identification was possible only from an inscribed bracelet the victim wore, and some tattered scraps of a note found on her body. Local papers dubbed the case, "the tragedy of the tango dance," lambasting "...the snaky, sinuous, sensual Argentina tango, the dance of the lawless Spanish-American underworld of Buenos Aires, trailed to the United States by way of Paris [which had] become in Chicago a veritable dance of death...."[76]

Spencer, nicknamed the "tango murderer" and "tango killer," was finally apprehended. He confessed not only to Mildred's murder but also to a score of other serial killings of young women across the country. At the trial, his defense lawyers pleaded insanity, and Spencer seemed to support their claims by making frequent outbursts of profanity during his trial. One time, he knocked down his own attorney and cried, "Let's cut this damned foolishness and put on a necktie party. I'm not nutty and willing to be hanged."[77]

On November 14, 1914, he was found guilty and sentenced to be hanged. His lawyers appealed, and the case ended up in the Illinois Supreme Court. On June 15, 1914, the Supreme Court upheld the lower court's decision. Spencer was executed on July 31, 1914.

Health Benefits from the Tango

Despite the many warnings that the tango was dangerous for one's health, other voices argued that the dance had benefits. On December 18, 1913, the *Sheboygan Press* in Sheboygan, Wisconsin, ran an editorial on its society page assuring its readers:

> We have the word of a well known physical culturist that the tango is the very best sort of tonic for good health. For the tango, danced properly, according to this authority, brings almost every muscle into play ... it is a great rejuvenator.[78]

Vernon and Irene Castle extolled the lasting benefits of tango dancing as healthy exercise. Gladys Beattie Crozier agreed. She wrote, "Many people find that ten minutes' rigorous practice of the Tango twists, dips and sudden turns after the morning bath form a most enlivening exercise in place of 'physical drill,' and is doing wonders for their powers of balance."[79] Crozier went on to say that "Business men, especially, who suffer from systematic overwork, find the close attention it requires to master and carry out the many steps and figures a splendid antidote for brain-fag and business worries after a trying day...."[80] The "butterflies" and "nuts" of society, as she calls various flighty women, can also find something to occupy themselves, whereas "the modern woman suffering from 'nerves' declares that in the dreamy, languorous movements of the French Tango just the soothing qualities she requires are to be found."[81]

The Gazette and Bulletin in Williamsport, Pennsylvania reported on May 12, 1914, that some medical authorities offered their professional opinions that dancing the tango was especially helpful to the elderly and middle-aged because it "joggled" the liver. Some said that to do the dance required looser clothing, which in itself carried enormous benefits. The article stated unequivocally that according to the Ohio Medical Association, "the tango promises to do as much for the western woman as unbinding the feet will do for her Chinese sister."[82] The thought was that since dancing the tango in high heels was out of the question, the tango ushered in the vogue of lower heels, which were more beneficial to foot health.

A butcher by the name of William Melago actually declared that he owed his life to the tango. When he accidentally locked himself in his meat freezer for three hours, he danced the tango to keep himself from freezing to death.

PART IV. THE CHARLESTON

14

Origins of the Charleston

As other dances had done in previous eras, the Charleston, quintessential symbol of the 1920's, ignited social controversy. The dance's wild, uninhibited movements were viewed by many as disgusting and decadent, yet the dance became so fashionable and popular, virtually all levels of society kicked up their heels to the Charleston's infectious beat. With flailing arms and legs, angular disjointed movements, and a reckless lack of control, the Charleston perfectly reflected the defiance, freedom, and turmoil of the period — its quick, syncopated rhythm mirroring the chaotic tempo of the Roaring 20's.

The second decade of the twentieth century was a period of great social change. A manic energy swept the American nation. Disillusioned with Woodrow Wilson's idealistic policies, and weary from the sacrifices of the Great War, Americans sought diversion. Sensationalism reigned; fads and crazes such as sitting on flagpoles or swallowing goldfish were all the rage.[1]

America enjoyed unprecedented prosperity — the largest economic boom the country had ever experienced. New developments in technology and automation saved time and reduced labor costs. Mass production was in full swing and materialism reigned.[2]

The rise in automobile use led to dramatic changes in the American social landscape as people in rural communities gained access to better medical care, higher education, and more varied forms of entertainment and leisure. Automobile use also offered a means of escape for young people wishing to be free of parental supervision. The youth of the period dubbed the car "the struggle buggy." Victorian courting rituals gave way to petting in a rumble seat.

Mass communication, in the form of radio and motion pictures, also grew rapidly, fostering the cult of celebrity. Names like Charles Lindbergh, F. Scott Fitzgerald, Admiral Richard Byrd, Amelia Earhart, Babe Ruth and Al Capone became known by millions. Movie magazines and confession tabloids aroused readers with lurid tales of romance and wild living. Movies advertised "brilliant men, beautiful jazz babies, champagne baths, midnight revels, petting parties in the purple dawn, all ending in one terrific smashing climax that makes you gasp."[3]

The novelty of the radio also grabbed Americans' attention in 1922 when KDKA, the first commercial radio station in the United States, broadcast out of Pittsburgh. Other stations quickly proliferated and households across country listened to the latest dance tunes beamed directly into their living rooms. Jazz music grew in popularity and became the hallmark of sophistication and modernity.

Social mores and moral beliefs were being challenged and changed at every angle. Women had just been given the right to vote in 1919 with the passage of the Nineteenth Amendment, and in 1922 this liberation was underscored with the Cable Act by which married women were granted U.S. citizenship regardless of their husband's legal status. In 1921, Margaret Sanger officiated over the inaugural meeting of the American Birth Control League, and in 1923 the National Women's Party was created to push through an Equal Rights Amendment to the U.S. Constitution.

During the Great War, women had filled in for men in the workplace, and many were not willing to return to subservient roles and give up economic independence after the Armistice.

Women who did remain within the sphere of the household found that with the advent of time-saving household appliances, they spent less time doing ordinary domestic chores and had more time for leisure activities. Many women, especially the young, began to venture beyond the roles traditionally assigned to them by society. More and more women danced and drank and smoked in public. Many adopted a carefree attitude about sex.

> [It was] an era of painful contradictions. Still reeling from the Great War and the worldwide wave of disillusionment that it inspired; both dazzled and bewildered by their sudden access to such technological wonders as radio, movies, the automobile, and the airplane; torn between the traditional life of simple rural virtue, and the exciting jazz age that beckoned to them from the streets of the cities (a lure of sexual experimentation and freedom from responsibility), people attempted to make sense of their lives.[4]

In the midst of this turmoil, the Roaring Twenties witnessed the rebirth of the Knights of the Ku Klux Klan which by 1924 had four million members and exerted powerful political leverage. As racism was growing in virulence in the United States, African American culture was also co-opted by large sections of white society. With the advent of the first all-black musicals on Broadway and the growing popularity of African American inspired music and dances, all things "black" were in vogue.

The 1920's began with much of the American nation in a furor over the enactment of the Eighteenth Amendment of the Constitution,[5] prohibiting the manufacture, sale, or transportation of alcoholic beverages. Social reformers who favored the Noble Experiment, as Prohibition was called, believed that it would ameliorate all manner of social evils: ridding the country of poverty, bringing a reduction in crime, and restoring family values. Evangelist Billy Sunday predicted that with the banning of liquor, "Men will walk upright now. Women will smile and children will laugh. Hell will be forever rent."[6] Sunday said that America would be "so dry, she can't spit."[7]

The results were not what Sunday and many others in the temperance movement had hoped. Consumption of alcohol increased dramatically. Large scale smuggling operations sprang up overnight,[8] and bathtub gin[9] and homemade spirits were concocted with such speed that authorities were unable to enforce the newly enacted Liquor Laws.[10] Speakeasies,[11] with their illicit liquor, scandalous jazz music, and provocative dancing, became symbols of a rebellious generation seeking to forget the recent war. It was in this chaotic social environment that the Charleston became the dance of the day.

African Dance

Dance historians believe that the roots of the Charleston can be traced to the ritual tribal dances of Africa. According to Marshall and Jean Stearns' seminal classic *Jazz Dance: The Story of American Vernacular Dance*, the Charleston bears a striking resemblance to an Obolo dance performed by the Ibo tribe in West Africa. Similarities are also found among dances of the Ashanti and Bari-speaking tribes, and the King Sailor Dance of Trinidad. W. G Raffé states in the *Dictionary of Dance* that the origin of the Charleston can be traced to a dance called the batuque from the Cape Verde Islands and Portuguese Guinea in West Africa.[12] Historian Frederick Kaigh said, "The children of Africa were doing the Charleston before Julius Caesar had so much as heard of Britain, and they still are."[13]

The African influence on the Charleston was clearly visible in the dance's use of polyrhythmic body movements. The juxtaposition of various rhythms created a seeming "looseness" in the Charleston. The wild articulation of the knees in the dance, called bee's knees, monkey knees, or the fan, was one of the by-products of this aspect of African dance.

Another connection between African dance and the Charleston was the use of improvisation. Although certain basic steps were recognized as common in the Charleston, invention, innovation, and individuality were expected while doing the dance, and improvisational breaks were common among early Charleston dancers. This type of breakaway improvisation pointed to the dance's African origins.

The importation of African dance movements to the United States occurred during the Atlantic slave trade when captured Africans brought their native dances to the Americas. These ritual movements eventually became more secularized as they were influenced by European stylistic elements introduced to the slaves on the plantations. Although many of the original African rhythms and steps were retained, other aspects were modulated and transformed as European and other influences cross-pollinated with them. This blending eventually morphed into the social dance called the Charleston.[14]

International star Florence Mills said, "I have heard as many stories of the origin of the Charleston as I have heard cures for colds. I believe one relating to Pickaninnies dancing it on Plantations outside Charleston, South Carolina in the late [eighteen] 'fifties, to the Negro tune called 'Take Your Foot Out of the Mud and Stick It in the Sand' to be the most authentic."[15]

In her book *Black Dance From 1619 to Today,* Lynn Fauley Emery states that the original Charleston was closely linked to a plantation dance called the Jay-Bird.[16] She adds, "...Harold Courlander, said that while the Charleston had some characteristics of traditional Negro dance, the dance itself 'was a synthetic creation, a newly devised conglomerate tailored for wide spread appeal.'"[17]

Many dance historians have suggested that the Charleston is descended from parts of a competition dance called the Juba.[18] The Juba was derived from an African step dance, the *Giouba*, in which one dancer challenged the technical skill of another in a series of bravura solos. Usually performed by two male dancers inside a circle of other participants,[19] the dance started with the outside ring of dancers circling counterclockwise around the two men in the middle using an eccentric shuffling step in which one foot was continually lifted. They followed the shuffling with a step called the Dog Scratch. Then, the two men in the center of the circle began a dance competition. As they performed increasingly difficult and intricate steps, they were urged on by the others who clapped, stamped, and slapped their thighs—keeping time, and encouraging the competitors in verse and song. Each new step was determined by the shouted and sung commands of the observers in a call-and-response format. The rhythmical slapping of the body was called patting.[20] Patting was often used to accompany the Charleston and was an integral part of the social dance. The practice eventually evolved into the Charleston signature display step called bee's knees, which involved crouching down and swinging the knees open and closed while simultaneously fanning the hands over them.[21]

The Branle

There have been efforts to trace the Charleston to European antecedents. In an article entitled "The Charleston Traces Its Ancestry Back 400 Years" which appeared in the *New York Times* on August 8, 1926, the author Fred Austin quotes Leo Staats, director of the ballet of the Paris Opéra, "...the Charleston of today is basically the Branle of the sixteenth century with a few frills added."[22]

Austin adds,

> Dancing masters may argue that the dance of the hour is a blood brother of some unholy ritual of the unredeemed African jungle, an off-shoot of cottonfield buck-and-wing or the invention of

Typical bee's knees position from 1925. In this publicity shot by the Nation Photo Company, Frank Farnum coaches Pauline Starke for her upcoming role in the MGM movie *A Little Bit of Broadway* (courtesy of the Library of Congress).

> negro roustabouts, merrymaking on the wharves of the city whose name it bears. M. Staat, with the annals of l'Academie Nationale de Musique et de la Danse at his back, says it is nonsense — that the Charleston is merely a variation, a recrudescence in new guise, but embodying the same underlying principle of the dance that was favored by noble and yokel alike for two centuries.[23]

Austin writes that Staat points out that the Charleston is not only descended from the Branle, but also contains other early dances such as *pas tortilles* or twisting steps which can be traced to Spain and "dates back to those dancers of Cadiz whose praises were sung in ancient Rome by Martial, Pliny the Younger and Petronius."[24] He adds that the lifting movements of *pas levés* are recognizable in the dance as well as *Rue de Vache* (literally translated as the "kick of the cow") that is seen in the side kick in the Charleston. He further suggests that elements of the Charleston are also found in the Sailor's Hornpipe. "The twisting movement of Jack Tar on the balls of his feet, as he moves backward and forward, simulating hauling a rope, is the Charleston wing of today, pure and simple."[25]

The article states,

> Jack Blue and Ned Wayburn may dispute as long as they please about who is entitled to laurel or hemlock, whichever is the fitting reward for introducing the Charleston to the stage. It doesn't matter, for the original Charleston, if M. Staats is right — and early records of dance bear him out — was publicly performed on the Field of the Cloth of Gold in 1520, when the court of Francis I and Henry VII held revel.... The Louvre was the home of the forefather of the steps with

which pickaninnies today charm nickels and dimes from the pockets of passers-by in Gotham, and roisters in the haunts of Francois Villon sang and danced the first Charleston to a tune that was not jazz. The floors of Versailles and the sward of Fontainebleau vibrated to the shock of thudding feet, but there was no fear expressed in those days that beams would collapse beneath the impact.[26]

Vague references to the origin of the Charleston are found in a few dance books which mention an illustration entitled "Pretty Caper" found in *Harper's Weekly*, October 13, 1866. The etching shows a gentleman with his right leg splayed out to the side in a typical Charleston move as he demonstrates the latest stage dance. Some historians have suggested that this indicates the Charleston was performed on stage earlier than during the 1920's.[27]

The Early Roots of the Charleston

After Emancipation, many former slaves regarded mobility as the greatest expression of their newly won freedom. As they left rural areas to find employment, some migrated to urban centers along the water, hoping to find work loading and unloading ships on the docks. They carried with them their dances.

Many dance historians believe that the dance known as the Charleston drew its name from the city of Charleston, South Carolina, where the dance was common among African-American dockworkers. As African-American workers migrated North after World War I, the Charleston spread to urban centers such as New York City.

This illustration entitled "The Pretty Caper," appeared in *Harper's Weekly* on October 13, 1866. The splayed arms and legs of the gentleman demonstrating a popular stage dance of his time suggest to some the movements of the Charleston.

Other historians more specifically trace the Charleston dance to movements drawn from the Gullah[28] culture of the Sea Islands that lie off Charleston Harbor.[29] Most of the inhabitants of these islands were either slaves or descended from slaves. These African Americans developed a unique language that combined pigeon English with African dialects and syntax. And, like African culture, Gullah culture, did not separate music from the dance. The unique rhythms and accompanying dance rituals of Gullah culture were often taken over by Charleston's early jazz and ragtime musicians.

One clear example of this was with the Jenkins Orphange Band,[30] which frequently utilized Gullah, or geechie music, as it was also called. True to tradition, the band featured young dancers who performed geechie steps in front of the musicians, conducting as they danced. Many scholars believe that the Jenkins Orphanage Band was largely responsible for spreading the Gullah inspired Charleston steps as they traveled the country trying to raise funds for the orphanage.

In his biography *Music on My Mind,* jazz piano great Willie "the Lion" Smith, recalled,

> One musician [from the Jenkins Orphanage Band], Russell Brown, used to do a strange little dance step and the people of Harlem used to shout out to him as he passed by "hey Charleston, do your Geechie dance." The kids in the Jenkins Orphanage Band also used to do Geechie steps when they came to Harlem on their annual tour.[31]

James P. Johnson, composer of the tune "The Charleston," remembered seeing the Gullah dances while playing piano at a club called The Jungles Casino[32] in New York City in 1913,

> The people who came to The Jungles Casino were mostly from around Charleston, South Carolina, and other places in the South. Most of them worked for the Ward Line as longshoremen or on ships that called at Southern ports.... They picked their partners with care to show off their best steps and put sets, cotillions, and cakewalks that would give them a chance to get off. The Charleston, which became a popular dance step on its own, was just a regular cotillion step without a name. It had many variations—all danced to the rhythm that everyone knows now. One regular at the Casino, named Dan White, was the best dancer in the crowd and he introduced the Charleston step as we know it. But there were dozens of other steps used, too. It was while playing for these southern dancers that I composed a number of Charlestons—eight in all—all with the damn rhythm. One of these later became my famous "Charleston" when it hit Broadway.[33]

Johnson was also exposed to Gullah musical motifs, rhythms, and dance steps in the form of the Ring Shout as a child. Johnson's parents frequently entertained in their New Brunswick, New Jersey home, performing shout dances with their friends. Johnson recalled,

> I'd wake up as a child and hear an old-fashioned ring-shout going on downstairs.... They danced around in a circle and then they would shove a man or woman out into the center and clap hands. This would go on all night and I would fall asleep sitting at the top of the stairs in the dark.[34]

The Ring Shout, whose roots can be traced back to African circle dances,[35] was used during Afro-Protestant worship services,[36] but eventually began to be performed in secular circumstances. The dance was common in the Gullah culture in South Carolina and Georgia, although forms of the shout were disseminated elsewhere. Performed in a circle, the Ring Shout, also called "running sperichils," was performed with the whole body and included the tapping of feet, flat-footed shuffles, clapping, waving of the arms, and shouting. Often during the dance, the worshippers lost control and "cut de pigeon wing" as they entered the trance state called "falling out." Spontaneity and communal participation were essential elements. Although the main form of the Ring Shout was a group dance, solo forms developed as well, especially in North Carolina and Virginia.

Musically, the Ring Shout consisted short repeated refrains that were interspersed with short melodic statements, in the African tradition of antiphonal call-and-response. These were improvisationally varied in intensity and rhythm. Johnson, known as the father of stride piano, later utilized this format in his composing. The stride style was originally called the shout style.[37] Another pianist of the time, Willie "The Lion Smith" Smith stated, "Shouts are stride piano—when James P. and Fats [Waller] and I would get a romp-down stomp going, that was playing rocky, just like the Baptist people sing."[38]

Although started as a religious dance, the Ring Shout eventually made its way to the secular stage of minstrel shows in the form of the Walk Around, the finale of the show during which the entire cast danced, sang, and paraded. Because of the wide appeal of minstrel shows, the dance received considerable exposure and eventually influenced other secular dances. It is believed that the Cakewalk was in some ways a derivative of the Ring Shout. Another offshoot of the Ring Shout was the Big Apple, with its call-and-response, shuffling steps, and improvisational nature. Others have recognized Shout steps that were later used in the Charleston.

Development and Dispersion
of the Charleston

Charleston on the Stage

The minstrel dance team of Golden and Grayton claimed to have been the first performers to bring the Charleston to the American stage. As early as 1890, the blackfaced duo did a
dance move in their act called patting rabbit hash,[1] which was directly related to a part of the
Charleston. It was described as;

> [A] brisk recitative accompanied by patting and slapping the hands on the knees, hips, elbows,
> shoulders, and forearms, producing triple time and rolls almost like a snare drum.[2]

Whether they were the first to present the dance on stage or not remains conjecture, however, years later the team again used patting in their vaudeville act. This act featured recognizable Charleston dance steps with the patting used in the form of the traditional bees knees with
the body crouched over and the arms fanning over the knees.

The Charleston gained national attention with the advent of the all-black musicals, popular on the New York stage in the early '20's. The dance was probably used in some form in the
groundbreaking Shuffle Along[3] although there is no definitive record of the dance being officially
inserted into the musical. Members of the original cast have been associated with "introducing" the dance in various ways. Chorus member Adalaide Hall,[4] for example, is said to have
taught the Charleston to Rudolph Valentino; Josephine Baker[5] is credited with introducing the
dance to Paris audiences. Stearns and Stearns mention that dancer Mae Barnes[6] did the
Charleston in one of the road companies of Shuffle Along "long before the dance became a hit."[7]

The first official documentation of the Charleston being used on Broadway was in the 1922
musical Liza,[8] the first all-black show to play during the regular Broadway season. The last number of the show was called "The Charleston Dancy," composed by Maceo Pinckard. The number was performed by a male tap dancer named R. Eddie Greenlee[9] and a chorus line of girls
lead by Maude Russell.[10] Greenlee said, "In that show [Liza] Maude Russell and I danced the
Charleston."[11] Russell proudly claimed that she was the one who had introduced the Charleston
to Broadway. She remembered, "I used to kick 32 times across the stage, and my legs would hit
my nose. I was a dancing fool."[12]

The following year on Broadway, a black dancer named Leonard Harper[13] did a few
Charleston steps in a musical called How Come?[14] The show, which opened on April 16, 1923,
featured two songs, "Charleston Cut-out" and "Charleston Finale," but the show was poorly
received and only lasted for 32 performances.

The Charleston didn't truly catch the public's attention until it was put in another all-black
show called Runnin' Wild,[15] which opened in New York on October 29, 1923. A specialty ragtime song written by James P. Johnson[16] and Cecil Mack[17] entitled "The Charston," later renamed
"The Charleston," was featured in the show. The number was sung by a fourteen-year-old

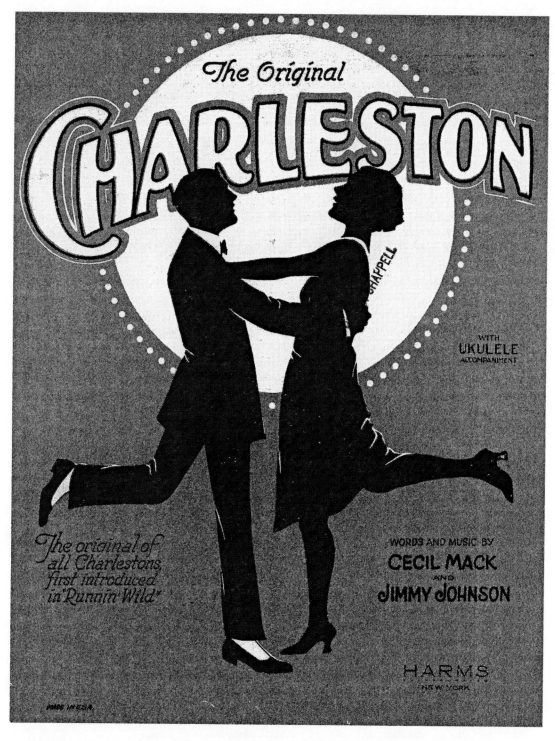

The cover of Cecil Mack's and James P. Johnson's "The Charleston" from the Broadway show *Runnin'*
Wild. The 1923 sheet music included printed directions by Oscar Duryea of how to correctly perform
the dance. The last line of the instructions warned, "Discretion should be used as to how pronounced
the Charleston 'kick up,' and 'toddle' movements are made for ballroom dancing."

chorine named Elisabeth Welch.[18] A chorus of boy dancers known as "The Dancing Redcaps"[19] did a wild Charleston dance to the tune, accompanying it with hand clapping, foot stomping and high-stepping energy. One eyewitness said,

> When Miller and Lyles introduced the dance in their show, they did not depend wholly upon their extraordinary good jazz band for the accompaniment; they went straight back to [early] Negro music and had the major part of the chorus supplement the band by beating out the time with hand-clapping and foot patting. The effect was electrical. Such demonstration of beating out complex rhythms had never been seen before on a stage in New York.[20]

"The 'Charston,' sung by Elisabeth Welch" was only briefly mentioned in *Variety's* review of the show on November 1, 1923, and didn't receive real critical raves until the show's Philadelphia run.[21] By 1924, however, critics were calling *Runnin' Wild* "the fastest dancing show ever produced."[22] One reviewer said,

> Its chorus dances with a religious fervor. Enthusiasm is the keynote. It is inspiring to watch them work. Bewildering. There is no soldiering on the job for this group — no affectations, just a group of dancing dervishes imbued with the joy of living and passing it on to the audiences. When they dance an inexplicable something fills the theatre and makes the audience gasp for breath.[23]

Accounts vary as to how the dance made its way into the show. One version states that before the opening of *Runnin' Wild*, the show's writer, Flourney Miller, had seen three youngsters performing an impromptu dance challenge when he had gone uptown to see a midnight show at the Lincoln Theater. The trio usually danced for pennies on the sidewalk outside of the theatre while audiences waited to get inside, but that night the Lincoln's producer (and Flourney's brother,) Irving C. Miller, had brought the boys inside and put them on the stage trying to eliminate his "outside" competition. The boys took turns trying to best each other at the Charleston in a traditional dance challenge as they beat out rhythms on garbage can lids and an overturned tub. They were a huge hit with the audience. Flourney Miller recalled, "The leader of the trio was Russell Brown but all we knew then was his nickname 'Charleston.' He had another colored boy with him and an Italian kid named Champ. Champ wore boots and did a little Camel Walk which the audience loved."[24] Miller convinced the boys to meet him at a rehearsal of *Runnin' Wild* the next day. "I had them dance for the cast," Miller remembered, "asked Jimmy [James P.] Johnson to add some music to the beat, and convinced our choreographer, Lida [Elida] Webb,[25] that it would make a fine number for the chorus."[26] Tap dancer Willie Covan and his dancing partner Leonard Ruffin were there that afternoon and eventually helped augment the routine. Covan said," The kids only had that first little step and a sort of Camel Walk, so we added an Airplane and a slide."[27]

A different account is found in Charleston champion Bee Jackson's article in *Collier Magazine* entitled "Hey! Hey! Charleston." Jackson states,

> The Negro girls and boys of Harlem had been dancing it on the streets of the uptown Negro section of New York for weeks when Miss [Elida] Webb saw Mary Scurdy, her ten-year-old niece, "stepping it" in her home. She had the child teach it to her. Then she took sixteen chorus girls and three chorus boys, showed them the fundamental steps, worked out the routine of it, and put it into *Runnin' Wild*.[28]

Despite Flourney Miller's enthusiasm about the new Charleston number, the producer of *Runnin' Wild*, George White, did not like the new routine. Miller recalled that White "brought his friends around to show them — in front of us— that the Charleston was nothing, and he tried everything but cutting the dance, which would have made us quit."[29]

White's low opinion of the number may have seemed justified judging by the audience's unenthusiastic response at the show's out of town tryout in Washington D.C. but, when *Runnin' Wild* officially opened in New York a few nights later, the crowd went wild for the Charleston.

The show became a huge hit and the Charleston the newest sensation. After playing Broadway, the show toured the United States. By 1925, two years after *Runnin' Wild* debuted, the Charleston was an international dance craze.

Other Contributors

Ned Wayburn, choreographer of the *Ziegfeld Follies*, often claimed credit for creating the Charleston and introducing it to the American public.[30] In an article published in *The Oakland Tribune* on April 7, 1926, Wayburn relates how he was traveling in the South and saw "a singular movement based on an off-beat which the negro pickaninnies were executing in their jubilees along the wharves and levees." He states that although "there was nothing definite in it as far as constituting a distinct dance, yet it did evince the 'something new — something different' which was in the air ... not merely peculiar to the black race, but as much related to the spiritual tone of the post-war period."[31]

According to Wayburn, he returned to New York in early August 1923, and arranged a meeting with the staff of his dance studio suggesting that a new dance be constructed out of the "inspiration" he had seen during his travels down South. Shortly after this meeting, Wayburn was hired by a Broadway producer to teach private lessons to a young African American boy for use in a stage routine. The boy began to demonstrate steps he already knew for the choreographer, and when the off-beat movement appeared, Wayburn asked the lad if the step had a name. Wayburn recounts, "I discovered that neither he nor anyone else had ever recognized it as anything of value in dancing. It was merely one of those steps which negroes did as a finish to their various types of jigging and merry-making."[32]

Wayburn claims that two weeks after this incident he and his staff created the Charleston by formulating a series of twenty distinct steps based on this off-beat movement. Planning to include the newly created dance in the newest edition of the *Follies* that he was mounting at the Amsterdam Theatre on 42nd Street, Wayburn decided to put the Charleston in the first act finale in a number called "Shake Your Feet."[33]

When popular *Follies* dancing star Ann Pennington balked at doing the unusual dance, Wayburn drafted a young dancer out of the chorus by the name of Bee Jackson.[34] Florence Ziegfeld, who did not like the wild dance when initially shown it in rehearsals, reluctantly agreed to have the number included in the opening night of the *Ziegfeld Follies of 1923*[35] on October 20, 1923, but then ordered it cut the next day.

In the article Wayburn states emphatically,

> Although many have reason to claim origination, development, and titling of the Charleston, I believe I am the one who has documentary evidence to substantiate his claims. It is not egotistical credit that I have sought for establishing the Charleston to the extent that the American Geographic Society at Washington, D. C., is considering its adoption as the American national dance, but a credit that is due anyone who has successfully assisted in the interpretation of an emotional era in the life of a great nation.[36]

Producer George White[37] is also sometimes listed as the first to bring the Charleston to the stage. As the producer of *Runnin' Wild,* White was certainly involved in some way with presenting the dance in the show that helped make it an international hit, although as stated earlier, the producer disliked the dance and initially fought to have it removed from the production. As the Charleston became a huge hit though, White sought to claim credit for bringing the dance to the public's notice and claimed that he had done so in one of the early editions of his revue *The George White Scandals.*

Many sources list Frances Williams,[38] a blonde singing and dancing star who appeared in three editions of the *Scandals*, as the performer most associated with presenting the Charleston under White's auspices. Williams, sometimes called "The Syncopated Songstress," was known as "one of the leading exponents of jazz crooning and fast time eccentric and jazz dancing."[39] She first appeared in *The George White Scandals* in 1926.[40] A review of the show in the June 28, 1926 issue of *Time Magazine* mentions "...Frances Williams, whose Charleston is notable."[41] The show also featured tap dancer Tom Patricola, who was well-known for his Charleston abilities, and singer/dancer Ann Pennington, who was credited with introducing the Black Bottom in this particular show. Since there is much documentation of the Charleston having been presented on the legitimate stage before 1926, Williams could not have been the first to introduce the dance in this production; however, she did become intimately associated with the dance in the public's eye. In clippings from papers of the era she is referred to as a "Charleston pioneer,"[42] and "the blonde song and dance lady, who made the Charleston famous."[43]

George White did present the Charleston in the 1925 edition of his *Scandals* before Frances Williams joined the revue in 1926. "Recognizing the dance's drawing power, *The George White Scandals of 1925* staged a mammoth theatrical representation of the Charleston put on by Tom Patricola[44] and five dozen women."[45] The song Patricola danced to had the following lyric that described the Charleston as,

> [A] new tune, funny blue tune with a peculiar snap!
> You may not be able to buck or wing
> Fox-trot, two-step, or even sing,
> If you ain't got religion in your feet,
> You can do this prance and do it neat.[46]

In theatre gossip columns from that same year, there were suggestions that George White himself might do the dance in the show. One such article states, "...on June 23 George White and his "Scandals" will frolic at the Apollo.... There is a persistent rumor, too, that George himself, will appear in the show, doing a Charleston, with taps."[47]

Frances Williams herself danced the Charleston on Broadway in 1925, but not in a George White show. She did the dance when she appeared with the Marx Brothers in *The Cocoanuts*, which ran at the Lyric Theatre from December, 1925 through November, 1926. A review by Alexander Wolcott in *The Stage* stated,

> Up to then the high moments had been pretty much the goings on of Groucho and Harpo, plus the singing and dancing of a startling girl named Frances Williams, who shuddered a devastating Charleston and vanished from sight, her head tossing like a chrysanthemum, all gold and agitation.[48]

The Cocoanuts included a song by Irving Berlin entitled, "Everyone In The World Is Doing The Charleston," which had been added to the "New Summer Edition" of the show.

Producer Lew Leslie, who presented many important black artists nationally and internationally, in such shows as *The Blackbirds, Dixie to Broadway*, and several revues at the Cotton Club, also claimed to have introduced the Charleston. In the program note for the Charleston Ball in London in 1926, Leslie wrote,

> It happened in my *Plantation Revue* six years ago when I hired a bow-legged colored boy from Charleston, South Carolina. I found similar steps in the routine and developed a dance from these.... The song "Charleston" was introduced after the dance was seen at my *Plantation* and its rhythm taken from a specially arranged number written for me.[49]

Black composer Will Marion Cook, in a letter to the editor dated December 19, 1926, suggested that when the *New York Times,* in an article in the Sunday edition earlier that week, credited producer George White and others with the creation of the Charleston and the Black Bottom, it was doing an injustice to African Americans who really originated the dances. In the letter,

Cook states that he personally knew of the Charleston being danced in the islands off the coast of Charleston, South Carolina for at least the past forty years, which would mean that the Charleston was being done by Blacks in the area in the 1880's. He said the dance migrated to New York around 1921 and was done by children in Harlem on the street corners as they danced for pennies. Cook says, that such dances are African in origin and that "...the American negro, in search of outlet for emotional expression, recreates and broadens these dances. Either in their crude state, or revised form, in St. Louis, Chicago, or New York the dance is discovered (?) and sold to the public as an original creation" (question mark is Cook's).[50]

Cook points out that the Charleston was first done on stage in a production called *How Come?*, and was performed by an African American man named Leonard Harper. He adds that the first music with a Charleston rhythm to appear on the scene was a tune that came out around 1922 called the "Charleston Strut" written by Tommy Morris. This was followed by James P. Johnson's "Charleston" in *Runnin' Wild*.

Cook states, "It is doubtful if Mr. White even saw a 'Charleston' until he attended the final rehearsal of 'Runnin' Wild.'" He continues, "Similarly, for many years, the 'Black Bottom' has been evolving in the South. Irvin Miller first produced the dance about three years ago in New York at the Lafayette Theatre. Two years ago Louis Douglass, famous in Europe, thrilled all Paris as he and Josephine Baker 'Black-Bottomed' at the Champs-Elysée Theatre." Cook closes, "Messrs. White et al. are great men and great producers. Why, with their immense flocks of dramatic and musical sheep, should they wish to reach out and grab our little ewe lamb of originality?"[51]

There is little doubt that the Charleston was first presented to the general public at large by African American performers in Broadway shows such as *Liza, How Come?*, and *Runnin' Wild*, or in revues and acts performed in clubs and cabarets in New York and other large cities; however, other performers and presenters of theatrical events did contribute to the development and popularity of the dance. In an undated essay from the period, Harlem Renaissance writer Wallace Thurmond summed it up:

> Most Negro dances originate in the cane brakes and cotton field settlements. They are introduced into the north by black migrationists and find their way into the theatrical world after they have been seen in some gin dive or cabaret. It is thus indeed hard to give credit where credit is due. Any number of people claim the honor of having originated this or that dance. All may have some ground on which to base their claim, for it is very possible that each one, having seen the raw material, has refined it for stage purposes.[52]

Cabarets, Nightclubs and Speakeasies

The Charleston, which first captured the public's notice with the advent of Broadway's all-black musicals, grew in popularity when it became a staple of top entertainers in cabarets, nightclubs, and speakeasies. In New York, Texas Guinan's[53] speakeasy, the *El Fey Club*, featured a young Charleston dancer whose trademark fast-paced moves earned him top billing as "The Fastest Dancer in the World." The young dancer was George Raft, who later gained fame as the stone-faced gangster in Hollywood films. Fred Astaire, a popular Broadway star at the time, saw Raft perform at the *El Fey* and said, "George did the fastest, and most exciting, Charleston I ever saw. I thought he was an extraordinary dancer...."[54] In 1925, Raft appeared in the Broadway show *The City Chap* at the Liberty Theatre on 42nd Street, performing his now-famous quick paced Charleston, as well as a new dance called the Black Bottom. He also did his Charleston in the Broadway show *Gay Paree*, performing the dance to the song "Sweet Georgia Brown," which was written for the show. One night Raft's lightning-fast dancing was even more speedy than usual, and he kept running in circles and looking up at the fly space while he danced. He admitted later that he had had an affair with one of his co-stars Winnie Lightner and when her husband, the assistant stage manager, found out, he feared the irate man might drop a sand-bag on him while he was dancing.[55]

Raft had spent part of his early dancing career working in "tea-rooms" as a gigolo, danc-ing for two dollars a day plus tips. He was paid to dance with lonely female patrons although the introductions often later led to sexual rendezvous. The work was physically demanding and sometimes dangerous. One jealous woman stabbed Raft with a hatpin when she saw him danc-ing with another client. He recovered quickly but was informed by the doctor that if the pin had been a few inches to the right, it would have pierced his heart and killed him. During his time as a gigolo, Raft shared an apartment with fellow gigolo Rudolph Valentino. When Valentino took the world by storm as a silent movie idol, Raft also began to gain national notice for his work in vaudeville and in clubs. One newspaper commented, "It is interesting to note that Raft and Valentino began their dancing life together at Rector's in the heyday of that smart restaurant. Valentino arose to fame on the tango and it looks like Raft is following with the Charleston."[56]

Bricktop[57] was a singer and dancer who gained fame performing in nightclubs in the 1920's and was one of the first to introduce the Charleston to Europe. Her given name was Ada Beat-rice Queen Victoria Louise Virginia Smith, and although her parents were African American, she was born with white skin and red hair. After performing in vaudeville, she ended up in New York City where she met Barron Wilkins, owner of the posh nightspot *Barron's Exclusive Club*. Wilkins hired the young singer/dancer and gave her the nickname Bricktop after seeing her flaming red hair. At the club, Bricktop got a chance to perform for such celebrities as Al Jol-son, John Barrymore, "Legs" Diamond, and a yet to be discovered chorus girl by the name of Lucille LeSeur, later known as Joan Crawford.[58]

Bricktop eventually left *Barron's* and, while she was performing at another nightclub, *Con-nie's Inn*, she was asked to sail to France to perform at a small club called *Le Grand Duc,* which eventually became the gathering place of writers and artists such as F. Scott Fitzgerald, Pablo Picasso, Ernest Hemingway, and T. S. Eliot, who included Bricktop in one of his poems. After hearing her sing early one morning at the club, she also won the admiration and enduring friendship of Cole Porter, who later wrote the song "Miss Otis Regrets" for her. One evening, Porter asked Bricktop if she could dance the Charleston, which had not yet been introduced to Europe. After her performance of the dance, Porter told her that she had "talking feet and legs." The next evening Porter returned with his wife Linda, society maven and hostess Elsa Maxwell, and a few other friends to view the dance. All were wowed by Bricktop's dancing. Porter came up with the plan of giving Charleston cocktail parties two or three times a week at his house at 13 Rue Monsieur. He proposed that Bricktop teach his guests the Charleston. The first evening, Bricktop taught the dance to the Aga Khan, and about fifty other individuals from the inter-national set. She later gave private Charleston instruction to high society individuals, charging ten dollars a lesson. Her clientele included the millionairess Dolly O'Brien (later linked roman-tically with Clark Gable), the Rothschilds, Daisy Fellowes, heir to the Singer Sewing machine fortune, interior designer, hostess, actress, and inventor of the Pink Lady cocktail, Elsie de Wolfe (Lady Mendl), Consuelo Vanderbilt, and even one of the prima ballerinas from the Paris Opera. She continued to demonstrate the Charleston at the top parties around Paris. In 1925, Brick-top met another African American whose name would become linked with the Charleston — Josephine Baker.[59]

Baker had come to Paris on the request of Mrs. Caroline Dudley Reagan, a producer whose husband was in the foreign service.[60] Reagan had the idea of bringing a black revue to Paris after seeing a rehearsal for a show at the Douglas Theatre in Washington, D. C. She recalled,

Eight black girls in black tights, one more superb than the next, dancing, dancing, dancing. It was the Charleston.... I was overwhelmed, drawn by the invisible magnet, to produce a company, to show such artists, to amaze, flabbergast, dumbfound Paris ... the elite, the masses, the artists from Picasso to the hippie painters of the streets ... and there is where the seed for this *Revue Nègre* sprouted. The germ possessed me and began to grow.[61]

Baker dazzled Parisian audiences with her magnetic personality and wild dancing when *Le Revue Negre* opened on October 2, 1925, at the Théatre des Champs-Élysées.[62] Baker was an overnight sensation. Even the stagehands were captivated by *le Charleston*. Baker recalled one of her first rehearsals in the theatre:

Hello! Charleston. The stagehands watch, the two firemen are amazed. They are not used to receiving trombone blows in their stomach. At the end, behind the scenery, the younger ones try to imitate, they would like to dance the Charleston: they shake flannel legs, they kick their feet in the air like cows, they also kick their neighbors.... The Charleston already possesses them. "Yes, sir, that's my baby."[63]

Baker's Charleston was uninhibited — she threw herself into it with utter abandon and the French audiences loved it. Her dynamic dancing was excitingly savage and effortlessly authentic. The freedom with which she expressed herself while dancing seemed to embody the spirit of the decade.[64] Although *Le Revue Negre* only ran for three months, the show made Josephine Baker an instant star.

Josephine Baker is often credited with introducing the Charleston to the people of France, but in addition to its having been done earlier by Bricktop, another performer had done the dance in Paris before Baker. Bee Jackson,[65] billed as the "Queen of the Charleston," had performed the dance at the *Music-Hall des Champs-Élysées* in July 1925 as the opening warm-up act for Paul Whiteman's orchestra.

Jackson, who Ned Wayburn claimed introduced the Charleston in a number he choreographed for *The Ziegfeld Follies of 1923*,[66] was also a favorite in speakeasies and nightclubs. Jackson had understudied *Follies* star Gilda Gray, and when Jackson left show after fifteen months, Gray recommended Jackson for a dancing spot in her nightclub *Rendezvous*. Jackson moved from there to a club called the *Question Mark*. According to an article she wrote for *Collier's Magazine* published on December 10, 1927, Jackson says that shortly after this, she was taken by her aunt and uncle to a performance of *Runnin' Wild* where she saw the Charleston for the first time. Jackson had the show's choreographer, Elida Webb, teach her the basic steps of the dance. Jackson took the steps that Webb had taught her and then created a routine on her own. She hired an agent who booked her in clubs around New York, such as the *Sliver Slipper*, Texas Guinan's *El Fey*, and the *Club Richman*. Jackson's beauty, personality, and talent quickly brought her recognition as a Charleston star. Webb said Jackson was "the best of all the 'Charleston' dancers, white or colored, and surely if anyone should know, I should."[67]

Jackson's popularity led to bookings on the Keith vaudeville circuit, and audiences around the United States were introduced to the Charleston. After a small role in the film *Lying Wives,* she went back to dancing in clubs, this time in Miami, Palm Beach and Havana. Success in these venues led to bookings in London and Paris. Some sources say that Jackson was responsible for introducing the Charleston to Great Britain. Whatever the case, Londoners loved her, giving her the title the "best dancer in the world," a sobriquet Jackson accepted "with becoming modesty."[68] Audiences couldn't get enough of the vibrant young American dancer. While in London, Jackson had dual engagements at the Piccadilly Hotel and the *Kit Kat Club*. "Bee Jackson is said to be the first white girl to exploit the Charleston, although others give credit to Bee Palmer[69], 'The Queen of Syncopation.' Miss Jackson took lessons from Lyda [Elida] Web at the Club Alabam and is now in London, where the new step is meeting wild approval."[70]

When Jackson won the World Championship Charleston Contest held in London, her popularity was cemented not only in Great Britain, but also internationally as well. As part of her prize, Jackson received a contract to perform on the London stage. She accepted the contract, but at the same time was approached by an Austrian producer who offered a lucrative contract to perform in Vienna, which she also accepted. In order to meet the terms of both contracts, Jackson commuted between London and Vienna. She was such a frequent passenger on the airlines, European newspapers dubbed her "the flying dancer."[71]

Jackson proved to be an equally great hit with Viennese audiences, where she "appeared on the stage in costumes as abbreviated as they [were] fetching."[72] One critic said, "[Jackson] dances with that inexplicable mixture of grace, energy and abandon which is the spirit of modern youth."[73] She became so popular the Viennese public voted her the prettiest woman in Austria. Some dance historians believe the phrase used to describe the signature step of the Charleston, "bee's knees," was named after Jackson.[74]

Charleston Contests

When the Charleston came into vogue, promoters scrambled to capitalize on its rising popularity. Charleston competitions proliferated. Many of these contests offered not only cash prizes, but also performing contracts, and young actors and dancers interested in having a career in show business entered their local Charleston competition hoping to find success. Two young girls from Texas were especially lucky; both Ginger Rogers and Joan Crawford began their careers by winning Charleston contests.

Ginger Rogers[1] was only fourteen years old when she won the Texas State Charleston Championships, organized by popular bandleader, Henry Santrey. Preliminary contests were held in cities across Texas with winners invited to participate in the finals in Dallas. After beating thirty other contestants in Fort Worth, Rogers traveled to the State Championships that were held on November 9, 1925 at the Barker Hotel. The competition was fierce. The elimination rounds left only two remaining dancers, Rogers and a local boy from Dallas. Each danced to break the tie, but the voting by audience applause ended in a draw again, so both youngsters had to Charleston one more time. Ginger Rogers won and was crowned the Texas State Charleston Champion.[76]

Her prize was an engraved silver medal and a four-week tour in vaudeville on the Texas Interstate circuit, part of the Orpheum Circuit, also known in show business as the "Death Trail." Her pay was $375 a week. Realizing that her daughter needed an act to perform, her mother, Lela Rogers quickly put one together, hiring two of the contest runners-up, Earl Leach and Josephine Butler. "Ginger Rogers and The Redheads," as the act was called, proved to be so popular, the engagement extended from four to twenty-one weeks. Reviews said that Rogers had "legs as fast as lightning."[77] The Galveston Daily News reported,

> The Charleston act itself as performed by Ginger, Earl Leach, formerly of Texas City, and Josephine Butler of Houston, is itself as clever and snappy as a dance act has been on the vaudeville circuit this year. Ginger herself is a clever little thing who has a distinctly attractive stage personality, wholly apart from her ability as a dancer. The Leach boy is a whiz, executing extraordinarily difficult steps, and "Red" Butler is a close second.[78]

The act played in theatres across the country, until "The Redheads," Leach and Butler, eventually left Rogers to join another act that paid more money. Rogers continued on as a solo act eventually joining the Paramount Publix circuit, playing in small musical revues in movie houses. After finding success on Broadway, she traveled to Hollywood where she gained international fame dancing with Fred Astaire and starring in many films.

Joan Crawford[79] won her first Charleston contest at a Kansas City café. Legend has it that her victory was partly due to her shoe's flying off in the middle of her dance. After winning, the young dancer moved to Chicago hoping to gain further success in the entertainment field and vowing in her own words "to be the best dancer in the world."[80]

After performing in clubs in Detroit and New York, she moved to Hollywood in 1925 and had small chorus parts and dancing roles in several pictures. Her break-through came in the film *Sally, Irene and Mary*, in which she did a featured Charleston dance. Louise Brooks recalled seeing Crawford in the picture, "...her legs were beautiful even though she used them to dance the Charleston like a lady wrestler."[81]

In 1928 she had another pivotal role as Diana Medford in *Our Dancing Daughters*. During one scene, Crawford ripped off her dress and clad only in her slip, danced a wild Charleston on top of a table. The movie not only made her a star, but also led audiences to see her as the personification of the carefree, mad-cap, jazz-loving flapper.[82]

While a young starlet, Crawford kept up a busy nightlife, frequently entering Charleston contests at local hot spots such as the Cocoanut Grove Nightclub at the Ambassador Hotel in downtown Los Angeles. She often competed against fellow Charleston-lover Carole Lombard.[83] Within her first two years in Tinsel Town, Crawford reportedly won 84 trophies.

Charleston contests were widespread and varied in size contingent upon the venue and the purpose for having the event.[84] The Governor of New York Alfred E. Smith started an impromptu Charleston Contest among the city's street urchins while waiting for a friend at the Abescon railroad station in Atlantic City. He showed a quarter to one young boy standing by the tacks and said, "How about a little Charleston there, young fellow?" When the boy obliged and gave him a dance, they were soon surrounded by other youngsters. After someone pulled out a harmonica, the youths had a competition, and the Governor finally chose a boy he dubbed "Charley," as the winner. After the train arrived, the Governor and his friend boarded a bus to leave the area, and Smith tossed out a handful of coins to the contestants.[85]

At the other end of the economic and status spectrum, Prince George of England frequently participated in Charleston contests. At one in particular, the heir to the British throne and his dancing partner, Lady Milford Haven, won a contest at the *Sporting Casino* in Cannes, competing against dozens of dancers. The Prince and the Marchioness kept their identities secret until after the judging. When they were awarded first prize, the crowd convinced them to present an exhibition dance. An account of the time reported, "...this will not help him at Buckingham palace, for it is recalled here that the King and Queen have frowned upon the eccentricities of the Charleston and have forbidden it at court functions."[86]

June 27, 1926 at the Polo Grounds in New York, a huge Charleston contest was put on by the United Jewish Campaign's Theatrical and Sports Field day. Twenty-thousand guests attended the event, and $75,000 was raised for European Jews. Music was to be provided by Ben Bernie and other famous orchestra leaders, and stage luminaries such as Al Jolson and Sophie Tucker performed and officiated at the event. Harry Houdini even performed his straight-jacket escape. Judges included Jolson and *Scandals* producer George White, among others. One thousand dancers were originally signed up to dance in the contest and professional Charleston dancers were barred from entering the competition. All ages were allowed to participate; children as young as four joined in the contest. One gentleman, an eighty-year old African American named "Chocolate," was said to be "among the more vigorous of the dancers"[87] The highlight, according to the *New York Times,* was a contest with 100 dancers that took place on a large piece of canvas that had been stretched and placed in the middle of a baseball field.

Mary Suchier won the $1,000.00 first prize presented by Al Jolson. In addition to the money, she was awarded a part in a Broadway show and a role in a Fox Film Company movie. Second place went to two brothers, George and Al Clayton. Third went to a Broadway actress Helen Dean.

Early twentieth century French postcard portraying the Charleston.

On December 15, 1926, at the Royal Albert Hall in London, England, British impresario Sir Charles B. Cochran presented perhaps the most memorable Charleston contest of the decade — a celebration that lasted for eight hours and gathered together some of the top dancers in the world. Prizes were awarded for the top Charlestoners in several categories, including Ballroom Amateur (Ladies and Gentleman), Ballroom Professional (Ladies and Gentleman), Stage Amateur (Ladies and Gentleman), and Stage Professional (Ladies and Gentleman). There was also a Troupe Dancing category with entrants such as the famous Tiller girls competing. In the Men's Amateur category, the prizes ranged from a "Trip to Paris on Imperial Airways" for the first place winner to a "Gillette Razor" for fourth.[88]

There were sixteen judges for the event. They included Fred Astaire, who was performing in London at the time, producer Lew Leslie, British ballroom dancer Josephine Bradley,[89] and championship dancer and London club owner Santos Casani,[90] who had recently created a sensation in the city by dancing a Charleston on top of a moving taxi. Guests for the evening included the full cast of Leslie's *Blackbirds of 1926* led by the enormously popular Florence Mills[91] who performed in the "Grand Finale." Cochran recalled the event:

> It was the unexpected and final entrance from the organ, down the steps, into the arena of Florence Mills, Johnny Hudgins, and the Blackbirds which sent the house wild with enthusiasm. Johnny Hudgins was encored and encored until it seemed as if his marvelously unattached limbs would fall off. One would have thought nobody could follow him. But the thunder increased as the slim body of Florence Mills went through more amusing contortions than you could imagine in a nightmare.[92]

An estimated 5,000 to 10,000 guests attended the event. One newspaper merely said, "All of London must have been there."[93] Lord Lew Grade,[94] who later became one of England's leading show business entrepreneurs, participated in the Amateur Men's Contest. He recalled, "The atmosphere was electric. I had never seen so many great dancers assembled under one roof and the tension backstage was almost too much to bear."[95] Grade won his division and was awarded the title of World Solo Charleston Champion. In addition to the prize money, he was given a four-week engagement performing at the Piccadilly Hotel at fifty pounds a week.

Charles Cochran, the promoter of the Charleston Ball at the Royal Albert Hall in 1926, summed up the furor of the Charleston craze, "The Charleston is more than a hobby. It is a disease rampant throughout the country."[96]

16

Fashion and Music of the Charleston

Reeling from the death, destruction, and devastation of the First World War, society in the 1920's tried to grapple with the emotional scars from that conflict. The younger generation in particular was disillusioned with old conventions and customs, and struggled to break free from the manners and mores of their parents. John F. Carter Jr. expressed his generation's disenchantment in his article "These Wild Young People, By One of Them," published in 1920. He wrote,

> I would like to observe that the older generation had certainly pretty well ruined this world before passing it on to us. They give us this Thing, knocked to pieces, leaky, red-hot, threatening to blow up; and then they are surprised that we don't accept it with the same attitude of pretty, decorous enthusiasm with which they received it....[1]

The war forced a generation of young men into early adulthood. It exposed them to brutality, chaos, and excitement. They developed a "live for today, for tomorrow we may die" attitude. When the Armistice came, they returned home bewildered, and often wounded both physically and psychologically.

Young women, who had joined the workforce to support the war effort, experienced a newfound sense of freedom and accomplishment. Those that served as nurses overseas were exposed to a more continental approach to behavior. These young women challenged the rigid standards and manners of home after being taken out of the cocoon of familial protection and placed in largely unchaperoned situations. When the war ended they were expected to return to their previous status as "obedient little girls." They had seen the horrors of war, and they returned confused and angry. One young girl wrote, "The war tore away our spiritual foundations and challenged our faith. We are struggling to regain our equilibrium."[2]

Disenchanted youth on both sides of the Atlantic rebelled against Victorian values and sparked a revolution in manners and morals. Throughout society, focus shifted to a youth-oriented culture. The flapper and the collegiate became the models of the day.[3]

Perhaps the most enduring iconic image of this tumultuous period in history is the madcap flapper, rouged and ready to Charleston. She was the "new woman"—independent-minded and rebellious. Typically between the ages of fifteen and nineteen, the flapper was seen as a frivolous nonconformist: bobbing her hair, adopting modern fashions, using make-up, smoking and drinking in public, going to "petting parties," and dancing to her heart's content. Flapper Ellen Welles Page described herself,

> If one judges by appearances, I suppose I am a flapper. I am within the age limit. I wear bobbed hair, the badge of flapperhood. (And, oh, what a comfort it is!), I powder my nose. I wear fringed skirts and bright-colored sweaters, and scarfs, and waists with Peter Pan collars, and low-heeled "finale hopper" shoes. I adore to dance. I spend a large amount of time in automobiles. I attend hops, and proms, and ball-games, and crew races, and other affairs at men's colleges. But none the less some of the most thoroughbred super flappers might blush to claim sistership or even remote relationship with such as I. I don't use rouge, or lipstick, or pluck my eyebrows. I don't smoke (I've tried it, and don't like it), or drink, or tell "peppy stories." I don't pet. And, most unpardonable infringement of all the rules and regulations of flapperdom, I haven't a line! But then—there are many degrees of flapper. There is the semi-flapper; the flapper; the super flapper.[4]

The Flapper's Dictionary, written in 1922, defined a flapper as the "ultra-modern, young girl, full of pep and life, beautiful (naturally or artificially), blasé, imitative, and intelligent to a degree, who is about to bloom into a period of womanhood and believes her sex has been and will continue to be, emancipated to a level higher than most mortals have been able to attain."[5]

There are several theories about the derivation of the word "flapper." Some sources claim that the term referred to the flapping of a girl's arms as she danced. Others suggest the word was first coined in Britain during World War I and referred to a young girl who wore her galoshes unbuckled causing the tops to flap when she walked.[6] The most likely derivation is from a British term that meant a young bird, especially a wild duck, just able to fly.[7] According to an article published in the *New York Times* in February 1922, the word "flapper," was a British sporting term, defined as a "young duck." The term was derived from the practice of young girls tossing their long hair as they strutted down the street, making them resemble preening ducks. When bobbing the hair became popular, the term continued to stick.[8]

The flapper was vilified by many and lauded by others. Newspaper editorials frequently appeared in the early 20's posing such questions as, "What does the flapper token? Is she a throwback to some primal cycle? A retrogression to the simian period? Or—Does she represent the leader—a trail-blazing pioneer heralding still greater freedom for women?"[9]

Opinions were divided. Progressives saw the flapper as a modern, female savior who could lead society into the twenty-first century. The establishment saw her as the downfall of society. "Something should be done to curb her. The ruin of the nation rests in the palm of her flippant hand. The future of the world swings on the pivot of her half-bare legs,"[10] said one critic. Another warned, "The flapper is an agency drunk with liberty and run amok from license. Something must be done to curb her. The ruin of a nation rests in the palm of her flapper hand."[11]

The Charleston was so popular that even motherhood couldn't keep flappers off the dance floor. An antique postcard of an etching by James Montgomery Flagg entitled "Jazz Babies—When the Modern Flappers Get Families of Their Own."

Flapper Fashions

Fashions during this period reflected the modern woman's desire to express freedom, youthfulness, and equality. The most prevalent example of this was a style known as *garconne*. Taken from the French word for "boy," but spelled with the feminine suffix, *garconne* de-emphasized the more mature, feminine silhouette of previous years and created a boyish look — broad shoulders, flat chest, and small hips.

Dresses with straight, cylindrical bodices and a dropped waistline came into vogue; the most popular variation was the *Basque dress* or *Robe de Style* with a dropped waistline and full skirt, as featured in the designs of the French couturière Jeanne Lanvin. The long shapeless shift hid feminine curves and created an androgynous look.[12]

Women with fuller busts resorted to either binding their breasts to achieve a flatter look or using other aids such as the Symington Side Lacer, a reinforced brassiere that had lacing on each side which could be pulled tight until the breasts were flattened.

In the quest for a more boyish figure, the modern woman may have bound her breasts, but she discarded another clothing constraint — her corset. The tightly cinched waist that emphasized feminine curves in the 1800's went quickly out of vogue. Those women that still chose to wear corsets during the day often abandoned them at night when they went out dancing. Dance halls and speakeasies made accommodations for their female patrons to "park" their corsets at the cloakroom so their Charleston kicks would be unencumbered. Conservatives were outraged at the practice. One detractor cried, "Young men like to have the girls remove their corsets.... This makes dancing a thing of passion. Corsetless dancing is nothing but passion."[13]

As more and more women abandoned the practice of wearing corsets, the Corset Manufacturers Association of America waged a well-organized and well-funded war against the trend. They campaigned tirelessly in ads and mailings for the properly corseted female. In one publication sent to retailers, the general manager of the Kalamazoo Corset Company explained why the sensible woman should always wear a corset:

> Fear! Fear of ill health, fear of sagging bodies, fear of lost figure, fear of shiftless appearance in the nicest of clothing, fear of sallow complexion. Fear sends them to the corsetiere, trembling; the same corsetiere from whom they fled mockingly a couple of years back, at the beck of a mad style authority who decreed "zat ze body must be free of ze restrictions, in order zat ze new styles shall hang so freely."[14]

The public and fashion designers largely ignored the industry's pleas for a tightly bound waist.[15] As views on corseting changed, department store sales of corsets and brassieres in Cleveland alone fell by eleven percent between 1924 and 1927. In 1925, one commentator observed, "The corset is as dead as the dodo's grandfather; no feeble publicity pipings by the manufacturers, or calling it a 'clasp around' will enable it, as Jane [the flapper] says, to 'do a Lazarus.'"[16]

Other undergarments also changed. Layered petticoats and dark heavy cotton stockings were replaced with silk or rayon step-ins and flesh-colored stockings. To keep stockings from falling down while dancing, garter belts were introduced. In hot weather, stockings were often abandoned completely.

Clothes that offered maximum freedom of movement were *de rigeuer*. Long, heavy skirts and tight bodices with full-length sleeves gave way to shorter, lighter garments with short sleeves and lower cut fronts and backs. In 1928, the Journal of Commerce estimated that over the course of the past fifteen years, the amount of material required for a woman's outfit had gone from about nineteen and a quarter yards of material to a mere seven. The freedom afforded by these lighter, less constricting garments allowed Charleston dancers to fling their arms and legs unencumbered by the bustles, trains, and heavy petticoats of the days of the waltz.

Perhaps the most obvious change in women's fashion came in skirt length. A hint of tantalizing calf was revealed when handkerchief hemlines and scalloped edges grew in popularity during the first part of the decade. In 1925, hemlines rose to about fourteen to sixteen inches off the ground, and in 1926, finally rose above the knee and stayed there until 1928. When asked his opinion about short skirts, American Ambassador to Britain Colonel George Harvey replied that they ought to be like "after-dinner speeches—long enough to cover the subject, but short enough to be interesting."[17] At the end of the decade, skirt length gradually began to drop again aided by the popularity of uneven and asymmetrical hemlines, and long sheer overskirts.[18]

One story that illustrates the frequently changing hemlines in the period concerns the court case of *Kutock vs. Kennedy*. New York actress Frances Kennedy sued her tailor, Morris Kutock, when he failed to deliver a gown on time. She had specially ordered the dress with the understanding that it would be delivered before she left town to perform in Chicago. When the gown was not completed the day before her departure, she hurriedly bought another gown elsewhere. When she returned from her out of town engagement, she refused to pay for Kotock's dress. The tailor sued. According to court testimony, Miss Kennedy stated that she should not have to accept the gown because "dresses go out of style about every three weeks." To illustrate her point, she had her husband and her lawyer, display three of her dresses as evidence for the judge and jury, showing that the most recent dress was longer than the others. Her expert witnesses, a fashion model and a costume designer, confirmed her findings. The jury, which was half female, all between the ages of eighteen and twenty-two, ruled in her favor after deliberating for only three or four minutes. After the verdict was read, "Kennedy reportedly hugged and kissed the jurors, invited them to her show and distributed autographed pictures of herself."[19]

Moral arbiters of the day were appalled by modern fashions, calling them vulgar, immoral, and injurious to a woman's character and health. One detractor cried, "The low-cut gowns, the rolled hose and short skirts are born of the Devil and his angels, and are carrying the present and future generations to chaos and destruction."[20]

In Philadelphia, in an effort to combat the modern fashions, a Dress Reform Committee drew up designs for a dress that was based on the suggestions of over a thousand clergymen in fifteen different denominations. The sleeves of the loose-fitting garment reached below the elbows, and its hem was no more than seven and a half inches off the floor. It was called the "moral gown."

Attacking flapper fashions from all angles, some opponents cautioned that the scanty nature of the dresses were dangerous to a woman's health. London surgeon Sir James Cantlie claimed that "[I]nsufficient clothing about the necks and throats of women is causing an increase in goiter." He warned that the new fashions threatened not only younger women, but also older ones who were tempted to "follow the evil example."[21] Dr. Florence Sherman warned women that wearing skimpier under-clothing provided less protection against diseases such as tuberculosis.

Amidst the uproar over improper dress, politicians tried to legislate the new fashions. In 1921, a bill was introduced in Utah mandating fines and imprisonment for women who wore "skirts higher than three inches above the ankle."[22] Another was put before Virginia lawmakers forbidding blouses or gowns that exposed more than three inches of throat. In Ohio, the legislature was even stricter, limiting décolletage to two inches. The same Ohio bill prohibited any "female over fourteen years of age" from wearing "a skirt which does not reach to that part of the foot known as the instep."[23]

Although most outrage was directed toward changes in women's fashions, there were those who felt that trends in male clothing were also going astray. More casual and sporty than in previous decades, men's fashion in the 1920's reflected the focus on youth. Around 1925, baggy pants were popularized by undergraduates at Oxford University.[24] Called Oxford Bags, the pants sometimes measured as much as forty inches around the ankle. These bell-bottoms quickly became the uniform of the modern young man and drew the ire of many.[25]

During World War I, American soldiers were issued front-buttoning underwear; after the war long-sleeved, long-legged underwear was abandoned for briefer garments, sometimes made of rayon or even silk. Men explored their more feminine side, even matching the color of their shirts to their boxers. Many viewed the changes in underwear as the emasculation of a whole generation.

Footwear

In the 1920's, as skirts shortened, shoes became more visible, and fashionable footwear became an important aspect of a woman's total "look." Advice columnist Emily Burbank suggested that a well-dressed modern woman should "keep in mind that your footwear is like the caption to a picture; it tells the beholder what is the meaning of the costume, what occasion the woman who planned it intended to grace. If the shoes are not the key to the costume then it means that they are wrong."[26] The stylish footwear for the flapper hoping to augment the garconne look was a narrow-toed, high-heeled shoe. The Charleston also influenced footwear. Comfortable dancing required a shoe with closed toes that could be securely fastened.

Many argued against the trend in women's shoes. "Men do not walk on pegs—why should women?"[27] According to Dr. Sara brown, a YWCA staff member,

> The wearing of tight shoes for appearance sake is harmful in many ways. Not only the physical but, the mental and spiritual side of the individual suffers. One cannot thoroughly enjoy a sermon at church on Sunday in tight shoes. Children are unable to pay proper respect to their elders by getting up and giving them their seat when their feet are cramped....[28]

Dr. Brown firmly urged women to "never wear ill-fitting shoes. They inhibit gentleness."[29] Dr. Florence A. Sherman warned that high heels not only caused all kinds of foot ailments, but also altered a woman's center of gravity. Besides poor posture, Sherman explained, to compensate for the destabilizing effects of high heels, the body could also develop "a train of misplacements and congestions such as prolapus of the stomach and bowels, constipation, indigestion, misplaced uterus, menstrual pain. We might add to this list accidents, decreased working capacity, deranged nerves, lack of exercise ... nor should we forget that the story of bad feet writes itself in wrinkles and a look of old age."[30] One critic of high-heeled shoes summed it up, "...practically every ill of womankind comes from the wearing of high heels."[31]

Hair Styles

The desire to look boyish led women of the 1920's to adopt another drastically innovative fashion trend—short hair. Throughout the Victorian era and before that, a woman's hair was viewed as her crowning glory. In the Roaring Twenties women chopped off their hair, and as the decade progressed, the most popular coiffures grew increasingly shorter—first the bob, then the shingle, and in 1926–7 the most severe, the Eton crop, a style considered truly shocking by more conservative people.[32]

Bobbed hair initially caught the public's notice when famed ballroom dancer Irene Castle cut her hair short in 1915.[33] The Castle Bob, as it was called, sparked a revolution in hairstyles that eventually took fire in the 1920's. Also called a 3/4 cut, the bob was a simplistic page-boy style with the hair blunt-cut straight around the head at the level of the ear lobes. The shearing off of one's locks in a 3/4 bob quickly became the symbol of the modern woman. When the *Saturday Evening Post* published a story by F. Scott Fitzgerald on May 1, 1921, called "Bernice Bobs Her Hair," the young heroine in the story, who had been transformed into a modern vamp, quickly became a role model for young women across the US and led many into their local barbershop to get their hair cut.[34] As the new hairstyle appeared on the Silver Screen on such stars as Louise Brooks and Clara Bow, the bob's popularity quickly spread, reaching its greatest popularity around 1923.

By 1924, the bob began to be replaced with a variation called the shingle, razor cut on the back. Shaped close to the head, this hairstyle was modified with Marcel waves or finger curls. Bruce Bliven, in his article "Flapper Jane," published in the *New Republic* in 1925, commented on the new flapper hairstyles. He wrote,

> Jane's haircut is also abbreviated. She wears of course the very newest thing in bobs, even closer than last year's shingle. It leaves her just about no hair at all in the back, and 20 percent more than that in the front—about as much as is being worn this season by a cellist (male); less than a pianist; and much, much less than a violinist. Because of this new style, one can confirm a rumor heard last year: Jane has ears.[35]

Around 1927, hair was cut even closer to the head and slicked back with Brilliantine in a style called the Eton Crop. The severe hairdo sometimes featured spit curls by the ears or was plastered down across the forehead, as worn by Josephine Baker.

As bobbed hair became the universal norm for women in the 1920's, the cloche hat that fit tightly to the head was adopted as the most popular form of millinery.

Makeup

In addition to changes in hair length, there were dramatic changes in the use of cosmetics during the Roaring Twenties. Makeup, previously considered improper for anyone but actresses and loose women to wear in public, became a necessary part of the flapper look. The modern woman used excessive powder to make her skin look pale, plucked her eyebrows to pencil thin dimensions, wore heavy blue and green eye shadow, and donned thick false eyelashes to create a "dragon lady" look. She painted her lips in a narrow cupid's bow, as if puckering up for a kiss. Using nail polish and coloring the hair also came into vogue.

As fashion dictated that the modern woman look more and more youthful, beauty shops sprang up in every town and city, offering facials and beauty treatments to prevent wrinkles. Cosmetic surgery also became popular; the woman who wanted to recapture her youth could now do so with a face-lift.

Bruce Bliven described the fashionable flapper:

> Beauty is the fashion in 1925. She is frankly, heavily made up, not to imitate nature, but for an altogether artificial effect—pallor mortis, poisonously scarlet lips, richly ringed eyes—the latter looking not so much debauched (which is the intention) as diabetic. Her walk duplicates the swagger supposed by innocent America to go with the female half of a Paris Apache dance.[36]

Moralists were concerned that wearing heavy makeup in public might damage a woman's reputation. Doctors in the 1920's had other concerns. In 1922, the *New York Times* ran an article entitled "Flapper's Cosmetics Alarming Physicians." One doctor was quoted as saying,

> The "flapper" of today may have to adopt the Asiatic veil twenty years hence if she does not want to be described as "frightful, fat and forty."... We practicing physicians cannot fail to view with alarm the increasing use of cosmetics by our young girls.... Many a girl has already ruined her complexion by these things. We tremble to think what many of the members of the growing generation will look like when they reach 40.[37]

In addition to being heavily made-up, the modern woman of the Jazz Age was also certain to be seen through a cloud of smoke. Women's acceptance of cigarette smoking in public led to a boom in tobacco sales in the 1920's as millions of young women took up the habit in an effort to be in vogue. Between 1918 and 1928 cigarette sales doubled. As the decade progressed, advertisements and billboards went from pictures of young ladies demurely asking men to please blow smoke their way, to portrayals of flappers with cigarettes hanging from their finely-painted lips.

Cigarette companies capitalizing on this trend started advertising campaigns that urged the modern woman to "reach for a Lucky instead of a sweet." To the modern movers and shakers of the Roaring Twenties, a woman who smoked was not only liberated, but also desirable.

The most fashionable flappers matched their cigarettes to their outfits. *The Wisconsin State Journal* reported that when one modern socialite spent a weekend in the country, she changed her frock several times, and each time appeared with a different colored cigarette that perfectly matched her gloves and dress.

As more and more women smoked, another barrier in the separation between the sexes broke down. The custom of men and women parting company after formal dinners so the gentleman could smoke became a thing of the past.

The Music of the Jazz Age

> The world went round before they discovered jazz, but it didn't go round so fast. Jazz and pep are just the same, except you can shake pepper. You can't shake jazz, no matter how hard you shimmy. Just when they made delirium tremens unconstitutional, jazz came along and gave us dancing tremens. A guy that's been up against a few bars of jazz now finds his head whirling in company with his feet.[38]

In 1922, F. Scott Fitzgerald dubbed the era of the flapper and the Charleston "The Jazz Age." It was a time when the dancing was wild and the music was hot. During this turbulent period from the end of the World War I to the stock market crash in 1929, the word "jazz" referred not only to the music, but also to the manners, the mood, and the morals of the day. *The New York Times* declared, "Jazz has become a state of mind — the emblem of the insurgent Young Generation."[39] But it was the music that had people up in arms.

Worried that jazz was exercising undue influence over its listeners and weakening their moral fiber, many expressed concern that the sound of a wailing saxophone was ruining the youth of America. The music of jazz came to represent not only the thrill and excitement of the Roaring Twenties, but also the downfall and danger of fast living.[40] On February 1, 1922, the *Brownsville, Herald*, in Brownsville, Texas, ran an article simply titled "Jazz." It stated,

> [T]he sound of jazz produces no more effect than a cheap flapper novel would have upon a person intellectually and morally sensitive to the beauties of the "Book of Ecclesiastes." Jazz music is an effect, not a cause, and is a result of the demand created by a jazz spirit which crept into other phases of life long before it invaded music. Jazz grammar, jazz spelling, jazz movies and even jazz business methods were in evidence years ago, yet jazz in music must bear the burden of abuse from the reformers of today. Jazz doubtless is all its enemies say of it — it is vulgar, degrading to young tastes, seductive, perhaps, to weak intellects, and its presence in the theater and dance hall brings it very close to a great number all the time. But compared to the evil wrought by a jazz newspaper or magazine, or a jazz preacher, its damage is slight, because young people do not look to a jazz orchestra for a good example.[41]

Jazz music differed from ragtime in that it emphasized improvisation over structured composition. In addition, the role of the solo performer in jazz took precedence over the composer.

Jazz, like ragtime, incorporated a mixture of European and African musical traditions. Its connection to African origins gave rise to a strong undercurrent of racist reaction, leading many to label the music as barbaric and primitive, and "designed for naked wriggling savages."[42]

Some believed that the syncopated rhythms of jazz stimulated sexual behavior. It was evident to most that the music of a good jazz band was almost irresistible when it came to dancing. This led detractors to campaign against the provocative music. They warned, "Dance music is wrong when it creates nasty steps. Then certainly it should be a matter of grave concern to the country that our dance music should not be wrong."[44]

Around the world the merits and dangers of jazz music caused bitter debate. In rural areas, it was generally rejected and seen as further evidence of the destruction of society. In urban settings, more progressive attitudes allowed jazz to flourish. Its acceptance was aided by prohibition, which fostered the growth of speakeasies and nightspots where jazz music and the Charleston came to represent rebellion, change, and the culture of youth. The availability of other entertainment venues and technological advancements in media also helped spread jazz in the cities. Educated urbanites tended to more readily accept minorities, allowing black culture to mingle with white. But even as modernists flocked to nightclubs and cabarets and thrilled to the syncopations and improvisations of jazz bands, the more conservative set looked upon jazz with shock and disdain.

Thomas Edison, the inventor of the phonograph, declared that jazz music sounded better when it was played backwards. Popular composer Jerome Kern denounced it. At his request, the producers of his new hit musical *Sitting Pretty* refused to allow "one note of its [the show's] music to be heard in cabarets, over the radio, on the phonograph, or most important, from the instruments of a jazz orchestra."[45] John Phillip Sousa declared, "Jazz lives because of those who cannot dance, but try to. Jazz enables those who cannot dance to strut around on the ballroom floor with everybody else. It is a refuge for the flat-footed, the knock-kneed and the awkward." Sousa also predicted the demise of jazz. He said, "We have a great many religious people in this country, and it is a good thing. Some time they are going to try to jazz 'Jesus, Lover of My Soul,' or 'Nearer, My God to Thee,' and that will be the end of jazz. The people will not stand for it."[46]

Irving Berlin, on the other hand, "asserted that out of the present day jazz would grow a national music and great national musicians."[47] Berlin stated:

> Jazz is a contribution of America to the arts. It is recognized the world over as part of the musical folk lore of the country. It is as thoroughly and typically American as the Monroe Doctrine, the Fourth of July, or baseball. Further, jazz is going to make the world safe for musical democracy. It is going to seat the highbrow beside the lowbrow at concerts. There will be endowed chairs for the dissemination of knowledge of jazz at the foremost conservatories of music. In that bright future, syncopation will doff its informal attire and don evening clothes, even to the high hat and the cape.[48]

The Word "Jazz"

The first documented use of the word "jazz" in the press appeared in the *Los Angeles Times* on April 2, 1912. The word did not allude to music, but to baseball. Referring to his new curve ball, pitcher Ben Henderson of the Portland Beavers remarked, "I call it the Jazz ball because it wobbles and you simply can't do anything with it."[49] A year later, the word appeared again in connection with sports, this time in reference to ball players who had extra energy, spirit, and vitality. On March 6, 1913, the *San Francisco Bulletin* ran an article by E. T. "Scoop" Gleeson who explained the term. He wrote, "What is 'jazz?' Why, it's a little of that 'old life,' the 'gin-i-ker,' the 'pep,' otherwise known as the enthusiasm."[50] From 1915 until 1918, "jazz" in the sense of enthusiasm was commonly used as a slang expression on the West Coast, especially on college campuses. The President of Berkley, Benjamin Ide Wheeler, used it so often many credited him with coining the word, although he denied creating it.

"Jazz," as a reference to a particular type of music, did not appear in common usage until around 1915 in Chicago,[51] although the music itself certainly was played well before that in New Orleans and other places.[52]

On July 11 of that year in the *Chicago Daily Tribune* the following appeared:

> Blues Is Jazz and Jazz Is Blues.... The Worm had turned — turned to fox trotting. And the "blues" had done it. The "jazz" had put pep into the legs that had scrambled too long for the 5:15.... "What are the blues?" he asked gently. "Jazz!" The young woman's voice rose high to drown the piano.... The blues are never written into music, but are interpolated by the piano player or other players. They aren't new. They are just reborn into popularity. They started in the south half a century ago and are the interpolations of darkies originally. The trade name for them is "jazz."[53]

The use of the word "jazz" as a musical genre continued to grow in popularity around Chicago and soon spread to other cities in the country. It was not until June 20, 1918, however, that the word was first seen in print in New Orleans, the city where jazz music got its start. The reference appeared in the *Times-Picayune*:

> Why [sic — what] is the jass music, and therefore the jass band? Indeed, one might say that Jass music is the indecent story syncopated and counterpointed. In the matter of jass, New Orleans is particularly interested, since it has been widely suggested that this musical vice had its birth in our slums.[54]

In his book *The Latin Quarter*, Herbert Asbury states that the first known example of the word "jazz" in print in New Orleans occurred much earlier, when the manager of the Haymarket dance hall posted a sign listing the billing for a band appearing at his place. According to Asbury, in 1895 seven boys ranging in age from twelve to fifteen formed a band in New Orleans and called themselves the "Razzy Dazzy Spasm Band." About five years later, a second group advertised an appearance at a local dance hall using the same name. When members of the original Spasm band arrived at the venue where the usurpers were scheduled to perform, with rocks in their pockets ready to battle for the name, the owner quickly painted over the billing to avoid trouble. He dubbed the second band the "Razzy Dazzy Jazzy Band." Asbury states that this sign was the first use of the word "jazz" in print.

There are many explanations of the etymology of the word "jazz." Dubose Heyward, the author of *Porgy*, stated that the word as it related to music might have taken its name from Jasbo Brown, an "itinerant negro player along the Mississippi and later in Chicago cabarets."[55] According to the New York orchestra leader Vincent Lopez, "jazz" got its name from Charles Washington, a black drummer who worked in a theatre in Vicksburg, Mississippi. The musician could not read music but was a wonderful improviser and was great at utilizing syncopated rhythms. "It was a practice to repeat the chorus of popular numbers and on the repeats 'Chaz' was called on to do his most fantastic ticks of rhythm. At the end of the first chorus, therefore, the leader would call out: 'Now, Chaz!' From this small beginning it soon became a widespread habit to call any form of exaggerated syncopation 'chaz,' which was eventually changed to 'jazz.'"[56] Musician Paul Whiteman said that he agreed with John Phillip Sousa who claimed it came from the word "jazzbo," an expression used in minstrel shows when the performers improvised or "jazzboed" the tune.

The *Historical Dictionary of American Slang* says that the word "jazz" is derived from "jasm," a term meaning "spirit, energy, vigor."[57] Jasm dated to 1842 and was related to the slang word "jism" or "gism," which also referred to semen. The connection to sex was established early and the word "jazz" was widely used to mean sexual intercourse. Its sexual connotations were so pervasive, many would not use the word in polite company. Even supporters of the music were loathe to utter the word. In 1924, *The Ogden Standard-Examiner* in Ogden, Utah explained,

> All friends of jazz agree that it has an unpleasant and unfortunate name. They expect it to lose its infant appellation and assume a more sober title somewhere along its progress toward establishment as a permanent form of music.[58]

"Jazz's" connection to sex is also found in other possible derivations of the word. Some suggest that the word was a reference to the jasmine perfume worn by prostitutes in the brothels of New Orleans, or that it was derived from "jezebel," a common name for a woman of the night.

Some etymologists believe that "jazz" could come from the French *jaser*; to chatter or chat, or *chaser*; to chase or hunt. It has also been suggested that the term could be related to Irish teas, pronounced "chass" and signifying heat.

The *Arcade Dictionary of Word Origins* states that the word is probably derived from African origins. The Mandingo, *jasi*, and the Temne *yas*, are possible sources. Walter Kinsley reported in the *New York Sun* on August 5, 1917, that the word was African. The article stated, "In his studies of the creole patois and idiom in New Orleans Lafcadio Hearn reported that the word "jaz," meaning to speed things up, to make excitement, was common among the blacks of the South, and had been adopted by the Creoles as a term to be applied to music of a rudimentary syncopated type." Kingsley added, "Jaz her up" was used on occasion by plantation slaves, and that in common usage in Vaudeville "jaz her up" or "put in jaz" meant to accelerate or add low comedy, while "Jazbo" meant "hokum."[59]

One unlikely explanation, that appeared in newspapers in the fall of 1919, said that the word was merely onomatopoeic, sounding like the bubbling of the effervescent waters at Boyes Hot Springs, in Sonoma County, California.

Reaction to Jazz

As with the Charleston, many looked upon jazz as a moral and medical threat. In 1922, one California newspaper announced, "Jazz is a musical rash that has broken out upon the youth of the land."[60] Reformer Jane Addams, the founder of Hull House, stated that jazz was "the greatest menace to child morality," adding, "...[jazz] music must be controlled. Until it is, a great many young boys and girls will dance to their moral doom."[61] In her magazine article "From the Ballroom to Hell," Mrs. E. M. Whitmore claimed that seventy percent of New York prostitutes "had been spoiled by jazz music."[62]

In Chicago, Judge Arnold Heap ruled that jazz music was immoral and fined a local café performer for dancing to it. A fellow judge in Chicago took a different tack. He stated that it was "impossible for music to be immoral." The twist came when he handed down his decision. He ruled that jazz [was] not music and therefore may be immoral."[63]

Cities across America drew up ordinances banning the playing of jazz in public places. These bans were not limited to the United States. In Tokyo, police declared that jazz was immoral and worked to bar American music and the dancing that went with it. One paper reported, "It's a wonder the Mikado does not send a flock of missionaries to the New York dance halls to convert wild America."[64]

In August of 1921, the *Ladies Home Journal* ran an article by Anne Shaw Faulkner entitled "Does Jazz Put Sin in Syncopation?" In it, Faulker warned of the moral dangers of jazz:

> We have all been taught to believe that "music soothes the savage breast," but we have never stopped to consider that an entirely different type of music might invoke savage instincts. We

have been content to accept all kinds of music, and to admit music in all its phases into our homes, simply because it was music.... Therefore, it is somewhat of a rude awakening for many of these parents to find that America is facing a most serious situation regarding its popular music. Welfare workers tell us that never in the history of our land have there been such immoral conditions among our young people, and in the surveys made by many organizations regarding these conditions, the blame is laid on jazz music and its evil influence on the young people of to-day.[65]

The saxophone — "the symbol of jazz" — was especially condemned. *The New York Times* quoted a Washington police sergeant who stated, "Any music played on the saxophone is immoral." He claimed that saxophones were "murdering peace." The outraged policeman concluded, "One would think the serpent wooed Eve with a saxophone."[66]

Musicians were divided. Many welcomed the exciting, innovative sounds of jazz. Others called it noise. Paul Whiteman achieved huge success as a proponent of jazz. Although many criticized the white bandleader, nicknamed the "King of Jazz," for sanitizing the art form, his popular recordings made millions of listeners fans of jazz. The music director of the Red Cross, on the other hand, urged members of the Texas Federation of Music Clubs not only to shun jazz themselves, but also to fight actively against it, calling the insidious music "poison."[67]

Following protests by its own musicians, France ordered American jazz players to be expelled from the country. Spanish and German musicians also denounced the new music, calling for it to be censored and demanding that any Americans who dared to play jazz be expelled.[68] Hungarian Gypsies also placed a ban on it, calling American jazz "immoral, inartistic, unpatriotic, and godless."[69]

Everyone had an opinion. The *Oakland Tribune* reported that even the National Association of Piano Tuners weighed in on the subject. The Association cited a specific reason for adopting resolutions condemning jazz:

> One would think jazz would be welcome noise to the piano tuner. What is there which may wreck the harmony, crack keys and jam the sharps all up with the flats any quicker than a jazz artist in full motion? The more jazz the more piano tuning, is an easy conclusion, but it does not work out that way. According to the piano tuners, and they should know, anyone who plays jazz does not care whether his piano is tuned or not.[70]

Opposition to Jazz for Medical Reasons

Some resisted jazz because they believed it ruined one's health. Anne Faulkner offered proof in her article "Does Jazz Put Sin in Syncopation?" She wrote,

> A number of scientific men who have been working on experiments in musico-therapy with the insane, declare that while regular rhythms and simple tones produce a quieting effect on the brain of even a violent patient, the effect of jazz on the normal brain produces an atrophied condition on the brain cells of conception, until very frequently those under the demoralizing influence of the persistent use of syncopation, combined with inharmonic partial tones, are actually incapable of distinguishing between good and evil, right and wrong.[71]

One particular case that grabbed the country's attention was the trial of 16-year-old Dorothy Ellingson, the "jazz maniac,"[72] who murdered her mother in San Francisco when Mrs. Ellingson tried to prevent her daughter from going to a "jazz party."[73] Local papers labeled the crime as the "latest product of jazzmania," and asked the question, "What Price Jazz?"[74] After her arrest, Miss Ellingson was heard to remark, "Jazz is all right but it drags you down."[75]

Mr. Duque, a man some credit with inventing the Maxixe, claimed, "Not one temperament in a thousand can stand an afternoon of jazz and remain sane. Jazz music produces a fevered disorder of the brain, leading to bad temper, slackness, lassitude and frequently bad health."[76]

Mr. Duque added, "[In Europe], husbands don't take their wives to dance, because they find it inevitably means a raggedy temper afterwards.... I look upon jazz as one of the direct causes of the increasing tendency toward divorce and ruined marital happiness. No man or woman is normal after he has danced to the music of a jazz orchestra for more than half an hour."[77] In addition to wrecking marriages, jazz also was credited with ruining household domesticity. Duque explained, "I have a friend who allowed his servants to dance during the slack afternoon hours to the music of a graphophone giving jazz airs. He had to stop it because the dinner was invariably badly cooked afterward and the whole house was disarranged."[78]

In Cincinnati, Ohio, the Salvation Army sued to prevent the building of a theatre adjacent to a maternity hospital. The group won a court injunction to stop construction by arguing that the new theatre might feature jazz music that "would have an unfavorable effect upon expectant mothers and influence the character of their babies." The suit stated, "We recognize that we are living in a jazz age, but we object to imperiling the happiness of future generations by inculcating in them before they are even born, the madness that now rules the country."[79]

In his article "The Jazz Path of Degradation," published in the *Ladies' Home Journal* in January 1922, John R. McMahon warned,

> It is likely the birth rate will be affected. The next generation will show certain physical consequences. There will be more weaklings and fewer stalwarts. The crop of human weeds will increase. Instead of real men and women, we may reasonably expect an augmented stock of lounge lizards and second-quality "vamps."[80]

Orchestra leader Paul Whiteman, on the other hand, praised the health-giving benefits of listening to jazz. He said, "Jazz is responsible for the health of young persons today. The more jazz, the more perfect race. And a generation of jazz will produce a race of perfectly developed men and women. Jazz is particularly good for the development of the perfect back."[81]

17

Reaction to the Charleston

The Charleston craze infected all levels of society from shop girl to debutante, from factory worker to royalty. It seemed like everyone everywhere was doing the Charleston. In 1925, the *New York Times* reported, "Dancers young and not so young enjoy the barbarous rhythm of its syncopation: they like the tricky steps and the recklessness that is somehow injected into them. It has life and vitality. You hear about it everywhere."[1] Clubs, speakeasies, and cabarets always had at least one Charleston specialty act. It seemed that on every corner in every major city, street urchins danced the Charleston for pennies. *Vogue* magazine reported that in Manhattan "'the westbound streets are clogged with smart motors bearing ladies to the Broadway dance emporiums' to learn the dance."[2]

Small's Paradise on 7th Avenue in New York City not only had Charleston dancing chorus girls, but also waiters who Charlestoned their way from table to table with bootleg liquor and trays of Chinese food. The dance was so popular even some non-dancing jobs required that applicants be well-versed in dancing the Charleston — just in case. St. Louis boasted of its own Charleston-dancing traffic cop. In Newcastle, England, hundreds of teens blocked traffic every Sunday evening as they filled the streets to dance the Charleston. The Charleston was the dance of the day.

Moral Objections

Despite the dance's far-reaching popularity, many viewed the Charleston with distaste — others with downright disgust. Articles, editorials, sermons, and speeches labeled the dance as vulgar, immoral, degenerate, and ugly. The Rev. E. W Rogers, vicar of St. Aidan's church in Bristol, England said, "Any lover of the beautiful will die rather than be associated with the Charleston. It is neurotic! It is rotten! It stinks! Phew, open the windows."[3] Dr. Francis E. Clark, the founder and president of the Christian Endeavor Society, stated that such indecent displays on the dance floor were "an offense against womanly purity, the very fountainhead of our family and civil life."[4] In 1922 the Morality League sought an anti-dance ordinance to combat the "cherry pickers, tack-hammers, cheek-pressers, hip-swingers, and lemon-rollers of the fierce jazz dance invaders."[5] The president of the League urged the youth of America to "dedicate themselves to bringing about the death of jazz."[6] He traveled around the country campaigning for teenagers to sign his no-dancing pledge. Elected officials,[7] clergymen, and parents tried to shield the innocent children of the world from the infectious jazz that was spreading like wildfire.[8]

Anti-Charleston diatribes appeared frequently in newspaper editorials, magazine articles, and sermons, denouncing the dance's erotic nature. *The Catholic Telegraph* of Cincinnati called the dance nothing more than a "syncopated embrace," admonishing, "The music is sensuous, the embracing of partners — the female only half dressed — is absolutely indecent; and the motions — they are such as may not be described, with any respect for propriety, in a family newspaper."[9]

Top and bottom: Vivian Marinelli giving Charleston lessons to members of the Palace Club basketball team of Washington, D.C. Photographs by National Photo Company entitled "The Charleston as an Aid to the Game" (courtesy of the Library of Congress).

New York stage actress Laurette Taylor agreed. She stated emphatically,

> I'm sick of seeing young people dance around as though they couldn't help it ... I really do think this jazz is a menace to the country. From the point of view of health, it is poisonous, nerve-racking, shattering, the din and clatter, the tomtom music — no rhythm, no melody — just sex and bedlam! And the young men! My word![10]

The Archbishop of Eastern Poland even went so far as to declare, "Dancing the Charleston is an unpardonable sin!" He added that he would "refuse absolution to women who confess indulging in this dance."[11]

Although most diatribes against the Charleston sprang from the dance's suggestive nature, such as the open and closing of the knees and the uninhibited kicking, shaking and jiggling, other objections resulted from racist responses to its African origins. Louis Chalif, one of the most highly respected dance teachers of the period stated that the Charleston was "of heathen African origin" and therefore should be banned.[12]

Dance masters meeting in Paris labeled the Charleston "Negroid, immoral, unspeakable and unworthy."[13] In England, the *Daily Mail* called the Charleston "a series of contortions without a vestige of grace or charm, reminiscent only of negro orgies."[14] In the U.S., the *Charleston Daily Mail* in Charleston, West Virginia declared it was a dance "which some drunken negro evolved from bodily contortions seen at a camp meetin' and a voo-doo ceremony...."[15]

Even the city for which the dance was named shuddered to be associated with the dance.

> The city of Charleston, South Carolina, objects to having a current dance of the "jazz" variety tagged with its name. The so-called "Charleston,"... far from flattering the justly proud Charlestonians, is causing them to blush more or less continuously with mortification.... [It is] a "rude dance, affected by a portion of the negro population" and being executed usually "in a spirit which is not polite." Let it be known, therefore, that Charleston indignantly disowns the "Charleston," whatever may be its intrinsic charm.[16]

Medical Objections

As the Charleston reached the zenith of its popularity, many physicians argued that the dance should be banned because its over-enthusiastic contortions were detrimental to one's health. "Dance the Charleston and dance yourself into physical collapse ... the ten million or so young people who nightly strut the latest dance craze ... are 'hoofing' their way to the hospital — and perhaps to the cemetery."[17] Doctors reported a variety of ills caused by too much Charlestoning — water on the knee, twisted ligaments, sprained or strained ankles and backs, fallen arches, foot deformities, weight loss, depleted energy, hernia, internal injuries, and overstrained heart.

In Paris, city officials concerned over the dance's safety denounced the Charleston "as highly dangerous to health, especially to women..." and debated banning the dance in public halls stating, "This is a result of the physical collapse of four professional dancing girls after having gone through the gyrations of the Charleston for several hours."[18]

The Charleston was physically active and dancers in the madness of the moment often violently threw their arms and legs about with utter abandon. There were several reported injuries sustained from either performing the energetic dance or being pummeled by a fellow dancer. On November 21, 1925, the *New York Times* reported, "Too much dancing of the Charleston is believed to be the cause of the serious illness of Thomas Duffy of White Street, who has been confined to his home for several days. An ailment of the back, doctors say, was caused by the constant jarring resulting from doing the dance step."[19] In Pennsylvania, "Another Charleston casualty went on record when Herman Wise of South Brownsville slipped and fell during the gyrations of an especially violent form of the Charleston on a Uniontown dance floor. He suffered a broken arm and other injuries but he continued in the dance until a doctor sent for by friends arrived."[20] *The Sheboygan Press* in Sheboygan, Wisconsin reported on a young woman who fell during the dance and broke her wrist. The paper warned, "Keep on and that dance will soon be as dangerous as football."[21]

A well-respected doctor in Paris condemned the Charleston, labeling it a "dangerous sport" because of "the violent strain [it] imposed on certain ligaments, especially those around the knee." He noted that he had treated 5,000 cases of sprained or dislocated knees and that many of those he diagnosed could be dubbed as "the Charleston knee."[22]

A London specialist admonished that the Charleston "would lead to a permanent distortion of the ankles."[23] The number of people suffering from flat feet became so common, some doctors dubbed the syndrome "Charleston feet.[24] One leading doctor stated, "...ninety percent of the present-day foot trouble is caused by too much Charleston dancing."[25]

Other physicians warned of more serious maladies.[26] They cautioned that "the shocks to the body may displace the heart and other organs ... [and that] ... paralysis and total collapse due to the contortions, shocks, jolts and jars of the Charleston are quite common."[27] On February 16, 1926, the *New Castle News* ran a story about a Kansas girl who died from dancing the Charleston. The article stated, "The recent death of 17-year-old Evelyn Myers was 'due to dancing the Charleston,' her physician, Dr. W. R. Boyer, of Pawnee City, Nebr., said yesterday. Dr. Boyer declared that the extreme physical exercise of the Charleston is particularly dangerous for young women and that it may easily induce inflammation of the peritoneum."[28] In Cincinnati, Ohio, Geneva Tully, sixteen years old, died of heart disease shortly after winning a Charleston contest. It was believed the strain of the contest had overtaxed the young woman.[29]

One physician, Dr. Harry Gilbert, was so eager to find scientific proof that the Charleston was dangerous, he performed examinations at one of the most popular night clubs in New York City. He tested the heart rates of dancers before and after dancing the Charleston and discovered that heart rates rose from an average of eighty pulses per minute to one hundred and thirty-four after performing the dance. He warned that "constant repetition of such exertion will cause permanent injury to the heart."[30]

In Chicago, a special Charleston clinic was opened by the YWCA with the purpose of studying the effects of the dance under strictly regulated laboratory conditions. A team of girl dancers, all members of a Charleston dance class, were the participants. Their weight was monitored and a record was kept of heart action and lung power. In addition, "accurate measurements of the twisting of pretty legs [were] being taken daily to determine what effect the dance has on their shape and size."[31] Photos were also taken to see if the girl's personal charms and beauty were adversely affected.

Some doctors simply disliked the Charleston because its rhythm was irresistible. The Medical Officer at one school in England described how "children of all ages now seem unable to keep their feet still."[32] He labeled the disease "Charleston Chorea."

Most medical complaints about the Charleston resulted from injuries related to the dance's constant kicking. "Many a time I have had a girl stop in the middle of a dance with a scream and go down in a little heap, clutching her ankle where it had been kicked by a No. 9 foot,"[33] said the proprietor of one dance hall. In Britain, one writer commented, "The trouble with the Charlestoners is that they exaggerate it and make a stunt of it. They stand in one spot on the floor and side-kick. The result is that other dancers are kicked, and the girls have their silk stockings torn."[34] Another critic of the dance observed,

> The dance is nothing but a series of kicks and stamps—bow-legged kicks, knock-kneed kicks, side kicks, back kicks, and stamps to correspond. This irresponsible kicking around, like a fly-pestered horse, makes it obvious why the dancers maintain the arm's-length position.[35]

The London District Council banned the dance because it was dangerous, and "a number of dancers received kicks resulting in a nasty dispute."[36] One member of the Council declared "...the man who invented the Charleston was a fit candidate for the lunatic asylum and that the 'fools' who attempted to dance it were 'balmy.'"[37] Many dance halls banned the dance outright, although one establishment in Brixton created a special roped off area so enthusiasts could dance all they wanted and only kick other Charleston fanatics. The manager of the hotel said, "As soon as we notice any couple about to succumb to the Charleston fever, we shove 'em behind the ropes, and make them stay there until they recover."[38]

The Piccadilly Hotel in London was one of the first in that city to prohibit the dance in any form under any condition, posting signs that read, "You are earnestly requested not to dance the Charleston." Other hotels did not officially forbid the dance, but informed their orchestra leaders to play music that made the Charleston "impossible, or at least difficult to the point of exterminating it by slow degrees."[39] Many establishments posted signs that read, "P.C.Q." which dancers understood to mean "Please Charleston Quietly!"

In addition to concerns about injuries sustained on the dance floor, physicians warned that the Charleston could affect a woman's beauty by leading to malformations of the skeletal system. Critics feared that the unnatural contortions of the Charleston, with knees and feet turned in, caused the bones and muscles to harden and would eventually create "...a race of knock-kneed, pigeon-toed, plier-handled females."[40] They predicted the dire consequences of "...Flo Ziegfeld diagnosing the charms of a bevy of beauties next year and failing to find one girlish figure which does not resemble that little instrument with which poppa gets under the fliver."[41]

One doctor disagreed. He saw the Charleston as beneficial to the bones of the body. He said, "...the Charleston could be accurately described as a self-inflicted osteopathic treatment. From that standpoint it is all to the good." He disliked the dance for other reasons. He went on to say, "...how any sane person can deceive himself or herself in the belief that it is fun is something else again."[42]

Despite calls to have the Charleston barred from ballrooms and dance halls on the grounds that it was immodest, tasteless, primitive, sinful, or injurious to health, the dance continued to grow in popularity. The youth of the 1920's loved the freedom and spirit of the dance. To be in step in the modern world, one had to dance the Charleston. As one realist declared, "For ban it as you will, condemn it as you will, frown upon it and call it vulgar if you are so inclined — you are merely marking yourself as out of step with the vogue. The Charleston is here to stay...."[43]

The Pickwick Disaster

Late in the early morning hours of Saturday, July 4, 1925, about 125 people in Boston, Massachusetts were celebrating the holiday at an "all-night China-town resort"[44] called the Pickwick Club. Several partygoers were turned away that night because the dance hall, located on the second floor of the old Dreyfus Hotel, on the corner of Washington and Beach, was so crowded it couldn't accommodate any more people.

Around 3 A.M. John Duffey finished crooning "West of the Great Divide." The crowd shouted for an encore of the song and the band struck up a snappy jazz version of the tune. The room full of revelers began to Charleston. Some set off firecrackers.

Frank Decker, another singer at the club recalled,

> At least fifty couples crowded on the floor and they danced like folks gone mad. Before the orchestra had played a dozen notes I could feel the floor swaying. I heard loud cracks but thought they were firecrackers. As the dance neared its close the orchestra speeded up the tempo and the dancers grew crazier than ever. It seemed as if they couldn't kick high enough or stamp their feet

hard enough to satisfy themselves. When the orchestra was blaring almost the last note of the piece, there came a deafening roar. The lights went out, and in the twinkling of an eye, the old Pickwick club was no more.[45]

The five-story building that housed the Pickwick Club collapsed.[46]

The front exit of the club had a "trick" lock so the crowd could not escape that way.[47] Some were able to scramble out the fire escape at the back of the building or leap out windows in the one wall that was left standing. A few were actually thrown from the building as it crumbled. Most were buried.

Two hundred firemen, elevated road workers, and members of the Public Works Department arrived to begin the rescue effort. They worked gingerly to avoid further collapse. "Under the concentrating glare of dozens of arc lights an army of men had patiently, brick by brick, stick by stick, worked their way down through the mass of debris, pausing now and again to lift another unfortunate."[48] The mayor of Boston, James M. Curley personally oversaw the recovery until he was so exhausted he was forced to go home.

Rescue efforts continued the next day. In a neighboring cabaret "on the second floor of an adjoining building ... an orchestra blared jazz while others danced alongside the scene of the disaster."[49] The huge crowd that gathered to watch the rescue efforts began to boo and hiss, and an officer was sent to order the music to stop.

The wreckage of the Pickwick Club in Boston after it collapsed. This photo appeared in the *Morning Herald* in Uniontown, Pennsylvania, on July 7, 1925 with the caption "Where Many Dancers Lost Lives." Reprinted with permission *Herald-Standard*.

The carnage within the five-story collapse was overwhelming. One bizarre account told of a man extricated from the wreckage:

> Inch after inch the corpse emerged, but when five feet of its length, and then six and seven feet continued to come the rescuers gasped. Not until a full nine feet of man had been pulled from the jagged mass of twisted steel and wood was the body freed.[50]

Reports stated the man's head and feet had been caught and pulled in opposite directions until his bones were pulled out of their sockets and his body stretched. Another victim, a woman, was severed at the waist. According to one account, a fireman named Edward F. Doyle "suffered a mental breakdown under the stress of the rescue work and it required eight of his comrades to put him in the ambulance that bore him to the hospital."[51]

Scores of seriously injured victims were pulled from the wreckage and rushed to local hospitals. Nineteen were confirmed dead, but the death toll quickly rose to thirty-seven. Workers ran out of the long wicker baskets they were using to transport the bodies and more had to be sent from a neighboring mortuary. A derrick and two steam shovels were brought in to remove the slabs of foundation stone and the remaining front wall that threatened to topple in on the recovery efforts. Workers tried tunneling into the basement of the Pickwick building from a construction site that was adjacent to the club.[52] Two more bodies were found. Fifty hours after the collapse, the bodies of Bart Chapman, Lillian McIssac, and Clara Fredrick were pulled from the wreckage and at 5:20 in the morning of the 6th, the last victim, Frank Driscoll, whose battered body was identified by the union card found in his pocket, was found. The final death toll would reach forty-four.[53]

The morning after the building's collapse, the police shot William Robinson in the arm for looting.[54] They arrested three others who were pillaging through the remains of the club's cloakroom, which was in the corner of the building and had survived mostly intact and was shielded by the fallen floors. Angelo Cook, a rescue worker, was also arrested for pocketing money he found on victims while digging through the ruins. He had collected $29.00.

On Monday, July 6, District Attorney Thomas C. O'Brien launched a grand jury investigation to look into the cause of the collapse.[55] In addition, all nightclubs and resorts in the city, as well as the theatre and all other buildings that surrounded the Pickwick, were shut down pending further inspection. "As a result of the Pickwick Club disaster, Police Superintendent Crowley has ordered the closing of the Lambs Club in the Back Bay district, and the Black and White Club in Roxbury, both which have been operated along lines similar to the Pickwick Club."[56] The owners of both nightclubs defied the order and remained opened for business as usual.[57]

The Pickwick Club disaster had far-reaching effects on how the Charleston was perceived. Many suspected that the collapse of the building was a result of the dancers' violent movements. Dance halls were closed and the dance was banned. The Charleston was called the "Dance of Death."[58]

"The Charleston dance may shake the foundations of public morality all it wants to, but when it weakens the foundations of buildings housing dance floors, it ought to be stopped,"[59] said city officials in Kansas City. After inspecting several buildings and finding them "thrown out of plumb by the vibrations and gyrations of Charleston enthusiasts," they looked "askance [at] the popularity of the violent pastime"[60] and prohibited it. Similar bans were called for in many other states. In Passaic, New Jersey, the Chief of Police stationed his men outside all dancing establishments to enforce his anti–Charleston edict. He banned the Charleston in all older halls, only allowing the dance in buildings that had been erected within the past month. He stated, "The Charleston is alright [sic] morally, so far as I know, but we do not want any casualties here because of it."[61]

" Where's Mary been lately?"
" I haven't seen her since the Pickwick Club crash."
" Oh, I was going too, but it fell through."

—*M. R. B.*

A cartoon by Ruth Wilson, with text by Mercedes R. Baker from the collegiate magazine *VooDoo* (1925 Girl's Number Issue, page 8). Reprinted with permission *VooDoo Magazine*, Massachusetts Institute of Technology.

One commentator in the San Antonio Light wrote:

> Reformers and moralists of all sorts look upon the Charleston as perhaps the most harmless of all dances since the stately minuet. It violates no laws, no codes of which they know anything. But to the structural engineer it is a menace and invention of the devil, monkeying with the laws of vibration and the building codes. The tango may be a home-wrecker, but the Charleston is a house-wrecker.[62]

Articles appeared in newspapers around the country offering scientific proof that the Pickwick had collapsed because "the newest crazy dance step causes vibrations which give the stamping heels of an average couple the destructive force of a giant twenty times their weight."[63] These articles stated that it was the scientific property of resonance that caused the crash. In other words, the amplitude of oscillation created by the repeated cadence of the Charleston dancers matched the natural frequency of the Pickwick building causing it to vibrate and shatter, similar to a glass shattering when a certain high pitch is sounded.[64]

> What the Charleston lacks in rhyme and reason, it makes up in rhythm, vicious brick-and-mortar destroying rhythm which the scientist calls "resonance".... It never occurred to any one that there was going among the molecules and atoms, millions of little divorces that were not recorded to human eyes, mortar that was more and more ready to become just lime powder and limp sand and wood and steel getting nearer and nearer to the snapping point. The Charleston makes some persons tired and it made that old building tired, more tired every day, until it could no longer stand up and flopped its weary bones on the street.[65]

The Charleston fad was relatively short. When Ann Pennington introduced the Black Bottom in George White's *Scandals of 1926*, a new craze caught the public's interest and rivaled the Charleston as society's favorite dance.[66] Nevertheless, the Charleston had a lasting impact on the world of social dancing.

The Charleston was the first dance to be readily accepted by men. College boys, athletes, policemen, waiters, princes—all wanted to learn the snappy dance. The relative simplicity of the steps made it accessible to a wider audience, both male and female, and because they didn't have to study with a professional teacher to learn the dance, men and women alike were drawn to the Charleston in huge numbers.

In their classic book *Jazz Dance: the Story of American Vernacular Dance*, the Stearns' also point out that the Charleston was important because "...the distinction between popular dances to watch, and popular dances to dance, was wiped out."[67] Contests were prevalent and anyone of any age or level of technical training could compete. This also led to the blurring of the line between professional stage performer and amateur. Most anyone could do the Charleston. The popularity and pizzazz of the dance also led to its being incorporated in many acts, especially

The Charleston Step, Showing How the Thumps Are Given at the Rate of Two Every Five Seconds.

Inset from an article in the *San Antonio Light* from Sunday, August 9, 1925, showing how the steps of the Charleston created a resonance that resulted in the Pickwick disaster. Copyright 1925 *San Antonio Light*. Reprinted with permission *San Antonio Express-News*.

An article in the *San Antonio Light* from Sunday, August 9, 1925, that explained how the vibrations caused by dancing the Charleston resulted in the collapse of the Pickwick Club in Boston. Copyright 1925 *San Antonio Light*. Reprinted with permission *San Antonio Express-News*.

tap dance routines, thus leading to new, innovative tap styles, and a merging of tap and ballroom on a professional level.[68]

The close dance hold that had marked earlier couple dances was abandoned with the Charleston and individuality was welcomed on the dance floor, foreshadowing the breakaway moves that later exploded in the Jitterbug and Break dancing. During the Jazz Age, cutting-in became more readily accepted, and dancers could change partners in the middle of a dance.

Because it did not cover the floor like other couple dances before it, such as the waltz, animal dances, and tango, the Charleston was also easy to film. The dance was frequently featured in the films of the fledgling motion picture industry.[69] The image of the madcap, dancing flapper has been seared into the consciousness of the world, insuring the Charleston's place as the quintessential iconic image of the Roaring Twenties.

18

Harmony and Disharmony

According to the *Oxford English Dictionary*, the word "ball," defined as "a social assembly for dancing," first came into common usage in the early 1630's. The word was derived from the Old French, *baler*, the Italian, *ballare*, and the Spanish *bailar*, all of which meant, "to dance,"[1] but "the etymology of the word had deep primal associations with confrontation and battle."[2] These connections are evident in other definitions of the word such as "a missile ... projected from an engine of war," "a globular case or shell filled with combustibles, intended to set buildings on fire, or to give light, smoke, etc.," and "a globular body to play with, which is thrown, kicked, knocked, or batted about"[3]—all definitions with connotations of violence and competition.

Dance historians point out that many dances evolved out of representations of fighting, military displays, or other forms of aggression. War dances are found in almost all cultures. The Scottish sword dance is one example of dancing based upon militaristic themes. The movements of the English Morris dance symbolically depicted the battle between the Moors and the Christians. The footwork of the galliard and the volta evolved from fencing positions.

In fact, the word "ball" is believed by some to be a corruption of the word "brawl," and during the Renaissance, the French court dance, the branle, was known as the brawl (or brawle) in England. Pyrotechnic displays, mock battles, and military parades frequently accompanied ceremonial dancing parties, and it was not uncommon for country dances to end in fisticuffs.

One macabre blending of violence and dancing occurred shortly after the French revolution in ballrooms and salons across the Continent. A practice developed called *bals à la victime*. Only the relatives of people who had died by the guillotine attended these events. The women adorned their throats with red ribbons to symbolize the effects of the blade. As the ball-goers danced, they shook their heads from side to side as if they were about to roll off.

Dancing has also often involved competition. In the Middle Ages, dancing accompanied tennis matches. At court, the minuet was used as an opportunity to outshine other members of the nobility. Men vigorously competed with each other in the schuhplattler, and vied for a maiden's attentions in the ländler. The competition to gain entry into the balls and dancing parties at Almack's was legendary.

Another definition of the word "ball" contains the concept of harmony versus disharmony; the word is defined as "any planetary or celestial body" which has associations with the ordering of the universe out of primordial chaos. The word was frequently used in reference to the sun, and the earliest roots of dancing can be traced to mimetic sun-worship rituals and primitive human's use of dance to insure the order and harmony in the world.

In his book, *Religious Dances in the Christian Church and in Popular Medicine*, Louis Backman describes a medieval dance that combined both the ancient aspects of the sun-worshipping ritual and a ball game. Called the pelota, this dance was usually performed by bishops or archbishops and their subordinates on Easter. The priests held hands in a long chain and did a three-step dance as they moved through a labyrinth set on the floor of the cathedral. As they performed the dance, the dean of the church tossed a ball to each of the participants. Historians surmise that the ball symbolized the sun and was associated with the legend that if people rose early enough on Easter morning, they would see the sun dancing in the sky.[4] The dance and ball game were used as a mystery play representing the Resurrection. The movement through the labyrinth represented Christ's journey into the underworld, his battle with Satan, and His escape from the Kingdom of the Dead.[5] The dance, therefore, represented both the forces of good and evil. It revealed both conflict and resolution.

These opposing aspects of conflict and resolution, or order and disorder, are both found within the various definitions of the word "ball;" they form an integral part of the word's meaning as well, as it is applied to social dancing. "The ballroom itself has been an arena wherein participants tacitly played with the term's duality of meanings—creation and destruction—through powerful and symbolic actions of ceremonial conduct and dancing."[6]

Therefore, to fully understand the cultural and historical impact of a social dance such as the waltz, one must balance its beauty, grace, and well-ordered harmony on the one hand with its many associations with turmoil and competition on the other.

The Waltz as Metaphor

Reactions to the waltz clearly embodied this duality. It was loved and hated; worshipped and feared; embraced and attacked. The dance contained both beauty and danger. Its paradoxical nature mirrored the equally dualistic nature of Victorian beliefs about class, economics, and gender.

As discussed earlier, the waltz democratized social dancing. Danced by all levels of soci-

"The Hunt Ball," an 1880's photogravure/engraving by D. Appleton & Co., New York, of an oil painting by Jules (Julius) L. Stewart. The original was exhibited at the World's Columbian Exposition of 1893.

ety regardless of pedigree or income, performance in the waltz was based on skill rather than on social status. Couples swirled around the room in any order, wherever they chose. Position on the dance floor was not determined by rank.

Those who pointed out the evils of waltzing warned that it was this very freedom that threatened morality. In the waltz, women danced with complete strangers. Unsuspecting females were therefore unwittingly subjected to all types of unsavory characters. The democratic waltz allowed even libertines and lotharios to be included.

Social conflicts played out in other ways in the waltz. To be allowed into Almack's or to dance with a duke at the Apollo Hall in Vienna could lead to acceptance in the right social circles or to a suitable marriage with someone of higher station. Giving a ball called attention to the host's social status and wealth, as did being included on the right guest list. Opponents of the waltz pointed to its lower class, primitive beginnings. In his book *The Lure of the Dance*, T. A. Faulkner wrote, "The so-called folk dance is the first rudiment of the waltz, and the notorious underworld round dance called the 'one-step.' [It] originated in the slums of Paris...."[7] Many late eighteenth century aristocrats were horrified by the waltz's crude, rural flavor. The waltz reflected these conflicting notions. For some it was the embodiment of grace, elegance, and beauty—an expression of civilization at its zenith. For others, it was a shameless exhibition and a proof of the downfall of society.

Conflicting economic issues were also embodied in the waltz. Unlike the minuet, the waltz was a simple dance to learn, not requiring the expensive services of a dancing master. Because the waltz posed a threat to their income, dancing masters shifted the emphasis from technique to manners and began utilizing the dance as a means of imparting moral training.

Economic interests led dancing teachers to form professional organizations that codified the teaching of round dances. They stated that money spent for lessons was a small price to pay for avoiding an embarrassing faux pas. The waltz initially threatened the dancing teachers' livelihood but eventually guaranteed their success.

There were other conflicts surrounding the economic impact of the waltz. The wasteful extravagance of dancing became the frequent subject of debate, and questions about the stewardship of time and money became one of the main themes in anti-dance literature. Ball-gowns and ballroom decorations cost money. Emperor Francis I of Austria even raised taxes by fifty percent to support the waltzing habit of the delegates to the Vienna Congress. Critics of the waltz asked, "How could these things be justified when money could better be spent feeding one's family or helping the poor?"

Perhaps the most obvious example of the waltz's ability to embody the turmoil of the Victorian era is how it expressed society's preoccupation with gender roles. The dance reflected conflicts that arose about how emotions and feelings should best be expressed between men and women in the context of proper social behavior. The physical enactment of these social interactions in the waltz mirrored the changing, paradoxical nature of nineteenth century ideologies.

These conflicting ideologies were most apparent in the complex societal and cultural sexual stereotypes that assigned the role of leader to the man and follower to the woman. In her book, *From the Ballroom to Hell: Grace and Folly in Nineteenth-century Dance*, Elizabeth Aldrich quotes Peter Shaw's essay on the subject. Shaw states,

> Each partner accepts the constraints and enjoys the prerogatives of a frankly-stereotyped role. The woman accepts that she must follow ... but she has the more desirable steps and a degree of freedom from care.... [The man's] is a role of responsibility, as it was once universally believed to be his sexual role in life.[8]

Yet, the roles that each assumed while dancing had even more subtle and profound meanings than what might first appear. In order to accomplish the rapid spinning of the waltz, both the man and the woman had to step in close to their partners. The waltz required a willingness to risk intimacy by both male and female. Both had to lean back, trusting in the support of their partners as they surrendered to the motion of turning. The man trusted the strength of the woman as equally as she trusted his. In order to waltz effectively, the couple had to share a common axis. They had to hold a continuous point of contact, and at the same time maintain self-sufficiency. If one overpowered the other, they would spin out of control. Both had to share a common center without losing identity or individuality. It was this dual approach to spatial intimacy — of proximity and distance — that allowed the greatest freedom while waltzing.

The waltz was a powerful metaphor, reflecting changing views about relationships during this period in history. It revealed new understandings about a woman's ability to contribute equally and a man's need to share power. The structured improvisational quality of the waltz required both partners to listen and respond appropriately on equal terms.

In this way, the waltz not only democratized social dancing by breaking down class barriers, but it also called into question gender stereotypes. The man was formally the leader, but the woman's role as follower demanded equal strength and support. In a very basic way the six-step pattern of the waltz footwork, with the man swinging around the woman as she swiveled on her own axis, then his swiveling as she swung across him, put the woman and the man on equal footing.

At first glance, the world of the nineteenth and early twentieth century ballroom seems ordered with the strictest rules regarding manners, behavior, and proper protocol, all created to insure social harmony and agreement. However, it was also a place where, according to dance detractors, danger and conflict lurked, morality was threatened, and people could spin out of control.

The waltz expressed this duality. It gave outer expression to inner experience, intimately revealing beliefs, philosophies, confusions, and concerns. At the same time, it reflected the turmoil of Victorian society and a rapidly changing world. The dance expressed both chaos and control. The wicked waltz symbolized both the heights of social attainment and the depths of degradation.

The Animal Dances, the Tango, and the Charleston

The aspects of violence, competition, and eventual resolution are also present in the dance crazes of the early twentieth century. These dances evoked both strong negative and positive reactions. They were hated and loved with equal passion. They mirrored the disorder and order of the times in which they appeared.

The steady trotting footwork of the dances of the ragtime era was embellished with the leans, lurches, and twitching of barnyard animals. Critics saw these simple, fidgety dances as expressions of social unrest. Psychologists and sociologists compared them to the dance epidemics of the Middle Ages. As with many social dances, however, animal dances were eventually refined, and they made their way into the salons of the social elite. The animal dance craze brought about a boom in exhibition ballroom dancers. When performed by the dancing feet of Vernon and Irene Castle, these dances became a youthful, joyous expression of elegance and class, and the symbol of a world moving hopefully into a new century.

The roots of the tango grew out of the milonga, a dance whose very name is derived from an African word meaning "argument." According to Robert Farris Thompson, however, the dance was not seen "as a predicament but as an amiable argument, an argument solved by generosity, shared values, and celebratory spirit."[9] The early duels between the compadritos and

"The Last Waltz" by Clarence F. Underwood, an early twentieth century Viennese postcard.

"The Dance," a 1906 lithograph by Howard Chandler Christy.

Italian immigrants, taunting each other with knives in the *duelo criollo*, became the elegant, ritualized footwork of the tango.

As a dance that featured individuality over matching steps with one's partner, the Charleston ignited a fire in the competitive spirit of young people around the world. Charleston contests were common. Besting someone on the dance floor was expected. It was a dance in which the body fought the constraints of control and fellow dancers were often kicked. The Charleston was seen by some as a brutal expression of a wounded generation, confused and angry after a devastating World War. It was violent — so violent that city officials feared it could bring down buildings. But it was also joyful — a release from tension and a proclamation of selfhood. When the flapper danced, she proudly proclaimed to the world that she deserved to be treated with respect and equanimity. The Charleston helped to level the playing field. In some ways, it was an expression of reconciliation between genders, classes, and races.

These dances reflected society. They revealed the era's conflicting notions about class, economics, and gender. Animal dances had their genesis in the dives and seedy dancehalls of the Barbary Coast. The tango was developed in brothels in the slaughterhouse district of Buenos Aires. The Charleston was a dance originally done by slaves brought over from Africa. All of these dances ended up in the salons and ballrooms of the rich and famous. They were greeted with shock and dismay, but they crossed social boundaries and shattered class distinctions. And like the waltz, they were democratic dances in the sense that anyone could do them. For many in the working class, keeping current with the latest trends in dancing became the symbol of modernity and a way of gaining status by imitating the moves of the wealthy. Hours spent in rigorous study with a dancing master gave way to learning the dance from friends, or a cheap dance manual, or a motion picture short. There were still instructors, of course, but the new dances were accessible to everyone. As the anthem of the ragtime age pointed out, everybody was "doing it."

Class distinctions were blurred by venue as well. The invitation-only, formal ballroom gave way to the public dance hall. Reformers may have warned that the dance halls could be dens of iniquity, but thousands flocked to them, radically changing the landscape of American urban culture. During the prohibition years, speakeasies flourished. Bankers, actors, criminals, and socialites intermingled in these smokey nightspots reflecting a dynamic shift in American class structure.

These dances brought financial success to some and left others deep in debt. They affected aspects of entertainment, fashion, and music — even influencing building codes. Business booms and busts reflected the economic impact of these dance crazes, and similarly the dances reflected the economic trends of the day.

Issues of gender were mirrored in the steps of the animal dances, the tango and the Charleston. As working class women crowded into dancehalls, they challenged old sterotypes about the roles of women in society. The sheltered Victorian maiden gave way to a more independent woman who could attend a dance without a chaperone and dance with a man of her own choosing. For many young immigrant women, dancing an animal dance was an expression of American individualism.

The tango and the woman who did it were provocative. She exposed her sexual nature openly by allowing the man to press his body over hers in a dip in public. In the book *Tango! The Dance, the Song, the Story*, the authors wrote,

> No dance plays command against subjugation as supremely and concisely as the tango does. More than any other dance, it is gender-led. The tradition of the male as leader who sets the protocol and the female as subordinate, subject to a few extroverted flourishes to enhance the male's decorum, is a long-standing etiquette of gender relations....[10]

While dancing the tango, however, the female had parity. The man and woman embraced with equal force and "...for every thrust of the male there [was] a female parry...."[11] As the woman kicked or stepped her leg between the man's legs, she symbolically invaded his domain and in doing so, suggested his vulnerability.

The tango brought important changes in women's liberation. These changes were signaled when women discarded their constricting hobble skirts, and replaced them with daring slit skirts and trouserettes so that they could match men's strides.

The Charleston changed women forever. Corsets and long curly locks came off; hemlines and spirits went up. It was a dance of joyous abandon and a symbol of physical freedom. The Charleston was energetic, optimistic, and openly erotic. It reflected the emancipation of women. It required strength, stamina, athleticism, and chutzpah. The dancing flapper was the modern woman.

The Charleston was also the first dance readily accepted by men. Up until this time, dancing was not considered a manly art. The Charleston made it acceptable for men to move their bodies in public without threatening their masculinity.

In Conclusion

On March 10, 1963, the *Independent Press-Telegram* in Long Beach, California, ran an interview with famed choreographer Eugene Loring, entitled "What's the Twist Doing to Us?" The interviewer observed that the twist seemed to be a reflection of the uncertainty and turmoil of the day, and questioned Mr. Loring about his reaction to the latest dancing fad. Loring responded, "Violence in dancing is as cyclical as wars and the social upheaval they bring...."[12]

Dance fads throughout the decades have been a manifestation of society's beliefs, values, attitudes, confusions, and concerns. Radical changes in dancing styles have portended radical changes in class structure, economics, and gender identity. They have reflected coming changes and mirrored society's resistance to these changes. Dance fads have given physical form to social confusion and offered a controlled outlet for this turmoil. They have often provided a solution for resolving crisis through a physical acting out of the issue.

The wicked waltz and other scandalous dances not only reflected society, but also shaped it. They compelled the world to decide what was beautiful, what was decent, and what was modern. They embodied both violence and grace, and they set the world dancing.

Chapter Notes

Chapter 1

1. Extracted from Billy Sunday's sermon "Backsliding" (available at several on-line sources).

2. Author unknown (available at several on-line sources)

3. Ann Wagner, *Adversaries of Dance: From the Puritans to the Present*. (Chicago: University of Illinois, 1997) p. 236, quoting Billy Sunday.

4. Members of the primitive Christian Church believed that angels danced in adoration around the throne of God, and after death, the blessed joined in this dance in Paradise. Ring dances were used in religious rituals to imitate this heavenly dance on earth. The use of dance was so common in the early Church that it was used after most prayers, during baptism rituals, during the ordination of priests, and on many other occasions.

5. Wagner, p. 10.

6. Louis E. Backman, *Religious Dances in the Christian Church and in Popular Medicine*. (London: George Allen & Unwin, 1952) p. 32, quoting St. Chrysostom.

7. Wagner, p. 7.

8. *Ibid*.

9. Wagner, p. 9, quoting Fabritius.

10. Wagner, p. 21.

11. Wagner, p. 14, quoting Henri Cornelius Agrippa's *Of Vanitie and uncertaintie of Artes and Sciences*.

12. Wagner, p. 27.

13. There were proponents of dancing during the Elizabethan era such as Sir Thomas Elyot, advisor to Henry VIII, who believed that the partner formations in proper dancing not only reflected the order and harmony of holy matrimony but was a model for it. The ideal wife followed her husband's lead, just a lady followed a gentleman on the dance floor. Sir John Davies reaffirmed this concept in his poem *Orchestra, or a Poem of Dancing* (1596). He wrote, "For whether forth or back or round he go, As doth the man, so must the woman do" (Wagner, p. 23).

14. Opponents to dancing felt that it was wrong to dance on the Sabbath since it was ordained as a day of rest and contemplation. In tandem with dancing's tendency to lead people into impure thoughts, participating in vigorous physical exercise, made dancing on a Sunday doubly sinful.

15. Wagner, p. 28.

16. Historians believe that Increase Mather was incited to write his anti-dance treatise after Francis Stepney, a Boston dancing master, claimed that he could teach more "Divinity" in "one Play" of his dance lessons than either the local Puritan preacher, the Reverend Willard, or the Old Testament. Area clergymen were outraged and took Stepney to court where he was ordered to stand trial for "Blasphemous Words; and Reviling the Government." Stepney was found guilty and was fined one hundred pounds. Stepney ran away without paying his debt, reconfirming the prevailing belief that dancing masters were of low character. Mather's anti-dance tract came out twelve days after Stepney's conviction.

17. Increase Mather, "An Arrow Against Profane and Promiscuous Dancing" (Boston: Printed by Samuel Green, and sold by Joseph Brunning, 1684) np.

"Mixt" or "gynaecandrical" (couple) dancing was especially frowned upon because the Puritans believed it led to sexual misconduct and therefore broke the Seventh Commandment, "Thou shalt not commit adultery." One Puritan, William Prynne wrote,

> Dancing serves no necessary use! No profitable laudable or pious end at all.... The way to heaven is too steep, too narrow for men to dance and keep revel rout. No way is large or smooth enough for capering roisters, for skipping, jumping, dancing dames but that broad, beaten pleasant road that leads to Hell.

(Richard Nevel, *A Time to Dance: American Country Dancing from Hornpipes to Hot Hash*. (New York: St. Martin's Press, 1977) p. 29, quoting William Prynne's *Histriomatrix*.)

18. Wagner, p. 49, quoting Increase Mather's *Testimony Against several Prophane and Superstitious Customs* (1668).

The Puritans objected to Maypole dancing because of its pagan origins. Dancing which was tied to drinking or feasting was also frowned upon. Certain mild forms of dance were accepted if they were used to teach manners to children. Group contra-dances that utilized formations were also accepted. In 1684, ministers in Boston issued a tract that stated that mixed dancing of any kind was sinful but did admit that dance could be used to teach children "due poyse and Composure of Body," if they were sent to the proper kind of teacher, "a grave person who will teach them decency of behaviour, and each sex by themselves." The tract reminded ministers that they were not even allowed to be a spectator at an event where dancing took place.

(Quotes from *An Arrow Against the Profane and Promiscuous Dancing, drawn out of the quiver of the Scriptures. By the Ministers of Christ at Boston in New-England* by Increase Mather, 1684.)

19. In the United States, issues of race and economics, especially in regards to African American culture deeply influenced society's negative perceptions about dancing. Many were opposed to dancing simply because the movements and rhythms were associated with blacks. In a similar way, folk traditions such as those that influenced the development of the waltz were sometimes viewed as too earthy and therefore uncivilized.

20. Wagner, p. 55.

21. Cotton Mather, "A Cloud of Witness; Darting out Light upon a Case, too Unseasonably made Seasonable to be Discoursed on" (Boston: [B. Green and J Allen], [1700]). Mather is actually quoting M. Rabutin, "in his Instructions to his Children."

22. Wagner, p. 93, quoting Oliver Hart's "Dancing Exploded. A Sermon showing the unlawfulness, sinfulness and bad consequences of balls, assemblies, and dances in general; preached in Charleston S.C., 22 March 1778."

23. Wagner, p. 93, quoting Oliver Hart.

24. Wagner, P. 107.

25. The desire to be part of the privileged class was a pressing concern for Americans trying to advance themselves dur-

ing the nineteenth century. As the nouveau riche attempted to buy their way into acceptance, sending their sons to the best schools, building huge mansions, and trying to outdo one another by purchasing expensive jewels and lavish apparel, they realized that to a certain extent, social acceptance could be "bought" with a few dance lessons. Knowing the correct way to move on the ballroom floor provided a certification of social standing. The urban elite rushed to the nearest dancing master for instruction in manners and deportment. They snatched up the latest books on how to dance and searched for tidbits of advice that would help them advance in society. The explanation of steps in these dance manuals was almost secondary; the main topic of interest was how dancing could express *savoir faire*. The obsession with polite social graces consumed a rapidly expanding prosperous middle class and fueled a prolific outpouring of courtesy literature. Myriad etiquette books and numerous dance manuals with extensive sections on self-improvement, manners, and deportment were written to teach the minute details of proper behavior on or off the dance floor. Careful study was required so that those striving to advance had an intimate knowledge of the customs and refinements that gracious living demanded. Strict standards regulated high society, and those who wished to be accepted in the *haut monde* had to play by the rules.

In 1879, the author of *Social Etiquette of New York* wrote,

> Etiquette is the machinery of society. It polishes and protects even while conducting its charge. It prevents the agony of uncertainty, and soothes even when it cannot cure the pains of blushing bashfulness.... It is like a wall built up around us to protect us from disagreeable, underbred people, who refuse to take the trouble to be civil.... If one is certain of being correct, there is little to be anxious about.

(Quote extracted from *Social Etiquette of New York*. (New York, 1879) pp. [7]–9. This version was taken from Elizabeth Aldrich's book *From the Ballroom to Hell: Grace and Folly in Nineteenth-century Dance*, p. 55.)

Although dance manuals and etiquette books helped many to achieve their goal of attaining higher social status, the stringent protocol set out in these books also created a barrier for some; the slightest faux pas could brand them forever, as outsiders. Dance manuals covered every subject of ballroom behavior: how to respond to an invitation; how to enter the room; how to converse; and of course, how to dance with grace and modesty. Victorian courtesy literature also offered explicit advice about how to give a proper ball. Elizabeth Aldrich cites many interesting and humorous examples in her book. On p. 117–118, she quotes *Manners and Tone of Good Society, By a Member of the Aristocracy*:

> Several fashionable ball-givers are beginning to perceive the folly of crowding two hundred to three hundred people together into rooms not properly ventilated, and have discovered that the only way in which to render the temperature of a London ball comparatively cool, is to remove the windows, and substitute lace draperies in lieu of bunting, with the addition of large blocks of ice placed in every convenient spot.

On p. 116, she quotes *The Habits of Good Society: A Handbook for Ladies and Gentlemen*:

> [A] polished floor, whatever the wood, is always the best thing to dance on, and, if you want to give a ball, and not only a crush, you should hire a man who, with a brush under one foot and a slipper on the other, will dance over the floor for four or five hours, till you can almost see your face in it.

26. Wagner, p. 113.

27. *Social Mirror* (St. Louis: 1888) p. 17, extracted from Aldrich, p. 59.

28. The Second Great Awakening was characterized by a spirit of energetic evangelical activism. Whereas leaders of the first Great awakening stressed the inherent sinful nature of man and his lack of power to overcome this nature without the direct intervention of God through the Holy Spirit, evangelicals of the Second Great Awakening focused on sin as a result of human action, preaching that man had the ability to resist sin consciously. This doctrinal stance significantly influenced anti-dance literature by placing emphasis on moral action.

29. Wagner, p. 117, quoting Charles Grandison Finney's *Hindrances to Revivals* (Boston: Willard Tract Repository, n.d.) p. 118.

In addition to condemning social dancing during this period, conservative revivalists criticized another disturbing threat to rational behavior. During the height of the Revivalist movement, frontier camp meetings often bordered on hysteria. Huge numbers of worshippers, drawn up in the fervor of the moment, manifested wild physical symptoms called "exercises." Although these spontaneous ecstatic movements were thought by many to be true manifestations of the Holy Spirit, they troubled conservative members of the Protestant Church because they were uncontrolled, unsightly, and too similar to dancing for comfort. These exercises took various forms, the most common being "jerking," in which first the arms and then the entire body twitched uncontrollably. In his autobiography, published in 1856, Methodist minister, Peter Cartwright described the practice:

> A new exercise broke out among us, called the jerks, which was overwhelming in its effects upon the bodies and minds of the people. No matter whether they were saints or sinners, they would be taken under a warm song or sermon, and seized with a convulsive jerking all over, which they could not possibly avoid, and the more they resisted the more they jerked. If they would not strive against it and pray in good earnest, the jerking would usually abate. I have seen more than five hundred persons jerking at one time in my large congregations. Most usually persons taken with the jerks, to obtain relief, as they said, would rise up and dance. Some would run, but could not get away. Some would resist; on such the jerks were generally very severe.

(Noel Rae, editor. *Witnessing America: The Library of Congress Book of Firsthand Accounts of Life in America 1600–1900*. (New York: Penguin, 1996) p.393, quoting Peter Cartwright's Autobiography, 1856.)

Moralists of the early nineteenth century placed great emphasis upon controlled, rational, reasonable behavior, and "dancing exercises" such as the "jerks" were seen as extremely vulgar and disturbing.

> Whenever a woman was taken with the jerks at a camp meeting her friends formed a circle about her, for the exercise was so violent that she could scarcely maintain a correct posture. Men would go bumping about over benches, into trees, bruising and cutting themselves, if friends did not catch and hold them. Some were ashamed of having the jerks, but most persons agreed that it was impossible to resist them.

(Marshall Stearns, *The Story of Jazz*. (New York: Oxford University Press, 1956) p.87, quoting G. G. Johnson, *Ante-Bellum North Carolina* (Chapel Hill: The University of North Carolina Press, 1937) p.399.)

30. Theories of evolution proposed by Charles Darwin and later discussed by Herbert Spenser and Edward Burnett Tylor dominated intellectual thought in the second part of the nineteenth century. These evolutionists touted a linear development of culture and viewed Africans as being on the lower end of the spectrum. European culture on the other hand represented the pinnacle of evolution. Social Darwinism taught that there was a progression from primitivism to

civilization and that primal, savage urges lay just below the surface. Succumbing to these urges in the dance was a dangerous slide backwards down the ladder of evolution and was thought to signify the downfall of civilization.

31. Fanny Essler was of Austrian decent. Her meteoric rise to international fame was largely due to the manipulation of the director of the Paris Opera, Dr. Véron, who manufactured a competition between Essler and another ballet star, Marie Taglioni. Véron masterfully fueled his publicity machine by pitting both ballerinas against each other until their rivalry was the talk of Paris. Eventually things reached such a fever pitch, both women had had enough of the petty sniping and comparisons and left Paris altogether. Taglioni toured to Russia, and Essler opted for the United States. Both had sensational success. Essler is credited with developing and popularizing balletic character dance. Her most famous dance was a solo entitled *La Cachucha*, inspired by Spanish dancers she had seen in Paris. It remained her most popular dance throughout her career. Essler was never married but had two children. She died in 1884, and was mourned by all Vienna. Taglioni died the same year in Marseilles. Her passing went virtually unnoticed.

32. Wagner, p. 141, quoting H. W. Beecher's *Lectures to Young Men on Various Important Subjects* (Cincinnati: Wm. H. Moore, and Asalem: John P Jewett, 1846) p. 248.

33. Wagner, 152, quoting William S. Potts, *A Sermon on Certain Popular Amusements of the Day* (St. Louis: Keith and Woods, 1848.)

34. Wagner, p. 120, quoting *A Few Reflections upon the Fancy Ball, Otherwise Known as the City Dancing Assembly* (Philadelphia: G. R. Lilibridge, 1828) p. 3–4. In his book *The Dance of Modern Society.* (New York: Funk & Wagnalls, 1892), p 39, William Cleaver Wilkinson also accused dance of being anti–American. He wrote, "...the dance being such has contributed to the creation of that meretricious taste in dress which seriously threatens, through its direct and indirect economic influence, to corrupt and deteriorate the very basis of our American society."

35. Professor T. A Faulkner was a former dancing master who gave up his profession to teach the world about the evils of dancing. His book *From the Ballroom to Hell* became a classic among the anti-dance literature genre and was frequently cited by other writers. In another of his books, *The Lure of the Dance: with Christ at the Ball.* (Chicago: George W. Noble, 1916), in the dedication and on p. 9, Faulkner explains his change of heart in two different stories. In the first, he says he stopped teaching dance after his eighteen-year old sister Ada, "a victim of dance-hall lust," said on her deathbed, "Sound the Warning, Tom, that other girls may be saved." Faulkner states that in obedience to her dying wish, he renounced the teaching of dancing and went on a mission to save other maidens from its horrible effects. In another version, Faulkner states that he ran into a former student of his who was "on her way to destruction," and he pleaded with her to return home. The woman turned on him and lashed out at him, saying, "Mr. Faulkner, when you close your dancing school and stop the business which is sending so many girls by swift stages on the straight road to Hell, girls who were pure and innocent when they entered your (and other) dance halls, then sir, and not until then, have you the right to ask me to reform, as you are doing, for your dancing school was the cause of my downfall — and mother was equally to blame, for she took me there." According to Faulkner, this event sparked in him a conversion experience and he realized that as a dancing master, he really was nothing more than the "Devil's Advance Agent," as he put it.

36. T. A. Faulkner, *From the Ballroom to Hell.* (Chicago: R. B. McKnight, 1894) p. 22.

37. Faulkner, p. 47.

38. T. A. Faulkner, *The Lure of the Dance: with Christ at the Ball.* (Chicago: George W. Noble, 1916) pp. 60–61, quoting Dr. Frank C Richardson.

39. Ernest Bell, *Fighting the Traffic in Young Girls or War*

on the White Slave Trade. (no city or publisher listed, 1910) p. 112.

40. H. W. Lytle, and John Dillon. *From Dance Hall to White Slavery.* (Chicago: Charles C. Thompson, 1912) introductory page, quoting Lester Bodine.

41. Lytle, p. 8, quoting the *Investigation of the Social Evil in Chicago by the Municipal Vice Commission.*

42. Lytle, introductory page, quoting Jane Addams.

43. Tom Sims, "New U.S. Dance Seen by Sims" *Reno Evening Gazette*, Reno, NV, September 28, 1925, p. 8, col. 3.

44. Catherine Rehart, *The Valley's Legends and Legacies.* (Sanger, CA: Quill Driver Books/Word Dancer Press, 1996) p.228.

45. Jim Dawson, *The Twist: The Story of the Song and Dance the Changed the World.* (Boston: Faber & Faber, 1995) p. 60.

46. Dawson, p. 61.

47. Dawson, p. 117.

48. Bruce Becker, *Penn State Daily Collegian*, April 30, 1979, p. 13, quoting Rod Fizz.

49. Wagner, p. 348.

Chapter 2

1. Desmond F. Strobel, "Waltz." In *International Encyclopedia of Dance.* Vol. 6. Ed. Selma Jeanne Cohen, p. 359–362. (New York: Oxford University Press, 1998) p.359.

2. Lloyd Shaw in *The Round Dance Book; A Century of Waltzing*, p. 101, suggests that the waltz's roots should be traced to Spain. He states, "...our modern waltz did develop from European modifications of an old step of the Basques...." In the web article "Opus No. 3/4 on the Origins and Early History of the Waltz," July 1998, Kim Mallet mentions that the French guillotine dance, the Carmagnole, was also one of the waltz's antecedents. In his anti-dance book *The Lure of the Dance: with Christ at the Ball.* (Chicago: George W. Noble, 1916), p. 18, T. A Faulkner explains that the waltz originated with a French dancing master named Gault in 1632. Faulkner writes, "He was licentious in the deepest sense of the word, and gloried in the fact that he had led many girls into lives of sin and shame. He had gone down so low in the moral scale that, finally, in an attempt to ruin his own sister he strangled her to death, for which he was guillotined in 1632."

3. The word volta was used in both Italian (*volta*—to turn) and French (*volte, voltare*—to turn) as part of the technical terminology of *escrime* (fencing), meaning to leap aside to avoid a thrust, in *dressage* (horsemanship), meaning the gait of a horse moving sideways then turning around a center, as well as in dancing. In her dance manual *The Dance, Ancient and Modern* (1900) p. 26, Arabella E. Moore says the word "volta" is derived from the word *voltiger* meaning "to flutter." Ms. Moores writes, "as one seems to do in the waltz, where the movements of the butterfly are imitated...." During the Renaissance, the term was used to refer to any turning couple dance. The word first appeared in dance manuals in Italy sometime in the 15th century. Although usually associated with France and Italy, the volta was also popular in other parts of Europe. Engravings show it in Westphalia as early as 1538. The volta is similar to another partner dance that was popular in France and Italy called la nizzarda, or the "The Girl from Nice," (also known as "The Dance of Nice.") Performed at court beginning in the fourteenth century up through the sixteenth century, this energetic dance is described in Cesare Negri's important dance manual, *Le gratie d'amore* (1602) reissued two years later as *Nuove inventioni di balli*. Although the partners performing la nizzarda also danced in a closed embrace, according to Negri's vague explanation of the dance, the turns were done with low hops and did not involve the high lift that characterized the volta. Later

descriptions do mention high lifts and greatly resemble the volta described by Negri's contemporary Thoinot Arbeau. Some dance scholars believe the two dances are one and the same.

4. Paul Nettl, *The Story of Dance Music*. (New York: Philosophical Library, 1947) p. 101, suggests that the root of the word "galliard" is *galleus* meaning "a gall-apple," which in turn indicates "in full bloom." The more common association was with the word "gay." Shaw, p. 102, states that the word "galliard" was used as an adjective such as in the phrase "Let's be galliard and brisk."

5. The pavane (pavan, paven, pavin) Ital. *Pavana, padovana,* Fr., *pavane,* Ger., *paduana,* was a solemn, ceremonial procession used to open a ball or accompany the entrance of the king. Many dance scholars suggest that the word "pavane" was derived from the Spanish word *pavón* (or Latin *pavo*) meaning "peacock," and that the dance's slow, stately movements were choreographed so that the courtier with his sword and robe and his partner with her long train could strut proudly like peacocks and show off all their fine regalia. One circular pattern in the dance also resembled the spreading of a peacock's tail. W. G. Raffé (*Dictionary of Dance*, p. 375) says this derivation is incorrect and the name of the dance springs from *pavi-ment* which means "path" or "way" or *pavimentum* or "pavement." Other sources state that "pavane" is probably derived from the name of the town of Padua, Italy. According to Troy and Margaret Kinney in *The Dance: Its Place in Art and Life.* (New York: Tudor, 1936) p. 56, the pavane was introduced by conquistador Hernando Cortez (1485–1547), who learned the dance in America, and brought it back to the Spanish court. The form of the pavane was utilized in the Grand March that began all formal balls in the nineteenth century, and today, parts of the ancient dance are still apparent when a bride walks down the aisle in all her finery.

6. When the caper was executed properly, the woman could spring into the air to surprising heights with the aid of the man. The movement created a certain syncopation, with the lift beginning with a preparation on count four, the lady airborne on count five, and the lady landing on the "and" count before six. The rhythm is easily understood if one sings the opening line of "My Country 'Tis of Thee." or "God Save the Queen." In the galliard, the caper, or cabriole, was an opportunity for the male dancer to demonstrate his athleticism with leg beats. Shakespeare mentions the caper in his play *Twelfth Night* when the character of Sir Tobey is asked about his ability to dance a galliard. He responds, "I can cut a caper."

7. The Cinque-pace or Cinq-pas was derived from fencing positions. The five steps consisted of:

  (a) *droite,* a straight move forward or back
  (b) *ouvert,* opening sideways
  (c) *ronde,* sweeping the foot on the floor
  (d) *glissé,* sliding the foot as in a glissade.
  (e) *tournée,* turning.

Other moves were added later including jumps and beats. The dance ended with *la salute,* a bow similar to the révérence.

8. Shaw, p. 103, relates that fifty-six year old Queen Elizabeth "took her morning exercise by dancing six or seven galliards as soon as she arose." The queen is reputed to have still been able to dance a lusty galliard at age seventy. Fond of all types of dancing, Queen Elizabeth is also reputed to have based her political favors on a courtier's ability to perform well in the pavane (Eng. pavin), rather than based upon his statesmanship. She frequently asked the members of her court point-blank who was the better dancer, her rival, Mary Queen of Scots, or their own monarch.

9. Arbeau, Thoinot, *Orchesography*. Translated by Mary Stewart Evans. (New York: Dover Publications, 1967) p.121.

10. Thoinot Arbeau, an anagram for the author's real name, Jehan Tabourot, was born into a distinguished family in Dijon, France around 1519 or 1520. His given name, Tabourot, is related to the word "tabor" and suggests that his family may have had something to do with drumming. Arbeau studied in Dijon, Poitiers, and possibly Paris eventually becoming the treasurer of the Chapter of Langres in 1542, and finally the vicar-general of the diocese. He wrote *Orchésocraphie (Orchesography)* at a time in history when religious dances were being re-introduced into the church and social dancing was growing in popularity following the *Ballet Comique de la Reine.* Arbeau completed the writing of *Orchésocraphie* at the age of sixty-nine and died the same year. The manuscript was discovered among his papers after his death and was published posthumously with permission from his family. His treatise on the dance remains one of the most detailed and important records of sixteenth century dance. According to Troy and Margaret Kinney, *The Dance: Its Place in Art and Life.* (New York: Tudor, 1936) p. 31, Arbeau commented on those who opposed dancing by remarking:

> We practice such merry-making on days of wedding celebrations, and of the solemnities of the feast of our Church, even though reformers abhor such things; but in this matter they deserve to be treated like some hind-quarter of goat put into dough without lard.

(Dough baked without lard hardens to the consistency of concrete.)

11. Arbeau, p. 122. On p.121 of the same translation, Arbeau states,

> ... after having spun around for as many cadences as you wish return the damsel to her place, when, however brave a face she shows, she will feel her brain reeling and her head full of dizzy whirlings; and you yourself will perhaps be no better off. I leave you to judge whether it is a becoming thing for a young girl to take large strides and separations of the legs, and whether in this lavolta both honour and health are not involved and at stake.

12. Eduard Reeser, *The History of the Waltz,* (London: Sidwick and Jackson, nd.) pp.4–5, quoting Johan von Münster's *Gottseliger Tractat von dem ungottseligen Tantz,* 1592.

13. Reeser, quoting Johann Praetorius' *Blocksberg-Verrichtungen,* 1668, p. 5–6. Julia Sutton in the *International Encyclopedia of Dance.* Vol. 6. (New York: Oxford University Press, 1998) p. 349–51, quotes Guillaume Bouchet, from his book *Les Serées* (1597) with almost the identical words;

> The *volta* [and] the *courante* ... which magicians have brought from Italy to France, besides their rude and bold movements, have the misfortune of causing an infinite number of murders and miscarriages, killing and destroying all who are yet unborn.

14. Lloyd Shaw, *The Round Dance Book: A Century of Waltzing.* (Caldwell, Idaho: Caxton Printers, 1948) p.104.

15. Allison Thompson, *Dancing Through Time: Western Social Dance in Literature, 1400–1918: Selections.* (Jefferson, NC: McFarland, 1998) p. 11.

16. Thompson, p. 11.

17. Joan Lawson, *European Folk Dance.* (London: Sir Isaac Pittman & Sons, 1953) p. 14, states that true couple dancing did not develop until the creation of the Provençal courts during the eleventh and twelfth centuries when the Provence area in southern France became an important center of culture. It was here that the troubadours, aristocratic poet-musicians, developed the idea of romantic courtly love from a mixture of Latin, Arabic and Christian sources. Adopting the sensuality of Arabic poetry from the Muslim courts of Andalusia and mixing it with the veneration of the Virgin Mary, these entertainers established the code of chivalry in which a knight offered humble, steadfast service to his lady even if that lady was unattainable. This concept of "loving from a distance," with no suggestion of infidelity, helped to

preserve decorum and at the same time heighten the romantic aspects. Called *fin amor,* or true love, this concept became an important theme that was carried through in literature, language, music, and in the development of new dance forms, eventually spreading through Europe and influencing culture for centuries. Lawson points out that the ideal of *fin amor* fostered the development of a strict code of social behavior. This in turn promoted the refinement of peasant dance movements that were appropriated by the aristocracy. She writes,

> For example, the man's forward thrust of the body and his embracing and carrying off the woman became the dignified kneeling before the lady of his choice, and the delicate giving of hands as he led her down the room; or the girl's violent gesture of repulse and attempt to escape became the admonishing shake of the finger and a shy turn of the head; and the triumphant flinging of the girl in the fertility leap became the dainty twist under the man's arm.

The concept of correct social behavior as expressed through the dance became a crucial aspect within the development of ballroom dancing. As ballroom dancing was being formulated, proper etiquette and correct manners were as important as the ability to dance well. It is possible to trace the connection between dancing and courtesy to practices that developed in the Provençal courts during the medieval period. In *Joseph Campbell: The Power of Myth with Bill Moyers.* Ed. Betty Sue Flowers. (New York: Doubleday, 1988) p. 193, Campbell points out that one of the five virtues of medieval knighthood was courtesy. Campbell states,

> And the medieval idea, in spite of the fact that these people were in protest against the ecclesiastical authorities, was respect for the society in which they were participating. Everything was done according to the rules. When two knights fought, they did not violate the rules of combat although they were engaged in *mortal* combat. This courtesy has to be held in mind.

Campbell relates how these rules of courtesy were equally important in regards to women.

> It was a very strange period because it was terribly brutal. There was no central law. Everyone was on his own, and, of course, there were great violations of everything. But within this brutality, there was civilizing force, which the women really represented because they were the ones who established the rules for this game. And the men had to play it according to the requirements of the women.

The correct treatment of women permeated various social dance forms, not only as demonstrated in the volta, but also later in the minuet. In his book *The Social Dances of the Nineteenth Century in England,* (London, Herbert Jenkins, 1960) p. 41, Philip J. S. Richardson states that the minuet was, "...originally a mid–seventeenth-century attempt to symbolize the chivalry of the Middle Ages and to revive the ideology of the Troubadours and Minnesingers...." The concept of "loving from a distance" in the minuet was also briefly explored by Ruth Katz in her article "The Egalitarian Waltz." In *Comparative Studies in Society and History.* (June 1973. Katz points out that the geometric uniformity and formality of the minuet did not allow for individual expression and therefore kept dancers at a distance. She adds, "The hoop skirt symbolized additional restraint and 'distance.'" (p. 173) In his book *World History of the Dance.* (New York: W.W. Norton, 1937) pp. 398–99, Curt Sachs comments,

> [T]he erotic is stylized to the last degree, everything is suggested, refined, and generalized to the point of formalism. Eros here is devotion, not love; discipline,

not impulse. To dance the minuet is to pay homage to the woman.

18. The Provençal troubadours were a literary community of wealthy aristocrats who wrote their poetry in a unique, medieval, southern French dialect called *langue d'oc. Langue d'oc,* which literally means "the language of yes," a reference to how the people of the region said "yes" (*oc*), had evolved from spoken Latin, and became the language with which troubadours created their innovative court poetry. The word "troubadour" is derived from the Provençal word *trobar,* "to find." These men were primarily interested in their literary pursuits and they relied upon assistants to perform their works. These assistants, known as *jongleurs,* were itinerant entertainers who juggled, sang, told stories, and attached themselves to troubadours at various courts. During the fourteenth century these jongleurs formed brotherhoods and began to adopt the name *ménétrier,* and later *ménestrel,* to denote a higher social class. It is from these words that the word "minstrel" is derived. In Northern France, troubadours were called *trouvères* and in Germany, they were known as *minnesingers.* German *minnesingers* began by imitating the Provençal troubadours, but during the thirteenth and fourteenth centuries, they expanded the art form and developed an original German style of courtly love poetry. Wagner's opera *Tannhäusser* is based upon the *minnesinger* tradition.

19. The Albigensian Crusade was a brutal, bloody war that lasted from about 1203 to 1229. The Crusade was called by Pope Innocent III, who wanted to eradicate a religious group that lived in south central France called the Cathars (or Cathari). The pope believed the group posed a threat to the Church's authority. The Crusade began as a war against heresy but evolved into a struggle for political and economic gain for an ambitious papacy. The Cathars held a dualistic view of the universe, believing in the coexistence of God, who ruled the spiritual realm, and Satan, who ruled the realm of the flesh, both entities being of equal power. Because of this belief, members of the sect believed that the most grievous sin was to perpetrate the world of the flesh or Satan. Therefore, Cathars abstained from sex and ate no food that was produced by sex, such as meat or eggs. One peculiar practice of the sect was suicide, often by starvation, to hasten the release from the evilness of the flesh. Members cultivated an aesthetic lifestyle and rejected the traditional priesthood and sacraments of the Catholic Church. They rejected prayer and viewed the veneration of holy images as useless. The Cathar church developed its own liturgy and elected its own bishops and deacons, believing that their religion was the only true Christian faith. After several futile attempts to root out the Cathars by sending various papal legates to the region to convert the heretics, Pope Innocent III finally ordered the use of force when one of his representatives was assassinated. The pope offered indulgences for any willing to fight for his cause and promised to offer the lands of the conquered Cathars to the victors. Many knights rushed to join the crusade in hopes of gaining wealth. The war became known as the Albigensian Crusade after the town of Albi that was a center of the Cathar movement. At the height of the Crusade, hundreds of Cathars were burned at the stake. Although the major part of the Crusade ended around 1229 with the Peace of Paris, sporadic fighting continued until 1255. Concern about the spread of Albigensianism and the Cathar sect led to the creation of the medieval Inquisition which specifically targeted the sect until 1279, continuing the practice in special tribunals even after that date.

20. In 1533, Catherine de Medici married the duc d'Orleans when both were fourteen-years-old. The duc d'Orleans, who later became Henri II, King of France, began a relationship with a thirty-five year old widow named Diane de Poitiers, (also known as Madame de Valentinois, or Duchesse de Valentinois) one year after his marriage. Valentinois became the king's confidante and wielded considerable influence at court for twenty-five years, even signing official

court documents. Arabella E. Moore, in her book *The dance, ancient and modern, translated from the French.* (Philadelphia: 1900) p. 26, wrote, "Madame de Valentinois, in the time of Francis the first, was very fond of this dance [the volta], and while dancing it sang the psalms translated by Clement Marot." (Francis I was Henri II's father.) Catherine de Medici was largely ignored during the reign of her husband and his successor, her eldest son Francis II. She gained prominence by assuming the role of regent for her second son Charles IX when he ascended the throne in 1560. She acted as Charles' advisor until his death in 1574. It was during reign of her third son, Henry III that the Italian dance, *la volta* became most popular. Catherine de Medici's influence upon the world of dance reached its zenith when the queen mother commissioned a spectacle to climax a two-week celebration honoring the marriage of Henry III's court favorite, the duc de Joyeuse to the queen's sister, Marguerite de Lorraine, daughter of Nicholas de Vaudemont. The royal entertainment was called *Le Ballet Comique de la Reine* (or *Le Balet Comique de La Royne*). This event is considered by most dance scholars to be the first ballet. The spectacle lasted five hours and cost an estimated six hundred thousand to one million dollars. The performance was a mixture of mythology, politics, and Old Testament tales presented in music, poetry, and dance called the *Ballet of Circe*. The revels were presented at the Louvre and featured elaborate costumes and scenic designs as well as special effects. It was choreographed by an Italian violinist named Baltazarini di Belgiojoso, who took the French name Balthazar de Beaujoyeulx. Beaujoyeulx became Catherine's *valet de chamber* and was responsible for staging her court entertainments. The ballet was presented on October 15, 1581 and was documented in a published work a few months later in the following year, indicating the spectacle's political and artistic importance at the time. These published notes on the choreography, along with the music and libretto were sent to every court and became the model for many other court entertainments in Europe.

21. Curt Sachs, *World History of the Dance.* (New York: W.W. Norton, 1937) p. 351.

22. Sachs, p. 352. Sachs also makes an interesting observation about the use of 3/4 rhythms in primitive cultures. On p. 194 he writes,

> [I]t is noteworthy that also in the cosmological concepts of these [primitive native] peoples the contrast between even and odd numbers is prominent.
> Among matriarchal, agricultural, moon-worshipping cultures the even numbers are regarded as sacred, while among the patriarchal, hunter, sun-worshipping cultures the uneven numbers are favored—as with rhythm.

23. The couple dance version of the schuhplattler was divided into different sections. The four sections were (a.) *nachsteigen*, (b.) *einlaufer*, (c.) *plattler*, and (d.) ländler. In the *nachsteigen* section, the man hissed, clicked his tongue, and clapped his hands as he leaped and somersaulted around his female partner in a display of technical virtuosity. The style of the dance was exaggerated; the man's body was kept erect so that the knees and feet had to be lifted up high to be hit by the hands. Arms were swung so that they flapped like wings. In the traditional form *einlaufer*, the dancer first hit the right thigh with the right hand, then the left with the left. This was repeated and then followed by hitting either foot with the right hand. Then, the left foot was hit once more with the left hand. During *plattler*, the man slapped his body continuously as his female partner spun around. The man was rewarded for his attentions to the woman in the last section of the schuhplattler, the *ländler*. According to Sachs, p. 221, there were some versions of the ländler in which the performers competed by balancing beakers of liquid on their heads while dancing.

24. Nigel Allenby Jaffé. *Folk Dances of Europe.* (North Yorkshire, England: Folk Dance Enterprises, 1990) p. 148.

Ruolieb's description of the male dancer's wooing and the female dancer's eluding of his advances is evocative of the way the ländler is still danced in remote mountainous regions of Germany today. Paul Nettl, *The Story of Dance Music.* (New York: Philosophical Library, 1947), p. 51, states that "Rudlieb" (Ruolieb) was the name of the poem, not the name of the author. Nettl relates that the poem follows the adventures of the hero Rudlieb as he visits a widow with a beautiful daughter. Two harpists perform poorly during his visit, so Rudlieb asks the widow if she has a harp he can borrow to demonstrate his ability on the instrument. He plays three songs, then is asked to play a reel. As he plays the dance music, a couple performs and Rudlieb describes their movements. Nettl points out that the poem was written in Southern Germany, "the home of the peasant dance, 'Laendler' and of the Waltz."

25. Originally, ländler melodies were rhythmical work songs that accompanied sowing, reaping, hunting, or other types of manual labor, such as that done by sailors or blacksmiths. Although the schuhplatter is based upon animal movements, certain rhythms and movements in the dance probably also developed as stylized versions of these work-based movements.

26. In her book *Dances of Austria*, (New York: Chanticleer Press, 1948) p. 8, Katherina Breuer writes, "The Ländler is thought to originate from a medieval Round dance. This, in its journey through the centuries, became a Pair dance in which the man leads the girl with complicated turns and twists to the final reunion of the pair in slow Waltz step."

27. Reeser, p. 6, quoting Sebastian Brant, *Das Narrenschiff*, chapter 61: "Von Dantzen," 1494.

28. Martin Luthur himself indicated that dancing was permissible as long as it was done modestly. He said that the sins associated with dancing were not inherent in the dance itself but rather born out of the "disorderly appetites of the dancers" Resser, p. 7.

29. Resser, p. 7, quoting Melchior Ambach, *Von Tantzen/ Vrtheil/ Ausz heilger Schrifft und den alten Christlichen Lerern gestalt*, 1543.

30. Reeser, p. 7–8, quoting Florian Daule von Fürstenberg, *Tantzteuffel d.i. wiver den leichtfertigen unverschempten Welttanz und sonderlich wider die Gotts Zucht und ehrvergessene Nachtenze*, 1567.

31. Resser, pp.10–12, quoting Böhme, *Geschichte des Tanzes in Deutschland*, 1686, stating a prohibition recorded in the Amberber Stadtbuch of 1554.

32. Kim Mallet, "Opus No. 3/4 on the Origins and Early History of the Waltz," July 1998. http://www.splittree.org/waltz/waltz.htm

33. Paul Nettl, "Birth of the Waltz" in *Dance Index*, vol. 5, number 9, November 1946, p. 214.

34. In his book *The Social Dances of the Nineteenth Century in England*, (London, Herbert Jenkins, 1960) p. 43, Philip J. S. Richardson suggests that the *allemande* might derive its name from Swabia, which was once known as Alemannia. He quotes Thomas Wilson who wrote in 1816, "Waltzing is a species of dancing that owes its origin to the Germans, having been introduced in Swabia, one of the nine circles of Germany." Nigel Allenby Jaffé. *Folk Dances of Europe.* (North Yorkshire, England: Folk Dance Enterprises, 1990) p. 156, suggests that various versions of the allemand traveled to France quite early through trade links. On p. 158, he states that the dance "was introduced into the royal court in Versailles when Alsace was incorporated into the French kingdom."

35. Rebecca Harris-Warrick, "Allemande" In *International Encyclopedia of Dance.* Vol. 1. Ed. Selma Jeanne Cohen, (New York: Oxford University Press, 1998) p. 47, quoting Giovanni Gallini, 1762.

36. Raffé, p. 21, states that the source of the *allemande* was an alms-giving ceremonial rite performed on Maundy Thursday by clerics. He traces this clerical rite even further back to two root sources; the first, an Iberian-Arabic source ref-

erenced in the Quaran, Chapter 107 entitled Al-Ma'Un, meaning "the Alms." This reference proscribed the regular collection of alms and is the etymology of the word "alimony." The second source was Sufi in origin and had to do with praying for "alms from Allah." Raffé states that the prophet Mohammed was called *Al-Min* meaning the "Faithful" or "True One." Muslim pilgrims would circle the Kaaba, the sacred stone at Mecca, seven times and chant ninety-nine of the "Hundred Names of Allah." *Al-Min* and other forms of Allah's many names became the source of the word "allemande," as well as other words such as "alumnus," "alma mater," and "almond." In a reference in Chaucer, another derivative was *leman,* or "dance partner." Paul Nettl, *The Story of Dance Music.* (New York: Philosophical Library, 1947), p. 107 states that the allemande movements were probably derived from pantomimic actions founded on primitive Germanic themes of jealousy and the kidnapping of a bride. He suggests that these themes are indicated when men cut in and stole partners.

37. A version of the allemande which utilized *tours de mains,* or "turns of the hands" was danced in France as early as the reign of Louis XIV, who was king from 1643–1715. By the 1760's, it was so popular in France that even though it was of German origin, it was virtually adopted as the French national dance.

38. According to Paul Nettl, "Birth of the Waltz," p. 214, "In colloquial German, *walzen* means *strolchen* (stamping), but can also signify *schleifen* (sliding or gliding). "Nigel Allenby Jaffé. *Folk Dances of Europe.* (North Yorkshire, England: Folk Dance Enterprises, 1990), p. 159, states that a ban of the ländler in 1748 contains the first reference to the word "walzen," and was used to describe turning or rolling movements. According to Andrew Lamb in his article "Waltz" from *The New Grove Dictionary of Music and Musicians.* Vol. 20. Ed. Stanley Sadie, (London: McMillan, 1980) p. 200, the earliest known example of music associated with the word *wälzen* is in a comedy by Felix Kurz entitled *Stegreifkomödie Der auf das neue begeisterte und belebte Bernardon (The Newly Revived and Inspired Bernardon)* from 1754. In this piece, there is reference to various styles of dancing with mention of the word *wälzen* and accompanying music, assumed to have been written by Joseph Hayden, in triple time. Lamb states that the word was first used in written form as the name of a dance in a booklet by C, von Zangen entitled *Etwas über das Walzen* in 1782. Resser, p. 1 says that the word *wälzen* was first found in print in Schiller's war-song *Graf Eberhard der Greiner von Wirtemberg,* part of the book, *Anthologie auf das Jahr,* which he mistakenly lists as published in 1882. Schiller's poem was actually published in 1782.

39. Despite the popularity of German folk dance at court, the waltz sometimes elicited negative responses. When the two Princesses of Mecklenburg first dared to do the dance at a court ball in 1794, the King was enchanted, but the Queen turned her face away in disgust and forbade her own daughters from doing the immoral dance. The Queen's ban on the waltz remained in effect at the Berlin Court until the reign of William II around 1888.

40. Mosco Carner, *The Waltz.* (New York: Chanticleer Press, 1948) p. 14.

41. One such folk tune, "Auch, du lieber Augustin," that has survived until today, is perhaps one of the earliest examples of a waltz.

42. John Playford (the Elder) was born in Norwich, England, in 1623, and made his living as a publisher of music and dance books. He began collecting country dance tunes with instructions about how to perform the accompanying dances, and published his first manual of 105 dances in 1651. Entitled *The Dancing Master, or Plaine and Easie Rules for the Dancing of Country Dances, with the Tune to Each Dance,* the book's enormous popularity led to seventeen subsequent editions. After the first edition, Playford shortened the title to *The Dancing Master* and added new dances. By the eighteenth edition the book contained more than 1,400 dances. The

importance of Playford's manual in the development of social dancing cannot be stressed enough. The effect of codifying and naming rural dances not only made them marketable to a wide audience, but also spurred a whole flurry of dance manuals that helped to further disseminate various dances.

43. Contre-dance (contredanse, contra-dance) did not draw its name from country dancing. Rather, the term referred to couples or quartets dancing in opposition or counter to each other, in figures such as two facing lines, as in the reel or longways, or in a square, as in the quadrille. Contre-dances featured active and inactive couples. The active couple started at the end of the column (or on one particular side of the square in a quadrille) and was the couple that did the most movement, progressing through various patterns until they eventually reached the opposite end of the column. Inactive couples moved up one position at a time until each one arrived at the head of the line and became the active couple. Although contre-dances emphasized relationships between the various dancers, they still did not allow for the intimacy inherent in the waltz when partners danced as an isolated unit.

44. Emphasis on rank and status was all consuming in French court dancing during the seventeenth and eighteenth centuries. One's place on the dance floor was determined by one's position at court in relationship to the king. Rigorous training with a dancing master and meticulous attention to proper etiquette and the prescribed protocol was strictly regimented. A misstep could lead to a loss of favor and therefore, a loss of one's place in the hierarchy. Describing one ball at Versailles in 1775, Horace Walpole explained how even Marie Antoinette made sure to execute the elaborate figures and patterns of the minuet without turning her back to her husband, King Louis XVI, when he decided not to dance that evening. Status was so important in the court at Versailles that every opportunity was taken to assert one's rank. This obsession with pedigree was even demonstrated in the practice of attending chapel. During services both dukes and princes could kneel on cushions, but only Princes of the Blood could place the cushions at a straight angle on the floor.

45. The exclusivity of the minuet was fostered in various ways. In addition to the proscribed social hierarchy that strictly dictated who could join the dance, participation in the minuet also required formal training in order to master the intricate steps and complex social graces that played an integral part of the display. Since only the wealthy could afford to hire dancing masters to train them in the art, those that danced the minuet were limited to the privileged few. A proper and pleasing physique was also required of those that wished to dance the minuet. In the book *Revolving Embrace: The Waltz as Sex, Steps, and Sound.* (Hillsdale, NY: Pendragon Press, 2002), p. 2, Sevin H. Yaraman writes,

> "Well shaped," "undeformed," and "well-proportioned" persons were encouraged to dance; those with "natural defects" were advised not to take part in court dancing of any sort. Indeed, it was considered absurd for people with "weak loins" or "very long arms" to attempt the minuet: "they are sure of being either laughed at, or pitied as idiots; instead of pleasure, it must be attended with the utmost anxiety; as soon as they hear the tittering of the room, or happen to be out in respect to the dance."

English contre-dancing marked a turning away from the segregated world of the minuet by democratizing social dancing. Because it encouraged self-expression and informality, participation in the dance was opened to all.

46. English country dances were eventually corrupted by dancing masters who began to embellish them with technical flourishes and more ornate steps taken from court dance. Although some of these changes did not affect the original character of the dance, the simplicity of many figures was lost. Society turned to other rural sources such as German dancing to recapture the naturalness of folk dancing.

47. Lamb, p. 201, quoting J. H Katfuss, *Taschenbuch für Freunde und Freundinnen des Tanzes* (1800).

48. Nettl, pp. 219–220, points out that in Mozart's opera *Don Giovanni* this aspect of the waltz is emphasized when Masetto and Leporello dance the *Deutschen*. "...the two men of the servant class symbolize the democratic principle, for in the waltz everyone can choose with who he wishes to *walzen*. A man can even *walzen* with a man.... Here we have a new and liberal philosophy of mankind where freedom in the choice of partner, and freedom of movement go hand in hand with the 'Freedom of Will.'"

49. Carner, p. 10.

50. Lamb, p. 201.

51. Sachs, p. 432.

Chapter 3

1. William H. Harris, and Judith S. Levey, editors, "Romanticism." In *The New Columbia Encyclopedia*, (New York: Columbia University Press, 1975.) pp. 2349–2350.

2. Ruth Katz, "The Egalitarian Waltz," In *Comparative Studies in Society and History*. (New York: Cambridge University Press, June 1973) pp. 176–7.

3. Allison Thompson, *Dancing Through Time: Western Social Dance in Literature, 1400–1918: Selections*. (Jefferson, NC: McFarland, 1998) p. 115.

4. Thompson, p. 115, quoting Wilson, *The Address; or, An Essay on Deportment*. (London: printed by the Author, 1821) p. 13.

5. A cultural revitalization movement began in Germany during the last half of the eighteenth century ignited by the teachings of philosopher Johann Gottfried von Herder. Herder's teachings idealized the pure, natural, unaffected spirit of the common man and promoted a return to native customs, traditions, and language as embodied in *das Volk* (the folk). These concepts sparked a growing trend towards nationalism in Germany and eventually spread across the European Continent to England where they were mixed with the aesthetics of the Romantic Movement. Nineteenth century intellectuals appropriated Herder's philosophy and embraced the idea of nationalism, seeing the return to an uncorrupted national culture as a remedy to the uncertainties that had resulted from the turbulent social transformations that occurred after the French Revolution. Romantic nationalism was especially strong in England and led to the rediscovery of country folk dances.

6. Katz, p. 178.

7. Katz, p. 174.

8. The purpose of the Vienna Congress was the reordering of Europe after the downfall of Napoleon I. The major players in the negotiations were Emperor Francis I of Austria, who hosted the event, his chief negotiator, Prince Fürst von Metternich, Charles Maurice de Talleyrand-Péigord of France, Lord Castlereagh of England, (and for a while his brother, the Duke of Wellington,) Czar Alexander I of Russia, and King Frederick William III of Prussia. Each of these men, along with several representatives from other European countries participated in the negotiations that were frequently held during nightly dances. Alexander I was passionately fond of dancing. A vain man with an eye for the ladies, he used to rub his face with a block of ice every morning to tighten his skin. Tallyrand attended the balls but was unable to waltz. He had been dropped as a baby by his wet-nurse, broken his foot, and was crippled for the rest of his life.

9. The nineteenth century began with the rise of Napoleon I (1769–1821) and his ambitious attempts to expand the French Empire. Napoleon was defeated in Spain in the Peninsular Campaign, and faced similar disasters in Russia that resulted in a humiliating retreat from Moscow. After another defeat at Leipzig, he finally surrendered control of the French government, and retreated into exile to Elba. On March 1, 1815, while the Vienna Congress was meeting to reorder a Europe that had been devastated by Napoleon's campaigns, the deposed monarch escaped from Elba, marched northward, and rallied a huge force behind him, attempting to reconstruct his empire. In June of that year, his armies were crushed at Waterloo by allied forces under the command of Arthur Wellesley, 1st Duke of Wellington. Napoleon surrendered and was shipped to the island of St. Helena where he was held prisoner. After a long battle with cancer, he died there on May 1, 1821.

After the annulment of his marriage to Josephine, Napoleon himself took lessons in waltzing in order to impress his new fiancé Marie Louise, the daughter of the Austrian Emperor, Francis I, host of the Vienna Congress.

10. The gathering given by the Czar's mistress, Princess Bagration, on October 1, 1814, provides a perfect example of how balls and entertainments were rife with political intrigue. After only two dances, Czar Alexander I approached Prince Hardenberg, the Prussian chancellor, to speak with him. The chancellor was hard of hearing, so the Czar took him to the hostess's private boudoir. The English, Austrian, and French diplomats, who were also attending the soiree, immediately met to discuss plans to deal with this troubling development. They wanted to avoid a united Russo-Prussian front during negotiations at all costs. Furthermore, the diplomats noticed that for the entire evening, the Czar refused to speak to Prince Adam Czartoryski, the advisor from Poland, an ominous signal to those hoping for an independent Polish state. With all the intrigue, the Czar still found plenty of time to waltz. Records state that he danced until four that morning.

11. The masked ball given at the Hofburg palace by the Austrian Emperor and his wife was held on October 2, 1814. The theme was red and gold, and the palace was draped with lush tapestries and hangings. All the guests wore elaborate costumes, and women were required to remain masked until midnight, at which time they could remove their disguises and reveal their identities. The ball opened with a polonaise. The Russian Czar led the dance with Maria Ludovica, Empress of Austria. The list of ten thousand invited guests was augmented by several gate crashers who bribed the doormen to get in to the event. These uninvited guests helped themselves to more than the rich food and drink. Three thousand silver spoons were stolen that evening. In her book, *The Congress Dances*, p. 126, Susan Mary Alsop includes a description of the ball given by the Comte Auguste de La Garde-Chambonas;

> The continuous music, the mystery of the disguises, the intrigues with which I was surrounded, the general incognito, the unbridled gaiety, the combination of circumstances and of seductions, in a word the magic of the whole vast tableau, turned my head, older and stronger heads than mine found it equally irresistible.

Negotiations, political maneuverings, and the waltz all played their parts that evening. At the end of the festivities, the exhausted Empress of Austria, who suffered from consumption, had to be carried to her bedchambers. Her husband, Emperor Francis I, was heard to remark, "If this goes on I shall abdicate. I can't stand this life much longer" (Alsop, p. 127).

12. During the Congress, the citizens of Vienna gave their Emperor, Francis I, the nickname "He who pays for everything." Yet, despite raising their taxes, they continued to hold the monarch in great affection. Their regard for "Papa Franz" only strengthened when the Emperor ordered his servants to set up trestle tables outside the palace after each weekly ball. All of the leftovers were set out for the poor. Nothing was wasted from a half-eaten roll to a piece of orange peel.

13. The phrase *"le Congress ne march pas, il danse,"* was supposedly coined by Prince Charles de Ligne, who was famous for his *bon mots*. The elderly Prince died in December as the Congress was being held. Apparently he caught pneumonia while waiting outside in the cold for "a midnight

assignation with a lady." He was eighty at the time. (Alsop, p. 176)

14. Although the Vienna Congress was perhaps the primary source of the waltz contagion, there were many other ways in which the dance was dispersed throughout the globe. French soldiers, who had been exposed to the waltz in their travels during the Napoleonic wars, were partially responsible for bringing the German folk dance back to France with them when they returned home after fighting abroad. Initially, French opposition to the closed position waltz was strenuous and vocal. In *The Social Dances of the Nineteenth Century in England*. (London: Herbert Jenkins, 1960), pp. 76–7, P. J. S. Richardson relates how in 1855, Gustave Boullay attacked the waltz in a booklet entitled *Reforme de la danse des Salons.*

Under the First Empire, and I even believe since the First Republic, the Waltz was the result of international wars, brought to us from Germany, but it only penetrated to the aristocracy after a long wait in the antechamber before it was allowed into the salon. From the beginning one saw that there was, in this intimacy between the dancer and his partner, something too familiar and one felt that this was not suitable for us. In France one thinks more than one acts.

15. Eduard Reeser, *The History of the Waltz*, (London: Sidwick and Jackson, nd.) pp. 22–23, quoting the *Journal des Luxus und der Moden*, March 1792.

16. Marcel Brion, *Daily Life in the Vienna of Mozart and Schubert*. (New York: Macmillan Company, 1962), p. 187.

17. The Mondschein, or "moonshine," was named after Margarete Mondschein, who had once owned a brick factory on the spot where the dancing palace was later built. As with the Apollo Hall, the ballroom was infamous for attracting prostitutes. In an attempt to maintain the decency of the establishment, police arrested any woman caught soliciting on the premises, even if the man she accosted did not object to her advances. Her punishment was to have her hair cut short, and then sweep the streets while wearing shackles on her feet. The punishment was abolished after the women of ill repute turned it into a game, and used their brooms to tease respectable citizens by sweeping dust onto their shoes. The punishment was changed to washing the dirty linens of hospital patients. After the Mondschein fell out of use as a venue for dancing, it was turned into a piano factory.

18. This quote is found in several sources, including Carner, p. 25, Resser, pp. 24–5, and Wechsberg, p. 51.

19. In 1701, the building that eventually became the Sperl was the home of the imperial hunter, Johann Georg Sperlbauer. A lavish public dance hall and tavern garden were added to the building by Johann Georg Scherzer, who was married to Sperlbauer's granddaughter. Georg Scherzer became one of the most prestigious and influential men in world of Viennese dancing, serving an elite clientele, and attracting top musicians such as Strauss and Lanner. (He was best man at Joseph Lanner's wedding.) On September 29, 1807, he officially opened his establishment to the public. Scherzer enforced rigid rules about how the ländler was danced in his establishment and gentleman were strictly forbidden to embrace their partners while doing the German folk dance. At the time of the Vienna Congress, the Sperl was considered one of the most elegant, distinguished, and prestigious dancing venues (after the Apollo). In the dining room patrons were treated to the famous Sperl baked chicken, the house specialty. Johann Strauss I performed there for the last time on September 25, 1849. The Sperl was closed in 1873 and the building was torn down.

20. Joseph Wechsberg, *The Waltz Emperors: The Life and Times and Music of the Strauss Family*. (New York: G. P. Putnam's Sons, 1973) p. 45.

21. Wechsberg, p. 45, quoting Heinrich Laube, 1833.

22. Just as there was a stiff competition between Joseph Lanner and Johann Strauss, there developed a similar rivalry between the Sperl and its competitor, Dommayer's Casino, another Vienna dancing palace. The quarrel was not resolved until Sperl's and Dommayer's children married each other.

23. This quote is found in several sources. This version was taken from Brion, p. 193.

24. Even the powerful influence of Johann Strauss, who frequently played at the Tivoli, could not save the pleasure gardens from decline. After only four years in business, the Tivoli was sold in 1834 and turned into a dairy farm.

25. Weschberg, p. 167. The premiere of *The Blue Danube* was performed by the Vienna Men's Choral Society, and accompanied by the combined orchestras of Josef and Eduard Strauss. The piece was conducted by Rudolf Weinwurm.

26. The Apollo was established by Sigmund Wolffsohn, an entrepreneur who had studied medicine. His other activities included manufacturing articulated artificial limbs for wounded soldiers, creating beauty creams for society ladies, and inventing a "health bed" made out of inflatable reindeer skins that was supposed to insure "delightful and amorous dreams." A few years after the heyday of Apollo, the dancing palace declined in popularity and was bankrupt by 1812. The citizens of Vienna all scrambled to buy souvenirs from the famous spot, but despite this, Wolffson could not pull himself out of debt and became totally destitute living on public charity until his death at eighty-five. The Apollo was bought in 1819 by a confectioner, and in 1831–32 was converted into a hospital during a cholera epidemic. By 1839, the building was turned into a soap factory (other sources say a candle factory). In 1876 the building that had housed the most lavish dance palace in Vienna was destroyed by fire, and the ruins were pulled down.

27. Marcel Brion, *Daily Life in the Vienna of Mozart and Schubert*. (New York: Macmillan Company, 1962) p. 193, quotes Auguste de la Garde's description of the Apollo:

The interior of the Apollo Palace, which occupied immense space contained magnificent halls and living shrubberies as in a garden. From a Turkish pavilion in glaring colours you could wander into a hut of a Laplander. Avenues bordered by fresh lawns planted with numbers of standard roses provided variations in the view. And all of this was indoors. In the centre of the dining-hall there towered an immense rock from which murmurous springs emerged in tumbling cascades, the waters then colleted in tanks full of live fish. All styles of architecture warred with each other in the decoration of these rooms; there was the capricious Moorish style, the pure Greek and the Gothic style with its rich carving.

28. In other sources, the capacity of the Apollo varies from 4,000 to 8,000. Marcel Brion in his book *Daily Life in the Vienna of Mozart and Schubert*. (New York: Macmillan Company, 1962), p. 189, states that there was room for 4,000 dancers but on opening night, 5,000 were admitted. Those that had been denied entrance protested outside and tried to break in. Brion indicates that despite these disturbances, the opening went off without a hitch, although the following year, a fight broke out in the cloakroom and several coats were lost. He also relates how there was confusion from all the carriages and several patrons had to walk home after their night of dancing.

29. Mosco Carner, *The Waltz*. (New York: Chanticleer Press, 1948) p. 18, quoting Michael Kelly, *Reminiscences*, 1826. Kelly was a friend of Mozart and the first to sing the role of Don Curzio in Mozart's *Le Nozze di Figaro*. In his book *Reminiscences*, Kelly himself is less enthusiastic about the waltz. He wrote, "For my own part, I thought waltzing from ten at night until seven in the morning, a continual whirligig; most tiresome to the eye and ear — to say nothing of any worse consequences."

30. The cotillion (or cotillon) was the French version of the contre-danse and consisted of figures performed by four couples who began in a square formation (as opposed to the

English version that was performed in two facing lines). Called the *contredanse française* in France and dubbed the cotillion outside of France, the dance utilized intricate footwork drawn from ballet and was much more difficult to execute than the typical country dance. It passed out of fashion after the French Revolution and was replaced with the quadrille, which was actually several cotillion figures linked together, although many dance manuals of the period still used the terms interchangeably. The name of the cotillion is derived from the French word for petticoat. Desmond F. Strobel in his article "Cotillon" in the *International Encyclopedia of Dance*. (Vol. 2. Ed. Selma Jeanne Cohen, p. 251–53. New York: Oxford University Press, 1998), p. 252 states that the name springs from an old French song which was popular in the eighteenth century. The lyric of the song read, "My gossipy companion, how does my petticoat look when I dance? It goes like this, it goes like that, like the tail of a cat." W. G. Raffé. *Dictionary of the Dance*. (New York: Barnes, 1964), p. 128 states that the name of the dance actually "referred to the dance of the *coterie*, originally a term meaning a gild or sharing company. As each member paid his quote (his quote or gild) so he received dividends or profits, as "gifts," when the disbursement was due, usually at annual, half-yearly, or quarterly meetings...." The dance mimicked steps of the successive phases of these meetings.

The cotillion evolved to include many steps and figures, some of which utilized the waltz. In the nineteenth century cotillions often lasted two or more hours and developed into games in which presents were offered or gentlemen competed for partners. These informal musical dance games had many inventive variations and utilized such diverse props as handkerchiefs, parasols, mirrors, chairs, and so forth. One version consisted of two gentlemen approaching a lady holding a parasol. She offered the parasol to one of the gentlemen, who then had to hold it over the heads of the lady and the other man as they waltzed around the room. Another consisted of a lady holding a fishing pole over several kneeling men and dangling a line that had a biscuit attached to the end of it, in front of their faces. The man who caught the biscuit with his teeth without using his hands received the honor of dancing with the lady.

31. The French version of the waltz was performed on the ball of the foot, as opposed to the flat-footed German and Viennese waltz. It was generally more complicated and often included pirouettes, intertwining of the arms, and other classical ballet adornments. The French waltz consisted of three different dances that were connected together. The first was the slow waltz that was repeated several times and increased in tempo until it led into the second dance. The second dance, which began allegretto and also increased in tempo, was called the Sauteuse waltz. It utilized leaps and springs. The final dance of the trio, the Jeté or Quick Sauteuse waltz, began allegro and increased to presto, and also included much leaping. The Sauteuse waltz and the Jeté waltz were performed in the manner of a valse à deux temps, with two main accents per bar of music. In a reference to whether one should waltz flatfooted or on the ball of the foot, Philip J. S. Richardson. *The Social Dances of the Nineteenth Century in England*. (London: Herbert Jenkins, 1960), p. 116, commented,

> At some popular assemblies dancers thought it was wrong to touch the floor with the heels in the course of the waltz, and I have seen a competition in which egg-shells were attached to the heels of the waltzers and the winner was the couple which kept these shells intact the longest.

32. Captain Rees Howell Gronow, *Reminiscences and Recollections*. London: Smith, Elder and Co., 18?) chapter entitled "Society in London in 1814," page unknown. This version of Gronow's book was taken from the online Library and edited by Tobias D. Robinson, 2001.

33. The celebration at Almack's was held to commemorate the defeat of Napoleon I following his calamitous invasion of Russia in 1812, retreat after the Battle of the Nations at Leipzig, and eventual abdication after the fall of Paris on March 31, 1814. This ball took place before Napoleon's escape from Elba and eventual defeat at Waterloo by Wellington.

34. Gronow, np. From the chapter in his memoirs entitled "Society in London in 1814."

35. Almack's Assembly Rooms on King Street, St. James's, were built by a Scotsman, William Almack, whose actual name was William Macall (MacCall or McCaul). The name of the establishment was created when the owner reversed the syllables in his surname. Macall, who had been the former valet of the Duke of Hamilton, and was married to the Duchess of Hamilton's lady-in-waiting, had saved some money after opening a coffee house in the West End in 1759, which catered to gentleman. In 1764, he opened an even more successful gaming club for young wealthy aristocrats who were looking for high-stakes gambling. It became especially popular as a gathering place for a group of dandies called macaronis. The marcaronis had gotten their nickname from a corruption of the Italian word *maccherone*, meaning "coxcomb," a reference to the way the young men affected foreign ways and wore their pretension like a badge. These young fops risked enormous sums of money at Almack's club, often bankrupting themselves after only one night of playing hazard. The stakes were so high that the men sometimes wore masks while gambling to conceal their emotions from the other players. The success of Macall's two ventures, led him to look for other opportunities to expand. He noticed that there was shortage of suitable public meeting places for the elite in London. Up to this point, Vauxhall Gardens and Ranelagh Gardens had been the most popular meeting spots in London. Both open-air pleasure gardens boasted pavilions for dancing, but more and more were starting to be overrun with prostitutes and pickpockets. Macall realized that by creating an elegant and reputable venue, he would meet the needs of fashionable society. In 1765 he built Almack's Assembly Rooms. The ballroom at Almack's was 100 feet long by 44 feet wide and boasted gilt columns and pilasters. The buildings were not even completed when the establishment opened on King Street on a rainy February night. Despite the inclement weather Macall was fortunate enough to attract at least a few distinguished guests, including the Duke of Cumberland. In *The Social Dances of the Nineteenth Century in England*. (London: Herbert Jenkins, 1960), p. 24, P. J. S. Richardson tells of a letter dated February 14, 1765, in which Horace Walpole wrote to the Earl of Hertford describing the event.

> The New Assembly Room at Almack's was opened the night before last, and they say is very magnificent, but it was empty; half the town is ill with colds, and many were afraid to go, as the house is scarcely built yet.... They tell me the ceilings were dropping with wet, but can you believe me, when I assure you the Duke of Cumberland was there? ...There is a vast flight of steps, and he was forced to rest two or three times. If he dies of it, — and how should he not?— it will sound very silly when Hercules or Theseus ask him what he died of, to reply "I caught my death on a damp staircase at a new club-room."

When Almack's first opened, members of society paid ten guineas to purchase a subscription that entitled them to dinner and dancing once a week for twelve weeks. After William Macall died in 1781, he willed Almack's to his niece who continued to operate the property with her husband, Mr. Willis, who served as manager and doorkeeper at the exclusive establishment. Almack's eventually became known as Willis' Rooms, and later was turned into an eating establishment called Willis's Restaurant. After that, Almack's was turned into an auction house and remained so until the buildings were heavily damaged in the bombings of London during World War II.

36. At one time, Almack's was the meeting place of an

exclusive London ladies' club, and it is likely that the patronesses that eventually controlled entrance into balls started as members of this club. The original committee included six women; Lady Pembroke, Lady Molyneaux, Mrs. Fitzroy, Mrs. Meynell, Miss Pelham, and Miss Lloyd. In 1814, when the patronesses attained their legendary status, the council was comprised of Lady Castlereagh, Lady Cowper (later Lady Emily Palmerston), Lady Sefton, Mrs. Drummond-Burrell (later Lady Willoughby De Eresby), Princess Esterhazy, and Countess (later Princess) Lieven. Lady Sarah Jersey was the leader of this group. She was the undisputed head of London society, which gained her the nickname of "Queen Sarah." It was "Queen Sarah" who personally refused entrance to the Duke of Wellington. In his memoirs, Captain Gronow described the women thus;

> The most popular amongst these *grandes dames* was unquestionably Lady Cowper, now Lady Palmerston. Lady Jersey's bearing, on the contrary, was that of a theatrical tragedy queen; and whilst attempting the sublime, she frequently made herself simply ridiculous, being inconceivably rude, and in her manner often ill-bred. Lady Sefton was kind and amiable, Madame de Lieven haughty and exclusive, Princess Esterhazy was a *bon enfant*, Lady Castlereagh and Mrs. Burrel *de tres grandes dames.*

According to accounts, the seven ladies rotated turns so that there was actually only one patroness at a time who controlled the distribution of tickets. Those fortunate enough to be honored with a voucher were allowed to bring one guest, but this guest had to meet with the patroness personally and be approved. If they were, the guest was given a "Stranger's Ticket." If they were not, they were blackballed. Tickets were especially sought after by mothers who wished to present their marriageable daughters in the hopes they might find suitable husbands at the elegant gatherings. This practice led Captain Gronow to refer to Almack's as a "matrimonial bazaar." Once the patronesses gave their stamp of approval to a young lady, her future was assured.

37. The Season in London was determined by the opening of Parliament in town, which in turn was determined by the closing of fox hunting season in the country. It usually began sometime before Christmas, and extended through the winter, spring and early summer. The greatest flurry of balls took place after the Easter holidays when a three-month whirlwind of parties and dances took place. The Season officially ended with the adjournment of Parliament and the simultaneous opening of grouse hunting season on August 12th. Curt Sachs in his book *World History of the Dance.* (New York: W.W. Norton, 1937), p. 68, suggests that the ballroom "dance season" that traditionally went from autumn to the end of winter can be traced to primitive fertility rites which tabooed dancing between sowing and harvesting

38. Lilly Grove, *Dancing.* (London: Longmans, Green, and Co., 1907) p. 402.

39. Gronow, np. From the chapter in his memoirs entitled "Society in London in 1814."

40. Besides setting the strictest guidelines regarding a gentleman's attire at each affair, the seven patronesses of Almack's declared that each ball would start precisely at 11:30 P.M. (Other sources say 11:00 P.M.) Doors closed at that time, and under no circumstances was anyone permitted entrance by the vigilant doorkeeper Mr. Willis. Kristine Hughes recorded the importance of this rule in her web article "The Lady Patronesses of Almack's" (2001). Hughes tells of an eyewitness account of the infamous incident in which the most famous military hero of the period was excluded. The story is recounted by a gentleman named Tricknor, who was standing next to Lady Jersey when the Duke of Wellington arrived late. He tells how an attendant informed the patroness of the Duke's arrival and his wish to enter. Lady Jersey asked what time it was, and the attendant answered, "Seven minutes after eleven, your ladyship." Tricknor recalled, "She paused, then

said with emphasis and distinctness, "Give my compliments to the Duke of Wellington, and say she is very glad that the first enforcement of the rule of exclusion is such that hereafter no one can complain of its application. He cannot be admitted." Captain Gronow's memoir reports how the Duke of Wellington "who had a great respect of orders and regulations, quietly walked away" when he was refused admittance.

In 1821, English author Pierce Eagan included in his book of tales, *Life in London,* a humorous set of verses that spoke of the rules at Almack's.

> "What sounds were those?— O, earth and heaven!
> Heard you the chimes—*half-past eleven*?
> They tell, with iron tongue, your fate,
> Unhappy lingerer, if you're late.
> Such is the rule, which none infringes;
> The door one jot upon its hinges
> Moves not. Once past the fatal hour,
> WILLIS has no dispensing power.
> Spite of persuasion, tears, or force,
> 'The LAW,' he cries, 'must take its course.'
> And men may *swear,* and women *pout,*
> No matter, — they are ALL SHUT OUT."

Later in Egan's tales of the happenings at Almack's, he explained how the Duke of Wellington was humbled when he tried to gain entrance to the Assembly Rooms.

> "Fair Worcester pleads with Wellington:
> Valour with beauty, 'Hence, begone!
> Perform elsewhere your destin'd parts,
> One conquer kingdoms, t'other hearts.
> My Lord, you'd have enough to do;
> ALMACK'S is not *like* WATERLOO.'
> For the first time in vain, his *Grace*
> Sits down in form before the place;
> finds, let him shake it to the centre,
> ONE fortress that he cannot enter,
> Though he should offer on its borders
> The *sacrifice* on HALF his orders."

(The above verses were extracted from Allison Thompson's book *Dancing Through Time: Western Social Dance in Literature, 1400–1918: Selections.* (Jefferson, NC: McFarland, 1998), pp.131–33, quoting Pierce Egan, *Life in London.* 1821; (New York: D. Appleton, 1904), pp. 231–233.)

41. The woman who introduced the waltz to England at Almack's Assembly Rooms was born in Riga, Russia in 1785 as Dorothea Christorovna Benckendorff. She married Count Lieven at the age of fifteen, and at the age of twenty-six, when he was made Russian Ambassador to the Court of St James's, she moved with her husband to England. She was reported to have a huge ego, and that she believed she had more political influence than either her own husband or the Czar of Russia. She was never hesitant to use her associations to gain power and was said to be a women who would betray anyone if it suited her purposes. Her husband was recalled to Russia in 1834, but she returned to England again in 1848, this time having been elevated to the status of Princess. She died in 1857.

42. Peter Buckman, *Let's Dance: Social, Ballroom and Folk Dancing.* (New York: Paddington Press, 1978) p. 125.

43. Various sources list the date for publication of Byron's poem as 1813, 1816, or 1821.

44. This poem is available in several sources. This version was extracted from Thompson, pp. 135–8.

45. George Gordon Noel Byron (1788–1824) had a much publicized affair with Lady Caroline Ponsonby Lamb, the wife of Viscount William Lamb, son of Byron's close friends, Lord and Lady Melbourne. (William Lamb, later Lord Melbourne, was the first prime minister to serve under Queen Victoria.) The two met when Bryon was 24, and he was already famous for writing "Childe Harold." Lady Caroline was 27, and the mother of an autistic son. The affair was tumultuous from the beginning. Byron was especially jealous when Lady Car-

oline waltzed with other men. Since the poet was lame and could not dance himself, the infatuated Lady Caroline gave up waltzing and sat with her lover despite the fact that she loved to dance and before the affair, was often considered the life of the party. After Byron abruptly ended the obsessive affair, the two ex-lovers happened to run into each other at a waltzing party given by Lady Heathcote in London on July 5, 1813. A wounded Lady Caroline approached Byron and said to the poet, "I conclude I may waltz now." Byron responded, "With every body in turn — you always did it better than anyone. I shall have pleasure in seeing you." Later after watching her dance with others Byron added sarcastically, "I have been admiring your dexterity." The hurt Lady Caroline seized a table knife (other sources say a broken glass) and when an amused and contemptuous Byron continued to taunt her, she fled the ballroom. She was eventually restrained by some ladies, but cut her hand as the knife was being taken away from her. The incident was reported in the papers and created a scandal.

46. Wilson's desire to cast a veneer of respectability over the waltz led him to create several sedate country dances that were performed in triple meter. These tamer versions of the waltz were designed so dancers did not utilize the notorious close embrace that so scandalized moralists.

47. The complete title of Thomas Wilson's dance manual was *A Description of the Correct Manner of Waltzing, the Truly Fashionable Species of Dancing, That, from the graceful and pleasing beauty of the Movements, have obtained an ascendancy over every other Department of that Polite Branch of Education.*

48. Carner, p. 21 and Thompson, pp. 118, and 133–4.

49. Philip J. S Richardson, *The Social Dances of the Nineteenth Century in England.* (London: Herbert Jenkins, 1960) pp. 56–57, states that the Princess Victoria was given a Birthnight Ball by King William and his wife Queen Adelaide on her twelve birthday, as well as one shortly before she ascended the throne at eighteen. The juvenile ball she attended at fourteen is mentioned in Elizabeth Longford's book *Victoria R.I.*, p. 28.

50. Elizabeth Longford, *Victoria R.I.* (New York: Harper & Row, 1973) p. 50.

51. Johann Strauss I also composed a piece called *The Myrtle Waltz* which he inscribed "for the wedding of Her Majesty Queen Victoria to His Royal Highness Prince Albert of Saxe-Coburg."

52. The most lavish and spectacular costume entertainment of the century was given by Spencer Compton Cavendish, the 8th Duke of Devonshire, and his portly wife, the Duchess Louise. The event was held on July 2, 1897, during the celebrations to commemorate Queen Victoria's Diamond Jubilee. Although the Queen was too old and infirm to attend herself, the names of several other members of the royal family graced the guest list, along with other aristocrats and visiting dignitaries. The invitations stipulated that guests dress in "allegorical or historical costumes before 1815." The eight hundred guests who received the coveted invitations and attended the Devonshire House Ball were organized into thematic groups and made ceremonial entrances in some of the most outrageously lavish and expensive costumes ever seen. The five groups were: the English Court of Elizabeth I led by Lady Tweedmouth; the Austrian Court of Maria Theresa led by Lady Londonderry; Queen Guinivere and the Knights of the Round Table led by Lady Ormonde; the Court of Louis XV and XVI, led by Lady Warwick as Marie Antoinette; and the Russian Court of Catherine the Great led by Lady Raincliffe. Three other loosely arranged groups consisted of the Italian procession, the allegorical costumes, and the Orientals, led by the stout, elderly hostess dressed as Zenobia, Queen of Palmyra, who made her entrance on a palanquin carried in on the straining shoulders of her servants posing as slaves. The Duchess' costume was designed by the famous Parisian couturier M. Worth. It had an under dress of silver cloth, stitched with silver thread and diamonds.

The gauze over-dress was green and gold and embroidered to the waist with metal work and covered with jewels. Her turquoise colored velvet train was also heavily studded with precious stones of every shade and hue, embroidered in gold and stitched in an Eastern design. The outfit was lavishly augmented by several pieces from the Duchess' extensive jewelry collection. Her headdress was made of diamonds ornaments and strands of pearls.

Other guests were similarly outfitted in costumes that spared neither expensive nor ingenuity. Alice Keppel, the mistress of the Prince of Wales, who was part of the Louis XVI group, went so far as to insist her dressmaker procure authentic material actually manufactured in the eighteenth century to insure her costume's authenticity. The Countess of Westmoreland, part of the allegorical group, appeared as Hebe, goddess of youth, and wore a huge stuffed eagle perched on her shoulder. One female guest had planned to make her entrance at the ball riding on an elephant borrowed from the London zoo, but at the last minute was dissuaded by the zoo keeper who warned her that the beast might not react well to all the commotion. Even all of the servants were dressed in either Elizabethan or Egyptian costumes.

The dancing that evening began and ended with grand processional marches, and was highlighted by quadrilles in which each group used steps from the country or historical period their court represented. These specialty dances were interspersed with the ever popular waltz for those not hampered by heavy, cumbersome costumes.

In the early Victorian era, opponents to dancing believed fancy dress balls were not only an ostentatious display of wastefulness and frivolity, but also, a breeding ground of vice which provided opportunities for sexual license under the anonymity of deceitful disguises.

53. The legend surrounding the polka states that it was discovered in Elbeleinitz, in Eastern Bohemia, by a local school teacher, Josef Neruda, who came across a peasant girl named Anna Chadimova (or Anna Slezak) singing and dancing one Sunday afternoon after she had received good news about her boyfriend, a soldier. Neruda copied down the girl's impromptu song and the next week, the peasant girl taught her improvised dance to some of Neruda's students. The dance began to be presented at various public festivals and in 1835, eventually found its way to Prague where it caught the public's attention. The dances true origins are more likely derived from the polska, a sixteenth century Polish folk dance, that was revived during the early nineteenth century when Bohemian nationalists were stirring up patriotic fervor. The polka was eventually taken to Paris around 1840, and presented at the Odéon Theatre by M. J. Raab, a dancing master from Prague, who performed the dance in Slavic costume. Recognizing the possibilities of creating the next fashionable trend, the top French dancing masters, Cellarius, Coralli, Laborde, and Petipa, took the peasant dance and refined it by adding French stylistic elements. The simple dance was expanded to include five figures around 1843–4, and each prominent dancing master developed his own version, proudly claiming that his and his alone was the best polka. Bitter rivalries developed, the most vociferous between the two schools of M. Cellarius and Eugene Coralli. The battle over who had the best polka reached such a fever pitch that a huge public contest was held between the two dancing masters. Coralli vanquished Cellarius at the contest, but the enmity only escalated as each camp continued to claim ownership of the superior polka. Polka mania quickly spread throughout the Continent, and then to England and America. Eugène Coulon, another French dancing master, is credited for first introducing the polka to the English in 1844, although the dance truly made its mark there when the more famous Cellarius presented the dance at Almack's in London the same year. Also that same year, famed ballet dancer Carlotta Grissi and her partner Jules Perrot, danced the polka on the stage of Her Majesty's Theatre to overwhelming response. The popularity of the dance cannot be overstated. Richard-

son, p. 83, quotes a piece in the *London Times* at the height of the polka craze, "Politics is for the moment suspended in public regard by the new and all-absorbing pursuit, the Polka."

The polka quickly spread to the United States, where it was received with similar enthusiasm, especially in New York. The popularity of the dance spawned a variety of merchandizing efforts associated with the polka. In America, fabric covered with circles began to be known as polka dotted. Politician James K. Polk took advantage of the dance craze as part of his 1844 presidential campaign. The word "polka" is derived from the Czech word *pulka*, meaning half, a reference to the small steps and half turns of the dance.

54. As with the waltz, the polka was met in some circles with shock and outrage. The *Illustrated London News* in April of 1844 included this commentary:

> It is a waste of time to consider this nonsense. The weathercock heads of the Parisians have been delighted always by any innovation, but they have never imported anything more ridiculous or ungraceful than this Polka. It is a hybrid confusion of Scotch Lilt, Irish Jig, and Bohemian Waltz, and needs only to be seen once to be avoided for ever!

(Richardson, p. 87–8.)

The polka craze arrived in Britain around 1844 and brought with it another craze, the *thé dansant*, or tea dance. These afternoon dancing parties became all the rage among the upper crust. Tea dances also brought with them a resurrection of the novelty dance-game that had first been introduced with the cotillion. One particularly popular variation used during the first set of the Congou quadrille was called *La Tasse*. During the dance, a gentleman approached his partner with a cup of tea that she took from him. He then retired. A second gentleman did the same with his partner. Then the two ladies would drink the tea while the two men chassezed around the floor. The women then balancezed to their partners who took their empty tea cups and retired.

55. Thompson, p. 150, quoting Charles Durang, *The Fashionable Dancer's Casket; or, The Ball-Room Instructor* (Fisher & Brother, 1856), p. 41.

56. Lorenzo Papanti lived from 1799–1873. Some sources state that he was the bandmaster on the U.S.S. Constitution. In the book *Romantic Days in Old Boston: The Story of the City and of Its People During the Nineteenth Century*, pp.314–315, author Mary Caroline Crawford states:

> Scion of a noble house of Colonna, Lorenzo Papanti, because a younger son, became an officer in the royal guard of the Duke of Tuscany as a means of making his own way in the world. While in this capacity he committed a political misdemeanor which soon obliged him to flee his native land in the night. With barely time to get letters of introduction and take clothing, — in which he did not fail to include his full court regalia, however, — he made his way to the old frigate *Ironsides*, the officers of which, knowing his story, took him aboard as a member of their band. In Boston he presented his letters and for a time eked out a scanty livelihood playing in the orchestra of the Boston Theatre. Then, with the help of his society friends, he founded Papanti's dancing academy. For a long term of years the little assembly room at 23 Tremont Street, opposite the old Boston Museum, was the scene of many juvenile trials and youthful triumphs. For there the two Papantis, father and son, successively taught little slippered feet to glide and not stumble, and awkward but well-meaning Boston youths how to bear themselves with courtly grace. Hundreds of memories centre about the tall spare man who there called out his directions over his violin bow and who was never visible save in the impressive elegance of a dress coat and a well-fitting wig.

57. Supposedly, Papanti's partner during the waltz was Mrs. Harrison Gray Otis. A scion of Boston society, Mrs. Otis, née Elizabeth Boardman, had married in to an influential family. Her father-in-law had been in Congress and was also the second mayor of Boston. Elizabeth was the second wife of the son William Foster Otis. The couple had five children. After, her husband died, she was romantically linked with several men including Daniel Webster and Henry Clay. It is highly unlikely that Papanti's demonstration in 1834 with Mrs. Otis was the first time the waltz was actually done in America. A more feasible explanation is that this event was the introduction of the Boston waltz, a slower, smoother version than the more widely popular Viennese waltz. It has been suggested that Papanti installed the sprung floor in his ballroom to accommodate Mrs. Otis who was a large, heavy-set woman.

58. Quote found in several online sources.

59. Quote from Cleveland Armory's book *The Proper Bostonians* (E. P. Dutton, 1947) extracted from the website "A Brief History of Scollay Square." Armory also wrote, "...By 1837 Papanti had has [sic] become so successful that he was able to move his academy to new and palatial quarters on Tremont Street. Here he built a hall with a $1200 chandelier, five enormous gilt-framed mirrors and the first ballroom floor in America to be built on springs." In Edward Everett Hale's book, *A New England Boyhood* (Boston: Little, Brown and Company, 1927, p. 5) the author writes, "It was a surprise to everyone when Papanti introduced it [gaslight] in his new Papanti's Hall. To prepare for that occasion the ground-glass shades had a little rouge shaken about in the interior, that the white gaslight might not be too unfavorable to the complexion of the beauties below" (extracted from the website National Park Services: Gaslighting in America"). Papanti's academy of dance on 21 Tremont Row was located next to Morton's dental office and was in existence from around 1837 until 1899. It was in Papanti's ballroom that Charles Dickens read from his book *The Pickwick Papers* when he first visited Boston in 1842.

60. Quote from Lucius Beebe's *Boston and the Boston Legend* (1935) extracted from the website "Historical Boy's Clothing — Dancing School and Social Dancing Lesson Routien [sic]" The same website says that Ronald Story's *The Forging of an Aristocracy* (1980) states "that 'Boston Assemblies' were held beginning in the 1830's at Papanti's ballroom, providing an opportunity for Harvard students to socialize."

61. Gretchen Schneider, "Social Dance: Nineteenth-Century Social Dance." In *International Encyclopedia of Dance*. Vol. 5. Ed. Selma Jeanne Cohen, p. 623–26. (New York: Oxford University Press, 1998) p. 626.

62. Gretchen Schneider, "United States of America: An Overview." In *International Encyclopedia of Dance*. Vol. 6. Ed. Selma Jeanne Cohen, pp. 230–53. (New York: Oxford University Press, 1998) p. 235.

63. Ted Shawn, *Every Little Movement: A Book about Francois Delsarte*. (New York: Dance Horizons, reprint 1974) pp. 31 & 28.

64. James Morrison Steele Mackaye, better known as Steele Mackaye, founded the first acting school in New York City, later known as the American Academy of Dramatic Arts.

65. Social movements such as abolition, suffrage, and nativism also influenced the style and substance of American dance forms.

66. Schneider, p. 235.

67. There were several versions of the Boston Waltz: the American Boston; the French Boston; the Spanish Boston; the Philadelphia Boston; the Imitation Boston; the Hesitation Boston; the Hesitation waltz; the Berceuse or Cradle Boston; the Herring Bone Boston; and the Valse L'Americaine. Today the Boston is commonly referred to as the American or Slow waltz.

68. The valse à deux temps, also called the valse à deux pas, or the Russian waltz, is believed to have originated in Russian and was first introduced to Europe around the mid-

dle of the nineteenth century in Paris, France. The following is an account of the dances' introduction in Paris:

> I know exactly what I am talking about when I speak of the Russian origin of the Two-step waltz, as my father was the second person to dance it in Paris in 1839 — I say "the second person" intentionally, for the first was one of his students. I can still remember the following curious and little known anecdote about the introduction of the Russian Waltz to France, for the Two-Step Waltz is not only Russian, but it is even their National Waltz. Let me add, in passing, that their ladies and gentlemen excel in dancing; their energy, their *brio*, often surpass ours. In January 1839, the Baron de Nieuken, attaché with the Russian delegation, took dancing lessons with my father, and took them as they were given at the time — composed of all the fundamental exercises of dance: *pliés, battements*, etc. Our baron had to go one evening to a great ball given by the Count Mole, then Minister of Foreign Affairs, and would have to dance the waltz with some charming Moscow ladies. He therefore asked his professor to rehearse it with him. My father was upset by the words "Two-step Waltz," which seemed in manifest contradiction with three-beat waltz time; but everything was promptly arranged when he saw our baron dancing the waltz with his first step on the first two beats of the measure, and the second step on the third beat. Right away my father understood that in dance, as in music, two notes can make up a three-beat measure, taking the notes here as movements. Pupil and teacher waltzed together, and the pupil that evening attracted the admiration of all the ladies for his two-step waltz. From that moment onward, the old three-beat waltz was but little honored in the salons; only the public balls kept it on; but, to follow the example above, the habitués of La Chaumière created a second, simplified kind of two-step waltz, contenting themselves with jumping sometimes on one foot, sometimes on the other, without paying much attention to the music. The prince of Galitzine, the baron and the count of Damas, and the marquis de La Baume were the first two-beat waltzers in Paris. The day after the ball at the Ministry of Foreign Affairs, they danced it at the home of Count Tanneguy Duchattel, Minister of the Interior.

(This account above is originally from an the dance manual *Traité de la danse, contenant la théorie et l'histoire des danses anciennes et modernes. Avec toutes les figures les plus nouvelles du cotillon*. Written by G. Desrat. (Paris: H. Delarue et cie, 190–?) pp. 80–83. The manual has digitalized by the American Ballroom Companion by the Library of Congress. The translation was taken from the Wikipedia listing "valse à deux temps.")

When dancing the valse à deux temps, the couple slid their feet on the floor instead of stepping. They made fewer revolutions and also reversed directions and revolved counterclockwise. The Viennese waltz only allowed the couple to spin clockwise. The ability to reverse directions cut down on the perpetual motion that created such vertigo.

69. Melvin B. Gilbert, *The Director: Dancing Deportment, Etiquette, Aesthetics, Physical Training*. (Portland, ME: Melvin Ballou Gilbert, 1898) (reprint by Dance Horizons 1975 or 1976) p. 17.

70. Thompson, p. 206, quoting Fred W. Loring, *The Boston Dip*. (Boston: Loring, Publisher, 1871.)

71. As the valse à deux temps gradually replaced the valse à trois temps, or Viennese waltz in popularity, American dancing masters expressed growing concerns. Connoisseurs of the waltz felt that true skill on the dance floor was only demonstrated if one did the valse à trois temps. This led dance instructors such as Allen Dodworth to refer to the simpler version as the "Ignoramus Waltz." Despite Dodworth's protests, the valse à deux temps grew in popularity in the United States.

72. Gilbert, p. 51.

Chapter 4

1. Elizabeth Aldridge, *From the Ballroom to Hell: Grace and Folly in Nineteenth-century Dance*. (Evanston, IL: Northwestern University Press, 1991) p. 24, quoting *The Mirror of the Graces*.

2. Susan Mary Alsop, *The Congress Dances*. (New York: Harper & Row, 1984) p. 166.

3. In his book *Reminiscences and Recollections*, Captain Gronow reported that when he attended a ball in London in 1816, the Prince Regent was offended that he wore trousers instead of knee breeches, but within the year, the Prince himself was wearing trousers whenever he appeared in public. In 1816, dancing master Thomas Wilson criticized the wearing of trousers instead of knee breeches and recommended that they be prohibited in the respectable ballroom.

4. Aldridge, p. 70, quoting *The Laws of Etiquette*. By a Gentleman. (Philadelphia: 1836) p. 29.

5. Cameron Kippen, "The History of Footwear — Dancing Shoes" 6/03 http://podiatry.curtin.edu.au/dance.html#long

6. Kippen, np.

7. The corset was believed to cause many health problems in women including migraines, melancholy, shortness of breath, tuberculosis and epilepsy (through friction of the lung and the rib), cancer, prolapsed uterus, atrophy of abdominal muscles, displacement of and damage to the liver, displacement of stomach and intestines, malformation of the ribs, scoliosis of the spine, and difficulty in childbirth. Although tight lacing certainly did present health risks, many of these claims were overblown. In 1859, one Paris newspaper reported that when a young lady had died when her liver was pierced by three of her ribs while trying to lace her corset too tightly. There were also rumors that one victim actually severed her liver in half by lacing her corset to tight. Opponents of tight lacing were numerous and vocal. In her web article *Fashion and Eroticism*. Chapter 9, "The Corset Controversy." Danielle Steel states that The Ladies' Sanitary Association announced "There ought to be the word *Torture*, or *Murder*, in large letters on every pair of stays." She also tells of Orson S. Fowler, an American phrenologist who denounced the corset for what he considered an even more insidious reason — it's ability to stimulate female sexuality. The web article reports that in his book *Intemperance and Tight-Lacing*, Fowler explained how by squeezing the liver, the corset tainted the blood, which in turn affected the brain and caused insanity. When this happened, he wrote, "[it] necessarily excites the organs of Amativeness, situated in the lowest point of the brain." Compression also "inflames all the organs of the abdomen which thereby excites amative desires." He concludes, "tight-lacing ... necessarily kindles impure feelings ... at the same time that it renders their possessors more weak-minded, so as the more easily to be led into temptation."

Dress reform gained momentum during the middle of the nineteenth century but was hampered by the widely held view that being frail, weak, or ill was fashionable, and a sign of higher social status. In addition, the dress reform movement was linked to the suffrage movement and therefore associated with an unpopular cause for many. In England there was at least one attempt to exhibit the advantages of dancing in the new pantaloons introduced by Amelia Bloomer. A ball was given and all female attendees were to arrive in the bloomer costume. When a large contingent of prostitutes crashed the dance though, it quickly degenerated into what many viewed as an orgy, confirming to the opponents of dress reform that any form of freedom for women foreshadowed the downfall of moral society. By 1857, even Amelia Bloomer herself gave up the costume named for her and returned to wearing crinolines.

The corset provided other challenges for dancing besides the more obvious health-related issues. The layers of stiffening also shielded a woman from the subtle pressure of the man's hand on her waist, and made it harder to interpret his hand signals as he was trying to lead her around the dance floor. Allison Thompson points out in her book *Dancing Through Time: Western Social Dance in Literature, 1400–1918: Selections.* (Jefferson, NC: McFarland, 1998), p. 152, that there were some advantages to the stiff corsets. They were "something to 'lean' against, providing support to women whose backs were weak due to lack of exercise." Thompson explains that when the man rested his gloved hand on the woman's waist, her layers of clothing and stiff corseting, actually presented the tactile feeling of something rigid and unmovable. She quotes one gentleman observer, who commented,

> To my mind, a non-stayed waist is horrid, and is often called fleshy, sticky, and other names by gentlemen at dances, and rightly too. What man enjoys a dance holding a flabby waist, where his fingers sink into fat? Has [the reader] ever noticed a tightly-laced girl at a ball? Invariably she has all the best partners, and with good reason. We love a stiff, hard, well-boned waist to hold.

(Thompson, p. 152, quoting Peter Farrer, *Men in Petticoats* (Liverpool: Karn Publications Garston, 1987) p.11.)

8. Aldrich, p. 25.

9. Aldrich, p.25, quoting John Robert Godley, *Letters From America*, p. 44.

10. Aldrich, p. 26.

11. Crinolines were used as underlining for several layers of petticoats, and were made of horsehair stiffening, reinforced with wood, wire, whale bone, or bamboo. These contraptions helped to carry the weight of the petticoats that sometimes weighed over nine pounds.

12. With the advent of the bustle, a large pad made out of horsehair, or whale bone and springs, skirts became tighter and more constraining. To deal with this new challenge, women sometimes tied their knees together with a piece of cloth so that they could maintain a graceful walk in which the movements were soft, undulating and almost imperceptible.

13. Aldridge, p. 74, includes a passage from Hudson K. Lyverthey's *Our Etiquette and Social Observances.* (Grand Rapids: 1881) p. 63, that describes the use of gloves.

> A gentleman cannot be too careful not to spoil a lady's dress. Gloves are not worn to a ball for looks alone but serve a practical purpose as well. The perspiration on the hand from dancing will ruin a lady's dress when gloves are not worn, then the gentleman should hold his handkerchief in his right hand so that his hands will not touch the lady's dress.

14. Aldridge, p. 72, quotes Cecil B. Hartley, *The Gentlemen's Book.* (Boston: ca.1860) p. 16,

> Never dance without gloves. This is an imperative rule. It is best to carry two pair, as in the contact with dark dresses, or in handling refreshments, you may soil the pair you wear entering the room, and will thus be under the necessity of offering your hand covered by a soiled glove, to some fair partner. You can slip unperceived from the room, change the soiled for a fresh pair, and then avoid that mortification.

15. Aldrich, pp. 103–105, offers fascinating examples of the language of glove, fan, parasol, and handkerchief flirtations.

16. Columbine, "The Language of Flowers" (web article). Extracted from *Collier's Cyclopedia of Commercial and Social Information and Treasury of Useful and Entertaining Knowledge*, 1882.

17. Aldrich, p. 30.

18. Joseph Wechsberg, *The Waltz Emperors: The Life and Times and Music of the Strauss Family.* (New York: G. P. Putnam's Sons, 1973) p. 61.

19. There were several inns and taverns along the Danube. Some of the most popular were "The White Lamb," "The Golden Bear," "The White Cockerel," "The Blue Star," and "The Good Shepherd." Johann Baptist Strauss I was born on the second floor of "The Good Shepherd" on March 14, 1804. His father, Franz Strauss was the tavern keeper. After his mother died when he was seven, and then his father died a few years later of an apparent suicide, Johann Strauss continued to frequent the taverns against his step-mother's wishes so that he could listen to the traveling musicians. Deciding that he wished to learn music, he begged his stepfather to buy him a violin. Legend has it that the young Strauss poured beer into his violin to improve its sound.

20. In addition to providing dance music, these musicians also frequently strolled table to table to provide music for the diners. This practice earned them the nicknames "beer fiddlers" and "roast-meat fiddlers."

21. The music-loving Viennese were avid collectors of "musical freaks," mechanical toys that played music. The most common example was the cuckoo clock. Other acoustical inventions included snuffboxes made with mechanical hummingbirds attached to the lid that popped up and sang every time snuff was taken, and a musical bed that was purported to encourage restful slumber by playing a lullaby as soon as one lay down, followed by muted horns to induce drowsiness. The bed also prevented oversleeping with its built-in alarm clock that startled the sleeper awake with a cacophony of playing instruments. Another musical freak was a pool table that played pleasing melodies during the game. The pool table whistled and laughed if a player missed a shot and greeted the victor with a fanfare of trumpets. Viennese dentists sometimes used a musical "soothing soundbox" which sang into a patient's ear during the more painful procedures, with gentle stress-reducing melodies and such catchy lyrics as "Let me come closer to your mouth and gaze at your pearly teeth!" One popular invention was a birdcage whose wires were musically tuned so when a bird landed on them, spontaneous melodies were created. Marcel Brion in his book *Daily Life in the Vienna of Mozart and Schubert.* (New York: Macmillan Company, 1962), p. 119 states, "It had become an obsession, and Schönholz reports that you could not open a door, touch a table, seize any object or even look at the clock without some spring immediately releasing floods of harmony."

22. The waltz music of Schubert, Strauss, Lanner, and others was strongly inspired by Austrian folk music. This influence was partially due to the melodic limitations and possibilities of rural instruments, and also by the vocal character of the alpine yodel. The "alp-cry," forced an abrupt transition across vocal registers so that the pitch jumped an octave, double octave, seventh, fifth, fourth, or third. Waltz composers frequently mimicked this yodel by inserting similar melodic jumps. The wide intervals commonly found in Austrian peasant dances expressed a strong, vigorous, masculine character, and contrasted sharply with the embellished Rococo and Baroque feminine quality of French music. This robust, lusty quality became an integral part of classical waltz compositions.

23. Mosco Carner, *The Waltz.* (New York: Chanticleer Press, 1948) pp. 25–6, quoting Nikolaus Lenau's "Styrian dance."

24. Aware of the conflicting social attitudes about the dance as an expression of both beauty and shame, many opera composers intentionally utilized the seductive strains of the waltz to illuminate a particular dramatic theme, especially taking advantage of the connection between society's disapprobation of the waltz and prevailing concepts about women.

The social connotations of the scandalous dance and it's various associations with both personal pleasure and public condemnation, led opera composers to utilize this paradox to convey to their audiences such dramatic themes as a woman's free-spirited vitality, her powers of seduction, and often, her eventual downfall. In the book, *Revolving Embrace: The Waltz as Sex, Steps, and Sound*, Sevin Yaraman explores this idea and cites *La Traviata* and *La Bomème* as just two examples of this musical device.

At the beginning of *La Traviata*, the two main characters, Violetta and Alfredo, sing a waltz duet. Verdi subsequently uses this theme throughout his opera to convey to his audience the "central motifs of love, joy, and Alfredo's dominance" (Yaraman, p. 46). Later at the end of the third act, the two lovers again sing a waltz duet as they face Violetta's impending demise. The waltz music then alludes to misery and a woman's ruin. In this way, Verdi employs the waltz's dual connotations to communicate his message to the audience by using it "to mark the key moments in the classical tragedic rise and fall, the moments of hope and despair" (Yaraman, p. 46). First produced in 1853, *La Traviata*, also known as "The Woman Led Astray" is a perfect example of nineteenth century society's attitudes towards women and the waltz. In *La Bomème* (1896) Puccini introduces his waltz theme in the character of Musetta. By choosing the waltz for Musetta instead of the frail main character Mimì, the composer reflects society's belief that women associated with the waltz are full of life. But, Puccini is also aware of the other social implications of the waltz, and uses the music to reveal that Musetta is flirtatious and seductive. She first arrives on the stage escorted by her benefactor, but quickly shows her true colors and attempts to seduce another man. Puccini clearly communicates that there is something inherently degenerate about this woman. As with the waltz, Musetta is the embodiment of all that is attractive, robust, beautiful, sexy, but also, all that is immoral.

25. Michael Pamer played nightly at *The Golden Pear Inn*. The inn was a favorite of Joseph Lanner's father, and the boy frequently accompanied his father when he visited the spot. It was there that Lanner first heard Pamer's style of Viennese dance music. Pamer was famous for one particular stunt. He would play a song entitled "Blissful Memories of the Good Hütteldorf Beer," and upon completing the number, chug a full stein of beer. If the audience egged him on, which they always did, he repeated the number and the beer guzzling again and again until he was totally intoxicated and the audience finally let him continue with the rest of the concert. Lanner joined Pamer's orchestra at age twelve but grew disgusted with the conductor's drunkenness that always resulted in rages, melancholy, or fits of crying. This childish behavior finally propelled Lanner to leave Pamer's group and form his own orchestra. Pamer's musical talent was undeniable, but his drinking along with heavy gambling eventually ruined him. He died an alcoholic at age forty-five. Johann Strauss also played for Michael Pamer. Both young men received invaluable practical experience with the talented but troubled Pamer.

26. Strauss had studied music against his father's wishes.

27. At the beginning of their friendship, Lanner and Strauss were almost inseparable. Wechsberg, p. 32, says that according to legend they were once down to their last clean shirt so they took turns wearing it. One wore the shirt out, while the other stayed home.

28. Lanner's and Strauss' famous fight took place in the ballroom of *Zum Bok*, (The Ram). It was early in the morning at the end of the concert, and both men were tired and slightly inebriated. Strauss grew irritated at Lanner's long-winded farewell speech and finally hit Lanner with his violin bow. Lanner lashed back and both began to battle until their bows broke. They then started to smash their instruments against each other, and as the fight escalated and dancing couples looked on in shock, chairs and furniture were also thrown. One chair hit a huge mirror that was the pride of the ballroom and renowned throughout Vienna. It shat-

tered, sending splinters of glass upon the audience. The suddenly sober Lanner and Strauss quickly disappeared from the building.

29. Weschberg, p. 32.

30. The men reconciled in 1828, when Lanner married. Gartenberg (p. 51) reports that the reconciliation took place at the marriage of Lanner's daughter, when Strauss "made an unscheduled appearance to congratulate the bride. As fate would have it, the wedding party took place in the same ballroom in which the final fracas had occurred. As Strauss appeared in the door all movement and conversation stopped. The music died away after a few hesitant bars as all eyes turned to the two men, Lanner and Strauss. The spirit of the happy occasion prevailed. Lanner's face lit up and he opened his arms to the unexpected but most welcome guest. The two rushed towards each other and embraced amid shouts and tears of joy." After reconciling the two friends frequently met and also played each other's compositions.

31. Weschberg, p. 37, quoting Chopin.

32. Lanner was first married at age twenty-seven to Franziska Jahns, the daughter of a glove-maker. He later took a mistress, Marie Kraus, a butcher's daughter, eventually divorcing his wife to marry her. An avid collector of smoking pipes, Lanner had a huge collection he had gathered from all over the world. His obsession with pipes would sometimes lead him to accost people on the street or at a dance if he saw a unique specimen he wanted to possess. He was known to spend exorbitant amounts on the spot if he desired one. Lanner had a hugely successful career as a composer and conductor of dance music. In addition to writing over one hundred waltzes, he also composed numerous other pieces of dance music. He was largely responsible for contributing to the waltz fever that swept Vienna during the nineteenth century. Josef Franz Karl Lanner died on Good Friday, April 14, 1843 at age forty-two from inflammation of the lungs due to typhus. Thousands and thousands came out to honor the man. Johann Strauss I conducted the music at his funeral.

33. Weschberg, p. 71.

34. In 1833, while still married to his wife Anna, who was the mother of six of his children, Johann Strauss met a hat-maker named Emilie Trambausch, and fathered six illegitimate children with her. He named his first son with Emilie, Johann, and Strauss' legal wife Anna was horrified at this blatant insult to her first born, Johann II. She confronted her wayward husband and gave him an ultimatum. Strauss chose the hat-maker, and in 1844, an angry Anna filed for divorce. The couple went through a bitter battle over money. Anna had band uniforms seized when Strauss refused to pay support to his first family. The divorce was finalized in 1846, and shortly after, Strauss changed his will to leave everything to Emilie and his children by her. Despite his musical successes, Strauss had enormous financial problems and difficultly supporting his two families. He fought with Anna constantly and threatened not to give her money if his sons followed him in to music field. On September 25, 1849, at the age of 45, Strauss died in near poverty from complications resulting in meningitis after contracting scarlet fever from one of his illegitimate daughters. Emilie was said to have beaten the little girl who gave him the disease nearly to death. The child's screams eventually prompted neighbors to call the police. According to Josef Strauss, he and his brothers discovered his father's dead body lying on hard wooden bed slats. The bed itself, and everything else in the house, had been hastily removed by Emilie, who had fled. Johann II was overcome after seeing his father's body and ran out of the apartment in horror, disappearing for two days until he finally showed up disheveled and exhausted. After this, he developed a morbid fear of disease and death. He was terrified of even seeing a hospital or cemetery from a distance. His phobia was so strong that he could not even attend his mother's funeral or that of his first wife. Anna Strauss and her sons eventually tracked down Emilie, and fought to get back the elder Strauss' instruments and scores. For a while, Emilie had a meager

existence as a water carrier, but soon she faded away in dire poverty. Johann Strauss II supported her children.

35. Anna Streim Strauss was the daughter of the innkeeper, who ran *The Red Rooster*, the tavern where Joseph Lanner and Johann Strauss I lived together as young men. She was pregnant with her first son Johann II when she married the elder Strauss on July 11, 1825. Throughout her live she was a powerful influence on her children's lives, and something of a legend around Vienna. Johann II was her favorite child and she worked tirelessly to support him in his music studies. She conspired with her son so that he could secretly study violin with Franz Amon, the first violinist in her husband's orchestra. Amon told the young Johann that a violinist was the star of the orchestra and urged him to practice his bow strokes in front of a mirror so they would be elegant and appealing to an audience. Johann I caught his son practicing like this one day and smashed the violin against the floor, forbidding his son to play. Anna Strauss went behind her husband's back and gave her son one of her husband's own violins so he could continue practicing.

36. Weschberg, p. 85.

37. Weschberg, p. 89.

38. Weschberg, p. 90.

39. Weschberg, p. 107.

40. *Ibid.*

41. *Ibid*, quoting Eisenberg.

42. Weschberg, p. 119.

43. Eduard had a son Johann III, who took over the directorship of the musical dynasty after his father's retirement. The grandchild of Josef, Eduard II, also continued in the family profession, as did his sons Eduard III and Johann IV. In the Strauss family, it was the tradition to name all male heirs Johann, Josef, or Eduard.

44. Gartenberg, p. 247, quotes Johann Strauss' description of his concert at the Peace Jubilee Festival Hall in Boston during his American tour. Strauss wrote,

> On the musician's platform there were twenty thousand singers; in front of them the members of the orchestra — and these were the people I was to conduct. A hundred assistants had been placed at my disposal to control these gigantic masses, but I was only able to recognize those nearest to me, and although we had had rehearsals there was no possibility of giving an artistic performance, a proper production. But if I had declined to conduct, it would have cost me my life. Now just imagine my position, face to face with a public of a hundred thousand Americans. There I stood at the raised platform, high above all the others. How would the business start, how would it end? Suddenly a cannon shot rang out; a gentle hint for us twenty-thousand to begin to perform the *Blue Danube*. I gave the signal, my one hundred assistant conductors followed me as quickly and as best they could and then there broke out an unholy row such as I shall never forget. As we had begun more or less together, I concentrated my entire energy on seeing that we should also finish together!— Thank Heaven, I managed even that. It was all that was humanly possible. The hundred thousand mouths in the audience roared their applause and I breathed a sigh of relief when I found myself in fresh air again and felt firm ground beneath my feet.

45. On one of Strauss's Russian tours in the 1850's, he was greeted with similar adulation. He received love letters and flowers daily from the women of St. Petersburg. One Russian officer confronted Strauss and regretfully informed him that he was honor bound to challenge him to a duel because his wife had sent the composer red roses every day. Strauss responded by taking the young officer to the back of the villa he was renting at the time to show him two unfurnished rooms that were overflowing with flowers. Strauss informed the officer that he had received all of these bouquets within the last two days from his numerous admirers. The officer realized that Strauss was not having an affair with his wife, apologized, and the two parted as friends.

46. According to Gartenberg, p. 244, Johann Strauss himself couldn't waltz.

47. Just one week prior to his death on May 26th Strauss had received a visit from Mark Twain, who traveled from the United States just to meet the famous composer.

48. The Strauss Society as founded in 1936 to collect and preserve the music of Johann Strauss. Two years later though, when doubts arose about the purity of Strauss's Aryan bloodlines, the Nazis prohibited all of the organizations activities, and worked to suppress the fact that Strauss' great-great-grandfather was Jewish. (Strauss's widow, Adele, was also Jewish.) Music scholars who knew of Strauss's ancestry were ordered to keep strict silence, and an elaborate scheme was perpetrated to confiscate old marriage documents that contained information about Strauss' Jewish heritage, and create forgeries to replace them. The incident caused great embarrassment to the *Auschluss* and would have been an enormous scandal to Hitler's regime if the information became known. Strauss's music had been used widely in Nazi propaganda to symbolize all that was purely German.

Chapter 5

1. Eduard Reeser, *The History of the Waltz*. (London: Sidwick and Jackson, nd.) p. 19, quoting the *Journal des Luxus und der Modern*, 1797.

2. There were a variety of holds utilized in the waltz. One variation required the man and the woman to place their hands on their partner's torso near the armpits. Another popular hold, described in Byron's poem "The Waltz," consisted of each partner putting one of their hands on the other's shoulder and the second on his or her waist, in mirror image. Both of these holds were considered even more shockingly intimate and rude than the traditional ballroom position (man with right hand on woman's waist holding her right hand in his left, woman's left hand on his shoulder) that was also viewed as improper.

3. Resser, p. 19, quoting the diary of Crabb Richardson.

4. Reeser, pp. 20–21, quoting Salomo Jakob Wolf, *Beweis daß das Walzen eine Hauptquelle der Schwäche des Körpers und des Geistes unser Generation sey. Deutschlands Söhmen und Töchtern angelegentlichst empfohlen*, (Various sources give three different publishing dates for the book — 1792, 1797, and 1799.) The translation of the title is, "Proof that the waltz is a main source of the weakness of the body and mind of our generation. Most urgently recommended to the sons and daughters of Germany."

5. In her book *Adversaries of Dance: From the Puritans to the Present*. (Chicago: University of Illinois, 1997) pp. 130–131, Ann Wagner conjectures that many women in the Victorian era did indeed have "delicate constitutions." She writes,

> Yet the ideal for the lady restricted her to hearth and home and encased her in a corset of steel and whalebone, rendering her relatively inactive, hence, physically unfit, by today's cardiovascular standards. A woman thus confined may have experienced some physical stress when first exposed to lively dancing. Under such circumstances, dance opponents may not have been overstating their charge that disease and death from exposure to cold followed vigorous or extensive dancing at an evening ball.

6. Elizabeth Aldrich, *From the Ballroom to Hell: Grace and Folly in Nineteenth-century Dance*. (Evanston, IL: Northwestern University Press, 1991) p. 19, quoting Dio Lewis, *Our Girls* (New York: Clarke Bros., 1871.) Lewis was the founder of a school for women of "delicate constitution" in Lexington,

Massachusetts. He was a proponent of other forms of social dancing, but felt that round dances such as the waltz were detrimental to a woman's health, and therefore should be avoided.

7. Allison Thompson, *Dancing Through Time: Western Social Dance in Literature, 1400–1918: Selections.* (Jefferson, NC: McFarland, 1998) p. 202, quoting Mrs. John Sherwood. *Manners and Social Usages*, 1884, extracted from pp. 150–155.

8. This quote originally came from Donald Walker's *Exercises for Ladies* (London: Thomas Hurst, 1836), p. 149. The version listed here was drawn from two sources— Sevin H. Yaraman. *Revolving Embrace: The Waltz as Sex, Steps, and Sound.* (Hillsdale, NY: Pendragon Press, 2002) p. 7, and Elizabeth Aldrich, *From the Ballroom to Hell: Grace and Folly in Nineteenth-century Dance.* (Evanston, IL: Northwestern University Press, 1991) pp. 19–20.

9. *Oshkosh Daily Northwestern*, Oshkosh, WI, June 16, 1988, p. 2, col. 3.

10. Dr. R. A. Adams, *The Social Dance* (Kansas City: 1921) p. 8.

11. James H. Brookes, *The Modern Dance.* (Chicago: The Church Press, nd.) p. 21.

12. Adams, p. 9.

13. Alfred Carroll, "Concerning 'Round Dances'" in *Harper's New Monthly Magazine*, vol. 32, issue 191, April 1866, pp. 614–616.

14. *Ibid.*

15. Reeser, pp. 18–9, quoting Ernst Moritz Arndt, *Reisen durch einen Teil Teutschlands, Ungarns, Italiens und Frankreich* (1804).

16. Ruth Katz, "The Egalitarian Waltz" in *Comparative Studies in Society and History.* (New York: Cambridge University Press, June 1973) p. 179.

17. Adams, p.12, quoting Dr. J. H. Kellogg.

18. The proper position for couple dancing was achieved by bending the body forward slightly, with hips back and heels elevated off the floor, in what was known in its more exaggerated version as the "Grecian Bend." This term referred to the line of the body being graceful and curved as in a Grecian statue.

19. Allen Dodworth, an Englishman turned American, was one of the most important teachers of social dancing in the United States. (He was also founder of the New York Philharmonic Society and one of its first violinists.) Dodworth believed that dance was a means of instilling good personal morals and gaining social manners. Always stressing the use of dance as a genteel art form, Dodworth was horrified by the vulgarity of the polka when it was first introduced in the United States in the early 1840's. In 1842, he opened his own dancing school, the Dodworth Academy in New York, and it remained in existence until 1920. He wrote *Dancing and Its Relation to Education and Social Life, With a New Method of Instruction Including a Complete Guide to the Cotillion (German) with 250 Figures*, which was first published in 1885, and which is considered one of the first real textbooks on dancing based on a specific teaching method. Dodworth's book contained diagrams, illustrations, and examples of musical phrases with the dance movements marked on them. Allen Dodworth died in 1896 and the dance studio was taken over by his nephew T. George Dodworth, who continued to foster his uncle's standards concerning deportment and the moral benefits of dancing. When ragtime dances such as the Bunny Hug and Turkey Trot came into vogue, T. George formed a group called The New York Society of Teachers of Dancing that worked to codify dance instruction and ban dances that were considered vulgar. The group railed against modern dances and also against the notion of "cutting in," a practice which was gaining acceptance among the general public. "Cutting in" went against the use of dances cards that well-bred ladies were expected to carry at each dance and undermined the control that could be exercised by sticking to an approved list of partners.

20. Allen Dodworth, *Dancing and Its Relations to Education and Social Life.* (New York: Harper, 1888) pp. 39 and 41.

21. Dodworth, p. 41.

22. Aldridge, p. 111, quoting *True Politeness, A Hand-Book of Etiquette for Gentlemen. By an American Gentleman* (New York: Leavitt and Allen, 1847) p. 37.

23. In *Adversaries of Dance*, p. 171, Wagner states,

> The Victorian code developed with a general distrust of the body. Daily dress completely covered it; women's fashions distorted it. The code carefully guarded sexual activity as well, even in marriage. The typical male on the eve of his wedding had seen only the face and hands of his bride except perhaps for a glimpse afforded by décolletage at a ball. Physical contact had been limited to a formal kiss on the hand, unless knees had touched daringly under a table. Further, marriage manuals commonly recommended sex only once a week and told the couple not to undress in front of each other. Thus, touching even within the bonds of marriage, was restricted by prevailing rules for health and morality. In this context, the closed dance position seemed a total breech of decorum and morality, for the lady danced with the man's hand on the small of her back. The position appeared like an embrace.

24. Melvin B. Gilbert, *The Director: Dancing Deportment, Etiquette, Aesthetics, Physical Training.* (Portland, ME: Melvin Ballou Gilbert, 1898) (reprint by Dance Horizons 1975 or 1976) p. 254.

25. Gilbert, 254.

26. Members of The American Society of Professors of Dancing were especially strong advocates of the proper position while waltzing. The President of the Society, Melvin Ballou Gilbert, wrote in the December, 1897 issue of his magazine *The Director*,

> The task of stamping out the tendency to degeneration in the waltz position is not an easy one. We feel that united action on the part of legitimate teachers of dancing is necessary, and to that end all members of the American Society are resolved to battle, so that the waltz shall stand pre-eminent, a position which it justly deserves....

27. Gilbert, p. 8.

28. "Latest in Dancing" *Hawaiian Gazette*, Honolulu, HW, October 7, 1898, p. 7, col. 1.

29. Henry W. Stough, *Across the Dead Line of Amusements.* (New York: Fleming H. Revell Co., 1912) pp.114–115.

30. Stough, p. 115.

31. In the anti-dance book, *Immorality of Modern Dances*, ed. by Beryl and Assoc. (New York: Everitt and Francis Co. [etc.], 1904) p. 31, the author writes, "It is a horrible fact, but a fact nevertheless, that it is absolutely necessary that a woman shall be able and willing to reciprocate the feelings of her partner before she can graduate as a perfect dancer, so that even if it is allowed that a woman may waltz virtuously she cannot in that case waltz well."

32. T. A. Faulkner, *From the Ballroom to Hell.* (Chicago: R. B. McKnight, 1894) pp. 14–15.

33. Aldrich, p. 20, quoting *The Illustrated Book of Manners* (New York: Leland Clay & Co., 1855) 397–98.

34. Originally from Mme. Celnart, *The Gentleman and Lady's Book of Politeness*, 2nd American ed. (Boston: Allen and Ticknor and Carter, Hendee, & Co., 1833). This version was drawn from two sources: Aldrich, p. 20, and Buckman, pp. 126–7.

35. Brookes, pp. 137–138.

36. Faulkner, p. 18.

Chapter 6

1. In their book *Down Memory Lane: Arthur Murray's Picture Story of Social Dancing*, (New York: Greenberg, 1954,

p. 66) Sylvia G. L. Dannett, and Frank Rachel state, "from 1912 through 1914 over 100 new dances had found their way in and out of our fashionable ballrooms." *The Syracuse Herald, Syracuse,* NY, December 28, 1913, p. 9 listed the following dances under the heading "Freak Dances in Vogue;"

> The Boston, The Grizzly Bear, Luncheon Lurch, Tennis Tango, Futurist Twirl, Banana Peel Glide, Turtle Dove, Wilcox Glide, Grape Juice Wallow, The Seasick, The Double Boston, Boston Dip, Pannier Waltz, The Kitchen Sink, Debutante Dip, Tango Dip, Bunny Hug, Frisco Rag, Frisco Glide, One Step, Grape Vine, Texas Tommy, Aeroplane Dip, Horse Trot, Brazilian Maxixe, Fish Walk, The Tiger, The "Cucia," Tango Dream, Hitchy-Koo, Hesitation Waltz, Boll Weevil Wiggle, and Diaphanous Dip.

Anti-dance critics were appalled at the dances and also at their names. In his book *The Social Dance,* Adams (Kansas City: 1921) p. 24, Dr. R. A. Adams wrote,

> God made man upright; He gave him pre-eminence and dominion over the beasts of the field and the creeping things of the earth; He gave to man reason and understanding, lifting him above other creatures of his hand-make. Yet, so utterly depraved has man become and so unappreciative of the distinction accorded him that he comes down from his high pedestal to imitate the beasts of the field and the chickens of the barnyard. It is a sad reflection of this Nation that they should run out of dance steps and dance names and come down to the level of the brutes whose sexual actions they imitate in what are called animal dances.

2. "All New York Now Madly Whirling in the Tango" *The New York Times,* January 4, 1914, Section: Magazine Section, P. SM8.

3. "Texas Tommy (dance)" November 12, 2006 http://www.barrypopik.com/index.php/new_york_city/entry/texas_tommy_dance/

4. "Origin and Spread of the Vivacious 'Turkey Trot'" *The Anaconda Standard,* Anaconda, Montana, February 11, 1912, p. 25.

5. *Ibid.*

6. *Ibid.*

7. "Tango Is Inherited From the Savages" *Anaconda Standard,* Anaconda, Montana, February 15, 1914, p. 31, col. 4. Professor Oscar Duryea also theorized that the modern dances were really "the outgrowth of the most barbaric of the dances the red overlords of North America participated in long before Christopher Columbus and for some time after him." The professor reasoned;

> [M]en and women of today who love the modern dances must be in reality savages at heart; that civilization has only glossed over their inherent instincts and that their inner selves are finding an outlet for their real inclinations through the dances that are really an outgrowth of the orgies in which their earlier predecessors indulged years ago.

Oscar Duryea fought to refine modern dances. Around 1914, he standardized the fox trot under the auspices of the "American Society of Professors of Dancing" and introduced the modified version to the public. The toned downed version replaced exhausting trotting steps with more accessible gliding steps. Duryea's promotion of the easier, less-vulgar fox trot probably saved the dance from dying out as the other rag dances eventually did.

8. Lew Purcell and Sam King started the club and named it The Ivy. When their partnership dissolved, Purcell opened his own place and called it Purcell's. It was located at 520 Pacific Street in one of the first buildings erected after the San Francisco earthquake. The dance-hall was next to a place called Spider Kelly's, considered at the time to be "the lowest, most rotten dive in the world" (James R. Smith. *San Francisco's Lost Landmarks,* Sanger, CA: Quill Books, 2005, p. 82). According to Smith, the Texas Tommy and Ballin' the Jack both originated at Purcell's. (p. 80.)

9. Marshall and Jean Stearns, *Jazz Dance: The Story of American Vernacular Dance.* (New York: Da Capo, 1994) p. 128, quoting Gene Harris, an impresario who worked at the Thalia.

10. After it closed as a dance hall, the Thalia became a garage.

11. Herbert Asbury, *The Barbary Coast: An Informal History of the San Francisco Underworld.* (New York: Alfred Knopf, 1933) p. 296. Belly dances were common in the dance halls of the Barbary Coast. On page 287 of Asbury's book he tells of a rather odd and humorous finale to the dance:

> The pièce de résistance of a Barbary Coast variety program was the lewd cavorting of a hoochy-coochy artiste, or the Dance of the Seven Veils as interpreted by a fat and clumsy Salome dancer, who simply wiggled a muscle dance to semi-classical music. Occasionally a few of the veils were omitted, and the dancer squirmed and twisted in very scanty raiment indeed. For some curious reason, perhaps to show that her strength and agility were not confined entirely to her abdominal muscles, the Salome dancer almost invariably concluded her performance by gripping a chair between her teeth and swinging it about her head.

12. In addition to the Thalia, other well-known dance halls in the areas included the Hippodrome, the U.S. Café, the Jupiter, Coppa's, the Golden City, the Folies Cabaret, the White House, the House of All Nations, the Dragon, the Bella Union, the Cave, the Comstock, the Golden Star, the Turkish Café, the O. K. Café, the Ivy Café, the Moulin Rouge, the California Dance Hall, Spider Kelly's, the Red Mill, the Bohemian Café, the Dance Hall, the Bear, the Manila, the Queen Dance Hall, the So Different, the Olympia Café, the Frisco, the Old California, the Scandinavian Dance Hall, Thorne's, the Criterion, the Headlight; the Belvidere, Lombardi's, Dew Drop Inn, Purcell's, Dutch Emma's, Squeeze Inn, the Owl Dance Hall; the Admiral, the Cascade, Menio's, the Palms, Marconi's, the Elko, and the Neptune Palace.

According to Erenberg's book *Steppin' Out,* p. 20, "San Francisco's Barbary Coast in 1910 had over 300 [dance halls] in a six-block radius, while the South Side of Chicago in the same year had over 285. New York's Tenderloin and Bowery and the French Quarter in New Orleans had similar numbers and types of dance halls."

13. Asbury, p. 287.

14. Asbury, p. 286.

15. *Ibid.*

16. "History of Turkey Trot and The Gavotte Pavlowa" *Wichita Daily Times,* Wichita, TX, February 22, 1914, p. 14, col. 1.

17. Asbury, p. 297.

18. Asbury, p. 298. In the last months of 1908, the Rev. Terence Caraher, known by Barbary Coast habitués as "Terrible Terry," began a crusade to close down the nickel dance halls. Supported by the secretary of the Board of Police Commissioners and several businessmen, by the end of 1910 Caraher was able to see the last of the nickel dance-halls abolished.

19. Johnny Peters had traveled East to New York with his dancing partner Mary Dewson in Al Jolsen's troupe. Upon reaching New York in 1912, Dewson became ill and Peters teamed up with Ethel Williams. The two entered many dance contests around the city and performed in a cabaret act at Bustanoby's on 39th and Broadway, where they danced the tango, maxixe, one-step, waltz, and Texas Tommy. According to Williams, Irene Castle saw the duo at the restaurant and hired Williams to teach her some steps. In 1913, Peters and Williams appeared *in My Friend From Kentucky,* better known as *The Darktown Follies,* at the Lafayette Theatre in Harlem, considered by some to be the most important musi-

cal of that decade. Peters and Williams performed a number called "The Texas Tommy." The show also featured the tango and the cakewalk, and in the finale of the show, in a number called "At the Ball, That's All," the cast introduced the dance Ballin' the Jack. The number was a circle dance based on the Ring Shout and as the cast snaked around the stage, Ethel Williams brought up the rear, pretending to be out of breath and improvising crazy steps and mugging, a practice later used by Josephine Baker in *Shuffle Along*. After seeing the production, Florence Ziegfeld bought the number in its entirety to put in his *Follies of 1914*. He hired Ethel Williams to teach the dance to his cast, but did not hire her to perform in his production uptown at the roof garden of the New York Theater.

20. "Origin and Spread of the Vivacious 'Turkey Trot'" *The Anaconda Standard*, Anaconda, Montana, February 11, 1912, p. 25.

21. "Turkey Trot Was a Cowboy Dance" *The Milford Mail*, Milford, Iowa, April 3, 1913, p. 2, col. 2.

22. "'Grizzly Bear' Old Greek" *The New York Times*, August 31, 1913, Section: Foreign News Financial Business Sports Want Advertisements, p. C1.

23. "Origin of Turkey Trot" *The San Antonio Light*, San Antonio, TX, September 14, 1913, p. 8, col. 7. The same article stated, "It was from this Pompeiian glide that the Spanish fandango originated, the French cotillion and the waltz, along with little parts of other terpsichorean creations." It also states women in ancient Abyssinia (present day Ethiopia) "danced in a circle, shaking their shoulders, wagging their elbows and wiggling after the manner of the exaggerated turkey trot."

24. "Turkey Trot New? Danced 500 Years in Borneo" *The Iowa Recorder*, Greene, Iowa, September 25, 1912, p. 2, col. 4.

25. "Origin of Modern Eccentric Dances Traced to Underworld" *The San Antonio Light*, San Antonio, TX, December 14, 1913, p. 34, col. 1. The quote continues, "The probability is that some unknown and unnamed burglar, picket-pocket, yeggman or police 'stool pigeon,' frequenter of the Barbary Coast, deserves the rather questionable honor."

26. "Turkey Trot Was a Cowboy Dance" *The Milford Mail*, Milford, Iowa, April 3, 1913, p. 2, col. 2.

27. "The Turkey Trot" *The Daily Courier*, Connellsville, PA January 22, 1912, p. 4, col. 3.

28. *Ibid.*

29. *Ibid.* According to the article, the turkey trot met with the agent's approval and he took the dance back to his ruler in Turkey.

Chapter 7

1. *The New York Times* claimed in one article that rag dances were first performed in the Bowery in New York. It stated, "...the 'rag' flourished in the east side dance halls, whence it was taken by sailors around the horn to the Barbary Coast of San Francisco." It is possible that rag dances developed concurrently on both coasts although San Francisco generally claims credit for being the instigator of the ragtime craze.

2. "Origin and Spread of the Vivacious 'Turkey Trot'" *The Anaconda Standard*, Anaconda, Montana, February 11, 1912, p. 25.

3. "Brought 'Tango' to America" *The New York Times*, January 17, 1914, p. 8.

4. *A Certain Party* opened at Wallack's Theatre on April 24, 1911 and ran through May 13, 1911. In the show Mabel Hite's character, Norah, danced with Mike Donlin's character, James Barrett, at the end of the second act to a song written by Tom Kelly. The review in *The New York Times*, April 25, 1911, p. 13, stated, "Mr. Donlin, it must be confessed, looked as if he'd much rather be on a ball field, but would

stick it out for her [Hite's] sake. What he may lack in histrionic ability — and that is little — he makes up for in an expression of benign good nature." In addition to starring in the production, Mabel Hite also wrote the music and lyrics to the third act finale entitled "You're Going to Lose Your Husband." This song later became fodder for the gossip columns when Hite and Donlin had marital troubles.

5. Joseph C. Smith was born in 1875, one of ten children of the famous American dancer George Washington Smith. His mother disapproved of the theatre and made each of her children promise they would not pursue it as a career. Nevertheless, Joseph's father gave him a thorough training in all the theatrical arts. He was trained as a harlequin, ballet dancer, and was proficient in the use of swords and the quarter staff. He was also a trick rider and could stand on a horse's back without support, a trick he quickly learned because he was whipped if he fell off. His training was rigorous and he became so adept and skillful at controlling his body, he once fell forty feet off a suspension wire and was able to land on the stage and only sustain a few bruises. He did not pursue his theatrical career until after his mother's death, when he became one of the most popular performers on the stage. His versatility allowed him to dance in classical ballets at La Scala in Milan and perform as a show dancer on Broadway. He choreographed and performed in several Broadway productions and claimed that he had introduced both the turkey trot and tango on the Broadway stage. In 1907 in the *Ziegfeld Follies* he introduced the apache dance with Louise Alexander. (This information is from Paul Magriel's book, *Chronicles of the American Dance*, p. 187. Neither Smith, nor Alexander are listed as performers in the *Ziegfeld Follies of 1907* credits on the Internet Broadway database, although Smith is listed as staging some of the numbers. The site does credit him as an apache dancer in *The Queen of the Moulin Rouge* which opened in 1908.) Smith is credited with being the first man to dance in public in formal evening clothes. The event took place in London when he arrived late to the theatre for a performance one evening and ran on stage without changing. The audience response was so favorable, the theatre manager asked him to continue wearing the outfit during the run. Smith was married to Frances Demarest, a singer. The two worked together in the Broadway production of *Madame Sherry*, a show in which Smith staged a polka for the hit number, "Every Little Movement Has a Meaning of Its Own." In 1910 Smith staged the floor show at Maxine's Café Madrid, said to be the first show of its kind in New York, setting a trend that fostered the spread of ragtime dancing. In December of 1932, Joseph C. Smith was killed by a truck while he was crossing the street at Madison Avenue and Thirty-Fourth Street.

6. Mabel Hite was born in Ashland, Kentucky and first appeared on the stage in an amateur production of Gilbert and Sullivan's *Iolanthe* at age eleven. A popular favorite in vaudeville, her professional credits also included *A Milk White Flag, The Telephone Girl, A Knight for a Day* and *A Certain Party*. In 1909, Hite married professional baseball player Mike Donlin and the two performed in vaudeville in a musical skit called "Stealing Home." She died on October 22, 1912 in New York at the home of her mother at age twenty-seven of intestinal cancer. In a bizarre twist to her life story, on November 28, 1915, a man walked into Murray's Restaurant on Forty-Second Street near Seventh Avenue and left a brown paper package at the checkroom, making an off-handed comment to Jack Bess the boy at the check counter. He said "Don't drop it, or it will blow up the place." Concerned that he had been give a bomb, the checkroom boy told the manager about the suspicious package. The manager gingerly took the parcel to an empty café next door and dropped it in a bucket of water, then called the police. They sent two detectives, who then summoned the Inspector of the Bureau of Combustibles, Owen Egan. Egan moved the suspicious package to an abandoned excavation site nearby and carefully removed the paper wrapping. Underneath he found a bronze

urn with the engraving "Mabel Hite Donlin, Died Oct. 22, 1912." The receptacle was Hite's cremation urn and still contained her ashes. The man who had checked the urn was Ray E. Frye, the manager of a mortuary who was personally entrusted with the ashes by Hite's husband Mike Donlin. He was moving the urn because his undertaking firm was moving to a new columbarium. (This information was extracted from *The New York Times*, November 29, 1915, p. 6.)

7. Mike Donlin was born on May 30, 1878, in Erie, Pennsylvania (other sources say Peoria, Illinois.) Known as "Turkey Mike" because of the way he strutted on the field, he became a professional baseball player in Santa Cruz, California in 1899 as a pitcher and later moved to San Jose in 1900 when the team franchise was sold. He was moved to the outfield and played with the St. Louis Cardinals until 1903, when he was sold to Cincinnati. In 1904, he joined the New York Giants, eventually becoming team captain. He played with the Giants until 1910 and was said to be, "...one of the greatest natural hitters in the game." He left baseball after he married Mabel Hite in 1909 and toured the vaudeville circuit with her as a singer and dancer. In 1914 he returned to the diamond to play with the Boston Braves, and then moved to the Pittsburgh Pirates. After the first World War, he moved to Hollywood and appeared in motion pictures. Athlete's heart led to his retirement in 1927 and motion picture and stage performers had a benefit minstrel show to raise money to send him to the Mayo Clinic for an operation. After Mabel Hite's death in 1912, Donlin remarried Rita Ross in 1914. Mike Donlin died at age fifty-six in Los Angeles, California on September 24, 1933 of a heart attack.

8. "Brought 'Tango' to America" *The New York Times*, January 17, 1914, p. 8.

9. *Ibid.*

10. *Over the River* ran at the Globe Theatre from 1/8/1912 through 4/20/1912 for a total of 120 performances. The show was produced by Charles Dillingham and Florence Ziegfeld, Jr., and starred vaudevillian Eddie Foy. Joseph C. Smith played a character named Charles Bigroll and was featured in a number called "The Tongo Dance." *The Anaconda Standard*, Anaconda, Montana, February 11, 1912, p. 25, wrote, "Lillian Lor[r]aine, with Joseph C. Smith, dances the tango, which is a variation of the turkey trot, every night at Eddie Foy's show, "Over the River," at the Globe theater, and extra help had to be hired to count the money." Exhibition dancer Monsieur Maurice also appeared in the show in a number called "The Maurice Rag."

11. "Origin and Spread of the Vivacious 'Turkey Trot'" *The Anaconda Standard*, Anaconda, Montana, February 11, 1912, p. 25

12. *Ibid.*

13. *Ibid.*

14. *Ibid.*

15. *Ibid.* Ziegfeld did credit Mabel Hite with being the first to introduced rag dancing on Broadway. The article states, "Miss Hite had beaten him to it by a few weeks. She had paid the San Francisco exponents of a new art $100 a week to teach her and Michael to rock and undulate. Therefore, Miss Hite was the first to put the dance on.... Even theater managers like Ziegfeld, who has [sic] nothing to gain by advertising an artist not in his troupe, admits that credit has to be slipped to Mrs. Dolin for introducing the turkey to New York"

16. *Little Miss Fix-It* opened on Broadway on April 3, 1911 at the Globe Theatre and ran through May 20, 1911. It later reopened at the Grand Opera House in November 27, 1911 and had a short run into December of the same year. It starred Nora Bayes. (Interestingly, this show opened three weeks before *A Certain Party*. It is uncertain when Lane's and Hunter's turkey trot was inserted into the show. James C. Lane is listed in the opening night credits but Edna Hunter is not. The only musical number that lists Lane is "no More Staying Out Late," but this is listed as being danced by Lane and the men of the chorus only. Edna Hunter was in the cast of *Over the River* in 1912.) The reference to the trot being done by Lane and Hunter is in the article "Origin and Spread of the Vivacious 'Turkey Trot'" credited earlier.

17. "Origin and Spread of the Vivacious 'Turkey Trot'" *The Anaconda Standard*, Anaconda, Montana, February 11, 1912, p. 25.

18. As one commentator in *The New York Times* observed in 1914, "If you wanted to keep your restaurant open, it seemed you were almost compelled to put in a cabaret show of some kind." An article in *The Atlanta Constitution*, (Atlanta, GA, September 13, 1914, p. 43, col. 3.), that spoke of how the dancing craze was gripping that city stated, "Unless we dine at home, our meals will be punctuated by trots...."

19. Lewis Erenberg, *Steppin'Out: New York Nightlife and the Transformation of American Culture, 1890–1930.* (Chicago: University of Chicago Press, 1981) p. 123.

20. Julie Malnig, *Dancing Till Dawn: A Century of Exhibition Ballroom Dance.* (New York: New York University Press, 1992) p. 8, quoting George Rector.

21. Erenberg, p. 132, quoting George Rector.

22. "All New York Now Madly Whirling in the Tango" *The New York Times*, January 4, 1914, Section: Magazine Section, P. SM8.

23. *Ibid.*

24. *Ibid.*

25. "Social Sanity Threatened, Says Our Foremost Psychologist" *Lima Daily News*, Lima, OH, May 31, 1914, p. 17, quoting Professor Hugo Muensterberg of Harvard University.

26. Joan Sawyer was born Cincinnati, Ohio around 1880. Her given name was Bessie J. Morrison. She was raised in El Paso Texas by a family called the Waltons and for a while took the name Bessie Walton. She returned to Ohio to attend school and at age fifteen decided to pursue a career in show business. In 1902, she had a short marriage to Alvah Sawyer, keeping his last name throughout her career. Success eluded her until 1907 when she appeared as a chorus girl in a production called *The Vanderbilt Cup*. This was followed by other small parts in *The Hurdy Gurdy Girl* in 1907 and *The Merry Go Round* in 1908. She first achieved real public notice when she hit the headlines by filing a $100,000 breach of promise suit against millionaire playboy Byron Chandler, claiming he had taken advantage of her with a promise of marriage. She lost the case when the defendant's lawyers pointed out that she was already married. In 1911, real success finally found Sawyer when she was discovered by popular ballroom dancer Maurice Mouvet. The two teamed up at Louis Martin's Café de Opera for a short time. After that Sawyer appeared in other top cabarets around New York. In 1913, agent William Morris signed her and she was offered a contract to dance at his Jardin de Danse at the New York Theatre. The engagement was hugely successful and she was soon in top demand around the city. While continuing to perform at the Jardin de Danse, she was offered a huge salary by Geroge Rector to do her act at his place. Rector also paid William Morris an enormous fee to "borrow" their star. She moved to the Shuberts' Persian Garden in January 1914 in an elegantly decorated room with an entrance sign in lights that read, "Joan Sawyer's Persian Garden." It was a huge hit and a popular spot for the upper set during afternoon teas or after the theatre. Sawyer herself danced nightly with a variety of partners from 11:00 P.M. to 1:00 A.M., except Sundays, sometimes performing at afternoon tea dances as well. In addition, she supervised all dance contests and taught lessons there. Sawyer had her own private black orchestra led by Dan Kildare. The Clef Club Orchestra, as it was called, not only accompanied Sawyers's dancing at the Persian Garden, but also recorded a series of dance records for Columbia. (Kildare was not credited and the recordings were marketed as Joan Sawyer's Persian Garden Orchestra, "recorded under the personal supervision of Joan Sawyer.")(Tim Brooks. *Lost Sounds: Blacks and the Birth of the Recording Industry.* Champaign, IL: University of Illinois Press, 2005, p. 305.) When Maurice

Mouvet and his partner Florence Walton began performing at The Persian Room, one floor below The Persian Garden, attendance at her club slipped and Sawyer did not renew her contract with the Shuberts. In the summer of 1914, she toured vaudeville, taking Kildare and his orchestra with her, until she was stopped by "appendicitis" and had to return to New York in mid–August of that same year. The real story involved a scandal when Joan abruptly dropped her fiancé Edwin Finney. Finney had met Sawyer at the Persian Gardens where she taught him how to dance. Finney showered the dancer with gifts, including spending $400.00 a month for an automobile for her. The two were engaged and plans were made for Finney to join her act as her dance partner for shows in Boston and Philadelphia. Plans were dropped when Sawyer suddenly took "ill" and broke off the engagement. In truth, she had learned that he did not have an income of $40,000 a year as he claimed, but only brought in about $3,000 annually. A staunch suffragist, Sawyer also grabbed national headlines in 1914 when, accompanied by a dance partner, chauffeur, mechanic and chaperon, she drove across country with a suffragist banner attached to her car. *The Fort Wayne Journal-Gazette*, (Fort Wayne, IN, July 4, 1915, p, 39, col. 6.) reported,

> Joan Sawyer, who is adding to her fame as a dancer a national reputation as a motorist and a advocate for suffrage, created considerable excitement in Detroit when she arrived there on her trans-continental tour across the continent from New York to San Francisco.

In 1917, Joan Sawyer appeared in a silent film entitled *Love's Law*.

27. According to an article in the *San Antonio Evening News*, (San Antonio, TX, January 27, 1923. p, 7, col. 2), John Jarrot (also spelled Jarrott, was one of the top dancers in the business. The article states, "Jarrott "made" Joan Sawyer, Bonnie Glass, Mae Murray and other stars of the Texas Tommy generation" According to one source Jarrot was married to Joan Sawyer at one time. He appeared in George M. Cohan's production of *The Yankee Consul* and was a sought after performer in vaudeville and on the cabaret circuit. Jarrot developed a serious drug habit that eventually ruined him. As one of society's top dancers he had commanded a salary of at least $1,000 a week, but his habit eventually made him destitute. In addition, Jarrot was heir to acres of land in the oil rich district of Texas, but lost it for non-payment of taxes. He hit bottom in 1923, when he was sentenced to six months in the workhouse on Blackwell's Island for stealing an overcoat worth $25.00. He confessed to the judge he had stolen the coat to sell it and make money to buy drugs. Near the end of his life, he worked as a doorman at some of the clubs where he had once headlined. In June of 1938, John Jarrot was admitted to Bellevue Hospital with pneumonia, giving his name as John Garrett. He succumbed to the disease on June 14, 1938 at age 55. Many sources credit Jarrot with introducing the turkey trot with his partner Louise Gruenning at Ray Jones café in Chicago around 1909.

28. While partnering Sawyer, Valentino became entangled in a sex scandal involving himself, Sawyer, athlete and real estate broker John "Jack" de Saulles, and de Saulles' millionaire wife Blanca. It is rumored that Joan Sawyer was having an affair with de Saulles, and Valentino, smitten with Blanca, agreed to testify for her in her divorce proceedings against her husband. De Saulles retaliated by having Valentino arrested at a nearby brothel. The charges against Valentino were bogus and eventually he was released, but the publicity hurt him and no one would hire him. Even worse, Blanca would not speak with him. In August of 1917, Blanca de Saulles got into an argument with her estranged husband over custody of their son. She held a gun to his head and demanded he hand over the child. In the ensuing struggle, she shot him five times. Charged with first-degree murder, the trial that followed created a national sensation, even bumping news of the First World War off the front pages.

Again, Valentino's name was dragged through the mud. He changed his name from Rodolfo Guglielmi and moved to Hollywood to avoid further scandal. After his success in motion pictures, the film studios arranged to have Valentino's police records concerning the event destroyed. In 1918, a silent movie was made based on the case. It was called *The Woman and the Law*. In 1940, Blanca de Saulles committed suicide.

29. Mae Murray was born Marie Adrienne Koenig in Portsmouth, Virginia, on May 10, 1889. She made her Broadway debut in 1906 in *About Town*, a show whose cast also included Vernon Castle. She was hired to be in the chorus of the *Ziegfeld Follies* in 1908 and later performed in other *Follies* productions. She eventually became a featured performer, and was nicknamed by Ziegfeld as "the girl with the bee-stung lips." Her biggest break came in 1910, when she replaced Irene Castle in *Watch Your Step*. She invented many dances. While doing a featured part in the *Ziegfeld Follies of 1915*, she was spotted by Adolph Zukor, who was scouting for new talent for the silent movies. She signed with Paramount Pictures and ended up starring in several films. Her biggest success came with the film version of *The Merry Widow* in 1923. She appeared in two films with Rudolph Valentino. In the late 20's her career began to falter and she eventually ended up destitute. Murray died on March 23, 1965 in Woodland Hills, California of heart failure. It is rumored that director Billy Wilder used Murray as the inspiration for the character of Norma Desmond in his movie *Sunset Boulevard*.

30. Malnig, p. 21.

31. The site of the Folies Marigny later became the home of Castles in the Air, the club owned by Vernon and Irene Castle.

32. Clifton Webb was born in Beech Grove, Indiana, on November 11, 1889. He was christened Webb Parmelee Hollenbeck. His mother left her husband, a railroad ticket clerk, because he didn't "care for the theatre" and moved with her son to New York where at age five, Webb began dance lessons. He made his stage debut at Carnegie Hall in a production of *The Brownies* at age seven. He then toured vaudeville, and landed leading roles in *Oliver Twist* and *Huckleberry Finn*. He studied voice as well as dancing and by seventeen was singing secondary leads with the Aborn Opera Company in Boston. At nineteen he adopted the stage name Clifton Webb and began his career as a professional ballroom dancer. He performed in numerous Broadway shows, toured in vaudeville, and also performed in a few silent movies. In his fifties, he was chosen to act in Otto Preminger's 1944 classic *Laura*, a role that won him an Oscar. He had a successful movie career, winning two other Academy Awards. He died of a heart attack at age 76 in Beverly Hills, California on October 13, 1966.

33. Malnig, p. 23.

34. John Murray Anderson was born on September 20, 1886 in St. John's, Newfoundland. He was educated at Bishop Field College and then studied at Edinburgh Academy in Scotland and Lausanne University in Switzerland. After working as an antiques dealer in New York City, he turned to theatre. He opened a dance studio called the John Murray Anderson school of Theater and Dance on East 58th Street and trained many young actors and dancers. In 1914, he met Genevieve Lyon of Chicago. The two wed and formed a dance act. When Lyon developed tuberculosis, the couple moved to Arizona for her health. She passed away from the disease in 1916. Anderson returned to New York and applied to enter the U.S. military and was accepted. Later he turned to producing and earned the nicknames, "King of the Revues," and "Uncle Broadway." During his career, he produced thirty-four major musical comedies and revues including three editions of the *Ziegfeld Follies* (1934, 1936, 1943), *Life Begins at 8:40* (1934), Billy Rose's *Jumbo* (1935), *One for the Money* (1939), *Two for the Show* (1940), *Three to Make Ready* (1946), and *New Faces of 1952*. He also staged seven circuses for Ringling Brothers, four Aquacades for Billy Rose, eleven pag-

eants, sixty-one stage productions for movie houses, and at least twenty-for major nightclub extravaganzas. In 1930 he directed the film *King of Jazz*. He also wrote the screenplay for *Ziegfeld Follies* (1946). Anderson died on January 30, 1954 in New York.

35. The Dolly Sisters were born Rosika (Rose) and Jansci (Jenny) Deutsch on October 25, 1892 in Budapest, Hungary. They emigrated to the United States in 1905, and began dancing in beer halls around 1907 in a tandem act. They toured on the Orpheum circuit until 1909, then joined the Keith circuit where they performed until 1911. They were eventually signed by Florence Ziegfeld and worked in the *Follies* for two seasons. The sisters also toured Europe, and made a few silent films. The two sometimes appeared with male partners in competing acts to boost ticket sales. Jenny married Harry Fox, who is credited with inventing the foxtrot. Known for their luck at gambling, they won $850,000 in one season at Deauville. Jenny later won 4 million francs at Cannes. She bought jewelry with her winnings and then went on to win another 11 million more. In 1933, Jenny was nearly killed in an automobile accident near Bordeaux, France, when her car fell over a cliff. Her recovery took six weeks and required at least fifteen surgeries, which she paid for her by selling most her jewelry. She never did recover emotionally from the accident and suffered from horrible depression afterwards. On May 1, 1941 she committed suicide, hanging herself in the shower of her apartment in the Shelton Hotel. Rosie herself attempted suicide in 1962, but failed. She died heart failure on January 1, 1970.

36. Erenberg, p. 165.

37. Maurice Oscar Louis Mouvet was born in the Chelsea district of New York on March 18, 1889. The family, of Belgian descent, moved to London when he was nine and at age fourteen to Paris where Mouvet worked as an auto mechanic and a chauffeur. On the way to work, he passed a famous French restaurant, and Mouvet wheedled the doorman into letting him look inside to watch the dancers. He had his first professional dance training at another cabaret, Noveau Cirque, at age 15, where he convinced the manager to engage him as a dancer after he demonstrated a few cakewalk steps. His love of dancing caused him to frequent the cafes and restaurants of Montmartre. He danced at the Royale and presented an act comprised of the cakewalk, polka, and two-step. He studied the waltz at the Bal Tabarin and began looking for a dancing partner. He was eventually offered a job dancing in Vienna at the Casino Theatre, where he performed with two female partners. Whenever he was not performing, he visited other clubs, studying the Viennese waltz. He later performed in Budapest and Monte Carlo. Upon returning to Paris, he formed a partnership with a woman by the name of Leona and the couple was hired to dance at the Café de Paris. His successes in Paris, especially as a proponent of the apache dance, led to invitations for Mouvet to dance before all the major crowned heads of Europe except the Emperor of Germany. In 1910, he was offered a contract with Louis Martin's Café de Paris in New York City with his new partner Madelaide D'Arville. (Leona had died of pneumonia.) Initially the team only danced the Viennese waltz and Argentine tango, fearing that if they did the apache, the club would be raided by the police, but later began including the dance in late-night performances. The team joined the cast of *Over the River*, but then D'Arville eloped after a Tuesday night performance leaving Mouvet unable to perform the following day for the matinee. The show's producer Florence Ziegfeld called Movet into his office at 7:00 P.M. the next evening and introduced him to Florence Walton. With only a half hour of rehearsal, the two went on that night. They went on to become one of the most successful ballroom exhibition teams, rivaling Vernon and Irene Castle. They married in 1911 and performed together around the world. Mouvet and Walton eventually divorced in 1920. (Mouvet also trained amateur dancer Joan Sawyer. They were engaged, but their partnership also dissolved when Sawyer married someone else.

Accounts differ as to when they danced together. Some say before he paired with Walton and others say before Madelaide.) His next partner was Leonora Hughes, a former telephone operator, but she left the act to marry Argentine millionaire Carlos Ortiz Balsualdo in 1925. Mouvet then teamed up with Barbara Bennett, sister of movie star Constance Bennett. They separated within the year after quarreling over money matters, and Mouvet hired Eleanor Ambrose, daughter of a Kansas City oil man, to replace her. In 1926, the two were wed in Paris and danced at the St. Moritz until consumption forced Mouvet to move to the Alps for his health. Mouvet died on May 18, 1927 of tuberculosis at the Hotel Savoy in Lausanne, Switzerland. His wife Eleanor Ambrose and his brother Oscar were with him. In October of 1927, Maurice Mouvet's father was arrested for trying to smuggle 750 pounds of opium into the United States. His wife, Mouvet's mother, claimed he had been acting strangely after his son's death and his actions were a result of grief. He was subsequently released because after his arrest, the seized drugs were analyzed, and it turned out there was no opium in the packages, just cheap chemicals created to look like opium with the intention of duping the opium buyers.

38. "Maurice and the New Dances" *The New York Times*, January 25, 1912, p. 10.

39. The *danse des Apaches* or Apache dance supposedly got its name after a Parisian journalist reported a scuffle outside a Montmartre nightclub. He wrote, "The fury of a riotous incident (a fight) between two men and a woman rose to the ferocity of savage Apache Indians in battle." The trio involved in the fight proudly accepted the association with savages and soon Parisian gangs were calling themselves *les Apaches*. The gangs, also known as "the Gunmen of Paris," recreated the fight scenario while dancing in Paris' many *caveau des innocents*, or underworld cabarets, and the dance was also dubbed the "The Dance of the Underworld." The pantomime dance, which told the story of a struggle between a pimp and his prostitute, or the raging jealousy of two lovers, was usually accompanied by tango or slow waltz music. It often involved violent pushing, slapping, dragging, throwing, or threatening the partner with a knife. Although a brutal dance, it was stylized to convey primitive passion instead of vulgarity. High society slummers became fascinated with the dance and for a brief while there were attempts to use it as a social dance, but its extreme physical demands caused it to remain an exhibition dance. Due to the dangerous lifts and throws utilized in presenting the apache, some women suffered broken necks and backs and died while performing. According to Irene Castle (*Castles in the Air*, p. 59.) Maurice Mouvet's first wife died performing the dance. The apache dance lifts were used in the Texas Tommy, and later became part of the Lindy Hop and Jitterbug. In his book, *Maurice's Art of Dancing*, p. 35, Maurice Mouvet wrote about the apache dance. He said, "It is I suppose, an intensely brutal dance, but it is not vulgar with deliberate vulgarity. It is a dance of realism, of primitive passion; as a picture of life in the raw it has beauty and artistic strength."

40. The "Gunmen of Paris" were real gang members and although most used knives instead of guns, they were a dangerous lot. Their women were used to distract unsuspecting men who were then attacked, robbed, and brutalized. The most famous of these gangs was *Les Apaches*. As the apache dance became popular, the ladies of Parisian high society would hire the most notorious hooligans to teach them to dance — the more bloodthirsty the criminal, the more they were paid. Some of these men included Jules Jacques, also called "the Tiger," Little Scarlip, Louis the Strangler, and Raoul the Butcher. The men not only taught the ladies to dance but also entertained them with sensational tales of the many throats they had cut.

41. The apache was supposedly brought to the United States by Joseph C. Smith around 1904.

42. Florence Walton was born in 1891 in Wilmington, Delaware. She first appeared on the stage in Philadelphia in

Miss Bob White as a young Quaker girl. In 1907, she appeared in the chorus of a musical comedy called *The Girl Behind the Counter*. Florence Ziegfeld then hired her as specialty dancer in his 1908 production of *Miss Innocence*. In 1911, she danced in *The Pink Lady* and in February 1912, while she was rehearsing for her next show, *The Rose Maid*, the show's producer, Florence Ziegfeld suggested her as a replacement for Maurice Mouvet's act, since Mouvet had lost his partner. The two became one of ballroom's premiere dance couples. They married in 1911 and dance together until their divorce in 1920. Walton died in 1981.

43. Malnig, p. 42.

44. Irene Castle described the couple as follows;

> Maurice was ill-tempered, a dark little man who looked Latin and had a hundred legends surrounding him. He waltzed beautifully and had undoubtedly taught Florence everything she knew. She was a little wooden from the waist up, but she had lovely legs and handled them beautifully [Castle, p. 60].

45. Newspaper accounts of the wedding of Leonora Hughes to cattle tycoon Don Carlos Ortiz Balsualdo reported that Maurice Mouvet wept uncontrollably during the ceremony, moaning over and over again, "I cannot bear it! How could she do this to me?" He was only mollified when after the ceremony, while processing down the aisle, the bride sat in the pew with him and consoled him. The couple then invited Mouvet to the wedding breakfast, with Maurice and the bride going in one car and the groom following in a second car. When he saw the couple off at the train station as they left for their honeymoon, he broke down again. Mouvet was heard to remark, "Losing your dance partner is much worse than losing your business partner or wife. If you lose your partner, you carry on your business somehow. If your wife leaves you, you go on with your work, even if your heart is broken. But when a man's dancing partner leaves him his heart and his business both go smash!" After the Balsuados went on their honeymoon, Mouvet held auditions for a new partner. The newspaper reported, "Girls came by the hundreds — tall girls, short girls, brunettes, blondes. Maurice danced with every one." But, Mouvet had no luck. "They have no fire," he said, "their feet move, but their hearts never. I could not make dancers of them — not in a hundred years." Mouvet was also heard to comment "I will have none but an American girl. They do not get fat." He then added bitterly, "Leonora was getting a little fat.... My new partner must be small and slim." Maurice Mouvet eventually hired Barbara Bennett. Upon hearing the news of his pick Mouvet's friends said, "Poor Maurice, he's in for trouble again" (quotes from an article entitled "In His Arms, But He Can't Keep Them There" *Galveston Daily News*, Galveston, Texas, April 14, 1925, p. 8).

46. Vernon Castle was born on May 2, 1887 in Norwich, Norfolk, England. His given name was William Vernon Blyth. Irene Castle was born on April 17, 1893 in New Rochelle, New York. Her given name was Irene Foote. After Vernon Castle graduated from Birmingham University School of Engineering, he worked as a magician in clubs and at private parties. He took the last name Castle to avoid confusion with his sister Coralie Blythe who was an actress. He first visited the United States with his sister and her husband, actor Laurence Grossmith. He was give a bit part in Grossmith's play and decided he liked show business. He went on to work as a chorus boy in several musicals. He was taken under the wing by producer Lew Fields, an ex-vaudevillian, who helped develop Vernon's comedic skills. In 1909 while vacationing in New Rochelle, he met Irene at the pool of the Rowing Club. She was not romantically interested in him when she first met him because she thought he was too skinny. Vernon was 5'11" and weighed only 118 lbs. Drama critics sometimes referred to him as "an attenuated green bean," or "a soda straw with legs." But, Irene had been taking dance lessons and was interested in show business, and hoped that he might help her gain a foothold in the business. Irene later recalled,

> My heart skipped a beat. My mind immediately began to make plans and weave schemes. I was meeting a real actor for the first time, and to further my excitement, he was associated with Lew Fields, one of the top names on the Broadway stage. I felt sure if Lew Fields could be persuaded to take one look at my dancing, my career would be on its way [Castle, pp. 31–32].

The two began dating, and Irene and Vernon quickly fell in love. They were married on May 28, 1911. Lew Fields discouraged Vernon from pursuing a career in dancing, believing he had more potential as a comedian. He did help Irene get small parts in various musicals. In 1911, they did decide to put a dance act together. They showed it to Fields who was not impressed and left the room without saying a word even before they had finished their demonstration. When confronted by Vernon, Field's retorted, "Who's going to pay to see a man dance with his wife?" They couple abandoned their plans for a dance act. In 1911, when the opportunity arose for Vernon to appear in comical sketches in Paris, the Castles traveled to France. Troubles hounded the production and the opening was delayed several weeks. Vernon Castle received no pay during the wait and soon the couple was out of money, depending on their servant's luck at craps to bring in enough funds to keep them fed. Vernon's show finally opened, but conditions at the theatre were so dreadful, Vernon quit in disgust. Desperation led them to hire themselves out as exhibition dancers at Louis Barraya's Café de Paris. Their first impromptu appearance was a huge hit, and after several successful successive weeks at the club, they received offers to perform at private parties attended by some of the most influential people in Europe. They also drew the attention of some of America's top theatrical producers. In May 1912, with the death of Irene's father, the couple left Paris and returned to the United States. They were approached to recreate their act at the Café de l'Opera in Manhattan, and there, met literary agent Elisabeth Marbury. Under her guidance, the couple became the darlings of New York. By 1914, the couple were at the height of their fame and popularity, starring in *Watch Your Step*, and embarking on their Whirlwind Tour of the United States to teach America the proper way to dance. In thirty theatres across the country they demonstrated and taught dances to packed houses. The twenty-eight day event climaxed at Madison Square Garden where the finalists from dance contests from the various cities performed, with an exhausted Vernon and Irene Castle. As World War I raged in Europe, Vernon Castle began to feel concerned about his native country being threatened by Germany. He enlisted in the military and after learning to fly was assigned to the Royal Canadian Flying Corps. He flew one hundred and fifty dangerous missions in Europe, and was decorated for his bravery. In 1917, he returned to the United States to train young aviators. He was killed during a training mission at Benbrook Field near Forth Worth, Texas, on February 15, 1918. After Vernon's death, Irene Castle continued to appear solo in several stage productions and in several silent movies before retiring. She remarried three more times. She became an avid campaigner for animal rights and formed an Illinois animal shelter called "Orphans of the Storm" that is still in operation. She died on January 25, 1969 in Eureka Springs, Arkansas. Vernon and Irene Castle are interred together at the Woodlawn Cemetery in the Bronx, New York.

47. Erenberg, p. 159, quoting the *Dramatic Mirror*, June 30, 1915.

48. Irene Castle, *Castles in the Air*, (New York: Da Capo, 1958) p. 54.

49. Castle, pp. 54–55.

50. Castle, p. 57.

51. A Russian gentleman offered them a three hundred franc tip after that initial performance; Vernon Castle wanted to refuse, but Irene made him accept the tip and soon their tips exceeded their salary. Irene recalled, "Men in the gentlemen's room would slip Vernon a thousand francs to show

their appreciation while their ladies came to my table and slipped me a thousand francs in case their escorts had forgotten to do so" (Castle, p. 58).

52. The Castles briefly left the Café de Paris when Maurice Mouvet and his partner Florence Walton were given a spot dancing at the cabaret at the same time. Mouvet's first wife, had been killed while doing an Apache dance when under the employ of the club's owner Louis Barraya, and Barraya had promised Mouvet that if he ever returned to Paris, he could dance at his club. Barraya hired the team even though the Castles were a huge success at the time. Mouvet did not like the Castles, considered them bitter rivals, and one night after too many drinks, he challenged Vernon to a fight. Castle refused, and then they informed the owner that they would no longer perform at the Café until Mouvet's engagement was finished. They took a short vacation and upon returning, were begged by Barraya to return to the club. They refused as long as Maurice Mouvet was still there. Barraya fired Mouvet and the Castles started dancing at the Café´de Paris again the next evening.

53. When Maurice Mouvet and Florence Walton returned from France, Mouvet finagled a contract from his old drinking buddy Louis Martin to dance on the same bill as the Castles. The rivalry escalated, this time with an added insult—Florence Walton copied Irene Castle's gowns down to the minutest details. The Castles informed Martin that they were considering a better offer from one of his competitors at the Knickerbocker. Martin promptly fired Mouvet and Walton and doubled the Castles' salary. Later, when the Castles were at the pinnacle of their success, Mouvet challenged them to a dance contest to be held at Madison Square Gardens to determine which couple was the best exhibition ballroom dance act in the world. Mouvet had rigged the panel of "impartial judges" with his old friends. The Castles refused the challenge and did not participate.

54. Elizabeth Marbury was a literary and theatrical agent representing such luminaries as Frances Hodgson Burnett, Oscar Wilde, George Bernard Shaw, Edith Wharton, W. Somerset Maugham, Eugene O'Neill, and later Jerome Kern She helped to mold the Castle's careers and turn them into household names. Marbury had an open lesbian relationship with Elsie de Wolfe, who became a well-known interior decorator after a failed career as an actress. Ms. De Wolfe decorated the Castle's various dancing establishments.

55. The Castle School of Dancing at Castle House, was located across from the entrance to the Ritz-Carlton on 46th Street. It had a marble foyer with a fountain and a double staircase that led up to the two large, mirrored studios. One studio was used for "jazz enthusiasts" and utilized an African American jazz orchestra. The second room was for tango and maxixe and featured a string orchestra. Tea was served daily by some of the top society women of the city who acted as hostesses. Before being purchased by the Castles, the building had been used by couturiere Madame Osborn.

56. Although they moved in the highest social circles, there were times when Irene and Vernon Castle were treated as hirelings. If a client mistreated them or demanded too much, Vernon Castle would quote an hourly fee for teaching lessons of one thousand dollars. They often received the exorbitant fee. At the height of their success, the Castles earned over $5,000.00 a week in a period when the average American earned between $10.00 to $15.00 a week.

57. One of the couple's most successful appearances on Broadway was in *The Sunshine Girl* which opened at the Knickerbocker Theatre on February 3rd, 1913 and ran until June 21st of the same year. (The show also reopened and ran from September 1st until the 20th of 1913.) In the theatre news of *The Evening Gazette*, Cedar Rapids, Iowa, March 22, 1913, p. 8. col. 2, the drama critic spoke of the couple's preparation for their performances in the musical;

> One of the really startling features in the Julia Sanderson musical comedy, "The Sunshine Girl," is

the dance performed by the two Castles—Vernon and Irene—in the second act. It is an extraordinary exhibition of agility, grace and that aerial quality which is the chief of all dancing. As preparation for their dances each night behind the scenes both Mr. And Mrs. Castle give a good ten minutes to a curious kind of limbering up. Before going on the stage each has a habit of firmly fixing the right foot on a table or the back of a chair in such a way that the leg is exactly at right angles with the body. Then standing rigidly each dancer bends forward until the face touches the knee—a feat in itself—impossible to the ordinary being. A half dozen of such "dips" renders each dance[r] as flexible as a stick of bamboo.

58. James Reese Europe was born in Mobile, Alabama in on February 22, 1881. His mother was free-born and his father was a slave who later went to law school. James was taught music by his mother and entered show business in 1904 as musical director for all-black musicals. He formed the Clef Club, an unofficial union and booking agency for black musicians. In 1912, Europe made history when his orchestra became the first jazz band to play at Carnegie Hall, an event that was repeated in 1913 and 1914. Europes' Society Orchestra became the first all-black orchestra to get an American recording contract when they signed with Victrola Records in 1913. Europe probably met the Castles in Newport, Rhode Island at a party given by Mrs. Stuyvesant Fish on August 22, 1913. They eventually became good friends and their close relationship allowed the Castles entrance into the inside world of black music and black dance. This in turn provided fresh and innovative material for the couple. During World War I, Europe was given a commission in the New York Army National guard. He directed the regimental band of the 369th Infantry, known as "Harlem's Hellfighters" which is sometimes credited with introducing the ragtime craze to France. The band made recordings in France and also upon their return to the United States. The vocalist on many of the recordings was Noble Sissle, who would later write the lyrics for *Shuffle Along*. On May 9, 1919, Europe was fatally stabbed in the neck during a dispute with a fellow band member, Herbert Wright. His jugular vein had been cut. He is buried in Arlington National Cemetery.

59. Erenberg, p. 168.

60. When Irene Castle decided to have her appendix out, she was concerned that after the operation, the nurses caring for her would comb her hair twice a day, something she dreaded. So, before she checked into the hospital, she took a pair of shears and chopped of her own hair, and then forbade the nurses to touch it. After she had recovered from surgery, Irene was invited to dinner by Elsie Janis. Instead of hiding her hair, she decided to wear it short, holding it in place by slipping a seed-pearl necklace, whose ends had been sewn together, around her head. Castle recalled;

> The first week there were two hundred and fifty Castle bobs; the next week twenty-five hundred. Stores began to feature the "Castle Band to hold your hair in place." Men's barbershops began to hang signs reading "Castle Clips here" and cartoonists pictured men dressing like women so they could stand a chance of getting a haircut in a barbershop filled with women. It was a departure from long-established custom and so radical that one Connecticut newspaper spread the news in bannered type across the front page. "IRENE CASTLE CUTS HAIR" [Castle p. 117].

Eve Golden states in her book *Vernon and Irene Castle's Ragtime Revolution*, p. 26, that Irene first cut her hair in 1909 while still in school so she could go swimming "during a vacant forty-minute period" and have her hair dry by the time she returned to class. Golden suggests that in addition to her hair's shorter quick-drying convenience, Irene enjoyed the sensation it caused among her classmates. When other students at the school followed her lead and began bobbing their hair as well, a scandal erupted and outraged parents wrote to the principal to stop the practice.

61. The Castle Walk was first done at a private birthday party for Elsie Janis held at the Castle's apartment above the Café de l'Opera. Vernon and Irene tried a variation of the one-step. As Irene recalled, "Instead of coming down on the beat as everybody else did, we went up. The result was a step almost like a skip, peculiar-looking I'm sure, but exhilarating and fun to do" (Castle, p, 79). After being introduced to the public at large, the dance became enormously popular. The couple was appearing in the Broadway show *The Sunshine Girl* during this time, and Vernon Castle was in such demand for teaching the Castles Walk, he taught from morning until curtain time. Then the exhausted dancer did the show, and after the curtain fell performed with his wife doing their exhibition dances at Louis Martin's. Vernon Castle did not claim credit for inventing the dance. He said he had taken the idea from Leon Errol, an acrobatic comic he had seen do the step. Eve Golden (pp. 46–47) relates,

> By 1915, when self-proclaimed originators of the fox trot and the Apache dance were quarreling with each other in the press, Vernon sent a letter to a show business trade paper: "My dear Mr. Errol: I read where it is said that you were the first to introduce the step that is known as the Castle Walk. In case it is any satisfaction to you, it is quite correct. I got the steps from you about four years ago, when you were doing a very wonderful dance called the Grizzly Bear at a burlesque theater in Pittsburgh. With best wishes and many congratulations to you on your art, I am a sincere admirer, Vernon Castle."

62. "Dancing Grips Gate City of South" *The Atlanta Constitution*, Atlanta, GA, September 13, 1914, p. 43, col. 3.

63. "Dancing Masters are in a Quandary Over What Bird or Beast to Imitate in Search of a New Dancing Sensation" *The Fort Wayne Journal-Gazette*, Fort Wayne Indiana, September 15, 1916, p. 9, col. 3.

64. Maurice Mouvet, *Maurice's Art of Dancing* (New York: G. Schirmer, 1915) p. 72.

65. From 1880 until 1920 in the United States, young, single, working class women made up a major part of the work force. In 1900, fourth-fifths of the women working were single, and one-third were between the ages of sixteen and twenty. Kathy Peiss examines this phenomenon in her excellent book *Cheap Amusements: Working Women and Leisure in Turn-of-the-Century.* (New York. Philadelphia: Temple University Press, 1986, p. 35.);

> New jobs in department stores, large factories, and offices provided alternatives to domestic service, house-hold production, and sweated labor in small shops. The employment opportunities, the changing organization of work, and the declining hours of labor altered the relationship between work and leisure, shaping the way in which leisure time was structured and experienced ... the workplace reinforced the wage-earner's interest in having a good time. Earning a living, an economic necessity for most young working-class women, was also a cultural experience organizing and defining their leisure activities.

66. Kathy Peiss, *Cheap Amusements: Working Women and Leisure in Turn-of-the-Century.* (New York. Philadelphia: Temple University Press, 1986) p. 6.

67. Although the culture of the dance hall fostered anonymous meetings and uninhibited behavior, young women often protected their reputations by attending in pairs or in groups of friends.

68. Peiss, p. 45.

69. "'Turkey Trot' Shocks Editor" *The San Antonio Light*, San Antonio, TX, July 7, 1912, p. 26. Most dance history books

that relate this story, including the Stearns' *Jazz Dance*, state that there were fifteen girls fired. Original newspaper accounts of the event reveal that there were actually sixteen.

Chapter 8

1. "Social Sanity Threatened, Says Our Foremost Psychologist" *Lima Daily News*, Lima, OH, May 31, 1914, p. 17, quoting Professor Hugo Muensterberg of Harvard University.

2. "Ragtime" — Wikipedia. http://en.wikipedia.org/wiki/Ragtime

3. Thomas L. Morgan's and William Barlow's *From Cakewalks to Concert Halls: An Illustrated History of African American Popular Music From 1895 to 1930.* (Washington D. C.: Elliott & Clark, 1992) p. 21, states:

> The roots of ragtime can be traced to the practice of "ragging" European dance music, a technique developed by slave musicians in the antebellum South. Playing banjos, fiddles, and an assortment of homemade rhythm instruments, they would overlay the basic rhythmic and/or melodic structures of European songs with alternative rhythmic schemes. This was accomplished by two or more musicians playing the competing rhythmic patterns simultaneously, or by one musician on a string instrument playing a separate pattern with each hand or with different finger and thumb combinations to achieve the desired cross rhythms. This polyrhythmic principle has always been prominently featured in the drumming traditions of West Africa, and the practice indeed may have come from there.

4. "Ragtime" — Wikipedia. http://en.wikipedia.org/wiki/Ragtime

5. A large number of ragtime dances were the result of music publishers taking advantage of the public's voracious appetite for new material. Songs were written specifically with the creation of new dances in mind, often including instructions in the lyrics for how to do them. In this way, a connection between songwriters and the dance hall was created, a trend that lasted into the 1930's. The popularity of dance songs led many composers to search for new material in African American honky-tonks and juke joints. Syncopation was in demand and many songwriters were eager to tap into the source and make a buck.

6. Ernest Hogan was born in Bowling Green, Kentucky around 1859. His given name was Ernest Reuben Crowders, but he changed his name to Hogan when he went into show business because Irish performers were in vogue at the time. As a minstrel, with his troupe, the Georgia Graduates, he introduced a comedy dance step called the Pasmala. Other dance steps were introduced in the song as well, such as the Saint-a Louis Pass and the Chicago Salute, which were both references to the World's Fairs held in those cities. One verse mentioned the Bumbishay (known by some as the Fanny Bump.) The Bumbishay, or as we know it, the Bombershay, is still commonly used in tap routines today. The song also mentioned the Turkey Trot at least fifteen years before it attained national popularity. Hogan was considered one of the most talented performers in the business and one of the best dancing comedians of his day. He toured with Black Patti's Troubadours, billed as the "Unbleached American," and also appeared in the road show *The Smart Set*. When he was cast in the black musical *Clorindy — The Origin of the Cakewalk* he achieved stardom. In 1907, Hogan joined the cast of *The Oyster Man,* but became ill from overwork and retired to a small home in Lakewood, New Jersey. He died there in 1909. (This information was extracted directly from my book *Tap Roots*.)

7. "Father of Rag-Time Music" *Spirit Lake Beacon*, Spirit Lake, Iowa, February 2, 1906, p, 2, col. 4. According to the

article, the "pas-ma-la" was a prompt used by a black dance caller from New Orleans during an African America dance in Belvidere Hollow, a section of Kansas City. The expression meant "pass and swing." Ernest Hogan then originated a dance by the same name. The dance became enormously popular in the black culture in Kansas City.

8. Hogan's song was originally entitled "All Pimps Look Alike to Me." After the song was published as "All Coons Look Alike to Me," some black singers of the era changed the lyric to "All Boys Look Alike to Me" to avoid using the racist word. The song was enormously popular and embraced by the public and the entertainment industry. It was sometimes used at ragtime piano contests in the semi-final rounds to eliminate players. Each contestant had to "rag" on the tune for at least two minutes.

9. In Morgan's and Barlow's book, p. 16, the authors write:

> The characterization of humorous minstrel novelty tunes as coon songs originated in the antebellum era in conjunction with the rising popularity of the 'Zip Coon' stereotype, a black urban dandy vainly trying to imitate the mannerisms of his former masters. The caricature and accompanying songs were first popularized by George Washington Dixon in the 1830s. They were then taken over by black minstrels like [Billy] Kersands, whose best known coon song, "Mary's Gone with a Coon," was actually a self-parody of the African American stigma associated with darker skin pigmentation.

10. Marshall and Jean Stearns, *Jazz Dance: The Story of American Vernacular Dance.* New York: Da Capo, 1994 Stearns, p. 120, quoting Edward B. Marks, *They All Sang* (New York: Viking Press, 1935) p. 91.

11. Everybody's Doin' It Now" words and music by Irving Berlin (New York: Ted Synder Co., 1911.) Eve Golden (p. 79) tells the story of a girl in Millwood, New York who was arrested for singing "Everybody's Doing It" and doing an improvised turkey trot as she walked past the house of the local justice of the peace. The official leveled charges against the girl for disturbing the peace. She was found not guilty after she explained to the jury that "she sang the song because she like it, and danced because she could not help it when she heard the catchy tune." The trial closed with the defense attorney singing Berlin's famous song and the jury calling for an encore.

12. "Foy in 'Over the River'" *The New York Times*, January 9, 1912, p.8.

13. Eve Golden, *Vernon and Irene Castle's Ragtime Revolution.* (Lexington, KY: University Press of Kentucky, 2007) p. 52.

14. *Ibid.*

15. "Hitting the Ragtime Dance" *The La Crosse Tribune*, La Crosse, Wisconsin, July 13, 1912, p. 3, col. 1.

16. "Anti rag-time girl." words and music by Elsie Janis, (New York: Jerome H. Remick & Co., @ 1913.)

17. *Ibid.*

18. Morgan and Barlow, p. 26.

19. "Attacks Slit Skirt" *The New York Times*, July 20, 1913, p. 2.

20. Mordecai Franklin Ham, *Light on the Dance.* (No publisher, 1916) p. 53.

21. "Slit Skirt Girl Driven Out" *The New York Times*, July 17, 1913, p. 1.

22. "Slit Skirt 'Disorderly'" *The New York Times*, June 29, 1913, p. 1.

23. *Ibid.*

24. "Mob a Woman Bather" *The New York Times*, September 12, 1913, p. 1.

25. *Ibid.*

26. "Judge Defends Slit Skirt" *The New York Times*, September 5, 1914, p. 1.

27. Mr. & Mrs. Vernon Castle, *Modern Dancing* (New York: Harper, 1914) p. 140.

28. Rayon was invented in 1910, and was the first artificial fabric to be used in clothing.

29. The Castles, p. 147. Many of Irene Castle's gowns were created by the couturier Lucile. Lucile, also known as Lady Duff-Gordon, was the younger sister of the actress Elinor Glyn. Castle was a huge supporter of the designer, despite scandal associated with the Duff-Gordon name. Lucile and her husband were on the Titanic when it sank. The couple and their maid ended up in lifeboat number one with only nine other people. The boat was equipped to hold forty. At the inquest after the sinking, the Duff-Gordon's were questioned as to how this occurred and why the boat did not go back to rescue others. Subsequent articles implied that Mrs. Duff-Gordon (Lucile) had been cruel, heartless, and blasé about the situation. She vehemently denied it, but the scandal sullied her reputation and many avoided her as a designer.

30. *Ibid*, p. 139.

31. *Ibid*, p. 142.

32. *Ibid*, p. 148.

33. *Ibid*, p. 143.

34. "Safety Dancing Pump Appears at Harvard for Use in Bunny Hug" *The Lowell Sun*, Lowell, MA, February 20, 1913, p. 23, col. 2.

35. *Ibid.*

36. The Castles, p. 145.

37. *Ibid*, p. 147. Castle said, "A top-heavy or uncomfortable head dress is as difficult to dance with as shoes that are painful ... if [a woman's hair] is in danger of sliding down, or she is wearing a heavy hat that will not stay in place, she is sure to hold her head stiffly an ungracefully" (Golden, p. 65, quoting Irene Castle).

Chapter 9

1. "Suzette's Views on Society and Dancing" *Oakland Tribune*, Oakland, CA August 24, 1913, p. 7. col. 1. The same article stated, "...only Americans can truly dance the trot.... In Germany they call the trot 'Truthahn Tanz,' and in France it is the 'Pas du Dindon.' Who would recognize the original under such appellations?"

2. "Origin and Spread of the Vivacious 'Turkey Trot'" *The Anaconda Standard*, Anaconda, Montana, February 11, 1912, p. 25.

3. "Prima Donnas Held Train" *The New York Times*, October 23, 1912, p. 1.

4. "Turkey Trot an Appeal to Real Sense of Rhythm" *Lincoln Daily News*, Lincoln, NE, September 27, 1913, p. 5, col. 1. The article continues; "The onestep makes a tremendous appeal because it is superlatively rhythmic. It makes an added appeal because its rhythm is not only regular, but occasionally irregular. Syncopation creeps in here and there with its mysterious fascination."

5. "The Dancing Mania"—an extract taken from *The Medical Times. The Anaconda Standard*, Anaconda, Montana, August 24, 1913, p. 21, col. 3.

6. Lewis Erenberg, *Steppin'Out: New York Nightlife and the Transformation of American Culture, 1890–1930.* (Chicago: University of Chicago Press, 1981) p. 81, originally extracted from "The Revolt of Decency," *New York Sun* quoted in *Literary Digest*, April 9, 1913, p. 894. In addition to objections concerning the close embrace and the jiggling of the body, some voiced concern that since it had "no regulated figures to hold the dancers within the bounds of decorum ... rag dance frequently degenerates into license and abandon" (quote from an article entitled "Ragtime and Morals," *The Oakland Tribune*, Oakland, Ca, August 15, 1913, p. 10, col. 1).

7. *Ibid.*

8. "Bishops Differ on New Dancing Steps" *The New York Times*, January 19, 1914, p. 6.

9. *Ibid.*

10. "Canon Assails Our New Dances" *The New York Times*, August 25, 1913, p. 3. The clergyman asked his congregation,

> Would indecent dances, suggestive of evil and destructive of modesty, disgrace our civilization for a moment if professed Christians were to say, "I will not allow my daughter to turn into Salome, even although Herod were to give me half his kingdom and admit me to the much-coveted society of a world which has persuaded itself that immodesty is artistic, and that anything is permissible in society which relieves the intolerable monotony of its pleasures."?

11. "Turkey Trot is Gait to Hell, Says Parson" *Atlanta Constitution*, Atlanta, GA, July 16, 1913, p.2.
12. "Bishops Differ on New Dancing Steps" *The New York Times*, January 19, 1914, p. 6.
13. "Bishops Differ on New Dancing Steps" *The New York Times*, January 19, 1914, p. 6.
14. "Billy Sunday Raps Nuptial Slackers" *The New York Times*, April 13, 1917, p. 7.
15. From "Theater, Cards and Dance" a sermon by Billy Sunday. In this sermon Sunday lambasted the close hold used in the modern dances. He said,

> When I danced on the puncheon floor in the log cabin on the frontier in Iowa, we used to be able to get a stick of wood between them, but now you can't get a piece of tissue paper between.... Most men don't care a rap for the dance; it is the hug that they are after.... You make men dance by themselves, and it will kill the dance in two weeks. You know that you don't care for the dance; it is the hug and the opposite sex.

16. Ann Wagner, *Adversaries of Dance: From the Puritans to the Present* (Chicago: University of Illinois, 1997) p. 259, quoting Billy Sunday's "A Plain Talk to Women."
17. "Abused Turkey Trot Spreads in London." *The New York Times*, February 18, 1912, Section: Transatlantic Wireless, Cable and Sporting Sections, p. C2. When choreographer and musician Uriel Davis visited to London, he was in great demand at all the top society events where he taught rag dances. When asked how London society was taking to the new steps, Davis responded,

> When I first arrived here I found society dancers knew nothing at all about trots and tangos. They were doing the waltz almost exclusively, and now and again jumping around somehow. The main trouble was an impression existing everywhere trotting dancers were vulgar. English people are good dancers, but the change was so radical it was hard for them at first to accustom themselves to it. Now they don't care much for the waltz and everyone is dancing trots, with the horse trot as a prime favorite.

(Quote from: *The Milford Mail*, Milford, Iowa, July 24, 1913, p. 6, col. 1.)
18. *Ibid*. The same society matron also said, "Nobody who waltzes well could possibly want anything more delightful than a waltz with a good partner to the music of a good band. We are asked to exchange this for jerks, slides, and grabs, all ungraceful and utterly, undignified." One particularly vocal opponent of ragtime dancing was Alice, Countess of Strafford, who declared, "The so-called dances can only be compared to the wild, abandoned frenzies of some ancient Bacchantic revel, although the modern versions are devoid of grace" (quote from: "London Dispute Over 'Turkey Trot'" *The New York Times*, May 21, 1913, p. 3).
19. "People in the Passing Show" *The Washington Post*, May 24, 1913, p. 7, col. 3.
20. "Temple Pictures London's Horror at 'Those Nasty American Hug-Dances'" by Herbert Temple. *The Syracuse Herald*, Syracuse, NY, December 8, 1912, p. 45, col. 6. In an article entitled "'Turkey Trot' Denounced" (*The New York Times*, February 25, 1912, Section: Transatlantic Wireless

Cable and Sporting Sections, p. C3.) it speaks of a piece in The *London Graphic* cautioning its readers about the lewd dances that were overtaking the nation.

> Dancing is in disgrace, the worst disgrace it has known since the priests of ancient Egypt evolved the first "rounds," or dances, under the burning sky of the East. It seemed that the fantasy and freakism could go no further than it did last season, but it could. We basely misjudged the powers of the modern dancers by supposing that the freaks of last year had resurrected the entire contents of the basket. Not at all. There were others, many others, and they are such that the mongrels of yesterday are as nothing compared to the hobgoblins of to-day. The latest dances are disgraceful.

21. "Fighting the 'Turkey Trot'" *The New York Times*, March 17, 1912, Section: Parts III and IV Transatlantic Wireless Cable and Sporting, p. C3.
22. "Ban the Turkey Trot" *The New York Times*, April 8, 1912, p. 3.
23. In Bellingham Washington, a young dance instructor by the name of H. O. Morrison was arrested for disobeying the city's dancing ordinances. At his trial, the judge asked the young man to be an expert witness in identifying others who had been arrested as perpetrators of the bunny hug and grizzly bear. Morrison agreed. At their trial, Morrison asked the judge if there could be a demonstration of some of the questionable moves of the bunny hug to show how despicable they actually were. When the judge agreed, Morrison asked two policemen to do the dance. Just as the two burly officers clasped arms around each other and were cheek-to-cheek, a reporter in the courtroom snapped a photograph. The next morning the photo ran on the front page of the local paper. The picture was also sent to other papers along with a copy of the judge's dance restrictions. A huge scandal erupted. As a result, the embarrassed judge dropped charges against the original dancers who had been arrested. It was found out later, that Morrison had actually engineered the whole brouhaha to thumb his nose at the dance restrictions.
24. "Society in War On Freak Dances" *The Fort Wayne Sentinel*, Fort Wayne, Indiana, September 20, 1912, p.15, col. 1.
25. "Chief Ryan Places Ban On the 'Hugging' Dance" *Dallas Daily Times Herald*, July 19, 1912, p. 1, col. 1–2. Society was deeply concerned about the threat that immoral dancing posed to young women. In certain cases drastic actions were taken to protect them. A young woman in Chehalis, Washington was actually sent to reform school for dancing the bunny hug, turkey trot, and angleworm wiggle.
26. "Mayor Gaynor Asks Ban Put on Bad Dance" *Fairbanks Daily Times*, Fairbanks Alaska, April 5, 1913, p. 1, col. 2.
27. *Ibid*.
28. "Southern Hotel Closed by Police" *The New York Times*, April 30, 1913, p. 1. At the hotel, the police interrupted "several hundred devotees of the cabaret and the tango and turkey trot who were dining and dancing in the main dining room." In addition to concerns about the dancing being done there, the police had been informed of "the presence of undesirable women in the lobby and dining room."
29. According to the article entitled "Broadway Sees Raid on Dance; 100 Seized" in *The New York Times*, February 15, 1921, p. 8, the owners of Wilson's Dance Studio were charged with maintaining a public nuisance and the dancers were charged with disorderly conduct. The thirty-nine young ladies who were arrested appeared before the judge and denied being "in the company of women of known bad character." The magistrate discharged them "and once more they were happy — and noisy."
30. "Turkey Trot Barred at Annapolis Dances" *The New York Times*, January 14, 1913, p. 17.
31. *Ibid*.
32. "Wilson Banned Ball Fearing Turkey Trot" *The New York Times*, January 21, 1913, p. 3.

33. Excerpt from Jane Addams, *The Spirit of Youth and the City Streets* (New York: The Macmillan Company, 1909), Chapter 1. Extracted from Nancy G. Rosoff's "Recreation and Social Chaperonage in the Progressive Era" (Lesson Plan). At the Organization of American Historians websitehttp://www.oah.org/pubs/magazine/progressive/rosoff.html

34. Dr. R. A. Adams, *The Social Dance* (Kansas City: 1921) p. 19.

35. Excerpts from Belle Lindner Israels, "The Way of the Girl," *Survey* 22 (3 July 1909): 494, 495, and 497. Extracted Rosoff.

36. Mordecai Franklin Ham, *Light on the Dance* (1916) p. 28.

37. "Welfare Inspector at Society Dance," *The New York Times*, January 4, 1912, p. 1.

38. *Ibid.*

39. *Ibid.*

40. *The New York Times*, (October 11, 1912, p. 9), ran an article that explained one of the ways the Committee tried to educate society members. "One of the foremost country clubs within the short radius of New York" sent for the Committee on Amusement Resources for Working Girls' dancing instructor to teach them the new tamer dances and asked that she "wean the young people of the club away from the unhallowed 'trot.'"

41. When Jolsen was asked about the origins of the dances, he explained that "he picked up the art as he saw it on the Barbary Coast, where he used to sell papers as a San Francisco boy. It's all the same ... call it 'Turkey Trot,' or "Bunny Hug,' as you will. Stripped of the variations, despoiled of the precautions, all the new variants drop insensibly into one thing. There in those fifteen or twenty dance halls, thriving as they did in his day on the patronage of the half-drunken sailors welcomed at port, the dance was born. The unsteady tar could only half skate about the floor to begin with. And then the orchestra would hit it up, and they would rag it a bit, and then strike out on the minors that are more seductive, I guess— and get closer and closer, and snap their fingers, and — and I guess I've said enough" Quote from: *The New York Times*, January 27, 1912, p. 1.

42. "Polite Dances Are Shown to Society" *The New York Times*, March 26, 1912, p. 13.

43. *Ibid.*

44. *Ibid.*

45. "Welfare Inspector at Society Dance" *The New York Times*, January 4, 1912, p. 1.

46. Despite efforts to regulate and refine dances, the results did not always go as expected. Two performers presented the turkey trot at the Hippodrome in London and advertised that any objectionable features of the dance had been removed. The response was not warm. "To remove objectionable features of one kind is not always to render a thing free from objection, and we have one very serious objection to urge against the 'turkey trot.' It is abominably ugly" (quote from: *The New York Times*. February 6, 1912, p. 3).

47. "Turkey Trot an Appeal to Real Sense of Rhythm" *Lincoln Daily News*, Lincoln, NE, September 27, 1913, p. 5, col. 1. Along with the Castles, Maurice Mouvet was a strong proponent of refining the popular dances. In his book *Maurice's Art of Dancing*, pp. 36–37, he writes, "...I also began to dance the Turkey Trot, but I never danced it with grotesque movements of the shoulders which made it so unpopular among people of refinement and good taste. My objection to it in the form in which it was danced in 1911 and the early part of 1912 was based purely on the ground of its ugly inartistic aspect."

48. In an article entitled "To 'Bunny Hug' and 'Horse Trot' in Unison in an Effort to Standardize Dancing" found in *The Evening Gazette*, Cedar Rapids, Iowa, December 2, 1913, p. 14, Uriel Davis states,

It seems like a tremendous undertaking, yet it is really very simple. The whole scheme depends upon having the instructions for dancing correctly standardized and sent from a recognized centre, so that they shall be everywhere uniform. I am not a teacher of dancing, but I can give the teachers of the country the proper information so they can teach their pupils. Naturally a dancing teacher does not want to confess that he is ignorant of any dance, no matter what it is, and if pupils ask for something that they have read of he does his best to teach it to them. The dancing masters want to teach the correct thing, but they do not always know where to get it. I am going to establish headquarters in some big city and from there will be sent exact directions for dancing the newest and most fashionable dances so that in the smallest town in the farthest West they may dance exactly as persons do in fashionable centres.

49. Mr. & Mrs. Vernon Castle, *Modern Dancing* (New York: Harper, 1914) p. 17.

50. Castles, p. 177. They also suggested; "Avoid low, fantastic, and acrobatic dips," and "Stand far enough away from each other to allow free movement of the body in order to dance gracefully and comfortably." The manual also explained proper arms positions, and informed the reader to "Remember you are at a social gathering and not in a gymnasium." They closed the list of rules with "Drop the Turkey Trot, the Grizzly Bear, the Bunny Hug, etc. These dance are ugly, ungraceful, and out of fashion."

51. "Turkey Trot Must Glide" *The New York Times*, January 31, 1913, p. 6.

52. "A Paris Decalogue to Guide Dancers" *The New York Times*, February 11, 1912, Section: Transatlantic Wireless, Cable and Sporting Sections, p. C4.

53. *Ibid.*

54. Eve Golden, *Vernon and Irene Castle's Ragtime Revolution* (Lexington, KY: University Press of Kentucky, 2007) p. 100.

55. "Dance Masters Denounce Jazz" *Reno Evening Gazette*, Reno, NV, January 23, 1920, p. 16, col. 3.

56. This contraption is described in *Castles in the Air*, p. 86. According to Irene Castle "It was against the law to dance too close to your partner at the time and bouncers in restaurants tapped their patrons on the shoulder when they get [sic] closer than nine inches."

57. "To Beat the Turkey Trot" *The New York Times*, October 11, 1912, p. 9.

58. During World War I, Davis led what was considered one of the best army bands, a corps of musicians from Camp Raritan, NJ. In addition to being a bandleader, songwriter, choreographer, and businessman, Davis served as musical director at the roof garden of the Bellevue-Stratford hotel. In the summer of 1915, he created a "mild sensation" when he presented a little canary named Andy who warbled to Davis' accompaniment on the piano. When the President Wilson announced his engagement to Miss Norma Galt, Davis began diligently training his "protégé" to warble passages from Mendelssohn's Wedding March and the Wedding March from Lohengrin. Davis would repeatedly pound out the passages on the piano and teach the bird. "The little bird took aptly to both tunes and has fairly well mastered them. Inside of several weeks in plenty of time for the wedding, the bird will be able to sing both numbers without hesitancy, [sic] Davis says" (quote from: *Trenton Evening Times*, Trenton, NJ, October 18, 1915, p. 11, col. 3).

59. The horse trot was a prancing-type dance which included kicks similar to the cakewalk. It replaced the turkey trot in popularity when it was first introduced, but its more strenuous nature and the difficulty women had in executing the kicks in long dresses, caused the dance to fall out of favor around 1914. Most sources state that the horse trot was first introduced at an event hosted by politician Hamilton Fish Jr., when he gave a Lenten Ball at the Copley Plaza in Boston for the top members of society from New York, Philadelphia, Chicago, Washington, and Boston on February 21, 1913. Orig-

inally 300 guests were invited, but the news of the event attracted a huge crowd and the ballroom was opened and 1,000 couples attended and saw the new dance. The *McKean Democrat* (Smethport, PA, August 7, 1913, p. 3, col. 1.) offered a different story. It reported that Davis's horse trot actually originated in Washington D. C. sometime in 1912. The newspaper stated,

> The horse trot was introduced last season at a ball given by the military attaché of the German embassy, Maj. Von Herwarth, and Mme. Von Herwarth. Both the music and the dance were originated by Mr. Uriel Davis, who, with his brother, is a favorite exponent of popular dance music in Washington. Mr. John Astor, then in the city, say [sic] the dance and took a fancy to it. At the behest of Mrs. Astor, Mrs. Ronalds, Mrs. Herbert Asquith and other well known ladies in London, Mr. Davis has gone to that city to teach the dance.

The paper added that after being introduced, the dance made its way from Washington to Newport and then Bar Harbor. (It is likely that the paper is actually referring to the introduction of the fish walk.)

In a story in *The Evening Gazette*, Cedar Rapids, Iowa, December 2, 1913, p. 14, Davis admitted, "I did not name the 'horse trot.' I was trying a variation of the aeroplane dip, worked out the steps and set them to music. I showed the steps to a German diplomatist and played the music. 'Why, it is just like a horse trotting,' he said. 'Why not call it that?' Soon afterward I introduced the 'fish walk' in London for the Duke and Duchess of Manchester."

60. The fish walk was introduced by Mme. Von Herwarth, wife of the military attaché of the German embassy in Washington, and danced to Uriel Davis' composition "The Walk of the Fishes." Instructions for the dance were as follows, "To do the fish walk, the new society dance originated here, one must strive to look and move like a mermaid in a hobble skirt. The idea is to perambulate in rhythmic hops just as you think a fish would" (quote from: *New Castle News*, New Castle, PA, May 1, 1913, p. 12, col. 3).

61. *The Portsmouth Herald*, Portsmouth, NJ, May 20, 1913, p. 7, col. 3, reported; "Mr. Davis claims he gets most of his ideas from the little dancers who follow the organ-grinders around and dance upon the sidewalks from morning until night enriching the owners of the organ by the contributions they draw from spectators." The article describes one situation in which an organ grinder in Hell's Kitchen was playing the "Horse Trot" music that Davis had written as Davis was passing by. He noticed some street urchins dancing the turkey trot, and stopped to teach them the actual horse trot. "Inside of thirty minutes [he] had twenty or more children enjoying the novel and invigorating steps of his dance ... the mothers of the children came out of the tenements and asked to be taught the dance and Davis had the busiest time of this life." According to the article, Davis was leaning against a lamppost exhausted when a limousine pulled up with four society ladies who were coming to do charity work. They recognized Davis because he had directed an entertainment at Sherry's the night before and the ladies had all attended. They called him to the car and Davis explained what had happened. Thrilled at the impromptu event, the ladies got out of their car and joined in the dancing and "by showering money among the throng kept the street in an uproar until three policemen came running down the street with clubs drawn and with visions of a riot to scatter the crowd. When they saw the ladies and Mr. Davis they apologized, but advised them to leave, for Hell's kitchen was no place for folks with jewels and money." Following the advice of the officers, Davis left with the ladies as the crowd ran behind the car shouting, "come back again some other day and do the 'Horse Trot.'"

62. "All London Crazy Over Turkey Trot; Hostesses Despair" *The Milford Mail*, Milford, Iowa, July 24, 1913, p. 6, col. 1.

63. *Vera Violetta* opened at the Winter Garden in 1911 and also featured in its cast, Al Jolsen, who according to reviews stole the show. The song "Tar-Rar-Rar-Boomdiay" was introduced in the show by actress Josie Collins.

64. Gaby Deslys claimed she was born in Marseilles, France on November 4, 1881. She gave her birth name was Marie-Elise Gabrielle Claire. A dispute about her heritage arose however when it was discovered that she might really have been of Czech peasant origins, her birth name being Hadwiga Nawrati, sometimes spelled Hedviga Navratilova. There is still confusion about the real truth. She took the name Gaby Deslsy, an abbreviation of "Gabrielle of the Lillies" as a stage name, and made her debut in Paris in 1905. She went on to become one of the most sought after performers of her day. She is credited with presenting the first striptease on Broadway. Well-known for her sense of fashion, Deslys never appeared in the same costume twice in the same theatre, and often changed gowns as many as ten times per show. She was romantically linked with Manuel II, King of Portugal, who showered her with jewels. Deslys claimed at her death that she owned her own weight in pearls. In World War I, she worked for the French government as a spy. She died on February 11, 1920 in Paris of pneumonia and a severe throat infection brought on by influenza.

65. Harry Fox was born on May 25, 1882 in Pomona, California. His birth name was Arthur Carringford. In 1897, he ran away from home to join the circus and, later, play professional baseball. He started in show business after a sheet music publisher heard him sing and hired him to be a song plugger, singing songs from the balconies of vaudeville theatres. In 1904 he gained notice when he appeared in San Francisco in a show called *Mr. Frisky of Frisco*, a production that later toured. After the earthquake of 1909, Fox moved to New York. He worked in vaudeville as a dancer and comedian and in 1907 teamed up with Beatrice Curtis. The two performed together and married. They divorced in 1912, when Fox joined the cast of *The Passing Show of 1912*. In 1914 he paired up with Yansci (Jenny) Dolly of the Dolly Sisters. The two did an act together and married. With the popularity of exhibition dance teams, Fox and his new wife used ballroom dancing as the centerpiece of their new act. Fox was hired to dance at the New York Theatre, which had recently been converted to a movie palace. Fox and his chorus of "American Beauties" performed between features there. The roof of the New York Theatre was converted into a cabaret, called the Jardin de Danse and the featured act in the revue there were the Dolly Sisters. It was in this show that Fox presented the foxtrot. Some sources state that Fox introduced his famous foxtrot in the *Ziegfeld Follies of 1913*, or 1914, but he is not listed in the opening night credits. Fox also appeared in silent films and a few talkies. He died in Woodland Hills, California on July 20, 1959.

66. Although most historians believe that the fox trot was named after Harry Fox, in his book *Maurice's Art of Dancing*, p. 82, Maurice Mouvet intimates that perhaps the dance earned its name from another source. He writes,

> Possibly the people who invented the title belonged to that rather slender class of persons who have leisure to hunt, and it may be that in their swift glimpses of the fleeing fox ... but who can say accurately? And does it really matter much, anyhow?

67. Joan Sawyer, "How to Dance the Foxtrot," Columbia Gramophone Company, November 23, 1914.

68. Marshall and Jean Stearns, *Jazz Dance: The Story of American Vernacular Dance* (New York: Da Capo, 1994, p. 98) quoting W. C. Handy.

69. Stearns, p. 98, quoting Irene Castle.

70. Ham, p. 52, quoting *The Houston Chronicle*.

71. "Turkey Trot Caused It" *The Fort Wayne Sentinel*, Fort Wayne, IN, June 7, 1913, p. 3, col. 4.

72. Castle, p. 85.

73. "Gibson Puts Ban on Wicked Dances" *The Syracuse*

Herald, Syracuse, New York, September 19, 1912, p. 18, col. 3.

74. "Dancing Masters are in a Quandary Over What Bird or Beast to Imitate in Search of a New Dancing Sensation" *The Fort Wayne Journal-Gazette,* Fort Wayne Indiana, September 15, 1916, p. 9, col. 3.

75. "Society Bars Turkey Trot" *Trenton Evening Times,* Trenton, NJ, November 8, 1912, p. 9, col. 4.

76. "Girl's Leg Broken Doing Turkey Trot" *Waterloo Evening Courier,* Waterloo, Iowa, September 24, 1912, p. 4, col. 5. *The Washington Post,* Washington DC, Feb. 14, 1912, p. 1, col. 4, reported on another incident of someone breaking a leg trying out one of the new ragtime dances. "Mrs. George Nelson of Snohomish, Snohomish County, broke her right leg in two places last night while trying to keep step to an original local dance called the "Snohomish."

77. "Dies After a Turkey Trot" *The New York Times,* June 11, 1912, p. 1.

78. *Ibid.* Mrs. Day was twenty-one. She was practicing the dance with her husband one Friday night before going to see some professionals do it at the pier. She had a sudden pain in her side so stopped dancing. Ten minutes later, when she was leaving the house, she collapsed. Doctors were summoned, but she died before they arrived.

79. Wagner, p. 263, quoting William Milburn Dye, *Popular Amusements and Their Substitutes,* Louisville: Pentecostal Publishing, 1912, p. 9.

80. "Riot at Preacher's Dance" *The New York Times,* September 18, 1913, p. 4.

81. "No 'Turkey Trot' For Her" *The Washington Post,* Washington D. C., January 15, 1912, p. 3, col. 4.

82. According to an account of the incident in the *McKean County Miner,* (Smethport, PA, January 23, 1902, p. 5, col. 2);

> Lillian Williams, a colored lady filled with sporting blood and booze, attended a pay-day dance in West Virginia last Saturday night. The orchestra was playing waltzy music when she wanted ragtime. She used a revolver in her argument for ragtime and as a result two colored musicians have departed this life, while a white spectator lies mortally wounded and Lil lies in jail. The police beat the mob on the scene or she would be hanging to a tree.

83. Ham, p. 27.

Chapter 10

1. Gladys Beattie Crozier, *The Tango and How to Dance It* (London: Andrew Melrose, 1913) pp. 7–8.

2. In a similar context, the word "tango" was also used by slave traders to indicate where slaves were held and also sold. Scholars suggest the word could be linked to the word *tambo,* an African word used to describe the pens and markets where slaves were kept and sold. In his book *Tango: The Art History of Love,* p. 81, Robert Farris Thompson has an extensive list of African Classical Ki-Kongo words that are related to the "tango" of Creole Buenos Aires idiom. For example, *tanga* (plural *matanga*), fete, festival, or a ceremony marking the end of a period of mourning; *tanga dungulu,* to walk, showing off, to swagger; *tangala,* to walk heavily and hesitatingly, to stagger, to toddle, to trot, to walk small steps, to walk like a chameleon, to march with the feet inward, to swagger, or a large drum, or a small drum; *tangala-tangala,* to walk like a crab; *tangalakana,* to walk zigzag, *tangama,* to take long steps, to leap or bound, to walk seriously or solemnly, to walk like a crab, to be thrown on one's back and be tightly held (as in wrestling), *tangana,* to walk like a chameleon, *taganana,* to walk.

3. The African deity of thunder and lightning known as *Shango, Sango, Xango, Chango,* and in Latin American,

Jakuta, became a symbol of African resistance to European enslavement. The god was worshipped in Haitian voodoo and in Brazilian condomblé. He is often represented in African art with one hand raised pointing to the sky while his other points to his reproductive organs. In my book *Tap Roots; The Early History of Tap Dancing,* I write about the similarities between the representations of this gesture by Shango, and representations of minstrel dancer Thomas Darmouth Rice performing the dance move that became known as truckin.'

4. Crozier, p. 14.

5. The music and dance of Andalusia was influenced by Arabic Muslim elements. These influences can be traced to the Moorish invasion of the Iberian Peninsula by North African Berbers in 711. The blending of Moorish court music with Gypsy folk songs was important in the development of Flamenco. The finger snapping and heel-stamping of Flamenco was brought to Argentina and became part of many folk dances of the pampas. They also filtered into parts of the tango, such as the heel-stamping breaks called *taconeos.*

6. In Spanish the word became *tangir*—"to pluck," as in "to pluck the strings of an instrument." The website To Tango—Tango Terms and Etymology, states that this etymology is doubtful. It explains that the 1899 edition of the dictionary of the Spanish Royal Academy of Letters, states the word could possibly be derived from the Latin *tangir,* meaning "to play instruments,"—*tango* in the first person would therefore mean "I play." Although the 1914 edition of the dictionary included *tangir* or *tangere* ("to play or to touch") as possible sources of the word, later editions omitted the reference.

7. The island of São Tomé is located off the western equatorial coast of Africa. It was discovered by Portuguese explorers sometime in the mid 1400s. In 1493, the first permanent settlement was established on the island. Because of the challenges of attracting new inhabitants to the remote spot, Portugal resorted to sending its "undesirables" there, mostly persecuted Jews. Robert Farris Thompson suggests in his book *Tango: The Art History of Love,* pp. 136–137, that Jewish elements can be found in the milonga, and also in the tango—for example, the rapid crossing front and back of the feet in the step *la vibrota* (the little snake) which is similar to the grapevine used in dancing the hora. Tracing these elements to the Jews of São Tomé is based only on conjecture.

8. The website ToTango—Tango Terms and Etymology states that music historian Carlos Vega mentions a solo dance called the tango that existed in the 18th century Mexico.

9. Crozier, p. 14. Crozier adds that in Jamaica the tango was first primarily danced only by children, but was later embraced by the adults of Kingston society.

10. Marilyn Grace Miller states in her book *Rise and Fall of the Cosmic Race: The Cult of Mestizaje in Latin America,* p. 84;

> In 1836, an entry appears in a dictionary from Matanzas Cuba, that not only associates the tango with a geographical site nearly antipodal to its current "birthplace" of Argentina, but also documents the presence of tango in institutionalized discourse almost a century before its so-called Golden Age in the 1920s. This Cuban dictionary defines tango as a meeting of black *bozales*—recently arrived enslaved Africans—for the purpose of dancing to the sound of their drums and other instruments.

This dictionary was published by Esteban Pichrdo.

11. According to the website ToTango—Tango Terms and Etymology, the dictionary of the Spanish Royal Academy of Letters, 1899 edition, gave two primary definitions of the word: first, "fiesta and dance of Negroes or *gente del pueblo* in America," and second, "Music for that dance." Colier, Cooper, Azzi, and Martin state in *Tango: The Dance, the Song and the Story,* that the two primary uses of the word were either as a place for blacks to dance or the dances themselves It was this second meaning, referring to tango specifically as

a black dance, that was taken to Spain and used to label dances which were African influenced.

12. In an article entitled "Dance Teachers Have Managed to Standardize the Tango" written by Helen Hoyt for the *Gazette and Bulletin*, Williamsport, PA, January 18, 1915, p. 10, col. 2., the author informed her readers, "...the tango comes you know originally from wild and wooly Africa."

13. On page 490 of his book, Raffé lists the twelve figures of the earlier forms of the dance as follows;

1. *El Paseo*— The promenade, arrival and round square space.
2. *El Marcha*— Setting to partners and slow march of the whole company.
3. *El Corte*— The company defines the circle of the Corte by moving around its circumference.
4. *El Medio Corte*— The leading couple demonstrate [sic] in the centre.
5. *El Chase*— is used to follow the first couple in figures, as they call.
6. *El Media Luna*— is halfway; as a half moon, the half circle now filled, defined.
7. *El Moulinet*— the mill, *Moulin*, by movement in two opposing circles.
8. *El Frottado*— Friction from the *Moulinet*, resolved by....
9. *El Ocho*— to centre, to "Eye" in smallest circle (=Oc; oke, oak-tree, etc.)
10. *El Abanico*— L'Eventail, the pigeon or "fanning out," to....
11. *El Ruade*— the Wheel, or Great Circle (the path, the Way) leading to....
12. *El Cruzado*— the Cross, or final balance

14. Mr. & Mrs. Vernon Castle, *Modern Dancing* (New York: Harper, 1914) p. 83.

15. Crozier, p. 9.

16. Jean Richepin, a prolific novelist, poet, and dramatist, was born on February 4, 1849 in Médéa, Algeria. He was the son of an army doctor, and initially planned to be a physician himself, but gave it up to study literature. He spent some years as an adventurer then turned to writing. His first book, a long poem entitled *Chanson des guex, The Song of the Hoboes* (1876) created such a scandal, it was censored. Richepin was arrested, fined 500 francs, and given a one-month prison sentence "for outrage to public decency and good morals" (Shipley, Joseph Twadell. *Modern French Poetry: An Anthology*. Manchester, NH: Ayer Publishing, 1972, p. 36). At one time, he was the lover of Sarah Berhardt. In 1908, he became a member of French Académie des Beaux Arts, an organization that was highly respected for its intellectualism. He died in Paris on December 12, 1926.

17. Crozier, p. 9. Richepin made these statements originally in a lecture he gave before the "Immortal Forty" entitled "a propos du Tango" on October 25, 1913 at a public gathering of the five Academies of the Institut de France in Paris. His lecture was attended by a large number of society women, but only four of his fellow Academy members. In addition to discussing the dance's origins, Richepin defended the tango as a suitable and respectable dance.

18. "Tango Captivates German Capital" *The New York Times*, November 9, 1913, Section: Editorial Foreign News Sports Want Advertisements, P. C3.

19. "Academicians Hear the Tango Praised" *The New York Times*, October 26, 1913, Section: Foreign News Sports Want Advertisements, p. C4. Richepin's declaration was contested by the Keeper of the Greek and Roman Antiquities at the British Museum who stated that there was no picture, representation, or record in the museum to support such a claim.

20. "Dance Craze is First Appearance of Social Hysteria in Centuries" *The Milford Mail*, Milford, Iowa, November 19, 1914, p. 6, col. 2.

21. Simon Collier, Artemis Cooper, Maria Susana Azzi,

and Richard Martin. *Tango!: The Dance, the Song, the Story* (London: Thames and Hudson Ltd.. 1995) p. 43.

22. The word "*candombe*" eventually came to signify all black dances of the Bantu people enslaved and brought to that country. Used generically, it also defined all aspects associated with the ancestral rituals of these suppressed people. The *candombe* was rooted in Bantu African drumming, but mixed with European influences. Blacks during this time, referred to their drums as *tangós*. By association, the term came to represent both the gathering places where the drums were played, and the dances that accompanied the drumming. In the early 1800's, the word "*candombe*" was interchangeably used with the words "*tambo*" and "*tango.*" The political establishment in Montevideo saw the African-based dances as a threat to public decency and tried to banish them, and by 1808, the governor was asked to ban such dances and "prohibit the tangós of the blacks" (quote taken from the book *El Candombe* by Ruben Carambula — extracted from the website "candombe" at www.candombe.com/english.html).

As European immigration grew after the midway mark of the nineteenth century, younger Afro-Argentines began abandoning the *candombe* in favor of imported European dance forms, such as the waltz, the polka, the mazurka, the schottische, and the habanera that had been brought from Cuba. White Argentinians reciprocated by adopting black forms of dance, such as the *candombe*.

23. The word habanera can be translated as "from the city of Havana." The dance, which originated in Havana, Cuba, was taken to Spain around 1850, and reached Argentina by way of sheet music as early as 1803.

24. Robert Farris Thompson states that the bass rhythm of the habanera was taken from a Kongo bass ngoma drum pattern known as *mbila a makinu*, which translates as "the call to the dance." He adds, "The use of the bass drum, as opposed to the treble, is deliberate: treble voicings represent our world, but bass patterns come from the spirit. 'They are sounds from beneath the horizon. They capture the deep part of what people are thinking.' Bass brings transcendence" (p. 115).

25. Collier, p.40.

26) In the ancient Angolan language the word "milonga" meant both "argument" and "issue." It also denoted using words to incite, rebel and stand up to authority. This tradition was later utilized in drum duels and challenge singing. However, the milonga in the most traditional sense was also about reconciliation. According to Thompson, p. 135, "Milonga in this sense sees cultural difference not as a predicament but as amiable argument, an argument solved by generosity, shared values, and celebratory spirit."

27. Collier, p.41.

28. Collier, p. 37.

29. Compadritos were sometimes called *guapos*, translated as "lady's men."

30. Collier, p. 38.

31. In the outer districts of Buenos Aires, many illegal brothels called *clandestinos*, flourished. Prostitution was rampant in the city and many of these women had been brought from Europe through the white slave trade. The "street tough" and the "tawdry woman" were common archetypes in tango lore.

32. Collier, p. 45, quoting Ventura Lynch. José Gobello, a noted writer on the history of the tango suggests that as the tango was given birth, African elements were added not only to the milonga, but also probably to the mazurka as well in the districts closer to the docks. In his book *Tango: The Art History of Love*, p. 130, Robert Farris Thompson writes,

He [Ventura Lynch] says, without evidence, that compadritos were the *only* persons who were dancing the milonga. But he certainly was not saying that *all* dancers of milonga, at *all* times, were making fun of the blacks in their dancing. For some compadritos *were* black. Others were mulatto. In the competitive spirit that was dominant in dancing ... blacks would inevitably have excelled. They lived and inherited battles of aesthetic inspiration.

33. In Kongo tradition cuts called *nzéngolo* symbolize change. They are inserted in African dance to challenge the dancer's wits and test whether if he can improvise. This tradition was used as the *corte* in the milonga and the tango at the end of the piece when the dancer struck a perfect pose and held it. In the tango, these held cuts or pauses were also used throughout the dance, challenging the performer to stay alert and constantly demonstrate the ability to adapt. The *quebrada* of the tango emerged from the Kongo tradition of *tyenga ye kanga makolo mu nabyu,* translated as "weaving the hips and tying knots quickly." This type of movement was used in the candombe and later found its way into the tango.

34. Collier, pp. 45–46.

35. Jo Baim, *Tango: The Creation of a Cultural Icon* (Bloomington: Indiana University Press, 2007) p. 45.

36. Robert Farris Thompson, *Tango: The Art History of Love* (New York: Vintage Books, 2005) p. 223, quoting José Gobello, *Breve historia crítica del tango* (Buenos Aires: Corregidor, 1999) p. 16.

37. Thompson, p. 158.

38. On p. 89 of his book, Thompson states, "In Kongo one interesting meaning of leaning far back and far forward is social defiance: 'we are palm trees, bent forward, bent back, but we never break.'" This type of leaning posture, used to suggest defiance was also found in the Cakewalk. In African culture, leaning and dipping also signifies "'Don't lean on the future without leaning on the past' ... In less formal contexts, leaning forward and back just means 'hi' and 'goodbye.'" Dancing in a deep plié also carried symbolic meaning. On p. 86 of the book, Thompson reveals, "Bending down with the knees pressed together is in Kongo an expression of honor. One may curtsy this way before the king, a god, or a spirit, the tomb of an ancestor, a medicine of God (*ukisi*), a magistrate (*mbazi a n'kanu*), or a healer of distinction (*nganga mbuki*)." In the African Bakongo language the knock-kneed position is named *fukama,* a word that means "bending the legs like a she-goat." This knock-kneed position played an important part of the Charleston with the use of bees knees, but "a trace of this inflection appears in the tango. Dancers in the early tango style, canyengue, danced close to the earth, inserting 'break patterns'—quebradas—with knees deeply bent" (p. 86). Another influence of African dance ritual found in the tango is the direction of movement. Tangos are traditionally danced moving counterclockwise around the floor. "This custom descends from the circle of the candombe, possibly reinforced by the waltz, but it ultimately goes back to counterclockwise-cycling dancers in Kongo. The original meaning: we are following the path of the sun, we are following the cycle of life everlasting" (p. 109).

39. Thompson points out that Italian culture also had an impact on the development of the tango. On p. 60 of his book, he quotes Viejo Tanguero, or "The Old Tanguero" who wrote in 1913,

> Around 1880 ... in the barrio of Corrientes ... tango [dancing] experienced ... a change, not only of figures but also in terms of the elasticity and swing [*contoneos*] that were the arresting characteristics displayed at the start. Now it was interpreted by young women who were for the most part Italian. So then it became known as "smooth tango" [*tango liso*].

40. Baim, pp. 38–39.

41. Thompson, p. 221 states, "Bars and bordellos were democratic venues, where blacks performed freely before admiring sets of people, like sailors and *tanos* (Italian immigrants). Passion of the dance transcended condition."

42. Acceptance of the tango by the upper echelon of Argentine society was partly due to the dance's immense popularity in Paris and its acceptance by European society. Buenos Aires in particular sought to imitate anything Parisian. Many French-flavored cabarets opened in Buenos Aires and flourished. That is not to say that the dance was readily embraced by all. Argentines living in Paris were often particularly resistant. "In Paris, members of the rich Argentine community saw the tango as symbolic of that strong anarchistic streak in their own society which was a threat to established order" (Collier, p. 96). In addition, they "were also deeply embarrassed by the tango's reputation of sexual and aggressive machismo, with its strong suggestion of tainted blood and prostitution" (Collier, p. 96).

43. The most renowned tango hall in Buenos Aries was the San Martín located on Rodríguez Peña Street. One of the most admired and famous professional tango dancer during the early years of the twentieth century in Buenos Aires was José Ovidio Bianquet. He was known as *El Cachafez,* (or *Cacha*) translated as "Barefaced Cheek," a nickname given to him by his father. "El Cachafez was an impeccable ballroom dancer, but one who could still dance the fiercer tango to spectacular effect — never quite able to forget the squalid surroundings from which his dance had sprung. He has always been taken as the paragon, the all-time master" (Collier, p. 59). Bianquet died on the dance floor at the age of 63. He had just finished doing one tango and was getting up to dance another.

Chapter 11

1. Jo Baim, *Tango: The Creation of a Cultural Icon* (Bloomington: Indiana University Press, 2007) pp. 52–53. One of those wealthy young aristocrats who came to Paris was poet Ricardo Güiraldes. According to Collier, p. 72, "...it was he more than anyone who was responsible for championing the tango in Paris. In 1911 he wrote a famous poem in honour of the dance [entitled "Tango"], and the following year gave a dazzling impromptu performance of tango in front of astonished guests at a fashionable Paris salon."

2. According to Collier, p. 67, "The first genuine tangueros to come to Paris from Buenos Aires were Angel Villoldo and Afredo Gobbi, the latter accompanied by his wife, the singer Flora Rodríguez de Gobbi." The three had come to Paris in 1907 to make records since the city had the most technologically advanced recording available. While there they recorded "some of the best-known early tangos."

3. Gladys Beattie Crozier. *The Tango and How to Dance It.* (London: Andrew Melrose, 1913) p. 10.

4. Mr. & Mrs. Vernon Castle, *Modern Dancing* (New York: Harper, 1914) p. 83.

5. In 1909,(some sources say 1908,) Mistinguett performed the "Valse Chaloupee," or Apache dance with partner Max Dearly at the Moulin Rouge. The rough style of dancing was closely associated with the tango. In 1911, she often presented the tango with her partner, a young Maurice Chevalier.

6. Maurice Mouvet, *Maurice's Art of Dancing* (New York: G. Schirmer, 1915) p. 86.

7. *Ibid,* p. 85. Mouvet states that there were 8 original tango steps: Promenade, Cortez, Media Luna, El Paso, L'eventail, Les Ciseau, El Pados, and the Single Three.

8. Crozier, p. 16.

9. Collier, Simon, Atemis Cooper, Maria Susana Azzi, and Richard Martin, *Tango! The Dance, the Song, the Story* (London: Thames and Hudson Ltd., 1995) p. 80.

10. A similar trend happened in other cities. In a *New York Times* article entitled, "All New York Now Madly Whirling in the Tango," (January 4, 1914, Section: Magazine Section, p. SM8,) the paper reported,

> Since the tango became popular an extraordinary number of dark-skinned young men have appeared in New York as teachers of the Argentinian dance, who claim to have come from south of the Rio de la Plata. Doubting Thomases assert the arrival of these

dusky young tangoists dates from the first of the Mexican revolutions, and unmask them as refugees from the other side of the Rio Grande.

The paper concluded, "Nowadays a young man who dances well may go far."

11. A confection known as *Le Gateau Tango* became a popular treat at tango teas. The name was bestowed on a variety of desserts and had many variations—from chocolate cakes with port-wine icing to biscuit-like cookies.

12. One major contest held at the Palais de Glace required the winning couple to dance an astounding sixty-two tangos.

13. Collier, p. 76.

14. "Tango Captivates Paris" *The New York Times*, February 16, 1913, Section: Part III, and IV, Editorial Section — Special Foreign Dispatches Sports Censored Want Advertisements, p. 29.

15. Camille de Rhynal, nicknamed Tod Cams, was a choreographer, dancer, manager, event organizer, writer, and composer. He created the first official dance competition in Europe by organizing the Tango-Tournament in Nice in 1907. Its success prompted him to repeat the contest in Paris later that same year. He also organized the first World Dance Championships in Paris in 1909, which later became an annual event.

16. Peter Buckman, *Let's Dance: Social, Ballroom and Folk Dancing* (New York: Paddington Press, 1978) p. 172.

17. "Super-tango Tea Enthralls London" *The New York Times*, April 26, 1914, Section: Editorial Section Foreign News Sports Want Advertisements, p. C4.

18. "Do You Tango?" *The Fort Wayne Sentinel*, Fort Wayne, Indiana, May 3, 1913, p. 26.

19. Crozier, p. 16.

20. "Berlin is Tango Mad." *The New York Times*, October 19, 1913, Section: Foreign News Special Dispatches Sports Want Advertisements, p. C2.

21. Collier, p. 86.

22. *Ibid.* One of the young men who demonstrated the tango to Tsar Nicholas II was Grand Duke Dimitri, who later participated in the assassination of Rasputin. While traveling to Paris with his Uncle Grand Duke Paul and his fifty-six year old aunt, the Grand Duchess Anastasia, Dimitri was often required to escort his aunt onto the dance floor. The woman loved to dance, but was dreadful at it and, being overweight and considered unattractive, could get few other men to partner her. Dimitri would often step on her feet and bump her knees on purpose to avoid the task. The Grand Duchess eventually took some lessons from Vernon Castle who was in Paris at the time. Although he supposedly taught the Grand Duchess the tango, she was always thought of as a horrible dancer. Irene Castle remarked that although she had not seen the woman do the tango herself, she imagined "It would be like watching an elephant waltz." Irene Castle, *Castles in the Air*. (Garden City, NY: Da Capo, 1980) p. 81.

23. Collier, p. 87.

24. Collier, p. 91.

25. "Tango Defeats Vatican" *The New York Times*, December 27, 1913, p. 1.

26. "Tango Mania Has New York in Its Grip" *Oelwein Daily Register*, Oelwein, Iowa, February 16, 1914, p. 2, col. 1. The same article laments about how even relationships are based upon whether a potential mate can tango or not.

> The debutante listens impatiently to mamma's accounts of the list of virtues of a certain eligible, and burst[s] out with: "Yes, yes, I know, — but does he tango?" The hostess, in her quest of that rare species, the social male, asks not whether he be fat or thin, old or young, gallant or boorish, good to look upon or homely as a barn, but — does he tango? And worse and more incredible than all, the intellectual, the college prof., the highbrow, the man of letters, the rigid financier care not whether a woman is lovely

as Venus, as wise as Minerva and as wonderful to look upon as a fashion plate; the only matter of any import is does she tango?"

27. "Tango-Itis" *The Lincoln Daily Star*, Lincoln, NE, October 5, 1913, p. 14. col. 1.

28. "Do You Tango?" *The Fort Wayne Sentinel*, Fort Wayne, Indiana, May 3, 1913, p. 26.

29. "Milady's Mirror" (a society column) *Sheboygan Press*, Sheboygan, Wisconsin, December 18, 1913, p. 4, col. 5

30. "Tangoing on Wheels" *The New York Times*, June 6, 1915, Section: Summer Resorts Fashions Queries and Answers Drama Automobiles Society, p. X1.

31. "Tango on Train" *The New York Times*, February 6, 1914, p. 1.

32. "Tango Tour From Toledo to Texas" *Indianapolis Star*, Indianapolis, IN, May 10, 1914, p. 50, col. 1.

33. Buckman, p. 173.

34. Castles, p. 84.

35. Castles, p. 85.

36. Castles, p. 20. On page 86 of their book, the Castles offer this advice to anyone who was interested in learning the tango;

> Take your lessons, if possible, from some one who has danced professionally in Paris, because there are so many good dancers there that anybody who can dance the Tango (and get paid for it) in Paris must really be a good dancer. American teachers go abroad for a few weeks, take a few lessons in the Abaye or some other places which live on the American tourist, come back home, and having forgotten all they learned coming over, start in teaching. There are others who go to one of our seaside towns, such as Narragansett, and read of a new dance and begin teaching it. There is, unfortunately, no way of stopping these people. You can only pay your twenty-five dollars an hour. If you don't learn the dance, you get a little exercise and a lot of experience.

Chapter 12

1. "New Dances Influence Paris Fashions for Spring Wear" *The New York Times*, April 12, 1914, Section: Society Drama, p. X10.

2. "Clothiers in Session" *The New York Times*, June 2, 1914, p. 15.

3. Gladys Beattie Crozier, *The Tango and How to Dance It* (London: Andrew Melrose, 1913) p. 129.

4. Crozier, pp. 129–130.

5. Crozier, p. 133.

6. Crozier, p. 135.

7. *Ibid.*

8. Mr. & Mrs. Vernon Castle, *Modern Dancing* (New York: Harper, 1914) P. 141.

9. *Ibid.*

10. "A Dance Alters Paris Gowns" *Indianapolis Star*, Indianapolis, IN, July 6, 1913, p. 45.

11. Castles, p. 142.

12. Castles, p. 147.

13. "Tango Craze Leads Fashion's Efforts" *Janesville Daily Gazette*, Janesville, Wisconsin, February 6, 1914, p, 10, col. 3.

14. Castles, p. 142.

15. *Ibid.*

16. "New Customs, New Costumes" *New Oxford Item*, New Oxford, PA, February 2, 1912, p. 4, col. 5.

17. *Ibid.*

18. In describing the tango trouserettes, the writer from *Janesville Daily Gazette*, February 6, 1914, explained,

> Over this foundation you may take one of three choices. The tango pantalets which start from the

waist and fasten snuggly with elastic about your ankles, the tango garter pantalets which are dainty lace and chiffon ruffles fastened to either knee with a stain garter, or the dainty lace incrusted tango petticoat, scant and diaphanous and slit at either side to allow your dip and glide full sway.

19. "*New Customs, New Costumes*" *New Oxford Item*, New Oxford, PA, February 2, 1912, p. 4, col. 5.
20. "*Tango Craze Leads Fashion's Efforts*" *Janesville Daily Gazette*, Janesville, Wisconsin, February 6, 1914, p, 10, col. 3.
21. Castles, pp. 148–149.
22. Castles, p. 145.
23. "*New Dances Are Influencing Fashions for Women*" *The New York Times*, December 28, 1913, Section: Society Fashions Drama Music, p. X10.
24. "*New Customs, New Costumes*" *New Oxford Item*, New Oxford, PA, February 2, 1912, p. 4, col. 5.
25. *Ibid.*
26. "*Tango Styles in Riot of Color*" *Oakland Tribune*, Oakland, CA, March 12, 1914, p. 4, col. 1.
27. "*Tango Craze Leads Fashion's Efforts*" *Janesville Daily Gazette*, Janesville, Wisconsin, February 6, 1914, p, 10, col. 3.
28. Castles, p. 147.
29. In his book *Light on the Dance*, p. 53, Mordecai Franklin Ham tells of one such case: "For the pleasure of dancing the tango, Brent Latimer of Greenville, S.C. paid the price of one eye, the sight being destroyed by a quill in the hat of the young woman with whom he was dancing."
30. Castles, p. 145.
31. Simon Collier, Artemis Cooper, Maria Susana Azzi, and Richard Martin, *Tango!: The Dance, the Song, the Story* (London: Thames and Hudson Ltd., 1995) p.78.
32. "*Tango Craze Leads Fashion's Efforts*" *Janesville Daily Gazette*, Janesville, Wisconsin, February 6, 1914, p, 10, col. 3.
33. *Ibid.*
34. "*A Valise for Dancers*" *The New York Times*, December 21, 1913, Section: Foreign News Sports Want Advertisements, p. C2.
35. "*Tango Craze Leads Fashion's Efforts*" *Janesville Daily Gazette*, Janesville, Wisconsin, February 6, 1914, p, 10, col. 3.
36. "*Tango Last Word*" *Evening Chronicle*, Marshall, MI, November 15, 1913, p. 4, col. 4.
37. Collier, p. 67 states, "They [the French] could not agree whether the dance's origins lay in the slums of Buenos Aires or in Uruguay, or whether its music was in origin a cross between Hispanicized Berber of the Flamenco and South American Indian music."
38. Collier mentions three early musicians of renown. The men, of African-Argentine descent included El Negro Casmiro, who played the violin, El Mulato Sinforoso, who played the clarinet, and El Pardo, probably the first to champion the bandoneón.
39. This combination of instruments was first put together by Roberto Firpo, bandleader of what many considered the premiere orchestra of the first decade of the twentieth century. Early recordings made by Vicente Greco featured six players, but Firpo replaced the flute with the double-bass.
40. The bandoneón was named after Heinrich Band, and most likely was a fusion of his surname and the word "accordion." Although some sources credit Band with inventing the instrument, other historians credit C. Zimmerman of Saxony with creating the first for the Industrial Exposition in Paris in 1849. It is known that Zimmerman's creation was advertised for sale at Band's music shop in Krefeld, Germany in December 1850. Band himself never claimed he invented the bandoneón, but in Germany, his named quickly became associated with the instrument. As its popularity spread throughout Germany, different sizes and models of the instrument were developed. One particular variety, the "Reinlander," was exported to Argentina and introduced there by German immigrants in the early 1900's. Unlike the traditional accordion, it does not have a keyboard, but rather

buttons. Some had up to seventy-one buttons, thirty-eight that were played by the right hand, and thirty-three by the left. Each button could produce two separate notes depending on whether the player was opening (inflating) or closing (deflating) the instrument. This made learning the instrument a difficult task for many.
41. Collier, p. 57.
42. Charles Romauld Gardes, better known as Carlos Gardel, was born on December 11, 1890. Some conjecture he was born in Uruguay, although there is strong evidence that he was born in Toulouse, France. He became a citizen of Argentina in 1923, and began singing in bars and clubs in Buenos Aires. In 1915, he was involved in a barroom fight at the Palais de Glace in Buenos Aires and was shot, most believe by Che Guevara's father Ernesto Guervara Lynch. The bullet was never removed from his body. In 1917, Gardel recorded "Mi Noche Triste" and by presenting this tango with lyrics in a genre that had previously been associated primarily with instrumental music, created the *tango-canción*. Gardel's popularity grew rapidly. He toured internationally, made many recordings, and appeared in numerous films for Paramount in France and the United States. He died on June 24, 1935 in a plane crash in Medellín, Columbia. Millions of fans around the world grieved. Several committed suicide after hearing of his death. He was nicknamed "The King of Tango," and also dubbed El Zorzal Criollo, "the songbird of Buenos Aires." In Argentina, Gardel is revered as the embodiment of tango and has achieved an almost saint-like status. A life-sized statue of the singer was erected in the cemetery where he was buried and present-day admirers frequently put a lit-cigarette in its hand to honor Gardel's memory.
43. Collier, p. 64.

Chapter 13

1. "Why Tango was Banned" *The New York Times*, December 2, 1913, p. 4. It was rumored that the Kaiser banned the tango because his daughter the Crown Princess was starting to learn the immoral dance. The Kaiser was also concerned that his son, who was "an ardent dancer," might also attempt the dance. As a result, he "...decided to put his imperial foot down on the dance by tabooing it for all officers of the army."
2. "Tango Flourishes Despite Boycotts" *The New York Times*, January 5, 1914, Section: Cable News Shipping Business Sports Want Advertisements, p. C3.
3. "Tango 'Absurd,' Says King" *The New York Times*, December 16, 1913, p. 3.
4. "Tango Defeats Vatican" *The New York Times*, December 27, 1913, p. 1.
5. Pope Pius X agreed to view the tango on the recommendation of one of his advisors, Cardinal Merry de Val. An Italian Prince, a friend of the Cardinal, had contacted the cleric, expressing concern that carnival time, a period of several balls, was nearing and members of society who loved the Argentine dance were ill-at-ease because the tango had been condemned by the Pontiff. The Prince assured the Cardinal that the tango had been refined by the well-known dancing master Professor Pichetti, and all objectionable features were eliminated. The new tango was now beyond reproach. When Cardinal Merry de Val approached the Pope the next day, His Holiness was in an audience with a brother and sister who were members of the Italian nobility. Pope Pius X asked the siblings if they would demonstrate the tango. They did. Although it is probable that the brother and sister offered a solemn and restrained demonstration, the Pope was less than enthusiastic. He suggested that if the young people wished to dance, they should choose instead a dance such as the furlana. The two did not know the dance, so the Pope had one of his servants demonstrate it. As the story circulated after the event, efforts were made to popularize the furlana, which earned the nickname, the "Pope's dance"

6. "Pope Saw Tango, Rome Story Says" *The New York Times*, January 28, 1914, p. 4.

7. "Tango Shame of Our Days" *The New York Times*, January 22, 1914, p. 4.

8. "All Denounce the Tango" *The New York Times*, January 7, 1914, p. 4.

9. "Bars 'Tango' as a Punishable Sin" *Waterloo Evening Courier*, Waterloo, IA, January 12, 1914, p. 2, col. 3.

10. "Tango Teacher Asks $4,000" *The New York Times*, January 29, 1914, p. 4. Some sources report dance teacher M. Stilson sued the cardinal for $4,000, others that he sued for $20,000. *The New York Times*, January 21, 1914, p. 4, reported, "M. Stilson says that since the formal prohibition of the tango by the Bishops he has lost students and money, that the zeal of the public has grown cold, and that therefore he intends to ask the court what legal redress he has against such an attack on his profession."

11. Simon Collier, Artemis Cooper, Maria Susana Azzi, and Richard Martin. *Tango!: The Dance, the Song, the Story* (London: Thames and Hudson Ltd., 1995) p.87.

12. Jo Baim, *Tango: The Creation of a Cultural Icon* (Bloomington: Indiana University Press, 2007) p. 88.

13. "Tango Flourishes Despite Boycotts" *The New York Times*, January 5, 1914, Section: Cable News Shipping Business Sports Want Advertisements, p. C3.

14. *Ibid.*

15. The exhibition was presented at a ball hosted by Grand Duke Michael of Russia at Kenwood in Hampstead. At first the tango was eliminated from Mouvet's and Walton's demonstration, but when the monarch expressed disappointment at not seeing the dance, the couple presented a seven-minute-long tango, which won the Queen's approval. As deference to the Queen, Walton did not wear a slit skirt, but a gown that reached to the ankles and even sported a small train which she held in her hand as the duo danced.

16. "No Tango 'Ads' Received" *The New York Times*, December 28, 1913, Section: Cable News Wireless Dispatches Sports Want Advertisements, p. C4.

17. "Tango Too Evil For Them" *Lincoln Daily News*, Lincoln, Nebraska, July 2, 1913. p. 4, col. 2.

18. "Pastors Approve Ban on the Tango" *The New York Times*, January 5, 1914, p. 5.

19. "More Church Heads Oppose New Dances" *The New York Times*, February 1, 1914, Section Foreign News Sports Want Advertisements, p. C6.

20. "Tango Barred in Vermont and Vindicated in Ohio" *Anaconda Standard*, Anaconda, Montana, October 18, 1913, p. 10, col. 6.

21. "Dancing of Tango Barred by Dean of the Cathedral" *Anaconda Standard*, Anaconda, Montana, March 7, 1914, p. 13, col. 3.

22. "Many Noted Tango Decision Made in Few Weeks" *Lincoln Daily News*, Lincoln, NE, January 19, 1914. P. 8. col. 1.

23. "Salvationists Halt Broadway Dancers" *The New York Times*, March 22, 1914, p. 1. According to the article, the dancers listened politely, applauded, and then offered the Army members donations. The Salvationists refused the money.

24. "New Nuggets" *New Castle News*, New Castle, PA, July 24, 1914, p. 11, col. 4.

25. "Tango Teacher Quits Choir" *The New York Times*, February 3, 1914, p. 1.

26. "Tango Barred in Vermont and Vindicated in Ohio" *Anaconda Standard*, Anaconda, Montana, October 18, 1913, p. 10, col. 6. *The New York Times* reported on the incident as well. In an article entitled "Dance Tango for Judge" that appeared on October 16, 1913, p. 1, it was reported,

So many men and women crowded in Judge Vickery's courtroom during the hearing of Anderson's petition for an injunction that the judge decided to hold the exhibition in more spacious quarters....

With music furnished by a graphaphone, Anderson and one of the young woman pupils danced "the only real tango," according to Anderson's description.

27. "Tango Barred to Harvard Athletes" *Syracuse Herald*, Syracuse, NY, May 11, 1914, p. 27, col. 4.

28. "No Tangoing to Result In No Teaching Pupils" *Titusville Herald*, Titusville, PA, July 17, 1914, p. 5, col. 5.

29. Mordecai Franklin Ham, *The Modern Dance* (1916) p. 27.

30. Social reformers warned that underneath their slick veneers, tango pirates invariably hid rather dubious pasts. "The veneer itself lured the unsuspecting, because this 'is all the rich girls ever see or try to see.'" (Erenberg, p. 83.)

31. "Tango Pirates Infest Broadway" by Richard Barry *The New York Times*, May 30, 1915, Section: Magazine Section, p. SM16.

32. *Ibid.*

33. *Ibid.*

34. *Ibid.* Social reformers viewed the tango pirate phenomenon as indicative of the destruction of proper Victorian values. These men were seen as doubly dangerous because they would not only seduce women away from respectable lives and marriages, but also damage otherwise respectable men by forcing them to imitate the tango pirate's low-class, sensual ways in order to hold on to their women, Reformers warned that the respectable men would therefore end up "lost and adrift, incapable of success" (Erenberg, p. 83).

35. "Eugenia Kelly Seen Again on Broadway" *The New York Times*, October 1, 1915, p. 5.

36. *The Syracuse Herald* on October 26, 1924, p. 12 called Albert J. Davis "among the great lovers of the present day," saying his romantic exploits might someday "supply themes for poets and novelist." The paper declared he was, "The tangoing hero whose light grace was so much admired in the Broadway cabarets in Pre-Volstead days [who] still lives to love and make helpless captive of girlish hearts." Davis was a professional dancer and partnered the popular Bonnie Glass, who later danced with Rudolph Valentino. (Eugenia Kelly stated that a jealous Bonnie Glass was actually the one who first contacted her mother about her daughter's lifestyle.) Davis was married three times. His first marriage was to Aimee Fogerty, daughter of a wealthy brewer; his second to heiress Eugenia Kelly; and his third to Marianne Conrad, daughter of a wealthy importer. *The Syracuse Herald* reporting on his last wife stated, "Once again the all-conquering Mr. Davis has shown rare skill in making beauty and riches fit ever so nicely into his marriage plans. It is quite as Broadway has come to expect in any romance where 'Al' is concerned."

37. "Eugenia Kelly Seen Again on Broadway" *The New York Times*, October 1, 1915, p. 5.

38. Lewis Erenberg, *Steppin'Out: New York Nightlife and the Transformation of American Culture, 1890–1930* (Chicago: University of Chicago Press, 1981) p. 78. *The Washington Post*, 5/26/15, p. 4, quoted Mrs. Kelly as stating, "What I am anxious to know is how much money these suede-top shoes, wrist-watch-wearing tango dancers have bilked my daughter of."

39. *Ibid.*

40. *Ibid.*

41. Eugenia Kelly defended her lifestyle, declaring that she would lose her social standing if she did party at night. She said, "No one but a 'dead one' could live in New York without visiting four to six cabarets and remaining out until 5 a.m. to tango" (*The Ogden Standard*, 7/10/15). Miss Kelly begged the friends that she knew from the clubs to speak in her defense at her trial and explain how nightlife was a necessary part of modern social expression, but none showed up to testify on her behalf. She was heard to comment later, "Oh, the cats. They say they are afraid of the notoriety and wouldn't come to court to help me prove my case. What do you think of them for friends?" (*The Ogden Standard*, 7/10/15)

42. Joshua Zeitz, *Flapper: A Madcap Story of Sex, Style, Celebrity, and the Women Who Made America Modern* (New York: Crown Publishers, 2006) pp. 3 & 4, quoting Eugenia Kelly. Shortly after the charges were dropped against her, Eugenia began seeing Al Davis again. Her mother, begged her personal attorney, John F. McIntyre "to take some sort of action against Davis personally to obliterate him from her daughter's life." At Mrs. Kelly's urging, McIntyre considered charging Davis with "enticement and inveiglement," charges he expected would "send him to State prison" (NY Times, 10/1/15). Mrs. Kelly also hired a private detective to watch Davis. Trying to shield her daughter from the tango pirate's influence, Mrs. Kelly took her daughter to a resort out West. According to the detective, Davis followed. The mother quickly took her daughter back to New York City, and again Davis followed them. Three months after the trial, Eugenia Kelly eloped with the recently divorced Al Davis. The two initially had trouble finding a minister who would agree to perform the marriage because of their notoriety after the court case. Eventually they found one who specialized in last-minute nuptials and were wed. Eugenia did inherit her fortune anyway. The couple had a daughter, but in 1922 were divorced.

43. "Hints Eugenia Kelly is Victim of a Plot" *The New York Times*, May 25, 1915, p. 8. *The Ogden Standard* in Ogden, Utah on July 10, 1915, reported that the Kelly case had a dramatic effect upon nightlife in New York. It stated;

> There is gloom six inches deep along Broadway, that great place of gayety in New York. The lights no longer shine brightly and are extinguished at 1 a.m., and the tangoists dance to subdued strains—since "Ma" Kelly put the lid on the nightlife of that great thoroughfare. Broadway is under the rigid inspection of the whole United States.

The paper explained that a "morality squad has placed a lid on Broadway and is sitting tightly upon it."

44. Mrs. Hilar secretly frequented tango parlors during the afternoons without her husband's knowledge, while he was occupied as a furniture salesman. There she flirted and danced with an assortment of men. She also attended vaudeville and at one theatre, met an Italian man, "with black hair and flashing black eyes." She invited him to lunch and over a meal of spaghetti, she arranged to have a tryst with him. Hilar registered at the Martinique Hotel as "Florence Gray, Boston" and was given room 726 on the seventh floor. After checking in, she returned to the restaurant and told the man where her room was and how to get to it without being detected. Hilar was discovered the next morning by the chambermaid, Salome Petit. She had been garroted with a cord (or ripped end of a towel.) Her windpipe was crushed. *The New York Times* (3/18/17) reported, that her "murderer, [displayed] the skill of a Parisian Apache." Hilar had come to the hotel wearing a large diamond ring, a diamond lavaliere, a diamond breastpin, and three other diamond rings, which were all missing when her body was discovered. Although her husband was a furniture salesman, he had once been wealthy and bought his wife jewels before his fortunes reversed. When asked to comment after his wife's murder, "he asserted that he was sure that she had always been a good woman and that she had never gone beyond harmless flirtations" (NY Times, 3/18/17). Benjamin Sternberg, a "favorite in 'tango parlors' because of his accomplishments as a dancer, (NY Times, 3/20/17) was charged with the murder. When he was arrested, "thousands of persons, anxious to see the alleged 'tango pirate,' gathered about the Second Branch Detective Bureau," (NY Times, 3/22/17) eventually causing a riot. Although he admitted meeting Mrs. Hilar on the day she was killed, he denied killing her. Sternberg was later released for lack of evidence. The case was complicated because the same maid who found Hilar's body later found a letter signed Florence Gray in the room of two young men. In the letter, Hilar wrote that she wanted a position dancing in a cabaret show, and asked the two men to help her find one.

45. These well-publicized cases brought to the forefront issues such as the widening of the generation gap, rebellion against parental control, a questioning of traditional family values, the loosening of moral standards, the rejection of traditional gender roles, and the disintegration of the social caste system.

46. "Tango Thieves Active" *The New York Times*, March 15, 1914, Section: Editorial Section, Foreign News Sports Want Advertisements, p. C2.

47. *Ibid.*

48. "Mayor Out to Stop 'Tea and Tango' Now" *The New York Times*, April 5, 1913, p. 2.

49. *Ibid.*

50. *Ibid.*

51. "Middle-aged Dancers Warned Against the Tango" *The New York Times*, December 28, 1913, Section: Magazine, p. SM2.

52. *Ibid.*

53. *Ibid.*

54. *Ibid.*

55. *Ibid.*

56. *Ibid.*

57. "A Result of the Tango" *The New York Times*, September 14, 1913, Section: Foreign News Special Dispatches Sports Want Advertisements, p. C2.

58. *Ibid.*

59. *Ibid.*

60. "Calls Dance Mania Psychic Epidemic" *The New York Times*, April 26, 1914, Section: Editorial Section Foreign News Sports Want Advertisements, p. C8.

61. *Ibid.*

62. *Ibid.*

63. "The Tango Face Spoils Women's Beauty, Latest Charge Against the Dance" *Waterloo Times- Tribune*, Waterloo, Iowa, August 7, 1914, p. 9, col. 1.

64. *Ibid.* The serious expression on a tango dancer's face was a prerequisite of the dance. Some found the expression absurd. "The Tango's solemnity is appalling. The dancers wear the corrugated brow of unaccustomed mental effort, or the final smile of a mechanical professor. There is no abandon. If there is, then it is not the Tango" ("Calls Tango 'Solemn'" *The New York Times*, November 2, 1913, Section: Foreign News Sports Want Advertisements, p. C2). The frozen face employed in tango dancing was an aspect that originated out of African ritual. It came from the belief that concentrated composure while dancing was a desirable attribute, indicating grace under pressure, and emphasizing equilibrium and control. In addition, silent concentration without distraction was an vital aspect of respectful spirituality. According to Robert Farris Thompson, *Tango: The Art History of Love.* (New York: Vintage Books, 2005) p. 222, "The rule of not dissipating the energy of the body by talking or smiling while dancing is strong too in Kongo. Here silence and concentration grant dancers leeway to spiritual ecstacy."

65. "The Tango Face Spoils Women's Beauty, Latest Charge Against the Dance" *Waterloo Times-Tribune*, Waterloo, IA, August 7, 1914, p. 9, col. 1.

66. *Ibid.*

67. "Expert Points Out Harm in the Tango" *The New York Times*, April 26, 1914, Section: Society Drama Foreign Resorts Music, p. X15.

68. "The Tango Face Spoils Women's Beauty, Latest Charge Against the Dance" *Waterloo Times-Tribune*, Waterloo, IA, August 7, 1914, p. 9, col. 1.

69. "Tangoist Hurls Furniture" *The New York Times*, February 7, 1914, p. 5.

70. Baim, p. 70, quoting Edward Marks memoir *They All Sang.*

71. *Ibid.*

72. "Tangoed to Death" *Fort Wayne News*, Fort Wayne, IN, February 12, 1915, p. 27, col. 4.

73. Baim, p. 57, quoting an unattributed article entitled "Man Killed by Tango," possibly from the wire service from Boston, dated January 23, 1914, found in the clippings file of the NYPL.

74. "The Tragedy of the Tango Dance" *The Fort Wayne Sentinel*, Fort Wayne, Indiana, October 6, 1913, p. 13, col. 1.

75. *Ibid.*

76. *Ibid.*

77. "Tango Killer Goes to Death" *Centralia Daily Chronicle-Examiner*, Centralia, WA, July 31, 1914, p. 7, col. 4.

78. "Milady's Mirror" *Sheboygan Press*, Sheboygan, WI, December 18, 1913, p. 4, col. 5.

79. Gladys Beattie Crozier, *The Tango and How to Dance It* (London: Andrew Melrose, 1913) p. 19.

80. *Ibid.*

81. Crozier, p. 20.

82. "Tango as a Health Promoter" *The Gazette and Bulletin*, Williamsport, PA, May 12, 1914, p. 5, col. 2.

Chapter 14

1. In 1924, professional daredevil Alvin "Shipwreck" Kelly sat on a flagpole in Los Angeles for thirteen hours and thirteen minutes. After his stunt, hundreds of amateurs across the U.S. imitated his feat, and tried to beat his record. Following the first World War, fads and record-breaking contests became especially prevalent. Sociologists suggest that their popularity grew out of three factors:

(a) yearning for thrills by those who had been exposed to the excitement and horrors of the war.

(b) an adventure for Americans seeking a "new frontier" to conquer

(c) a desire for the common man to prove himself by achieving the impossible.

The dance marathons of the 1920's and 30's grew out of this type of phenomenon. Other contests included endurance kissing, handholding, gum chewing, roller skating, rocking in a chair, piano playing, as well as all manner of food eating contests. The inventiveness of these competitions was seemingly limitless. One fellow by the name of Bill Williams spent thirty days pushing a peanut up Pike's Peak with his nose trying to win a five hundred dollar bet. The *United Press Dispatch* in Warsaw, Indiana had the following report, "Clarence Tillman, 17, local high school student, put 40 sticks of chewing gum in his mouth at one time, sang, 'Home, Sweet Home,' and between verses of the song, drank a gallon of milk." This quote is found in *This Fabulous Century: Sixty Years of American Life*, Vol. III — 1920–1930, New York: Time-Life Books, 1970, p. 240.

2. Of course not all Americans experienced such prosperity. Many, especially those living in rural parts of the country, continued to live simple lives virtually unaffected by trends and fads that have come to symbolize the Decade.

3. Frederick Lewis Allen, *The Revolution in Manners and Morals*. http://xroads.virginia.edu/~hyper/Allen/ch5.html

4. Peter Jennings and Todd Brewster, *The Century* (New York: Doubleday, 1998) p. 100. Sexual standards were also shaken up by the popularity of the teachings of Sigmund Freud. The dictum that sexuality was the motivating force behind all actions led many in the 20's to proclaim that an uninhibited sex life was healthy and that self-control was out of date.

5. The Eighteenth Amendment grew out of the turmoil caused by the Temperance Movement, which preached against the ill health, poverty, crime, and immorality caused by alcoholism. Two powerful groups in the United States, the Woman's Christian Temperance Union, founded in 1879, and the Anti-Saloon League, founded in 1893, wielded considerable political clout in Washington and began to demand governmental controls of alcoholic beverages. Support of

Prohibition gained momentum after the great influenza epidemic of 1918 which resulted in the deaths of over 20 million people worldwide, twice the number of deaths that resulted during the entire four years of World War I. Evangelicals suggested that the flu had been a punishment for man's wickedness. Prohibition was looked upon as one way to atone for society's sins and return to the path of righteousness. Backed by church groups around the country, reformers were finally able to secure the passage of federal liquor laws when Congress adopted and submitted legislation to the states for ratification on December 18, 1917. Within thirteen months, enough states had finally ratified the amendment by January 16, 1919, and the Eighteenth Amendment became law. Its implementation was secured by the passage of the Volstead Act, despite the veto of President Woodrow Wilson. Initially many interpreted the prohibition of intoxicating spirits to mean only distilled liquors, but a strong anti–German sentiment which flourished after World War I soon led to a ban of beers and ales as well. As the efforts to control manufacture, sale, transportation deteriorated as the decade went on, support for prohibition waned and on December 5, 1933, the Eighteenth Amendment was officially repealed with the passage of the Twenty-First Amendment.

6. Jennings, p. 100, quoting Billy Sunday.

7. Peter McWilliams, PROHIBITION: A LESSON IN THE FUTILITY (AND DANGER) OF PROHIBITING. "Ain't Nobody's Business If You Do" PART IV: SIX CHAPTERS IN SEARCH OF A SHORTER BOOK http://www.sky.org/data/aint/402.htm, quoting Billy Sunday.

8. Senator Shepard Morris, who authored the Eighteenth Amendment, professed to be an ardent Prohibitionist, once stating, "There's as much chance of repealing the Eighteenth Amendment as there is for a hummingbird to fly to the planet Mars with the Washington Monument tied to its tail." Shortly after the passage of the amendment though, federal enforcement agents found a still on the outskirts of Morris' Texas ranch. The still produced more that 130 gallons of illegal alcohol a day. In another example of how prohibition laws were often completely disregarded, federal enforcement agents set up their own speakeasy in the center of Manhattan that they ran for nine months without getting caught. Speakeasies could be found in most cities across the country. There were between thirty thousand and one hundred thousand in New York City alone.

9. Like grain alcohol, wood alcohol, can lead to intoxication, but it is extremely dangerous to drink. Many Americans in an attempt to create cheaper homemade liquor used wood alcohol in a practice called "cutting," mixing it with the more expensive grain alcohol to make it go further. Some unscrupulous bootleggers also simply rebottled wood alcohol and sold it as pure and safe. As a result, more than 10,000 people died from wood-alcohol poisoning during Prohibition (1,565 in 1928 alone.) Many also went blind or developed severe kidney and liver problems due to the effects of wood alcohol poisoning. Other horrendous concoctions used in creating homemade liquor included using anti-freeze and embalming fluid.

10. Peter McWilliams offers the following quote from Herbert Asbury's "The Great Illusion" about Prohibition;

> The American people had expected to be greeted, when the great day came, by a covey of angels bearing gifts of peace, happiness, prosperity and salvation, which they had been assured would be theirs when the rum demon had been scotched. Instead they were met by a horde of bootleggers, moonshiners, rum-runners, hijackers, gangsters, racketeers, triggermen, venal judges, corrupt police, crooked politicians, and speakeasy operators, all bearing the twin symbols of the eighteenth amendment — the Tommy gun and the poisoned cup.

11. According to the Online Etymology Dictionary, the speakeasy got its name from joining the two words "speak"

and "easy." This referred to the practice of talking quietly when mentioning the illicit club in public, or when inside the club so that authorities would not be alerted. Unlike the "men-only" saloons that had existed before prohibition, speakeasies welcomed women as well.

12. According to W. G. Raffé, the batuque (also called the butuque or batucada) was descended from Portuguese West African tribal dances. It was performed as both a solo and a couple dance inside a surrounding circle of spectators. The dance featured handclapping and percussive accompaniment, and included shuffling feet and violent wiggling of the hips. The dance is believed to have moved from Africa to Portugal during the 16th century where it became a popular couple dance. Due to its wild movements, the dance was forbidden during the reign of Emperor Manuel I. The batuque later became more refined and was used in Spain during the 18th century as a flirtation piece featuring finger snaps. Portuguese colonists who settled along the east coast of South America in the 16th century, brought slaves from south-west Africa to work their plantations, and the batuque was transported to Brazil, the country that it is now most associated with. In some cases, the Brazilian batuque was performed as a game. One dancer was surrounded by a circle of others, who rushed at him during the dance, attacking him and trying to throw him to the ground using only their legs. In its most common form though, the dance was performed as one of seductive exhibitionism. Usually a soloist or couple performed within a circle showing off their choreographic prowess. After dancing for a while the soloist or one of the partners would indicate who would replace them by giving them an *umbigada*, the most unique feature of the Brazilian batuque. The *umbigada* consisted of touching one's belly, specifically the naval, against someone else's. The dance was also done in two opposing lines, and again, partners were replaced by performing an *umbigada*. After 1814, tracts began to appear in Brazil prohibiting the dance on the grounds that it promoted indecency. The Catholic Church was especially opposed to the dance's sensuality believing the batuque was associated with ritual dances of procreation. Despite the warnings, the batuque grew in popularity among all classes in Brazil and as it became more accepted by whites, the dance transformed and became more refined. The word "batuque" is now used as a generic term for a whole variety of dances and rhythms with percussive instruments. It is also used as another name for Candomblé, the Afro-Brazilian religion, in which rhythms are used to call forth the gods. By the end of the nineteenth century, dances that had previously been called batuques began to be known as sambas. The Brazilian word "samba" is linked to the African word "semba" which referred to a belly bounce, similar to the batuque's *umbigada*.

13. Marshall and Jean Stearns, *Jazz Dance: The Story of American Vernacular Dance* (New York: Da Capo, 1994) p.13, quoting Frederick Kaigh's *Witchcraft and Magic in Africa*, p.21.

14. In an article in *The Bridgeport Telegram,* Bridgeport, CT, December 16, 1925, p. 12, col. 2., Dr. F. L. Deane, the Bishop of Aberdeen and Orkney states, "...the Charleston is a combination of southern steps and an African snake dance."

15. Bill Egan, *Florence Mills: Harlem Jazz Queen* (Lanham, MD: Scarecrow Press, 2004) p. 182, quoting Florence Mills. The quote originally appeared in the program for the Grand Charleston Ball held at the Royal Albert Hall on December 15, 1926. The book (pp. 270–271) also features a 1926 interview with Mills in which she comments on the Charleston. She says,

> I smile to myself when I see you do it so sedately, with such good taste, the Charleston in your ballrooms. It is the dance of my people, of our piccaninnies, the happiest dance in all the world. They were Charlestoning in Kentucky before the Civil War. Do you know how the Charleston came to New York? It came on the feet of the coloured piccannies. The pic-

cannies used to play around the plantations of the South. Today they play around the subways of New York. Years ago you could see them dancing the "Take Your Foot Out of the Mud and Stick It in the Sand" step outside the subways of 42nd and 50th Streets. Their grandfathers did it to the "[Rubato] Pulse" rhythm long ago, when they came, as slaves, from the plantations. The pix would do it for money. They'd stop. Throw them a quarter and they'd Charleston till Doomsday. So it got to the clubs, dance restaurants, and cabarets. I like to see it, especially the nice new quiet way you do it, because it reminds me that there is somewhere a common tie linking all the races which make up mankind.

16. Lynn Fauley Emery, *Black Dance: From 1619 to Today.* (Pennington, New Jersey: Princeton, 1988) p.226, quotes Roark Bradford's article "New Orleans Negro Declared Not Guilty of the Charleston" (no publication given,) January 3, 1926. In the article, Bradford states that the Jay-Bird "...seems to have been a vague basis of distortion for the Charleston." He qualifies the statement by adding that, "...no Negro ever originated anything that required as much physical exertion as the present brand of Charleston." Emery states that she believes Bradford was perhaps correct in suggesting the Charleston was related to the Jay-Bird, but she also points out that Bradford demonstrated in other statements that he had biased, uninformed, racist opinions about the Charleston's relationship to African and African-American dances.

17. Emery, p.227, quoting Harold Courlander, *Negro Folk Music U.S.A.,* p.189.

18. In the book *Step It Down: Games, Plays, Songs, and Stories from the Afro-American Heritage,* by Bessie Jones and Bess Lomax Hawes, (New York: Harper & Row, 1972) p.37–40 there is a description of the Juba dance game which has recognizable Charleston steps in it. The basic Charleston step is referred to as "jump for joy" and utilizes the traditional Charleston footwork except it is more restrained with the feet being kept close to the ground and the flicking up of the feet to the side eliminated. The word "juba" was probably derived from the African word *giouba*, the name of the original dance form. Bessie Jones and Bessie Lomax Hawes give an alternate explanation, stating that the word was derived from "jibba" which was a modification of the word "giblets." The remains and leftover ends of foods, called the "giblets," were mixed together with milk in a mush, and the name was given to the dance and patting game because they were similarly composed of a mixture of various elements. In Charles Earle Funk's book, *Heavens to Betsy!*, there is an explanation of the colloquial phrase, "to dance juba." Drawing from the interpretation of Dr. Mitford M. Mathews originally given in *American Speech,* Funk suggests that Juba was a common name given to African-American girls who were born on a Monday. Tradition stated that girls born on this day were inclined to mischievous behavior so they had to be regularly punished. The movements that were later taken over by minstrels and called the Juba, were an imitation of the involuntary motions that resulted from these girls being hit with a switch. It is doubtful that this is the real explanation for the development of patting juba and the Juba dance in the United States. The name Juba is prominently featured throughout African history. Juba I (Joob) was the name of a Numidian King who ruled from 85 BC- 46 BC. An ally of Pompey and Metellus Scipio in their attempt to wrest the Roman army from Julius Caesar, he committed suicide after Caesar's victory at Thapsus. His son, Juba II was educated in Rome and reinstated as king in Numidia and later Mauretania. The Roman Emperor Augustus gave Cleopatra Selene, the daughter of Antony and Cleopatra to him in marriage. In Genesis 4:21 there is a reference to Jubal, the son of Lamech, as the inventor of musical instruments. ""He [Jubal] was the father of all those who play the lyre and pipe." Sonny Watson on his web site www.SwingStreet.com suggests there could be a

possible connection between this reference and a plantation dance step called the Jubal Jew. (Much of the information cited in this chapter and accompanying notes about the Juba dance, patting juba, and the Ring Shout was taken directly from my book *Tap Roots: The Early History of Tap Dancing*.)

19. The Juba as it was done in Africa and later in the United States was almost always performed as a circle dance. In Haiti, it was done as a set dance with two lines facing each other. Performed like this, the dance was also called the Martinique. This version of the Juba was clearly influenced by European elements.

20. Patting was sometimes called "body music." While patting, the dancer leaned forward in a crouched position and then struck his left knee and then his right, followed by slapping his two hands together. Variations included using double strokes on the left while continuing with just one hit on the right, and also hitting the shoulders. In his article "Jazz at Home," In *Survey Graphic*, Harlem Number (March 1925), p.665, J. A. Rogers quotes J. A. Jackson of the *Billboard*,

> Poverty compelled improvised instruments. Bones, tambourines, make-shift string instruments, tin can and hollow wood effects, all now utilized as musical novelties, were among early Negroes the product of necessity. When these were not available 'patting juba' prevailed. Present day 'Charleston' is but a variation of this. Its early expression was the 'patting' for the buck dance.

Patting was also done by hitting rhythms on an instrument, such as a fiddle or banjo. Using the hands, stiff straws, quills, knitting needles, or sticks, people called "beaters" sat at right angles from the instrumentalist and hit the strings between the bridge and the player's left hand. These polyrhythms were even more complicated because the fiddler or banjo player also stomped his feet while playing. In Juba beating, or Jubilee beating, as it was sometimes called, the performer also improvised rhymes, similar to modern rap music. He accompanied the words with the complex rhythms he beat out on the instrument or on his body. Lyrics would often conceal satirical jabs at whites that were accented with sharp percussive hits on the instrument or body. The rhythms of patting in this way conveyed covert messages. The word "patting" also came to represent other forms of slave communication. When patting Juba became popular in the U.S., its rhythms so intrigued the poets, Edgar Allan Poe and Sidney Lanier, they experimented with the same complex rhythms in their verses. A later version of patting Juba was called Hambone, and in the 1950's, patting hand rhythms were used in a dance called the Charley Bop.

21. Some dance historians believe the crouched over, feet-apart-and-knees-together position of bees knees, (also spelled bee's knees or bees' knees) is derived from a gesture of obeisance used in Kongo dance rituals, similar to a curtsy. The knock-kneed position is also found in parts of the Russian Czardas and some conjecture that the movement may have came through Finland and was brought to the United States by Finnish sailors who stopped off in New Orleans in their travels. In addition to the Charleston, the knock-kneed position is also found in other dances such as the Argentinian cayengue and the milonga.

22. Fred Austin, "The Charleston Traces Its Ancestry Back 400 Years" *The New York Times*, August 8, 1926, Magazine Section, SM2.

23. *Ibid*. To back up his claims, Staat quotes Thoinet Arbeau's book *Orchésographie* to show how similar the movements are to the basic Charleston step:

> Spring on one foot to support the body and at the same time carry the other in the air to in front of the shin, then change feet. Hold yourself on tiptoes, then bring the heels together, then turn them right, then turn them left, then turn them right again. The dancer stands on one foot to support the body and raises the other in the air as if he wished to kick some one.

24. *Ibid*.

25. *Ibid*. During the Charleston Ball in London in 1926, British choreographer Max Rivers was asked to give his thoughts on the origins of the Charleston. He stated,

> This dance has been credited to nearly every part of the world except to that from which it really sprang. I believe the British Sailor, of some four hundred years ago, was its originator, for it is obvious to anyone with a knowledge of the Charleston to see that all its principal steps and ninety percent of the minor movements are nothing more than adaptations from the Sailor's Hornpipe.

The above quote was extracted from the web article "Center for Jazz Arts Announces Initiative Promoting Jazz Appreciation Month in Britain," Embassy of the United States—London http://london.usembassy.gov/culture/jazz_appreciation_2006.html

26. *Ibid*. The mention of the beams collapsing at the end of the quote refers to the Pickwick Club collapse. Jack Blue, who is mentioned at the beginning of the quote owned a popular dance studio in New York City and coached professional stage dancers. One reference found in *The Decatur Review*, Sept 4, 1921, p. 9, col. 2, called Blue the "dancing master for the *Ziegfeld Follies*." According to the *Charleston Daily Mail*, July 29, 1928, P. 11, col. 3, "Jack Blue [was] one of America's foremost teachers of tap and eccentric dancing"

27. There is reference to this in Sylvia G. L. Dannett's and Frank Rachel's book *Down Memory Lane: Arthur Murray's Picture Story of Social Dancing* (New York: Greenberg, 1954) p. 107.

28. The terms "Gullah" and "Geechee" refer to both the language and the culture of people who inhabit the Sea Islands of South Carolina and Georgia—an area that extends from Georgetown, SC to the Golden Isles of Georgia above Florida. At the height of the Atlantic Slave Trade during the eighteenth century, approximately 40 percent of the Africans who were enslaved were brought to mainland North America in South Carolina, most through Charleston Harbor. Due to the remoteness of the Sea Islands, blacks who settled on the Sea Islands had little contact with races other than Native Americans. This fostered the preservation of African culture and language forms. Gullah language combines elements of West African dialects and syntax with pidgin English. Referred to as a Creole language, it remains today the only surviving English-based Creole language in America. Although the words "Gullah" and "Geechee" are used interchangeably, academicians generally use "Gullah" to refer to those living on the South Carolina Sea Islands, and the word "Geechee" to those living on the Sea Islands of Georgia and northern Florida. Historians suspect the word "Gullah" is either derived from the word "Gola," an African tribe found in Liberia, or a corruption of the word "Angola," where many of the culture's ancestors originate. The derivation of the word "Geechee" is believed to either be a reference to the Ogeechee River located near Savannah, Georgia, or a transliteration of the name "Gidzi," an ethnic group from the Windward Coast of Africa. Others suggest it originates from a Liberian tribal name.

29. In the article "Hey! Hey! Charleston," *Colliers Magazine*, December 10, 1927, p.34, Bee Jackson states,

> The Charleston is distinctly a Negro dance which originated on the islands of Beaufort County on the South Carolina Coast. The "Buford" Negroes have been doing it at outings and picnics for years. It reached the mainland about six months before I saw it [in 1923], probably carried there by Negro laborers or sailors, and spread among the colored people coming north via Charleston, from which city it got its name.

30. The Jenkins Orphanage was started in 1891 by the Rev. Daniel Jenkins after he found four homeless waifs liv-

ing in an abandoned building on the outskirts of Charleston, South Carolina. A former slave who had been orphaned himself, Jenkins approached the Charleston city council with a plan to found an orphanage for African-American boys. He received permission to use an abandoned warehouse that was next to the prison on the waterfront. Within one year, Jenkins had 360 boys in his care, ranging from the ages of five to eighteen. (He later accepted children as young as three and as old as twenty.) After failing to get permission to buy land for farming, so the boys could learn a trade and the orphanage could become self-sufficient, Jenkins decided to raise money by forming a military band. He hired two music teachers who tutored the boys in reading music and trained students to become proficient on several instruments at a time. The "Pickinanny Band" as it was called, toured to New York to raise funds but was initially unsuccessful. Jenkins borrowed money to take himself and the band of thirteen boy musicians to London. Unable to secure bookings while in England, the band played on street corners until the group was arrested for disturbing the peace. Several churches, hearing of the arrest, raised funds for the band's release, and as stories of the band's plight began to surface, the British pubic began flocking to hear performances at various meeting rooms around London. The Jenkins Band was able to return to the United States and as news of their British successes spread, they began to tour regularly to cities such as New York on the east coast during the summer and to cities in Florida during the winter. The band's reputation grew. In 1902, they played at the Buffalo Exposition, and two years later they had their own stage at the St. Louis World's Fair. The same year the Jenkins Band was invited to play at the Hippodrome in London. Tours also took them to Paris, Berlin and Rome. In 1905, the band played in the Presidents Roosevelt's inaugural parade, and in 1909 they played for President Taft's. The group's repertoire consisted of Sousa marches, as well as cakewalks and ragtime tunes. Because of the band's popularity and heavy touring schedule, they were instrumental in spreading the popularity of early jazz and ragtime. The Jenkins Orphanage Band also served as the training ground for many talented musicians who later went on to play in the some of the most famous jazz bands and dance orchestras during the 1920's.

31. Julie Hubbert, SYMPOSIA: "Jenkins Orphanage," quoting Willie "the Lion" Smith. http://www.sc.edu/orphan film/orphanage/symposia/scholarship/hubbert/jenkinsorphanage.html

32. The Jungles Casino was a dank, seedy dance hall located on 62nd Street in an area that today is known as Hell's Kitchen. Because it was difficult for black businesses to get a dance hall license, the establishment was licensed instead as a dancing school. James P. Johnson played there once a week for the "classes." There were no dance teachers and the patrons danced as they liked. The establishment had a cement floor that flooded when it rained, forcing the dancing to be stopped on wet days while the floor was mopped up. Candles had to placed around the piano to keep it dry in the fetid air. Illicit liquor was hidden in the furnace and the coal bin. The clientele of the Jungles Casino was largely made up of gullah longshoremen who had migrated from South Carolina to find work on the docks up North. In his book *James P. Johnson: A Case of Mistaken Identity,* pp. 56–6, Scott Brown quotes Johnson as he recalled;

The dances they did at the Jungles Casino were wild and comical — the more pose and the more breaks, the better. These Charleston people and the other southerners had just come to New York. They were country people and they felt homesick. When they got tired of two-steps and schottisches (which they danced with a lot of spieling), they'd yell: "Let's go back home!" ... "Let's do a set!" ... or "Now put us in the alley!" I did my "Mule Walk" or "Gut Stomp" for these country dances. Breakdown music was the best

for such sets, the more solid and groovy the better. They'd dance, hollering and screaming until they were cooked. The dances ran from fifteen minutes to thirty minutes, but they kept up all night long or until their shoes wore out — most of them after a heavy day's work on the docks.

33. Allen Woll, *Black Musical Theatre: From Coontown to Dreamgirls* (New York: Da Capo Press, 1989) p. 90, quoting James P. Johnson form a 1959 interview with Tom Davin in the *Jazz Review,* "Conversations with James P. Johnson, " pp. 10–14.

34. Scott E. Brown, *James P. Johnson: A Case of Mistaken Identity* (Metuchen, NJ: The Scarecrow Press, 1986) p. 13, quoting James P. Johnson.

35. It is believed that the Ring Shout's origins lay in the BaKongo practice of tracing cosmograms on the ground and dancing over the drawn figures in order to invoke spirits. Patterns were drawn to represent the cosmos. Most often the symbol consisted of a circle surrounding a cross. The horizontal bar of the cross represented the division between the living and the dead. The vertical bar of the cross represented the connection between God and the underworld. By circumscribing the circle, the dancer symbolically moved through life to death and then into rebirth. The pattern also mirrored the rising and setting of the sun. The origin of the name Ring Shout is not what it first may seem. The word "shout" in this context is derived from the Arabic word *saut,* which is pronounced like the English word "shout." The word referred to the counterclockwise circling of the sacred stone of Mecca by Muslim pilgrims until they were exhausted. In the Protestant Churches in America, the Ring Shout was done circling the alter; a synthesis of Protestant Christianity with Islamic practices.

36. The original close to the floor, dragging, step-together-step of the religious version of the Ring Shout, was always performed so that the feet did not cross, which was of critical importance because the Baptists defined dancing as a crossing of the feet. Secular dancing was considered sinful and banned by Methodist, Baptist, and Presbyterian churches. Despite this regulation, African-Americans were able to keep alive their dance traditions under the auspices of the church by developing forms of movement that got around the religious requirement of not having the feet cross.

37. Stride piano was also known as rent-party piano, or parlor social piano among other names. It was a transitional style of music which some believe bridged ragtime and jazz.

38. Brown, p.15, quoting Willie "The Lion" Smith.

Chapter 15

1. In *The Century; a popular quarterly.* Vol. 25, Issue 3, January 1883, p. 480, in an article called "Uncle Remus's Christmas Dance-Songs," there are songs by Noel Chandler Harris. The first song is called "Rabbit-tum-a-hash." The first verse of that song is,

RABBIT foot quick, Rabbit foot light,
Tum-a-hash, turn-a-heap!
Hop, skip, jump! Oh, mon, he's a sight!
Kaze he res all de day en run all de night,
Turn-a-hash, turn-a-heap,
Oh, Rabbit-tum-a-hash!

The song includes the following instructions;

[The songs] are sung with what Uncle Remus would call the knee-racket; that is to say, they are patting songs.

2. Douglas Gilbert, *American Vaudeville: Its Life and Times* (New York: Whittlesey House, 1940) p. 171.

3. *Shuffle Along,* with music by Eubie Blake, lyrics by

Noble Sissle, and book by Flourney E. Miller and Aubrey L. Lyles opened at the 63rd Street Music Hall on Broadway on May 21, 1921. It ran for 504 performances. After struggling with difficulties during out-of-town tryouts and arriving in New York $18,000.00 in debt, the show took New York by storm. The show became such a smash, New York police had to convert 63rd into a one-way street to ease the nightly traffic jams. The first major production in more than a decade to be produced, written and performed entirely by African Americans, *Shuffle Along* helped to legitimize the black musical and shattered many long held racial stereotypes. The musical presented the first sophisticated, serious, African-American love story. It demonstrated that white audiences would pay to see legitimate black entertainment, and it allowed black audiences to sit in the orchestra rather than being relegated to the balcony. It featured several African American luminaries during its various incarnations and tours including Florence Mills, Josephine Baker, Ulysses S. "Slow Kid" Thompson, Mae Barnes, Adalaide Hall, and Paul Robeson. *Shuffle Along* sparked interest in African American source material, spawning a flurry of black musicals, and introducing the use of jazz in musical scores. It had a huge impact on stage dancing by making it more rhythmic, intricate, and authentic.

4. Adalaide [Adalade] Louisa Hall was born in Brooklyn, New York on October 20, 1901. She first appeared on Broadway in the chorus of *Shuffle Along*. In 1923, she was cast in *Runnin' Wild* and was featured as a solo singer, where she appeared under the original spelling of her first name, Adalade. In 1925, Ms. Hall toured Europe as the lead in a show called *The Chocolate Kiddies Revue*. During this period, she is believed to have introduced the Charleston to Europe preceding the more commonly credited Josephine Baker. Hall performed the dance to Duke Ellington's "Jig Walk." She recorded Ellington's "Creole Love Song" in 1927, one of the first recording to feature scat singing. The recording brought international recognition to both Hall and Ellington. In 1928, Ms. Hall appeared on Broadway again in *Blackbirds of 1928*, replacing Florence Mills after her untimely death. She introduced the classic song "I Can't Give You Anything But Love," among other favorites. She later reprised her role in *Blackbirds of 1928* in Paris. She returned to Broadway, appearing opposite legendary tapper Bill Bojangles Robinson in *Brown Buddies* in 1930. During this time, she also appeared at the Cotton Club with the Duke Ellington Orchestra. Beginning in 1931, she toured Europe for approximately two years, becoming one of the wealthiest black women in the United States. Ms. Hall continued to perform in various venues, including the famous Cotton Club. In 1939, she moved to Europe with her husband Bert Hicks. She lived in France and then moved to Britain where she lived until her death on November 7, 1993.

5. Josephine Baker first auditioned for *Shuffle Along* during its out of town tryout in Philadelphia hoping to move with the show when it went to Broadway. She was fourteen years old. When asked for her age, she lied, and said she was fifteen. The producers did not hire Baker, not only because the minimum hiring age for chorus girls under New York State law was sixteen, but also, they thought she was too thin, small, and dark-skinned (Noble Sissle and Eubie Blake in an attempt to appeal to white audiences initially cast the ensemble girls as light skinned as possible.) At age fifteen, a penniless Baker moved to New York and again auditioned for the show, this time applying light powder and giving her age as seventeen. She was rejected again. She was offered the job of being a dresser on one of the tours and reluctantly agreed. While on the road, she learned the routines and eventually got the opportunity to fill in for one of the chorus girls who had gotten ill. When she first appeared on stage, she ad-libbed and clowned, winning hateful glances from her fellow chorus dancers, but huge laughs and applause from the audience. She repeated her outrageous behavior in subsequent performances, and her reputation grew and favorable reviews flowed in. Sissle and Blake, hearing stories of the chorus girl

who stopped the show every night on the tour, came to a performance and asked to speak with Baker after the show. Convinced they had come to fire her, Baker pleaded with the two men to keep her on, begging them to remember that she was now sixteen. (She was actually only fifteen at the time.) Instead of firing her, Sissle and Blake offered Josephine Baker a position in the main company of *Shuffle Along*, which was to tour after closing its Broadway run at the end of that summer. Baker stayed with that touring production for almost two years.

6. Edith Mae Barnes, nicknamed "the bronze Ann Pennington," was born Edith Mae Stith on January 23, 1097 in New York City. She began her career touring with shows such as *Bon Bon Buddy, Jr.* in 1922, and *Dinah* in 1923. She made her Broadway debut in *Runnin' Wild* in 1924 as the featured dancer in the Charleston number. In 1927, she danced in the national tour of *Shuffle Along*, leading the legendary tapper Bill Robinson to dub her "the greatest living female tap dancer." In the 30's she starred in the long-running song-and-dance revue *Hot Rhythm* and then toured on the Keith vaudeville circuit. In 1938 she fractured her pelvis in an automobile accident and she turned to singing. She died in Boston on Dec 13, 1996 of cancer at the age of 89.

7. Stearns, Marshall and Jean, *Jazz Dance: The Story of American Vernacular Dance* (New York: Da Capo, 1994) p. 143.

8. *Liza*, with lyrics and music by Maceo Pinkard and book by Irvin C. Miller, had its tryout in Harlem under the title *Bon Bon Buddy Jr.*. The show was renamed and then opened on Broadway on November 27, 1922 at Daly's Theatre and ran there until March 11, 1923. It then reopened at the Nora Bayes Theatre on March 12, 1923 and ran until April 21, 1923 for a total of 172 performances, making it the most successful African American musical of the 1922–1923 season. The song "The Charleston Dancy" opened the second act of the show and was performed by Maude Russell (in the part of Mandy,) and the girls chorus. The song was written by Maceo Pickard, music and Nat Vincent, lyrics. Although most historians accept the musical *Liza* as the first official presentation of the Charleston on the Broadway stage, there is documented evidence that the dance was around well before the show's premiere in 1922. Thaddeus Drayton, the vaudeville partner of the man who did the Charleston in *Liza* in 1922, said that he saw the dance in his hometown of Charleston, South Carolina in 1903 when he was on a visit there. He commented, "They dolled it up later."(Stearns, Marshall and Jean. *Jazz Dance: The Story of American Vernacular Dance*. New York: Da Capo, 1994. p. 112.) Nobel Sissle, who wrote the lyrics for the ground-braking *Shuffle Along* claimed, "It's a real old Southern dance.... I remember learning it in Savannah around 1905."(Stearns, p. 112.) Dancer Coot Grant saw the Charleston being danced in 1909,and the Whitman Sisters, dancing luminaries on the African American vaudeville circuit, were said to have been using the dance in their act as early as 1911. James P. Johnson stated that he knew of people dancing the Charleston around 1913 as a "regulation cotillion step" (Stearns, p.112). He added, "...it had many variations—all danced to the rhythm that everybody knows now" (Stearns, p. 112). Billy Maxey claimed he first saw it in 1917 and two years later was giving Charleston lessons to movie stars. Rubberlegs Williams stated that he won a Charleston contest in Atlantic City as early as 1920.

9. Rufus Eddie Greenlee (1863–1963), and his partner Thaddeus (Teddy) Drayton, were famous in vaudeville for their elegant class act. Donning top hats, tails, monocles, and carrying canes, they danced a sophisticated version of the Virginia Essence. Both men studied dance at Miss Hattie Anderson's Dance School on 53rd Street in New York City as young boys. They began performing together around 1909, when they traveled to Europe to join the famous dancing team of Johnson and Dean. They returned to the United States in 1914 and toured extensively in vaudeville, appearing at the top houses including the Winter Garden and the

Palace Theatre in New York. The duo was approached about appearing in *Shuffle Along* but the producers would not meet their asking price. In 1922, at the height of their popularity, they were asked to dance in *Liza*. They also performed in *Aces and Queens* (1924–1925) and *Lovin' Sam From Alabam* (mid–1920's) They danced at the opening of the Cotton Club, and in 1926 took their act to Russia, giving a special performance for Joseph Stalin. The act dissolved in the 1930's and Greenlee began performing with his wife for about six more years. He retired to run a café in New Haven, and lived there until his death in 1963. Because of his penchant for collegiate dress, and since he lived in New Haven Connecticut, home of Yale University, Greenlee earned the nickname "Rah! Rah!."

10. Maude Russell Rutherford, was born in Texas to a black mother, Margaret Lee, and a white father, William McCann, who because of racial prohibitions of the time, never lived together. Russell met Josephine Baker in 1921 while working in a show in Philadelphia and later the two toured together in one of the companies of *Shuffle Along*. She commented, "I was the dancer and she was the clown. But she could out-clown my dancing!" (Stephen Bourne, The Independent, London, "Obituary: Maude Russell," May 9, 2001) Known as the "Slim Princess," Russell appeared in the chorus of *Liza* (1922) where she led the line of dancers in the Charleston. In addition to dancing in *Liza*, she appeared in *Dixie to Broadway* (1924), where she worked with Florence Mills, *Chocolate Scandals* (1927), and *Keep Shufflin'* (1928). She was also a favorite at the Cotton Club. In 1936, she appeared in *Lew Leslie's Blackbirds of 1936* in London with a cast that included the Nicholas Brothers. She continued to perform in the 1940's but left the entertainment business in the 50's and began to work as a hotel switchboard operator in Atlantic City. She was married five times. At age ninety-eight, Russell commented on any younger men that might think about dating her for her money. She said, "I ain't spending nothing but the evening, and I ain't putting out nothing but the lights." Russell died at the age of 104 in Atlantic City on March 4, 2001.

11. Stearns, p. 144, quoting Eddie Greenlee.

12. Joyce Wadler, "Maude Rutherford, High-Kicking Songster of 20's, Dies at 104" *The New York Times*, March 29, 2001, np. Obituary

13. Leonard Harper was born in Birmingham, Alabama in 1889. As a young man he became a founding member Freeman-Harper-Muse Stock Co., a theatrical company that performed at Frank Crowd's Globe Theatre in Jacksonville, Florida. He then began touring in vaudeville with a dance act called "Harper and Banks" with Osceola Banks (who later became his wife.) The couple also performed in the enormously successful *Plantation Days* when it toured London. In 1923, he produced, choreographed and performed in a show called *The Frolics*, which ran at the Lafayette Theatre in Harlem. Next he worked as dance director on *Lucky Sambo*, which had a short Broadway run and then toured for a year. In 1925, he danced in Lew Leslie's *Brown Skin Quinan Revue* at the Plantation Club in Harlem and then joined the cast of *Blackbirds of 1926*, which played at the Alhambra Theatre in New York, and then toured to Paris and London. Other credits as a dancer or choreographer included *Club Kentucky Revue* (1927), *Midnight Steppers* (1927), *Hot Chocolates* (1928), *Leonard Harper's Revue* (1928), *Cotton Club Parade* (1935) and others. Harper died of a heart attack in 1943 while rehearsing for a nightclub show in New York City.

14. *How Come?,* with book by Eddie Hunter, opened at the Apollo Theatre at 223 W. 42nd St., in New York on April 16, 1923 and ran through May 19, 1923. The Philadelphia run of the show featured singer Bessie Smith. Smith was later replaced by Alberta Hunter. Marshall and Jean Stearns, p. 112, hint that *How Come?* featured Charleston dancing by the vaudeville team of Chapelle and Stinnette.

15. *Runnin' Wild* had its out of town tryout in Washington D.C., opening at the Howard Theatre on August 23, 1923.

Despite good reviews, box office sales languished and the producer threatened to close the show after the first week unless the cast agreed to work without pay. The cast refused, but a compromise was reached when writers Miller and Lyles gave up their salaries so the chorus members could receive partial payments. Attendance gradually improved largely due to an increase in white audiences whose interest was piqued by the favorable reviews and good word of mouth. The show began to add special midnight performances to bring in previously untapped black audiences. The show moved to Boston in September for a successful six week run, although the Charleston number sung by Elisabeth Welch, went largely unnoticed in reviews. The show opened at the New Colonial Theatre in New York on October 10, 1924. It ran until May 3, 1924, then re-opened as a new edition at the Colonial Theatre on June, 23, 1924 running for five days until June 28, 1924. The show later toured around the New York area in Brooklyn, the Bronx and Long Island and in 1928 a road company took the show to London. *Runnin' Wild* was produced by George White, with music and lyrics by James Johnson and Cecil Mack, and book by Flourney E. Miller and Aubrey L. Lyles. Miller and Lyles, a comic vaudeville duo who had previously written and performed in the groundbreaking *Shuffle Along*, also performed in *Runnin' Wild*. Because of the popularity of the Charleston number, by 1925, the order of the musical numbers in *Runnin' Wild* was rearranged to include the song and dance before the end of each act, re-choreographed to include the entire cast.

16. James Price Johnson was born in New Brunswick, New Jersey on February 1, 1894. As a child he was blessed with perfect pitch. He began piano lessons with his mother and later studied classical piano and was introduced ragtime. At age eight, when his family moved to a rough neighborhood in Jersey City, the young boy would perform buck-dances and sing and play the guitar on the streets outside the local bawdy houses and saloons. Musicologists believe Johnson absorbed the sounds of the ragtime music that he heard coming from inside these establishments, which later influenced his piano playing. Known as the father of stride piano playing, (or sometimes as the grandfather of hot piano,) Johnson gained the reputation of being the best piano player on the East Coast. He recorded hundreds of piano rolls on his own and also made over 400 recordings from 1916 onward as an accompanist, backing up such artists as Bessie Smith and Ethel Waters. Johnson's musical style influenced such greats as Fats Waller, (who took private lessons from Johnson,) Duke Ellington, Count Basie, George Gerswhin, Art Tatum, and Thelonious Monk. Known by his colleagues as "The Brute," Johnson was a prolific composer and wrote eleven musicals for Broadway including *Plantation Days, Shuffle Along* and *Runnin' Wild*. He is believed to have recorded the first jazz piano solo, entitled "Carolina Shout." Later in his life he composed several symphonic works, including "Yamekraw," the first genuine African American Rhapsody. His song "The Charleston" became one of the most popular songs of the 1920's. Johnson suffered a stroke in 1940, which left him partially paralyzed. In 1951, a second stroke left him bedridden and unable to speak. He died four years later in Jamaica, New York on November 17, 1955.

17. Cecil Mack, born Richard C. McPherson in Norfolk, Virginia in 1883, was a writer, lyricist, composer, director, and performer. In addition to providing the lyrics for *Runnin' Wild*, he was involved in such Broadway musicals as *Bandanna Land, Lew Leslie's Blackbirds, Rhapsody in Black*, and *Swing It*. In 1905 he was responsible for organizing the Gotham Music Publishing Company, which merged four months later with the Attucks Music Publishing Company. The newly formed company became the first African-American owned music publishing company in the United States. This company helped to further the dissemination of music written by black composers, and provided sheet music that did not portray racial stereotypes on the cover art. He was also a founding member of Frogs, Inc., the most important

African American Theatrical Club of the period (1908 to the mid 1920's). Mack died in 1944 in New York City.

18. Elisabeth Margaret Welch was born in Manhattan on February 27, 1904, (she gave the date as 1908) in an area called San Juan Hill, the site of which is now the location of the Lincoln Center. Her father was African-American /Native American and her mother was Scotch/Irish. As a child, Welch was a member of St. Cypian's Episcopal Church choir. She had a booming voice that earned her the title "loud alto." The choir was invited to sing in the Broadway production of *Runnin' Wild,* and in the show, Welch, billed as "Ruth Little," sang the song "The Charleston" (referred to as "Singing Charleston" in her *New York Times* obituary 7/18/03). She was fourteen years old. Welch joined the cast against her strict Baptist father's vehement objections. Some sources state that her father was so outraged with his daughter's behavior, he walked out on the family, saying "Girlie's on the boards. She's lost!" (According to an interview in the *Daily Telegraph,* Welch stated she held herself responsible for the desertion. She said, "He associated show business with low life, and he thought I would become a whore."—"Elizabeth Welch"— Brief Biographies: African American biographies, vol.6 — accessed on internet) The year before Welch appeared in *Runnin' Wild* she had also been in the cast of *Liza* in 1922. Some sources say she actually debuted the Charleston in that show. In 1924, Welch joined the cast of *The Chocolate Dandies,* under the name Jessie Johnson. She later joined the cast of Lew Leslie's *Blackbirds of 1928,* and *The New Yorkers* (1930) where she introduced the Cole Porter classic "Love for Sale." In the early 1930's she performed at the Moulin Rouge in Paris, becoming a successful cabaret performer in France. In 1933, she moved to London where she remained a popular star in musicals, nightclubs, radio and films until her death on July 15, 2003 at the age of 99. In a The New York Post review of her one-woman show, Clive Barnes wrote,

> With her sweetness, her gentility, arsenic-laced with a sense of roguish innuendo and pagan sensuality, she is like no one else. She has class, and class, and class. A saloon singer who would make any saloon into a salon.

19. Stearns, p. 145, state that some of the chorus boys in the "Dancing Redcaps" went on to be well-know performers of their time. They included Sammy Dyer, Derby Wilson, Pete Nugent and Chink Collins.

20. Jacqui Malone, *Steppin' On the Blues: The Visible Rhythms of African American Dance* (Chicago: University of Illinois Press, 1996) p. 77, and Allen Woll, *Black Musical Theatre: From Coontown to Dreamgirls* (New York: Da Capo Press, 1989) p. 90, quoting James Weldon Johnson, *Black Manhattan* (New York: Alfred P. Knopf, Inc., 1930), p. 190.

21. This information is found in Woll's book, p. 89.

22. "Miller and Lyles in 'Runnin' Wild'" *The Bridgeport Telegram,* Bridgeport, CT, December 27, 1924, p. 6, col. 2.

23. "Miller and Lyles in 'Runnin' Wild'" *The Bridgeport Telegram,* Bridgeport, CT, December 31, 1924, p. 14, col. 2.

24. Stearns, p. 145, quoting Flourney Miller.

25. Elide [Elida] Webb Dawson was in the cast of *Shuffle Along* and also performed at Ziegfeld's *Club Alabama.* She was a dancer and choreographer at the Cotton Club from 1923–1934, and one of the only female, black choreographers used at the club. In 1932, she appeared in the Broadway production of *Showboat.* She was married to dancer George Dawson, Jr., known as "The Strutter." Webb was one of the first African American choreographers to work on Broadway and many claim she "invented" the Charleston. Her work on *Runnin' Wild* certainly popularized the dance and helped propel it into the international craze it later became. She was also responsible for teaching the Charleston to Bee Jackson and Josephine Baker. She died at age 79 in New York.

26. Stearns, p. 145, quoting Flourney Miller.

27. Stearns, p. 146, quoting Willie Covan.

28. Bee Jackson, *Colliers Magazine,* "Hey! Hey! Charleston,"

December 10, 1927, p. 34. In Fred W. Emiston's book *The Coon-Sanders Nighthawks: The Band That Radio Made Famous,* pp. 151–152, the author gives Lida Webb's account of how the Charleston made it into *Runnin' Wild.* (Emiston mistakenly refers to Ms. Webb as a man throughout the piece.) It states,

> He [sic — Elida Webb] had been on the road with the famous black show Shuffle Along. Upon returning to New York in May of 1922, he [sic] saw some black children on the streets doing a simple dance they called "the Charleston," because they had learned the steps from neighborhood children whose family had just moved up from Charleston, S.C.. Said Webb, "There was something fascinating, and it caught me." He [sic] took that simple one-routine movement that the youngsters were doing and added some complementary steps. Later, when in July 1922, he [sic] was engaged to stage the chorus numbers in the black revue *Runnin' Wild,* he [sic] used the dance in a number with sixteen women and three men. They opened in Washington on 20 August 1922, the first opportunity the public had to see the Charleston as a finished product.

29. Stearns, p. 146, quoting Flourney Miller.

30. Edward Claudius Wayburn was born in Pittsburgh, Pennsylvania on March 30, 1874. The son of an inventor and manufacturer, Wayburn began his career in amateur productions and later when working as an usher at the Chicago Grand Opera House, appeared as a walk-on in many productions. He performed in vaudeville as a singer and ragtime piano player and first appeared in New York in 1897 in a play called *The Swell Miss Fitzwell.* In 1901 he directed the Four Cohans in *The Governor's Son* and subsequently was known primarily as a director. He created the staging for several editions of the Ziegfeld Follies from 1916 to 1919 and then again from 1922 to 1929. He developed what became known as the "Ziegfeld Walk," a sideways strut that allowed showgirls to descend stairs without falling. He also staged many shows for the Shuberts, Oscar and William Hammerstein, and Lew Fields. Wayburn ran one of the most popular dancing schools in New York City for thirty-seven years and trained many, many professionals as well as amateurs, He worked with many celebrities including Fred Astaire, Ann Pennington, Gilda Gray, Marilyn Miller, Mae West and Fanny Brice. Wayburn was also an author and a song-writer. He died on September 2, 1942 in New York at age 68.

31. Ned Wayburn, "Ned Wayburn Writes About the Dance of Today — The Charleston" *Oakland Tribune,* Oakland, CA, July 4, 1926, pp. 46–47.

32. *Ibid.*

33. The listing in the opening night program read: "SCENE 20 — FIRST ACT FINALE — SHAKE YOUR FEET. Sung by Brooke Johns and Follies Chorus, Introducing a new dance invented by Ned Wayburn called the Charleston."

34. Ned Wayburn initially hired Bee Jackson as a chorus dancer for the *Ziegfeld Follies.* According to Jackson, she was eventually given the position of understudy to *Follies* star Gilda Gray, in Gray's South Sea Isle dance. In an article entitled "From Little Egypt's Hootchy-Kootchy to the Strip Tease" found in *The San Antonio Light,* San Antonio, TX, May 9, 1937, p. 107, col. 3., it states,

> Ned Wayburn, who for fifteen years directed all Ziegfeld's dances, brought it [the Charleston] up from the South and taught it to Bee Jackson. Ziegfeld liked it in rehearsals, but threw it out after the opening night as "too vulgar," but that one night of it was the making of Bee. The following year, George White put the Charleston in the Scandals. It proved to be the most popular dance crazes. During its height, declares Wayburn, he had as many as 1,500 pupils a day taking lessons at his school.

35. In the book *Down Memory Lane: Arthur Murray's Picture Story of Social Dancing* by Sylvia G. L. Dannett and Frank R. Rachel, page 106, the authors state,

> In October, 1923, on the stage of the New Amsterdam Theatre, the Ziegfeld Follies introduced a dance which truly expressed the restlessness of the era.... It happened while Ned Wayburn was rehearsing the new edition of the Ziegfeld Follies. Sissle and Blake, authors and composers of *Shuffle Along*, the first of a great number of Negro musicals to hit Broadway, brought a young colored boy to see the director. The boy executed what later became the best-known, characteristic step of the Charleston, and Wayburn knew a stage hit when he saw one. He used this step as the foundation and developed a new dance, for which Sissle and Blake wrote the music.

This reference seems to correlate with Wayburns's newspaper account to some extent, although there is no evidence that Sissle and Blake provided music for any of the *Follies* productions. I did find an interesting reference in *The Davenport Democrat and Leader*, November 1, 1925, p. 18, col. 2. The article states,

> In 1923 Ned Wayburn, the New York dancing master, introduced the Charleston on the stage of the New Amsterdam theatre in New York City in "Shuffle Along," but at that time it did not catch the popular fancy.

I could find no evidence in my research that Wayburn had anything to do with *Shuffle Along*.

In his web article about Noble Sissle and Eubie Blake, Thomas L Morgan writes that white producers Florenz Ziegfeld, Jr., and George White were so impressed with the dancing in *Shuffle Along*, they hired members of the cast to teach dance steps to the chorines of their own revues. Stearns and Stearns do not mention this incident in their book *Jazz Dance*, although they have a very thorough chapter on *Shuffle Along*. They do mention that Ziegfeld purchased a dance routine called "At the Ball" from a black musical entitled *Darktown Follies*. In the book (p.130) dancer Ethel Williams states that she taught the white cast how to dance the routine, but none of the black dancers were hired to appear in Ziegfeld's show. The "At the Ball" number was a Circle dance similar to the minstrel Walk Around and based upon the Ring Shout dance. As the chorus did the Texas Tommy and serpentined around the stage with each dancer's hands upon the waist of the person in front of them, the final person in the line, Ethel Williams, improvised crazy steps and brought the house down. This same type of stepping-out-of-the-line approach was used by Josephine Baker in *Shuffle Along*.

36. Wayburn, *Oakland Tribune*, Oakland, CA, July 4, 1926, pp. 46–47. On Sonny Watson's Streetswing.com, he states that a man name Willie Higgie of the vaudeville act "Higgie and Brown" said "that he had invented the Charleston (aka Charleston Walk) in a back stage Theatre in Washington before Wayburn and was mad that Wayburn was taking the credit." Will Higgie also performed with an act called "Willie Higgie and the Five Magnetic Girls," mentioned in vaudeville ads as "a Sextette of Smart Steppers— Willie Higgie and His Bevy of Beauties in 'Rhyme and Rhythm'— Personality, Appearance, Pep." In the *Davenport Democrat and Leader*, March 6, 1927, p. 18, col. 1, there is a mention that Higgie invented a dance called the "Higgiejig." The paper calls it "the latest ballroom sensation ... unusually refined and fascinating."

37. George White was born on March 12, 1892 in New York (other sources listed the birthplace as Toronto.) His birth name was George Weitz. As a youngster, he danced for pennies in New York clubs. He was part of a dancing team in burlesque and later did his own solo act. In 1912, he went to Paris and saw the French *revue à grand spectacle*. He returned to the U.S. and decided to mount his own opulent extravaganzas, called *George White's Scandals*. He also produced several conventional musicals. Despite his dislike of the Charleston number in *Runnin' Wild*, he later recognized its potential and tried to steal the number for one of his *Scandals* shows. Throughout his career as a producer, White had a reputation of being pretentious and of always trying to tone down any African-American styles of dancing in his shows. During the Great Depression, White stopped his series of *Scandals* and tried to put his revues into films and nightclubs but had only limited success. An excessively wasteful man, White often filed for bankruptcy throughout his life. He was once jailed for causing a fatal auto accident. White died in Hollywood, California on October 7, 1968 of leukemia.

38. Frances Williams was born in St. Paul, Minnesota November 3, 1901. Her birth name was Frances Jellinek. She began performing at age 14 and by the age of 16, she had left home to tour with an acrobatic troupe. Williams appeared in vaudeville in an act called "Vanessi and Williams." She sang in nightclubs in New York such as "The Wigwam" and others, and at "Ciro's" she performed in a revue called "The Rhapsody in Blue," with music by George Gershwin. Irving Berlin heard her sing in this production and suggested her for "The Coconuts" starring the Marx Brothers. After this, she was hired for the George White's *Scandals* where some sources suggest she introduced the Charleston. She had her first role in a book show in *International Revue* where she sang the classic "Exactly Like You." Roles in other productions included George M. Cohan's *Mary*, *Artists and Models*, *DuBarry Was a Lady*, *Panama Hattie*, and *The New Yorkers*. In 1932, she appeared in a show called *Everybody's Welcome* in which she introduced the song "As Time Goes By." A popular celebrity, William's love life was frequently discussed in the gossip columns. *The San Antonio Light*, San Antonio, TX, May 22, 1932, p. 47, reported on her divorce from her husband, saxophonist and orchestra leader, Lester Clark. Williams was granted the divorce on the grounds of "professional cruelty" when Clark missed a beat while accompanying her on his sax during a performance in "The New Yorkers." Clark had hit his wife earlier and given her a black eye. She forgave him for this, but a husband who "spoiled her song by missing a beat, playing off-key, or sounding a sour note, was not to be forgiven." Two other members of the cast testified in court that they had seen evidence of Williams' physical abuse but that the "professional cruelty" in missing beats was the one unforgivable offense committed buy the saxophone player. The judge granted the divorce. After the trial, Williams gave this advice, "Don't marry part of the orchestra." Williams made several films and five recordings. She died January 27, 1959 of cancer.

39. "Exceptional Vitaphone Numbers at State" *Daily News Standard*, Uniontown, PA, September 14, 1927, p. 2, col. 3.

40. The extravaganza opened on June 14, 1926 at the Apollo Theatre and ran until June 18, 1927 with a total of 432 performances. The songs in *George White Scandals of 1926* were written by DeSylva, Henderson, and Brown, and in addition to "The Black Bottom" included the classic "Birth of the Blues." The show also featured special music by George Gershwin. His "Rhapsody in Blue" closed the first act. In one edition of the *Scandals* (either 1926 or 1928), Williams starred with another female singer, Rose Perfect. During one performance, Williams decided to wear a gardenia on her gown. The next night, Perfect appeared on stage with two pinned to her dress. Not to be outdone, Williams wore three the following night. Columnists and drama critics began to cover what became known as "The Battle of the Gardenias." The feuding escalated until producer George White put a stop to it because "audiences wanted to hear songs, not count flowers." By that time, Rose Perfect was wearing six gardenias and was declared the victor by newspapers. At Frances Williams' funeral, a package was sent containing seven gardenias. It was sent by the former press agent of *George White's Scandals*, Nanette Kutner.

41. "New Plays," *Time Magazine*, Monday, Jun. 28, 1926.

Extracted from Time Magazine.com http://www.time.com/time/magazine/article/0,9171,846604,00.html

42. *The Wisconsin Rapids Daily Tribune*, Wisconsin Rapids, WI, January 23, 1931, p. 3, col. 5.

43. "'Scandals' Will Open Tomorrow," *Syracuse Herald*, Syracuse, NY, March 4, 1928, p. 6, col. 3. In her obituary in *The New York Times*, January 28, 1959, p.31, entitled "Frances Williams, Actress Dies; Introduced Charleston On Stage," it mentions that Williams performed in various editions of George White's *Scandals* from 1926 through 1929, and that it was in one of the early editions of the show that "the song 'Charleston' and the dance started the vogue."

44. Tom Patricola was born on January 22, 1891 in New Orleans, Louisiana. A popular staple of vaudeville, he was famous for the comic characters he imitated in his dances, and many credit him with furthering the widespread use of character pantomime as a valid source of material for tap routines. Patricola, who played the ukulele while he danced, contributed many original steps still used by tap dancers today, including one series of moves that utilized the Suzi-Q and was later named for him. According to the Stearns, (p. 210) Harland Dixon called Tom Patricola "a mop gone crazy." Patricola appeared in five editions of the *Scandals* and achieved international recognition as a top Charleston and Black Bottom dancer. He appeared in several films, often portraying himself. He died on January 1, 1959 in Pasadena, California after undergoing brain surgery.

45. Nicholas E. Tawa, *Supremely American: Popular Song in the 20th Century: Styles and Singers and What They Said About America* (Lanham, MD: Scarecrow Press, 2005) pp. 58–59.

46. Tawa, pp. 58–59.

47. "Tenth Row Center" *The Lima Sunday News*, Lima OH, June 14, 1925, p.22, col. 7.

48. Woollcott, Alexander, "Laughter at the Lyric" in *The Stage*. Extracted from *The Cocoanuts*—Reviews. "Why A Duck?" @ marx-brothers.org http://www.marx-brothers.org/whyaduck/info/broadway/coco-reviews.htm

49. Bill Egan, *Florence Mills: Harlem Jazz Queen* (Lanham, MD: Scarecrow Press, 2004, p. 182) quoting Lew Leslie.

50. Will Marion Cook, "Spirituals and Jazz" *The New York Times*, December 26, 1926, Section: Drama Music Art Society Fashion Screen Resorts Steamships Travel, p. X8.

51. *Ibid.*

52. Wallace Thurman, *The Collected Writings of Wallace Thurman: A Harlem Renaissance Reader,* ed. by Amritjit Singh and Daniel Scott III (New Brunswick, NJ: Rutgers University Press, 2003) p. 72. (an excerpt from an undated essay written by Wallace entitled "The Bump (A Dance They Do in Harlem)."

53. Mary Louise Cecelia Guinan was born on a ranch outside of Waco, Texas in 1884. She began acting at the convent school she attended in Waco, and then became a stock actress in amateur theatricals. She eventually went to Hollywood and acted in silent Westerns, where she was the first movie cowgirl and dubbed the "Queen of the West" Using her notoriety in motion pictures to get bookings in vaudeville, she also made a career as a torch singer and worked on Broadway. She started as a night club hostess in a small café in Greenwich Village where the headwaiter was a young Eric Von Stroheim. Her greatest fame came with the opening of her club the El Fey financed by gangster Larry Fay. Many famous people performed at the El Fey including fourteen-year old dancer Ruby Keeler, and a young comedian, Milton Berle. Guinan was well-known for coining many phrases and always greeted her customers with her most famous line "Hello, Suckers!" "Sucker," said La Guinan, "is a smart guy who can afford to be trimmed—and likes it!" (*The Port Arthur News*, November 24, 1929, p. 22, col. 3.) She had many run-ins with the police, often opening new clubs after they had closed down her establishments for violating prohibition. In 1927, she was put in jail after a wealthy college student she had fleeced out of $7,000 later got a job as a federal prohibition agent. He gathered evidence against the club

hostess, raided her 300 club and had Guinan arrested. According to the *Nebraska Star*, February 17, 1927, p. 1, col. 3, when bail was refused, the hostess responded, "How sweet. What a thrill! Texas Guinan is going to jail!" She then proceeded to entertain the hundreds of club patrons who had followed her to jail after her arrest. After her performance, "she retired in her elaborate ermine cloak and brilliant headdress to spend what remained of the night perusing a magazine." In 1929, she was also put on trial for "maintaining a nightclub nuisance" at her club the Salon Royale. A few days later the same thing happened at the Club Intime where she was also hostess. October 1930 brought another raid at the Club Argonaut, but Guinan talked the agents out of arresting her. She was arrested in July 1931 along with singer Helen Morgan for violating prohibition regulations. She was indicted but won an acquittal. The same year she left New York, taking a troupe of girls with her to open a club in London but was barred from entering the country. She planned to also perform in France, but she was stopped by the French police upon landing and ended up returning to the United States, losing $50,000 in the failed venture. One of Guinan's last public appearances was at the Angelus Temple in Los Angeles when she spoke from the pulpit after being converted by Aimee Semple McPherson. Guinan was touring with her troupe of 40 girls when she suffered severe bout of ulcerated colitis in Vancouver. As the condition worsened, she was operated on, but never recovered. She died on November 5, 1933 at age 49.

54. Lewis Yablonsky, *George Raft.* (New York: McGraw-Hill, 1974) p. 40.

55. Yablonsky, p.47, implies that Raft appeared in *Gay Paree* at the Wintergarden Theatre with Winnie Lightner and cast members Sophie Tucker and Oscar Levant, and danced the Charleston to "Sweet Georgia Brown." According to Internet Broadway Database, a production of *Gay Paree* ran from August 1925 to January 1926 at the Shubert Theatre, and the cast did include Lightner, and interestingly enough, Texas Guinan, but Raft, Levant, or Tucker are not listed in the opening night credits. Nor is there a listing for the song, Sweet Georgia Brown." A production called *Gay Paree* did open at the Wintergarden in November 1926 and closed in April 1927, but Lightner, Raft, Levant and Tucker are not listed in the credits. Neither is the song.

56. "Charleston—Everybody is Trying to Do It!" *New Castle News*, New Castle, PA, January 7, 1926, p. 18, col. 7.

57. Bricktop was born on August 14, 1894 in Alderson, West Virginia. Her father was an African-American barber, and her mother was Scotch-Irish and African-American, who had been born a slave. Their daughter was born with white skin and bright red hair. She was given the name Ada Beatrice Queen Victoria Louise Virginia Smith because her mother had asked the neighbors for suggestions for names for her daughter and didn't want to offend any of them by not using their suggestions. After her father died when she was four, the family moved to Chicago. She began singing and dancing at an early age and at sixteen met Flourney Miller and Aubrey Lyles who were performing at the Pekin Theater. Miller and Lyles were casting a tour of a new vaudeville show and hired Smith as one of the chorus girls. She later toured on the TOBA vaudeville circuit with the Oma Crosby Trio and the Kinky-Doo Trio. In 1926, Bricktop opened her own club, *Chez Bricktop* and cemented her role as the darling of the Paris café-society. Bricktop's club became one of the most popular gathering spots of the glitterati including Noel Coward, Tallulah Bankhead, and the Prince of Wales. Since the Prince already knew the Charleston when he met Bricktop in 1928, she taught him the Black Bottom, although some sources mention that she also coached him in the Charleston. In 1939, when German troops were advancing on Paris during World War II, she was aided in her escape by the Duchess of Windsor. Later Bricktop opened clubs in Mexico City and Rome. She died at age 89 in New York City.

58. While performing at Barron's, Bricktop convinced

the owner to hire a young piano player named Duke Ellington. She also brought in her friend Florence Mills to perform there. When the lead in *Shuffle Along* was being replaced, Bricktop recommended Mills who eventually conquered Broadway in the role in that groundbreaking black musical.

59. Josephine Baker was born Freda Josephine McDonald on June 3, 1906 in St. Louis, Missouri. She began in show business as a dancing street performer. She traveled in vaudeville and at fifteen moved to New York. She was eventually hired as a chorus girl in *Shuffle Along*. Performing as the last girl in the line, traditionally a comic spot, Baker grabbed attention with her energetic and charismatic mugging. In 1925, she went to Paris and met Bricktop, who took the young Baker under her wing, often giving her advice. Because Baker was barely literate and had trouble writing her name, she was overwhelmed with autograph seekers. Bricktop suggested she have a rubber stamp made of her name, which Baker did. The two grew cold to each other when Baker did not heed Bricktop's warnings about a man Baker was dating. Baker became the most successful American performer in France with a career that lasted many years. She starred in three films, with her movie debut in the silent film *La Sirène des Tropiques* featuring a memorable Charleston dance. During World War II, she work in the Underground and for her service she was awarded the Croix de Guerre, Légion d'Honneur, and the Rosette of the Résistance. A strong supporter of the Civil Rights Movement, she adopted twelve orphans of differing ethnicities, which she called her "Rainbow Tribe." She died at age 68 on April 12, 1975.

60. On the trip to Paris aboard the *Berengaria,* Josephine agreed to participate in a charity show for children of sailors that had been lost at sea that was being held on board the ship. She insisted on singing two sentimental ballads and flopped terribly. The show was saved by Louis Douglas' five-year-old daughter Marion who was thrown on stage at the last minute to dance a Charleston. Ms. Douglas later remembered the experience; "I remember dancing until I saw stars. I had an out-of-body experience. I danced, I danced, I danced, my legs kept going. And the audience was raving, people were screaming, and I was so excited I couldn't calm down afterwards. My father tried to take me downstairs, my mother tried to, but I wouldn't let anyone except Josephine put me to bed" (Baker and Chase, pp. 100–101, quoting Marion Douglas). Josephine sweetly put the little girl to bed but inwardly was seething with rage. She threatened to return to New York, but later Mrs. Regan convinced her that the Paris audiences would love her.

61. Jean-Claude Baker and Chris Chase, *Josephine: The Hungry Heart* (New York: Random House, 1993) p. 91, quoting Caroline Reagan.

62. After failing to secure the talents of Florence Mills or Ethel Waters, who were too expensive to hire, Reagan approached Josephine Baker whom she had seen perform at the Plantation in New York. Baker also asked for more than Mrs. Reagan was able to pay, but eventually a deal was reached and Reagan convinced her to travel to France. The show was advertised as "*Une Revue Nègre avec Josephine Baker et Louis Douglas...*" with "Les 8 Charleston Babies."

63. Baker and Chase, p. 107, quoting Josephine Baker.

64. *Ibid.* Josephine Baker explains how the Charleston should be done:

> The Charleston should be danced with necklaces of shells wriggling on the skin and making dry music.... It is a way of dancing with your hips ... to bring out the buttocks and shake your hands. We hide the buttocks too much. They exist. I don't see what reproach should be offered them.

65. Bee [Beatrice] Jackson was born in Flushing, New York and grew up in Bound Brook. She danced in amateur productions locally and at age fifteen auditioned for Ned Wayburn. She was hired as a chorus dancer for the *Ziegfeld Follies,*

and was eventually given the position of understudy to *Follies* star Gilda Gray, in her famous South Sea Isle dance. She left the *Follies* after fifteen months. She had a brief stint performing in clubs and then was hired as one of the models in *Artist and Models.* After her successes in London and Vienna she performed other dances with which she became associated, such as the rhumba. An article in *The San Antonio Light,* January 31, 1932, p. 49, col. 3, "Vienna, in spite of the fact that it is the home of the graceful and modest waltz, finds the sensuous movements of the rhumba very much to its liking — and it prefers Bee Jackson to interpret the dance for them." Jackson followed up her engagement in Austria with ones in Constantinople and Berlin, where she appeared in a German talkie. A celebrity of the highest degree, Jackson had her legs insured for $100,000, and her name frequently appeared in newspapers around the globe. Her betrothal for example was announced in the *Syracuse Herald,* October 10, 1925, p. 22, col. 3. It read;

> Bee Jackson, musical comedy blonde who made the Charleston famous, is going to put chains on Carl Foreman professional swimmer and former lifeguard, as soon as he is free from the present Mrs. Foreman according to Zit's weekly. She is Isabel Bennett, 17-year-old dancer, who is suing for the annulment on the grounds that she picked his name out of a hat one night and woke up the next morning an unwilling bride.

Another juicy bit of gossip spoke about the time Jackson was propositioned by the notorious womanizer King Ahmed Zog [Zogu, Zogue] of Albania. When he asked her to come "visit" him in his palace, Jackson supposedly responded to the offer by "giving him a great big biff on the nose. How dare he!" (San Antonio Light, September 11, 1932, p. 51) Jackson died in Chicago on July 18, 1933 at age 24, from complications after having an appendectomy.

66. As mention earlier in this chapter, *Follies* choreographer Ned Wayburn claimed that it was Bee Jackson who introduced the Charleston during a one night only performance of a number called "Shake Your Feet." Jackson does not mention this in her biographical article in *Colliers Magazine,* entitled "Hey! Hey! Charleston," (December 10, 1927, p.34.) In my research I found many photo caption and articles, including her obituary that did list Jackson as the originator of the Charleston. Her international celebrity certainly led many who associated her with the dance to claim that she was the first to introduce it to the general public.

67. Fred W. Emiston, *The Coon-Sanders Nighthawks: The Band That Radio Made Famous* (McFarland: Jefferson, NC, 2003) p. 152. Elida Webb also coached William Reardon, Dorothy Clark and Josephine Baker in the Charleston.

68. "Must Fly to Keep Her Jobs" *The San Antonio Light,* San Antonio, TX, March 22, 1931, p. 58, col. 5. The article states that Jackson "...smilingly informed her admirers that she would try to live up to their estimate of her Terpsichorcan talents, although she was certain that Europe and America are full of dancers who would question her right to such an all-inclusive and high-sounding title."

69. Bee Palmer was best known for popularizing shimmy dancing. Born in 1894, she began in vaudeville and by 1914, had dubbed herself the "Shimmie Queen." In 1918, she became a Ziegfeld Girl, introducing a song in the *Ziegfeld Midnight Frolics* entitled "I Want to learn to Jazz Dance." She appeared in other editions of the *Frolics* and various Broadway productions until she toured with her own show called *Oh Bee!.* Palmer often ran into controversy because her shimmy was considered too risqué. In addition, critics were not always kind to her. The *Milwaukee Journal* for example had a review that read;

> Miss Palmer is a buxom, exceedingly blond young person, with the best of intentions, but an exceedingly unfortunate method of putting them to effect. Her dancing is not quite bad enough to be shocking,

and not quite good enough to be passable. Now and then she sings, which she shouldn't.

Despite this less than flattering notice, Palmer continued to be a popular singer and dancer throughout the 20's and 30's. She appeared with the Paul Whitman Orchestra and made several recordings. She co-wrote the song "Please Don't Talk About Me When I'm Gone." Palmer died at age 73 on December 23, 1967. (Above quote extracted from the web site: www.redhotjazz.com/beepalmer.html.

70. "Charleston — Everybody is Trying to Do It!" *New Castle News*, New Castle, PA, January 7, 1926, p. 18, col. 9.

71. "Must Fly to Keep Her Jobs" *The San Antonio Light*, San Antonio, TX, March 22, 1931, p. 58, col. 5.

72. "Queen 'Bee's' Scantiest Costume" *The San Antonio Light*, San Antonio, TX, November 20, 1932, p. 40, col. 5.

73. *Ibid.*

74. Historians debate the etymology of the expression bee's knees. One camp suggests that it referenced the dancing legs of Bee Jackson. Another held that it referred to the pollen sacks found on the backs of bees' legs—as in goodness or sweetness lay behind the knees. A third group hints that the word could possibly be a corruption of the word "business." Another states that bee's knees is a shortening of the phrase "Be all and end all of everything"—condensed to "b's and e's." Some say the phrase was coined by American cartoonist Tad Dorgan, who also invented "cat's pajama's" and "Yes, we have no bananas." The expression bee's knees (also spelled bees knees or bees' knees) not only referred to the crossing and uncrossing of the hands over the knees during the Charleston, but, was also frequently used in flapper slang to refer to something wonderful. In the book *Flappers 2 Rappers: American Youth Slang*. Springfield, MA: Merriam-Webster, Inc., 1996, pp. 20–21, Tom Dalzell states that it was a common practice in flapperese jargon to link the name of an animal with a part of the anatomy to signify "outright perfection" (Flea's eyebrows and elephant's adenoids are just two other examples of the colorful lingo). In Eric Partridge's *The Dictionary of Slang and Unconventional English*, New York: MacMillan, 1961, p. 44, bee's knees is defined as "The acme of perfection, beauty, attractiveness, skill, desirability, etc." An article in the *Daily Northwestern*, Oshkosh, WI, October 16, 1922, p. 6. col. 1, states "'The bee's knees' is an expression in flapper jargon signifying a thing of small consequence...." In the 1797 version of the *Oxford English Dictionary*, the phrase is defined as "something insignificant." In the 1920's with the shortening of skirts and dresses, knees became a worldwide topic of fascination. In an article in *The Olean Evening Herald*, Olean, NY, February 6, 1926, p.15, col. 4, about a local beauty contest, the author writes of how the winner of the contest had a plain face, but the judges had to award her the trophy because she had bee's knees, meaning she had perfect knees. He wrote, "No more shall alabaster brows and lily throats and ruby lips and Grecian proboscis be rated above beautiful kneecaps...." The author praised the young beauty queen and reminded other young ladies about the importance of preserving their knees. He warned, "High heels have murdered beautiful knees. They cause the girl in walking to put most of her weight upon her knees instead of dividing the weight between calf, thigh and knee, as it should be. This weight upon the knees, widens them, and ruins the shape of the kneecap. They look more like hard-boiled eggs or mustache cups than knees!" In the Jazz Age, flappers, wishing to enhance their knees' beauty, started the practice of applying powder or rouge to their kneecaps. One fashion trend was to actually attach little stuffed bees to the stockings to make it look like the insects were resting on each knee. Some in the period took adornment of knees even further. A picture in the *Olean Evening Herald*, which appeared on June 7, 1924 with the caption "Sweetheart Knees Replace Bee's Knees," showed young girls in Baltimore demonstrating the latest fad — painting pictures of their boyfriends' faces on their kneecaps.

75. Virginia Katherine McMath (Ginger Rogers) was born on July 16, 1911 in Independence, Missouri. Her mother, neé Lela Emogen Owens, had separated from her husband, William Eddins McMath, before Ginger was born and so the child was raised with the aid of her maternal grandparents. When her mother remarried in 1920, the family moved to Fort Worth, Texas and Ginger adopted her stepfather's surname. Her nickname Ginger was bestowed upon her by her cousin Helen who had troubled pronouncing the name "Virginia," and called her "Ginja." In Fort Worth, Lela Rogers worked as theatre critic for the local newspaper, *The Fort Worth Record* and often took her daughter along with her as she reviewed shows. While waiting for her mother, Ginger would spend the time backstage, learning bits of song and dance routines. It was here she says that she first learned the Charleston from Eddie Foy. Jr. Foy was part of the legendary family vaudeville song and dance act "Eddie Foy and The Seven Little Foys." Ginger herself had once performed with the group when one of the children was ill and unable to go on. In 1929, at seventeen, she married a vaudeville hoofer who was twelve years older than her named Edward Jackson (Jack) Culpepper whom she had known from her childhood days in Texas. Culpepper was an alcoholic and they divorced a year later. Rogers started performing in a solo act. At age eighteen she had landed a role on Broadway in a show called *Top Speed*. The review in *The New York Times* called her "charming, although the Herald-Tribune commented that Rogers was "unlikely ever to disturb the Terpsichoreon Hall of Fame" (Morley, p.17). Paramount sent a talent scout to see the show, but he reported back to his bosses that Ginger Rogers was "just another Charleston dancer who can't act...." Despite this, Rogers began to shoot a series of musical short films as well as small parts in other films. This eventually led to the offer of a contract with Paramount. Rogers declined the offer though because she was offered the lead in a new Gershwin musical called *Girl Crazy*. She introduced two songs in the show, "Embraceable You" and "But Not for Me" that later became classic musical standards. It was while doing this show that she first met Fred Astaire who had been hired to choreograph one of her numbers. Another member of the *Girl Crazy* cast was Ethel Merman. After *Girl Crazy* closed, Rogers signed with Pathé films and traveled to Hollywood. After a few disappointing roles, she and the studio agreed to drop her option. She began to work for other studios until she ended up at RKO. It was here after nineteen films to her credit, she was featured in *Flying Down to Rio*, the film that reunited her with Fred Astaire. Their on-screen chemistry led them to dance together in ten films and propelled them into becoming the most famous dancing couple in movie history. Rogers made many other films and in 1940, won the Best Actress Academy Award for her role in *Kitty Foyle*. By 1945, she was the highest paid actress in Hollywood. She died on April 25, 1995 at the age of 83 at her home in Rancho Mirage, California. She is buried in Chatsworth, CA in the Oakwood Memorial Park, the same cemetery where Fred Astaire lies.

76. In February of the following year (2/8–9/26), Rogers entered the National Charleston Dance Contest of the World held at the Trianon Ballroom in Chicago, Illinois. She came in second. The husband and wife team of Jim and Louise Sullivan carried away the First Prize of $10,000.00. Jim's hometown paper, the *El Paso Herald-Post*, in an article about the dancer on January 25, 1974, p. 9, quotes Sullivan as claiming "the holes in his shoes at the time — he'd been out of work — had something to do with their winning." Sullivan explained that he had put a thin piece of rubber in the shoe to cover the hole and that gave him extra traction during the fast-paced competition. Apparently the floor was extra slippery and other dancers kept falling. (One contestant broke his ankle.) The couple was inadvertently listed as "a brother-and-sister team" in newspaper accounts of their victory, but in fact had recently been married before the contest. A newsreel of their winning the contest had been filmed, and when

the duo played in vaudeville they started their act by showing the footage on a large piece of paper. They then broke through the screen and began dancing. Louise Sullivan had also won a singles Charleston contest held two months earlier on Christmas eve in 1925. After winning the National Championships, the Sullivans toured in vaudeville and nightclubs. In 1968, they appeared in the movie *The Night They Raided Minsky's.*

77. Sheridan Morley, *Shall We Dance: The Life of Ginger Rogers* (New York: St. Martins Press, 1995) p.14.

78. "Three Boys Win in Contest at Martini; Girl is Fourth" *Galveston Daily News,* Galveston, TX, January 15, 1926, p.3, col. 4

79. Joan Crawford was born Lucille Fay LeSueur in San Antonio, Texas on March 23, 1904. (After she was famous, the date of her birth mysteriously changed to 1906 or 1908.) When her father deserted the family, Crawford's mother Anna married Henry Cassin, a music hall owner from Lawton, Oklahoma. At her stepfather's urging, Crawford took the stage name Billie Cassin and began to pursue a career as a dancer in her stepfather's theatre. After Cassin's music hall closed, the family moved to Kansas where Crawford won the Charleston contest. She was hired as part of a line of dancing chorines at the Oriole Terrace, a club in Detroit , where she was seen by J.J. Schubert, who offered a part in his New York revue *Innocent Eyes.* In 1924, while in New York, Crawford met Nils T. Granlund, who with his partner, singer Harry Richman, had opened a speakeasy called *Club Richman.* Crawford begged Granlund for a job, claiming that her mother was ill and needed financial support. Granlund hired her as a featured Charleston dancer for $50.00 a week, and also became her sugar daddy. He eventually arranged a meeting between his protégé and M.G.M. talent scout Marcus Loew, who set up a screen test for Crawford. Because he felt LeSeur sounded like "sewer" and was difficult to pronounce (and to distance the young woman from her notorious sexual past), studio mogul Louis B. Mayer came up with the idea of having a contest for fans to pick a new name for his starlet. Dubbed "Name Her and Win $1,000," the contest was part of a promotion run by the fan magazine *Movie Weekly.* The winning entry resulted in Lucille LeSeur being re-christened, Joan Arden, but a few weeks after taking the new name, an extra with the same name who also working on the M.G.M. lot threatened to sue and so the second place entry, Joan Crawford, was adopted. Mrs. Louise M. Artisdale of Rochester, New York, won a prize of $500 for inventing Joan's new name. In the 1920's Crawford was well-known for her many roles as the Charleston-loving flapper. In the 1930's she frequently appeared in films as the working woman struggling to survive. She left MGM in 1942 and went to Warner Brothers and in 1945 appeared in *Mildred Pierce,* winning an Academy Award for Best Actress. She made her last film in 1970. Joan Crawford died on May 10, 1977.

80. As an child, Crawford had severely injured her foot while jumping off of a porch onto a broken milk bottle. The cut was so serious, she was unable to attend school for a year and a half and had at least three operations on her foot. Despite this, the young Crawford was determined to pursue a career in dancing.

81. Louise Brooks, from a 1957 unpublished essay originally intended for a book by Brooks called *Women in Film.* The book was never published. Extracted from the website: http://www.joancrawfordbest.com/brooksessay.htm

82. Later in her career, Crawford was hired to perform on *The Lucy Show.* The episode called for her to dance a Charleston. She was rehearsing the number when Lucille Ball, stopped the number and yelled at Crawford that she was off the beat. On the second try, Ball snapped, "I don't like the way you're dancing—how did you win a Charleston contest in Texas? You can't dance!" Crawford tried the dance once more, but Ball cut the number and left Crawford collapsed on the floor in tears.

83. An article in *Photoplay Magazine,* October 1940 states

that on Friday nights, the Ambassador Hotel in Los Angeles held Charleston competitions and "these contests almost always ended as a private contest between Jane Peters (Carole) and Lucille LeSueur (Joan Crawford)." It was while she was dancing at the Cocoanut Grove (also spelled Coconut) in 1925 that Lombard was seen by a Fox Studio executive who arranged for her first screen test.

84. Charleston contests were so common and widespread that it is impossible to list all of them here. Two in particular though did strike my interest. Chief Yellowhorse and his wife Oggie won the Cinderella Roof Contest at the ballroom of the Biltmore Hotel in Los Angeles, and afterwards claimed to be the best "redskin" Charleston Champions in the world. The couple lived in Saugus, CA on actor Harry Carey's Trading Post, which was used as a movie set at times and also featured live performances. In another case, a huge Charleston contest occurred at the Hippodrome in New York City. It was held on April 6, 1925 and Miss Belle Davy was crowned the top Charlestoner. Fourteen finalists had been chosen out of nearly 300 entrants, but Miss Davey won by getting the most applause from the audience. She won $250.00 in gold, a week's engagement at the Club Richman, and a pearl necklace. As the decade progressed marathon Charleston contests became more common. In 1926, a girl in Oakland, CA set the world's record for continuous Charleston dancing after hearing that on the East coast, some girls had claimed the title by dancing for thirty-three minutes. Addressing the exhausted musicians who accompanied her in a contest of Charleston endurance, Doris Conover who danced for 47 consecutive minutes without stopping told the weary players, "You two will have to eat more iron if you expect to play for Charleston dancers." Conover wore a bathing suit, shoes and stockings informing others that the bathing costume gave her freedom of movement that was "absolutely essential in dancing America's newest steps" (*Oakland Tribune,* Oakland, CA, January 15, 1926, p. 12, col. 1). *The New York Times,* June 17, 1928, p. 18, reported on one such contest held at Madison Square Gardens. Among the contestants were a dozen long distance runners with "steel-sinewed legs" who pitted themselves against "waxy-complexioned trotters from the night clubs and dance academies." As the derby progressed the professional athletes began to falter. By the seventh day of the competition, "many of the slim, shiny-headed tangoers, who looked like hospital cases besides the whiskered mahogany-faced runners, are still in the derby, but the men from the open spaces are gone." The remaining couples were "thrown into despair late in the afternoon when Couples 3 and 7 began to Charleston with great vim, for no reason except to show how fresh and gay they were." Many detractors complained that the excesses of marathon dancing were undesirable. The *Lancaster Daily Gazette,* Lancaster, Ohio, January 28, 1926 p. 5, col. 5, reported on one contest which was banned in Detroit. It stated, "In denying a permit for a Charleston endurance contest here, President John C. Lodge of the Detroit City Council branded the proposal "silly," while one other member of the council said he would "rather grant permission to hold a prize fight with sledge hammers."

85. This story is found in the article "Smith Starts Urchins Doing the Charleston While He Waits in Station at Absecon" *New York Times,* November 27, 1926, p. 1.

86. "Prince George Wins Charleston Contest with Lady Milford Haven at Cannes Casino" *The New York Times,* March 28, 1927, p. 1. The Prince was an avid and accomplished dancer. The *Modesto News-Herald,* November 9, 1926, p. 6, col. 4, reported, "The Prince of Wales has mastered the Charleston and dances it with the skill and rhythm that only professional dancers can equal."

87. "20,00 Attend Fete for Jewish Relief" *The New York Times,* June 28, 1926, P. 3.

88. Second prize was "One case of John Jameson's 'Three Star' Whiskey, and One case of Black and White Liqueur Whiskey;" third prize was a "Set of six Official Mustard Club Pots, including Official Membership to Club."

89. Josephine Bradley was born in Dublin on March 24, 1893. She studied ballet but transitioned into ballroom dancing, winning the World Foxtrot Championship in 1924 with her dancing partner G. K. Anderson. The same year, Bradley was asked by the newly formed Ballroom Branch of the Imperial Society Of Teachers of Dancing to help formulate the basic techniques of the foxtrot, tango, quickstep, and waltz. Her career in the world of dance led her to be called the first lady of Ballroom.

90. A pioneer of early ballroom dancing in England, Santos Casani opened a dancing school after the first World War. He achieved notoriety by dancing the Charleston on top of a taxi as it drove down Kingsway. Casani made dance instructional films and in 1926 acted in a movie entitled "The Flat Charleston." In 1933, he opened Casani Club in Regent Street.

91. Florence Mills was born on January 25, 1896 in Washington D.C.. She was the daughter of former slaves. Her given name was Florence Winfrey. By age five, she was winning medals for her cakewalk dancing. She then performed in vaudeville with her sisters and also on the burlesque circuits, and in clubs and cabarets. At the Panama club she became friends with Bricktop, who later recommended her for her breakthrough role in *Shuffle Along*, where she caused a sensation with her accomplished dancing and her lilting, birdlike soprano voice. She was offered a part in the Ziegfeld Follies but instead accepted a role in the all-black revue *Dixie to Broadway*. She then did the lead in Blackbirds and when the show traveled to London she achieved international recognition. She was frequently asked to demonstrate or teach the Charleston to the glitterati of the city or judge the many Charleston competitions held during the craze in London. In Paris she performed with Black Birds (*Les Oiseaux Noirs* in French) to rave reviews and was frequently compared to Josephine Baker. French Ballet critic André Levinson wrote in *Theatre Arts Monthly*;

> The mad arabesques of the incomparable Josephine can give us an almost shocking insight into our more somber depths, but Florence Mills, for instance, is developing into an almost precious elegance. It is no longer the tigress who stands before us but the marquise, who has rubbed a little burnt cork on her cheeks, instead of her customary rouge, before dancing a Court Charleston. (Egan, p. 162, quoting André Levinson)

Mills was married to dancer Ulysses "Slow Kid" Thompson, one of the top legomania dancers of the time. A versatile performer, Mills excelled in all varieties of jazz, tap, eccentric and acrobatic dancing. Often called one of the greatest black entertainers in history, she was a major figure in the Harlem Renaissance and one of the first international superstars of the twentieth century. She was an intellectual woman who fought for Civil Rights and did many charitable works. Her nicknames included the "Queen of Jazz" and the "Queen of Happiness." She died at age 31 in New York City on November 1, 1927 of complications from pelvic tuberculosis. Her funeral attracted more than 150,000 mourners.

92. Egan, p. 182.

93. *Ibid.*

94. Lew Grade was born Louis Winogradsky in Tokmak, Ukraine on December 25, 1906. He emigrated in England in 1913 and worked in the embroidery business with his father. He became interested in dancing after being introduced to the faced-paced dances like the Charleston at the East Ham Palais de Dance where he had gone to meet girls. Because he had a photographic memory, the young man picked up steps easily and quickly. A friend who recognized his talent, persuaded him to enter a Charleston contest being held at the Hippodrome. His chief competition at the event were the Reubens, a brother and sister team who had recently won the European Charleston Championship held earlier in Paris. According to Grade, he went to a bar across from the Hippodrome and while drinking a lemonade, created a new Charleston step which he called the "Crossover." The flashy step helped him to beat the Reubens and he danced away with the first prize of 25 pounds. Grade continued to enter small contests around London while still working in the garment industry, but after winning the championship at Albert Hall in 1926, he decided to dance professionally. Grade formed a dance act with one of his former rivals, a young Charleston dancer by the name of Al Gold. The two had moderate success but the act eventually broke up and Grade went solo. He co-headlined at the Moulin Rouge in Paris and it was here that the French press misspelled his first name as "Lew." He liked the mistake and kept the name. He continued to dance professionally until he developed water on the knee and gave up performing. In 1933, he founded a talent agency and represented such British stars as Sir Ralph Richardson and Lord Laurence Olivier, as well as American talent including Frank Sinatra, Bob Hope and Jack Benny. He became a television producer and was responsible for the British hits "The Saint," "The Prisoner," and "The Avengers," among others. Also a movie producer, Grade financed such films as "The Return of the Pink Panther," "The Boys From Brazil," "On Golden Pond," and "Sophie's Choice." He also produced the big screen version of *The Muppet Show*. As a thank you, Jim Henson created the muppet character Dr. Bunsen Honeydew in Grade's likeness. On Broadway, Grade produced Stephen Sondheim's "Merrily We Roll Along" and Andrew Lloyd Webber's "Starlight Express." Lew Grade died on December 13, 1998 at age 92.

95. Egan, p. 182.

96. "Says 'Charleston' is a Disease" *The Lowell Sun*, Lowell, MA, December 14, 1926, p. 19, col. 4.

Chapter 16

1. John F. Carter, "These Wild Young People, By One of Them," *Atlantic Monthly*, 126, September 1920, pp. 301–304, extracted from the web site: http://eagle.clarion.edu/~faculty/tpfannestiel/carter.html. Carter's essay provides a powerful insight into the mindset of the youth of his day. He writes,

> Now my generation is disillusioned, and, I think, to a certain extent, brutalized, by the cataclysm which their [the older generation's] complacent folly engendered. The acceleration of life for us has been so great that into the last few years have been crowded the experiences and the ideas of a normal lifetime. We have in our unregenerate youth learned the practicality and the cynicism that is safe only in unregenerate old age. We have been forced to become realists overnight, instead of idealists, as was our birthright. We have seen man at his lowest, woman at her lightest, in the terrible moral chaos of Europe. We have been forced to question, and in many cases to discard, the religion of our fathers. We have seen hideous speculation, greed, anger, hatred, malice, and all uncharitableness, unmasked and rampant and unashamed. We have been forced to live in an atmosphere of "tomorrow we die," and so, naturally, we drank and were merry. We have seen the rottenness and shortcomings of all governments, even the best and most stable. We have seen entire social systems overthrown, and our own called in question. In short, we have seen the inherent beastliness of the human race revealed in an infernal apocalypse.

2. Ellen Welles Page, "A Flapper's Appeal to Parents," *Outlook*, December 6, 1922, p. 607. (available at several online sources). Page also wrote,

> And do you know who is largely responsible for all this energy's [sic] being spent in the wrong direc-

tions? You! You parents, and grandparents, and friends, and teachers, and preachers—all of you! "The war!" you cry. "It is the effect of the war!" And then you blame prohibition. Yes! Yet it is you who set the example there! But this is my point: Instead of helping us work out our problems with constructive, sympathetic thinking and acting, you have muddled them for us more hopelessly with destructive public condemnation and denunciation.

3. A flapper was also sometimes called a sheba, a barlow, a beasel, a chicken, a harmonica, a jalopy, a mama, a hot mama, a whoopee mama, or a jazz baby. More specific labels were a beaut (a cute flapper,) a biscuit (a pettable flapper,) a no-soap (a flapper who didn't go to petting parties,) a bookie (a flapper who was easy to date,) a hooker (a flapper who didn't like to work,) a weed (a flapper who took risks,) a jeweler (a flapper who collected fraternity pins,) a Princess Mary (a flapper who planned to marry soon,) and a twister (a flapper taken to a dance.) Her male counterpart was referred to as a flipper, a sheik, a goof, a Jazzbo, a sharpshooter, a slicker, a stroller, or a lounge lizard. More specific labels for men were a cake-eater, angel child, ballroom golfer, bunduster, crumb-gobbler, crumpet-muncher, Eskimo pie eater, grummy ostrich, parlor Bolshevik, pastry snake, porcupine, puddle jumper, snake, sponge cake and tea-crasher (all defined as the opposite of he-man,) a beasel hound, scandal-walker, or subchaser (a lothario,) a cuddle cootie (a man who took his girl in a car,) a brooksy boy (an over-dressed man) and a dud (a modern man who did not live up to his name.) Flappers and collegiates developed their own colorful lingo, and were the first youth generation to actually create specific slang dictionaries. "Flapperese," as the slang was sometimes called, has mostly faded from general use today, although certain expressions still survive. The wide variety of terms flappers used is too vast to list here, but a few choice words that relate to dancing deserve mention. "A drag" was a dance, "to drag" or "drag a sock" meant to dance, "a hopper" was a dancer, "a sip" and "a sloppy" were names for a female dancer, "an Oliver Twist" was a good dancer," "a horse prancer" was a bad dancer, a "floorflusher" was an insatiable dancer, "absent treatment" referred to dancing with a timid partner, "a canceled stamp" was a shy girl at a dance, "a heeler" was an inferior dancer, "a corn shredder" was a man who was an awkward dancer, "feet" referred to a very clumsy dancer, "button shining" meant dancing close, "give the knee" meant to dance cheek-to-cheek and toe-to-toe, "an egg harbor" was a free dance, "horn in" meant to get into a dance without an invitation, "rug shaking" and "wrestle" referred to dancing the shimmy, "struggle" referred to modern dances, and "Get hot! Get hot!" was a common phrase shouted out to a flapper doing the Charleston. (This information was extracted from Tom Dalzell's book *Flappers 2 Rappers: American Youth Slang*. Springfield, MA: Merriam-Webster, Inc., 1996, pp. 8–23.)

4. Page, p. 607.

5. Tom Dalzell, *Flappers 2 Rappers: American Youth Slang* (Springfield, MA: Merriam-Webster, Inc., 1996) p, 22, quoting *The Flapper's Dictionary: As Compiled by One of Them* (Plattsburgh, NY: The Imperial Press, 1922.)

6. In the article "Pastor Defends Flapper and Criticises [sic] Men's Dress," *The New York Times*, April 10, 1922, p. 1, the Rev. Frederick E. Hopkins of the First Presbyterian Church of Michigan City, IN, said,

> The flapper is told she does not look graceful scuffling along in unbuckled galoshes ... she can reply, men look slouchy in soft shirts with sometimes a ruffle cascading between the bottom of the vest and the waistband. Don't be surprised if she says to men; "When you wear suspenders I will buckle my galoshes."

The Reverend went on to observe that flappers "will stop bobbing their hair like a pineapple when men stop having theirs like a chrysanthemum" The second part of the quote was found in "Champions of Flapper Cause Parry Menacing Thrusts of Critics in United States," *Fort Wayne Journal-Gazette*, May 7, 1922, p. 34, col. 4.

7. This particular definition of "flapper" can be found in the *English Dialect Dictionary* and dates to 1856. It is also traceable to a listing in the *Oxford English Dictionary* as early as 1773. An article in *The Evening News*, August 20, 1892 stated "... a 'flapper' is a young wild duck which is unable to fly, hence a little duck of any description, human or otherwise." In 1986, author Robert Chapman wrote that the connection between a young bird and a girl in the 1920's were perhaps linked "from the idea of an unfledged bird flapping its wings as one did while dancing the Charleston." (This information was extracted from Dalzell, p. 22.)

8. In an editorial in *The New York Times* dated June 25, 1922, the author wrote that the word flapper as it was used in 1922, had an entirely different connotation than when the term was first coined. He wrote,

> The term [flapper] and the type it describes were first of all outgrowths of the World War—that both signified in the first instance a girl who engaged in war work and thereby, tasting the sweets of independence of and equality with man, became a destroyer of established custom and the sole arbiter of her own destiny. As a matter of fact, the flapper, as we know her today, is the complete antithesis of her on whom the title was first bestowed. In 1910 American visitors to England heard of the flapper. Those who inquired into the meaning of this unusual and previously unheard appellation found that it designated a girl, varying in age form 14 to 17, who had not yet 'come out,' who rode in the side car of a motorcycle, and because she had not reached the debutante stage of doing her hair on the top of her head wore it hanging down her back, braided or loose, so that it flapped in the wind. Hence the name flapper. This girl was in type anything but radical or unusual. In speech, manners and dress she was modest, unassuming and refined, the personification of a well-bred, well-reared, well-educated daughter in a family of means and social position. She wore her skirt half way to her ankles. She was thoroughly conventional. She had none of the assurance, none of the independence, none of the impudence, none of the defiance of social laws, none of the slang, none of the freedom with those of the opposite sex, none of the scorn for parental advice, none of the derision for respectability, none of the daring in dress, none of the imperviousness to criticism which had made the American flapper a by-word.

Above quote extracted from "Exit the Flapper Via Longer Skirts," *The New York Times*, June 25, 1922, Section: Editorial, p. E2. Interestingly, there were early uses of the word flapper in reference to "loose" behavior. Farmer's and Henley's *Dictionary of Slang* from the 18th and mid-19th centuries lists a flapper as "a very young prostitute." In 1909, J. Redding Ware defined the word in his *Passing English of the Victorian Era* as "a very immoral young girl in her early teens." IN 1957, Eric Partridge defined flapper as "a young harlot." (This information was extracted from Tom Dalzell's book *Flappers 2 Rappers: American Youth Slang*. Springfield, MA: Merriam-Webster, Inc., 1996, pp. 22–23.)

9. "Is Today's Girl Becoming a Savage?" *Modesto Evening News*, Modesto, CA, June 14, 1924, p. 26, col. 1.

10. *Ibid.*

11. *Ibid.* In an article entitled "What Makes the Flapper Go Round?" in the *Oakland Tribune*, Oakland, CA, November 9, 1929, p. 27, author Velva G. Darling lists three reasons why women become flappers. She writes,

> a. Physical Freedom — her sudden breathless winning of freedom of the knees, freedom of affection, freedom that only earning your own living can give.

b. Nervousness— an unusual and excessive nervousness which has never before descended upon a nation of girls— nervousness forced upon tiny little girl babies— three years old, five years old, ten years old — by last year. Everywhere they turn they heard talk of "atrocities," Hooverizing, death-lists, boys "over there" being shot to death daily.

c. Motherhood — the sub-conscious realization that comes instinctively to the most brainless flapper that she is the embodiment of the new race now developing in America.

In the *Fort Wayne Journal-Gazette*, May 7, 1922, p. 34, col. 4, ("Champions of Flapper Cause Parry Menacing Thrusts of Critics in United States,") the author gives more humorous reasons why the youth of America become flappers;

Mrs. Emma Chase, the district superintendent of schools, in Sullivan county, New York, said that boys and girls become flappers because they have their breakfast in bed.... Dr. Alfred E Stearns, head master of Phillips Academy, Andover, Mass., blamed parents who surround their children with home brew and jazz.

12. The quest for a boyish figure led many flappers to starve themselves in an effort to look thin and boyish. In her article "What Makes the Flapper Go Round?," *Oakland Tribune*, Oakland, CA, November 9, 1929, p. 27, Velva G. Darling wrote, "[The flapper is] devoted to frail unhealthiness, immaculate emaciation, and genteel starvation."

13. "What is Jazz Doing to Our Boys and Girls?" *Atlanta Constitution*, Atlanta, GA, January 15, 1922 Sunday Magazine, quoting Dr. M. C. Pearson, executive secretary of the Council of Churches in Detroit, Michigan.

14. Bruce Bliven, "Flapper Jane," *New Republic* 44, September 9, 1925, p. 65. This quote was extracted from the website The Jazz Age: http://www.geocities.com/flapper_culture/jane.html

15. Other factors that brought about the demise of the corset were the growing athleticism of women with the such sports as cycling and tennis, and the increasingly short supply of metal used in steel-laced corsets, due to the first World War.

16. Bliven, p. 65. In addition to less confining underwear, abbreviated swimwear also created a furor in the 1920's. Perhaps the most scandalous outfit was the one-piece bathing suit. In Atlantic City there was a beach patrol that enforced bathing suit restrictions. Laws stated that swimsuits were to be "neither too low in front or back" and the attached skirts " of reasonable length — at least halfway to the knees. Bare limbs will not be tolerated; full length hosiery must be worn" (Latham, p. 71). Trying to get around these rules, flappers would roll their stockings down below the knee. "Beach cops" were used to enforce the hosiery rule "with a curt 'Roll 'em up sister..."(Latham, p. 73) Louise Rosine, who was visiting from Los Angeles, was arrested on the beach in Atlantic City when she refused to roll her stockings up to cover her knees when she was confronted by the beach police. "Miss Louise Rosine ... most emphatically declared to-day it was "none of the city's business whether she 'rolled her stockings up or down,'" and is now in the City Jail in a state of mutiny and uncovered knees" (Latham, p. 83). Rosine continued her protest in jail, stripping herself completely and refusing to re-robe until she was set free. The embarrassed jail's warden, Wes Brubaker, who had dealt with hunger strikes, but never nudity, was flummoxed. Eventually he had two female assistants pin blankets around the outside of the rebellious bather's cell. Atlantic City also hired "undercover 'copettes' attired in nifty bathing suits," whose job it was to "nab ogling male bathers and break up love matches on the beach" (Latham, p. 77). On Chicago Beaches, to help swimmers to comply with the laws, Mrs. A. M. Loucks was hired as a "beach tailor." The older woman roamed the beaches during the summer with a small sewing kit and a tape measure. Each female swimmer had to pass her inspection. If the swimsuit failed the test, Mrs. Loucks would quickly remodel the costume by sewing on extra material, reminding the woman to reinforce the stitches when they got home. Despite efforts to regulate swimming suits, "When municipal authorities discovered that, worn by local "bathing beauties," these swimsuit styles attracted tourism ... the decency dilemma in some towns and cities was quite quickly dismissed in the interests of capitalism" (Latham, p. 65).

17. "Champions of Flapper Cause Parry Menacing Thrusts of Critics in United States" *Fort Wayne Journal-Gazette*, Fort Wayne, IN, May 7, 1922, p. 34, col. 5.

18. Professor Paul H. Nystrom actually graphed the length of skirts during this period and published his findings in *The Economics of Fashion*. The statistician measured fashion plates in the *Delineator* each month and determined the ratio of the height of the skirt hem above the ground to the total height of the figure. The graph demonstrated the constant fluctuations of dress length beginning in 1919, when the average distance of the hem above the ground was six or seven inches above the ground or about 10 per cent of the woman's height. In 1920, the graph curved upward to about 20 per cent, then dipped down again to ten percent for the next three years, reaching its low point in 1923. In 1924, it rose between 15 and 20 per cent, and in 1925 to more than 20 per cent. The curve continued to rise until by 1927 it had passed the 25 per cent mark when skirts had reached the knee.

19. Angela J. Latham, *Posing a Threat: Flappers, Chorus Girls, and other Brazen Performers of the American 1920s* (Hanover: Wesleyan University Press, 2000) p. 27.

20. Frederick Lewis Allen, *The Revolution in Manners and Morals*, quoting President Murphy of the University of Florida. Extracted from the website: http://xroads.virginia.edu/~hyper/Allen/ch5.html

21. Latham, p. 57, quoting Sir James Cantlie "The Bare-Neck Evil," *Literary Digest* 65, April 3, 1922, p. 116.

22. Allen.

23. *Ibid*.

24. Bell-bottoms were created by Oxford students because they could easily be slipped over short knee-pants or knickers which were forbidden in the classroom on campus.

25. Later skin-tight pants replaced baggies and became the symbol of "jazz clothing." Long tight-waisted, form-fitting jackets with long, single back vents, worn with stovepipe pants were a sign that the wearer was a fan of jazz music.

26. Latham, pp. 54–55, quoting Emily Burbank, *The Smartly Dressed Woman: How She Does It* (New York: Dodd, Mead and Company, 1925) p. 104.

27. Latham, p. 55, quoting Young Women's Christian Association (YWCA), *The Girl Reserve Movement: A Manual for Advisors* (New York: Woman's Press, 1923), pp. 281–284

28. Latham, p. 55, quoting Dr. Sara Brown in Walton's, "Y.W.C.A. Stamps."

29. *Ibid*.

30. Latham, pp 55–56, quoting Florence A. Sherman "Hygiene of Clothing," *Journal of Home Economics* 17, January 1925, p. 25.

31. Latham, p. 57, quoting Reese Carmichael, "The Ladies," p.45.

32. The trend towards shorter hair began during the first World War when women began to take over men's jobs and work in factories to support the war effort. In the web article at "Costumer's Manifesto" Dr. Tara Maginnis states, "The Pope even issued a bull during the war declaring that short hair for women was not immoral, and was a necessity for many factory workers." Despite the Pope's announcement, many were offended by the new hairstyles. The superintendent of schools in Atlantic City for example forbade teachers to bob their hair.

33. According to the web article featured on Christy's Fashion Pages "Flapper Fashion"— Irene Castle cut her hair after seeing the new shorter fashion in Paris.

34. In Michael Warner's web article "The Bob" the author writes, "In some cities, long lines of women were reported

standing outside barbershops while inside, many women patiently sat on floors waiting their turn to be bobbed. In New York City, reports of up to 2,000 heads per day were being clipped." The new styles caused furor not only among those who were shocked that a woman would consider cutting her hair, but also among those doing the cutting. In May 1922, the *American Hairdresser* reported on the battle that raged between professional hairdressers and barbers. The hairdressers objected to women going to barber shops viewing them as unsuitable places of a woman's delicate nature (and no doubt, upset at the loss of business,) and the barbers tried to force legislation that would forbid hairdressers from cutting hair (hoping to hold on to all the added revenue themselves.)

35. Bliven, p 65.

36. *Ibid.*

37. "Flapper's Cosmetics Alarming Physicians," *The New York Times,* April 13, 1922, p. 10, quoting Dr. William L. Love.

38. "Just Jazz" by Neal R. O'Hara in his column "Live Wires," *The Post-Standard,* Syracuse, NY, April 13, 1920, p. 13, col. 3.

39. "Putting the Music Into the Jazz," *The New York Times,* February 19, 1922, Section: Book Review and Magazine, p. 41.

Jazz music came to represent the discontent of an unsettled generation reeling after the Great War. It symbolized physical and sexual freedom and individual expression. As stated in the *Oakland Tribune,* May 22, 1922:

> Jazz is the protest of the mass of humanity against the failure of civilization. Jazz is the snarl of the rebelling savage against the faith which has cheated him. Jazz is the hunger cry for color and joy and power and peace—for the fullness of life.

40. The following diatribe against jazz was extracted from a letter to the column "What They Say to Geraldine," in the *Oakland Tribune,* Oakland, CA, November 19, 1922, p. 15, col. 1.

> Jazz!
> I hate it.
> The girls run around
> Short on clothes
> And long on experiences.
> The men eagerly slink
> Along behind—
> Their greased hair clinging sleekly
> To their thick skulls.
> Bell-bottomed trousers flap
> About bony ankles, while
> A nauseating simper distorts
> The human face.
> Girls who read "The Sheik"
> And smell of cigarettes
> Are rivaled only by boys
> Whose orchid silk B.V.D.'s
> Are finished off with lace and rosebuds.
> Conversation runs to "damns"
> "Hells," newly invented epithets,
> And bootleg hootch.
> Where are the youths of yesterday?
> Where will we get the parents of tomorrow?
> Where, oh, where?
> Not from the youths of today—
> I hate 'em!
> Them—and
> Jazz!

41. "Jazz" *Brownsville, Herald,* Brownsville, TX, February 1, 1922, p. 4, col. 2. (originally printed in the *Kansas City Star.*)

42. "Mayor of Wilkes-Barre Would Put Ban on Jazz" *Wisconsin Rapids Daily News,* Wisconsin Rapids, WI, August 27, 1924, p. 8, col. 2, quoting Dan Hart, the mayor of Wilkes-Barre, PA. Hart drew up an ordinance banning the playing of jazz music on streets or other public places within the city. Violating the law resulted in a fine of up to one hundred dol-

lars. When asked to comment, the mayor said, "first of all, tell the people I am not a nut." He then added, "I'll tell you how it is. Deep down in their hearts people don't want it.... That music is savage; it has a direct brute appeal." In her article "Does Jazz Put the Sin in Syncopation?" published in the *Ladies Home Journal,* (August 1921, pp. 16–34), Anne Shaw Faulkner commented on the primitive roots of jazz. She wrote:

> Jazz originally was the accompaniment of the voodoo dancer, stimulating the half-crazed barbarian to the vilest deeds. The weird chant, accompanied by the syncopated rhythm of the voodoo invokers, has also been employed by other barbaric people to stimulate brutality and sensuality.

Although most music historians do point out jazz's connection to African tribal rhythms, *The Eau Claire Leader,* January 23, 1920, p. 7, col. 5., reported that jazz originated among primitive tribes in the Philippines. It stated;

> Where did jazz originate? The answer has been laid at the door of the South Sea Islanders, the Wild Men of Borneo, the nautch dancers of India, and the tamasha wallahs of the Malay Peninsula. But according to a group of Uncle Sam's soldiers, who returned last week from a visit to the dog-eating Igorottes of Baguio, north of Manila, it is the Igorottes who are responsible for the famous American jazz.

According to the story, American soldiers were in the area and were given a feast by the local chiefs. As entertainment, the chiefs offered "their zippiest dancers and the loudest tom-tom beaters to furnish the music." The article reported, " A captain in the party, who is a relative of one of the Mroadway [sic] theatrical managers, announced that he would at once recommend that a band of the dog eaters he [sic] brought to New York to show the American people what original jazz looks like, as well as settle once and for all the question of where jazz got its start."

44. "Putting the Music Into the Jazz" *The New York Times,* February 19, 1922, Section: Book Review and Magazine, p. 41. In "Does Jazz Put the Sin in Syncopation?" Anne Shaw Faulkner added:

> Realizing the evil influence of this type of music and dancing, the National Dancing Masters' Association, at their last session, adopted this rule: "Don't permit vulgar cheap jazz music to be played. Such music almost forces dancers to use jerky half-steps, and invites immoral variations. It is useless to expect to find refined dancing when the music lacks all refinement, for, after all, what is dancing but an interpretation of music?"

45. "Jerome Kern Hits at Jazz Orchestra" *The New York Times,* April 12, 1924, Section: Amusements, Hotels and Restaurants, p. 18.

46. "End of Jazz Not Far Off, Declares Sousa" *Charleston Daily Mail,* Charleston, WV, March 21, 1922, p. 2, col. 6.

47. "Berlin Calls Jazz American Folk Music" *The New York Times,* January 10, 1925, p. 2.

48. "Jazz Here to Stay Say Music Experts" *Ogden Standard-Examiner,* January 27, 1924, p. 21, col. 1.

49. "Jazz" (word)—From Wikipedia, the free encyclopedia.

50. *Ibid.*

51. The online encyclopedia Wikipedia states that the use of the word "jazz" in relation to music could have first been implemented by musician and bandleader Bert Kelly, who picked up the term on the West Coast and used it as early as 1914 to refer to his dance band, then brought the term with him to Chicago when his band played there in 1915. This story seems to be confirmed by an article that appeared in the *Literary Digest* on April 26, 1919 that stated, "[t]he phrase 'jazz band' was first used by Bert Kelly in Chicago in the fall of 1915, and was unknown in New Orleans." There is also

conjecture that the term made its way to Chicago with trombonist Tom Brown, who appeared as the front man for a band that played in Chicago in 1915. The band from New Orleans dubbed itself as a "Jass Band." Other possible contenders for originating the term in reference to a type of music are the Stein's Dixie Jass Band and The Original Jass Band. Legend has it that the latter was named by Chicago cafe manager Harry James. An article that appeared in the magazine *Song Lyrics* in November 1937 explained, "A dance-crazed couple shouted at the end of a dance, 'Jass it up boy, give us some more jass.' Promoter Harry James immediately grasped this word as the perfect moniker for popularizing the new craze."

52. The origins of jazz have deep connections to the musical traditions of New Orleans. The numerous marching bands that were prevalent in the city influenced the instrumentation of early jazz bands (brass, reeds, and drums), and small traveling bands of local musicians were vital in spreading early jazz throughout the South and elsewhere. Black musicians who played piano in the city's brothels, especially in the infamous Storyville district, had a profound influence on the early art form. Storyville was created in January of 1898 when an ordinance was introduced that limited brothels, saloons and other businesses of vice to a five block area of the city. The law was introduced by Alderman Sidney Story and much to the horror of the conservative politician, newspapers quickly dubbed the area Storyville. During its peak years Storyville contained 2,000 prostitutes and 30 piano players, including King Oliver, Clarence Williams and Jelly Roll Morton, by many considered to be the father of jazz. Storyville was closed down during World War I when the federal government issued an order prohibiting prostitution within a five-mile radius of military sites. Legal protests against the closing went all the way to the Supreme Court but were not successful.

53. "Jazz" (word)— From Wikipedia, the free encyclopedia.

54. *Ibid.*

55. *Ibid.*

56. "Notes and Half Notes" *La Crosse Tribune and Leader-Press*, La Crosse, WI, p. 7, col. 5.

57. "Jazz" (word)— From Wikipedia, the free encyclopedia.

58. "Jazz Here to Stay Say Music Experts" *Ogden Standard-Examiner*, Ogden, UT, January 27, 1924, p. 21, col. 1.

59. "Jazz" (word)— From Wikipedia, the free encyclopedia.

60. "Jazz Affects People Differently; Chief Lack Harmony is Internal" *Woodland Daily Democrat*, Woodland, CA, March 16, 1922, p. 5, col. 1.

61. "Jazz Music Declared Greatest Menace to Morals of Children" *San Antonio Light*, San Antonio, TX, January 29, 1922, p. 8, col. 5.

62. Joshua Zeitz, *Flapper: A Madcap Story of Sex, Style, Celebrity, and the Women Who Made America Modern* (New York: Crown Publishers, 2006) p. 23.

63. "Jazz Affects People Differently; Chief Lack Harmony is Internal" *Woodland Daily Democrat*, Woodland, CA, March 16, 1922, p. 5, col. 1.

64. "Knocking Jazz" *Mansfield News*, Mansfield, OH, August 2, 1925, p. 27, col. 2.

65. Anne Shaw Faulkner. "Does Jazz Put the Sin in Syncopation?" *Ladies Home Journal*, (August 1921, pp. 16–34.)

66. "Our Moaning Saxophone is Now Called Immoral" *The New York Times*, September 13, 1925, Section: Magazine, p. SM2.

67. "Magee Urges Ban on Jazz Music Pieces" *San Antonio Evening News*, San Antonio, TX, April 29. 1920, p. 1, col. 3.

68. Outraged at the treatment of American musicians being expelled from countries opposed to jazz, U.S. Representative Vaile of Colorado, a member of the Committee on Foreign Affairs, proposed a bill that would retaliate against any nation that denied admission to or restricted the activities of American jazz musicians. Many politicians became involved in the dispute over jazz. The U.S. Labor Department was pulled in to the fight when Joseph Weber, the President of the American Federation of Musicians petitioned the government agency to designate jazz musicians as laborers instead of musicians. He claimed that since jazz was not really music, jazz musicians were not really musicians.

69. "Ban on Jazz" *Lima News*, Lima, OH, September 27, 1928, p. 14, col. 2.

70. "Daily Almanac" *Oakland Tribune*, Oakland, CA, September 7, 1922, p. 20, cl. 3. Many considered jazz to be nothing more than a lot of noise. On March 2, 1922, the *Monessen Daily Independent* in Monessen, PA, included the following in an article about jazz:

> Then came jazz, which went one step farther in the direction of incoherence and satisfied the demand for mere noise. There are some folks who would rather get out on the streets and yell than hear a fine orchestra perform, and such people enjoy the thumping upon and blowing into eccentric instruments and the general noise and confusion of jazz music.

In an article in *Star Publications* in Chicago (2/5/20), the reporter humorously explained how the cacophony called jazz was born.

> The jazz band idea, according to a French paper, originated in the time of the Directory. At the concerts of the Cat orchestra were twenty cats, heads in a row on the keyboard of a harpsichord. The performer by striking the keys pulled the cats' tails, causing a caterwauling which sounded like a jazz band.

71. Anne Shaw Faulkner, pp. 16–34.)

72. "Ellingson to Aid Girl" *Evening State Journal and Lincoln Daily News*, Lincoln, NE, January 21, 1925, p. 2, col. 7.

73. "Dorothy Waits in Cell for Sentence to Prison" *Nevada State Journal*, Reno, NV, August 24, 1925, p. 1, col. 2.

On the day of the murder, Dorothy's mother suggested that her daughter look in the newspaper for a job. Dorothy explained that she already had plans to go out to a "jazz party," where she was to meet her friends, many of them male musicians. Mrs. Ellingson demanded her daughter stop her excessive nightlife, but Dorothy refused and the two argued. Dorothy then went into her brother's room, got his gun, and shot her mother as she was sitting on the bed putting on her shoes. Dorothy packed a suitcase, took whatever money she could find in the house, took a trolley into town where she checked into a cheap lodging house, and then went to the party. She danced the night away and the next day went shopping and to a movie. She was finally arrested after a fellow "night life companion" revealed her whereabouts. The girl showed no remorse and confessed to the shooting. During her first murder trial, Dorothy was so emotional, the trial was halted and a sanity hearing was held. During the hearing, Dorothy's father revealed that when his wife was six months pregnant with Dorothy, she tried to choke her husband to death while he slept. The defense claimed that this pre-natal event undoubtedly influenced Dorothy in later years. Dorothy was ruled to be insane and committed to the State Hospital in Napa, California for a month of observation. Psychologists at the hospital determined that Dorothy was in fact sane, and able to stand trial. In her second murder trial, the jury determined that the murder was without malice and unpremeditated. Dorothy was convicted of manslaughter and sentenced to prison at San Quentin. She calmly chewed gum while the verdict was read. As a result of the sensation created by the trial, the San Francisco Federation of Women's Clubs declared that it would take immediate steps "to stop moral infections" ("Life Term for Slayer of Mother" *Independent*, Helena, MT, January 18, 1925, p. 4, col. 3).

74. "Girl Admits Wild Revelry After Slaying Mother" *Oakland Tribune*, Oakland, CA, January 15, 1925, p. 1, col. 1.

75. "She Was the Life of the Party" *Sheboygan Journal*, Sheboygan, WI, January 19, 1925, p. 3, col. 4.

76. "French May Ban Jazz in Dancing" *The Washington Post*, Washington, D.C., June 13, 1920, p. 62, col. 7.

77. *Ibid*. In his article "The Jazz Path of Degradation" (*Ladies Home Journal*, 1/22, p. 22) John R. McMahon expanded on the effects of jazz music and jazz dancing in regards to ruined home-life. He wrote:

> Jazz is lewd to the physiological limit.... It is a path of degradation.... For the women it may mean impairment or defeat of motherhood. For the young man of marrying age it may spell a postponement into the infinite future of the undertaking of marital responsibilities.... If jazzing were an innocent and wholesome pastime it would still be a crime because of its injury to the home. How many married folk who dance are skulkers and deserters from their own firesides? If they do not neglect each other they are probably neglecting their children. It is a mania of selfish amusement. The idle female jazzer is a poor sort. Worse is the married male who side-steps his family obligations while practicing the newest movements with strange partners upon the waxed floor.

One popular fad during the 1920's was the jazz wedding. Accompanied by snappy jazz music, the bride and groom literally danced down the aisle. The marriages didn't always last. One husband sued for divorce because he realized his wife was "jazz crazy." The man lamented:

> I'm fond of dancing, but I don't want to dance every minute. My wife does. She jazzes out into the kitchen to get breakfast, one-steps while she's setting the table, fox-trots from the cupboard to the stove and jazzes while she's pouring out the coffee. She hums rag tunes all the time, and she's worked out a jazz orchestra with the dishpan and the carving knife for the main instruments and the glasses and the spoons for a kind of pep variation. I'm tired of it—myself!

(Quote from the *Oakland Tribune*, May 16, 1920, p. 6.)

78. *Ibid.*

79. "Oppose Jazz Near Hospital" *Portsmouth Daily Times,* Portsmouth, OH, February 5, 1926, p. 18, col. 1.

80. John R. McMahon. "The Jazz Path of Degradation" *Ladies Home Journal*, January 1922, p. 22.

81. "Jazz Dance Builds Healthy Race, Paul Whiteman Tells Flappers" *Wisconsin Rapids Daily Tribune*, Wisconsin Rapids, WI, March 3, 1925, p. 7, col. 4.

Chapter 17

1. Jane Grant, "Charleston Prances into Favor" *The New York Times,* August 30, 1925, Magazine Section, p. SM2.

2. "Mrs. Berlin Writes on the Charleston," *The New York Times,* February 7, 1926, p. 6.

3. Frances Rust, *Dance in Society: An Analysis of the Relationship between Social dance and Society, in England, from the Middle Ages to the Present day* (London: Routledge & Kegan Paul, 1969) p. 90.

4. Frederick Lewis Allen, "The Revolution in Manners and Morals." Many objected to the Charleston not only because it was believed to be immoral, but also because it was seen as a waste of time. *The New York Times*, March 8, 1929, p. 22, reported that in Bellaire, Ohio, nineteen-year-old schoolteacher Ruth Timmon was accused of teaching her students the Charleston and ignoring more scholarly pursuits in the classroom. She was brought before the school board to face the allegations. Others protested that the dance had no aesthetic redeeming qualities at all—that it was just stupid and ugly. As reported in the *San Antonio Light*, November 29, 1925, p. 19, col. 7, a judge in Washington D.C. fined a man for doing the Charleston on the street because "no one would dance the Charleston unless he had been drinking or was crazy." Hearing of the ruling, the chairman of the annual debutantes ball that year in Washington announced that "Since there'll be neither cocktails or lunatics at the bal de fete. I guess we'll have to ban the Charleston."

5. Marshall and Jean Stearns, *Jazz Dance: The Story of American Vernacular Dance.* (New York: Da Capo, 1994) p. 114, quoting an article in the *New Orleans States* from July 8, 1922.

6. Stearns, p. 114. According to article in the paper, at the time of publishing, the president of the Moral League, Generalissimo Leslie Schroeder, was only able to enlist one teenage girl in his anti-dance campaign.

7. Official restrictions against jazz dancing were widespread. In Russia, the Charleston was banned and American dances were denounced as "indecent products of the fat American Bourgeosie" (*The Helena Independent*, Helena, MT, January 4, 1927, p. 10, col. 2). In Rome, dance halls were raided by a special anti-dance police squad after officials in Italy "declared war against jazz dancing known as wicked hip wiggling" (*Gastonia Daily Gazette*, Gastonia, NC, January 28, 1926, p. 5, col. 7). In Vienna, Austrian authorities banned the dance and fined any who disobeyed the edict. In Bucharest, "the Charlestonian wiggle proved too much for [the city's] sense of propriety," and the Rumanian government levied a tax on the immoral dance. (*Charleston Daily Mail*, Charleston, July 11, 1927, p. 11, col. 2.) The Charleston caused an uproar wherever it was danced. Advocates of the dance vociferously defended their right to do it, while opponents fought for its demise. The *Dunkirk Evening Observer*, Dunkirk, NY, March 7, 1927, p. 17. col. 3. reported, "The Charleston is blamed for a riot in a Rio de Janeiro club in which three policemen were injured, a number of Charleston dancers arrested, and the interior of the club extensively damaged." The event took place in the "Club Gymnastico Portuguez" when several young Brazilians started to dance the Charleston. When the music was stopped they protested and "in a few minutes a free-for-all was in progress.... Finally the Charleston forces were surrounded and taken to the police station, but the advocates of less strenuous dances were by that time too weary to continue the program." When outright bans were not enacted, there would often be official chaperones to at least monitor the dancing. The *Charleston Gazette*, Charleston, WV, October 7, 1924, p. 7, col. 6, reported;

> In New York City, a dance hall czar was appointed to oversee local establishments and make sure dance halls presented "the proper environment for young people." The post was created by the Metropolitan Dance Hall Association in response to threats from the Women's City club. The ladies were concerned that such places fostered immoral behavior, and suggested the dance halls be "wiped out." A czarina, who was a member of the Women's club, was also appointed to assist the czar. The article added, "It is not known who the czardines will be, unless the men who frequent the dance halls may be called that."

The New York Times, April 14, 1928, Section: Business & Finance, p. 34, ran an article that told of how one official got caught in his own net;

> The mayor, and also acting President of the Board of Education and Chief of Police in Lodi New Jersey, Mr. Nicholas V. Monett, was arrested at a dance hall and charged with "aiding and abetting in the maintenance of a disorderly house." Immoral dancing was allegedly taking place at the establishment and the joint was raided. The mayor said that he "had visited the hall in the capacity of Chief of Police of the township."

Politicians and religious leaders were not the only ones who tried to regulate dancing. Dance teachers formed a powerful lobby in hopes of preventing unseemly influences in the dance. At the New York convention of Society of Dancing Teachers of America on August of 1925, the members "agreed that the flapper and sheik mode of doing the dance was to be combated...." In an effort to create rules to tone down the dance, they declared, "kicks, 'suggestive movements' and complex motions were eliminated. The feet must not be more than 45 degrees out of line with the body and there must be no leaning backwards." The dancing masters were demonstrating the new form of the dance when a woman who called herself "Hard-hearted Hannah from Savannah" broke into the convention and protested "in the name of the South" that kicks should not be taken out of the dance. (Quotes From: *The Fitchburg Sentinel*, August, 25, 1925, p. 3, col. 1.)

8. An article in *The New York Times*, June 13, 1926, p. 21, entitled "Arrest Of Dancers Bring Street Row" demonstrates the typical response of city officials trying to monitor the moral corruption they associated with the Charleston. In Canarsie Village, New York, 8-year-old Denora Cardona heard music coming from a loud speaker outside of a radio supply store and began to dance the Charleston. She attracted a crowd who tossed coins at her. Her friend, twelve-year old Anna Zalezo joined her and the crowd grew until the police arrived. Two policewomen pushed through the wall of onlookers in order to arrest the two girls and turn them in to the Children's Society "for improper guardianship." The crowd of spectators was not happy. One woman reportedly screamed, "Let 'em alone. They ain't no law against Charlestoning. Why don't you arrest some o' them society women. They dance it." The police ignored the protests and grabbed the children. A small riot resulted. A third police officer, patrolman William Dunn arrived and the melée was eventually broken up. Denora's mother was arrested for endangering the morals of a minor, and Anna's mother was arrested for interfering with an officer in performance of her duty. The eight-year-old was released to the custody of her parents but had to appear in Children's Court. Anna was turned over to the Children's Society. After the disturbance had been quelled, the radio outside the store began to play a waltz.

9. Allen. In the *Hamilton Evening Journal*, Hamilton, OH. August 8, 1925, p. 1, col. 2, choreographer Ned Wayburn declared that the Charleston was actually a very moral dance because those dancing it had to stand at least four to six inches away from each other in order to do the movements.

10. Margaret O'Leary, "More Ado About the Flapper" *The New York Times*, April 16, 1922, Section Book Review, p. 49.

11. "Condemns the Charleston" *The New York Times*, March 9, 1927, Section: Hotels and Restaurants Resorts, p. 28.

On February 25, 1924, p. 1, *The New York Times* quoted representatives of the Vatican denouncing jazz dances such as the Charleston;

> ... one of the causes of recent flagrant immorality, perhaps the most pernicious because the less apparent, is the modern dance ... this new industry of the feet, performed by the stimulus of distorted, panting notes of orchestra, should be watched severely.

Although many church leaders labeled the Charleston as immoral, others disagreed. In an article in *The New York Times* entitled "Dance the Charleston at Revival," January 19, 1926, p. 13, the following story was reported,

> At a religious revival in Chicago, three girls danced before the congregation and one, Sarah Riezinger performed a Charleston. The evangelist overseeing the event commented that he could not find Biblical evidence to support the banning of "harmless dancing."

12. "Origin of the 'Charleston' in Doubt but Its Popular" *Charleston Daily Mail*, Charleston WV, September 9, 1925, p. 28. Even seemingly enlightened individuals were offended by the Charleston's association with primitive African dance. Isadora Duncan was a groundbreaking dancer who celebrated in breaking the rules, but she detested the Charleston, saying it was nothing more than "tottering ape-like convulsions...." She protested that it echoed "the sensual convulsion

of the Negro ... ignoble [and] wiggling from the waist down" (Daly, p. 219). Impressario Sol Hurok lambasted the Charleston. He said, "Aside from the fact that it is the worst dance ever created, that it is condemned by intelligent people and that physicians have pointed out the harm it does the body, the Charleston is the most vulgar orgy a human being can indulge in" (*New Castle News*, June 24, 1926, p. 2).

13. "The Charleston will never do...." *The Modesto News-Herald*, Modesto, CA, July 1, 1926, p. 27, col. 7.

14. Rust, p. 90.

15. "Origin of the 'Charleston' in Doubt but Its Popular" *Charleston Daily Mail*, Charleston WV, September 9, 1925, p. 28. *The Abilene Daily Reporter*, Abilene, TX, March, 17, 1927, p. 18, col. 1, had a typical racist view of the Charleston's connection to African dance, when is reported the following story:

> The tale is told of an Australian composer who was surrounded by yelling cannibals in one of the darkest of the cannibal isles, and how he used one of the "modern" inventions of society to stave off disaster. The composer began to dance the Charleston, and pretty soon all the cannibals joined in the dance — men women and children. You see, here's proof if needed, that many of the modern dances aren't modern at all, but came direct from savagery.

The *New Castle News*, New Castle, PA, January 7, 1926, p. 18, col.1, had another offensive explanation of the dances origins;

> A fat Southern mammy stood in the doorway of her white folks drawing room watching the couples swaying in mad rhythm over the floor. She had raised Miss Cah'line and her mother before her and they had brought her in tonight to see the Charleston, the new step over which the world has gone wild. She stood an instant, her wide hips shaking with the syncopated air. And then she chuckled softly. "Lawd bless yo' chile," she said, "is dat the Chahlston yo'all is ravin' about. Why honey, Ah've done dance dat all mah life, and mah old daddy befoh me. Only we didn't know it was the Chahleston. But evah since Ah can remember ouah niggahs down in Chahleston have been doin' it down on the levees. Ah spects dat's how it got its name. But we nevah lowed the quality up No'th would be dancin it."

16. "1925: Dance Disowned: In Our Pages: 100, 75 AND 50 Years Ago, *International Herald Tribune*, Saturday, September 23, 2000. http://www.iht.com/articles/2000/09/23/edold.t_36.php. In the article "Origin of the 'Charleston' in Doubt but Its Popular," *Charleston Daily Mail*, Charleston WV, September 9, 1925, p. 28, there was a similar story:

> The origin of the dance is shrouded in mystery. Some of the teachers insist that it is an adaptation of negro steps and that is why they attribute it to the south. Charleston S.C. however, arises in its wrath and repudiates the pesky thing. It will have none of it. It's boys and girls remain aloof from such a dancing frolic. Charleston, W. Va., says it is not guilty and insists the South Carolina must deal with the "pest" one way or another. There are several other Charlestons in the postal guide, but there is no doubt that in the popular mind that Charleston, S.C., is intended, although it is clear that the dance, as it is danced today, did not have its beginnings in that city of culture and chivalry.

17. "How Science Says the Charleston 'Churns Up' Your Insides" *The Zanesville Signal*, Zanesville, OH, February 28, 1926, p. 31.

18. "Paris Authorities to Ban Charleston" *The Times*, San Mateo, CA, May 12, 1927, p. 5, col. 2.

19. "Ill, Charleston Dance Blamed" *The New York Times*, November 21,1925, p. 4, col. 3.

20. "Man Slips, Fall Breaks Arm Doing Charleston Dance"

New Castle News, New Castle, PA, April 4, 1928, p. 10, col. 5.
The New York Times, August 16, 1925, p. E15, reported that William Franken, a Volunteer Fireman in Union City, New Jersey, broke his leg while doing the Charleston for his fellow firemen. After the accident, it was recommended that the Charleston be avoided at the upcoming Volunteer Firemen's Ball.

21. "Office Cat" ("A woman fell and broke her wrist....") *The Sheboygan Press,* Sheboygan, WI, January 25, 1926, p. 14, col. 2. Another sad story in *The New York Times,* which appeared on June 21, 1926, p. 2, reported how six teenagers drowned after Arther Tessier, a local Charleston contest winner, was demonstrating the dance to his friends while they were in a rowboat on the St. Mary's River near Sault Ste. Marie, Michigan. The boy lost his balance and the rowboat capsized, killing all six.

22. "Jazz Dances 'Dangerous Sports,' Says Doctor, Adding 'Charleston Knee' To Mankind's Ills" *The New York Times,* April 29, 1928, Section: Editorial, p. E1.

23. Rust, p. 90.

24. Dancer and teacher Arthur Murray claimed that the Charleston actually cured his fallen arches.

25. "How Science Says the Charleston 'Churns Up' Your Insides" *The Zanesville Signal,* Zanesville, OH, February 28, 1926, p. 31.

26. According to *The New York Times,* November 20, 1926, p. 19 the Charleston was banned by the municipal authorities in Turkey "as a hygienic measure." *The New York Times,* August 8, 1926, p. E1, mentions uproar in Mexico over the issue;

The Department of Health has issued orders forbidding the dancing of the Charleston in public dance halls. The ground taken is that it constitutes such violent exercise that it is likely to cause heart failure. The department order adds that the dance is ugly and ungraceful; that it consists of contortions and the loosening of the joints, which are prejudicial to health, and that it is antagonistic to all artistic appearances.

27. Rust, p. 90.

28. "Charleston Dance Kills Schoolgirl, Doctor Declares" *New Castle News,* New Castle, PA, February 16, 1926, p, 6, col. 2.

29. Tully's death was reported in *The New York Times,* June 6, 1926, p. 15. The Charleston did require a lot of energy to perform. In an article in *The New York Times,* July 10, 1927, p. XX2, it was reported that Carl Tigerstedt, a doctor at the University of Helsinfors in Finland, had designed a machine to measure the energy utilized in dancing. The tests were performed on two medical students dancing in a small sealed chamber to the beat of a metronome since radio music was unavailable. The subjects danced for fifteen minutes. Five hundred and thirty-six calories of energy were expended by the subjects in that time dancing a Charleston, an expenditure of energy he stated that was "more tiring than a laborer sawing wood by hand." A waltz on the other hand only used two hundred and eighty calories. To put this in perspective, Dr. Tigerstedt stated when dancing a waltz "a person of normal weight expends in an hour as much bodily heat as would raise the temperature of five pints of water from freezing to boiling." The doctor pointed out that the limited space used in testing the subjects prevented maximum movement and so dancing in a dance hall or ballroom would take even more exertion. He listed the Charleston and the Mazurka as the two most taxing dances.

30. "How Science Says the Charleston 'Churns Up' Your Insides" *The Zanesville Signal,* Zanesville, OH, February 28, 1926, p. 31.

31. *Ibid.*

32. Rust, p. 90.

33. "Charleston — Everybody is Trying to Do It!" *New Castle News,* New Castle, PA, January 7, 1926, p. 18, col. 4.

34. "Charleston Banned in London's Dance Halls" *Oxnard Daily Courier,* Oxnard, CA, June 3, 1926, p. 4, col. 6.

35. "How the Charleston Wrecked the Dance Hall" *San Antonio Light,* August 9, 1925, p. 66.

36. "Vote to Ban Charleston" *The New York Times,* September 30, 1926, p. 15.

37. *Ibid.*

38. "Charleston Banned in London's Dance Halls" *Oxnard Daily Courier,* Oxnard, CA, June 3, 1926, p. 4, col. 6.

39. *Ibid.*

40. "Will the Charleston Bring That Plier Handle Silhouette" *The Port Arthur News,* Port Arthur, TX, January 10, 1926, p. 11, col. 3.

41. *The Port Arthur News,* p. 11. When interviewed for this article, World Charleston Champion Bee Jackson disagreed. She stated, "The Charleston is the modern fountain of youth and eternal health, to say nought [sic] of everlasting beauty." Jackson went on to say that the dance was "not only conducive to beauty and long life," but that it was "highly moral, ethical religious and pure." She was convinced of this because "not one single professional reformer or minister had chided her for her dance."

42. "Just Dumb" *La Crosse Tribune,* La Crosse, WI, April 27, 1926, p. 3, col. 1.

43. "Charleston — Everybody is Trying to Do It!" *New Castle News,* New Castle, PA, January 7, 1926, p. 18, col. 4.

44. "Ruins Yield Two Score" *Los Angeles Times,* July 6, 1925, Part I, p.1, col. 1.

45. "Why the 'Charleston' Was a Dance of Death" *The Galveston Daily News,* Galveston, TX, August 19, 1925, p. 8, col.2.

46. The Pickwick was located on the second floor of a five-story building on 12 Beach Street that was formerly the site of the Dreyfus Hotel. The rest of the building was vacant except for the club, which had about forty tables scattered throughout the establishment and featured a waxed linoleum dance floor. The Pickwick had been open about one year before its collapse. A popular gathering spot for all types of patrons, it was frequented by "politicians and bankers [who] brought parties there from the theatres and early closing dance places. Theatrical persons, boxers, sporting men, and a wide variety of others dropped in frequently. The club served light meals and much ginger ale. Patrons brought their own or bought liquor from bootleggers they met there. An orchestra played for dancing and a cabaret program from just before midnight to 3 o'clock. On holidays the time was extended." Quote from *The Charleston Gazette,* July 6, 1925, p. 2 , col. 3.

47. This fact was exposed during the grand jury testimony of the club's doorman George F. Callahan, and was reported in *The Fitchburg Sentinel,* July 23, 1925, p. 13, col. 1. Twelve of the victims were found near the front door trapped in a pocket under the rubble.

48. "12 Known Dead in Dance Hall Crash" *The Galveston Daily News,* July 5, 1925, p.10, col. 5.

49. *Ibid.*

50. *The Sheboygan Press,* Sheboygan, WI, July 6, 1925, p.1, col. 8. The nine-foot corpse was originally identified as Lieutenant Inspector "Benny' Alexander, but acquaintants of the police officer later said that the body was not that of Alexander. The account also gives graphic details of finding other victims in the rubble. In one, the paper reports on workers finding the body of a boxer, probably either Frank Tillo or "Neddo" Flannagan.

It was a fighting man, stiff and cold in death, but still crouched in a battle pose with left fist clenched and arm raised in guard, and with right arm drawn back and its knuckles gripping for a knockout. The stance was perfect ring stance and as if this were not enough to mark him as a fighter, he had a cauliflower ear. He was a grim battler, in a club of many battles, but death had won.

51. "Bodies Found in Club Ruins" *Los Angeles Times,* July 6, 1925, Part I, p.2, col. 6.

52. According to an account in *The Chicago Daily Herald,* July 10, 1925, p. 5, col. 5, most of the bodies were buried at least 15 to 20 feet below street level and were actually found in debris that had slide into the pit next to the Pickwick. The excavation site, where a garage was being built, was at least forty feet deep and was believed to have been partially responsible for the club's collapse. It was the wall along this side of the building that was the first to split and topple. At the trial, engineer Hugh Stanley Urquhart testified that he had actually inspected the building supports, on Friday, the day before the catastrophe and discovered that the earth surrounding the concrete piers had been dug away. He further stated that he had warned Hyman Bloomerg, who was lessee of the building, that this presented an imminent danger. Other contributing factors to the building's collapse were a fire that had occurred about four months earlier on April 13th. Firemen who had put out the fire testified before the grand jury that they had dumped at least 7,000 gallons of water on the second floor to extinguish the flames. William F. Glennon, who was the orchestra leader and brother of the club's manager testified that after the fire the dance floor had been moved from the center of the club to the side near the Beach Street Wall. James J. Hendrick, Boston building inspector had actually inspected the structure forty-eight hours before the disaster and pronounced it safe. After the accident he stated, "Although some of the woodwork was charred, the supporting timbers were not sufficiently damaged to warrant installation of new beams" (*The Kingston Daily Freeman,* Kingston, NY, July 6, 1925, p. 1, col. 7). On Wednesday, July 1st, three days before the collapse on the 4th, there was a heavy wind and rain storm in Boston, and part of the building's roof had blown off soaking the dance floor with water. A hole had been chopped in the floor to let the water drain off into the basement. Former Lieut. Governor Barry, who helped with the rescue efforts commented, "I had feared this disaster weeks before it happened. Several days ago I passed by the building, and its condition shocked and astounded me. I could not understand why the building had not been condemned. I saw that fifty supporting timbers and a side wall had been damaged by the recent fire. Ever since that I thought the building should be condemned. Its condition suggested a crash" (*The New York Times,* July 5, 1925, page 2, col. 1). At the trial, engineer General George W. Goethals, who had supervised the construction of the Panama Canal, revealed that the collapse was due to Pier Two giving away, triggering the breaking of the other building supports. In his testimony he stated that Pier Two was constructed of "the rottenest concrete I have ever seen" (*The Bridgeport Telegram,* August 12, 1925, p.4, col. 5.) Police and city officials had wanted to close the club earlier but didn't because it had a State Charter. After the collapse, it was discovered that the charter was issued for The Commercial Men's Club, which had shut down long ago and therefore, the charter was expired. Secretary of State, Frederick W. Cook defended his issuing the charter saying that he had been sent a report from the Boston police commissioner assuring him that the petitioners had never been found guilty of illegally selling liquor or of creating a gambling nuisance.

53. Some of the victims were first time visitors to the club, others were habitués. By Monday morning, July 6, 1925, the following were confirmed dead:

Stuart Henderson, 37
William Cochrane, 28
Frank Tillo, Boston boxing favorite
William Grossman, 36
James Glennon, 29, the floor manager of the club
John Mclaughlin, 30
Margaret (Peggy) Lawson
Francis McLean, 19
Henry Glavin, 33, a waiter at the club
James Congdon, 46, a waiter at the club
Loretta Keegan, 36
Frank (Teddy) Vara, 24

Pauline DeLuca, 35
Carl (Red) Paulsen, 23, taxi cab driver
Bartholomew O'Donnell, 24
Edward (Neddo) Flannagan, Boston boxing favorite
Edith Jordon, 28, a newlywed of just a few months was extricated from the tangled wreckage after nine hours. After being taken to the hospital, she asked to see her husband who had survived, but shortly afterwards, she died of shock
Margaret Murphy, 29
John (Johnnie) Scales, 21, who had been singing when the building collapsed
Paul Halleran, 33, patrolman who was there guarding the club
W. H. Marr, 30, coast guard cutter
Doris Stern, 24
Benjamin (Benny) Alexander, 41, police lieutenant-inspector, who was waiting in the club to apprehend a jewel thief he had been trailing
Joseph Phaneuf
Charles Smith
John Duffey, 30, singer and former boxer
William (Toots) Murray, 35, a criminal who was indicted for gas bombing the Rhode Island State Senate chamber in 1924
Esther Wilson
May Moore
Jere Longobardi, 38
Miss Nixon
Clara Frederick
Sarge Penta (or Lanza)
John Murphy
Calofaro
Celia McEachern, 22, sister of Lillian McIssac
Lillian McIssac, (listed as McGinnis in some accounts)
Ella Colley, a waitress
Bert Chapman
Francis Driscoll.

The following were missing and believed dead — Ella Cauley, 25, a waitress at the club, James (Bubba) Murray, a singer, Charles De Costis, Louis Lupo, Gusto Sylvester, Ethel Dixon, Mary McDonald, George Bell, Charles Smith, Charles Dicicco, Morris Black, Rose Cadigan.

Several patrons of the club that night were seriously injured sustaining cuts, abrasions, and broken bones, including fractured spines and skulls.

54. *The Kingston Daily Freeman,* Kingston, NY, July 6, 1925, p. 1, col. 7, stated that Robinson, a boxer, was shot in the leg. The man denied looting and told the police that he was entering the wreckage to get a better view of the rescue efforts. Police suspected that he and the others arrested "were after the stakes of a gambling game said to have been in progress in a vacant room above the dancers at the time the big building crumbled."

55. Ten defendants were eventually charged with manslaughter in the death of police officer Paul Halloran. One of the ten and an eleventh man were charged with maintaining a common nuisance. Those indicted for manslaughter were: John I. Pultz, the building contractor of the garage being erected on the lot next to the Pickwick, John M. Tobin, his superintendent, Harry M. Haven, contractor for the excavation, Lawrence J. Perkins, the foreman on the site, Nathan Fritz, a contactor who had made repairs on the Pickwick after the fire two weeks earlier, George C. Funk, the architect on the repair project, Hyman Bloomberg, lessee of the club building, Edward W. Roemer, city building department construction supervisor, and James J. Hendrick, city building inspector. Timothy Barry, president of the Pickwick was charged with manslaughter and maintaining a public nuisance. His brother Daniel Barry, was only charged with maintaining a public nuisance. Judge Henry P. Lummus presided

over the trial. By August 7, 1925, all of the defendants were acquitted in the indictments for manslaughter. The charges against the building inspector, James J Hendrick, the city building inspector, and the garage site foreman, Lawrence Perkins were held pending further evidence. In September of the same year, two civil suits were brought by the sister of boxer "Neddo" Flannagan for $15, 000 each against the Pultz Company claiming that it was their negligence in excavating the site next to the club that had caused the Pickwick's collapse.

56. *The New York Times*, Sunday, July 5, 1925, page 2, col. 1.

57. On November fourth of the same year of the Pickwick disaster, a second dance club in Boston actually collapsed, although no patrons were seriously injured. An account in the *New Castle News*, New Castle PA, November 4, 1925, p.11, col. 3, stated, "With a roar that reverberated through the south end, the three-story building at No. 576 Shawmut Avenue, not far from the site of the ill-fated Pickwick night club building, collapsed and tumbled into the street today."

58. "Death Toll Reaches Forty-Three" *The Sheboygan Press*, Sheboygan, WI, July 6, 1925, p.1, col. 8. The reference to the Charleston as the "dance of Death" can also be found in numerous other sources.

59. "Charleston Throw Building Out of Plumb" *San Antonio Express* October 16, 1925 p. 19, col. 8.

60. *Ibid.*

61. *The New York Times*, August 30, 1925, Section 2, p. 1, col. 7. In Denver, one dance hall was closed because the Charleston "not only shook the joists and rafters, but threatened to shimmy the whole building to destruction." *The Fresno Bee*, Fresno, CA, December 2, 1925, p. 5, col. 2. In Hoboken, New Jersey when one policeman outside the Grand street dance hall reported, "the cavorting of the Charlestonians made the building sway menacingly [sic]," city officials put a conditional ban on "the new flapper dance." *The Bridgeport Telegram*, Bridgeport, CT, August 27, 1925, p. 1, col. 2. *The Morning Herald*, Uniontown, PA, January 18, 1926, p. 15, col. 4, it stated,

> The Charleston joined the radio, bare knees and cigarets [sic] on the list of things banned at Goucher college. The latest ban was placed by Miss Elizabeth Mason, Midgard Hall mistress. Miss Mason followed her edict with an explanation that since the advent of the Charleston at Goucher, Midgard Hall's plaster was being jazzed off the ceilings and pictures, too, were tumbling down.

62. "How the 'Charleston' Wrecked the Dance Hall" *The San Antonio Light*, August, 9, 1925, p. 65, col. 1.

63. *Ibid.*

64. *Ibid.* The same article states,

> The Charleston had been danced in Boston about three months, and it appears to have been a special favorite in that hall. Probably the first time it was done the music and the performers hit the fundamental rhythm of the building, and without knowing what it meant, felt the structure respond. There is a feeling of subconscious satisfaction and an exhilarating sense of power in making big inanimate objects sway to the magical motions of puny human beings. This may account for the fact that the dancers at the Pickwick Club at once became addicts of the crazy Charleston.

65. *Ibid.* The same article continued:

> It is asserted that it was by resonance that Joshua and his host tumbled the walls of Jericho.... By blowing exactly the right note on all the bugles it is quite possible that the masonry might have been caused to disintegrate, just as the Pickwick Club did. The difficulty of this explanation lies in how Joshua got all his bugles in such perfect tune and how he knew just the right note. That in itself would be something of a miracle. More probable is the theory that it was a

coincidence of the tread of the marching host happening to hit the fundamental note of the wall.... For all we know, Joshua's host may have done a few steps out there not unlike the Charleston.

66. The Black Bottom (also sometimes called the Swanee Bottom) almost supplanted the Charleston as the most popular dance of the 1920's, after it was presented by the diminutive dance star Ann Pennington in George White's *Scandals of 1926*. Pennington, one of the most popular dancers of the period, stood only four feet, eleven and a half inches tall in heels. Her nickname was Tiny. According to the *Davenport Democrat and Leader*, Davenport, Iowa, October 3, 1926, p. 16, col. 5, Pennington "perfected [the dance] under the Mr. [Ned] Wayburn's guidance." In the *San Antonio Light*, May 9, 1937, p. 107, col. 3, it states,

> White looking for a successor to the Charleston, brought out "the Black Bottom," introduced by Ann Pennington. It also had Southern antecedents and was supposed to be based on the movements of a cow lifting her feet out of the black mud of the Mississippi. But that wasn't all, as interpreted by Miss Pennington, it was likewise the writhing of eels, the squirming of worms, the antics of crabs, the flight and pursuit of love-minded fish and the graceful waving of weeds on the muddy bottom.

Although the dance gained national attention when Pennington did it in the *Scandals*, it had been around for much longer before the production premiered in 1926. Henry "Rubberleg" Williams said, "That dance is as old as the hills.... Done all over the South — why, I remember doing it myself around 1915" (Stearns, p. 110). African American songwriter Perry Bradford had written a song describing the movements of the dance in a song entitled "Original Black Bottom Dance," which he composed in 1907 and which was published in 1919, long before the dance was presented in the *Scandals*. Interestingly, Bradford also references the Charleston in the lyric of the song;

> Now listen folks, open your ears,
> This rhythm you will hear —
> Charleston was on the afterbeat....

(Ned Wayburn actually described the Black Bottom as "one of the four hundred versions of the Charleston," in an article in the *Hamilton Evening Journal*, Hamilton, OH. August 8, 1925, p. 1, col. 2)

The Stearns points out that it was a commonly known that a black dancer, Freddie Taylor taught the Black Bottom to Ann Pennington. Charleston dancer Mae Barnes stated, "I introduced Ann Pennington to Freddie Taylor ... and she gave him a Cord automobile." Bradford related that George White had seen the Black Bottom danced in the Broadway production of *Dinah* in 1924 and hired three white composers (DeSylva, Henderson, and Brown) to come up with a song for the dance. Dance historians say the Black Bottom first made its appearance in New Orleans. Others claim it came by way of Georgia. It is likely that the dance grew out of an African American dance called the Jacksonville rounders dance, although other sources say that it was derived from a dance called the Echo. The hopping movements and slapping of the backside were believed to be based on the wigglings of the rear end of a cow trying to extricate itself from the mud. Some sources state that the dance was an adaptation of a dance called the Deep Muddy, and was popular in seedy saloons around 1905. *The Charleston Gazette*, Charleston, WV, November 25, 1927, p. 4, col. 3, quotes Mrs. Esther Gagnet as stating that the Black Bottom was originally performed by the cannibals of Sumaria. The article states, "The 'Black Bottom' did not come from Georgia or the Congo; it was not brought from Africa to America by old slaves; it is not an invention of dusky workers in the cotton fields of the south ... but a native dance of Sumatra which has been inexistence for some 800 years." The dance was immensely popular and young people scrambled to learn it. In an article entitled "Dancers! Get Ready for Instruction in Nifty Black Bottom" in *The Davenport Democrat and Leader*, Davenport Iowa, December 5, 1926, p. 19, col. 5, the writer tells of how the important it is to master the new fad. He writes, "The dancer who doesn't know the Black Bottom is going to be out of luck. Or, to borrow a recent wise crack, about as much use as a glass eye at a keyhole, and boys and girls, that's about the most useless thing a guy could picture without a kodak." As with the Charleston, the dance also had many opponents. *The San Antonio Light*, San Antonio TX, February 20, 1927, p. 10, col. 1, wrote, ""With fervor in her voice, Aimee Semple McPherson, famous Los Angeles evangelist, tonight declared that 'Satan has a strangle-hold on New York,' and that many of its young people — and old ones too, are 'black bottoming' on the road to hell.... 'Oh that Black Bottom,' she cried, 'the Black Bottom of hell, with every night club floor a trapdoor for innocence and youth.... It is all so cheap and gaudy." The evangelist went on to declare that patrons of nightclubs were following a will o' the wisp and falling into the bogs and quicksands of destruction." The article describes how MacPherson had visited Texas Guinan's Three Hundred Club in New York and invited the night club hostess and twenty-five of her dancing girls to hear her preach at the Glad Tidings Tabernacle. Guinan accepted and in return asked MacPherson to stay and see the entertainment at her club telling her, "We've got a Charleston dancer who is the best in the world, and that's taking in a lot of territory."

67. Stearns, p. 112.

68. Some source suggest that Leonard Reed was the first to blend tap and Charleston. Others such as Bill Robinson also utilized the Charleston while tapping.

69. Bessie Love is credited with performing the first onscreen Charleston in a film called *The King on Main Street* (1925). Two memorable films that featured the Charleston were Jean Renoir's *Sur un Air de Charleston* (1926) and *Fatal Footsteps* (1926). Renoir's film (also released under the title *Charleston Parade*) tells the story of a blackfaced space traveler who comes to Earth and discovers a young wild woman. She teaches him a native dance — the Charleston, and he decides to take her back home with him on his spaceship. Performed by African-American dancer Johnnie Huggins and his nearly nude white female lead, Renoir's wife, Catherine Hessling. Censorship boards in the United States and Europe criticized the film for its provocative sensuality. *Fatal Footsteps* tells the story of a man named Charley who is practicing for a Charleston contest. Despite setbacks, he invents special shoes that will guarantee his success in the competition.

Chapter 18

1. After the sixteenth century, the French *baler* was changed to *baller*. Scholars trace the origins of the word to the Late Latin word *ballare*, that in turn was derived from the Greek *ballizein*. The word "ball" is also related to the word "ballet." In *The Dictionary of the Dance*, pp. 49–50, W. G. Raffé provides fascinating information about some of the roots of the word. He states that "ballet" is derived from the Italian *Balia*, which was

> ... the ruling committee of the Medici family in Florence during the 14th century. The *balletto* was the "little ball" or *ballo* — in effect the display of power ceremonially by make it a "show of arms" — the *balia* was the fact of rule, the *ballo* was its visual form....

He goes on to say that in its most ancient form, "ballet" is descended from *boulé*, a Greek word for a town council of elders that "had its own especial ceremonial, notably the solemn entry into session, in procession and costume, prefaced by heralds." He adds on page 75,

... in demands for precedence, this social expression of place and position was always claimed and used — from processional to ritual dance in ceremonial occasions of public character. What happened in the secret meetings, whether of policy or of mystical and religious proceedings, is little known; and must be derived from the known link with Sparta: and with the grand affirmation of Lucian: "They dance out their religion."

The council dealt with secular matters, laws, revenues, and wars, and issued edicts, a practice that which Raffé points out was adopted in Rome as *Bullae*, later known as the "Papal Bull."

This legalistic aspect founded a long tradition, which endured in parallel with the aspect of display of princely courts in Europe, as the bailey, bailiff, and bail (deposit of prisoner for release). Its religious aspect continues in many ball games, from the method of voting for *boulé* by beans (black and white or red) into bowls, bowling, (*ballein*, throwing the ball) and fades into ballistics.

Raffé states that the word is also related to the word "bully" and "baloney."

2. Gretchen Schneider, "Ball." In *International Encyclopedia of Dance*. Vol. 1. Ed. Selma Jeanne Cohen, pp. 277–79 (New York: Oxford University Press, 1998) p. 277.

3. Oxford English Dictionary Online, "ball." http://www.oed.com

4. The sun as a symbol for Jesus Christ was often used by the early Christian church. References to the Latin term sol *justitae*, or "sun of righteousness" and the term *sol resuurectionis*, or the sun of resurrection are commonly found in early hymns and other writings.

5. Christians adopted the symbology of the labyrinth from the Greek legend of Theseus. In early Christian art, Satan was portrayed as the Minotaur complete with horns. Christ assumed the role of Theseus, who conquered Satan and emerged from the maze of death with the saved. Inlaid labyrinths of multi-colored stones were frequently built into church floors or walls, usually in the western-most portions of the church. The West was associated with the underworld and the setting of the sun in the West was compared to Christ's decent into Hell. The East was associated with the Resurrection and the rising of the sun. Labyrinths can still be seen in many of the great cathedrals in Europe. When the Muslims captured Palestine in medieval times, Church authorities allowed Christians to make symbolic pilgrimages to Jerusalem by crawling on their knees through the labyrinth. In France, this practice earned the labyrinth the name "Road to Jerusalem," or sometimes just "Jerusalem" or "Heaven." There are therefore two distinct usages of the labyrinth as a Christian symbol: first, as a representation of the underworld, and second, as the *Sancta Ecclesia* or Heavenly city. Labyrinth dances can be traced back to ancient times and were prevalent throughout the ancient world in Greece, Italy, and other places, although most were based on the Cretan legend of Theseus. One version in which the participants were dressed in armor and performed on horseback is mentioned in the *Aneid*. The dance was used in ritual ceremonies to symbolize the battle of good against evil.

6. Schneider, p.277.

7. T. A. Faulkner, *The Lure of the Dance: with Christ at the Ball* (Chicago: George W. Noble, 1916) pp. 49–50.

8. Elizabeth Aldrich, *From the Ballroom to Hell: Grace and Folly in Nineteenth-century Dance* (Evanston, IL: Northwestern University Press, 1991) p. xv, quoting Peter Shaw's essay in *Commentary*, 1988.

9. Robert Farris Thompson, *Tango: The Art History of Love* (New York: Vintage Books, 2005) p. 135.

10. Simon Collier, Artemis Cooper, Maria Susana Azzi, and Richard Martin. *Tango! The Dance, the Song, the Story* (London: Thames and Hudson Ltd., 1995) p. 172.

11. Collier, p. 176.

12. "What's the Twist Doing to Us?" *Independent Press-Telegram*, Long Beach, CA, March 10, 1963, p. 108, col. 1.

Bibliography

Publications

Adams, Dr. R. A. *The Social Dance*. Kansas City: 1921.

Aldrich, Elizabeth. *From the Ballroom to Hell: Grace and Folly in Nineteenth-century Dance*. Evanston, IL: Northwestern University Press, 1991.

Alsop, Susan Mary. *The Congress Dances*. New York: Harper & Row, 1984.

Arbeau, Thoinot. *Orchesography*. Translated by Mary Stewart Evans. New York: Dover Publications, 1967.

Armstrong, Lucile. *A Window on Folk Dance*. West Yorkshire, England: Springfield, 1985.

Asante, Kariamu Weish, editor. *African Dance: An Artistic, Historical, and Philosophical Inquiry*. Trenton, NJ: Africa World Press, 1996.

Asbury, Herbert. *The Barbary Coast: An Informal History of the San Francisco Underworld*. New York: Alfred Knopf, 1933.

Ayto, John. *Dictionary of Word Origins*. New York: Arcade, 1990.

Backman, E. Louis. *Religious Dances in the Christian Church and in Popular Medicine*. London: George Allen & Unwin, 1952.

Baim, Jo. *Tango: The Creation of a Cultural Icon*. Bloomington: Indiana University Press, 2007.

Baker, Jean-Claude, and Chris Chase. *Josephine: The Hungry Heart*. New York: Random House, 1993.

Bell, Ernest. *Fighting the Traffic in Young Girls or War on the White Slave Trade*. 1910.

Beryl and Associates, editors. *Immorality of Modern Dances*. New York: Everitt and Francis Co. [etc.], 1904.

Bowen, Eza, series editor. *This Fabulous Century: 1920–1930*. Time-Life Books, vol. III. New York: Time-Life Books, 1969.

Breuer, Katharina. *Dances of Austria*. Part of the series *Handbooks of European National Dances*, Ed. Violet Alford. New York: Chanticleer Press, 1948.

Bricktop, with James Haskins. *Bricktop: Prohibition Harlem, café society Paris, movie-mad Rome — the queen of the nightclubs tells the exuberant story of a fabulous life*. New York: Antheneum, 1983.

Brion, Marcel. *Daily Life in the Vienna of Mozart and Schubert*. New York: Macmillan Company, 1962.

Brookes, James H. *The Modern Dance*. Chicago: The Church Press, 1890s.

Brooks, Tim. *Lost Sounds: Blacks and the Birth of the Recording Industry*. Champaign, IL: University of Illinois Press, 2005.

Brown, Alan. "Pavan." In *The New Grove Dictionary of Music and Musicians*. Vol. 14. Ed. Stanley Sadie, pp. 311–14. London: McMillan, 1980.

Brown, Scott E. *James P. Johnson: A Case of Mistaken Identity*. Metuchen, NJ: The Scarecrow Press, 1986.

Buckman, Peter. *Let's Dance: Social, Ballroom and Folk Dancing*. New York: Paddington Press, 1978.

Campbell, Joseph. *Joseph Campbell: The Power of Myth with Bill Moyers*. Ed. Betty Sue Flowers. New York: Doubleday, 1988.

Carner, Mosco. *The Waltz*. New York: Chanticleer Press, 1948.

Cass, Joan. *Dancing Through History*. Englewood Cliffs, NJ: Prentice Hall, 1993.

Castle, Irene. *Castles in the Air*. Garden City, NY: Da Capo, 1980 — reprint of 1958 edition.

Castle, Mr. & Mrs. Vernon. *Modern Dancing*. New York: Harper, 1914.

Cohen, Selma Jeanne. *Dance as Theatre Art: Source Readings in Dance History from 1581 to the Present*. New York: Harper Row, 1974.

Collier, Simon, Atemis Cooper, Maria Susana Azzi, and Richard Martin. *Tango! The Dance, the Song, the Story*. London: Thames and Hudson Ltd., 1995.

Crawford, Mary Caroline. *Romantic Days in Old Boston: The Story of the City and of Its People During the Nineteenth Century*. Boston: Little, Brown and Co., 1910.

Crozier, Gladys Beattie. *The Tango and How to Dance It*. London: Andrew Melrose, 1913.

Cullen, Frank and Florence Hackman. *Vaudeville, Old and New: An Encyclopedia of Variety Performers in America*. Vol. I. New York: Routledge, 2006.

Daly, Ann. *Done Into Dance: Isadora Duncan in America*. Bloomington, IN: Indiana University Press, 1995.

Dalzell, Tom. *Flappers 2 Rappers: American Youth Slang*. Springfield, MA: Merriam-Webster, Inc., 1996.

Dannett, Sylvia G. L., and Frank Rachel. *Down Memory Lane: Arthur Murray's Picture Story of Social Dancing*. New York: Greenberg, 1954.

Dawson, Jim. *The Twist: The Story of the Song and Dance the Changed the World*. Boston: Faber & Faber, 1995.

Desmond, Jane C., editor. *Meaning in Motion: New Cultural Studies of Dance*. Durham: Duke University Press, 1997.

Desrat. G. *Traité de la danse, contenant la théorie et l'histoire des danses anciennes et modernes. Avec toutes les figures les plus nouvelles du cotillon*. Paris: H. Delarue et cie, 190-?.

Dodworth, Allen. *Dancing and Its Relations to Education and Social Life*. New York: Harper, 1888.

Donington, Robert. "Volta (i)." In *The New Grove Dictionary of Music and Musicians*. Vol. 20. Ed. Stanley Sadie, pp. 74–5. London: McMillan, 1980.

Driver, Ian. *A Century of Dance: A Hundred Years of Musical Movement, from Waltz to Hip Hop*. London: Octopus Publishing Group, 2001.

Duggan, Anne Schley, Jeanette Schlottman, and Abbie Rutledge. *Folk Dances of European Countries.* New York: Barnes, 1948.

Egan, Bill. *Florence Mills: Harlem Jazz Queen.* Lanham, MD: Scarecrow Press, 2004.

Ellfeldt, Lois. *Folk Dance.* Dubuque: Wm. C. Brown, 1969.

Erenberg, Lewis. *Steppin' Out: New York Nightlife and the Transformation of American Culture, 1890 -1930.* Chicago: University of Chicago Press, 1981.

Faulkner, T. A. *From the Ballroom to Hell.* Chicago: R. B. McKnight, 1894.

_____. *The Lure of the Dance: with Christ at the Ball.* Chicago: George W. Noble, 1916.

Fonteyn, Margot. *The Magic of Dance.* New York: Afred A. Knopf, 1979.

Franks, A. H. *Social Dance: A Short History.* London: Routledge and Kegan Paul, 1963.

Friedland, Lee Ellen. "Folk Dance History." In *International Encyclopedia of Dance.* Vol. 3. Ed. Selma Jeanne Cohen, pp. 29–38. New York: Oxford University Press, 1998.

Funk, Charles Earle. *Heavens to Betsy! And Other Curious Sayings.* New York: Harper & Row, 1983.

Gilbert, Melvin B. *The Director: Dancing Deportment, Etiquette, Aesthetics, Physical Training.* Portland, ME: Melvin Ballou Gilbert, 1898, (reprint by Dance Horizons 1975 or 1976).

Golden, Eve. *Vernon and Irene Castle's Ragtime Revolution.* Lexington, KY: University Press of Kentucky, 2007.

Gottschild, Brenda Dixon. *Waltzing in the Dark: African American Vaudeville and Race Politics in the Swing Era.* New York: Palgrove, 2000.

Gronow, Captain Rees Howell. *Reminiscences of Captain Gronow, Formerly of the Grenadier Guards, and N. P. for Stafford: being Anecdotes of the camp, the court, and the clubs, at the close of the last war with France. Related by himself.* (commonly known as *The Reminiscences and Recollections of Captain Gronow.*) London: Smith, Elder and Co,. 18?) This version of Gronow's memoirs was taken from the Online Library and edited by Tobias D. Robinson, 2001.

Grove, George, and Stanley Sadie. *The New Grove Dictionary of Music and Musicians.* London: McMillan, 1980.

Grove, Lilly. *Dancing.* London: Longmans, Green, and Co., 1907.

Guilcher, Yves. "France: Recreational Dance." In *International Encyclopedia of Dance.* Vol. 3. Ed. Selma Jeanne Cohen, pp. 63–65. New York: Oxford University Press, 1998.

Ham, Mordecai Franklin. *Light on the Dance: The Modern Dance; A Historical and Analytical Treatment of the Subject Religious, Social, Hygienic, Industrial Aspects As viewed by The Pulpit, the Press, Medical Authorities, Municipal Authorities, Social Workers, etc.* (No publisher listed), 1916.

Harris, William H., and Judith S. Levey, Editors. *The New Columbia Encyclopedia.* New York: Columbia University Press, 1975.

Harris-Warrick, Rebecca. "Allemande" In *International Encyclopedia of Dance.* Vol. 1. Ed. Selma Jeanne Cohen, p. 45–7. New York: Oxford University Press, 1998.

Haskell, Arnold. *The Wonderful World of Dance.* Garden City, NY: Garden City Books, 1960.

Hillgrove, Thomas. *A Complete Practical Guide to the Art of Dancing.* New York, 1863

_____. *Hillgrove's Ballroom Guide and Practical Dancer.* New York, 1863 (reproduction 1992).

Hughes, Kristine. *The Writer's Guide to Everyday Life in Regency and Victorian England, From 1811–1901.* Cincinnati: Writer's Digest Books, 1998.

Jaffé, Nigel Allenby. *Folk Dances of Europe.* North Yorkshire, England: Folk Dance Enterprises, 1990.

Jennings, Peter, and Todd Brewster. *The Century.* New York: Doubleday, 1998.

Jones, Bessie and Hawes, Bessie Lomax. *Step It Down: Games, Plays, Songs, and Stories from the Afro-American Heritage.* New York: Harper & Row, 1972.

Katz, Ruth. "The Egalitarian Waltz." In *Comparative Studies in Society and History.* New York: Cambridge University Press, June 1973. Also in *What is Dance? Readings in Theory and Criticism.* Ed. Roger Copeland and Marshall Cohen. Oxford: Oxford University Press, 1983.

Kirstein, Lincoln. *Dance: A Short History of Classic Theatrical Dancing.* Princeton: Dance Horizons/ Princeton Book Co., 1987.

Knowles, Mark. *Tap Roots: The Early History of Tap Dancing.* Jefferson, NC: McFarland, 2002.

Lamb, Andrew. "Waltz." In *The New Grove Dictionary of Music and Musicians.* Vol. 20. Ed. Stanley Sadie, pp. 200–6. London: McMillan, 1980.

Latham, Angela J. *Posing a Threat: Flappers, Chorus Girls, and other Brazen Performers of the American 1920s.* Hanover: Wesleyan University Press, 2000.

Lawson, Joan. *European Folk Dance.* London: Sir Isaac Pittman & Sons, 1953.

Longford, Elizabeth. *Victoria R.I.* New York: Harper & Row, 1973.

Lytle, H. W. and John Dillon. *From Dance Hall to White Slavery.* Chicago: Charles C. Thompson, 1912.

Malnig, Julie. *Dancing Till Dawn: A Century of Exhibition Ballroom Dance.* New York: New York University Press, 1992.

Malone, Jacqui. *Steppin' On the Blues: The Visible Rhythms of African American Dance.* Chicago: University of Illinois Press, 1996.

McDonagh, Don. *Dance Fever.* New York: Random House, 1979.

_____. "Social Dance: Twentieth-Century Social Dance before 1960." In *International Encyclopedia of Dance.* Vol. 5. Ed. Selma Jeanne Cohen, p. 626–31. New York: Oxford University Press, 1998.

McGowan, Margaret M. "Balet Comique de La Royne, Le" In *International Encyclopedia of Dance.* Vol. 1. Ed. Selma Jeanne Cohen, p. 275–7. New York: Oxford University Press, 1998.

Miller, Marilyn Grace. *Rise and Fall of the Cosmic Race: The Cult of Mestizaje in Latin America.* Austin: University of Texas Press, 2004.

Miller, Nathan. *New World Coming: The 1920s and the Making of Modern America.* Cambridge, MA: Da Capo Press, 2003.

Mish, Frederick C., Editor. *Merriam-Webster's Collegiate Dictionary,* Tenth Edition. Springfield, MA: Merriam-Webster, Inc., 1994.

Moore, Arabella E. *The dance, ancient and modern, translated from the French.* Philadelphia: A. Moore, 1900.

Morgan, Thomas L., and William Barlow. *From Cakewalks to Concert Halls: An Illustrated History of*

African American Popular Music From 1895 to 1930. Washington D. C.: Elliott & Clark, 1992.

Morley, Sheridan. *Shall We Dance: The Life of Ginger Rogers.* New York: St. Martins Press, 1995.

Mouvet, Maurice. *Maurice's Art of Dancing: an autobiographical sketch with complete descriptions of modern dances and full illustrations showing the various steps and positions.* New York: G. Schirmer, 1915.

Murphy, Sophia. *The Duchess of Devonshire's Ball.* London: Sidgwick & Jackson, 1984.

Nettl, Paul. *The Story of Dance Music.* New York: Philosophical Library, 1947.

O'Neill, Rosetta. "The Dodworth Family and Ballroom Dancing in New York" In *Chronicles of the American Dance.* Ed. Paul Magriel, 81–100. New York: Henry Holt, 1948.

Partridge, Eric. *Origins: A Short Etymological Dictionary of Modern English.* New York: MacMillan, 1959.

_____. *The Dictionary of Slang and Unconventional English.* New York: MacMillan, 1961.

Peiss, Kathy. *Cheap Amusements: Working Women and Leisure in Turn-of-the-Century.* New York. Philadelphia: Temple University Press, 1986.

Petermann, Kurt. "Germany: Traditional and Social Dance." In *International Encyclopedia of Dance.* Vol. 3. Ed. Selma Jeanne Cohen, pp. 138–143. New York: Oxford University Press, 1998.

Peterson, Jr., Bernard L. *Profiles of African American Stage Performers and Theatre People, 1816–1960.* Westport, CT: Greenwood Press, 2001.

Poole, Daniel. *What Jane Austen Ate and Charles Dickens Knew: From Fox Hunting to Whist — the Facts of Daily Life in 19th-Century England.* New York: Simon & Schuster, 1993.

Quirey, Brenda. *May I Have the Pleasure? The Story of Popular Dancing.* London: Dance Books, 1987.

Quirk, Lawrence J., and William Schoell. *Joan Crawford: the Essential Biography.* Lexington: University of Kentucky Press, 2002.

Rae, Noel, editor. *Witnessing America: The Library of Congress Book of Firsthand Accounts of Life in America 1600–1900.* New York: Penguin, 1996.

Raffé, W.G. *Dictionary of the Dance.* New York: Barnes, 1964.

Reeser, Eduard. *The History of the Waltz,* translated from the Dutch by W. A. G. Doyle-Davidson. London: Sidwick and Jackson (nd.)

Rehart, Catherine. *The Valley's Legends and Legacies.* Sanger, CA: Quill Driver Books/Word Dancer Press, 1996.

Richardson, Philip J. S. *The Social Dances of the Nineteenth Century in England.* London: Herbert Jenkins, 1960.

Rogers, Ginger. *Ginger: My Story.* New York: Harper Collins, 1991.

Rose, Phyliss. *Jazz Cleopatra: Josephine Baker in Her Time.* New York: Vintage Books, 1991.

Royce, Anya Peterson. *The Anthropology of Dance.* Bloomington: Indiana University Press, 1977.

Rust, Frances. *Dance in Society: An Analysis of the Relationship between Social dance and Society, in England, from the Middle Ages to the Present day.* London: Routledge & Kegan Paul, 1969.

Sachs, Curt. *World History of the Dance.* New York: W.W. Norton, 1937.

Sanders, Coyne Steven, and Tom Gilbert. *Desilu: The Story of Lucille Ball and Desi Arnaz.* New York: Harper Collins, 1994.

Schneider, Gretchen. "Ball." In *International Encyclopedia of Dance.* Vol. 1. Ed. Selma Jeanne Cohen, pp. 277–79. New York: Oxford University Press, 1998.

_____. "Social Dance: Nineteenth-Century Social Dance." In *International Encyclopedia of Dance.* Vol. 5. Ed. Selma Jeanne Cohen, pp. 623–26. New York: Oxford University Press, 1998.

_____. "United States of America: An Overview." In *International Encyclopedia of Dance.* Vol. 6. Ed. Selma Jeanne Cohen, pp. 230–53. New York: Oxford University Press, 1998.

Scholes, Percy A. *The Concise Oxford Dictionary of Music.* London: Oxford University Press, 1977.

Sharp, Cecil J. *The Country Dance Book,* Part II. London: Novello & Co., 1927.

Shaw, Arnold. *The Jazz Age: Popular Music in the 1920's.* New York: Oxford University Press, 1987.

Shaw, Lloyd. *The Round Dance Book: A Century of Waltzing.* Caldwell, Idaho: Caxton Printers, 1948.

Shawn, Ted. *Every Little Movement: A Book about Francois Delsarte.* New York: Dance Horizons, reprint 1974.

Shipley, Joseph Twadell. *Modern French Poetry: An Anthology.* Manchester, NH: Ayer Publishing, 1972.

Sorell, Walter. *The Dance through the Ages.* New York, Grosset & Dunlap, 1967.

Stearns, Marshall. *The Story of Jazz.* (New York: Oxford University Press, 1956.

Stearns, Marshall and Jean Stearns. *Jazz Dance: The Story of American Vernacular Dance.* New York: Da Capo, 1994.

Stough, Henry W. *Across the Dead Line of Amusements.* New York: Fleming H. Revell Co., 1912.

Stratyner, Barbara. *Ned Wayburn and the Dance Routine: From Vaudeville to the Ziegfeld Follies.* (Studies in Dance History, No. 13) Madison, WI: Society of Dance History Scholars, 1996.

Strobel, Desmond F. "Cotillon." In *International Encyclopedia of Dance.* Vol. 2. Ed. Selma Jeanne Cohen, p. 251–53. New York: Oxford University Press, 1998.

_____. "Polka." In *International Encyclopedia of Dance.* Vol. 5. Ed. Selma Jeanne Cohen, p. 221–23. New York: Oxford University Press, 1998.

_____. "Quadrille." In *International Encyclopedia of Dance.* Vol. 6. Ed. Selma Jeanne Cohen, p. 285–87. New York: Oxford University Press, 1998.

_____. "Waltz." In *International Encyclopedia of Dance.* Vol. 6. Ed. Selma Jeanne Cohen, p. 359–362. New York: Oxford University Press, 1998.

Suskin, Steven. *Show Tunes 1905–1991: The Songs, Shows and Careers of Broadway's Major Composers.* New York: Limelight Editions, 1992.

Sutton, Julia. "Arbeau, Thoinet." In *International Encyclopedia of Dance.* Vol. 4. Ed. Selma Jeanne Cohen, p. 579–83. New York: Oxford University Press, 1998.

_____. "Negri, Cesare." In *International Encyclopedia of Dance.* Vol. 1. Ed. Selma Jeanne Cohen, p. 103–7. New York: Oxford University Press, 1998.

Sutton, Julia, with Patricia Weeks Rader. "Volta." In *International Encyclopedia of Dance.* Vol. 6. Ed. Selma Jeanne Cohen, p. 349–51. New York: Oxford University Press, 1998.

Tawa, Nicholas E. *Supremely American: Popular Song in the 20th Century: Styles and Singers and What They Said About America.* Lanham, MD: Scarecrow Press, 2005.

Thompson, Allison. *Dancing Through Time: Western Social Dance in Literature, 1400–1918: Selections.* Jefferson, NC: McFarland, 1998.

Thurman, Wallace. Ed. by Singh, Amritjit, and Scott, Daniel III. *The Collected Writings of Wallace Thurman: A Harlem Renaissance Reader.* New Brunswick, NJ: Rutgers University Press, 2003.

Thompson, Robert Farris. *Tango: The Art History of Love.* New York: Vintage Books, 2005.

Wagner, Ann. *Adversaries of Dance: From the Puritans to the Present.* Chicago: U. of Illinois, 1997.

Wallace, Carol McD., McDonagh Don, Druesedow, Jean L., Libin, Laurence, and Old, Constance. *Dance: A Very Social History.* New York: Rizzoli, 1986.

Wechsberg, Joseph. *The Waltz Emperors: The Life and Times and Music of the Strauss Family.* New York: G. P. Putnam's Sons, 1973.

Wilkinson, William Cleaver. *The Dance of Modern Society.* New York: Funk & Wagnalls, 1892.

Woll, Allen. *Black Musical Theatre: From Coontown to Dreamgirls.* New York: Da Capo Press, 1989.

Yablonsky, Lewis. *George Raft.* New York: McGraw-Hill, 1974.

Yaraman, Sevin H. *Revolving Embrace: The Waltz as Sex, Steps, and Sound.* (Monographs in Musicology No. 12) Hillsdale, NY: Pendragon Press, 2002.

Zeitz, Joshua. *Flapper: A Madcap Story of Sex, Style, Celebrity, and the Women Who Made America Modern.* New York: Crown Publishers, 2006.

Ziegfeld, Richard and Paulette. *The Ziegfeld Touch: The Life and Times of Florenz Ziegfeld, Jr.* New York: Harry N. Abrams, 1993.

Articles

"Abused Turkey Trot Spreads in London" *The New York Times*, February 18, 1912, Section: Transatlantic Wireless, Cable and Sporting Sections, p. C2.

"Academicians *Hear the Tango Praised*" *The New York Times*, October 26, 1913, Section: Foreign News Sports Want Advertisements, p. C4.

"All Denounce the Tango" *The New York Times*, January 7, 1914, p. 4.

"All London Crazy Over Turkey Trot; Hostesses Despair" *The Milford Mail*, Milford, Iowa, July 24, 1913, p. 6, col. 1.

"All New York Now Madly Whirling in the Tango" *The New York Times*, January 4, 1914, Section: Magazine Section, P. SM8.

"Another Tragedy in the Fateful Sage of America's Idolized Dance Stars" *The Port Arthur News*, Port Arthur, TX, January 19, 1936, p. 52.

"Approve Modern Dances" *The New York Times*, August 30, 1925, p. 16

"Arraign Boston Architect on Charge of Manslaughter" *The Lowell Sun*, Lowell, MA, July 14, 1925, p. 1, col. 5.

"Arrest Of Mouvet Shocks Wife in Paris" *The New York Times*, October 27, 1927, p. 5.

"Attacks Slit Skirt" *The New York Times*, July 20, 1913, p. 2.

Austin, Fred. "The Charleston Traces Its Ancestry Back 400 Years" *The New York Times*, August 8, 1926, Magazine Section, SM2.

"Ban Charleston in Mexico" *The New York Times*, August 8, 1926, Section: Editorial General News Financial and Business News Business Opportunities, p. E1.

"Ban 'Grizzly Bear' at Yale" *The New York Times*, January 21, 1912, Transatlantic Wireless Cable and Sporting Sections, p. C2.

"Ban on Jazz" *Lima News*, Lima, OH, September 27, 1928, p. 14, col. 2.

"Ban the Turkey Trot" *The New York Times*, April 8, 1912, p. 3.

"Bans Turkey Trot at Panama" *The New York Times*, May 21, 1913, p. 3.

Barry, Richard. "Tango Pirates Infest Broadway" *The New York Times*, May 30, 1915, Section: Magazine Section, p. SM16.

Becker, Bruce. *Penn State Daily Collegian*, April 30, 1979, p. 13.

"Being Jazz Crazy" (Winifred Black Writes About Folks and Things) *Oakland Tribune*, Oakland, CA, May 16, 1920, p. 6. col. 8.

"Berlin Calls Jazz American Folk Music" *The New York Times*, January 10, 1925, p. 2.

"Billy Sunday Raps Nuptial Slackers" *The New York Times*, April 13, 1917, p. 7.

"Bishops Differ on New Dancing Steps" *The New York Times*, January 19, 1914, p. 6.

"Black Bottom Facing Mile-step in Dance Battle" *The Bridgeport Telegram*, Bridgeport, CT, October 26, 1926, p. 9, col. 3.

"'Black Bottom' Finds Great Vogue in East" *Davenport Democrat and Leader*, Davenport, Iowa, October 3, 1926, p. 16, col. 5.

"Bodies Found in Club Ruins" *Los Angeles Times*, July 6, 1925, Part I, p.2, col. 6.

"Bodies of 39 are Taken From Ruins of Wrecked Club" *Charleston Gazette*, July 6, 1925, p.1, col.6

"'Bomb' in Murray's in Mabel Hite's Urn" *The New York Times*, November 29, 1915, p. 6.

"Boston Bans the Tango" *The New York Times*, October 12, 1913, p. 1.

"Boston Hotel Collapses While Holiday Party in Progress; 12 Known Dead, 17 in Hospital" *Albuquerque Morning Journal*, Albuquerque, NM, July 5, 1925, p. 1, col. 1.

Bourne, Stephan. "Obituary: Maude Russell" *The Independent*, London, May 9, 2001.

"Breaks Arm in Tango" *The New York Times*, March 12, 1913, p. 4.

"Breaks His Leg Dancing" *The New York Times*, August 16, 1925, Financial and Business News Business Opportunities Editorial, p. E15.

"Broadway Sees Raid on Dance; 100 Seized" *The New York Times*, February 15, 1921, p. 8.

"Brought 'Tango' to America" *The New York Times*, January 17, 1914, p. 8.

"Building Death Cases Dismissed" *The Charleston Gazette*, Charleston, WV, August 8, 1925, p.1, col.7

"Bury Pickwick Club Victims" *The Lowell Sun*, Lowell, MA, July 7, 1925, p. 16, col. 4.

"Calls Dance Mania Psychic Epidemic" *The New York Times*, April 26, 1914, Section: Editorial Section Foreign News Sports Want Advertisements, p. C8.

"Calls Tango 'Solemn'" *The New York Times*, November 2, 1913, Section: Foreign News Sports Want Advertisements, p. C2.

"The Cannibals of Sumatra Credited (or Blamed) for the 'Black Bottom'" *The Charleston Gazette*, Charleston, WV, November 25, 1927, p. 4, col. 3.

"Canon Assails Our New Dances" *The New York Times*, August 25, 1913, p. 3

"Capitol Gives Double Header in Vaudeville" *Davenport Democrat and Leader*, Davenport, IA, March 6, 1927, p. 18, col. 1.

Carroll, Alfred. "Concerning 'Round Dances'" *Harper's New Monthly Magazine*, vol. 32, issue 191, April 1866, pp. 614–616.

"'A Certain Party' an Amusing Farce" *The New York Times*, April 24, 1911, p. 13.

"Challenges a 'Trotter'" *The New York Times*, July 10, 1913, p. 3.

"Champion Dancer of Vienna" *The San Antonio Light*, January 31, 1932, p. 49, col. 3.

"Champions of Flapper Cause Parry Menacing Thrusts of Critics in United States," *Fort Wayne Journal-Gazette*, Fort Wayne, IN, May 7, 1922, p. 34, col. 4.

"Charleston—Everybody is Trying to Do It!" *New Castle News*, New Castle, PA, January 7, 1926, p. 18, col. 7.

"Charleston as Wrestling Aid Swells West Virginia Squad" *The New York Times*, January 39, 1926, Section: Sports, p. 10.

"Charleston Banned As Joists, Rafters Rattle" *The Fresno Bee*, Fresno, CA, December 2, 1925, p. 5, col. 2.

"Charleston Banned by Debs as Judge Makes Hard Remarks" *The San Antonio Light*, San Antonio, TX, November 29, 1925, p. 19, col. 7.

"Charleston Banned in London's Dance Halls" *The Oxnard Daily Courier*, Oxnard, CA, June 3, 1926, p. 4, col. 6.

"Charleston Causes Death" *The New York Times*, June 6, 1926, p. 15

"Charleston Contest Banned in Detroit" *The Lancaster Daily Gazette*, Lancaster, OH, January 28, 1926 p. 5, col. 5.

"Charleston Dance Barred" *The New York Times*, July 26, 1925, p. 23.

"Charleston Dance Kills Schoolgirl, Doctor Declares" *New Castle News*, New Castle, PA, February 16, 1926, p, 6, col. 2.

"Charleston in Rowboat Costs Lives of Six; Boy Demonstrating Dance Capsizes Craft" *The New York Times*, June 21, 1926, p. 2

"The Charleston is Destined to be Popular and Lasting, Says Local Dance Instructor" *The Davenport Democrat and Leader*, Davenport, IA, November 1, 1925, p. 18, col. 2.

"Charleston is Tough On Plastering" *The Morning Herald*, Uniontown, PA, January 18, 1926, p. 15, col. 4.

"Charleston Splits Dancing Teachers" *The New York Times*, June 29, 1926, p. 3.

"'Charleston' Sways Building, Police Order Dance Ban" *The Bridgeport Telegram*, Bridgeport, CT, August 27, 1925, p. 1, col. 2.

"Charleston Throws Building Out of Plumb" *San Antonio Express*, San Antonio, TX, October 16, 1925 p. 19, col. 8.

"Charleston Tower to Immortalize Dance" *The New York Times*, September 8, 1926, p. 2.

"The Charleston Traces Its Ancestry Back 400 Years" *The New York Times*, August 8, 1926, Magazine Section, SM2.

"The Charleston will never do..." *The Modesto News-Herald*, Modesto, CA, July 1, 1926, p. 27, col. 7.

"Chief Ryan Places Ban On the 'Hugging' Dance" *Dallas Daily Times Herald*, Dallas, TX, July 19, 1912, p. 1, col. 1–2.

"Clothiers in Session" *The New York Times*, June 2, 1914, p. 15.

"Collapse of Boston Dance Hall" *Davenport Democrat and Leader*, July 5, 1925, 0.1, col. 5.

"College Ban the Charleston" *The New York Times*, January 8, 1926, Section: Amusements Hotels and Restaurants, p. 19.

"Concord's Mayor Bars Charleston" *The New York Times*, February 16, 1926, p. 12.

"Condemns the Charleston" *The New York Times*, March 9, 1927, Section: Hotels and Restaurants Resorts, p. 28.

"Costly Tango" *Des Moines Daily News*, Des Moines, IA, January 19, 1914, p. 2, col. 3.

"Daily Almanac" *Oakland Tribune*, Oakland, CA, September 7, 1922, p. 20, col. 3.

"A Dance Alters Paris Gowns" *Indianapolis Star*, Indianapolis, IN, July 6, 1913, p. 45.

"Dance Charleston in Louis XV's Court" *The New York Times*, July 20, 1926, Section: Amusements Hotels and Restaurants, p. 17.

"Dance Craze is First Appearance of Social Hysteria in Centuries" *The Milford Mail*, Milford, IA, November 19, 1914, p. 6, col. 2.

"Dance Masters Denounce Jazz" *Reno Evening Gazette*, Reno, NV, January 23, 1920, p. 16, col. 3.

"Dance Tango for Judge" *The New York Times*, October 16, 1913, p. 1.

"Dance Teachers Hold A 'Henry Ford' Night; Continue Efforts To Discourage Charleston" *The New York Times*, August 26, 1926, Section: Social News, p. 10.

"Dance the Charleston at Revival" *The New York Times*, January 19, 1926, p. 13, col. 2.

"Dance Winner Bows on 1926 TV Newsreel" *El Paso Herald-Post*, El Paso, TX, January 25, 1974, p. 9, col. 3.

"Dancer Drops Dead" *The New York Times*, April 22, 1914, p. 24.

"Dancers! Get Ready for Instruction in Nifty Black Bottom" *The Davenport Democrat and Leader*, Davenport, IA, December 5, 1926, p. 19, col. 5.

"Dancing Grips Gate City of South" *The Atlanta Constitution*, Atlanta, GA, September 13, 1914, p. 43, col. 3.

"The Dancing Mania" (an extract taken from *The Medical Times*) *The Anaconda Standard*, Anaconda, MT, August 24, 1913, p. 21, col. 3.

"Dancing Masters are in a Quandary Over What Bird or Beast to Imitate in Search of a New Dancing Sensation" *The Fort Wayne Journal-Gazette*, Fort Wayne Indiana, September 15, 1916, p. 9, col. 3.

"Dancing Masters Move to Purify Charleston" *The New York Times*, May 15, 1926, Section: Amusements, Hotels and Restaurants, p. 19.

"Dancing Masters Uplift Charleston" *The New York Times*, August 25, 1925, p. 11.

"Dancing of Tango Barred by Dean of the Cathedral" *Anaconda Standard*, Anaconda, Montana, March 7, 1914, p. 13, col. 3.

Darling, Velva G. "What Makes the Flapper Go Round?" *Oakland Tribune*, Oakland, CA, November 9, 1929, p. 27.

"Death Followed Turkey Trot" *The Star Publications*, *The Chicago Heights Star*, Chicago, IL, July 12, 1912, p. 3, col. 1.

"Death Toll Reaches Forty-Three" *The Sheboygan Press*, Sheboygan, WI, July 6, 1925, p.1, col. 8.

"Declares Charleston Dance is Vulgar" *New Castle News*, New Castle, PA, June 24, 1926, p. 2, col. 5.

"Diagnoses 'Tango Foot'" *The New York Times*, May 31, 1914, Section: Foreign News Sports Want Advertisements, p. C2.

"Differ One Charleston As a 'Vulgar' Dance" *The New York Times*, August 25, 1926, Section; Amusements, Hotels and Restaurants, p. 19.

"Don't Worry About the Young Folks—Jazz—Keynote of the Century" Wisconsin Rapids Daily Tribune, Wisconsin Rapids, WI, March 3, 1925, p. 7. col. 1.

"Dorothy Waits in Cell for Sentence to Prison" *Nevada State Journal*, Reno, NV, August 24, 1925, p. 1, col. 2.

"Dozen Bodies Taken From Debris of Night Resort in Boston Chinatown Area" *Charleston Gazette*, Charleston, WV, July 5, 1925, p. 1, col. 6.

"Duel over Turkey Trot" *The New York Times*, July 26, 1913, p. 1.

Duranty, Walter. "Proletarian Dance Invented For Soviet" *The New York Times*, January 19, 1927, p. 7.

"Elide Webb Dawson, 79, Cotton Club Dancer Dies" *The New York Times*, Obituary, May 2, 1975, p. 38.

"Ellingson to Aid Girl" *Evening State Journal and Lincoln Daily News*, Lincoln, NE, January 21, 1925, p. 2, col. 7.

"Employes [sic] Testify in Pickwick Case" *The Fitchburg Sentinel*, Fitchburg, MA, July 24, 1925, p. 1, col. 4.

"End of Jazz Not Far Off, Declares Sousa" *Charleston Daily Mail*, Charleston, WV, March 21, 1922, p. 2, col. 6.

"England to Bar Texas Guinan" *The Oakland Tribune*, Oakland, CA, May 22, 1931, p. 23, col.3.

"Eugenia Kelly Seen Again on Broadway" *The New York Times*, October 1, 1915, p. 5.

"Exceptional Vitaphone Numbers at State" *Daily News Standard*, Uniontown, PA, September 14, 1927, p. 2, col. 3.

"Exit the Flapper Via Longer Skirts" *The New York Times*, June 25, 1922, Section: Editorial, p. E2.

"Exits and Entrances" ("England reports as a pair of 'wows'...") *The Oakland Tribune*, Oakland, CA, October 7, 1925, p. 12, col. 3.

"Expert Points Out Harm in the Tango" *The New York Times*, April 26, 1914, Section: Society Drama Foreign Resorts Music, p. X15.

"Father of Rag-Time Music" *Spirit Lake Beacon*, Spirit Lake, IA, February 2, 1906, p, 2, col. 4.

"Find 44 Bodies in Boston Club House Ruin" *Newcastle News*, Newcastle, PA, July 6, 1925, p. 1.

"Find the Charleston as Popular as Ever" *The New York Times*, June 30, 1926, p. 12.

"Fire in Pickwick Club is Described" *The Fitchburg Sentinel*, Fitchburg, MA, July 23, 1925, p. 13, col. 1.

"Fish Walk is Latest Dance" *New Castle News*, New Castle, PA, May 1, 1913, p. 12, col. 3.

"Folk Dance Revival Is Aim Of Teachers" *The New York Times*, August 24, 1926, p. 9.

"44 Bodies Are Found" *Hamilton Evening Journal*, Hamilton, OH, July 6, 1925, P. 1, col. 7.

"Foy in 'Over the River'" *The New York Times*, January 9, 1912, p. 8.

"France Orders Our Jazz Players Expelled" *The New York Times*, May 31, 1924, p. 1.

"Frances Williams, Actress Dies; Introduced Charleston On Stage" *The New York Times*, January 28, 1959, p.31

"Frances Williams, Charleston pioneer..." *The Wisconsin Rapids Daily Tribune*, Wisconsin Rapids, WI, January 23, 1931, p. 3, col. 5.

"French May Ban Jazz in Dancing" *The Washington Post*, Washington, D.C., June 13, 1920, p. 62, col. 7.

"From Little Egypt's Hootchy-Kootchy to the Strip Tease" *The San Antonio Light*, San Antonio, TX, May 9, 1937, p. 88

"Fur Salesman Held in the Hilar Case" *The New York Times*, March 20, 1917, p. 7.

"Gibson Puts Ban on Wicked Dances" *The Syracuse Herald*, Syracuse, NY, September 19, 1912, p. 18, col. 3.

"Girl Admits Wild Revelry After Slaying Mother" *Oakland Tribune*, Oakland, CA, January 15, 1925, p. 1, col. 1.

"Girl Dead From Charleston; Doctor Calls Dance Dangerous" *The New York Times*, February 16, 1926, Section: Amusements, p. 27.

"Gives Charleston's Origins" *The New York Times*, January 19, 1926, p. 8.

"Grand Jury in Disaster Probe" *The Charleston Gazette*, July 7, 1925, P.1, col. 3.

Grant, Jane. "The Charleston Prances Into Favor" *The New York Times*, August 30, 1925, Magazine Section, SM2.

"'Grizzly Bear' Old Greek" *The New York Times*, August 31, 1913, Section: Foreign News Financial Business Sports Want Advertisements, p. C1.

"'Grudge' Brings Police Raid on New York Club" *Nebraska Star*, Lincoln, NE, February 17, 1927, p. 1, col. 3.

"Hamilton Fish, Jr., Gives Lenten Ball" *The New York Times*, February 22, 1913, p. 11.

"Has Plain Face But Bees' Knees" *The Olean Evening Herald*, Olean, NY, February 6, 1926, p. 15, col. 4.

"Heiress is Penitent" *The Washington Post*, Washington D.C., May 26, 1915, p. 4, col. 4.

Hoyt, Helen. "Dance Teachers Have Managed to Standardize the Tango" *Gazette and Bulletin*, Williamsport, PA, January 18, 1915, p. 10, col. 2.

"Hilar Case Inquiry Tangled by Letter" *The New York Times*, March 25, 1917, p. 19.

"Hints Eugenia Kelly is Victim of a Plot" *The New York Times*, May 25, 1915, p. 8.

"His Drug Not Opium, Mouvet Released" *The New York Times*, November 17, 1927, p. 4.

"History of Turkey Trot and The Gavotte Pavlowa" *Wichita Daily Times*, Wichita, TX, February 22, 1914, p. 14, col. 1.

"Hitting the Ragtime Dance" *The La Crosse Tribune*, La Crosse, WI, July 13, 1912, p. 3, col. 1.

"Honey Flow Too Heavy; Knees of Bees Are Weak" *Modesto News-Herald*, Modesto, CA, June 6, 1930, p. 9, col. 2.

"Hootchy-Kootchy to Strip Tease" *The San Antonio Light*, May 9, 1937, p. 107, col. 3.

"Houdini to Aid Jew's Drive; Charleston Contest With 1,000 Entrants Also Listed for Field Day" *The New York Times*, June 12, 1926, Section: Amusements Hotels and Restaurants, P. 13.

"How the 'Charleston' Wrecked the Dance Hall" *The San Antonio Light*, August, 9, 1925, p. 65.

"Ill, Charleston Dance Blamed" *The New York Times*, November 21, 1925, p. 4, col. 3.

"In His Arms, But He Can't Keep Them There" *Galveston Daily News*, Galveston, TX, April 14, 1925, p. 8.

"Is Today's Girl Becoming a Savage?" *Modesto Evening News*, Modesto, CA, June 14, 1924, p. 26, col. 1.

"Italy Makes War on Jazz Dance Halls" *Gastonia Daily Gazette*, Gastonia, NC, January 28, 1926, p. 5, col. 7.

Jackson, Bee. "Hey! Hey! Charleston" *Colliers Magazine*, December 10, 1927, p. 34.

"Jazz" (from a letter to the column "What They Say to Geraldine") *Oakland Tribune*, Oakland, CA, November 19, 1922, p. 15, col. 1.

"Jazz" (originally printed in the *Kansas City Star*.) *Brownsville, Herald*, Brownsville, TX, February 1, 1922, p. 4, col. 2.

"Jazz Affects People Differently; Chief Lack Harmony is Internal" *Woodland Daily Democrat*, Woodland, CA, March 16, 1922, p. 5, col. 1.

"Jazz Dance Builds Healthy Race, Paul Whiteman Tells Flappers" *Wisconsin Rapids Daily Tribune*, Wisconsin Rapids, WI, March 3, 1925, p. 7, col. 4.

"Jazz Dances 'Dangerous Sports,' Says Doctor, Adding 'Charleston Knee' To Mankind's Ills" *The New York Times*, April 29, 1928, Section: Editorial, p. E1.

"Jazz Here to Stay Say Music Experts" *Ogden Standard-Examiner*, Ogden, UT, January 27, 1924, p. 21, col. 1.

"Jazz Music" *Monessen Daily Independent*, Monessen, PA, March 2, 1922, p. 6, col. 1.

"Jazz Music Declared Greatest Menace to Morals of Children" *San Antonio Light*, San Antonio, TX, January 29, 1922, p. 8, col. 5.

"Jerome Kern Hits at Jazz Orchestra" *The New York Times*, April 12, 1924, Section: Amusements, Hotels and Restaurants, p. 18.

Joel, Lydia. "The Waltz: The Dance That Wouldn't Stay Banned." In *Dance Magazine* (Nov. 1950), pp. 30–31.

"John Jarrott: Former Dancer and Vaudeville Actor Is Dead at 55" *The New York Times*, June 17, 1938. p. 21.

"Judge Defends Slit Skirt" *The New York Times*, September 5, 1914, p. 1.

"Just Dumb" *La Crosse Tribune*, La Crosse, WI, April 27, 1926, p. 3, col. 1.

"King Zog's Comic Opera Kingdom" *San Antonio Light*, San Antonio, TX, September 11, 1932, p. 51.

"Knocking Jazz" *Mansfield News*, Mansfield, OH, August 2, 1925, p. 27, col. 2.

"Latest in Dancing" *Hawaiian Gazette*, Honolulu, HW, October 7, 1898, p. 7, col. 1.

"Launch 'Budapest' Dance; Hungarians, Disliking Charleston, Seek to Check its Spread" *The New York Times*, November 26, 1926, p. 14.

"Lillian Williams..." (Local and General) *McKean County Miner*, Smethport, PA, January 23, 1902, p. 5, col. 2.

"Listen World" *Oakland Tribune*, Oakland, CA, May 22, 1922, p. 11, col. 1.

"London Dispute Over 'Turkey Trot'" *The New York Times*, May 21, 1913, p. 3.

"London is Amazed by 'Turkey Trot'" *The New York Times*. February 6, 1912, p. 3.

"Magee Urges Ban on Jazz Music Pieces" *San Antonio Evening News*, San Antonio, TX, April 29. 1920, p. 1, col. 3.

"Man Slips, Fall Breaks Arm Doing Charleston Dance" *New Castle News*, New Castle, PA, April 4, 1928, p. 10, col. 5.

"Many Killed in Dance Hall Crash" *The Chicago Daily Herald*, July 10, 1925, p. 5, col. 5.

"Many Noted Tango Decision Made in Few Weeks" *Lincoln Daily News*, Lincoln, NE, January 19, 1914. P. 8. col. 1.

"Maurice and the New Dances" *The New York Times*, January 25, 1912, p. 10.

"Maurice is Dead; Was Famed Dancer" *The New York Times*, May 19, 1927, Section: Sports, p. 27.

"Mayor Gaynor Asks Ban Put on Bad Dance" *Fairbanks Daily Times*, Fairbanks Alaska, April 5, 1913, p. 1, col. 2.

"Mayor of Wilkes-Barre Would Put Ban on Jazz" *Wisconsin Rapids Daily News*, Wisconsin Rapids, WI, August 27, 1924, p. 8, col. 2.

"Mayor Out to Stop 'Tea and Tango' Now" *The New York Times*, April 5, 1913, p. 2.

"A Mayor Seized in Raid" *The New York Times*, April 14, 1928, Section: Business & Finance, p. 34.

"Middle-aged Dancers Warned Against the Tango" *The New York Times*, December 28, 1913, Section: Magazine, p. SM2.

"Mike Donlin Dead; Once with Giants" *The New York Times*, September 25, 1933, p. 15.

"Milady's Mirror" *Sheboygan Press*, Sheboygan, WI, December 18, 1913, p. 4, col. 5.

"Miller and Lyles in 'Runnin' Wild'" *The Bridgeport Telegram*, Bridgeport, CT, December 27, 1924, p. 6, col. 2.

"Miller and Lyles in 'Runnin' Wild'" *The Bridgeport Telegram*, Bridgeport, CT, December 31, 1924, p. 14, col. 2.

"Miss Bee Jackson, Early Exponent of 'Charleston' Was Internationally Known" *The New York Times*, July 19, 1933, p. 17.

"Mob a Woman Bather" *The New York Times*, September 12, 1913, p. 1.

"Morals Court Judge Says Jazz Music Obscene Revival of Barbarism and Fines Café Dancer for Bad Actions" *Waterloo Evening Courier*, Waterloo, IA, January 28, 1922, p. 2, col. 2.

"More Church Heads Oppose New Dances" *The New York Times*, February 1, 1914, Section Foreign News Sports Want Advertisements, p. C6.

"Mrs. Berlin Writes on the Charleston" *The New York Times*, February 7, 1926, p. 6.

"Murder Dancing Teacher" *The New York Times*, September 28, 1913, p. 2.

"Musical College to Open Sept. 12" *The Decatur Review*, Decatur, IL, Sept 4, 1921, p. 9, col. 2.

"N.Y. Dancing to Hell" *The San Antonio Light*, San Antonio TX, February 20, 1927, p. 10, col. 1.

"Ned Wayburn" *The New York Times*, September 3, 1942, Section: Obituaries, Page 19.

"Ned Wayburn Writes About the Dance of Today — The Charleston," *The Oakland Tribune*, Oakland, CA, April 7, 1926, pp. 46–47.

"New Charleston Vogue; Adele Astaire Predicts Winter Craze for Kickless Variety in London" *The New York Times*, September 27, 1926, Section: Social News, p. 25.

"New Customs, New Costumes" *New Oxford Item*, New Oxford, PA, February 2, 1912, p. 4, col. 5.

"New Dances Are Influencing Fashions for Women" *The New York Times*, December 28, 1913, Section: Society Fashions Drama Music, p. X10.

"A New Kind of Cruelty Wins Her Divorce" *The San Antonio Light*, San Antonio, TX, May 22, 1932, p. 47.

"New Nuggets" *New Castle News*, New Castle, PA, July 24, 1914, p. 11, col. 4.

"New York Public Dance Hall Will Be Ruled by Czar" *The Charleston Gazette*, Charleston, WV, October 7, 1924, p. 7, col. 6.

"New Yorkers Sure Do Like Grizzly Bear" *The Cedar*

Rapids Evening Gazette, Cedar Rapids, IA, December 8, 1911, p. 6, col. 3.

"Nine Killed in Collapse of Dance Hall." *Oakland Tribune*, Oakland, CA, July 4, 1925, p. 1, col. 8.

"No Tango 'Ads' Received" *The New York Times*, December 28, 1913, Section: Cable News Wireless Dispatches Sports Want Advertisements, p. C4.

"No Tangoing to Result In No Teaching Pupils" *Titusville Herald*, Titusville, PA, July 17, 1914, p. 5, col. 5.

"No 'Turkey Trot' For Her" *The Washington Post*, Washington D. C., January 15, 1912, p. 3, col. 4.

"None Injured in Club Crash" *New Castle News*, New Castle PA, November 4, 1925, p.11, col. 3.

"Notes and Half Notes" *La Crosse Tribune and Leader-Press*. La Crosse, WI, p. 7, col. 5.

"Oakland Girl Charlestons to World's Record" *Oakland Tribune*, Oakland, CA, January 15, 1926, p. 12, col. 1.

"Office Cat" ("A woman fell and broke her wrist...") *The Sheboygan Press*, Sheboygan, WI, January 25, 1926, p. 14, col. 2.

"Oh Busy Little Bees, Decorate Shapely Knees" *The San Antonio Light*, San Antonio, TX, July 1, 1925, p. 11, col. 2.

O'Hara, Neal R. "Just Jazz" (In Column "Live Wires") *The Post-Standard*, Syracuse, NY, April 13, 1920, p. 13, col. 3.

"Ohio Faces Charges of Teaching the 'Charleston'" *The New York Times*, March 8, 1929, p. 22.

"Old Halls Not Strong Enough, Charleston Barred in Passaic" *The New York Times*, August 30, 1925, Section: Financial and Business Opportunities Editorial, p. El, col. 7.

"Once Rich Woman Slain in Hotel" *The New York Times*, March 18, 1917, p. 1.

"One More Love Match for Society's Famous Lover" *The Syracuse Herald*, Syracuse, NY, October 26, 1924, p. 12.

"Oppose Jazz Near Hospital" *Portsmouth Daily Times*, Portsmouth, OH, February 5, 1926, p. 18, col. 1.

"Origin and Spread of the Vivacious 'Turkey Trot'" *The Anaconda Standard*, Anaconda, MT, February 11, 1912, p. 25.

"Origin of Modern Eccentric Dances Traced to Underworld" *The San Antonio Light*, San Antonio, TX, December 14, 1913, p. 34, col. 1.

"Origin of the Jazz Band" *Star Publications*, Chicago IL, February 5, 1920, p. 6, col. 4.

"Origin of Turkey Trot" *The San Antonio Light*, San Antonio, TX, September 14, 1913, p. 8, col. 7.

"Originator of the Charleston Dance is Dead After Illness" *The Gleaner*, Zanesville, OH, July 20, 1933, p.5, col. 2.

"Our Moaning Saxophone is Now Called Immoral" *The New York Times*, September 13, 1925, Section: Magazine, p. SM2.

"Pale Faces Excel Runners in Dance" *The New York Times*, June 17, 1928, p. 18.

"Paris Authorities to Ban Charleston" *The Times*, San Mateo, CA, May 12, 1927, p. 5, col. 2.

"Paris Bars the Tango" *Humeston New Era*, Humeston, IA, April 14, 1915p. 12, col. 1.

"A Paris Decalogue to Guide Dancers" *The New York Times*, February 11, 1912, Section: Transatlantic Wireless, Cable and Sporting Sections, p. C4.

"Paris Forbids the Tango" *The New York Times*, April 10, 1915, p. 2.

"A Pastor Agrees" *The Bridgeport Telegram*, Bridgeport, CT, December 16, 1925, p. 12, col. 2.

"Pastor Defends Flapper and Criticises [sic] Men's Dress," *The New York Times*, April 10, 1922, p. 1.

"Pastors Approve Ban on the Tango" *The New York Times*, January 5, 1914, p. 5.

"People in the Passing Show" *The Washington Post*, May 24, 1913, p. 7, col. 3.

"Personal" (Mrs. Elizabeth Barger Embleton...") *Charleston Daily Mail*, Charleston, WV, July 29, 1928, P. 11, col. 3.

"Pickwick Club Collapsed Due to Weak Pier" *The Bridgeport Telegram*, Bridgeport, CT, August 12, 1925, p.4, col. 5.

"Pickwick Club Death Lists Mounts to 44" *The Fitchburg Sentinel*, Fitchburg, MA, July 6, 1925, p. 1, col. 6.

"Pickwick Club Ruins Yield More Bodies to Searchers" *The Lowell Sun*, Lowell, MA, July 6, 1925, p. 1, col. 3.

"Pickwick Probe Halts to Await Engineer's Report" *The Fitchburg Sentinel*, Fitchburg, MA, July 8, 1925, p. 1, col. 3.

"Police Take Census of 'Tango Pirates'" *The New York Times*, March 28, 1917, p. 13.

"Polite Dances Are Shown to Society" *The New York Times*, March 26, 1912, p. 13.

"Pope Saw Tango, Rome Story Says" *The New York Times*, January 28, 1914, p. 4.

"President's Aide to Be Married Too" *Trenton Evening Times*, Trenton, NJ, October 18, 1915, p. 11, col. 3.

"Prima Donnas Held Train" *The New York Times*, October 23, 1912, p. 1.

"Prince George Wins Charleston Contest With Lady Milford At Cannes Casino" *The New York Times*, March 28, 1927, p. 1.

"Prince Knows How" *Modesto News-Herald*, Modesto, CA, November 9, 1926, p. 6, col. 4.

"Put Ban on Charleston" *The New York Times*, November 7, 1926, Section: Editorial General News Financial and Business News Business Opportunities, p, E6.

"Puts Ban On Charleston" *The New York Times*, October 26, 1926, Section: Wholesale Market, p. 44.

"Putting the Music Into the Jazz" *The New York Times*, February 19, 1922, Section: Book Review and Magazine, p. 41.

"Queen Bars Charleston" *The New York Times*, March 5, 1927, p. 3.

"Queen 'Bee's' Scantiest Costume" *The San Antonio Light*, San Antonio, TX, November 20, 1932, p. 40, col. 5.

"Queen Mary Sees Tango and Likes It" *The New York Times*, June 13, 1914, p. 3.

"Ragtime and Morals" *The Oakland Tribune*, Oakland, Ca, August 15, 1913, p. 10, col. 1.

"Rescuers Recover 43 Bodies from Ruins" *The Kingston Daily Freeman*, Kingston, NY, July 6, 1925, p. 1, col. 7.

"A Result of the Tango" *The New York Times*, September 14, 1913, Section: Foreign News Special Dispatches Sports Want Advertisements, p. C2.

"Retaliation Is Proposed in Congress Bills On Countries That Bar Our 'Jazz' Players" *The New York Times*, January 26, 1926, p. 4.

"Riot at Preacher's Dance" *The New York Times*, September 18, 1913, p. 4.

Robbins, Jerome. "From the Castles To the Creep" *The*

New York Times, March 21, 1954, Section: Magazine, Page SM24.

Rogers, J. A. "Jazz at Home," In *Survey Graphic*, Harlem Number (March 1925), pp. 665–7, 712.

"Ruins Yield Two Score" *Los Angeles Times*, July 6, 1925, Part I, p.1, col. 1.

"Saloonkeeper's Wife Is Prince's Partner; He Does The Charleston and Enjoys Himself In One Of The Poor Quarters of London" *The New York Times*, December 3, 1926, p. 5

"Salvationists Halt Broadway Dancers" *The New York Times*, March 22, 1914, p. 1.

"Salzburg Shocked By The Charleston" *The New York Times*, August 13, 1926, Section: Amusements, Hotels and Restaurants, p. 12.

"Saw Dance, Wrote Music; Oscar Straus in Vienna Composes for the Charleston by Watching It" *The New York Times*, March 31, 1927, Section: Sports, p. 20

Sawyer, Joan. "How to Dance the Foxtrot." Columbia Gramophone Company, November 23, 1914.

"Says 'Charleston' is a Disease" *The Lowell Sun*, Lowell, MA, December 14, 1926, p. 19, col. 4.

"Says Jazz Players are not Artists" *The New York Times*, August 1, 1927, p. 21.

"'Scandals' Will Open Tomorrow" *Syracuse Herald*, Syracuse, NY, March 4, 1928, p. 6, col. 3.

"Set Charleston Record" *The New York Times*, January 10, 1925, Section: Classified Advertisements Apartments to Let Houses and Estates, p, W19.

"She Was the Life of the Party" *Sheboygan Journal*, Sheboygan, WI, January 19, 1925, p. 3, col. 4.

Silverman, Sime. "Large Shows Continue to Make Hits in Large Cities" *San Antonio Evening News*, San Antonio, TX, January 27, 1923. p, 7, col. 2.

Sims, Tom. "New U.S. Dance Seen by Sims" *Reno Evening Gazette*, Reno, NV, September 28, 1925, p. 8, col. 3.

"Slit Skirt 'Disorderly'" *The New York Times*, June 29, 1913, p. 1.

"Slit Skirt Girl Driven Out" *The New York Times*, July 17, 1913, p. 1.

"Smith Starts Urchins Doing the Charleston While He Waits in Station at Absecon" *New York Times*, November 27, 1926, p. 1.

"Social Sanity Threatened, Says Our Foremost Psychologist" *Lima Daily News*, Lima, OH, May 31, 1914, p. 17.

"Social Workers See Real 'Turkey Trots'" *The New York Times*, January 27, 1912, p. 1.

"Society Bars Turkey Trot" *Trenton Evening Times*, Trenton, NJ, November 8, 1912, p. 9, col. 4.

"Soldiers Track Jazz to its Lair" *The Eau Claire Leader*, Eau Claire, WI, January 23, 1920, p. 7, col. 5.

"Some women it appears..." *Wisconsin State Journal*, Madison, WI, August 10, 1924, p. 10. col. 7.

"Southern Hotel Closed by Police" *The New York Times*, April 30, 1913, p. 1.

"Spirituals and Jazz" *The New York Times*, December 26, 1926, Section: Drama Music Art Society Fashion Screen resorts Steamships Travel, p. X8.

"Stage Dances Shown at Teachers' Meeting" *The New York Times*, August 27, 1925, Section: Sport, p. 20.

"Sternberg Admits He Met Mrs. Hilar" *The New York Times*, March 21, 1917, p. 6.

"Sternberg Charged with Hilar Murder" *The New York Times*, March 22, 1917, p. 8.

"Sternberg is Set Free" *The New York Times*, June 30, 1917, p. 7.

"Suits for $30,000 in Pickwick Deaths" *The Lowell Sun*, Lowell, MA, September 17, 1925, p. 14, col. 4.

"Sure Companion Killed Mrs. Hilar" *The New York Times*, March 19, 1917, p. 18.

"Suzette's Views on Society and Dancing" *Oakland Tribune*, Oakland, CA August 24, 1913, p. 7. col. 1.

"Sweetheart Knees Replace Bee's Knees" *The Olean Evening Herald*, Olean, NY, June 6, 1924, p.14, col. 1.

"Tango 'Absurd,' Says King" *The New York Times*, December 16, 1913, p. 3.

"Tango as a Health Promoter" *The Gazette and Bulletin*, Williamsport PA, May 12, 1914, p. 5, col. 2.

"Tango Barred in Vermont and Vindicated in Ohio" *Anaconda Standard*, Anaconda, MT, October 18, 1913, p. 10, col. 6.

"Tango Barred to Harvard Athletes" *Syracuse Herald*, Syracuse, NY, May 11, 1914, p. 27, col. 4.

"Tango Captivates German Capital" *The New York Times*, November 9, 1913, Section: Editorial Foreign News Sports Want Advertisements, P. C3.

"Tango Craze Leads Fashion's Efforts" *Janesville Daily Gazette*, Janesville, WI, February 6, 1914, p, 10, col. 3.

"Tango Defeats Vatican" *The New York Times*, December 27, 1913, p. 1.

"The Tango Face Spoils Women's Beauty, Latest Charge Against the Dance" *Waterloo Times-Tribune*, Waterloo, IA, August 7, 1914, p. 9, col. 1.

"Tango Flourishes Despite Boycotts" *The New York Times*, January 5, 1914, Section: Cable News Shipping Business Sports Want Advertisements, p. C3.

"Tango Is Inherited From the Savages" *Anaconda Standard*, Anaconda, MT, February 15, 1914, p. 31, col. 4.

"Tango is Tabooed by Kaiser's Order" *The New York Times*, November 18, 1913, p. 4.

"Tango Killer Goes to Death" *Centralia Daily Chronicle-Examiner*, Centralia, WA, July 31, 1914, p. 7, col. 4.

"Tango Shame of Our Days" *The New York Times*, January 22, 1914, p. 4.

"Tango Styles in Riot of Color" *Oakland Tribune*, Oakland, CA, March 12, 1914, p. 4, col. 1.

"Tango Teacher Asks $4,000" *The New York Times*, January 29, 1914, p. 4.

"Tango Teacher Quits Choir" *The New York Times*, February 3, 1914, p. 1.

"Tango Thieves Active" *The New York Times*, March 15, 1914, Section: Editorial Section, Foreign News Sports Want Advertisements, p. C2.

"Tango Too Evil For Them" *Lincoln Daily News*, Lincoln, Nebraska, July 2, 1913. p. 4, col. 2.

"Tango Tour From Toledo to Texas" *Indianapolis Star*, Indianapolis, IN, May 10, 1914, p. 50, col. 1.

"Tangoed in His Freezer" *The New York Times*, February 12, 1914, p. 1.

"Tangoed to Death" Fort Wayne News, Fort Wayne, IN, February 12, 1915, p. 27, col. 4.

"Tangoist Hurls Furniture" *The New York Times*, February 7, 1914, p. 5.

"Tangoist to Sue Prelate" *The New York Times*, January 21, 1914, p. 4.

"10 on Trial for Manslaughter as Result of Pickwick Club Disaster" *The Fitchburg Sentinel*, Fitchburg, MA, July 20, 1925, p.7, col. 5.

Temple, Herbert. "Temple Pictures London's Horror at 'Those Nasty American Hug-Dances'" *The Syracuse Herald*, Syracuse, NY, December 8, 1912, p. 45, col. 6.

"Texas Guinan Defines Sucker as a Guy Who Can Afford to Be Trimmed" *The Port Arthur News*, Port Arthur, TX, November 24, 1929, p. 22, col. 3.

"Texas Guinan Enjoys Trial" *The Havre Daily News*, Havre, MT, April 10, 1929, p. 8, col. 5.

"Texas Guinan's Bizarre Career Ended by Death." *San Antonio Light*, November 6, 1933, p 4, col. 1.

"Texas Guinan's Club Raided by 2 Dry Agents" *The Lima News*, Lima, OH, October 29, 1930, p. 7, col. 4.

Tigerstedt, Carl, M.D. "Dancers Use Up Great Energy" *The New York Times*, July 10, 1927, Section: Special Features, Page XX2.

"This Day in History" *Daily Herald*, Chicago IL, July 12, 2002, p. 16, col. 2.

"This Girl Turned the Light Out on the Great White Way" *The Ogden Standard* in Ogden, UT, July 10, 1915, p. 16.

"To Beat the Turkey Trot" *The New York Times*, October 11, 1912, p. 9.

"To 'Bunny Hug' and 'Horse Trot' in Unison in an Effort to Standardize Dancing" *The Evening Gazette*, Cedar Rapids, Iowa, December 2, 1913, p. 14.

"A Toll of Thirty-nine Taken in Boston Horror" *The Renwick Times*, Renwick, IA, July 16, 1925, p. 2, col. 2.

"The Tragedy of the Tango Dance" *The Fort Wayne Sentinel*, Fort Wayne, IN, October 6, 1913, p. 13, col. 1.

"Trial of Pickwick Club Defendants" *Kingston Daily Freeman*, Kingston, NY, July 20, 1925, p.1, col. 3.

"38 are Killed on Independence Day" *The Lima Sunday News*, Lima, OH, July 5, 1925, p.1, col. 6.

"Turkey Bars Charleston as Menace to Health" *The Gleaner*, Kingston, Kingston, November 29, 1926, p. 15, col. 3

"The Turkey Trot" *The Daily Courier*, Connellsville, PA January 22, 1912, p. 4, col. 3.

"Turkey Trot an Appeal to Real Sense of Rhythm" *Lincoln Daily News*, Lincoln, NE, September 27, 1913, p. 5, col. 1.

"Turkey Trot Barred at Annapolis Dances" *The New York Times*, January 14, 1913, p. 17.

"'Turkey Trot' Denounced" *The New York Times*, February 25, 1912, Section: Transatlantic Wireless Cable and Sporting Sections, p. C3.

"Turkey Trot is Fatal to a Youthful Bride" *The Daily Courier*, Connellsville, PA, June 11, 1912, p. 1.

"Turkey Trot is Gait to Hell, Says Parson" *Atlanta Constitution*, Atlanta, GA, July 16, 1913, p.2.

"Turkey Trot Must Glide" *The New York Times*, January 31, 1913, p. 6.

"Turkey Trot New? Danced 500 Years in Borneo" *The Iowa Recorder*, Greene, IA, September 25, 1912, p. 2, col. 4.

"'Turkey Trot' Shocks Editor" *The San Antonio Light*, San Antonio, TX, July 7, 1912, p. 26.

"Turkey Trot Was a Cowboy Dance" *The Milford Mail*, Milford, Iowa, April 3, 1913, p. 2, col. 2.

"Turks Ban the Charleston as a Menace to Health" *The New York Times*, November 20, 1926, Sports, p. 19.

"12 Known Dead in Dance Hall Crash" *The Galveston Daily News*, July 5, 1925, p.10, col. 5.

"20,000 Attend Fete for Jewish Relief" *The New York Times*, June 28, 1926, P. 3.

"Two Score Dead In Boston Crash" *The Newport Mercury*, Newport, RI, July 11, 1925, p. 5. col. 4.

"Vale the Turkey Trot" *The McKean Democrat*, Smethport, PA, August 7, 1913, p. 3, col. 1.

"Valencia is Successor of The Charleston" *Hamilton Evening Journal*, Hamilton, OH. August 8, 1925, p. 1, col. 2.

"A Valise for Dancers" *The New York Times*, December 21, 1913, Section: Foreign News Sports Want Advertisements, p. C2.

"Vatican Organ Condemns Jazz Dances as Immoral" *The New York Times*, February 25, 1924, p. 1.

"Vienna Will Bar Tango" *Ogden Examiner,* Ogen, UT, December 31, 1913, p. 2, col. 5.

"Vote to Ban Charleston" *The New York Times*, September 30, 1926, p. 15.

"War On Charleston As Old Kaffir Dance" *The New York Times*, December 10, 1926, p. 8. *Washington Post*, Washington, D.C., February 16, 1926, p, 1.

"Welfare Inspector at Society Dance" *The New York Times*, January 4, 1912, p. 1.

"Where He Gets His Ideas" *The Portsmouth Herald*, Portsmouth, NJ, May 20, 1913, p. 7, col. 3.

"*Where Many Dancers Lost Lives*" *Morning Herald*, Uniontown, PA, July 7, 1925, p. 3, col. 5.

"Why Tango was Banned" *The New York Times*, December 2, 1913, p. 4.

"Why the 'Charleston' Was a Dance of Death" *The Galveston Daily News*, Galveston, TX, Aug. 19, 1925, p. 8, col. 2.

"Will Put Ban on Improper Dances" *The Daily Commonwealth*, Fond du Lac, Wisconsin, December 9, 1912, p. 5, col. 6.

"Will the Charleston Bring That Plier Handle Silhouette" *The Port Arthur News*, Port Arthur, TX, January 10, 1926, p. 11, col. 3

"Wilson Banned Ball Fearing Turkey Trot" *The New York Times*, January 21, 1913, p. 3.

Winchell, Walter. "Walter Winchell on Broadway" *Eureka Humbolt Standard*, Eureka, CA, February 11, 1959, p. 4, col. 5.

"Women Assail Charleston; Nebraska Societies Want Vulgarity on the Dance Floor Curbed" *The New York Times*, February 21, 1926, p. 13.

Websites

The African Registry. "She could "Do It All," Elisabeth Welch!" 2005. http://www.aaregistry.com/african_american_history/2268/She_could_Do_It_All_Elisabeth_Welch

_____. "Mae Barnes, a true stage original!" 2005. http://www.aaregistry.com/african_american_history/2072/Mae_Barnes_a_true_stage_original

Alexander, Scott. The Red Hot Jazz Archive. "James Price Johnson." http://www.redhotjazz.com/jpjohnson.html

"Almack's" at *London Clubs*. http://homepages.ihug.co.nz/~awoodley/regency/club.html

"Almack's Assembly Rooms." http://www.britainexpress.com/History/almacks.htm

"Almack's Club History" at *Almack's — The Exclusive Online Gaming Club. 2001.* http://195.149.39.241/club_history/club_history.php

"American Vintage Blues: History of Fashion, 1910–1920" http://www.vintageblues.com/history1.htm

Aslan, Pablo. "The Evolution of Tango Music" (adapted from "Tango Stylistic Evolution and Innovation," UCLA Masters thesis, 1990. www.avantango.com/Pages/Articles/musichist.html

Associated Press: NY Times Obituary, July 18, 2003. "Elisabeth Welch." http://www.nytimes.com/2003/07/18/obituaries/18WELC.html?ex=1128744000&en=3d668135b5e3a4de&ei=5070

Avery Research Center for African-American Culture and History at the College of Charleston http://www.cofc.edu/avery/archives.htm

"Bee Palmer" http://www.redhotjazz.com/beepalmer.html.

Book Rags—"Joan Crawford" http://www.bookrags.com/Joan_Crawford

"A Brief History of Scollay Square" bambinomusical.com/Scollay/History

Carter, John F. "These Wild Young People, By One of Them," Atlantic Monthly, 126, September 1920, pp. 301–304. http://eagle.clarion.edu/~faculty/tpfannestiel/carter.html

The Celtic Connection "Twentieth Century Texas"—Chapter Eight http://users.ev1.net/~gpmoran/20THTX.htm

"Center for Jazz Arts Announces Initiative Promoting Jazz Appreciation Month in Britain," Embassy of the United States—London http://london.usembassy.gov/culture/jazz_appreciation_2006.html

Center for Jazz Arts—Feature Exhibition—"Royal Albert Hall" (December 2005) http://www.centerforjazzarts.org/albert_exhibition2.html

Collins, Russ. "Oc Language—Langue d'Oc." 1996–2003 http://www.provencebeyond.com/history/oc.html

The Columbia Electronic Encyclopedia. "Langue d'oc and langue d'oïl." 1994, 2000 http://www.infoplease.com/ce6/society/A0828822.html

Columbine. "The Language of Flowers" http://www.apocalypse.org/pub/u/hilda/flang.html

"Candombe" www.candombe.com/english.html

"Carlos Gardel" http://comunidad.ciudad.com.ar/ciudadanos/herman/Gardel/gardel_eng.htm

Corry, John. "Adelaide Louisa Hall." http://www.findagrave.com/cgi-bin/fg.cgi?page=gr&GRid=7979544&pt=Adelaide%20Hall

The Dance Card Museum http://www.drawrm.com/dance.htm

Doktorsji, Henry. "The Clasical Bandoneon," 1998. www.ksanti.net/free-reed/history/bandoneon.html

Edwards, Audrey. "The ages of beauty—old and young African American women of beauty," Essence Magazine, Jan, 1995. http://www.looksmartmom.com/p/articles/mi_m1264/is_n9_v25/ai_16427919/pg_2?pi=gbl

Ellis, Carl. "Lew Grade Part I: the early years and Part II; the pre-war years"—Transdiffussion.org http://www.transdiffusion.org/emc/tvheroes/lewgrade/indexl.php

"Extravagant Crowd: Carl Van Vechten's Portraits of Women: Bricktop—Nightclub Owner and Entertainer." http://beinecke.library.yale.edu/cvvpw/gallery/bricktop.html

Fields, Jill. "Fighting The Corsetless Evil: Shaping Corsets And Culture, 1900–1930."From the *Journal of Social History*, Winter, 1999. From *Find Articles.* http://www.findarticles.com/p/articles/mi_m2005/is_2_33/ai_58675450

"George Raft" on BookRags http://www.bookrags.com/George_Raft

Ginger Rogers Official Site. http://www.gingerrogers.com/about/photo.html

Harriman, Margaret Case. "Starlight Starbright," Originally appeared in Vanity Fair, February 1936. Extracted from The Best of Everything.com, http://www.joancrawfordbest.com/articlevanfair36feb.htm

Herbert Hoover Presidential Library and Museum Gallery Three: The Roaring Twenties http://hoover.archives.gov/exhibits/Hooverstory/gallery03/gallery03.html

Hetzler, Sid. "Old Vienna Dance Photo Album." 2000. http://www.splittree.org/misc_pages/ovphotos.htm

"Historical Boy's Clothing—Dancing School and Social Dancing Lesson Routien [sic]" histclo.com/act/dance/danceschr

Howell, Anthony. "Tango with an axe to grind." Times Online, April 19, 2006. http://content1.clipmarks.com/content/8E0930B5-4AD3-473C-BB0C-84CBE6003E8C/

Hubbert, Julie, SYMPOSIA: "Jenkins Orphanage." http://www.sc.edu/orphanfilm/orphanage/symposia/scholarship/hubbert/jenkins-orphanage.html

Hughes, Kristine. "The Lady Patronesses of Almack's." 2002. http://members.aol.com/LONDON20/mysite_005.htm

Huntington Herald-Dispatch, February 2, 1984. "Cabaret Queen, Bricktop Is Dead." West Virginia Division of Culture and History, 2005. http://www.wvculture.org/history/notewv/bricktop2.html

Internet Movie Database—Biography for Carlos Gardel http://www.imdb.com/name/nm0306624/bio

Internet Movie Database—Biography for Elida Webb http://www.ibdb.com/person.asp?id=113400

Internet Movie Database—Biography for Frances Williams (II) http://www.imdb.com/name/nm0930590/bio

Internet Movie Database—Biography for Lew Grade http://www.imdb.com/name/nm0333528/bio

Jackson, Lee. *The Victorian Dictionary*. "Victorian London: Entertainment and Recreation—Dancing at Almack's." http://www.victorianlondon.org/entertainment/dancingatalmacks.htm

James Price Johnson Foundation Website. 2005. http://www.jamespjohnson.org/jamespjohnson.htm

January, Bob. "The Waltz." 12/2001. http://www.bobjanuary.com/waltz.htm

Jarrett, Charles W., and Lucas, David M. "Introducing Folknography: A Study of Gullah Culture" A Paper Presented at the 65th Annual Meeting of the Rural Sociological Society, August 14–18, 2002. http://www.southern.ohiou.edu/folknography/gullah/finishedproduct.htm

Jones, Kenneth. "Elisabeth Welch, Tony Nominated Star of Musicals, Revues and International Cabaret, Dead at 99." From *Playbill News*, 7/16/03. http://www.playbill.com/news/article/80699.html

"Josephine Bradley" extracts taken from a selection of articles that appeared in previous editions of Memory Lane. http://www.memorylane.org.uk/previous_articles.htm

Kelly, Susan. "Ginger Rogers" http://www.things-and-other-stuff.com/movies/profiles/ginger-rogers.htm

Kenrick, John. Stage Musical Chronology: "The 1920s." 2003. http://www.musicals101.com/1920s.htm

Kippen, Cameron. "The History of Footwear—Dancing Shoes" 6/03 http://podiatry.curtin.edu.au/dance.html#long

Knauff, Margie. "The Move Towards Rational Dress." http://www.mpmbooks.com/amelia/RATIONAL.HTM

"Lady Caroline Ponsonby Lamb" Written 1997, revised 7/22/2003. http://www.englishhistory.net/byron/lc lamb.html

Lamb, Andrew. "Strauss Dances" (Excerpts from the sleeve notes.) 2000. http://www.hyperion-records.co. uk/notes/67169.html

"Leonard Reed" — MAXWELLDEMILLE.com, http:// www.maxwelldemille.com/leonard/

"Lew Grade" Hollywood.com, http://www.hollywood. com/celebrity/Lew_Grade/192449

Looney, Andrew. 2000. "Thought Residue." http:// www.wunderland.com/WTS/Andy/ThoughtResidue 00.html

"Louise Brooks." Excerpt from a 1957 unpublished essay originally intended for a book by Brooks called *Women in Film.* The book was never published. http://www.joancrawfordbest.com/brooksessay.htm

Lupic, Jack. "Bandoneon History," 2004. www.gardel-web.com/bandoneon.htm

Maginnis, Tara, Ph.D. "The Costumers Manifesto: The History of Fashion and Dress— WWI to WWII"

Theatre 355 — Week 14: Online Version University of Alaska Fairbanks http://www.costumes.org/classes/ fashiondress/WW1toWW2.htm

Mallet, Kim. "Opus No. 3/4 on the Origins and Early History of the Waltz.," July 1998. http://www.split tree.org/waltz/waltz.htm

"Maude Russell (The Slim Princess)" obituary. http:// www.tip.net.au/~wegan/newsarchive1.htm

McWilliams, Peter. PROHIBITION: A LESSON IN THE FUTILITY (AND DANGER) OF PROHIBIT-ING "Ain't Nobody's Business If You Do" PART IV: SIX CHAPTERS IN SEARCH OF A SHORTER BOOK http://www.sky.org/data/aint/402.htm

Mencken, H.L. *H.L. Mencken on Music,* "Tempo di Valse" From: http://www.dancers-archive.com/rec-arts-dance/topics/memorable-quotes.txt

Mensing, Christian. "Christian's Bandoneon Page" www. inorg.chem.ethz.ch/tango/band/bandoneon.html

Morgan, Thomas L. "Cecil Mack (R. C. McPherson)," 2000. http://www.jass.com/cmack.html

_____. "Noble Sissle and Eubie Blake," 1997. http:// www.jass.com/sissle.html

National Archives. "The Emergence of Modern America (1890–1930)" http://www.archives.gov/education/ lessons/modern-america.html

National Park Services: Gaslighting in America (Plates) nps.gov/history/history/online_books/hcrs/myers/ plate2.

"New Plays," *Time Magazine, Monday, Jun. 28, 1926.* Extracted from Time Magazine.com http://www.time. com/time/magazine/article/0,9171,846604,00.html

Online Etymology Dictionary http://www.etymonline. com

Oxford English Dictionary Online — "ball" http://www. oed.com

Page, Ellen Welles. "A Flapper's Appeal to Parents by," *Outlook,* December 6, 1922, p. 607. http://www.oran ge.k12.oh.us/teachers/ohs/Tjordan/Pages/flapper's appeal.html

Pascoe, Christine. "Christy's Fashion Pages— Flapper Fashion" 2002. http://www.rambova.com/fashion/ fash4.html

Pfeiffenberger, Sylvia. "The blackness of tango: Dance's dark roots in a country 'without blacks,'" The Independent Weekly, May 10, 2006. http://www.indy week.com/gyrobase/Content?oid=oid%3A31481

Photoplay Magazine, October 1940 — extracted from http://www.geocities.com/cactus_st/article/article56. html

"Poiret and Eastern Influence— Women's Fashions of the 1910s" http://www.vintagevixen.com/history/ 1910s.asp

Phrase and Word Origins: "What is the origin of "the bee's knees"? http://www.yaelf.com/questions.shtml

Red Hot Jazz. "Alberta Hunter." http://www.redhot jazz.com/hunter.html

Reel Classics: The Classic Movie Site — "Ginger Rogers: She Adds New Chapter to Her Success Story" from LIFE Magazine March 2, 1942 pp. 60–68. http:// www.reelclassics.com/Actresses/Ginger/ginger-article.htm

Reformed Presbyterian Church (Covenanted) Homepage — Assorted anti-dance sermons:

Heckman, George C. *Dancing as a Christian Amusement.* Philadelphia: Presbyterian Board of Publication, 1879.

Mather, Cotton. *A Cloud of Witnesses; Darting Out Light upon a CASE, too Unseasonably made Seasonable to be Discoursed on.* Circa 1700.

Mather, Increase. *An Arrow Against the Profane and Promiscuous Dancing, drawn out of the quiver of the Scriptures.* Boston: By the Ministers of Christ, 1684.

Mesick, John F. *A Discourse on the Evils of Dancing; Delivered.... Before the Congregation of The German Reformed Salem Church of Harrisburg* Harrisburg: The. Fenn, 1846.

Palmer, B. M. *Social Dancing Inconsistent with a Christian Profession and Baptismal Vows:* a Sermon, in the Presbyterian Church, Columbia, S.C. June 177, 1849. Published by request of the Church Session. Columbia: Printed at the office of the South Carolinian, 1849.

Sikes, Rev. J. R. *A Time to Dance: A Sermon on Dancing.* Second Revised Edition. York, PA: Office of the Teacher's Journal, 1879. http:// www.covenanter.org/index.htm

Richards, Stanley. "The Troubadors and Courtly Love." From the essay by the same name. http://www.her mes.gen.nz/troubadors.htm

Robinson, Tobias D., editor. Chapter entitled "Society in London in 1814" from *Reminiscences of Captain Gronow.* (London: Smith, Elder and Co,. 18?) Free Online Library, 2001. http://www.db3nf.com/library/ 876–1.html

Scott, Donald. "Evangelicalism, Revivalism, and the Second great Awakening." http://www.nhc.rtp.nc.us: 8080/tserve/nineteen/nkeyinfo/nevanrev.htm

Sears, Christopher. "The Tango and Its Origins," 1999. www.mola-inc.org/PressRoom/TangoOrigins.pdf

The Silent Collection: Featuring: MAE MURRAY http://www.things-and-other-stuff.com/movies/pro files/mae-murray.htm

Steel, Danielle. *Fashion and Eroticism.* Chapter 9, "The Corset Controversy." 2000. http://www.corsets.de/ node59.html

Stone, Tammy. "1910s in fashion" http://en.wikipedia. org/wiki/1910s_in_fashion

The Strauss Dynasty "Former Performing Places" http:// www.cva.ahk.nl/composersmusic/muziekgeschiede nis/strauss_spielorte_e.html

Sublette, Ned. "Tango and its Origins"— Times Online.

May 3, 2006. www.timesonline.co.uk/article/0,,110 69-2163593,00.html

Sutton, Allan R. Mainspring Press: Award winning research in historic recordings. "Bert Williams' Imitators," 1996. http://www.mainspringpress.com/williams.html

Thomas, Pauline Weston. "Flapper Fashion—1920s Fashion History" For Fashion-Era.com, 2001–2006. http://www.fashion-era.com/flapper_fashion_1920s.htm

ToTango—"The Bandoneon" http://www.totango'bandoneo.html

Trachtenberg, Leo. "Texas Guinan: Queen of the Night" From *City Journal*, Spring 1998. www.city-journal.org/html/8_2_urbanities-texas.html

Variety— Obituaries. "Joan Crawford remembered: *Variety* takes a look back at the memorable actress" (By the *Variety* Staff) May 10, 1977 (re-posted May 10, 2007) http://www.variety.com/article/VR1117964648.html?categoryId=25&cs=1

Victorian Lace...Victorian Lifestyles. "A Brief History of Ballroom Dancing." 2003 http://www.geocities.com/victorianlace10/home.html

Wadler, Joyce. *New York Times*, March 29, 2001. Obituary. "Maude Rutherford, High-Kicking Songster of 20's, Dies at 104" http://www.tip.net.au/~wegan/newsarchive1.htm

"Waltz." April 2003. http://www.centralhome.com/ballroomcountry/waltz.htm

Warner, Michael. "The Bob" http://www.hairarchives.com/private/1920s.htm

_____. "The Boston" (Dance History Archive) 6/2003. http://www.streetswing.com/histmain/z3bostn1.htm

_____. "Juba Dance" 8/2/2005. http://www.streetswing.com/histmain/z3juba.htm

Watson, Sonny. Sonny Watson's StreetSwing.com, http://www.streetswing.com/histmain/z3chrlst.htm

Wikipedia—"Bandoneón" http://en.wikipedia.org/wiki/Bandoneón

Wikipedia—"Batuque" http://www.absoluteastronomy.com/encyclopedia/b/ba/batuque.htm

Wikipedia—"Carlos Gardel" http://en.wikipedia.org/wiki/Carlos_Gardel

Wikipedia—"Dolly Sisters" http://en.wikipedia.org/wiki/Dolly_Sisters

Wikipedia—"James Reese Europe" http://en.wikipedia.org/wiki/James_Reese_Europe

Wikipedia—"Joan Crawford" http://en.wikipedia.org/wiki/Joan_Crawford

Wikipedia—"Josephine Baker" http://en.wikipedia.org/wiki/Josephine_Baker

Wikipedia— Mae Murray http://en.wikipedia.org/wiki/Mae_Murray

Wikipedia—"Texas Guinan" http://en.wikipedia.org/wiki/Texas_Guinan

Williams, Iain Cameron. "Biography for Adelaide Hall." http://indie.imdb.com/name/nm0355263/bio

Yami, Reyza & Karina. Salsa Site. "Samba."2002 http://www.salsasite.com/dances/samba.htm

Index

Numbers in **bold italics** indicate pages with illustrations

259